Howard Thomas

THE JOURNAL OF EUGENE DELACROIX

THE JOURNAL OF EUGENE DELACROIX

TRANSLATED FROM THE FRENCH
BY WALTER PACH

*Illustrated with Reproductions of the Paintings
and Drawings of the Artist*

CROWN PUBLISHERS · NEW YORK

CONTENTS

ILLUSTRATIONS

Illustrations

For obvious reasons no attempt has been made to change the notations of the pre-war locations of the works of art mentioned in the foot-notes to the text and on the plates.

Delacroix

INTRODUCTION
Eugène Delacroix and His Journal

INTRODUCTION

EUGENE DELACROIX AND HIS JOURNAL

To APPRECIATE the importance of the book which is here offered for the first time in English, it is necessary to consider the position of Eugène Delacroix as an artist and as a thinker. That position was affirmed by his work from its early period, and the hundred years since then have steadily increased its prestige. A single look about the great room in the Louvre which contains the masterpieces of French painting in the nineteenth century will suffice to declare the esteem in which that museum — the chief spokesman of the world's thought on art — holds the man whom Renoir called the greatest artist of the French School. Delacroix's pictures, transferred from less important galleries in the same building, descending from the less advantageous spaces high on the walls to the place of honor, "the line," and now occupying more than one third of it, owe their ever greater consideration to the pivotal role they have played in shaping the talent of artists and the judgment of connoisseurs from the time they were painted till today.

'And, if prophecy is ever allowable, that today will continue through a long tomorrow.

The *Journal* is an intimate record of what occurred in the mind of the painter from 1822 till his death in 1863. Some months before he began to write down his daily or nightly thoughts in the notebooks which he carefully kept by him and re-read, he had electrified the world of art with his first masterpiece, the *Dante and Vergil*. Only twenty-four years old at the time (he was born in 1798), he already showed his faculty for giving general significance to a particular subject. It was through the same genius that he was, later, to raise color from an accessory to a completely expressive role; and if, in the *Dante and Vergil*, the painter's art had not yet attained this greater expansion, his intellectual power was such as to vivify the limited means of his youth, and to impose an image upon the excited mind of the time with all the force of a symbol.

The poet of Christian Europe and his guide from the classical world are shown standing together in a boat which rides the waters of the infernal lake, while behind them a city burns and desperate souls attempt to board the craft. Thus art and learning had come through the terrors of the Revolution and had given fresh evidences of vitality, even in the years when Napoleon was sweeping the continent with armies which carried to every land the sense of a new period. The imperial epic still of a mere yesterday, its court-painter, David, still dominating schools and exhibitions with a harshly classicist art as yet barely challenged, the younger generation nevertheless knows that a different style, a wider range of ideas are necessary. To seek refuge, as Ingres did, in the art of the museums will not suffice, even if breathless perfections are the result. The new adventure of humanity finds prophecy and a first realization in the arts of Goya in Spain, and Constable, Turner, and Blake in England. Perhaps it is the English poets who give the clearest statement of character to the period — which reaches supreme heights and depths in the later Beethoven, in Schubert and in Schumann. The world-wide scope of the Romantic movement, as it came to be called, is evidenced by the rise, at this very time, of Edgar Allan Poe and his contemporaries and successors among the poets and painters of America.

In France, Gros, the painter of Napoleonic history, had already forecast the tendencies of the new school by the fiery drama of his rendering, and by his color, an element which knew but small favor in the art of his master, David. Unable to reconcile the ideas of the older man, whom he adored, with those of the young painters whom he strongly influenced, Gros put an end to his life: the most illustrious and tragic of the many who, at this time, found escape in suicide. At the Salon of 1822, when Delacroix was unable to afford a proper frame for the *Dante and Vergil,* Gros, a member of the jury, had recognized the genius of the new man, and had ordered the work framed at his own expense. By so doing and by the words he spoke afterwards, he had given his young admirer the first of those accolades from the great which were to be his fortune throughout his life, and were to steel him against hostility and misunderstanding.

Three years earlier, a work instinct with the *Sturm und Drang* of the new time had already told decisively of its urge. This was Géricault's *Raft of the Medusa.* The younger painter had seen the vast canvas evolve, for he had posed for one of the figures in it. Devoted to the man who had thus at the outset given a titanic expression to the Romantic spirit, Delacroix was imbued throughout his whole first period with the influence of Géricault, and the memory of it was never to depart from his mind or his work.

In glancing back at these astounding years of his youth, we may well recall again the words which Goethe spoke to Eckermann on seeing Delacroix's illustrations to *Faust.* No friend of Romanticism, as we know, the old poet (he was approaching eighty) had his thoughts of over half a century before vividly brought back to him, and he marveled at the fullness with which, in a foreign land, his meanings had been rendered. Without for a moment setting the genius of Ingres above that of Goethe, one may consider that the antagonism toward Delacroix of the chief of the Classical School is to be ranked as an even more striking testimony to the position of the younger master. The world needed a balance for the formidable movement of Romanticism, and Ingres, with his almost religious invocation of the art of the past, supplied this need. I shall try to show later that Delacroix himself was renewing qualities inherent in many of the greatest classics. It was difficult, at the time, to recognize this aspect of his work, and to Ingres, seeing truth only in certain manifestations of the eternal elements of art, the ideas of the man he correctly recognized as the embodiment of a new spirit were anathema: he avoided mention of his name, referring to him in his writings as "the apostle of ugliness."

The error involved in this case, as in almost all others where men have sought to fix limits for the beautiful, has been demonstrated by the admiration for Delacroix of an unbroken line of later masters. The discoveries of the Impressionists as to the relation of light and color are based on study of Delacroix; Renoir and Cézanne are deeply influenced by him; van Gogh makes variants of his pictures; Seurat ponders deeply over his aesthetics; Matisse and Derain are devoted upholders of his authority. Thus there was the most ample justification for André Suarès when he said that all modern art issues from Delacroix. He was but continuing the literary homage to the painter which reached its greatest heights in the writings of Baudelaire, and has given us splendid pages of criticism by Théophile Silvestre and Taine, not to mention the voluminous and always more enthusiastic tributes of the later decades. The best among them are those of Herr Meier-Graefe, M. Moreau-Nélaton and M. Escholier.

The *Journal*, supplemented by the letters of Delacroix, gives us perhaps the most complete record we have of any artist's life, even though the notebooks covering certain years are lost, probably forever. One would give much to have the impressions of his one visit to London, in 1825, of its then young National Gallery, and of the British Museum. Sketches of landscape and of certain antique sculptures, together with a few letters, are all that we possess. In contrast, we have an extraordinarily full and vivid account of what must be regarded as the greatest outer event of Delacroix's life, the journey to Morocco in 1832.

Though it occupied less than six months, its memories lasted on with the painter for the thirty-one years he had still to live. Till the very end of that time we find explicit or indirect allusion to the scenes of the river Sebou, of Alcassar-el-Kebir, of Meknez, and of Algeria, which country he also saw. Recorded with all the fervor of discovery, and yet with control and reserve, the Orient appears in innumerable pencil or water color sketches and in the closely packed words of the *Journal,* as if created for his mood and his needs. Its mystery (even greater in that less traveled day than now, when we know it ill enough), its fire, and, for the European, its freedom were such stuff as Byron had sought in Greece, and Géricault had treated in his horse-men, seamen and battles. Here was romance in its most intoxicating form. But observe how, at this very moment, the balance is kept in a mind formed by the profoundly classical heritage of Delacroix. At Tangier he writes in his journal, "This people is wholly antique," and the thought recurs again and again in these pages and in the *Letters.* The wearing of a burnous with its graceful folds, the dignity of bearing of the Moors, the beauty and modesty of the women (whom he sees chiefly in the Jewish households), the "majesty which is lacking among ourselves in the gravest circumstances," all bring before his mind the life of Greece and Rome in their great time. In later years he writes to Théophile Silvestre "It was among these people that I really discovered for myself the beauty of antiquity."

In his painting the special beauty he mentions was to express itself anew. The color-sense which Orientals had kept alive through the centuries opened up to him vistas of an art in which the classical unity, variety, and harmony should appear in the realm of color as fully as the Greeks embodied them in form. There had been colorists in Europe before, to be sure. Delacroix had looked deeply into the painting of Titian and had made copies from Rubens and Veronese. But even such masters had never used color as a free element, in the way the Moors did in their weaving and building and decoration. Europe's conception of picture-making, while affected by the marbles of Venice and the textiles of the northern countries, had never permitted itself to accept the delight of the senses as a sufficient reason for the existence of either form or color. The illustrative and expressive function of art on one side, and scientific research on the other, had given such importance to modeling, perspective and, above all, to chiaroscuro that the aesthetic qualities survived only as a kind of by-product. If they are so pure and powerful, notwithstanding, that we are compelled to rank European painting as the highest reach of the art, it is so only at the price of constant renewal, of a refusal to continue with forms whose vitality it has exhausted.

And so, the eighteenth century having come to its violent close, the ideals of grace, naturalness and charm peculiar to that time became abhorrent to the stern men who made the Revolution. When David, a member of the Convention of the Revolution, refused to continue with the Academy and used the word academic as a term of reproach to those of his pupils whose works recalled in any way the manner of Boucher or Lancret, he did so in the name of an art of pure reason, one which was to bring back the simplicity of the antique. To be sure the antique as understood by David was a latter-day product, resulting from the work of various men in Italy, after the unearthing of Pompeii, and of other men in Paris, later on.

Ingres, even though revolting against the narrowness of David's conception of the classical qualities, never extended them beyond the elements of form. When he touched on Oriental themes, as he frequently did, it was to submit them to the discipline of the Greeks and the Romans, whose yoke was made hateful to successive generations. As to that "beauty of antiquity" which Delacroix speaks of rediscovering, all but the clearest minds were misled, even as the school of David was misled, in the matter of men like Watteau. That proscribed master, a Fleming by descent, was the object of a lifelong homage from Delacroix, who was thus naturally led to the source of Watteau's heavenly color in an older Flemish painter — in Rubens. And so when Morocco laid before the traveler's eyes its harmonies, new to European understanding even while so ancient, he was ready to grasp their significance, to see them as something not merely decorative, but united with the antique grace and "majesty" which he recognized in the people of the land.

A year after the Moroccan journey, Delacroix painted the first of the great murals which were to occupy so much of his later life. Géricault had passed on to him, about twelve years before, a commission for a church decoration, that he executed in the manner for which his schooling (based on Davidian ideals) had prepared him. Without knowing of his contact with the Orient, one could be sure that something more than the development due to time and practice had intervened between this early, immature mural painting and those of the Chamber of Deputies. The ceiling of the Galerie d'Apollon in the Louvre and the chapel at the church of Saint Sulpice, the masterpieces of his work on an architectural base, show the painter advancing in knowledge with the passing of the years but still utilizing the sense of harmony that was so purified and strengthened by his sight of an art wherein color plays an almost exclusive role.

During the lifetime of the master and for many years afterward, color was the one quality that most critics would concede to him. Théodore Rousseau expressed his generous and deep admiration for Delacroix in terms which do not exclude mention of "exaggerations and faults," though he says that the art in its ensemble is "as powerful as a voice from the *Inferno* of Dante." Doubtless it is Baudelaire who utters the appraisal nearest to that of today. Aroused by constant objections to Delacroix's drawing, he retorted that there were but two men in Paris who could draw as well: they were Ingres and Daumier. The placing of the great classicist's name between those of his rival and of a newspaper cartoonist, must have seemed about the furthest reach of Satanic paradox to the public of the time. But as Daumier has risen in general esteem to his mighty place among draftsmen, so the penetrative critical genius of the poet has been vindicated: the elements in Delacroix's drawing which even Rousseau could consider to be lapses, have come to take their place as necessary to this conception of form, one more complex and rich than that of a mere master of line.

Of particular interest, as regards the quality of drawing in Delacroix's work, are the references he makes to the conception of the *oves*, the ovoids which gave him the essentials of the form. If the volumes are right, he argues, the contours will always find their true place and quality afterward. The idea made a deep impression on van Gogh at a later time, when he wrote down the fact that Delacroix got the tradition from Géricault, and that it is to be followed back to the Greeks. In Delacroix's own time, we find so able a draftsman as Jean Gigoux telling of the wonderful way in which his friend grouped a series of rapidly traced ovoids, thereby obtaining the masses of a running horse; the drawing may very well be the one reproduced in the present volume. So that it was not merely the colorist but the master of form whom people compared with Ingres.

Without reopening this futile comparison between the giants of the two schools of the earlier nineteenth century, we may at least mention the historical fact that it is Delacroix who has left us the great monuments of mural painting of the time. And the fact has a significance, for painting on the walls of public buildings is evidently the form of the art which addresses itself to a collective audience: the easel picture, to which Ingres devoted himself particularly, is better adapted to solitary enjoyment, as in an individual's apartment, and is indeed at a disadvantage, frequently, in the vast galleries of a museum. Delacroix's mastery of the great walls which represent some of his ultimate achievement is a proof that the impersonality of classical art belongs to his nature as well as the introspection that marks the Romantic School.

The employment of assistants, in which practice he followed the authors of extensive decorations in earlier centuries, takes away no whit from his individual title to his murals. And yet, to know the most personal aspects of his art, to understand its researches, to feel its hopes and doubts and triumphs most intimately, one must dwell with the easel pictures and with the almost numberless studies. Even today no one can give a definitive editing to the catalogue in which Robaut made his splendid attempt to record the work of Delacroix, but it has been estimated that the paintings (exclusive of the decorations) run to over a thousand, the water colors and pastels to more than two thousand, the drawings and sketches in various mediums to some nine thousand. When one adds to this enormous production the *Journal;* the *Letters* (which contain only a small part of those actually written), and the two volumes of essays which have been republished from old magazines, one can form an idea of the energy seething in the artist — who, as these pages reveal, was often kept from his work by poor health.

What compensated for the time thus lost; what tells the secret of the boy of fourteen who already drew superbly, and of the man of sixty whom we find delighting in the great stores of new strength he found ready for his work is the clarity of mind that made each effort count and the intensity of purpose that unifies the whole. From the first he knows, if only in a general way, what he wants. The *Dante and Vergil* was the result of the concentrated effort of but a few months. The immense number of sketches prepared him to carry through his decorations and large canvases in the manner that he describes in the present volume. Instead of being a mere improviser, as was frequently asserted, he planned his work so thoroughly that when he came to the final execution, he brushed it in with the seeming impetuosity of a sketch. One notes the satisfaction he feels on hearing from Corot, whom he admires, that "despite my desire to systematize, instinct will always have the upper hand with me."

He will accept to the full the guidance of the masters, from whose work he made so many copies, and will frankly learn from contemporaries or in their company. Thus we find him at the Jardin des

Plantes with Barye (observe at the Metropolitan Museum, in New York, the close resemblance of Delacroix's horse, in his *Rebecca* picture, to Barye's Centaur in the *Theseus* group nearby); he will frequent the Englishmen, Fielding and Bonington, who initiate him into uses of water color which had developed in their country earlier than in France; and he will give close attention to Constable's theory of the intensification of a color by dividing it into its components. Later, he will listen eagerly to the scientists who can help him on the same score, and when Paul Signac comes to write the book in which he summarizes the century's research into the science of color, a good third of it is devoted to the contribution of Delacroix.

The *Journal*, however, testifies to a far deeper interest of the master's, one which has not been sufficiently regarded by the critics. In the present pages we see Delacroix as a constant student — probably the deepest of all modern students, of the classical element in art. We have spoken of him as the Romanticist, the man on fire with the new genius of a period which released a veritable phalanx of great men. But had he been merely a man of his time, his importance would be no more than historical, and would long since have declined beyond recovery, instead of mounting higher, as we have observed from his position in the museums and from his ever renewing influence on later artists. We have seen him as a colorist able to increase the whole of Europe's heritage of color through acquaintance with an Islamic people whose temperament and whose religious law alike cause them to restrict themselves to the abstract elements of art. But Delacroix is even less Oriental than he is transitional.

I have attempted elsewhere to show the derivation and effect of the Greek elements in his work ("Notes sur le Classicisme de Delacroix," published in *L'Amour de l'Art* for June, 1930). Suffice it to recall that the firm grounding in the poets of antiquity he received during his boyhood induced a lifelong fidelity to them and to the character of thought they represent. And so we have the spectacle of a man who never set foot on the soil of Greece or Italy, who knew the slight vestiges of ancient painting only by reproduction or by a few weak fragments in Paris or London, and yet who reaches back, through Poussin and Veronese, or, as I prefer to think, through the mysterious instincts of genius, to the central tradition of the whole art of his continent. While less clear than in ancient sculpture, this tradition is still accessible to us in Greek painting as it comes down through its late representatives at Pompeii and Herculaneum (decadent ones, to be sure, but grand ones). For anybody well acquainted with this art, it is enough to glance at certain passages in Delacroix (Jacob's hat in the mural at Saint-Sulpice for example) to be back in the days of those Greeks who, through Alexandria and the Italic colonies, carried on the painting which had evolved in Athens. And ere anyone tries to explain the resemblance as fortuitous, let him consider these lines from the entry in the *Journal* dated March 11, 1850, at the very time when its author was preparing his studies for the great decoration just referred to. After noting how, in Persia, the architecture is peculiar to the country while in Europe "from Cadiz to Petersburg" everything now looks as if designed in the same *atelier,* he proceeds:

"Our architects have but one procedure, that of returning forever to the original purity of Greek art. Not to speak of the maddest of them, who do the same for Gothic, these purists perceive every thirty years that their immediate predecessors made a mistake of appreciation as to this exquisite imitation of the antique. Thus Percier and Fontaine, in their day, thought they had settled the matter forever. The style, of which we see the remains in certain clocks dating from forty years ago, shows itself today as what it really is: dry and mean, without one of the qualities of the antique. . . . The sculpture of Phidias is held in the same honor by the painters. You may not so much as mention to them the antiques of Rome or of Greece before or after Phidias!"

Having penetrated so far into the qualities of the classical schools as to see that blindness to the beauty of the early or the late periods means falsifying the qualities of the golden time as well, Delacroix would not be of those misled by superficial matters. His classicism was of the spirit, and as accessible to manifestations of the eternal laws when they appeared in Racine or Mozart as when they appeared in Raphael — or Rubens!

Such capacity for seeing relationships where lesser men see none (to refer once more to William James's definition of genius) is evidently of the essence of Delacroix's position as a thinker. The forty years covered by the *Journal* include acquaintance with most of the great artists and writers of that brilliant period of French culture. Delacroix, with his important family connections and the distinction as a painter which he achieved at the outset of his career, knew everyone of note in the Paris of his day, and in these pages, destined, as he believed, for no eyes save his own, he wrote down freely his impressions of the men and events — intellectual and artistic — by which he was surrounded. He can say things about other artists that his sense of propriety did not permit him to say in his letters or even, as far as report informs us, in conversation. The frequently disjointed character of the entries in his notebooks shows us the man at work, seizing impressions white-hot; often it is across a series of years that we see him pursuing the understanding of some problem.

The result of these musings was to have been a Dictionary of the Fine Arts, a work so vast that even the energy of a Delacroix could not carry it through without too great sacrifice of the thing to which his life was dedicated and to which every other interest was subordinate: his painting. And so the dictionary never came to existence as a separate book, but remains as part of the *Journal*, paragraph after paragraph, page after page of intensive reflection by a mind whose immense native power was steadily developed through contact with the great men of the past and the most distinguished of his day.

Indeed the present volume has a value as reflecting the world of letters, politics, music, and the theater which is exceeded only by its importance among writings on art. Delacroix's youthful intimacy with the prodigious character and talent of Géricault was followed by his association with one great painter after another; and we listen to him discuss music with his friend Chopin and literature with Balzac, Gautier, and George Sand. We imagine the pride that even he must have felt in the homage of Baudelaire who, seeing him at once in his pivotal importance, told of it in *Les Fleurs du Mal,* where he gave to Delacroix an equal place with Michelangelo, Rembrandt, and those other masters — *Les Phares* — whom he treats as the beacons which illumine the sea of human life.

In the *Essays,* Delacroix gives his own statement as to the great artists. What he says is of capital importance as history in such cases as that of Gros, whom the author knew personally, and it is the most masterly existing critique of others, like Poussin (as Desjardins, one of the recent biographers of that master, has testified); yet these writings will not take rank with the *Journal* of Delacroix, because the painter's respect for an art not his own caused him to keep them within the narrow limits of a style which he considered proper for the pages of serious reviews. Hence, despite the light the essays shed on men and problems, despite the fact that a paper like the one on Prud'hon is also a revelation of the life of the man who wrote it, there is nothing (save of course the paintings) that brings us so close to Delacroix as does the *Journal.*

Its reappearance is a token of the enduring interest in the master. And that enduring quality is to be explained in only one way, it seems to me. The things that last are the great things, the ones that are always true. If one point stands out from this book, it is that from youth to old age, Delacroix's effort was to know these permanently true things and to build his own work upon them. The romance of his period, which gives its name to the school with which he is always classed, resided in the discovery of beauty in unsuspected places of the past as well as in the present. Delacroix, writing here of his admiration for Géricault, Corot and Rousseau, for Beethoven and Chopin, is one of the moderns of his time. He expresses the Romantic adventure through the courage with which he places contemporary men on a level with those whose work hangs in the museums. I have endeavored to show how deeply he belongs to the Classical School as well. But as we read these pages expressive of his love for Mozart and Cimarosa, for Racine and Shakespeare, for Rembrandt and Raphael and Titian, for Rubens and Homer — whom he associates so boldly — and above all as we see him referring all things to the Antique and scrutinizing the essential likeness to it of the best latter-day productions, we become aware that he passes beyond the limits of the two contending schools of his period to become one of the men who must have significance for all time.

This, more than the technical matters I referred to previously, is the explanation of his influence on succeeding masters. Indeed the painting of Delacroix is more known through its reverberations amid the mountain-chain of artists that stems from it than through direct acquaintance, even by visitors to museums. This condition, however, is changing. Time was needed to convert appreciation of the painter as an innovator to an understanding of him as a classic, and some time must yet intervene, perhaps, before the forbidding aspect we are prone to associate with a classic gives way to a seeing of him as one whose love of life and art affords the deepest, most inexhaustible delight.

Delacroix, with his immense activity, production and influence, has already passed, or nearly passed, into the realm of legend. There are few alive who knew him and who can give us even a glimpse, at first hand, of the man as he appeared to the people of his time. I had an acquaintance with such a one, Odilon Redon, and I know that no memory of his long and rich life was dearer to him than that of his single meeting with the man whom he ranked highest among all the moderns. I tell the story as the artist told it to me. "In 1861, Delacroix attended a ball at the Hôtel de Ville, where my brother and I were presented to him. I was then twenty-one years old, my brother was younger; so we did not venture to speak much to him, but all evening we followed him from group to group in order to hear every word he should say. Famous men and women became as silent as we when he spoke. He was not what one would call handsome, but in his distinction — a prince. When he left the ball my brother and I still wanted to see more of him, so we walked behind him through the streets. He went slowly and seemed to be meditating, so we kept at a distance in order not to disturb him. There had been a rain, and I remember how he picked his steps to avoid the wet places. But when he reached the house on the Right Bank where he had lived for so many years, he seemed to realize that he had taken his way toward it out of habit, and he turned back and walked, still slowly and pensively, through the city and across the river, to the Rue de Furstenberg where he was to die, two years afterward."

Odilon Redon was already an artist in 1861, and part of the devotion that he and his brother (a musician) felt for Delacroix was due to the latter's great achievement. But the significance of the tiny incident is perhaps more to be understood if we look on it as revealing the effect produced by the painter as a man. And in this light we may re-read passages in the *Journal*, such as the one in which he compares Raphael and Rembrandt — to the advantage of the latter, a violent piece of audacity at that time — or that one in which he records his visit to a great collection where, after seeing Rubens and Watteau, his idols for a lifetime, he feels that it is Ruysdael who, in his simplicity, possesses the supreme quality. "Beside him, here, those other men are too much the artists," he observes. Delacroix is the master of Romanticism that he has always been considered; he is, as we see always more clearly, an inspired continuer of the classical qualities; no one can read this book without recognizing in him the humanity that held the two elements of art in their perfect and beautiful association.

The *Journal*, as it appears in the second French edition, contains some fifteen hundred pages. Yet in reducing that mass of material to about half its bulk, as I have done in the present volume, I am confident that the work has suffered no real loss because, very simply, the pages omitted are not worth reprinting. Leaving aside the fact that the reader's approach is made not fifty percent but immeasurably easier by eliminating so much inert material, it is clear that what remains must only gain by the absence of pages which could have had no interest save for Delacroix and those immediately around him. I have met but few persons who have even tried to go through the three solid volumes of the French editions. Most of those who have begun, with whatever pious intentions, to read the famous work have given up after floundering among allusions to permanently forgotten people, among pages of expense accounts (I give some examples of them), and among interminable lists of colors — the data from which the master's assistants worked on the great decorations — but of no use to artists today when Delacroix is no longer here to direct the proportions of colors used in one combination or another. I believe my thirty-five years of admiration for the great artist have prevented me from sacrificing any detail which, when extracted from pages of dross, might throw light on his theories, his character, or the essentials of life in his time. The editor of the first edition, M. Paul Flat, omitted the many pages that Delacroix extracted from the books he was reading and copied into the notebooks which were to become the *Journal*. M. André Joubin, the editor of the second edition, restored the extracts, though it seems that even he refrained from expanding his volumes to the extent of including everything. I have made the freest use of both editors' notes, omitting some and adding others of my own. As to quotations from Voltaire, Chateaubriand and others in which Delacroix found his own thought expressed, they seem to become an integral part of the *Journal*, and so are in a different category from numberless other extracts, which help us no more in a study of Delacroix's genius than his observation of the weather, or the notations on diet and medicines, which the frequently ailing old bachelor sets down at length. I must indeed express the hope that readers who share Delacroix's dislike for long books will agree that all the material here included does possess, at the very least, a certain value.

The second French edition, which I follow in the present text, is doubtless based on a correct theory when it separates the earlier and later parts of the *Journal*. From 1824 there is a complete break, until we reach the Moroccan journey of 1832. Although M. Flat attempts to bridge the gap, as also the longer one from 1832 to 1847, with material taken from notebooks or from loose sheets of writing that have come down to us, I believe the division into separate chronological sections is more reasonable. Delacroix himself indicates by certain entries of 1847 that he is beginning anew; and, by adopting the idea of two well-separated divisions of the *Journal*, we see far more clearly the difference between the youth and later life of the artist. The affairs with women and the rebellion against difficult material conditions (caused by the loss of the family fortune) make way for sobriety of living and for a deepening of his lifelong inquiry into the causes and effects of art.

The illustrations here offered were chosen not only with the idea of showing landmarks in the great painter's career and other works of particular beauty, but because they, like his text, show the unceasing development of his mind. A salient characteristic of this is the tenacity with which, over many years, he held to the working out of an idea. It is not enough to see him making innumerable studies for a work like the *Massacre at Scio* or the different paintings of the *Christ on the Lake of Genesareth,* (there are at least nine of them that I have come on, so far); far more illuminating is it to see him in 1862, the year before his death, return to his theme of nearly twenty years earlier, the *Education of Achilles,* and do a picture of it that is not alone absolutely fresh in inspiration, but so perfect that it seemed to some of his admirers the most beautiful of all the thousand and odd works in the exhibition at the Louvre in 1930. It offered new evidence as to the rightness of a sentence of Elie Faure's: "Every author writes but one book, every painter does but one picture." Or as Duchamp-Villon put the idea, "The life of an artist is always a process of perfecting."

In what is regarded by many as Delacroix's supreme effort, the decoration of the chapel at Saint-Sulpice, we have, on one side the *Jacob Wrestling with the Angel,* a Romantic subject from a Romantic book such as had fired his youth, and on the other wall, the *Heliodorus,* a subject drawn from Raphael, whose figure of the angel he has quite openly appropriated — and as that word means — made it his own, revivifying it in the light that Raphael himself, in his Roman period, was carrying on from Classical art, as Sir Charles J. Holmes has so admirably pointed out in his book on this subject.

If our illustration thus shows Delacroix drawing on a Latin source of inspiration and paralleling, in this way, the preference for Classical drama revealed by the *Journal,* it is imperative to show him also as the man of the North. His love for Ruysdael, mentioned above, his own seeing of landscape, and then the two pictures by Rubens described by him in these pages and here reproduced, corroborate our knowledge that from his mother — French by nationality but of pure German blood — he had a strain of descent to connect him with Holland, Flanders, and the land of Shakespeare, the poet to whom he owes so much.

Yet he is French. I know no summing up of the matter like that which ended a conversation I once had with M. Paul Jamot, now the Curator of Paintings of the Louvre, and himself so distinguished a student of Delacroix's art. I had recalled a sentence from the remarkable analysis of Poussin, the essay mentioned earlier in this Introduction. After telling how that master spent his whole mature life in Italy, where his work, in its external appearance, came to be almost identical with that of the Bolognese painters around him, Delacroix risks the accusation both of chauvinism and of paradox by exclaiming "Poussin is the least Italian of all artists!" M. Jamot smiled and observed, "At least we may say that he is the most French of all artists." And these pages, with their simple love of the things and the thoughts of France, tell us that Delacroix himself, with all his debt to Italy, Flanders, England, and the Orient, is of his own soil.

A word may be said as to certain artists and certain processes of art, notably fresco, which he often discusses. We need to recall once more that he never visited Italy; and it may be added that the few but fine frescoes of the Louvre, the murals by Fra Angelico and Botticelli, came to France only after his death. He never saw the great walls of Cimabue, Giotto, and Masaccio, and what he says of Michel-angelo and Raphael is based on the sculpture by the former artist to-gether with engravings after his painting, and on the easel pictures of the latter. He therefore knew of fresco by little more than hearsay, which had given him, in the matter of another art that he loved — I mean music — only the slightest idea of one of the supreme masters: no other than Bach. A little research is all we need, however, to find out that, in Delacroix's period, almost nobody heard more of the music of that "All-Father" than he did; indeed I am told that the name was more often used at the time to refer to Philip Emanuel Bach than to the mighty Johann Sebastian. As near as that day is to our own, we must have some historical fact, like this example drawn from music, to make us aware of the change of ideas that has come about. The same is true in the field of painting, especially as artists have arrived at a new understanding of the Primitives. Those of France were discovered by so recent an exhibition as the one of 1904, save in the case of a few specialists. Delacroix barely mentions so pivotal a figure as van Eyck, knows nothing of Breughel, and so little of the early Italians that his interest is confined almost entirely to the Golden Age. Yet no apologies need be made. The power of his mind renders ample the material for thought which he possessed, and it is with a permanently modern outlook that he couples the names of Vergil and Mozart in his entry of February 23, 1858, after a consideration of the way that Greek art, because of rather than despite its perfection, retains its aspect of peren-nial freshness; the idea stands as an absolute anticipation of the best thought of today.

Often, in coming on his references to the incompleteness of the Primitives, we must remind ourselves that what he had in mind was the version of their art introduced by Ingres and his school. With this fact before us, the *Journal* becomes invaluable once more through the light that it throws on the differences between the two great men. As a postscript to the history of that famous rivalry, let me quote again from Chenavard, who is to appear so often in these pages. He is writing of an occasion when he and Delacroix were going together to the Institute for one of its sessions.

"Chance willed it that Ingres should be only a few steps ahead of us. As we were approaching the door, and those two irreconcilable enemies were just meeting and measuring each other with a look, Ingres suddenly extended his hand to Delacroix, moved by an impulse of secret sympathy which for a long time had been drawing together the natures of the two great artists, both revolutionaries in their way and both sterling men. . . .

"I cannot tell you the joy that gripped my heart when I stood beside those two splendid athletes whom the French School had watched in their proud struggle, when I saw their two flags finally united by the embrace of friendship, when I evoked the memory of so many fallen comrades, who, could they have seen, as I did, Ingres and Delacroix — irreproachable draftsmanship and the life inseparable from it — meeting and clasping hands on the landing of the Institute of France, would have asked no more for the moment of their death as conquered men."

There is the voice of the Romantic period, that we are to hear throughout the book we are about to enter. In order that the reader may leave behind him the phraseology of today and recall that of a time when strong men could speak with emotion and the language of emotion, I leave the final words of this Introduction to Théophile Silvestre, thereby following the example of M. Moreau-Nélaton and of M. Escholier, who, in their definitive books, give over the description of the master's last moments to one who had loved him so early and so well.

"Thus died, almost with a smile, on August 13th, 1863, that painter of great race, Ferdinand-Victor-Eugène Delacroix, who had a sun in his head and storms in his heart; who for forty years played upon the keyboard of human passions, and whose brush — grandiose, terrible or suave — passed from saints to warriors, from warriors to lovers, from lovers to tigers, and from tigers to flowers."

Eugène Delacroix and His Journal

For many years artists and art lovers have been urging an English edition of the *Journal*. I was finally led to undertake it by Mrs. J. Caesar Guggenheimer's interest in the great painter and his book. In presenting it in its new form, I wish to acknowledge Mr. Wallace Brockway's work on the first section, and I must offer thanks to my wife, above all, and to my friends Arthur L. Strasser and J. E. Spingarn for the generous advice with which they have assisted me.

WALTER PACH

New York, July 26, 1937

THE JOURNAL OF EUGENE DELACROIX

THE JOURNAL

1822

Louroux, Tuesday, September 3, 1822.

I AM carrying out my plan, so often formulated, of keeping a journal. What I most keenly wish is not to forget that I am writing for myself alone. Thus I shall always tell the truth, I hope, and thus I shall improve myself. These pages will reproach me for my changes of mind. I am starting out in a good humor.

I am at my brother's. The Louroux clock has just struck nine or ten o'clock. I have been seated in the moonlight five minutes, on the little bench outside the door, in order to collect my thoughts. But though I am happy today, I cannot recapture last night's sensations. There was a full moon. Seated on a bench against my brother's house, I spent some delightful hours. After seeing some neighbors home who had dined with us, and taking a turn around the pond, we returned. My brother read the papers, while I studied some sketches of Michelangelo's which I had brought with me. The sight of his grand drawing moved me profoundly and disposed me to the most favorable emotions. The moon, vast and red in the cloudless sky, rose little by little among the trees. In the midst of my reverie, and while my brother was speaking to me of love, I heard Lisette's voice in the distance. It has a sound that makes the heart beat faster; it is more compelling than all the other charms of her person, for she is not truly pretty; but she has a quality that Raphael understood so well — arms like bronze and a form both delicate and robust. Not truly pretty, this girl has, however, a certain finesse, a bewitching blend of allure and maidenly modesty, as when she came in while we were at dessert two or three days ago. It was Sunday. Although I do not like her in that finery, which binds her too much, she did please me mightily that day, especially with her divine smile, called forth by

35

certain over-free words which troubled her and made her lower her tell-tale eyes. There was, indeed, emotion both in her person and in her voice, for in answering certain trivial questions, her voice was somewhat changed, and she never once looked at me. Her throat rose and fell under her neckerchief. I think that was the evening I kissed her in the dark passage of the house, after returning from the village through the garden. The others had gone on ahead; I had remained behind with her. She repeatedly bade me stop, ever in a low, sweet voice. But all this means nothing. What does it matter? This memory, which will not haunt me like a passion, will be a lovely flower on the road of life and in my memory. Her voice is like that of Elizabeth Salter, whom I am beginning to forget.

Sunday morning I received a letter from Félix, saying that my picture had been hung at the Luxembourg.[1] Today, Tuesday, I am still much excited. I admit that this makes me very happy, and the thought, when it returns to me, colors my days most agreeably. Now it dominates me and has quickened my desire to return to Paris, where I shall find only dissembled envy, satiety after triumph, but never a Lisette like mine, never moonlight and the peace I breathe here.

To revert to the pleasure of last Monday night, I could not resist devoting a drawing in my album to that sweet evening — recapturing the delightful view from the bench where I was so happy. I hope to get back as much as I can to my former ideas and pleasures. But in God's name, let me get on! I must remember the ideas I had about what I want to do in Paris in order to keep busy, and the ideas I've had about subjects for pictures.

To paint my *Tasso in Prison,* life size.

Thursday, September 5.

I have been hunting with my brother in the sweltering heat. On the way back I killed a quail in such a way as to gain my brother's

[1] The picture referred to is Delacroix's first masterpiece, the *Dante and Vergil,* exhibited at the Salon of 1822, purchased by the government for 1200 francs, and now in the Louvre.

praises. It was the sole trophy of the chase, moreover, though I shot thrice at rabbits.

This evening we met Mlle Lisette, who had come to mend my shirts. As she was slightly behind, I took her in my arms. Her resistance wounded me, for I saw that it came from her heart. On a second visit, I saw her again. She put me off flatly by saying that *if she wanted it*, she would let me know. I repulsed her, my feelings being hurt, and took a turn or two down the path before moonrise. I met her once again. She was going to draw water for supper. I had a mind to sulk and not go back, but I gave in once more. "Then you don't love me?" "No." "Do you love someone else?" "I love no one," or some absurd reply meant for *enough*. This time I let her hand fall angrily and turned my back, wounded and chagrined. She breathed a laugh that wasn't a laugh. It was the echo of a protestation made half seriously. But the unpleasantness of it remained. I resumed my walk, affecting not to look at her. I can't bear to think of this any longer. Though not in love with her, I am indignant and want to make her sorry for her conduct. Just now, I simply have to vent my spleen. I had planned to watch her washing tomorrow. Shall I give in? All is really not yet over — shall I be ass enough to go back to her? I certainly hope not.

Little of interest yesterday, the 4th. The day before yesterday was the anniversary of my beloved mother's death: the day I started my journal. May she be with me as I write, and may she never have cause in it to blush for her son!

I wrote to Philarète this evening.

The following idea had never come to me until yesterday, when my brother called it to my notice. We had just killed a hare and, rested from the chase, we began to wonder at the influence of the state of mind on one's physical condition. I cited the Athenian who died on hearing of the victory of Plataea (I think), the French soldiers at Malplaquet, and a thousand others. It argues eloquently for the loftiness of the human soul, and I don't see how one can refute it. How the trumpets and, above all, the beating drums incite to battle."

Even the gaiety so easily excited by light music is not vulgar and lacking in imagination. Back of the joys it brings, there are poetic sensations, an agreeable reverie that spoken pleasantries can never inspire. Music is so transient a pleasure, one feels it escaping even while experiencing it, and to such a degree that a melancholy impression mingles with the gaiety it creates. But also, when it expresses sorrow, it still evokes a tender emotion, and the heart's beat quickens to it. The pleasure caused by the regularity of the measure, in reminding us that our span is brief, enjoins us to revel in the music.

September 7.

These past few days I have decided to visit M. Gros,[2] and the plan is most attractive to me.

We spoke this evening of my worthy father. I recalled, in detail, the various events of his life. My father in Holland, surprised at dinner with the directors by the rebels stirred up by the French government itself; he harangues the drunken, brutal soldiery without the least emotion. One of them takes aim at him but the shot goes astray when my brother intervenes. He talks French to them — to those Dutch boors. The French general, in league with the rebels, offers him an escort. He replies that he refuses an escort from traitors.

The operation. Previously lunching with his friends and physicians, then directing the workers. The operation was done in five stages. He said, after the fourth: "My friends, here are four acts done — may the fifth not be a tragedy!"

On my return next year, I want to copy my father's portrait.

Boerhave[3] said that he had never been awakened to treat a man who had gone to bed without his supper.

[2] Baron Gros (1771-1835). The great painter had perceived the importance of Delacroix's *Dante and Vergil* at the Salon, and in complimenting the young artist on his work, had spoken of it as the painting of Rubens in a chastened spirit.

[3] Boerhave (1668–1738), a celebrated Dutch physician. The meaning is that those who go without supper have a better chance of sleeping through the night. Delacroix's delicate health caused him to take a constant interest in matters of hygiene.

A celebrated man said to a young and impertinent braggart, who was boasting that he had never been afraid of anything: "Monsieur, then you have never snuffed a candle with your fingers!"

Think of strengthening your principles. Think of your father and overcome your native frivolity. Do not be polite to hypocrites.

On the eve of my departure from Louroux.

I am carrying away a painful estimate of my brother's situation. I am young and free, while he, the soul of truth and candor, and endowed with a character which should place him in the vanguard of estimable men, lives surrounded by brutes and rabble. This woman [*] has a good heart, but should he consider that alone as the means to bring peace to the end of his troubled career? Henri Hugues has explained his position to me in a way I had always sensed myself, but my feeling about it has become blunted by familiarity. I do not dare to guess the stormy future awaiting him — what a sad business not to be able to own to his companion in the presence of gentlefolk, or to be reduced to making of that evil a weapon for defying what he comes to regard as prejudices! The day before yesterday there was a kind of ball preceded by a dinner which made the awkwardness of his position clearer to me.

This morning Uncle [Riesener] and his son, Henry, left. The separation, though doubtless brief, pains me. I am fond of Henry. He is a bit of a scoffer, so that he is at first received with scant favor; but he is an honest fellow. Yesterday night, on the eve of departure, which should have meant something to my brother — above all — we dined late and luxuriously. The day before the dinner I was reconciled to Lisette, and so danced with her late into the night. Charles' girl and Henry were with us. I was greatly vexed. Henry was saying crude and filthy things in front of a woman who was already heated with wine, etc. I have respect for women; I couldn't say anything obscene to them. Whatever their depravity, I can't help blushing if I do violence to that modesty whose externals, at least, they should never lose. I think, my

[*] A woman of low position with whom General Delacroix, the artist's brother, had a liaison.

poor shy lad, that this is not the way to get on with the ladies. And perhaps Henry, the weary libertine, is more pleasing than another for this very reason. There were not, in the entire gathering, two worthy people. My poor brother! You won't admit your sad state, even to yourself, and so your friends can't cure you.

At Paris, Tuesday, September 24.

I arrived here Sunday morning. I made the wretched journey atop the coach. Frightful cold and penetrating rain. I cannot say why the pleasure I was promising myself of seeing Paris once more waned as I approached. I embraced Pierret, and I find myself sad. The news of the day is to blame. During the day I went to see my picture at the Luxembourg and returned to dine with my friend. The next day I saw Edouard with much pleasure; he told me that he was studying Rubens passionately. I am enchanted. Edouard lacks color, above all, and I am rejoiced at those studies which will lead him to his true talent and to the success I am so eager to see him achieve. He has had no success at the Salon — it is a shame! We promised to see each other this winter.

Paris, October 5.

Fedel, Uncle Riesener and I, with Rouget, whom we took with us, went to see the prizes on exhibition. The torso and picture by Debay, Gros' star pupil, disgusted me with his master's way of teaching, and only yesterday I was still hankering after it.

My uncle seemed moved and charmed by my picture. They advise me to go on alone, and now I have a great mind to do so.

Something odd, which has bothered me all day, is that I have been thinking constantly of the suit I tried on this morning, which fitted me badly. I was looking at all the styles in the streets. I went with Fedel to the meeting at the Institute, where they gave out the prizes. I like Fedel a lot. I am sorry that he doesn't work harder.

My uncle has offered to take me to M. Gérard's. Do a water color after Van Ostade's *Winter Landscape,* and the *Painter in His Studio*

by I don't know whom, and some other little Flemish master besides.
Go to see the stage off, to make some studies of horses.

October 6.

It must not be thought that just because I rejected a thing once, I must
ignore it when it shows itself today. A book in which I had never found
anything worthwhile may have a moral, read with the eyes of a more
mature experience.

I am borne, or, rather, my energy is borne, in another direction.
I will be the trumpeter of those who do great things.

There is in me something that is often stronger than my body,
which is often enlivened by it. In some people the inner spark scarcely
exists. I find it dominant in me. Without it, I should die, but it will
consume me (doubtless I speak of imagination, which masters and
leads me).

When you have found a weakness in yourself, instead of dis-
sembling it, cut short your acting and idle circumlocutions — correct
yourself. If the spirit had merely to fight the body! But it also has
malign penchants, and a portion of it — the most subtle, most divine
—should battle the other unceasingly. The body's passions are all
loathsome. Those of the soul which are vile are the true cancers:
envy, etc. Cowardice is so loathsome it must needs be the child of body
and soul together.

When I have painted a fine picture, I haven't expressed a thought.
Or so they say. What fools people are! They deprive painting of all its
advantages. The writer says nearly everything to be understood. In
painting a mysterious bond is established between the souls of the
sitters and those of the spectator. He sees the faces, external nature;
but he thinks inwardly the true thought that is common to all people,
to which some give body in writing, yet altering its fragile essence.
Thus grosser spirits are more moved by writers than by musicians and
painters. The painter's art is all the more intimate to the heart of man
because it seems more material; for in it, as in external nature, justice is
done frankly to that which is finite and to that which is infinite — that

is, to whatever the soul finds to move it inwardly in the objects which affect the senses alone.

Paris, October 12.

I return from the *Marriage of Figaro* full of sublime ideas. . . . Found a letter from my brother.

I saw M. Hénin this morning. I am ever as bewildered as a little child. How unstable I am! In a single moment an idea upsets everything and turns the strongest resolutions topsy-turvy. Through an inner conscientiousness, I should not care to seem better than I am. But what's the use? Everyone is more disturbed by his least trouble than by the most signal disaster of a whole nation.

Do only what is exactly needed.—You are wrong.—Your imagination has misled you.

This music inspires me with splendid thoughts. I have a great desire to create when I hear it. What I lack, I fear, is patience. I would be a totally different man if I had the self-restraint to work like several people I know. I am too eager to get results.

We dined together — Charles, Piron, and I. Then to the Théâtre des Italiens. How deliciously these women move me! Their grace, their physique, all those divine charms I see but can never own, fill me equally with delight and chagrin.

I should like to resume piano and violin study.

I thought again of the lady of the Italiens.

Same evening, half past one at night.

I just saw Orion shining for a moment amid black clouds and a raging wind. I thought first of my vanity, in comparison with those suspended worlds. Then I thought of justice, of friendship, of the divine sentiments engraved on the heart of man, and I no longer found anything great in the world save man and his Creator. This idea impresses me. Can it be that He does not exist? Can chance, by combining certain elements, have created the virtues — reflections of an unknown grandeur? If chance had made the universe, what would *conscience, remorse,* and *devotion* signify? Oh, if you can believe, with all the strength of your being, in that God who invented duty, your indecision will be settled. For admit that it is always this life — fear for it or for your comfort—that troubles the fleeting days, which would pass peacefully, if, at the end of the journey, you saw the bosom of your Heavenly Father waiting to welcome you.

I must leave this to go to bed—but I have dreamed most pleasantly.

I see some progress in my study of horses.

Tuesday, October 22.

After helping Pierret home because of his bad knee, I sat down awhile. I could see his maid almost in half-profile: a charmingly pure and lovely profile. What a contrast a straight nose presents with the turned-up nose like that of his wife! There was a time when one of my weaknesses was thinking the turned-up nose a misfortune, and the straight nose a compensation for many disadvantages. They are actually ugly. It's a matter of instinct.

As usual, my slight build abashes me. I cannot see my nephew's beauty without feeling envy. I am often ill; I cannot speak for a long time.

This evening I again admired Riesener's little portrait of Félix. I am envious. Nevertheless, I should not care to change what I can do for that, but I should like to have his simplicity. It seems to me so difficult, without hard work, to paint the eye — the space between eyelash and eyebrow.

Last Tuesday morning, [October] 15, a little baggage named Marie — nineteen years old — came to pose. I took a big chance of a disease with her.

I went to see Henri Hugues. I read the taking of Constantinople with him. Admired the heroic courage of Constantine, the last emperor.

The next day, Wednesday, I had friends over in the evening. We had burnt brandy and hot wine to drink.

I want to paint *Milton and His Daughters* for the Society of the Friends of Art.

Sunday—the day before yesterday—dined with M. de Conflans, whom I had been to consult some days before. I had an amusing time. We sang from the score of the *Marriage of Figaro*.

I bought *Don Juan*. I am painting the portrait of a woman in exchange for some engravings. I have resumed my violin.

I always let myself blush; I haven't enough poise. I suffer for the model, and I don't observe closely enough before actually starting to paint.

My sister returned Tuesday evening.

Sunday, October 27.

My beloved Soulier is back. I greeted him today. The first moment was all happiness for his return. Then I felt a pang. As I was about to ask him over to my rooms, I thought of an accursed letter whose writing he would have recognized. I hesitated. That chilled the joy I got out of seeing him again. I tried shams — I pretended to have lost my key. Any pretext. At last I put him off. He left, promising to meet me again this evening. We went for a walk. I hope that my wrong to him will not affect his relations with J. . . .[5] May the good Lord keep him from ever knowing about the affair! And why do I, this very moment, feel something like satisfied vanity? Oh! if he knew anything, I would be desolate. He busies himself with music; this pleases me. I am promising myself some charming evenings. I had noted that it was difficult for happy impressions, intensely felt, to recur under the same circumstances and to the same people. I still do not see what would prevent the charming moments spent with him, which I have treasured so tenderly in my heart, from returning. Yet, I feel a kind of sadness. He is not my sort of man. Also, I know what annoys me, when I am near him: It is something about which I have made up my mind and

⁵ Soulier's mistress, a woman of fashion, who, during his absence in Florence, deceived him with Delacroix. The latter seems to have retained a deep affection for her during several years.

want to hear about as little as possible. Yesterday I spoke to M——
about it. He agrees with me: There is some sort of trickery involved.
He considers us free. Since this conversation with him, I am more carefree. I dined with him and two friends, Guillemardet and Champion.
Then Mme Pasta in *Romeo,* which I saw again with pleasure.

Yesterday I saw Edouard and Lopez at Mauzaisse's studio. Superb
atelier. The idea came to me that there was no need to have such fine
surroundings in order to do good things. Perhaps the contrary.

I was still undecided, these past days, whether I would go to see the
lady of the Italiens. Every time I go there, I recall it with rapture. I
dream of her — joys beyond attainment and of which I can but dream
— a token of another life. My happiness was wan enough when I had
it — today it is colored by imagination; it is that which evokes my
sorrows and my joys.

I think I dined at Uncle Pascot's Thursday or Friday. I had not
drunk much, but enough to be dizzy. It is a pleasant state to be in, no
matter what the puritans say. Félix was there; Henri showed up later.

1823

Paris, Tuesday, April 15, 1823.

I RESUME my undertaking after a long lapse of time. I believe it is a way of calming the emotions that have troubled me so long. I think I see that, since Soulier's return, I am more troubled, less master of myself. I am as frightened as a child. All my troubles are combined, that of my expenses as well as the use of my time. Today I made several good resolutions. Let these pages, at least, if my memory fails, reproach me for forgetting them — a folly that has served only to make me unhappy.

If M. Verninac of Marseilles does not remedy my sister's situation in some way, I shall go to live with her. I want more than anything else under the sun to give my nephew a great eagerness for work and that extreme fortitude inspired by an unhappy and insecure position. Until that is settled, I want to fence; that will help to regulate my life from day to day.

Today I was lost in admiration of Andrea del Sarto's *Charity*. This painting really moves me more than Raphael's *Holy Family*. One can paint well in so many styles. How noble, elegant, and strong his children are! And his women — what a head — and the hands! I should like to have time to copy it. That would be a reminder for me, so that in copying from nature without the influence of the masters, I should remember that one ought to have a grander style.

I must absolutely begin to draw horses. I must go to the stables every morning, go to bed very early, and get up very early.

"I believed that I could see you again with impunity.[1] I had hoped that you would receive me coldly. Through kindness you have not done so. Why make two people wretched? I almost thought I had forgotten

[1] Draft of a letter to J.

46

you. Whatever your feelings for him, he is your friend and your family's friend.[2] He can see you when he wishes.[3]

"I ought not to have seen you again — yet all is reawakened in me! In your kindness you did not receive me coldly. What can come of it — endless torments which already have begun for me? A sharing! Whatever your feeling for another, he is your friend and your family's. How could I pace back and forth under your windows while he is with you? I had counted on my will power, but you have ruined everything. It doesn't matter. Deprived of seeing you, I will cherish the memory of your last good-bye. You, too, remember a loving friend.

"Why did you welcome me the way you did? To bring me back to my madness!"

It was Saturday, May 10, when I saw her again. I shall not say how she received me: I shall remember. This has troubled me greatly.

I am completely calm now. Jealousy was beginning to growl. I dined with Pierret the same day.

Friday, May 16.

Today I saw Laribe and brought him the description of the subject matter for my proposed picture, derived from the history of France. What I foresaw is happening. They will stall, they will prune the idea, eliminate competitors. I spoke to him unceremoniously, perhaps too much so. I fell back on the promise of an order for a church, but as a man who had little faith in the scheme. He answered me like a man who scarcely wants to do the same.

Fortify yourself against first impressions; preserve your presence of mind.

Neither the ardent promises of your best friends nor the offers of service by the powerful nor the interest a man of honor accords you ought to make you believe that there is anything real in what they say, as to results, I mean: because so many promisers mean well when they

---

[2] Soulier.
[3] The first paragraph is crossed out, and the letter begun over again in the next.

are talking with you, like false heroes, or those folk who start up in a fury, like women, but whose ardor evaporates on the approach of action. On your side, be prudent in receiving more particularly those absurd attentions that are merely the fruit of a momentary whim.

Habitual orderliness of ideas is your sole road to happiness, and to reach it, orderliness in all else, even the most casual things, is needed.

How weak I am, how vulnerable and open to surprise on all sides, when I am face to face with those people who do not speak aimlessly, and whose resolution is always ready to support the word with the deed! . . . But are there any such, and haven't people often taken me for a man of firm will? The mask is everything. I must admit that I fear them, and is there anything more ruinous than being afraid? Even the most constant man is by nature a poltroon, when his ideas are wavering, and presence of mind, the first of his defences, comes only when surprise has no access to the soul, which has seen everything beforehand. I know that this determination is immense, but by dint of going back to it, one naturally advances a great deal.

I saw Sidonie last Tuesday. Ravishing moments! How lovely she was, nude and in bed! Mainly, kisses, delightful games. . . .

She returns Monday.

Géricault[4] came to see me Wednesday, the day before yesterday. I was upset by his coming: how absurd! Thence to the royal riding school, where I tarried to no great good; then to see Cogniet.

In the evening to the Fieldings.[5]

Yesterday, Thursday, Taurel came to see me; he made me yearn

[4] Théodore Géricault (1791–1824), though only seven years older than Delacroix, was as much his teacher as his comrade. They had both studied under Guérin. Delacroix had posed for one of the figures in *The Raft of the Medusa*. In 1820 Géricault passed on to Delacroix the order for a picture afterward placed in the Cathedral of Ajaccio.

[5] Four English artists, brothers. They were Theodore, Copley, Thales, and Newton Fielding. Delacroix came to know them through Soulier. Thales, whom he knew best, induced him to come to England in 1824.

for Italy. Dined with Félix — long talk at Monceaux and on the way back. Some of the above ideas are its fruit.

Here are some of the silly things I wrote down some days ago, in pencil, while working on my little picture of *Phrosine and Melidor*. This was after a session of high jinx which had given me a moderate dose of bad humor.

"Why have you not received me as coldly as you love me? What rights have I over you? Why do you want to see me? You tell me to come to see you! What sharing, O heavens! Leaving you, I flattered myself that your eyes had told me the truth. It sufficed to treat me as a friend: it was the least concession. Further, what have I asked for? I would be a sorry sort if I had returned to you in the hope of loving and being loved. I thought I had completely conquered. I was counting, above all, on your help. What was the meaning in your eyes?

"You were cruel enough to kiss me! Do you think that I will live with this man if I begin loving you, or that I will suffer him near you, where out of pity, no doubt, you will grant him everything? This pity does not suit a loving heart. My heart is not so soft. Do you therefore despise me? . . ."

Now I am no longer mad. Socrates says we must fight love with flight.

I should read *Daphnis and Chloe:* It is one of the old stories we must willingly tolerate.

Don't forget the allegory of the *Man of genius at the portals of the tomb*, and of *Savagery dancing around the pyre*, in which the Mohammedan followers of Omar throw books, holy effigies, and the man himself. A suspicious eye follows his last sigh, and the harpy holds him by his mantle or winding sheet. As for him, he throws himself into the arms of Truth, the supreme deity. His regret is deep, for he leaves error and stupidity behind him — but he goes to find rest. One might use Tasso to personify him. His shackles fall off and remain in the monster's hands. The crown of immortality escapes his attacks and the poison which drools from his lips onto the pages of the poem.

Saturday, May, 1823.

I return from a fine walk with my dear friend Pierret. We spoke, of course, of those delicious follies that interest us so much. At present I am mad about the lovely figure of Mme de Puységur's maid. Since her employment in the house, I have greeted her in a friendly way. The day before yesterday, in the evening, I met her on the boulevard; I had just paid some fruitless calls. She was walking arm-in-arm with a girl also in service at her mistress'. I had a good notion to take them under my wing. A thousand stupid considerations crossed my mind, and all the time I was getting farther and farther away from them, telling myself angrily that I was a fool and should profit by the occasion . . . to speak to her, hold her hand, anything . . . finally, to do something. But her girl friend — two servant-girls at my side — I could scarcely stand them to ices at Tortoni's. So I walked off most hurriedly to M. Hénin's, where I was informed of his return. Then at last, when it was too late to overtake them, I ran after them and walked uselessly around the boulevards.

Yesterday I went with Champmartin[6] to study the dead horses. I nearly went with him to the brothel with our friend Sanson, who luckily was not at home. I say luckily, though I wanted to go at the time. But men don't know what they ought to desire. On my return, little Fanny was with our estimable janitress, Mme F. . . . I settled down, talked a good hour, and contrived to go upstairs when she did. I felt in all my being the deep and delicious thrill that ushers in joyful times. My foot pressed against her foot and her leg. My emotion was delightful. Putting my foot on the first step of the stair, I did not know yet what I was going to say or do, but I anticipated something decisive — I put my arms tenderly around her waist. The landing gained, I

[6] Charles-Henri Callande de Champmartin (1792–1883), a pupil of Guérin's, one of the good portrait-painters of the time, remained a life-long friend of Delacroix's.

embraced her warmly and pressed my lips to hers. She did not repulse me. She said she was afraid to be seen. Should I have gone further? How cold words are in painting the emotions! I kissed her again and again, I pressed her to me time and time again. Finally, I left her, promising myself to see her the next day. Alas! It is today — I have had but a single thought all day. I have seen her, but I don't know what she means to do. She seemed to shun me or to feign not to see me. Tonight, this very minute, my door is ajar — I hope for I know not what . . . that which cannot happen. I foresee an infinitude of obstacles. But how sweet it all could be! This is not love: That's too much to call it — a strange, nervous tickling moves me when my thoughts are concerned with a woman. For she is not very attractive, as a matter of fact. Nevertheless, I will treasure the delightful memory of her lips pressed to mine.

I want to write her a little note that demands a reply, then another. I don't have to write anything she can take seriously. I will simply tell her, considering how rarely we see one another, to write me when I can see the portrait she promised to show me. O folly, folly! Folly that we love and would escape! No! This is not happiness. It is better than happiness, or it is very poignant misery. Wretch that I am! If I really should fall passionately in love with a woman! My craven heart does not dare to prefer the peace of an indifferent soul to the delicious and excruciating pangs of a tumultuous passion. Flight is the sole remedy. But we persuade ourself that there will be time to flee, and one would be indeed desperate to flee even misery itself.

I was with Pierret this evening to retouch a family portrait poor old Petit was finishing when he died. I felt a throb of pain in this humble refuge of a poor old painter who was not without talent, and at the sight of the wretched work of his languishing old age.

I decided to paint scenes from the *Massacre at Scio*[7] for the Salon. I go to see Cousin tomorrow.

[7] Exhibited at the Salon of 1824, bought by the government for six thousand francs. Now in the Louvre.

Monday, June 9.

Why not profit by the antidotes of civilization — good books? They strengthen and diffuse serenity through the soul. I cannot doubt that which is truly good, but with zealots and plotters, caution is needed.

Too often do we reproach ourselves with having changed: It is the object itself that has changed. What is more desolating? I have two, three, maybe four friends. So! I have to be a different man with each of them or, rather, to show to each the face he recognizes. It is one of the greatest calamities that one can never be known and sensed completely by one and the same man; and when I think of it, I believe that here is the sovereign evil of life — it is this inevitable loneliness to which the heart is doomed. A wife of your own stature is the greatest of all blessings. I should prefer her superior to me in all ways, rather than the contrary.*

Sunday, November 9.

Saw my darling again.[s] She came to my studio. I am much more tranquil and yet most deliciously thrilled. I am mildly dear (as she understands the expression) to her, for I am convinced that she has for me approximately the same tender feeling I have for her. Strange emotion! I held her leg and even ventured to move along up. *Eh bien!* In the evening I went to the house of Mme——, my cousin, and all the time never ceased to. . . . Dear lady, at least do not try to awaken new torments in my heart. . . . I found so many things to tell her when she was no longer there. It seemed to me that the secret told all, since there is no longer a question of making anyone unhappy. But I no longer wish her to tell me that she loves me while she has dealings with someone else.

I also saw Piron that evening. . . . I see *her* again Thursday.

God! but things are in arrears! And my little Emilie. Already she

---

* This page retraces the emotions connected with that idea. I should like to go through life with it; it is good. [Marginal note written by Delacroix at a later date.]

[s] This is still J.

is forgotten — I do not speak of her. I had charming times with her.

I was with her last Monday, the same day I went to see Régnier, where I saw a sketch by Constable[9]— an admirable bit, unbelievably fine.

I finished a design for *Scio* this week, and almost finished one for *Tasso*.

November 10.

"I want only a woman[10] who has the candor, with a man who is her friend, to explain herself, just as men do to each other. Why did you come to the Rue de Grenelle? It was more than mere courtesy. It's uncertainty that I hate most. Tell me, dear friend, that we are equally dear to you. Why blush? Is woman made differently than we are? Do we hesitate to court someone who captivates us momentarily? So, declare your love. Say that your heart is big enough for two friends, since neither of us is your lover. Then I won't be jealous; then, I believe, I will not think myself guilty in possessing you. I should like to be your master in all respects. With what delight I have pressed you to my heart! Your own words rang true. You said to me, 'How long it has been since I have seen you thus, dear friend'! Ah, never more to see you! Can I not, if you are ill, come myself for news of you? Is there no way through your brother?"

And you, my poor friend: You are to be pitied. One does not suffer what you suffer. I think I am happier, for at least I am satisfied with myself. She does not blame us at all for abandoning each other. "I leave it to your discretion," she said. I sincerely hope that he can stop loving her. Thus Thursday I await her impatiently, but afterwards there will be nothing further. As for her, she has decided, very simply, to dispense with me. Let her tell me that herself, and my mind will be at rest. Can no one suggest to her brother or her godchild to invite me?

[9] As is so often told, the art of Constable made a great impression on Delacroix, and caused him to repaint the sky and other parts of the *Massacre at Scio* at the last moment.

[10] J. again.

December 17.

"I have only now received your letter. For some days I remained at home and did not go to my studio. J., your memory will be ever dear to me, and what you suffer I suffer with you. I too have my vexations, and a battle to wage against more than one kind of adversity. Time, need — both press and gall me. Do not add to these hardships the idea I am indifferent to what affects you. Lately you were so kind as to be interested in me, though in vain. I would have been to see you, but I feared that you might, on that occasion, interpret my visit as a mere act of politeness, such as people do. Now I can thank a friend whole-heartedly. You may well imagine that I have not waited on your letter to get news of you. Your poor child! I pity you very much. Farewell! My sad face could scarcely console you. Farewell and tender regards."

December 22 or 23, midnight.

I return home with feelings of goodwill and resignation to fate. I passed the evening with Pierret and his wife in their modest home. We resign ourselves to poverty. In fact, when I complain of it, I am outside of myself, outside of the state proper to me. One needs, for wealth, the kind of talent I don't have at all, and when one hasn't it at all, there must be something else to supply the lack. Let us do everything calmly, let us react emotionally only to fine works of art or noble deeds. Let us work tranquilly and without haste. As soon as I begin to sweat and my blood to boil, beware. Cowardly painting is the painting of a coward.

    I am going to see Leblond tomorrow evening. I quite enjoy these evenings, and besides, I like Leblond very much. He is a good friend. Last Saturday I spent the evening at Perpignan's. English tea, punch, ices, etc., pretty girls, etc.

Tuesday, December 30.

Today with Pierret. I had a date at the Friends of Art to go to see a picture gallery, almost all Italian, among which is M. Guérin's *Marcus Sextus*. We were late, thinking that we had but one canvas to see and that we should find these old pictures mediocre. On the contrary, few pictures, but these admirably chosen, and above all, a Michelangelo cartoon. O sublime genius! How stamped with majesty are the features, though almost effaced by time! I felt a passion for great things aroused in me once more. Let us, from time to time, gain renewed strength from great and beautiful creations. This evening I worked on my Dante again. Decidedly, I was not born to paint stylish pictures.

Leaving there, we went to a dyer's where we saw a girl whose figure and head were wholly in accord with the feelings those lovely Italian works had inspired in me. If I can, I shall return there often. There are some admirable Venetian portraits. A Raphael and a Correggio. . . . And Raphael's beautiful *Holy Family!*

This evening Félix came to see me — he had arrived this morning or last night. What a good friend he is! We talked most pleasantly all evening. Tomorrow, Saint Sylvester's Day. The year is ending. Last Saturday — the 27th. . . . Dined with Edouard and Lopez at the picture restorer's. In the evening they introduced me to M. Lelièvre, their friend. I accompanied Edouard to his door. Much talk and good fellowship.

Meanwhile I have sold my wretched *Ivanhoe* to M. Coutan, the collector of Scheffer's work. Poor man! And he says he will buy others from me. I am much more inclined to believe that he is not greatly pleased with this one.

Some days ago I was at Géricault's in the evening. What a sad time! He is dying — his emaciation is horrible. His thighs are as big as my arms. His head is that of an aged and dying man. I sincerely want him to live, but I no longer hope. What a frightful change! I recall that I returned full of enthusiasm for his painting, especially a study for the head of a rifleman. Remember it. It is a landmark. What beautiful studies! What firmness! What superiority! And to die amid all that one has created in all the vigor and passion of youth, when one cannot move an inch in bed without the help of others!

Thursday, January 1.

As is ever the case, if I remember rightly, I carried away from the fine New Year's Eve party Pierret gave us only a profound melancholy. Those serenades, above all, those trumpets and horns are suitable only for the fleeting moment, instead of preparing you joyfully for the coming one. This day — I mean *today* — is the saddest of the year; yesterday the year was not yet over. Edouard spent the evening with us. I saw Goubaux again — we talked over college days. . . . Several have become swindlers and have gone wrong.

Sunday, January 4.

Poor devil! Who can create grandly amid these everlasting links with all that is vulgar? Think of the great Michelangelo. Feed yourself on grand and severe ideas of beauty which feed the soul. I am ever turned from their study by foolish distractions. Seek solitude. If your life is well-ordered, your health will not fail.

Here is what the great Michelangelo wrote on the brink of the grave: "Borne on a frail bark to the middle of a stormy sea, I draw near to the close of my life. I touch the common bourne where everyone goes to account for the good or evil that he has done. Ah! how clearly I now perceive that art, my idol, the tyrant of my imagination, plunged it in error. All is error here below. Amorous thoughts, sweet and empty imaginings, what will become of you, now that I am doubly near to death — one that is certain, the other menacing me? No, sculpture, painting, cannot suffice to calm a soul turned towards divine love — a soul laved by sacred fire." (Verses at the end of his collected poems.)

Monday, January 12.

The *Massacre at Scio* all this last month.

After lunching with Raymond Verninac and M. Voutier, went to the Luxembourg. I returned to my studio bubbling over with enthusiasm, and, Hélène coming in a bit later, I made some studies for my picture one after another. Unhappily, she carried off part of the energy that I wanted for the day's work.

In the evening Dimier treated us to punch at Beauvilliers'.

Last Tuesday — January 6 — dined at Riesener's with Jacquinot and the daughter of the colonel, his brother. She does not have beautiful features, but I keenly wish to remember, and for a long time, her Italian face and, above all, that clearness of complexion (yet it isn't precisely a good complexion) and that purity of outline. I refer to that even texture and firmness of the skin that is peculiar to virgins. It is a valuable thing to keep in mind for painting, but I feel it slipping away already.

Yesterday, Sunday, [January] 11, dined at the house of Leblond's mistress — no impression except one of vulgarity. This past week did a sketch of the prefect.

I am really beginning my picture today—Monday, [January] 12.

Sunday, January 18.

Dined today at M. Lelièvre's with Edouard and Lopez. Fine, excellent fellows. Heavy discussion about the arts, and especially valiant efforts to clarify the worth of Raphael and Michelangelo.

Today, Emilie Robert.[1]

Yesterday — Saturday — and Friday — the day before yesterday, partially painted in or prepared the woman in the foreground.[2] Leblond visited my studio.

Yesterday — Saturday — *Don Giovanni,* played by Zucchelli. Spent Friday evening at Taurel's.

I had Provost, the model, Tuesday, [January] 13, and began with the head of the dying man in the foreground. The next day — Wednesday — and Thursday, [January] 15, at Mme Lelièvre's with Edouard in the evening. She has asked me to dine today.

To Provost, about . . . . 8 fr.
To Emilie Robert, today . . . . 12 fr.

I read recently, in the *Journal des Débats,* about an original book that treats all sorts of things. It is signed with a pseudonym, *Philemneste,* and tells that an English judge, wishing to live a long time, began to question all the old men he met on the kind of life they led and on their regimen and as to whether or not their longevity was due either to food or intoxicating liquor, etc. The only constant element among them was rising early in the morning and, above all, not taking a nap once they were awake. *Very important.*

Saturday, January 24.

Today I set to work on my picture again — I stopped work on it last Saturday, the 18th. The preceding Monday or, rather, Tuesday, the 13th, I had only done a few sketches. Today, I drew and painted in the head, breast, etc. of the dead woman in the foreground.

Again I had *la mia chiavatura dinanzi colla mia carina Emilia.* It did not slacken my eagerness for the work. You have to be young to do

[1] Model for the nude figure in the *Massacre at Scio.*
[2] The old woman in the *Massacre at Scio.*

both things at one time. With the exception of the hand and the hair, everything is finished.

This evening presented at M. Raoul's, and tomorrow to dine at Mme Lelièvre's. I said to Edouard this evening that, unlike most people who make their progress in the battle of life with the help of their reading, it happens that I have read only to sanction those things I have made part of myself. For since I have left college I have read nothing or, rather, I have never read. Further, I marvel at the fine things I come across in books; I am never bored or sated with them.

Yesterday — Friday, [January] 23 — I was to go to Taurel's in the evening. After leaving Rouget's, after dinner, laziness propelled me to the library, where I skimmed through the life of Rossini; I surfeited myself with it, and made a mistake in doing so. As a matter of fact, that Stendhal is rude, arrogant when he is right, and often nonsensical.

Rossini was born in 1792, the year of Mozart's death.

Sunday, January 25.

Dined today at M. Lelièvre's. A peppery colonel, prating of his exploits in Spain, bored us tremendously.

Returning with Edouard, I had more ideas than I had had all day. People who have ideas breed them in you. But my memory flits so from day to day that I am no longer master of anything, neither of the past, which I forget; nor scarcely of the present, when I am usually so immersed in one thing that I lose sight of what I should do, or fear that I shall — I am not even master of the future, since I am never sure but that my time has been disposed of in advance. I want to undertake to learn much by heart, in order to have my memory at my disposal. A man without a memory doesn't know on what to rely; everything betrays him. Many things I should like to have remembered from our conversation on the way home, have escaped me.

I was telling myself what a sad thing in our wretched condition it is to be constantly face to face with oneself. That is what makes the society of pleasant folk so charming; they make you believe, for an instant, that they are you to a certain extent, but then you fall back quickly enough into your unhappy unity. Thus, can the dearest friend, the woman most beloved and worthy of being so, never assume part of your burden? Yes, but only for a few moments. They have their own cross to bear.

I come back to another one of my ideas: the one that preceded the last. Every night, I said to Edouard, after leaving M. Lelièvre's, I return home in the frame of mind of a man to whom the most diverse events have happened. That too always leads to a state of mental chaos that stuns me. I am a hundred times more stupid, a hundred times more incapable, I believe, of busying myself with the most ordinary affairs than a peasant who has ploughed all day. I said to Edouard that one is interested in one's friends when they have made as much progress as oneself; the proof of this is that the charming events of life whose memory we cherish tenderly would not be very good to relive in actuality, and precisely in the way they occurred; witness the friends of childhood whom we see after a long time.

Today, as I was beginning the woman dragged along by the horse, I was visited by Riesener, Henri Hugues, and Rouget. Imagine how they treated *my poor creation,* which they saw in the most chaotic state, when I alone can guess how it is going to turn out. Look, as I said to Edouard: I have to battle against ill fortune and the idleness that is natural to me, I need my enthusiasm if I am to earn the bread I eat, and then a lot of mental paupers like those come, even into my den, to nip my inspirations in the bud and measure me with their glasses — they who would not deign to be Rubens! Happily — and I offer you my thanks for this, kind heaven — you give me the presence of mind I need in my poverty to keep at a distance the doubts their stupid criticisms often create in me. Even Pierret made some criticisms, but they affected me not in the least, for I know what my work needs. Henri was not as exacting as the other gentlemen.

After they left, I relieved my mind by a volley of curses on mediocrity, after which I got back to balance.

The praises of M. Rouget, who should not care to be Rubens, bored me. Meanwhile, he is borrowing my study, and I made the mistake of promising it to him. Perhaps it will be useful to me.

On returning to the studio, I thought of doing a pensive girl cutting a pen, and standing in front of a table.

Monday, January 26.

I gave Emilie Robert 1 2 francs for three sittings for my picture. Passed the evening at Félix's.

I forgot to note that I had a mind to keep a kind of memorandum-book on painting,[3] where I could set down the differences among the arts. For example, in music, form predominates over substance, in painting, quite the contrary is the case. One makes allowances for things that belong to all time, in favor of the beauties of genius.

Dufresne came to see me at my studio.

Ho fatto una chiavata graziosissima. I find in Mme de Staël the exact way I develop my ideas about painting. This art, and music also, are above thought; hence their advantage over literature, through their very vagueness.

Tuesday, January 27.

This morning I got a letter at my studio announcing the death of my poor Géricault. I cannot get used to the idea. In spite of the certainty everyone must have had of losing him soon, it seemed to me that we could almost conjure death away by keeping the idea out of our minds. But death did not forget its prey, and tomorrow the earth will hide the little that remains of him. What a different destiny so much bodily strength, so much fire and imagination, seemed to promise! Although he was not precisely my friend, this unhappiness pierces my heart. It made me leave my work and paint out everything that I had done.

[3] First mention of what was to be the *Dictionary of Painting* which Delacroix undertook in his later years and which is part of this *Journal.*

I dined at Tautin's with Soulier and Fielding. Poor Géricault, I will think of you very often! I imagine that your spirit will often come to hover about my work. . . . Farewell, poor young man! Your suffering is at an end, in any event.

From what Soulier told me, it seems that Gros spoke about me to Dufresne in a very favorable manner.

Tuesday morning, February 2.

I got up about seven o'clock. A thing I ought to do more often. Ignorant, common people are very happy. Everything in nature is plainly laid out for them. They understand whatever there is, because there it is. And, for that matter, are they not more reasonable than all the dreamers, who go so far that they suspect even their own thoughts? Suppose their friend dies? According to their conception of death, they do not add to the grief of tears that cruel anxiety of not being able to explain so natural a happening. He was living, he no longer lives; he spoke to me, his spirit heard mine: nothing of all that is left. Except that grave. Is he resting in that grave, as cold as the tombstone itself? Does his spirit wander round his tomb? And, when I am thinking of him, does his spirit still stir my memory? Habit reduces everyone to the level of the common people. When the prints are effaced, he is dead, and so the thing no longer upsets us. Wise men and thinkers seem much less advanced than ignorant people, since what would serve them as proof is not even proved for them. I am a man. What is this *I*? What is *a man*? They spend half their life in attacking piece by piece, in verifying, whatever they find; the other half in building the foundations of an edifice that never rises above the level of the ground.

Tuesday, February 17.

Today dined at Tautin's with Fielding and Soulier. I am making progress in my English.

Today painted the drapery of the woman in the corner; yesterday, retouched her. Also did the foot and hand of the woman on her knees.

Gave Marie Aubry, after Géricault's
   death . . . . 7 or 8 francs
To the beggar-woman who had posed
   for the study in the cemetery 7
To old Nassau 5
To young Nassau 1.50
To Jucar 5
To Emilie Robert, Monday, Sunday,
   Saturday, February . . . . 12, 14, 15, and 16

Midnight is striking. Time to go to bed.

Friday, February 20.

Every time that I see the engravings of *Faust*,[4] I feel overcome with a desire to use a totally new style of painting, which would tend, so to speak, to a literal tracing of the outlines in nature. Through the extreme variety of the foreshortenings one could lend interest to the simplest of poses; thus, for small pictures one could draw in the subject and rub in the color on the canvas, and then copy the exact pose from the model. I ought to try this in what work remains for me on my picture.

   Today I began to sketch what still remains to be done.
   Gave Milie . . . . 3 francs

Sunday, February 22.

Dined at Riesener's with Henri Hugues, who came to fetch me at the studio.

   Sketched the background, with Soulier.

Tuesday, February 24.

Had Bergini today: 5 francs. Used him for a sketch of the man on horseback, and redid the man lying down. The intoxication of work.

   In the evening, at Pierret's. The Salon put off.

[4] He refers to the twelve plates by Peter von Cornelius which had appeared in 1810.

Friday, February 27.

Dined at Perpignan's.

What pleases me is that I am acquiring reason without losing the emotions evoked by beauty. I certainly do not want to deceive myself, but it seems to me that I am working more calmly than ever before, and I have the same love for my work. One thing distresses me, and I do not know its cause; I need distractions, such as gatherings of friends, etc. As to the enticements that disturb most people, I have never been disquieted by them, and today less than ever. Who would believe it? What are most real to me, are the illusions that I create with my painting. The rest is shifting sand.

My health is bad, as capricious as my imagination.

Yesterday and today, painted the legs of the young man in the corner. What thanks do I not owe heaven for not plying any of those charlatan's trades, which are used in order to impress the human race! I can laugh at them, anyhow.

Thursday, February 28.

Painted the head of the youth in the corner.

To Nassau	11 fr. 50
To Prévost	1 fr. 50

I was thinking of the happiness Gros has had of being entrusted with works so suitable to his kind of ability.

This evening I have the desire to make some sketches for Goethe's *Götz von Berlichingen*, about which Pierret spoke to me.

Monday, March 1.

I have not worked at all today.

Wrote to Philarète Chasles the following:

"I can imagine your extreme amazement: 'What, that painter fellow writing me! *Che impensata novità!* And why so?' Perhaps you

Study of a Nude Model (1823). Collection of Dr. Viau, Paris

Study for The Massacre at Scio (1824). The Louvre

Horse Frightened by a Storm (1824). Museum of Buda-Pesth

A Tiger (probably 1830). Private Collection, New York

An Arab (1832). Collection of Walter Pach, New York

Moorish Musicians (1833). The C. W. Kraushaar Art Galleries, New York

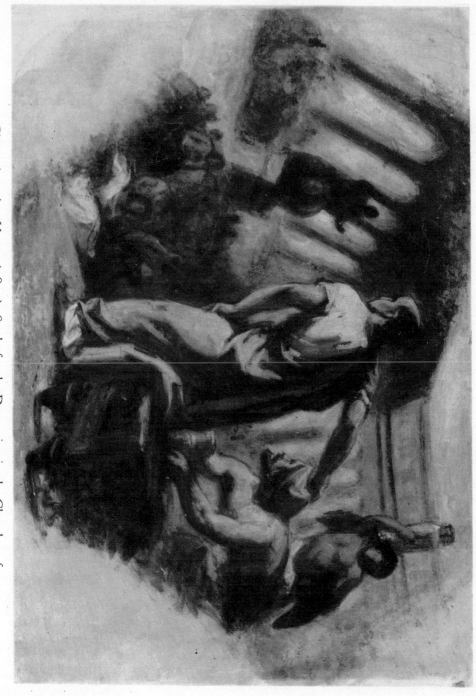

Cicero Accusing Verres (1844). Study for the Decoration in the Chamber of Deputies, Paris. Private Collection, New York

Study for a Ceiling in the Hôtel de Ville, Paris, which was destroyed in 1871
(this sketch was made between 1849 and 1853). Collection of
Mr. Grenville L. Winthrop, New York

make it too complicated, while the most natural explanation escapes you.

"I am writing you, my old friend, for reasons we formerly understood better. We have both progressed in that career that unrolls its measured way before us. Certain feelings become absurd. On the contrary, the objects our naive imaginations so philosophically disdained when we were sixteen or seventeen years old have become the very serious objects of our worship. I have spent the evening re-reading all my old letters, for I am more addicted to keeping things than a Senate, and that keeps only its plaster casts. While you are at the Opéra ball (or at least I suppose you are), at two o'clock in the morning I am buried in sweet and affecting memories. In the old days, you were disgusted with life and the so-called vanities of life; today, I have caught your malady of that period, and probably you have caught the philosophical carelessness I used to have then. Nevertheless, what am I doing with these letters? And Sousse? In reading one from him my heart bled at the thought of all which that man inspired in me. This life of ours, so brief for the slightest undertakings, is an arduous and long-winded test of human friendships. In the career you pursue, you cannot find many friends, and, above all friends for life, as we were with Sousse, before reality changed each of our lives. If you find friends, so much the better; you are happier than I. In spite of fleeting coolnesses, I think we must, at long intervals and by fleeting signs, keep our friends. Above all, let us enjoy our friendship while it can still be disinterested. If you were a minister of state, I would not have written to you this evening. I would have re-read your letters, stifled my emotion, and said, 'He's a dead man — think no more of it.' I am not saying that I would sooner have written to my old comrade who had lagged behind, had I been the minister of state or the *parvenu*. The human heart is an ugly pigsty; I am not to blame. But who dares to answer for himself? Write me, make my heart open to certain emotions of youth — which come no more. Even if this would be only an illusion, it would still be a pleasure. Farewell, etc."

I re-read also some letters from Elizabeth Salter. What a strange effect, after so long a time!

Found Philarète's letter with the theme for a *Death of Bias* at the age of eighty-five. After having defended vehemently, at the Theban bar, a friend accused of a capital crime, Bias died with his head resting on his daughter's knees.

Wednesday, March 3.

This morning, at the Luxembourg. I am amazed at Girodet's inaccuracy, especially in the young man in his *Deluge*. This man knows literally nothing about draughtsmanship.

Was at Emilie Robert's. Unwell. Stomach trouble.

Not knowing what else to do, I planned the *Condemned at Venice*.[5] Emilie dropped in, and I made use of the occasion; this made me feel somewhat better.

Work hard at your picture. Think of Dante. Re-read him. Constantly exert yourself to return to great ideas. What fruit can I reap from my almost complete solitude, if I have only commonplace ideas?

Yesterday, on the go, invited to Dec[amps';][6] terrible painting. Saw Edouard. Once more felt a desire to paint the *Castaways* of Lord Byron, but to paint them on the seashore, in safety.

Was at Henri Scheffer's in the evening.

Today, Wednesday. This evening, I came home from Leblond's. Fine evening party; he had done an uncommon thing: punch, etc. Some music that pleased me. Dufresne is scarcely ever dull.

Am I really such a poor thing? It takes the prods of a pitchfork to stir me; I go to sleep when these stimulants are lacking.

Thursday, March 4.

Today, went to see Champion. Dined with him.

Fedel came to see me at the studio. Dined together. In the evening

[5] First thought for the *Marino Faliero*, which is now in the Wallace Collection.

[6] Probably Decamps, who was very young at the time; later on Delacroix praised him highly.

to *Moïse en Egypte,*[1] alone; I found many delights in it. La Bonsignori recalled certain dear features to my mind. Admirable music! One must go alone to enjoy it. Music is the luxury of the imagination.

Medea engrosses me. Also some theme from *Moïse,* for example, the Scene of the *Shadows.*

Friday, March 5.

Did the head and torso of the young girl fastened to the horse. *Dolce chiavatura.* Dined with Soulier and Fielding and went to the Ambigu to see *Les Aventuriers;* very interesting and done in a new style. Natural.

The impression of *Moïse* still remains, and I have the desire to see it again.

Saturday, March 6.

I passed the day at my studio. Emilie R. *Chiavatura anche.* Bad work. Dined with Fielding and Soulier at Tautin's.

Thought of doing some scenes from *Jane Shore* and the plays of Otway.

At Tautin's met Fedel and some other friends who were on their way out. Agreed that we would go around together sometimes. To do some incidents of the Inquisition. *Philip II.*

Sunday, March 7.

Saw Mayer a moment about Pasta's portrait. It's not very good.

Fielding and Soulier at my studio. Fielding arranged my background for me.

Leblond dropped in with his sweetheart, and in the evening was at Pierret's. Excellent tea and puns all evening long.

Thursday, March 18.

Finished the *Turk Mounting a Horse.*

Friday, March 19.

Spent an excellent day at the Museum with Edouard. The Poussins! The Rubens! and, above all, Titian's *Francis I!* Velásquez.

[1] Opera by Rossini.

Afterwards, saw the Goyas, at my studio, with Edouard. Then saw Piron. Met Fedel. Dined together.

A good day.

Thursday, March 25.

Was with Leblond to look at pictures. Titian's *Marchesa di Pescara* and an admirable Velasquez, which engrosses my mind completely.

Saturday, March 27.

Early to the studio. Lopez. Pierret came there. Dined at his place; read some Horace. Longing for poetry, no reference to Horace. Allegories. Reveries. Singular situation of man! An endless subject. Create, create!

Yesterday, Tuesday, March 30.

In the morning, at my studio.

The repairing of my stove made me take a walk to the Museum, admired Poussin, then Paolo Veronese, standing on a stool.

Tried to repaint the head of the dying man.

In the evening, at Pierret's. A good evening discussing good things. In the evening, on return, received the unpleasant news from Thiffeneau.

Wednesday, March 31.

At Leblond's. Returned in the evening with Dufresne. He infused me with a new ardor. Spoke of Veronese: he too portrays strong emotion.

I must eat little and work alone in the evening. I believe that seeing society people, or merely people, from time to time, is not such a danger to work and the progress of the mind as it is claimed to be by many pretended artists; to consort with them is certainly more dangerous. Their whole talk is on a low level; I must return to solitude. Moreover, I must live soberly as Plato did. How is one to retain one's enthusiasm about anything when one is at all times at the mercy of other people, and when one has constant need of their society? Dufresne is right: the things one experiences when alone with oneself are much stronger and much fresher. Whatever the pleasure of communicating one's emotion to a friend, there are too many nuances to explain to oneself though perhaps each feels them, but in his own way, which thus weakens each one's impression. Since he advises me, and since I acknowledge the necessity, to see Italy alone and to live alone, when I am established there, let us begin from now on to get accustomed to such a program: every happy reform will be born of it. Memory will return and presence of mind, and order, too.

Today Emilie. *Due chiavature . . . ossia una prima, poi una . . .* 5 francs.

Dufresne said, about Charlet, that he was not sufficiently simple in his way of working: that he makes you feel his cleverness and his processes. Something to think about.

Thursday, April 1.

This morning was with Champmartin at Cogniet's, where I lunched.

I have seen the death mask of my poor Géricault. O revered monument! I was tempted to kiss it. His beard, his eyelashes. . . . And his sublime *Raft.*[8] What hands, what heads! I cannot express the admiration it inspires in me.

Paint with small, short brushes. Beware of oil washes.

I got the desire to make a sketch of Géricault's picture. Let us hurry to do it. What a sublime model and what a precious reminder of that extraordinary man.

Saturday, April 3.

Today, to Emilie, 8 francs: *chiav.* Was with Decamps at the Duc d'Orléans' to see his picture gallery. Charmed with Schnetz's picture of the wife of the brigand. Met Steuben. Want to do some little pictures, particularly in order to buy something at the Géricault sale.

In the evening, *Jane Shore.*

Sunday, April 4.

I am completely concerned with my need to retreat further into solitude. The loveliest and most precious moments of my life flow away in distractions which, at bottom, bring me nothing but boredom. The

[8] *The Raft of the Medusa,* Géricault's masterpiece.

possibility or the expectation of being interrupted is already beginning to impair the little strength left to me by the badly spent hours of the night before. Memory, having nothing important to exercise itself on, perishes or languishes. I beguile the hours with fruitless projects. A thousand precious thoughts miscarry through lack of continued effort. They devour me, they give me up to pillage. The enemy is within the walls, in the heart; he stretches forth his hand everywhere. Think of the wealth that awaits you, instead of the emptiness that constantly carries you outside of yourself, away from inner satisfaction and a clear memory; think of the presence of mind a well-regulated life affords; health that will not be shattered by endless concessions to passing excesses that the society of others entails; and then the steady, plentiful work.

I have been to my studio. Scheffer came and began his portrait. Dined together at Bossi's. It does not matter by the way and in this way. Last year, it was the habit of going to those dinners on certain fixed and expected days which was so harmful.

I must get the *Panhypocrisiade*.[9] I could make some drawings from it. Also a series on *René*, also on *Melmoth the Wanderer*.[10]

Try to recover the artlessness of the little portrait of my nephew.

Wednesday, April 7.

Worked on the little *Don Quixote*. In the evening, Leblond, and tried some lithography. Superb ideas for that subject. Caricatures in Goya's manner.

The first and most important thing in painting is the contours. The rest could be quite ignored since, if they are there, the painting is strong and finished. I, more than others, need to check up on myself on this matter: think constantly of it and always begin that way.

[9] Satirical poem by Népomucène Lemercier.

[10] A novel by an English author, Robert Maturin. In 1831, Delacroix derived from it the subject of his picture *L'Amende Honorable,* now in the Willstach Collection, Philadelphia.

It is to this that Raphael owes his finish, and so does Géricault, often.

I have just re-read hurriedly all the preceding: I deplore the gaps. It seems to me that I am still master of the days I have set down, though they are passed. But those not mentioned in this paper are as if they had never been.

In what depths am I plunged? Need this weak and fragile paper turn out to be, through my human frailty, the sole monument of existence that remains to me? The future is all black. The past that has not been preserved is the same. I grumble at being obliged to have recourse to that; but why always be shocked at my weakness? Can I pass a day without sleeping and without eating? That is for the body. But my mind and the record of my soul, all that will be annihilated, because I do not want to owe what remains of them to the obligation of writing. On the contrary, nothing is better than the doing of a little chore that recurs daily.

A single occupation, periodically fixed in a life, orders all the rest of that life: all tends to revolve around that. In preserving the story of what I experience, I live doubly; the past will return to me. The future is always there.

Begin to sketch many men of my time. Many medals,[11] for the sake of the nude.

The people of the present time: Michelangelo and Goya. Lemercier, not Charlet. The lash of satire.

Read the *Panhypocrisiade.*

Thursday, April 8.

I'll soon be in financial straits. I must work hard. Worked on *Don Quixote.*

Tancredi, in the evening. Moderately entertained. Poppleton and Soulier came to see me.

Bought some German engravings of the time of Louis XIII.

[11] Delacroix's admirable lithographs after antique medals date from 1825; many of them do contain nude figures.

Friday, [April] 9.

Today, Bergini. Gave him 3 francs. Redid the man in the corner. In the evening, Pierret. Finished the *Leicester*.

Instead of another picture of fairly large size, it occurs to me to do several little pictures, but all labors of love.

I still have about 240 francs. Pierret owes me 20 francs.

Today, lunched on eggs and bread . . .	0 fr. 30
To Bergini	3 fr.
Belot, paints	1 fr. 50
Dinner	1 fr. 20
Total . . .	6 fr.

Saturday, [April] 10.

At the studio early. Hélène came with her pals. Bergini. Retouched the man clinging to the horse. To him, 3 francs.

Dined with Poppleton, Lelièvre, Comairas, Soulier, and Fedel. Was at Comairas'. Astonishing painting. A little drinking-bout. This evening my hand could scarcely write.

Discussed philosophy in the street with that fool of a Fedel.

Dinner	2 fr.
Engraving	1 fr. 16
	3 fr. 16
Bergini	3 fr.
Total . . .	6 fr. 16

In the morning, Pierret dropped in. Comairas came for the horse's head. Luncheon.

At the Luxembourg: *Rebels of Cairo,* by Girodet, full of vigor, great style. Ingres charming and then my picture,[12] which gave me great pleasure. There is still a defect that turns up in what I am doing,[13] especially in the woman bound to the horse; it lacks vigor, the full depth of the paint. The contours are still a wash, and not clean-cut. I must remember this constantly.

Worked at the studio touching up the kneeling woman.

Saw the Velasquez and got permission to copy it. I am carried away with it completely. It has what I have been looking for so long — an impasto that is firm and yet blended. What I must chiefly remember are the hands. It seems to me that by combining this style of painting with firm and bold contours, one should be able to make some small pictures easily.

Was at the Turk's, in the Palais-Royal. What a wretched Jew, with his cloak that he didn't even want to let me look at! Be that as it may, I almost have its cut. Dined with Rouget and went to M. Lelièvre's.

I returned early, congratulating myself on copying the Velasquez, and full of enthusiasm.

What folly always to keep for the future would-be subjects that are more beautiful than others!

As to my picture, I must leave what is done well, although it is in a style I am abandoning. The next will show variety at least, if not progress.

But to return to my preceding observation, with this stupid mania, one always does things in which one is not vitally interested, and are therefore bad; the more of them one does, the more one finds to do. Excellent ideas come to me every moment, and instead of executing them at the very moment they are clothed with the charm imagination lends to them in the form they assume at that moment, one promises oneself to do them later, but when? One forgets, or what is worse, one

[12] The *Dante and Vergil.*
[13] The *Massacre at Scio.*

no longer finds any interest in what seemed inspiring. This is what happens in so wandering and impressionable a mind — one fancy drives another out more quickly than the wind changes and turns the sail the other way. Assuming that I have plenty of subjects, what shall I do with them? Keep them in storage, waiting in the cold for their turn, and never will the inspiration of the moment quicken them with the breath of Prometheus: I will have to take them from a drawer when I need to make a picture. It is the death of genius. What is happening this evening? For a whole hour I have been wavering between *Mazeppa, Don Juan, Tasso,* and a hundred others.

I think that what would be best to do when one needs a subject, is not to have recourse to the ancients and to choose of them. For what is more stupid? Among the subjects that I have kept, because they seemed lovely to me one day, what determines my choice of one over another, now that I have the same feeling for all? The mere fact that I can hesitate between two of them implies lack of inspiration. Really, if I took up my palette at this moment, and I am dying to do so, the beautiful Velasquez would be on my mind. I should want to spread out some good thick, fat paint on a brown or red canvas. What I would need, then, in finding a subject is to open a book that can inspire me and let its mood guide me. There are those that are never ineffective. Just the same with engravings. Dante, Lamartine, Byron, Michelangelo.

At Drolling's, this morning, I saw several fragments of figures by Michelangelo, drawn by Drolling. God! what a man! What beauty! A strange thing, and a very beautiful one, would be joining Michelangelo's style to that of Velasquez. That idea came to me right after seeing the drawing. It is gentle and it is full. The forms have that softness which, so it seems, only a heavy loading of the paint can give, and at the same time the contours are vigorous. The engravings after Michelangelo give no idea of this. Therein lies the sublimity of the execution. Ingres has something of that. The spaces within his contours are smooth and but slightly cluttered up with details. How that would facilitate labor, especially in small pictures! I am glad to remember that impression. Bear well in mind those heads by Michelangelo. Ask Drolling to let you copy them. The very remarkable hands! The grand way that the parts of the body are connected. The smooth cheeks. The pure noses. All this is what I have always been seeking. There was some of it in that little portrait of Géricault which was at Bertin's, a bit in my portrait of Elizabeth Salter, and in that of my nephew. I should have achieved it much sooner had I seen that this could go only with the firmest contours. This is eminently so in the standing woman in my copy of Giorgione, *the nude women in the fields*.[14] Leonardo da Vinci has some of this, Velasquez some, but it is very different in Van Dyck: there one sees too much oil, and the contours are soft and languishing. Giorgione has much of this. There is something analogous, and very alluring, in the famous back in Géricault's picture,[15] in the head of the beardless youth, and in the thumb of the small child squatting at the end of the raft. Remember the arm of the figure he drew from me. What joy it would be to have, from his sale, one or two of Géricault's copies after the old masters! His family group after Velasquez, etc.

Luncheon	0 fr. 17 sous
Dinner	16 sous
Soap	1 fr. 10 sous
Sugar	7 sous
Total . . .	3 fr. 10 sous

Tuesday, April 13.

Fleeting humors that almost always come to me in the evening. Sweet philosophical contentment, could I but stay you! I do not complain of

[14] The *Concert Champêtre*, in the Louvre. Delacroix's copy of it. (No. 158 in the catalogue of his posthumous sale), brought 1200 francs.

[15] The *Raft of the Medusa*. The "famous back" is doubtless the one for which Delacroix posed.

my lot. Yet I need still more of that good sense that resigns itself to the inevitable. I must no longer keep for a more opportune time what I can do pleasurably now. What I shall have done cannot be taken from me. And as for the ridiculous fear of making things below one's potential abilities. . . . No, there is the root of the evil. There is the hiding-place of stupidity I must attack. Vain mortal, you are limited by nothing, neither by memory that eludes you, nor by the forces of your body, which are feeble, nor by the fluidity of your mind, which wars against these impressions as they reach you. Always, at the back of your soul, there is something that says to you, "Mortal, drawn from eternal life for a short time, think how precious these moments are. Your life must bring you everything other mortals draw from theirs." But yet, I know what I mean. . . . I believe that everyone has really been more or less tormented by this.

Dimier dropped in at Leblond's: he is going to leave for Egypt.

Paints and canvases	11 fr.
Porter	1 fr.
Doorman at the studio	10 fr.

Dufresne promised me the *Panhypocrisiade* and some poems by M. de Lamartine.

This morning, Velasquez. Interrupted. At my uncle's. Dined with him. In the evening, at Pierret's. He is resolved to be a portrait painter: he is right. Beginning next month, he is to come to my studio every morning.

Breakfast	1 fr.	4 sous
Paints	2 fr.	10
Chestnuts		15
Total . . .	4 fr.	9 sous

April 14.

This morning worked on the Velasquez. Began the head over again; it was too big for the body. Stopped in order to go to luncheon and was right to do so. Then I worked until half past four. Leblond came in.

Thursday, April 15.

In the morning, went to fetch the Turkish robe at M. Jal's, which made me arrive too late at my rendezvous with Hélène and Laure.

Progressed a lot with the little *Don Quixote,* and began to paint *The Penance of Jane Shore.*

Returned home. Prepared the *Jane Shore* for lithographing. Dined at Lack's and went back home. Read *Le Diable au corps* by André de Nerciat and slept a bit.

April 19.

Wish to do some subjects from the Revolution, such as the *Arrival* of Bonaparte at the Army of Egypt, the *Farewell at Fontainebleau.*

Tuesday, April 20.

I have come from Leblond's. There was a lot of talk about Egypt: one can go there for little or nothing. God grant that I may go there! Let us think plenty of this, and whether my beloved Pierret will come with me. He is the man I need. In the meantime, let us strive to free ourselves from the shackles that bind the spirit and shatter health. Rise early. Think of learning Arabic (to use in Egypt). Soon I will go to Dimier's and ask him some news of his studies.

What is it like: going to Egypt? Everyone praises it to the skies. And whether it does not cost more than going to London. For three hundred francs, De Loche and Planat have gone there. I should have to go in March and return in September; there would be time to see Syria. Is living merely vegetating like a mushroom attached to a rotten stump? The mean habits are consuming me quite. Besides, I must make preparations in advance. As long as I have legs, I hope to live positively. Would to God the Salon would enable me to go on my travels soon! Scheffer owes me a favor. He passed part of the day at my studio.

I have almost finished the *Don Quixote* and progressed much further on the *Jane Shore*.

The girl came to pose this morning. Hélène slept or pretended to. I do not know why I stupidly think myself obliged to act of the rôle of a worshiper. But the natural aptitude was no longer there. I excused myself on the pretext of a headache; when she was ready to go and there was no longer any time, the wind had changed. Scheffer consoled me in the evening, and he has found himself in precisely the same situations. I am afraid of everything, and still think that an inconvenience will last forever. I myself, I will pass away, too. This also is a consolation.

My lithograph I made at Leblond's has not come out badly.

Félix came to my studio a moment, and Henry was at Leblond's. There were trios for wind instruments. Yesterday Batton afforded me more pleasure with his wild improvisations at the piano. Edouard is enchanted with my Velasquez; he says that it is the most beautiful he has seen. My good Pierret enchanted me in being as absorbed as I in all the plans that have interested me this evening. He is as intoxicated as I am.

Dinner, myself and Scheffer	2 fr. 7 sous
Coffee	17 —
Total . . .	3 fr. 4 sous

Wednesday, April 21.

At the Velasquez early: could not work at it. Lunched and went to see Cogniet. Made a bad sketch, from nature, to please him. Did a drawing after Géricault. I must study contours, as Fedel is doing at the Académie. Cogniet advised me to go to see Méhul's *Joseph*. This evening, at Pierret's. Enchanted, as I was, too, with some sketches after Géricault.

Breakfast and dinner	2 fr.
Belot, paints	1 fr.
Maréchal	1 fr.
Prints, Raphael's *Massacre of the Innocents* .	10 sous
Total . . .	4 fr. 10 sous

Thursday, April 22.

Henry Scheffer said that today, when Didot was at his brother's and speaking to him of my plan to take apprentices, Didot said that I myself would be the first of my apprentices. I do not know whether that influenced my disposition all the rest of the evening, but I am plunged in the deepest melancholy.

April 24.

One thing which struck me in the work of Allier and which Champmartin recalled this evening, was that it was like the painting of Géricault, which may help to make me see the weak as well as the fine side of it. I have compared the emotions this type of style generates with that of Michelangelo, when noticing Allier's modeling of legs and breasts. Think of it that I may do neither one nor the other; the right way is between the two.

Lunched	1 fr.	
Dined	1 fr.	4 sous
Punch	12	
Pistol	1 fr. 10	
Billiards	1 fr. 10	
Total . . .	5 fr. 16 sous	

It is too much for one day, and a foolish one at that.

The memory of the little group in stone by Géricault enchants me. It would be amusing to do some. But I would have to be a tireless worker. How can I find time to do everything?

Sunday, [April] 25.

At the studio, about eleven o'clock. At Pierret's first, then at Soulier's. Pierret came to join me.

Worked on the Turk in the middle distance, who can be seen through the fire. Henry came and read the *Diable au corps*. Félix a moment. Dined with Pierret. Then was at M. Lelièvre's. Found no one at home. At M. Guillemardet's. Louis seemed to me very ill. Seeing him so gave a painful impression, mingled with that solemn and banefully poetic feeling of human frailty, inexhaustible source of the strongest emotions. Why am I not a poet? But at least let me feel as much as possible in each of my paintings, what I wish to produce in the souls of others. Allegory is a fine field! *Blind destiny dragging along all the suppliants who hope, by their cries and their prayers, to stay his inflexible arms.* I believe, having worked the thing out elsewhere, that it would be excellent to fire the imagination by doing some verses, rhymed or not, on a given subject, in order to help oneself to enter into the spirit of painting it. By dint of accustoming myself to rendering all my ideas in verse, I could easily do them, or at least in my own way. I must try to do some about my Scio subject.

Monday, April 26.

The outcome of my days is always the same: an infinite desire for what one never gets; a void one cannot fill, an utter yearning to produce in all ways, to battle as much as possible against time that drags us along, and the distractions that throw a veil over our soul; almost always, too, a kind of philosophical calm that prepares us for suffering and raises us above mere nothings. But there, perhaps, imagination still leads us astray; at the least accident, goodbye to philosophy! I should like to identify my soul with that of another.

M. Rivière, at Perpignan's, was talking about Godwin's novel *Saint Leon;* he found the secret of making gold and of prolonging his life by means of an elixir. All possible woes become the consequences of his fatal secrets, and yet, in the midst of his afflictions, he feels a secret pleasure in the strange powers that isolate him in nature. Alas! I could not find the secrets, and I am reduced to deploring in myself what was this man's sole consolation. Nature has put a barrier between my soul and that of my most intimate friend. He feels the same thing. If only I could savor, at my leisure, those impressions that I experience in my own way when alone. But the law of variety makes sport of that last consolation. Years are not needed to destroy the innocent enjoyments that each event brings to light in a vivid imagination. Every passing moment either bears them away or impairs them. The moment I write, I have begun to feel twenty things which I no longer recognize once they are expressed. My thought escapes me. The laziness of my mind, or rather its feebleness, betrays me rather than the slowness of my pen or the insufficiency of my tongue. It is torture to have feeling and imagination if memory lets them evaporate as promptly as they appear. If I only were a poet all would be an inspiration to me! To strive to battle against my rebellious memory — would that not be a way of making poetry? For what is my position? I imagine. Then the only question is that of my laziness in investigating and recapturing the idea that escapes me.

I got up early this morning and went immediately to the studio: it was not yet seven o'clock. Pierret was already at work.

Laure broke her word with me. I worked feverishly all day. I was tired out by night. At Perpignan's. That M. Rivière very amusing and interesting. He is a philosopher, moreover, just a bit discouraging and tending toward materialism. We spoke of Lord Byron and of that mysterious type of work which peculiarly captivates the imagination.

Tuesday, [April] 27.

At Leblond's. Interesting discussion about genius and unusual men. Dimier thought that great passions were the source of genius. I think that it is imagination alone, or better still, what amounts to the same thing, that delicacy of the organs that makes one see what others do not see, and which makes one see in a different way. I was saying that even great passions joined to imagination lead most often to disorder in the mind, etc. Dufresne said a very true thing: what made a man unusual was, fundamentally, a way utterly peculiar to himself of seeing things. He applied it to the great captains, etc., and finally to the great minds of all sorts. So, there are no rules for great souls: rules are only for people who have merely the talent that can be acquired. The proof is that they do not transmit this faculty. He was saying: "How much reflection is needed to create a beautiful, expressive head, a hundred times more than for a problem, and yet at bottom, the matter is merely one of instinct, for it cannot explain what brings it about." I note now that my mind is never more excited to create than when it sees a mediocre version of a subject that is suitable to me.

Wednesday, April 28.

Not up to the mark all day. Silly melancholy. It would be very beneficial to go to bed early, now that the evenings are boring. How fine it would be to get to the studio at daybreak!

Worked on the child.

Thursday, April 29.

Glory is not an empty word to me. The sound of praise fills me with true happiness. Nature has set this sentiment in the hearts of all. Those who forego glory or who cannot achieve it, are wise in showing for this phantom — the ambrosia of great spirits — a disdain that they call philosophical. Of late men have been possessed with an incomprehensible impulse to strip themselves of what nature has given to them rather than to the animals they load with the heaviest burdens. A philosopher is a gentleman who makes his four meals the best possible, for whom virtue, glory, and lofty sentiments are to be indulged in only so long as they do not curtail these four indispensable functions and their little bodily and individual comforts. In this sense, a mule is a much more acceptable philosopher since, in addition, he accepts blows and privations without complaint. What these people regard as the thing to take pride in, above all, is that voluntary renunciation of the sublime gifts that are beyond their reach.

For my painting of *Christ,* the angels of death, sad and stern, cast their melancholy glances at Him. Think of Ezekiel. A *Passage of the Red Sea* would be a beautiful thing.

Saturday, May 1.

Played billiards, or rather, gossiped while I pushed the balls around. Egypt! Egypt! Through General Coëtlosquet, I am to have some Mameluke weapons. This morning, I was in a frenzy of creation at my studio, and I again caught my feeling for the *Christ,* which had meant nothing to me. The same for *Botzaris.* This evening I caught a glimpse of those lovely nudes, simple in form and modeled in Guercino's manner, though more solid. I am not at all cut out to do small pictures, but I could do some of that sort.

Tuesday, May 4.

Here it is, the fourth month gone since the beginning of the year. Have

I spent this time dreaming? It has gone like a flashing of lightning. I haven't finished my picture, by any means. I am kept back at every step. I touched up the background today. Félix came to the studio.

This morning I saw Thil at his house; he lent me a little Bible which is a rich mine of motifs. I stopped in at Edouard's a minute. Dined with Fielding and Soulier at Rouget's, then at Leblond's. Dufresne is a very amusing and honest fellow. Hypnotism. His trick on a physician who put a woman to sleep. Her friend whispers certain things to the woman that she has the good nature to repeat. He himself pretends to be hypnotized and replies wonderfully well to the questions of the delighted physician, who is citing the case in his work. How much faith should one have in these dreams? On the way back, planned with Soulier to do aquatints together, after my drawings: I will retouch with a needle.

Friday, May 7.

I must forge ahead, and stop only to finish the *Velasquez*. The human mind is strangely made! I would have consented, I believe, to work at it perched on a belfry; now I can think of the finishing of it only as the greatest bore. All this, simply because I have been away from it for so long. It is somewhat the same with my picture and all works that are possible to me. There is a thick crust that must be broken before I can take heart in anything; a rebellious piece of ground that resists the ploughshare and the hoe. But with a little tenacity, its unfriendliness suddenly vanishes. It is prodigal with flowers and with fruit. One simply can not gather them all.

The nightingale. The fleeting instant of gaiety throughout nature. Those so fresh leaves, those lilacs, that rejuvenated sun. Melancholy takes flight during these brief moments. If the sky is covered with clouds and darkens, it is like the pretty pouting of one's sweetheart: we are sure she will be herself again.

On my way home this evening, I heard the nightingale. I hear him still, though very far away. This warbling is really unique, rather on account of the emotions it evokes than for itself. Buffon goes into a naturalist's ecstacies over the flexibility of the throat and the varied notes of the melancholy springtime songster. As for myself, I find in him that monotony, the inexhaustible source of all that makes a lively impression. It is like a view of the vast sea. One waits always for still another wave before breaking away from the sight; one cannot leave it. How I hate all these rhymers with their rhymes, their glories, their victories, their nightingales, their meadows! How many of them really describe what a nightingale makes one feel? But if Dante speaks of it, it is as fresh as nature, and we have heard only that. Yet all is artificial and dressed up, a product of the mind. How many of them have described love? Dante is really the first of poets. One thrills with him, as if before the thing itself. Superior in this to Michelangelo, or rather, different, for in another fashion, he also is sublime, though not through his truth. *Come columbe adunate alle pasture,* etc. *Come si sta a gracidar la rana,* etc. *Come il villanello,* etc. Therein lies what I have always dreamed, without being able to define it. Be just that in painting. It is a unique course to follow.

But when a thing bores you, do not do it. Do not pursue a fruitless perfection. There are certain faults (faults, that is, to the vulgar) which often impart life.

My picture is acquiring a twist, an energetic movement that I must absolutely complete in it. I need that good black, that blessed dirt, and those limbs that I know how to paint and few even try to get. The mulatto model will serve my purpose. I must get fullness. If my work loses in naturalness, it will be more beautiful and more fruitful. If it only holds together! O smile of the dying! The look of the mother's eye! Embraces of despair, precious domain of painting! Silent power that at first speaks only to the eyes, and which wins and makes its own all the faculties of the soul! There is the spirit, the real beauty that is proper to you, beautiful painting, so insulted, so misunderstood, delivered up to the blockheads who exploit you. But there are hearts who will still receive you devoutly; souls who will not be satisfied with phrases, any more than with fictions and ingenuities. You have only to appear with your manly and simple vigor, and you will please with a pleasure that is pure and absolute. Admit that I have worked with reason. I do not care for reasonable painting at all. I can see that my turbulent mind needs agitation, needs to free itself, to try a hundred different things before reaching the goal whose tyrannous call everywhere torments me. There is an old leaven, a black depth that demands satisfaction. If I am not quivering like a snake in the hands of Pythoness, I am cold; I must recognize it and submit to it, and to do so is happiness. Everything I have done that is worth while, was done this way. No more *Don Quixotes* and things unworthy of you! Concentrate intensely before your painting and think only of Dante. Therein lies what I have always felt in myself.

Sunday, May 9.

Already the 9th. How time flies! I was at the studio about eight o'clock. Not finding Pierret, I went to breakfast at the Café Voltaire. I dropped in to see Comairas, in order to borrow his Pinellis.

I felt a desire to do some contemporary pictures. The life of Napoleon swarms with subjects. I have read the poems of one Belmontet which, full of pathos and romanticism, have perhaps more than ever set my imagination to work.

My picture is taking on a different style. Somberness is replacing the confusion that held sway in it. I worked on the man in the center, the seated one, from Pierret. I am changing the plan.

Left the studio at half past seven. On my way to the monastery, dined at a restaurant that was new to me. Then at my cousin [Lamey's].

Yesterday, Saturday, [May] 8.

Breakfasted with Fielding and Soulier. Then to Dimier's, to see his antiquities: four magnificent alabaster vases of fine workmanship; a very old sarcophagus. Remember the style of the feet of the two seated Egyptian figures which are supposed to date from remotest antiquity.

Monday, May 10.

I read part of the *Giaour* at Schroth's place. I must do a series from it.

Walk in the Tuileries. Met Fedel, etc. Boulevards. At Gihaut's — got Gros' lithographs. At M. Guillemardet's: Louis is getting along nicely. Going out, I met Félix and Caroline returning. They had been at my studio.

Paint the *Giaour*.

Brought to Félix's the drawing that I made of him.

Tuesday, May 11.

So there will come a time when I will no longer be agitated with thoughts and emotions and desires for poetry and effusions of all sorts. Poor Géricault! I saw you go down into the narrow house, where there are no longer even dreams. And yet I cannot believe it. How I should like to be a poet! But at least, create in painting! Make it simple and daring. How many things there are to do! Make engravings, if painting is too much for you, and big pictures. The life of Napoleon is the epic of our century for all the arts. But I must hurry. Painting — I have said it a thousand times — has its favors that are peculiar to itself alone. The poet is very rich: remember eternally certain passages from Byron to inflame your imagination for all time. They suit me well. The end of *The Bride of Abydos, The Death of Selim,* his body tossed by the waves and that hand above all, that hand lifted up by the billow that has just spent itself on the beach. That is most sublime and it is his alone. I feel those things in the way that painting can render them. *The Death of Hassan* in *The Giaour.* The Giaour contemplating his victim and the curses of the Mussulman on the murderer of Hassan. The description of Hassan's deserted palace. The vultures whet their beaks before the conflict. The grapplings of the warriors who seize each other. In doing which one dies, biting the arm of his enemy.

The curses of Mazeppa[16] on those who have tied him to his

[16] Several of these images from Byron were used by Delacroix as the subjects of paintings.

charger, with the castle of the Count Palatine crumbling on its foundations.

This morning, I read some pages which got a prize from the Société des Bonnes Lettres. Dialogue between Fouché, Bonaparte, Fontanes and Carnot. There are some fine things in it, but also some masterpieces of asininity.

Worked at Fielding's on his *Macbeth*. At the studio towards noon. Began the *Fight of Hassan and the Giaour*.

This morning I was reading in the *Pandore* this incident: an English officer, during the war with America, finding himself at an advanced post, sees an American officer absorbed in his observations and seeming so absent-minded as not to notice him, although only a very short distance away. He takes aim at him, but, stayed by the horrible idea of firing at a man as if he were a target, he holds his finger on the trigger ready to fire. The American gallops away and disappears. It was Washington!

Wednesday, [May] 12.

At the studio at nine o'clock. Breakfasted at the Café Desmares. At Soulier's afterwards. Soulier came with M. Andrews. Cogniet came about three hours later; he seemed to me very satisfied with my painting. He seemed to see, he said, the beginning of a picture of the great old time. And then how that poor Géricault would like this painting! The old woman, without her mouth wide open, and no exaggeration in the eyes, [as he said]. The device of the young people in the corner, simple and touching. He seemed astonished that anyone does that sort of picture at present, etc. He pleased me very much, rightly enough.

Dined at half past six in the Rue de la Harpe. *Fielding is come there and we are returned together at his home. I was then very sleepy and slept a little bit on the bed of Soulier while he was abed.*[17] Returned at ten o'clock.

Saturday, May 15, during the day.

What makes men of genius, or rather, what they make, is not new

[17] These two sentences written by Delacroix in English.

ideas, it is that idea — possessing them — that what has been said has still not been said enough.

Yesterday, Friday, May 14.

Intense sadness and despondency all evening.

This morning, reading the review of Lord Byron at the beginning of the volume, I felt again awakening in me that insatiable desire to create. Can I tell whether that would be happiness for me? At least, it seems so. Happy poet and happier still in having a tongue that submits to his imaginings! Yet, French is sublime. But I should have to give battle many times to this rebellious Proteus before subduing him.

What torments my soul is its loneliness. The more it expands among friends and the daily habits or pleasures, the more, it seems to me, it flees me and retires into its fortress. The poet who lives in solitude, but who produces much, is the one who enjoys those treasures we bear in our bosom, but which forsake us when we give ourselves to others. When one yields oneself completely to one's soul, it opens itself completely to one, and then it is that the capricious thing allows one the greatest of good fortunes, that of which the account of Lord Byron speaks, that of sympathizing with others, of studying itself, of painting itself constantly in its works, something that Byron and Rousseau have perhaps not noticed. I am not talking about mediocre people: for what is this rage, not only to write, but to be published? Outside of the happiness of being praised, there is that of addressing all souls that can understand yours, and so it comes to pass that all souls meet in your painting. What good is the approbation of friends? It is quite natural that they should understand you; so what importance is there in that? What is intoxicating is to live in the mind of others. What is so devastating! I ask myself. You can add one soul more to the number of those who have seen nature in a way that is their own. What all these souls have painted is new for them, and you will paint them new again! They have painted their soul, in painting things, and your soul asks its turn, also. And why should you resist when it does so? Is its request more absurd than the need for repose that your limbs ask, when they and all your physical being are fatigued? If they have not done enough for you, neither have they done enough for others. Those very ones who believe that everything has been said and done, will greet you as new and yet will close the door behind you. And then they will say again that everything has been said and done. Just as man, in the feebleness of age, believes that nature is degenerating, so men with commonplace minds and who have nothing to say about what has already been said, think that nature has allowed certain ones, and those only in the beginning of time, to say new and striking things. What there was to say in the times of those immortal spirits, attracted the notice of all their contemporaries, just as in our time, but for all that not many tried to seize the new thing, to enter their name hastily, in order to steal for themselves the harvest that posterity was to reap. Novelty is in the mind that creates, and not in nature, the thing painted. The modesty of him who writes always keeps him from including himself among the great minds of which he speaks. He always speaks, we agree, to one of those luminaries, if there are any, whom nature. . . .

. . . Thou who knowest there is always something new, show it to them in that which they have disregarded. Make them believe that they have never heard of the nightingale or the vast ocean, and everything that their gross senses try to feel only when others have first taken the trouble of feeling it all for them. Don't let words embarrass you. If you nourish your soul, they will find an occasion to come forth. They will unite in language which will be well worth the hemistiches of this man or the prose of that one. Look — you are original, you say, and yet your verse takes fire only at reading Byron or Dante, etc! That fever, you take it for the power to create, but it is, rather, a mere need to imitate. . . . Ah, no. The fact is that they have not said the hundredth part of what there is to say; the fact is that with a single one of the things that they skim over, there is more material for original geniuses than there is . . . and that nature has put in safe keeping in the great imaginations to come more new things to say about her creations than she has created things.

What shall I do? I am not allowed to do a tragedy: the law of the unities is against that. A poem, etc.

Tuesday, May 18.

Do you think that Byron would have created his energetic poems in the midst of turmoil? That Dante was encompassed by distractions when his soul was voyaging among the shades? Without the soul, nothing connected, nothing productive. Projects constantly interrupted; and the sole cause of it is associating with many people.

Saturday, [May] 15.

Left at two o'clock with Riesener, my aunt, Henry, Léon, and Rouget.

The next day, Sunday [May] 16.

In the forenoon practised jumping and casting the javelin. Walked in the woods. Construed *Childe Harold* with my aunt.

Friday, May 28.

At least admire the great virtues, even if you are not strong enough yourself to be truly virtuous! Dufresne said that he is capable of devotion to all great things, etc., but that he sees the emptiness of them, that they are nothing, in fact. I feel the contrary. I pay them homage, but I am too weak to do them. My business is quite different.

Saturday, [May] 29.

Worked on the drapery of the old woman.

In the evening, rejoined Félix and Pierret at the Palais-Royal. Saw Mme de Conflans. Desires.

Monday, [May] 31.

This evening saw the *Barber [of Seville]* at the Odéon. It was very satisfying. I sat next to an old gentleman who has seen Grétry, Voltaire, Diderot, Rousseau, etc. He saw Voltaire in a certain salon, paying his famous gallantries to the ladies. In leaving, he said, "I see in you a century that is beginning; in me, one that is ending: the century of Voltaire." We see that the modest philosopher took the trouble of naming his century for posterity in advance. He was taken by one of his friends to breakfast with Jean-Jacques in the Rue Plâtrière. They went out together. In the Tuileries, some children were playing ball. "There," said Rousseau, "that is how I should like Emile to play," and then more in that vein. But the ball of one of the children happened to strike the philosopher's leg. He flew into a passion and chased the child with his cane, abruptly leaving his two friends.

Worked little today and on the old woman. Yesterday, dined at Ruffi's with Leblond.

Tuesday, June 1.

I saw myself in the glass, and I was almost scared by the wickedness in my features. Yet that is the man who must carry into my soul a fatal torch which, like the wax tapers burned for the dead, lights only the obsequies of what was once sublime.

Lover of the muses, you who vow to their cult your purest blood, ask these learned divinities to give you back that lively eye sparkling with youth, that lightness of an untroubled mind. These chaste sisters have been worse than courtesans to you. Their perfidious delights are more illusory than the cup of pleasure. It is your soul that has unnerved your senses, your twenty-five years without youthfulness, your fervor without strength. Your imagination embraces everything, and you haven't memory of a common shopkeeper. The true wisdom of the philosopher ought to consist in enjoying everything. Yet we apply ourselves to dissecting and destroying everything that is good in itself, that has virtue, albeit the virtue there is in mere illusions. Nature gives us this life like a toy to a weak child. We want to see how it all works; we break everything. There remains in our hands and before our eyes, stupid and opened too late, the sterile wreckage, fragments that will not again make a whole. The good is so simple. We need to take so much trouble if we want to destroy it with sophisms. And should all this goodness and beauty be only a sublime varnish, only a shell to help us in enduring the rest, who can deny that it exists to that extent at least? How strange men are, not to let themselves delight in the beauty of a painting, because the back of it is a worm-eaten panel! All is not good: but all cannot be bad, or rather, and for that reason, all is good.

Who has committed an egoistical deed without reproaching himself with it?

Friday, June 4, morning.

I live in company with a body, a silent companion, exacting and eternal. He it is who notes that individuality which is the seal of the weakness of our race. My soul has wings, but the brutal jailer is strict. He knows that it is free only to be enslaved again, weakling that it is: it forgets itself in its prison. Only very rarely does it catch a glimpse of the blue of its native home in the sky. Oh! sad destiny! to yearn endlessly for release, spirit that I am, lodged in a mean vessel of clay. You use your strength only to torment yourself in a hundred ways.

It seems to me that the body may be the organization that tones down the soul, which is more universal, yet passes through the brain as through a rolling mill which hammers it and stamps it with the stamp of our insipid physical nature, and what weight is more insufferable than that of this living cadaver which we inhabit? Instead of dashing towards the objects of desires that it cannot grasp, nor even define, it spends the flashing instant of life submitting to the stupid situations into which its tyrant throws it. As a bad joke, doubtless, heaven has allowed us to view the sight of the world through this absurd window: its fieldglass, out of focus and lusterless, always turned in the same direction, spoils all the judgments of the other, whose native good faith is corrupted, and often horrible fruits are the result! From such a point of view, I can very easily believe in the influences on you, and in the hump on your back. But doing so will make me mourn them forever. What are the soul and the intelligence when separated? The pleasure of naming and classifying is the fatal thing about men of learning. They are always overreaching themselves and spoiling their game in the eyes of those easy-going, fair-minded people who believe that nature is an impenetrable veil. I know very well that in order to agree about things, we must name them; but thenceforth they are specified, they are neither constant species, nor . . .

Sunday, June 6.

Early to bed and early rise
Makes a man healthy, wealthy, and wise.
(Franklin)[18]

Do not forget to buy *Poor Richard's Almanac.*

What will my fate be? Without fortune and without inclinations suitable for acquiring one, much too lazy, when it is a question of bestirring myself to such a purpose, although worried, at intervals, about the outcome of it all. When one is prosperous, one does not feel pleasure in being so; when one is not, one wants the enjoyments which prosperity ensures. But as long as my imagination is my torment and my pleasure at the same time, what matters comfort or lack of comfort? It is a nuisance, but it is not the worst.

As soon as a man is intelligent, his first duty is to be honest and strong. It is no use to try to forget, there is something virtuous in him that demands to be obeyed and satisfied. What do you think has been the life of men who have raised themselves above the common herd? Constant strife. Struggle against the idleness that is common to them and to the average man, when it is a question of writing, if he is a writer: because his genius clamors to be manifested; and it is not merely through some vain lust to be famed that he obeys it — it is through conscience. Let those who work lukewarmly be silent: what do they know of work dictated by inspiration? This fear, this dread of awakening the slumbering lion, whose rearings stir your very being. To sum up: be strong, simple, and true; there is your problem for all times, and it is always useful.

[18] Delacroix copied the words down in English.

There is no merit in being truthful, when one is naturally so, or rather, when one cannot be otherwise; it is a gift just like being a poet or a musician. But there is some courage in being so by dint of thinking it over, or through a kind of vanity. Just like the person who says to himself, "I am ugly," and who says to others, "I am ugly," that they may not seem to have found it out before him.

Dufresne is truthful, I believe, because he has completed the circle. He must have started by being affected, when he was only partly enlightened. He is truthful because he sees the stupidity of not being so. He had, I still suppose, enough sense to try to dissemble his weaknesses. At present, he prefers not to have them, and he will accuse himself of them with the best will in the world, not really thinking that he has them, if he takes care to hide them when he feels them in himself. In his case, I haven't yet reached that frankness and serenity that I find in myself when I am with those to whom I am used; I am not sufficiently his friend yet to have an opinion completely opposed to his, or to listen carelessly or, at least, not to feign an interest when he speaks to me. If I stop and search for a reason, perhaps there is (and this is certain) that fear of passing for a man of less intelligence, if I do not think as he does. Absurd stupidity! Even if you were sure of retaining the upper hand with him, does anything equal the hardness of a face constantly turned toward deception? He is a man, after all; and above all, respect yourself. You respect yourself only by being open and above-board.

Wednesday, June 9.

Laure brought me a splendid Adeline, sixteen years old, large, well made, and with a charming head. I will do her portrait and have good hope of it; I have it on my mind.

I went to see the drawing by Gros at Laugier's; nothing can be more pleasing. Has made less impression on me, however, than the picture. In strange contrast with the real warmth in so many things by Gros is the general coldness of the execution; rather flat. Besides, no individuality of drawing in the various portions, hands, feet, etc. More

or less the convention of the studio. One feels that the draperies are
arranged, that the whole effect is preconceived, as when he puts the
black in the foreground, etc. Just the same, I am not too much disheartened by it.

But it is important always to make a sketch.

Monday, [June] 14.

In the evening went to the house of M. de Conflans. He was alone.[19]
Café de la Rotonde.

Received a note from Laure; very amusing.

On leaving the house about eight o'clock at night, met the tall,
pretty working girl. I followed her as far as the Rue de Grenelle, always
meditating what course to pursue and almost miserable because I had
the chance. I am always like that. I found, afterwards, all sorts of ways
to use in accosting her, and when it was the right time for them, I
opposed them with the most absurd difficulties. My resolutions always
evaporate when there is need of action. I need a mistress who would
keep my flesh up to pitch. I am much tormented with the idea, and
turn it into high-minded bouts with my work. Sometimes I long for
the first woman to come along. Heaven grant that Laure come tomorrow! And then, when a girl falls to my lot, I am almost annoyed; I
don't want to be obliged to act; therein lies my cancer. To make a
decision or simply to rouse myself from my sloth. When I am waiting
for a model, every time, even when I am most busy, I am enchanted
when the hour is up and I tremble when I hear her put her hand on the
key. When I leave a place where I am the least bit ill at ease, I admit
that there is a moment of extreme delight in the feeling of the liberty
to which I have returned. But there are moments of sadness and boredom, which certainly try me severely; I experienced that this morning
at my studio. I have not enough simple, commonplace energy to
overcome the thing by busying myself some other way. As long as
inspiration is lacking, I am bored. There are some people who, in order

[19] Delacroix had hoped to see Mme de Conflans.

to avoid boredom, know how to set themselves a task and accomplish it.

I was thinking today that despite our little spats, I like Soulier very much: I understand him, and he understands me. I like Leblond very much. And, too, I like my good old brother; I know him well; I wish I were richer, so that I might give him some pleasure from time to time. I must write him.

Tuesday, June 15.

Worked on the old woman, on her shoes.[20] Prévost in the afternoon. My sister came to see me this morning. In the evening, Leblond. To Prévost (for posing), 2 francs, 50 centimes. Thil came this morning. He prefers my painting to Géricault's: I like them both very much.

Thursday, June 17.

At the studio at noon. The lady of the Italiens came.[21] Much moved. Perpignan came, and so did M. Rivière. A letter from Laure. To the Italiens with Fielding. Ricciardi. Mme Mombelli and husband. The lady was there. *I am very fond of this pretty scenery. I was looking at her incessantly.*[22]

I absolutely must make compositions of all interesting subjects as they come to me. I know from experience that I cannot make the best of them if I wait about carrying them out.

Saturday, [June] 19.

With Pierret and Fielding, at Montfaucon. Saw Cogniet, and Géricault's picture. Saw the Constables. It was too many things in one day. That Constable did me much good. Returned towards five o'clock. I was at my studio two hours. Great lack of sex. I am quite shameless.

"May I hope, lovely lady, to see you Thursday, and will you pardon me for not having been to see you? I dare to flatter myself that you will not be as stern as you say, and that you will not be cruel enough

[20] Still the *Massacre at Scio*.

[21] Mme de Conflans.

[22] Delacroix writes these two sentences in English.

to pass the yellow door without coming in. I suppose it will be in the afternoon, as before. If it is not presuming too much, I would permit myself to ask you for a little more time."

The battle starts: shall I see her or not?

Friday, June 25th.

Went with Dorcy to see Géricault's studies. At Cogniet's. Saw the Constable again. At Montfaucon. Dined thereabouts.

Wednesday, June 30.

At M. Auguste's.[23] Saw some admirable paintings after the masters: costumes, especially horses, admirable, quite beyond those of Géricault. It would be very useful to have some of these horses and copy them, as well as the Greek, Persian, and Indian costumes, etc.

Also saw there some painting copied from Haydon. A very great talent. But, as Edouard very properly said, absence of a strong personal style. Drawing in the style of West. I was forgetting M. Auguste's beautiful studies, after the Elgin marbles. Haydon spent a considerable time copying them; but nothing of that shows in his own work. The beautiful thighs of the men and women! What beauty without excess! inaccuracies that are never noticed.

In the evening, with Fielding. Had tea in the Rue de la Paix.

Wednesday, July 7.

Today, M. Auguste came to the studio; he is much charmed with my painting. His praises have given me new life. Time is flying. Tomorrow I will go to look for some costumes. Passed the evening with Pierret. Yesterday, Leblond. I saw Edouard who is ill and who worries me.

[23] Jules-Robert Auguste, usually referred to as M. Auguste (1789–1850), painter, sculptor, and collector of objects of art which he lent to Delacroix. (Cf. Charles Saunier, *Monsieur Auguste,* in the *Gazette des Beaux-Arts,* 1910).

July 20.

Thought much of M. d'Houdetot's drawing and style. Make many sketches and take time: in this, especially, I need to improve. On this account, I must get some fine Poussin engravings and study them. The great point is to avoid that confounded facility given us by the brush. Take, rather, some hard material to work in, such as marble: that would be quite new. Work in an obstinate medium in order to subdue it patiently.

August 19.

Saw M. Gérard[24] at the museum. The most flattering praises. He asked me to dine in the country tomorrow.

In the evening, at Soulier's with Leblond and Pierret. Dined at Pierret's yesterday.

Lunched today with Horace Vernet and Scheffer. Learned one of Horace Vernet's chief rules. *Finish a thing when you have got a grasp of it.* Only way of accomplishing much.

Yesterday, Monday, October 4.

Saw the gallery of the masters again. Made some studies at the riding school and dined with M. Auguste. Saw some superb sketches from the Neopolitan tombs. He speaks of the new aspect one could give to religious subjects by drawing inspiration from the mosaics of the time of Constantine. Saw at his house Ingres' drawing after his bas-relief and his composition, *Saint Peter Delivered from Prison.*[25]

Tuesday, October 5.

Passed the day with M. de Conflans at Montmorency. Walk in the forest. In the evening returned with Félix. The lady in between the two of us. Leblond. Received a letter from Soulier this evening.

[24] Baron Gérard (1770–1837). The famous pupil of David was one of the first to speak in favor of the work of Delacroix.

[25] Doubtless M. Auguste's bas-relief, the *Battle of the Amazons,* mentioned in the catalogue of his sale.

NOTE BY THE EDITOR

The French conquest of Algeria in 1830 had given to France a turbulent and dangerous neighbor, the Sultan of Morocco, who was tempted to intervene in what had become French territory. In 1831, the government of France decided to negotiate with Sultan Muley-abd-el-Rahman and to conclude a treaty of good neighborliness with him. The mission was entrusted to Count de Mornay, a young diplomat of great intelligence and culture. Delacroix was presented to him in the world of journalism, the opera, and the theater, which both frequented. The painter no doubt pleased the diplomat, who attached him to his mission.

The experience had an incalculable effect on the artist's development. To the last days of his life, Delacroix was still evoking memories of his unforgettable vision. But the following pages have an even wider significance. They show the man whose previous training had been exclusively European face to face with a world new to him — physically and in its conception of art. His own painting is modified at once by the contact with the Orient, and the intensification of color so afforded is passed on to the whole line of his successors.

Really to appreciate the written record of the journey to Morocco, one needs to see the notebooks themselves, filled as they are with sketches for which the words are often no more than titles. The reproductions herewith give some idea of the quality of the drawings and water colors that accompany the notes, but they would need to be multiplied several hundreds of times for us to realize their quantity.

1832

Tangier, January 26.

WITH the *pasha*. The entrance to the castle: The guardsmen in the court, the façade, the lane between two walls. At the end, under a sort of vault, men seated, making a brown silhouette against a bit of sky.

The handsome man with the green sleeves.

The mulatto slave who poured the tea, yellow caftan and burnous attached in back, turban. The old man who gave the rose with *haik* and dark blue caftan.

The pasha with his two haiks or hoods, and the burnous beside. All three of them on a white mattress with a long square cushion covered with printed calico. A long narrow cushion of checkered cloth, another in horsehair, of various patterns; tips of the feet visible, the inkwell made of horn, various small objects lying about.

The head of the customs house[1] leaning on his elbow, his arm bare, if I remember rightly: very wide haik on his head, white turban on top, amaranth-colored cloth hanging over his breast, his cowl not in use, his legs crossed. We had met him mounted on a gray mule as we came up. A great deal of his leg was to be seen; a little of his colored breeches; his saddle covered in front and behind by a scarlet cloth. A red band went around the hind quarters of the horse and hung down. The red halter or rather the breastpiece of the harness also hanging down. A Moor led the horse by the halter.

The handsome man with the green sleeves, his outer shirt in dimity, bare-footed in the presence of the pasha.

The garden divided by alleys covered with trellises. Large orange trees covered with fruits; on the ground fruit had fallen; high walls enclosed the garden.

[1] Amin Bias, the minister of foreign affairs and of finance, delegated by the Sultan to treat with the Count de Mornay. Delacroix had done his portrait in the album of water colors of the Count de Mornay (Catalogue Robaut, 50).

Entered all the byways of the old palace. Marble court, marble fountain; capitals in a bad composite style, the very simple attic storeys built of stone: complete dilapidation.

The ceilings of the niches and even of the small rooms are filled with painted sculptures, scalloped like the opening of a mandolin. The columns of the tower in the court are of white marble with which, also, the court is paved.

When returning by a fine staircase at the right, noticed a fine-looking man who followed us, disdainful in his manner.

Went out through the room where the pasha is supposed to dispense justice. To the left of the door in the rear through which we entered the room, a sort of drum built of boards, about two and a half feet high, and going from the door to the corner, where the pasha sits. The lengths of the walls, in the spaces between the pilasters which go up to the vault, ledges of stone to serve as seats. The soldiers, without guns, were awaiting us at the door, drawn up in two lines leading to the guard room through which we had entered.

Saw a very good-looking Jewess resembling Madame R ———.

Mornay called my attention to a Negro; he seemed to me to have a special manner of wearing the haik.

While going to one of the consuls saw the mosque from the side. A Moor was washing his feet in the fountain which is in the center of it; another one was washing himself as he squatted on the brink.

January 29.

Enchanting view while descending the length of the ramparts; after that the sea. Cactus and enormous aloes. Bamboo enclosure; patches of brown grass on the sand.

When returning, the contrast between the yellow and dry bamboo with the verdure of the rest. The mountains more nearly a brown green, dotted with blackish dwarfed shrubs. Huts.

The scene of the fighting horses.[2] From the start, they stood up and fought with a fierceness which made me tremble for those gentlemen, but it was really admirable for a painting. I witnessed, I am

[2] This episode inspired the picture known as *Rencontre de Cavaliers Maures*, refused at the Salon of 1834 (Catalogue Robaut, 469).

certain, the most fantastic and graceful movements that Gros and Rubens could have imagined. Then the gray got his neck around the other one. For a time that seemed endless, it was impossible to make him let go. Mornay managed to dismount. While he was holding him by the bridle, the black reared furiously. The other kept on fiercely biting him behind. In all this struggle the consul fell down. We then let the two horses go; they kept on fighting with each other as they got to the river, both falling into it as they continued fighting and at the same time trying to get out of the water; their feet slipped in the mud at the edge; they were all dirty and shiny, wet to the mane. After repeated beatings, the gray let go his hold and went toward the middle of the water; the black came out of it, etc. . . . At the other side the soldier trying to tuck up his clothes so as to get the other horse out.

The dispute of the soldier with the groom. Sublime, with his mass of draperies, looking like an old woman and yet with something martial about him.

On our return, superb landscapes to the right, the mountains of Spain in the tenderest tones, the sea a dark greenish blue like a fig, the hedges yellow at the top because of the bamboo, green at the base on account of the aloes.

The hobbled white horse that wanted to jump onto one of ours.

On the beach, when about to come back, met the sons of the *caid*, all on mules. The oldest one, his dark blue burnous; haik about like that of our soldier, but very clean; caftan of a canary yellow. One of the young children all in white with a kind of braided cord from which a weapon was probably hanging.

January 30.

Visit to the consuls of England and Sweden. The garden of Monsieur de la Porte (Consul of France at Tangier). The tomb in the country.

January 31.

Drew the Moor of the consul of Sardinia. Rain. While going to the English consul, took note of quite a clean-looking merchant in his shop;

the floor and the passage-way garnished with white mats, pots and merchandise on one side only.

February 2, Thursday.

Drew the daughter of Jacob in Moorish costume. Went out about four o'clock. A Moor with a very remarkable head who had a white turban over his haik. Heads of Moors like those of Rubens, nostrils and lips rather coarse, bold eyes; noticed the rusty cannon.

The old Jew in his shop when I was going down to the house (like a picture by Gerard Dou). Women with their heels and, I think, their feet painted yellow.

Friday, February 4.

The *gelabia,* the costume of the common people, of merchants, of children. I remember that gelabia, exactly the costume of antiquity, in a little figure at the Louvre: hood, etc. The cap is the Phrygian cap.

The palimpsest is the tablet on which the school children write. Mutual teaching is native to this country. In moments of relaxation the children go in troups, carrying this tablet on their heads. It is covered with a species of clay on which they write with a special ink. Erasures are made, I think, by wetting it and letting it dry in the sun.

The Gate of the Danish consul.

In the Jewish quarter I saw some remarkable interiors while passing by. A Jewess standing out in vigorous relief; red skullcap, white drapery, black dress.

It is the first day of Rhamadan. At the moment when the moon rose, and while it was still daylight, guns were shot off, etc.; this evening they are making an infernal noise with their drum-beating and their trumpets of ram's horn.

Saturday, February 25.

In the garden of the Swedish consul after breakfast; to Abraham[3] at noon. Noticed, while passing in front of his sister's door, two little

[3] Abraham ben Chimol, dragoman of the consulate of France. Delacroix had made a study from him in the album of Moreau-Nélaton, and a portrait in the album of Monsieur de Mornay (Catalogue Robaut, 499).

Jewish girls sitting on a carpet in the court. On entering his house, his whole family in a kind of little niche and on the balcony above, with the door to the staircase. The woman on the balcony, charming subject.

Sunday, February 12.

Drew the Jewess Dititia in Algerian costume.

Then went to the garden of Denmark. The charming path. The graves amid the aloes and the iris *(aegyptiaca)*. The purity of the air. Mornay as much impressed as I by the beauty of nature here.

The almond trees in flower. The lilacs of Persia, big tree. The beautiful white horse under the orange trees. Interior of the court of the little house.

When we came out, the black and yellow orange trees across the door of the little court. As we went away the little white house in the shadow amidst the dark orange trees. The horse through the trees.

Dinner at the house with the consuls. In the evening Monsieur Rico sang some Spanish melodies. The South alone produces such emotions.

Feeling indisposed, I remained alone in the evening. Delightful reverie in the moonlit garden.

Wednesday, February 15.

Went out with Monsieur Hay.[4] Saw the muezzin at the top of the mosque.

The school with the little boys. All the tablets with Arab writing. The word *table of the law,* and all the ancient indications as to the manner of writing show that these were tablets of wood. The inkwells and the slippers before the door.

Tuesday, February 21.

The Jewish wedding.[5] The Moors and the Jews at the entrance. The two musicians. The violinist, his thumb in the air, the under side of

[4] Consul General of England.
[5] This scene inspired the famous *Jewish Wedding* of the Salon of 1841 (Catalogue Robaut, 867), now in the Louvre.

the other hand very much in the shadow, light behind, the haik on his head transparent in places; white sleeves, shadowy background. The violinist; seated on his heels and on his gelabia. Blackness between the two musicians below. The body of the guitar on the knee of the player; very dark toward the belt, red vest, brown ornaments, blue behind his neck. Shadow from his left arm (which is directly in front of one) cast on the haik over his knee. Shirtsleeves rolled up showing his arms up to the biceps; green woodwork at his side; a wart on his neck, short nose.

At the side of the violinist, pretty Jewish woman; vest, sleeves, gold and amaranth. She is silhouetted halfway against the door, halfway against the wall; nearer the foreground, an older woman with a great deal of white, which conceals her almost entirely. The shadows full of reflections; white in the shadows.

A pillar cutting out, dark in the foreground. The women to the left in lines one above the other like flower pots. White and gold dominate, their handkerchiefs are yellow. Children on the ground in front.

At the side of the guitarist, the Jew who plays the tambourine. His face is a dark silhouette, concealing part of the hand of the guitarist. The lower part of his head cuts out against the wall. The tip of a gelabia under the guitarist. In front of him, with legs crossed, the young Jew who holds the plate. Gray garment. Leaning against his shoulder, a young Jewish child about ten years old.

Against the door of the stairway, Prisciada; purplish handkerchief on her head and under her throat. Jews seated on the steps; half seen against the door, strong light on their noses, one of them standing straight up on the staircase; a cast shadow with reflections clearly marked on the wall, the reflection a light yellow.

Above, Jewesses leaning over the balcony rail. One at the left, bareheaded, very dark, clear-cut against the wall, lit by the sun. In the corner, the old Moor with his beard on one side; shaggy haik, his turban placed low on the forehead, gray beard against the white haik. The other Moor, with a shorter nose, very masculine, turban sticking out. One foot out of the slipper, sailor's vest and sleeves the same.

On the ground, in the foreground, the old Jew playing the tambourine; an old handkerchief on his head, his black skullcap visible. Torn gelabia; his black coat visible near the neck.

The women in the shadow near the door, with many reflections on them.

February 21, evening.

On our way to the Jewish wedding, the merchants in their shops. Lamps, sometimes on the wall, but more often suspended in front by a cord, pots on a board, *palancos*. They take butter with their hands and put it on a leaf. On entering the street to the right there was one whose lamp was concealed by a piece of cloth which hung from the shed.

Before dinner, on our way to the garden of Sweden, guns hanging up and the scabbard hanging beside it; big pitcher at the side.

In the evening, dressing the Jewess. The form of the miter. The cries of the old women. The face painted, the young married women who held the candle while she was being dressed. The veil thrown over her face. The girls standing on the bed.

During the day, the newly married women against the wall, their near relative as a chaperone; the bride brought down from the bed. Her companions remain upon it. The red veil. The newly married women when they arrive in their haik. The beautiful eyes.

The arrival of the relatives. Wax torches; the two torches painted in different colors. Tumult. Faces lit up. Moors mixing in. The Jewess held on both sides; one, behind, holds up her miter.

On the way, Spaniards looking out at the window. Two Jewesses or Moorish women on housetops silhouetting against the blackness of the sky. Gave M. Hay's daughter the drawing of the Moorish woman seated. The old Moors climbing on the stones of the road. The lanterns. The soldiers with the staves. The young Jew who held two or more torches, the flame going up to his mouth.

Friday, March 2.

Outing with M. Hay. Dined at his house.

The foot sidewise in the stirrups sometimes.

The flag with its support planted in front of the tent.

The plain, and the mass of the tribe going off into the distance. In front half a dozen horsemen in the smoke. One man further in front: dark blue burnous. Ahead, turning their backs to us, the line of our soldiers preceded by the caid and the flags.

The race of the five or six horsemen. The bareheaded young man, yellow green caftan. The almost pure Negro, pointed cap, blue caftan.

The light from the side on the edge of the men's faces. The shadow on white objects has a strong blue reflection. The red of the saddles and of the turban, almost black.

Crossing the ford, the men climbing; a white horse at the side.

March 5, 1832.

First day. Ain-el-Daliah. Left Tangier at one o'clock.

The arrival at the camp. Mountains black and wild to the right, the sun overhead. Walking through underbrush of dwarfed palms and stones. The whole tribe drawn up to the left crowning the height; further off, following, horsemen against the sky; further off the tents.

Took a walk through the camp in the evening, contrast of garments against the background.

The Iman calling to prayer in the evening.

March 6.

At Garbia. Started about seven or eight o'clock. Climbed a hill, the sun to the left. Mountains very clear cut, one behind another, against a pure sky.

Found various tribes. Men firing off guns as they leap into the air. Crossed a mountain (Laclao), very picturesque. Stones. I stopped for a moment.

Very fine view at the top of the mountain, half an hour before reaching camp; the sea to the right and Cape Spartel.

Powder-play[6] in the plain before the river. The two men who ran

[6] This subject of the powder-play, the ceremonial firing of guns, was treated several times by Delacroix; see the Robaut catalogue.

up against each other: the horse of one of them touched the ground with its haunches. One especially, with a black-blue caftan and the sheath of his gun slung over his shoulder; later on a man with a sky blue caftan.

The tribe following us; disorder, dust; the cavalry in front. Powder-play: the horses in the dust, the sun behind. Sleeves rolled up as they rush forward.

As we went down from Laclao, very black green meadow to the left; mountain the same; in the distance, mountain of a raw blue.

At the camp. The soldiers running in confusion, their guns over their shoulders, in front of the tent of the pasha and drawing up in a line. The pasha says. . . .

The soldiers coming, four or five at a time, in front of the tent of the cavalry general and bowing. Then all in line receiving orders in small squads; the others squatting while they await their turn.

The tribes going to render homage to the pasha and bringing provisions.

March 7.

At Tleta dei Rissana. The plain terminated by very large olive trees on the hill. We lunched beside the Aiacha river.

The meeting with the other pasha. Damask on the crupper of the pasha's horse. Musicians on horseback.

The prayer near the tent of the commander.

Spent the evening with Abou[7] in our tent. Conversation about the horses. The music box which would not stop. Felt like laughing.

Thursday, March 8.

Alcassar-el-Kebir. Before reaching Alcassar. The population, music, powder-play without end. The pasha's brother giving blows with his staff and with his saber. A man breaks through the crowd of soldiers and fires at us point-blank. He is seized by Abou. His fury. They

[7] The caid Ben Abou, chief of the military escort. His portrait in water color was in the Mornay album (Catalogue Robaut, 509).

drag him off by his turban, which has come unwound; they lay him out further off. My fright. We run. The saber was already drawn. . . .

On the hilltops to the left, various standards; designs on the various backgrounds red, blue, green, yellow, white; others with the foot soldiers in various uniforms.

The long trumpets as we entered Alcassar.

Friday, March 9.

Camped at Fouhouarat.

Late departure from the Alcassar camp. Rain. Entered Alcassar and crossed the town. Crowd, soldiers striking heavy blows with straps; horrible streets; pointed roofs; storks on all the houses, on the tops of the mosques. They seem very large for such buildings. All in brick. Jewesses at the garret windows.

Went through a big passage-way lined with hideous shops, roofed with badly joined bamboo.

Reached the edge of the river. Big olive trees at the edge. Dangerous slope.

In the middle of the river, musket shots from both sides. On reaching the other bank, we went for more than twenty minutes through a hedge of riflemen who looked threatening enough. Musket shots at the feet of our horses. Men half naked.

The man thrown down on his back with his horse on top of him. Picked up half dead; got back on his horse a moment afterward.

Voracity of the Moors; in the evening Abraham told us stories in the tent.

Saturday, March 10.

El-Arbadi Sidi Eissa Bel-hacen.

Sick last night. We were uncertain whether we would remain on account of the weather. The Jews did not want to leave. The sun came out. Crossed the river Emda, which winds in three branches. Paid a visit to Ben Abou. He had a coat of white cloth.

He told us that the emperor sometimes joins in the powder-play, sometimes with twenty or thirty horsemen whom he designates.

Their horses spend the night in the open air, rain or heat, and are only the better for it.

Some children threw stones at us. Men were sent to arrest the whole village. They will perhaps not get out of this for fifty piasters. Probably the two cows given this evening to Mornay came from this.

Sunday, March 11.

At the river *Sébou*, at the passage of El-Aitem.

When the Moors want to obtain something, as a boon, etc., so as not to be refused they come and bring a sheep near your tent, or even an ox as a present, and slaughter it in sacrificial fashion to show that it is an offering. One is very strongly bound by the obligation which this act imposes. The horses rolling on the river bank.

The day when we camped at Alcassar, they came and killed three sheep, one before the tent of Bias, the second before that of the caid, the third before our tent, to obtain mercy for a man accused of murder. Bias is looking into the matter.

In the meantime, the whole evening was spent over the question of a poor Jew who had been beaten on account of some brandy that he had refused to deliver to Lopez, the French agent at Larache, who was to have given it probably to the brother of that caid in whose tent we were this evening. They would not let the Jew go unless he paid four piasters and ten ounces to the man who gave the beating.

Monday, March 12.

At ——— on the banks of the river Sébou.[8]

Crossed the Sébou this morning. Ridiculous embarkation. The horses running away and beaten to make them enter the boats. Naked men driving the horses in front of them. While crossing the river with us, Bias said that they did not build any bridges in order to arrest rob-

[8] *The Banks of the River Sébou*, Salon of 1859 (Catalogue Robaut, 1346).

bers more easily and to collect taxes and to arrest seditious people. It is he who said that the world is divided into two parts, "Barbary," and "the rest!"

In a race one of the chiefs came up to us; Abou went toward him, and the man made a small tear in his mantle. When we arrived at the camp, Abou tore his mantle to pieces, preferring to burn it rather than let anyone else get the benefit of it. They broke his pipe also. He was furious, and the soldiers could do nothing with him.

March 14.

Arrived in the plain and saw Zar Hone from the distance. Descended to the bank of a pretty river. The edges covered with small laurel. Continued along the flank of the mountain amidst stones and ruins. On approaching Zar Hone, saw ploughmen; the plough. The fountain seen from a distance.

Thursday, March 15.

Meknez.

Started out in the morning. Fine weather. The city of Zar Hone with its smoke. The mountains at the horizon to the right, half covered with clouds. Entered the mountains and, after a certain distance, discovered the great valley in which Meknez is situated.

Crossed a swift brook in the midst of confusion. The pasha of Meknez and the chief of Mescouar had already come to meet us. We climbed the hill. Met the emissary of the emperor, a horrid mulatto with mean features: very fine white burnous, pointed cap without turban, yellow slippers and gilt spurs; violet belt embroidered in gold, heavily embroidered cartridge belt, the bridle of his horse violet and gold. Races by the black guard, caps without turban. Fine sight on looking behind us at that mass of tanned or black faces; the white of clothing dull against the background.

Went through the tiresome promenade. Racing to our left all the time; to the right musket shots from the infantry; from time to time we came upon groups of seated men, who arose at our approach and fired point-blank. Preceded by musicians. Marching behind the flags.

Fine effect as we ascended, the flags etc., silhouetting in dull color against a sky of purest azure.

About twenty flags. Passed beside the tomb of a saint. A palm tree over it. Built of bricks. The gate of the city very high. Varied porcelains, etc. Once we had entered, the horsemen on the ramparts.

Within the gate, immense crowd. To the right, the big gate, which is colossal. In front of us a street. To the left, a long and broad square and, drawn up in a semi-circle before us, the infantry, who fired off their guns. The cavalry behind the men on foot. The mob behind, on hillocks and on the houses.

Thursday, March 22.

Audience with the emperor.[9]

About nine or ten o'clock, started out on horseback, preceded by the caid on his mule, with some soldiers on foot and followed by those who bore the presents. Passed in front of a mosque, fine minaret that one sees from the house. A little window with fine woodwork.

Went through a passage covered with bamboo, as at Alcassar. The houses are higher than those of Tangier.

Reached the square opposite the great gate. The crowd, which got blows with ropes and sticks. Iron plates on the gate, studded with nails. Whitewashed half way up.

Entered a second court after getting down from our horses and went through a line of soldiers; to the left a great esplanade where there were tents, and soldiers with their horses tied.

Advanced after a wait and reached a great square where we were to see the king.

[9] Delacroix evoked that scene in the famous picture, *The Reception of the Emperor Abd-el-Rahman,* which was exhibited in the Salon of 1845, and which is today in Museum of Toulouse (Catalogue Robaut, 922). A small version of it is in the Vanderbilt collection, New York; it dates from 1862 (Catalogue Robaut, 1441).

Before he came out, there were cries of *Ammar Seidna* "Long live our Lord" (God understood). From the gate, which is mean and without ornaments, there first came small detachments of eight or ten black soldiers in pointed caps; they arrived at brief intervals and drew up in lines to the left and right. Then two men bearing spears. Then the king, who advanced toward us and stopped very near by. Great resemblance to Louis-Philippe, younger, thick beard, fairly dark complexion. Burnous of fine dark cloth closed in front. A haik underneath on the upper part of his chest and almost completely covering his thighs and legs. White chaplet with blue silk around his right arm, of which one saw little. Silver stirrups. Yellow slippers which hung loose in back. Harness and saddle of pinkish color and gold. Gray horse, with cropped mane. Parasol with unpainted wooden handle; a small golden ball at the tip; red on top and in the folds, red and green underneath.

After having answered with the customary compliments and having remained longer than is usual in these receptions, he ordered Mushtar to take the letter from the king of the French and accorded us the unheard of favor of visiting some of his apartments. He wheeled about, after having made us a sign of adieu, and was lost in the crowd to the right with the musicians.

The vehicle which had come out after him was covered with green cloth, and was drawn by a mule caparisoned with red; the wheels were gilded. The men who fanned him with white cloths as long as turbans.

Entered through the same gate. There, remounted our horses. Passed through a gate which led to a kind of street between two big walls lined with soldiers on both sides.

There we got down from our horses in front of a small gate; knocking on the gate for a while. We soon entered a court of marble, at the center of which a fountain, shaped like a vase, dripped water; above, small painted shutters. Went through several small rooms with young children, Negroes mostly and none too well dressed. Came out on a garden terrace. Doors in bad condition, paint wearing off. Found a small kiosk of unpainted wood, a kind of couch, a drum-shaped object of cabinet work, with a species of rolled-up mattress. To the left entered a door that was better painted. Very fine court with fountain in the middle; at the back a door in green, red and gold; the walls tiled to the height of a man. The two walls leading to the rooms had a peristyle of columns; delightful painting in the interior and on the vault. Tiles up to a certain height. To the left a bed somewhat in the English fashion. To the left a mattress or bed on the ground, very clean and very white; in the corner to the right, a mirror. Two beds on the ground. Pretty carpet toward the back. In front, matting up to the entrance. Saw, from that room, Abou and one or two others leaning against the wall near the entrance door. Netting above the court.

The commander-in-chief of the cavalry, squatting before the door of the stables. From that door, on looking back, fine effect; the lower part of the walls whitewashed.

There we found our horses and our armed troops again, and went into a more rustic garden. Went out through the place where the emperor's horses grazed; accompanied by soldiers and the people. The child with the picturesque shirt.

Friday, March 23

Went out for the first time. The door with the woodwork above it.

Kind of market for dried fruits, potteries, etc. Bamboo huts up against the walls of the city. Bamboo partitions in the shops, like the trellis work of the gardens. Man in the shadow of a cloth held up by two sticks. The door closed for prayer. Men beating on the wall of tapia[10] and uttering cries in measure each time that one of them gave the signal.

Saturday, March 24.

Entered the house of Abraham's friend. Jews on the terraces silhouetted

[10] Wall of tapia, wall of beaten earth. They put damp earth between boards which form a sort of mold, and they press it together by beating. When the earth is dry, they take off the covering of boards.

against a sky slightly clouded and azured, as Paul Veronese paints it. The pretty little woman came in and kissed the hands of all of us. The Moors were eating. Painted table.

Jews playing in the house of the bride. One of them was in the center, one foot in an old slipper and kicking at any whom he could reach among those surrounding him, who gave him terrible blows with their fists.

In winter as in summer, the king's horses are allowed to remain in the open air. Only during about forty of the coldest days do they put a blanket over them.

Mushtar, who was sent among other presents a piece of white cashmere, had a yard more of it sent yesterday the 27th, because he is counting on two suits of it.

The emperor orders the presents for his ministers brought to him and chooses whatever suits his fancy.

On the 30th, the emperor sent us Jewish musicians from Mogador.[11] They are the finest in the empire.

Abou came to hear them. He took a little paper from his turban in order to write down our names. My name was very difficult for him to pronounce.

Jewish cemetery.

Abraham told us that the masons generally build walls without a plumb-line entirely by instinct; he said that a given workman was incapable of doing over a thing that he had done previously.

April 1.

In the morning, went to the court where the ostriches are; one of them had been wounded by the horn of the antelope; it was difficult to stop the flow of blood.

[11] Delacroix represented this scene in the picture entitled *Jewish Musicians from Mogador,* exhibited in the Salon of 1847, now in the Louvre (Catalogue Robaut, 1011).

Went out about one o'clock. The gate of the city beyond the mosque on leaving the house. Another gate on the street.

Child with the flowers at the tip of the braid of his hair.

Arrived at the market, looking back into the dark passage-way. Mussulmans squatting, I singularly lighted; man in his shop, bamboo behind him, a knife suspended.

April 2.

Bias sent to us for a sheet of paper in order to write the emperor's reply.

April 5.

Left Meknez about eleven o'clock. Worked a great deal the day before. Big arcades against the wall to the left between two gates; the same gate, as one turns back to the big square. Door covered with sheet iron.

Fine valley to the right, stretching back as far as one can see.

Crossed a Moorish bridge. Faded paint. The city in the distance. At the river Sébou.

Crossed many mountains; big squares, yellow, white, and violet with flowers. The place where we camped at the edge of the river. During the day, while we were resting before our arrival, met a courier who brought us letters from France. Very great pleasure.

April 7.

At Reddat.

Crossed the Sébou. Mounted on my horse, I went along the Sébou, very agreeable water. Tents to the left, *douars*. The crossing of the Sébou. The ostrich.

On horseback etc. After lunch we entered beautiful mountains. Descended into a superb valley with many fine trees. Olive trees on gray rocks.

Crossed the Wharrah river, not deep; great big toad. Later on, great heat before reaching camp in a beautiful spot called Reddat.[12]

---

[12] Souvenir of this camp in a picture (Catalogue Robaut 688).

Mountains in the distance. Went out in the evening after sunset. Melancholy view of this immense and uninhabited plain. Sounds of the frogs and other animals. The Mussulmans made their prayer at that time.

Evening. The quarrel of the servants.

April 8.

At Emda.

Fatiguing day. Heavy sky and nervous weather. Crossed a beautiful and fertile country, many douars and tents. Flowers without number, of a thousand kinds, forming the most variegated carpet. Rested and slept in a water hollow.

In the morning met another pasha who is going about his duties with soldiers; on our first trip, we had had his assistant, who was here. The bridle of his horse covered with wrought steel. Arabs. Abou dined with us.

April 9.

At Alcassar-el-Kebir.

Mountains. Went near a place where we had lunched on our first trip, in a hollow, near a fountain. Odorous broom plants. Blue mountains in the distance. When we came in sight of Alcassar, we saw soldiers from Tangier camping in the distance; they are going to Marakech. They were in line. Our soldiers formed a line also. Powder-play. The chiefs and soldiers came to see their chief again, kissing their hands after having taken their other one. Some soldiers kissed his knee. River of Alcassar. Fragments of tapia construction.

Milk offered by the women. The staff with a white cloth. The milk given first to the standard-bearers, who dipped their fingertips in it. Then to the caid and to the soldiers.

The children who went to meet the caid and kissed his knee.

The saber on the road; get Abraham to explain this to me.

April 10.

Mounted the horse of M. Desgranges. Beautiful country, very blue mountains, violet to the right; the mountains are violet in the morning and evening, blue during the day. Carpet of yellow flowers, violet before reaching the river of Wad-el-Maghzen.

Went again through the entrance of the narrow and winding valley called the Camel's Neck. Long fatiguing day.

April 11.

Ain-el-Daliah.

Mounted Cadour's horse, mine being sick. Again saw the fine olive trees on the slope of a hill. Observed the shadows formed by the stirrups and the feet. A shadow which always draws the outline of the thigh and of the leg below it. The stirrup coming out while the straps remain invisible. The stirrup and the clasp of the breastpiece very white without any gloss. Gray horse, a bridle at his head; worn, white velvet.

I must mass the human figures in dark color, and then put light touches on to bring them into relief.

Lunched at the place on the edge of a brook where we lunched on our outward trip. Going on, soldiers to the left detached against the sky. The men in half-tint, charming color; the blacks, figures etc. The dark note of the horses very marked.

Saddle with a powderhorn, breastpiece with a pummel, guncase green. Head like a Michelangelo, white blanket.

The women who came to present milk to the standard-bearers and to the caid.

Next day, April 12.

Left Ain-el-Daliah with the son of the pasha, escorted on each side by two men with guns. The cavalry sack slung around the neck. The infantry sometimes carries it that way.

Halfway along the road, some women and men placed a saber in front of him. Get Abraham to explain this.

Nearer the city, children came to pay compliments to Abou, who questioned them and gave them money.

Tangier. After the return from Meknez.

Went to the house of Abraham with M. de Praslin and M. d'Haussonville. The girl with the little kerchief on her head; her dress. The Negroes who came to dance at the consulate and through the city. Woman in front of them covered with a haik and bearing a staff with a cloth at the end to collect money. A touch of fever about the 16th of April. On the 20th took a walk. My first outing with M. D. and M. Freyssinet along the waterfront. The black man bathing the black horse; the Negro as black and as shiny as the horse.

Tangier, April 28.

Yesterday, April 27th, there passed under our windows a procession with music; drums and oboes, it was for a young boy who had just finished his school and who was being escorted about with ceremony. He was surrounded by his comrades who sang, and by his parents and teachers. People came out of the shops and houses to compliment him. He was enveloped in a burnous, etc.

At times of distress, the children come out with their school tablets and carry them with solemnity. These tablets are of wood coated with clay. They write with reeds and a sort of sepia which can easily be wiped off. This people is wholly antique. This exterior life and these carefully closed houses: the women withdrawn, etc. The other day, quarrel with sailors who wanted to enter a Moorish house. A Negro threw his wooden shoe in their faces, etc.

Abou, the general who conducted us, was seated the other day on the doorstep; our kitchen boy was seated on the bench. He bent over to the side only the least bit so as to let us pass. There is something democratic in such offhand manners. The big men of the country will squat down in the sun on a street corner and chat together, or stretch out in the shop of some merchant.

These people have a small number of legal cases, anticipated or possible: for certain cases, a given punishment in a given circumstance; but the whole business is arranged without those endless and tiresome details with which our modern authorities overwhelm us. Custom and ancient usage govern everything. The Moor gives thanks to God for his poor food and his poor cloak. He considers himself only too happy to have them.

Certain quite common and antique customs possess a majesty which is lacking among us in even the gravest circumstances. The custom of having the women go on Friday to the graves with the branches that are sold in the market. The weddings with music, the presents borne behind them by the relatives, the *couscous,* the bags of wheat on mules and asses, an ox, clothes on cushions, etc.

It must be difficult for them to conceive of the turbulent mind of the Christians and that restlessness of ours which urges us on to novelties. We notice a thousand things which are lacking with these people. Their ignorance produces their calm and their happiness; but we ourselves, are we at the summit of what a more advanced civilization can produce?

They are closer to nature in a thousand ways: their dress, the form of their shoes. And so beauty has a share in everything that they make. As for us, in our corsets, our tight shoes, our ridiculous pinching clothes, we are pitiful. The graces exact vengeance for our science.

May 16.[12]

On the 16th of May in the evening, after a wearisome quarantine of seven days, we were permitted to enter Cadiz; great joy. The same thing next morning on going about.

The mountains on the other side of the bay very distinct and of beautiful color. On approaching, the houses of Cadiz were white, and gilded against a beautiful blue sky. Saw some handsome Greeks on entering the city.

Cadiz, Friday, May 18.

Midnight is sounding at the church of the Franciscans. Singular emo-

[12] On May 15th Delacroix started out for a two weeks' excursion to Cadiz and Seville, after which he returned to Tangier.

tion in this country which is so strange. This moonlight. These white towers under the light of the moon. In my room there are two engravings by Debucourt: *Les Visites* and *L'Orange;* on one of them is inscribed: published on the first day of the nineteenth century; that reminds me that I was already of this world! What a long time since my early youth!

Took a walk in the evening; at the house of Mme Carmen, met Signora Maria Josefa.

M. Gros, the chancellor, dined with us. He is a man of the gentlest appearance and he drank nothing but water with his dinner. As he refused to smoke after the desert, he told us simply that his moderation was a matter of regimen; a few years ago he smoked three or four dozen times a day, he drank his bottle of brandy, and kept no account of his bottles of wine. Some time ago he let himself go with drinking beer; he drank six or eight bottles in no time at all; he was just the same way with women, he has gone to the greatest excesses with them. There is something for Hoffman in this character.

The strange make-up of this man, who has permitted himself every indulgence and every excess. He told me that being deprived of his cigar was the greatest hardship of all for him. He constantly had a dream that he had gone back to his old habit, that he reproached himself severely for having departed from his regimen, and that then, when he woke up, he was very much pleased with himself. What a life of pleasure this man really has led! Wine and, above all, tobacco gave him a perfectly voluptuous enjoyment.

About four o'clock, went to the monastery of the Augustinians with M. Augrand. Staircases lined with tiles. The choir of the brothers in the upper part of the church and the long room with the pictures as one approaches it. Even in the bad portraits with which the walls of the cloister are papered, influence of the fine Spanish school.

Saturday, May 19.

At the monastery of the Capuchins. The father who acts as caretaker, when showing us his garden, tells us to take some flowers, if not for ourselves, at least for the ladies. He did not think that the garden of the monastery was worthy of our visit, since the wind had spoiled the fruits.

On entering, a very simple square court, images on the walls, etc., the church to the right, opposite. The Virgin of Murillo: the cheeks perfectly painted and the eyes celestial. The church very dark. The sacristy; wardrobes of blackish wood, benches. (Made sketches.) The little garden of the father in charge — the choir in the rear, the corridor leading from it. Picture of a recumbent skeleton, to the right of the door to the corridor of the infirmary. (Sketch.) Corridors as far as one could see; staircases; geographical maps on the walls. Small sculpture of a *Pieta* set into the wall under a small painting of a monk in ecstacy, his hands clasped as he contemplates the crucifix. Cloister below, paintings above each arch; death amidst the riches of the earth. The garden.

On the 20th, in the morning, went to the monastery of the Dominicans. The church very beautiful.

The cathedral in ruins without ever having been finished. Devilish hot sun.

The bull.

Seville, Wednesday, May 23.

Relationship with the Moors. Great gates everywhere. Compartments of the ceiling of cabinet work. The garden; the brick path bordered with tiles, the ground lower. Crenelated walls. Enormous keys.

Alcala. The night. The moon on the melancholy waters. The cry of the frogs. The Moorish gothic chapel near the aqueduct before entering the city.

(Seville). In the morning went to the cathedral: magnificent obscurity. The Christ above on the red damask. The great grill which surrounds the high altar. The back of the altar with little windows and entrance to a crypt.

Arcades on the houses. The woman lying on the ground at the

door of the church; brown arm against the black of the mantilla and the brown of the dress. Singular character arising from the fact that one sees almost no white, especially around the head.

Took a walk in the evening; terrace which reminds me of my childhood at Montpellier.

Banks of the Guadalquivir. Before that, the Capuchin preaching. Windows covered with colored cloth and draperies.

Friday, May 25.

M. Baron came early to call for me. Ascended the tower, the Giralda. No steps. The environs resemble those of Paris. Dined with M. Hartley and M. Muller, and went with them in a carriage to see the Cartuja (the Carthusian Church). Fine Zurbarán in the sacristy. Fine tombs. Arcanum behind the altar. Graveyard. Orange trees. Moorish court. Paintings and tiles on the walls, benches of tiles.

At noon made a drawing of Signora Dolores. Before that to the church of the Capuchins. On their coat-of-arms, the five wounds of Jesus (sketch), the one in the center is the largest, and two arms, one of them bare. Fine Murillos; among others the saint with the miter and the black robe, giving alms. The pink chapel to a Madonna.

In the evening went to the cemetery. (Sketch.)

On returning from the Capuchins, went along the walls of the city; double enclosure, one lower than the other at a distance of about six or eight feet. (Sketch.)

In the evening to the house of M. Williams. M. D. Melancholia. Guitar. When returning, the soldier who was playing the guitar in front of the guard house. Brief moments of varied emotions during the evening. The music, etc. In the morning, two saints by Goya in the sacristy of the cathedral.

The horses led in troops over the bridge. The men with sheepskin coats and breeches; that would make a picture. (Sketch.) Chains on the door, at every place where the king has entered.

The refectory of the Carthusians.[14] The bishop; green hat. (Sketch.)

Saturday, 26.

Alcazar: superb Moorish style, different from the buildings in Africa. The garden remarkable, and the hanging gallery which partially surrounds it. Finished the study of the mantilla at the house of M. Williams. Embarrassment.

The famous Romero, matador and instructor in bullfighting, made scarcely any movements in avoiding the bull. He could lead him up in front of the king in order to kill him and, after having delivered his thrust, he swung about at the same instant to salute without looking behind him.

The famous Pepillo, a very celebrated matador, was killed in Madrid by a bull. He was caught in the side by the horn; he tried in vain to free himself by raising himself with his arms over the very head of the animal who was carrying him all around the arena—and at a slow gait so that the horn was penetrating deeper at every moment. It carried him suspended in that fashion and already dead. Romero was inconsolable not to have been there; he was persuaded that he would have been able to free him.

Sunday, 27.

At the house of M. Williams in the evening.

Dancers. The little one who lifted her leg. The biggest one very graceful. At the beginning of the evening I was bored. Mme Ford corrected the music for me and I was near her. Then the sister of M. Williams explained to me the words of the air which she gave me. The dancers explained the castanets to me. The pretty child who sat down between the legs of M. D.

[14] The Carthusian church of Seville inspired Delacroix for at least four drawings (Catalogue Robaut, 1645 and 1647) and, in 1838, for a composition: *Columbus at the Monastery of Santa Maria de Robida* (Catalogue Robaut, 659).

Mme Ford; adieu in the English fashion. Coquette. I had been there during the day without finding her in; I had wandered through the streets like a Spanish lover. Streets covered over with cloths.

Before that, made a drawing in a big hall, near the cathedral. Dined at Hartley's house and went to the monastery of Saint Jerome with those gentlemen; the famous Cevallos[15] is there. Saint Jerome by Torrigiani.[16]

Monday, the 28th.

Went to the Casa de Pilata.[17] Superb stairway. Tiles everywhere. Moorish garden.

Farewell to M. Williams and his family. I cannot leave, probably forever, these excellent people. Alone a moment with him. His emotion.

The boat; departure. The lady in officer's clothing. The banks of the Guadalquivir, sad night. Solitude amidst these strangers who were playing cards in the dark, uncomfortable space between the decks. The lady who rolled up her sleeve to show me her wound.

Bad feelings on waking up; debarkation at San Lucar.

Returned in a carriage with the maid from the Cadiz hotel. Deserted country. The man on horseback with his blanket round his neck.

Algiers, June 25.

Landed about eleven o'clock. The waterfront. Street going uphill. Narrow streets that run into each other. Called on the general. Called on the naval commander. Went to the Kasbah. The entrance dark, the gate

[15] Pedro Cevallos, Spanish statesman (1764–1840), retired to the monastery of Saint Jerome in Seville.

[16] Torrigiani, Italian sculptor, contemporary of Michelangelo, born in 1472, died at Seville in 1522. The statue of Saint Jerome mentioned by Delacroix is in the museum of Seville.

[17] The Casa de Pilata is one of the finest examples of the Moorish style which are preserved in Seville.

painted, fountain. (Sketch.) The roofs in Turkish style on the inside. (Sketch.) The ceiling painted, often with boards, not with beams. The cypress trees above. (Sketch.) In front of the dark passage-way where the Arabs are (Sketch.). The room of the Dey. Balcony. The rich people hang brocaded tapestries over the doors and windows, etc. (Sketch.) At Oran. Coats of arms in the white walls (Sketch.)

NOTE BY THE TRANSLATOR

FROM 1832 we are obliged to leap to 1847, reserving for the supplement those scattered fragments, written on loose leaves of paper or more often in sketchbooks, which relate to this interval of fifteen years, but which are not part of the *Journal* itself.

The *Journal*, interrupted on the 5th of October 1824, does not really start again until the 19th of January 1847, as is witnessed by the following lines, written that same day: "I write this by my fireside, happy to have gone and bought this notebook before I came home; I am beginning it under good conditions. May I frequently continue to take note of my impressions! I shall frequently see in it what one gains when one notes one's impressions, and how one deepens them in recalling them."

Tuesday, January 19.

WENT at half past ten to see Gisors,[1] about the project for the stairway in the Luxembourg. Then to the gallery of the Luxembourg to meet M. Masson;[2] he gives up the idea of engraving the picture himself. Went to the Panthéon. Saw the cupola with the decorations by Gros; alas what thinness and uselessness. The pendentives by Gérard which I did not know. The whole thing frightful in color. Slaty skies, tones that stab one another, on all sides; the shiny surface of the painting gives one the final shock and makes the whole thing unbearably thin. A gilt frame badly suited in its character to that of the monument, taking up too much room as compared with the painting. *Prometheus on the Rock,* with nymphs who are consoling him. It is lacking in the sense of the ideal.

From Vimont's studio to the Jardin des Plantes. The natural history collection open to the public on Tuesdays and Fridays. Elephants, rhinoceros, hippopotamus, strange animals! The way Rubens has rendered this is marvelous. On entering this collection I had a feeling of happiness. The further I went along, the more this feeling increased: it seemed to me that my being was rising above the commonplaces, the small ideas, the small anxieties of the moment. What a prodigious variety of animals, and what a variety of species, of forms, and of destinations! At every moment, what seems to us deformity side by side with what seems to us grace. Here are the herds of Neptune, the seals, the walruses, the whales, the immensity of the

[1] Alphonse-Henry de Gisors (1796–1866) architect. There had been a question of having Delacroix decorate the walls of the great staircase, to the left of the court of the Luxembourg palace. The project was not carried out.

[2] Alphonse Masson (1814–1898), engraver. In 1854 he executed a portrait of Delacroix for *L'Histoire des Peintres Vivants* by Théophile Silvestre. He also engraved several pictures by Delacroix, including the *Massacre of Scio,* then in the Luxembourg.

fishes with their insensitive eyes, and their mouths stupidly open; the crustaceans, the crabs, the turtles; then the hideous family of the serpents. The enormous body of the boa, with his small head. The elegance of its coils wound around a tree; the hideous dragon, the lizards, the crocodiles, the alligators, the monstrous gavials with their jaws tapering suddenly and ending at the nose with a curious protuberance. Then the animals which are nearer in their nature to our own: the innumerable deer, gazelles, elks, bucks, goats, sheep, with forked feet, horned heads, the horns being straight, twisted or in curls; the bovine race, with the wild ox and the bison; the dromedaries and the camels, the llamas, the vicunas, which are related to them; finally the giraffe, the ones from Levaillant, sewn together and patched up; but also the one of 1827 which, after having been the delight of all idlers and having shone with incomparable splendor, had to pay mortal tribute in his turn, dying in obscurity as complete as his entry into the world had been brilliant. Here he is, all stiff and clumsy as nature made him. The ones that preceded him in the catacombs had doubtless been stuffed by men who had not seen the appearance of the animal during its lifetime: they had made it rear its neck proudly, not being able to imagine the bizarre turn of that head pushing forward, the characteristic movement of a living creature.

The tigers, the panthers, the jaguars, the lions, etc.

Whence comes the impression which the sight of all that produced on me? From the fact that I got out of my everyday ideas which are my whole world, that I got out of my street which is my universe. How necessary it is to give oneself a shaking up, to get one's head out, to try to read in the book of creation, which has nothing in common with our cities and with the works of men! Certainly, seeing such things renders one better and calmer. When I came out of the museum, the trees got their share of admiration, and they had their share in the feeling of pleasure that this day has given me. I returned by way of the far end of the garden on the quay. On foot a part of the way and the rest in the omnibuses.

I write this by my fireside, happy to have gone and bought this notebook before I came home: I am beginning it under good conditions. May I frequently continue to take note of my impressions! I shall frequently see in it what one gains when one notes one's impressions, and how one deepens them in recalling them.

Statue of Buffon,[3] not bad, not too ridiculous. Busts of great French naturalists, Daubenton, Cuvier, Lacépède, etc. etc.

January 20.

Worked on the picture of *Valentin*.[4] Did the background. In the evening went to the house of J.[5]

M. Auguste lent me a water color, a *Black Horse* and also two volumes of *Souvenirs de la Terreur;* he gave me back the notebook of the little gallery of Algiers, and a portmanteau.

January 21.

I am reading the *Souvenirs de la Terreur* by G. Duval. The effort to render the scenes, and the supposititious, imagined conversations, and to give color and reality, takes away all one's confidence in him. His systematic hatred of the Revolution is too plainly shown. The historian, notwithstanding, could profit from this book, not on account of the small facts which are reported but, looking past the partiality of the writer, he would see that we must discount the enthusiasm and spontaneity of the movements which are most admired in that period. What one sees in this book of the working of the minor mechanisms reduces to the proportion of conspiracies what often appears in history as the effect of national sentiment.

January 23.

Composed the *Christ Bearing the Cross*. Continued my pastel of *Christ in the Garden of Olives*.

[3] The statue of Buffon referred to is by Pajou.
[4] The *Death of Valentin,* exhibited in the Salon of 1848 (Catalogue Robaut, 1008).
[5] Mme. de Forget, his cousin.

I must consider, for my pictures, the fine exaggerations of horses and of men in Rubens, especially in the *Hunt* by Soutman.[6]

January 24.

In the evening went to the house of M. Thiers.[7]

Saw D'Aragon[8] again. When only a few people were still there, he told us about Marshal Soult.[9] He said he would challenge anyone to find a single brilliant action in the man's life. Very laborious, etc. At the camp of Boulogne, he was one of those who made Napoleon Emperor. They did not know how they were to go about it. The Senate would probably have refused to take the step even though the army was completely devoted to the First Consul. Someone got the idea, and I think it was General Soult, of having a petition signed by a disorganized corps of dragoons, which, deprived of its horses and having nothing to do, was getting very near the stage of demoralization common among soldiers reduced to idleness. They signed the petition, which was presented to the Senate as the will of the army. Cambacérès was against it. Fouché, who was also eager to get back into favor, bestirred himself actively. Under the circumstances, the Senate followed the example of the Senate of Rome in the time of the emperors: they hastened to name in advance the man whom they saw as about to be named by the soldiers.

January 25.

The influence on a composition of the principal lines is immense. I have under my eyes the *Hunts* by Rubens, among others, the *Lion Hunt* etched by Soutman, where a lioness, springing forward from the depth

---

[6] Pieter Claesz Soutman (1580–1657), one of the engravers who reproduced the pictures of Rubens.

[7] Louis-Adolphe Thiers (1797–1877), the statesman and historian, was an early and vigorous admirer of Delacroix. His long-continued power in the government permitted him to render many services to the painter.

[8] Member of the Chamber of Deputies, a friend of George Sand's.

[9] Marshal Soult (1759–1851) was at that time President of the Council.

of the picture, is stopped by the spear of a horseman who turns about in his saddle: one sees the spear bend as it plunges into the chest of the furious animal. In the foreground, a Moorish horseman has been thrown to earth; his horse, also overthrown, is already seized by an enormous lion. But the animal turns with a horrible grimace toward another fighter lying flat on the ground who, in a final effort, buries a dagger of terrifying width in the body of the monster; the man is as if nailed to the earth by one of the hind feet of the animal, which claws his face in frightful fashion as it feels itself stabbed. The rearing horses, the bristling manes, a thousand accessories, shields torn from the arms, tangled bridles, the whole thing combines to strike the imagination, and the execution is admirable. But the picture has an aspect of confusion, the eye does not know where to stop, it gets the feeling of a frightful disorder; and it seems that art has not presided sufficiently to augment, by prudent distribution or by sacrifices, the effect of so many inventions of genius.

On the contrary, in the *Hunt of the Hippopotamus,* the details do not demand anything like the same effort of the imagination. In the foreground one sees a crocodile which, in the painting, must assuredly be a masterpiece of execution; but its action could have been more interesting. The hippopotamus, the hero of the action, is a formless beast that no execution could render bearable. The action of the dogs as they spring forward is full of energy, but Rubens has frequently repeated that effect. From a description, this picture will seem inferior at all points to the preceding one. However, from the manner in which the groups are disposed, or rather from the single and unique group which constitutes the picture as a whole, the imagination receives a shock, which is renewed every time that one's eyes fall on it, even as, in the *Lion Hunt,* one is always thrown into the same uncertainty as to the lines.

In the *Hunt of the Hippopotamus,* the amphibian monster occupies the center; riders, horses, dogs, all throw themselves upon him with fury. The composition offers approximately the shape of a Saint

Andrew's Cross, with the hippopotamus in the middle. The man thrown to the ground and stretched out among the reeds under the feet of the crocodile, prolongs a line of light below, and so prevents the composition from having too great importance in the upper part; what is of incomparable effect is that large space of sky which frames the whole on both sides, especially at the left side which is entirely bare, and so gives to the ensemble, through the simplicity of this contrast a movement, a variety, and at the same time a unity, which are incomparable.

January 26.

Worked on the *Arab Horsemen*. Dined at the house of M. Thiers. I don't know what to say to the people that I meet at his house, and they don't know what to say to me. From time to time, noticing the deep boredom produced in me by those conversations of politicians about the Chamber, etc., they talk painting with me.

How cold and tiresome is this modern style of dinners! Those lackeys who, in some respects, do the whole work, and who really give you your dinner. The dinner is the thing least considered: it is despatched, as one gets rid of a disagreeable function. Good-bye to cordiality, farewell to good humor. The fragile glassware, what a stupid luxury! I can't touch my glass without spilling it and getting half of its contents onto the tablecloth. I escaped as soon as I could. Princess Demidoff[10] was there. M. de Rémusat was at the dinner; he is a charming man, but after "good morning" and "good evening," I don't know what to say to him.

January 27.

Worked at the *Arab Horsemen* and at the *Valentin*.

In the evening went to Labbé, and then Leblond. Garcia[11] was

[10] Princess Demidoff (Princess Mathilde), daughter of King Jerome, had married Prince Anatole Demidoff in 1841 and had separated from him in 1845.
[11] Manuel Garcia (1805–1906) musician, son of the celebrated singer, and brother of the two singers, Marie (la Malibran, who died in 1836) and Pauline (Mme Viardot).

there. Spoke of the opinion of Diderot on the actor. He affirms that the actor, even while controlling himself, should be passionate. In reply, I maintain that everything takes place in the imagination. Diderot, when he refuses all sensibility to the actor, does not sufficiently state that imagination replaces it. What I have heard Talma[12] say explains well enough the two combined effects: those of the inspiration necessary to the actor, and of the mastery of himself which he must at the same time preserve. He said that when on the stage, he was perfectly able to direct his inspiration and to judge himself, even though having the full appearance of giving himself up to his part; but he added, that if, at that moment, someone had come to tell him that his house was on fire, he could not have torn himself from the scene: it is the condition of any man engaged on work which occupies all his faculties, but whose soul is not, on that account, overcome by an emotion.

Garcia in defending the role of sensibility and of true passion, thinks of his sister, Mme Malibran. He tells us as proof of her talent as a great actress that she never knew how she would play. Thus, in *Romeo* when she reaches the tomb of Juliet, she would sometimes stop at a pillar, on entering, in a burst of grief; at other times she would throw herself down sobbing before the stone, etc.; she thus achieved moments full of energy and seemingly full of truth, but it also happened that she would seem exaggerated and faulty in her timing, and as a consequence unbearable. I do not recall ever having seen her *noble*. When she came the nearest to the sublime, it was only to such a conception of it as a bourgeoise might possess; in a word, she was completely lacking in the sense of the ideal. She was like the young people who have talent, but whose turbulent time of life and whose inexperience always make them think that they cannot do enough with it. It seems that she was endlessly seeking new effects in a situation. If one takes that course, one is never finished: that is never the way of consummate talent; when such a person has done his study and found

[12] Talma, the celebrated tragedian.

his personal note, he breaks away from it no more. That was the distinguishing feature of the talent of Mme Pasta.[13] It characterizes the art of Rubens, Raphael, and all the great composers. Outside of the fact that with the other method the mind finds itself in perpetual uncertainty, one's whole life would be spent in trying over the same thing. When la Malibran had finished her evening, she was exhausted: mental fatigue was added to physical fatigue, and her brother agrees that she could not have lived for long in that way.

I tell him that Garcia, his father, was a great actor, constantly the same in all his roles, despite his apparent inspiration. He had seen him, for Othello,[14] study a grimace before the mirror; sensibility would not proceed in such fashion.

Garcia related to us that la Malibran, when she was puzzled as to the effect that she should seek for the moment when the unforeseen arrival of her father interrupts the transports of joy that she feels on learning that Othello is alive after his combat with Roderigo, she asked advice on this point from Mme Naldi, the wife of that Naldi who was killed by the explosion of a shell, and the mother of Mme de Sparre. That woman had been an excellent actress. She told her that, having to play the role of Galatea in *Pygmalion,* and having remained motionless in astounding fashion for all the time necessary, she had produced the greatest effect, at the moment when she makes the first movement which tells of the spark of life.

Mme Malibran, in *Mary Stuart,* is brought before her rival, Elizabeth, by Leicester, who implores her to humiliate herself before her rival. She finally consents to do so, and, falling on her knees, gives herself to the deepest supplication; but, outraged by the inflexible hardness of Elizabeth, she would rise up impetuously and throw herself into a fury which, he said, produced the greatest effect. She tore her handkerchief and even her gloves to tatters. There again is one of those effects to which a great artist will never descend: they are the

[13] The Italian singer.
[14] Opera by Rossini (1814).

kind which delight people in the boxes and afford a passing reputation to those who are willing to indulge themselves that way.

There is this unfortunate thing about the talent of the actor: after his death it is impossible to establish any comparison between him and his rivals, those who competed with him for applause during his lifetime. Posterity knows nothing of an actor save the reputation which his contemporaries made for him; and for our descendants, la Malibran will be placed on the same line as la Pasta; perhaps she will even be preferred, if one takes into account the exaggerated praise of her contemporaries. Garcia, in speaking of la Pasta, classed her among the cold and controlled talents, *plastic,* as he said. As to that word "plastic," what he should have said was ideal. At Milan, she had created *Norma* with extraordinary brilliancy; people no longer talked of la *Pasta,* but la *Norma.* Mme Malibran arrives, she demands that role for her début, and she succeeds, with that piece of childishness. The public, divided in the beginning, carries her to the clouds, and la *Pasta* was forgotten; it was la Malibran who had become la *Norma,* and I have no difficulty in believing it. The people whose minds do not rise very high, and who are not at all difficult in matters of taste — which is to say, unfortunately, the majority, will always prefer talents of the type possessed by la Malibran.

If the painter left nothing of himself, and if we were obliged to judge him, on the testimony of the people of his time, how different reputations would be from those that posterity has established! How many names, obscure today, must have been shining lights in their time, thanks to the caprice of fashion and to the bad taste of contemporaries! By good fortune, however fragile it is, painting or, replacing it, engraving preserves the documents of the case, places them under the eyes of posterity which can thus give back his place to the man of real eminence who has been underesteemed by the foolish public that comes and goes and is always fascinated by tinsel, and by the husks of truth.

I do not think that one can establish a satisfactory parallel between the execution of the actor and that of the painter. The former has had his moment of violent and almost passionate inspiration, during which he has been able to place himself, by imagination always, in the role of the character he portrays: but once his effects are arrived at, he must, at each performance, become more and more cold in producing his effects. To some extent he does no more each time than give a new example of his original conception, and the more he gets away from the moment when his ideal, only half evolved, could still appear before his mind with a certain confusion, the more he approaches perfection: he makes tracings, so to speak. The painter has, indeed, that first passionate seeing of his subject. But that trial of himself is more formless than that of the actor. The more talent he has, the more beauties the calmness of study will add; not that he will conform to his first idea in the most exact way, but he will emphasize that idea by the warmth of his execution.

Execution, in painting, should always have about it something of improvisation, and therein lies the capital difference between it and the execution of the actor. That of the painter will be fine only if he has saved himself up for a certain abandon later on, for discoveries made as the work advances, etc.

January 28.

How rare the musical temperament is among the French!

Dined at the house of Mme Marliani. Chopin[15] was there; he told me of his new treatment by massage. That would be very fortunate. During the evening, a certain General Ameilher played on a queer guitar which he had constructed according to his own ideas. In my opinion he does not get the advantages from it to produce his effect. He plays too weakly. The mania of all the guitarists is to be making little trills the whole time.

[15] Chopin, for whom Delacroix professed himself in the liveliest accord, and with whom he had for ten years been friends, was gravely ill at that time. He had just broken off his affair with George Sand.

Walked home with Petetin who talked to me about economics and the investing of money. He told me that it is surprising how quickly one can increase one's fortune when one has a good understanding of such matters.

January 29.

Tired from my evening of yesterday.

It is probable that when one works often without a model, however happy one's conception, one does not attain those striking effects which the great masters arrive at in simple fashion, merely because they naively rendered an effect in nature, even an ordinary one. And just there will always be the pitfall; effects like those of Prud'hon or like those of Correggio will never be those of Rubens, for example. In the little *Saint Martin* by Van Dyck, as copied by Géricault, the composition is very ordinary; notwithstanding, the effect of the horse and the rider is immense. It is very probable that that effect was achieved because the subject was seen by the artist in nature. My little Greek (Comte Palatiano) has the same accent.[16] One might say that, with the reverse process, you arrive at effects which are more tender and penetrating, even if they have not that striking and masterful look which at once commands admiration. The white horse of the *Saint Benedict* by Rubens[17] seems like a thing done purely from the imagination, and yet makes a most powerful effect.

Dined with Mme de Forget.

January 31.

Yesterday evening J. (Mme de Forget) gave me an article by Gautier on the Luxembourg which is full of praise.

February 2.

Went to see Muller in the morning. Dupré and Rousseau came in

[16] *Le Comte Palatiano* (Catalogue Robaut, 170).

[17] In 1841 Delacroix had made a copy of the picture, now in the museum of Brussels where it is placed beside the original by Rubens (Catalogue Robaut, 736).

during the day. They repeated a whole lot of arguments in favor of their famous society; but I had made my decision and I declared to them my complete aversion for the project.[18]

What can one do after a day, or rather a morning like that? First going out in the morning, and then the coming of those two talkers at the moment when I might have got back some disposition for work left me half exhausted till the evening. Called on M. Thiers.

February 3.

Muller returned my visit very promptly; the nerve of that young cock is remarkable. I had criticized certain parts of his pictures with an extreme reserve; as a rule I can't help doing so, and I don't like to hurt people. In my studio he seemed to me quite at his ease: "This is good, I don't like this." That's the way he spoke; Hédouin got angry about it. He told me about the extreme self-confidence of Couture.[19] It is the mark of that school; Muller belongs to it. The other mark of it is that eternal white which they plaster on everywhere and their rendering of light which, in their pictures, looks as if they made it out of flour.

On account of what those gentlemen said to me, I painted out the window in the background of the *Moroccans Sleeping.*[20] Worked at

[18] The question was of founding a society which should give annual exhibitions, to balance those of the official Salon, and avoid the rigors of the jury. Jules Dupré and Théodore Rousseau were the promoters of it.

[19] Thomas Couture (1815–1879), the famous painter of the *Romans of the Decadence* which we shall see Delacroix appreciating later on (entry of May 7, 1847) with measure and exactitude, distinguished himself by his high opinion of himself, and his lack of comprehension of the genius of Delacroix: "Intelligent and insufficient at the same time," he wrote about Delacroix in the *Revue Libérale* for April 10, 1867, "the mediocrity of his execution constitutes for him a false originality." (This was written more than three years after Delacroix's death).

[20] This picture, the *Corps de Garde à Mequinez* of the Salon of 1847, is now in the Museum at Chantilly (Catalogue Robaut, 1018). The window is still there.

the *Arab Horsemen:* the darkness compelled me to stop with it: I then began to sketch the *Christ au Tombeau,*[21] the sky only.

Rivet[22] came at four o'clock. I was happy to see him; his considerateness is charming. Soon we were as in the old days. I find him changed and that makes me feel badly. He is very well pleased with my article on Prud'hon.[23]

Stayed at home this evening. My state of mind was melancholy, if I may say so, and not sad. The various people whom I saw today were doubtless the cause of this state. I made bitter reflections on the profession of the artist; this isolation, this sacrifice of almost all the feelings which animate the generality of men.

February 4.

Reached the Chamber of Deputies at half past eleven. On arriving, saw the decoration on the walls by Vernet.[24] One could write a volume on the frightful decadence in the art of the nineteenth century that this work shows. I do not speak only of the bad taste and of the mean execution in the crudely colored figures; but the grisaille and the ornaments are deplorable. In the poorest village, and at the time of Vanloo, they would still have seemed detestable.

I saw my hemicycle[25] again, and with pleasure; I perceived at once

[21] This is the *Christ au Tombeau* of the Salon of 1848, now in the Boston Museum (Catalogue Robaut, 1034).

[22] Baron Charles Rivet (1800–1872), prominent in politics for many years. He was a great friend of Delacroix's.

[23] An article which appeared in the *Revue des Deux Mondes* for December 1st, 1846, reprinted in the *Œuvres Littéraires* of Delacroix (published in the series of the *Bibliothèque Dionysienne*).

[24] Horace Vernet, by reason of his intimate relations with the royal family of Orléans, had been commissioned to decorate a ceiling in the Palais Bourbon, the seat of the Chamber of Deputies.

[25] Delacroix had painted *Orpheus Bringing Civilization to Greece* in one of the hemicycles of the library of the Palais Bourbon. The decoration of the Library, for which Delacroix received the order in 1838, was finished in 1847. It is composed of two hemicycles and five cupolas, each of the later being divided into four pendentives. The paintings in the hemicycles are executed

what was necessary to get back the effect. Merely changing the drapery of the *Orpheus* gave vigor to the whole thing.

What a pity that experience comes at just the age when one's strength is leaving one! It is one of nature's cruel derisions, this gift of talent, since it comes only through time and study, and they wear out the vigor one needs for executing.

In the omnibus, when returning, I observed the effect of the half-tone on the horses, bays and blacks, that is to say on a shining skin. One has to paint them as a mass, like the rest, with a local color midway between the high-light and the tone of warm color. On this preparation all that is necessary is a warm transparent glaze for the change of plane in shadow or with reflections and on the projections in this halftone color the high-lights are marked out with light, cold tones. In the bay horse, this is clearly to be seen.

February 5.

I spent the whole day resting and reading in my room. Began *Monte Cristo;* it is very entertaining except, however, the interminable dialogues which fill the pages; when one has read that, one has read nothing.

After dinner went to Pierret's house. We were talking of the jokes and cock-and-bull stories of M. de Conflans.

I said that in literature the first impression is the strongest; in proof, the *Memoirs* of Casanova, which produced an immense effect on me in 1829, when I read them for the first time, in the abridged edition. Since then I have had an opportunity to look through passages in the more complete edition, and have got a different impression.

directly on the wall, coated with a preparation of wax. The paintings on the cupolas are executed on canvas, which was applied to the wall. These admirable paintings, the finest decorative ensemble in French art, were so badly lit as to be almost invisible. Electric lighting installed in 1926, followed by a recent cleaning (1930), revealed them to the public. Before doing them Delacroix had been commissioned by M. Thiers to decorate the vestibule called the *Salon du Roi* or Throne Room of the Palais Bourbon. This magnificent decoration was executed between 1833 and 1837.

Young Soulié tells me that M. Niel, having read the *Neveu de Rameau* in the French translation made from Goethe's rendering of it into German, preferred it to the original. Undoubtedly this derives from the effect of that vivid impression that Goethe's words produce on the mind, and that is not to be found in the original work on returning to it.

(I am re-reading this in 1857. I am re-reading the *Memoirs* of Casanova now while I am sick; I find them more adorable than ever; hence they are good).

February 6.

Worked but little in the morning. In the afternoon, sketched in the whole of the figures of the *Christ au Tombeau*. Dined and spent the evening with J . . . (de Forget).

Planet[26] came at four o'clock; he seemed very taken with my sketch; he would have liked to see it on a large scale. The sincere admiration that he evinces gives me great pleasure. He is of those who reconcile me with myself. May heaven reward him for it! The poor lad is totally lacking in confidence, and that is a pity, for he has fine qualities.

February 8.

Excellent day.

I began by going to the Rue Taranne to see the picture of *Saint Just* by Rubens;[27] an admirable painting. The two figures of the

---

[26] Louis de Planet, (1804–1877), a pupil of Delacroix's; one of his collaborators in the decoration of the library of the Chamber of Deputies. He worked on several of the pendentives, laying in the color broadly on the drawings of Delacroix, who then completed the work.

[27] A picture from a monastery in Antwerp, which was for sale when Delacroix saw it in 1847. It was purchased some years later by Napoleon III for 16,000 francs and given by him in 1853 to the museum of Bordeaux where it is today. Delacroix made a copy of this picture; it is today in the museum of Freiburg (Catalogue Robaut, 1942). In the original, only the head of the saint was painted by Rubens.

spectators, with his broad drawing, have a frankness in the chiaroscuro and the color which belongs only to the man who does not seek, and who tramples under foot all crazy researches, and the even more silly demands which people make.

Then to the Chamber of Deputies. Worked at the woman carrying the little child, at the child on the ground, and then at the recumbent figure of the man above the centaur; I think I have gone far ahead. Very long session. Returned without fatigue.

To complete the day, I learned when I got home that Mme Sand was back and sent word to tell me that she was. I shall be glad to see her again.

Stayed at home in the evening; I was wrong to do it. The following day showed the effects. I should have gone for a walk. Just the fresh air, perhaps, contributes to quicken the circulation; and so the next day I did nothing. The upset stomach commands as a master, but as a master very unworthy to rule, for he fulfills his functions badly, and stops all the rest.

February 9.

Hence ill disposed.

Demay came. While he was there M. Haussoullier came. All those young men of the school of Ingres have something pedantic about them. It seems that there is already a very great merit on their part in having joined the party of serious painting: that is one of the words of the *party*. I told Demay that a whole lot of men of talent had done nothing worth while, with that mass of fixed opinions that they impose on themselves, or that the prejudice of the moment imposes on you. That is the case, for example, with that famous idea of *beauty*, which is, as everybody says, the goal of the arts. If it is their only goal, what becomes of the men like Rubens, Rembrandt, and all the northern natures generally, who prefer other qualities? Demand purity, in a word beauty, from Puget — good-bye to his verve! This is an idea to develop. In general the men of the north tend less in this direction.

The Italian prefers ornament. One gets a confirmation of this in music.

Saw *Don Juan* in the evening. Disagreeable impression on seeing the piece. The bad Don Juan (the actor)! Is that the execution, the looseness to give to an ancient work? But how its grandeur grows in memory and, next day, with what happiness I remembered it! What a masterpiece of romanticism! And that in 1785! The actor who plays Don Juan takes off his mantle so as to fight with the Father. At the end, not knowing what expression to put on, he gets down on his knees before the Commander. I am sure that not two people in the theater noticed it.

I was thinking of the modicum of imagination necessary to the spectator who is to be worthy of hearing such a work. It seemed evident to me that almost all the people who were there were listening inattentively. That would be a small matter, but the parts most fit to strike the imagination did not arrest them any more than the others. It takes a great deal of imagination to be vividly impressed at a performance. The combat with the Father and the entrance of the Ghost will always strike a man of imagination. The larger part of the spectators sees nothing in that of any more interest than the rest.

February 13.

Worked at the composition of the *Foscari*.[28] Tried it on a No. 80 canvas; I think it will be all right so.

February 14.

The Beautiful is assuredly the meeting-place of all the parts when each is in proper balance. Develop this, remembering *Don Juan*.

Rossini does not vary his characters so much.

February 15.

Got up in bad humor, set to work to go over the sketch of the *Christ au*

[28] *The Two Foscari*, finished only in 1855; this celebrated picture is now in the Musée Condé at Chantilly (Catalogue Robaut, 1262).

Tombeau. The good qualities I found in it made me feel better, but I paid for it with a stiff neck in the evening and on the next day. My sketch is very good. It has lost some of its mystery; that is the drawback of the methodical sketch. With a good drawing for the lines of the composition and the placing of the figures, one can do away with the sketch, which represents a needless repetition of the work. One obtains the qualities of the sketch in the picture itself, by means of the vagueness in which one leaves the details. The local color of the Christ is raw umber, Naples yellow and white; over that, certain tones of black and white, slipping in here and there the shadows with a warmer tone.

The local color of the sleeves of the Virgin: a slightly russet gray. The lights with Naples yellow and black.[29]

Tried the *Foscari* on the number 80 canvas. Decidedly it is lost on that. I shall try it on size number 60.

February 19.

T. . . tells me very rightly that the model lowers the man who works from him, a foolish person makes you feel like a fool. The man of imagination, in his endeavor to raise the model to the ideal which he has conceived, also takes some steps, in spite of himself, toward the commonnesss which presses in upon him, and which he has before his eyes.

Saw two acts of the *Huguenots:* where is Mozart? Where is that grace, expression, energy, all in one — inspiration and science, the comic and the terrible? Out of this tormented music there come forth efforts which surprise you; but it is the eloquence of a man in a fever, flashes followed by chaos.

Piron gave me news of Mlle Mars,[30] who is very ill. Charles[31] was extremely sad to hear that.

[29] The foregoing notation of colors, one among innumerable such passages in the *Journal,* could be of use to Delacroix but to no one else. Hence other passages of the kind will be omitted.

[30] Mlle Mars, the celebrated tragedienne.

[31] The Count de Mornay, with whom Delacroix made the trip to Morocco. He was the friend of Mlle Mars.

February 20.

The moralists and philosophers, I mean the real ones, like Marcus Aurelius and Jesus, never talked politics, since they did not consider it save from the standpoint of humanity. Equal rights, and twenty other chimeras, did not concern them; all they recommended to men was resignation to fate, not to that obscure *fatum* of the ancients, but to that eternal necessity which no one can deny, and against which the philanthropists will not prevail when they try to escape from the severe laws of nature. To follow those laws, and to play his part in the place assigned him amidst a general harmony, is all that the philosophers have demanded of the wise man. Sickness, death, poverty, the torments of the soul, all are eternal, and will torture humanity under every kind of government; the form, democratic or monarchical, has nothing to do with the case.

Dined at the house of M. Moreau.[32] Returned with Couture. He reasons very well. It is surprising what an eye we have for characterizing one another's faults. Everything that he told me about each person he mentioned is very true and very finely observed, but he does not take account of their good qualities; above all, just like the rest, he sees and analyzes *qualities of execution* alone. He tells me, and I can well believe it, that he feels the best thing for him is to work from nature. He says he makes preparatory studies, so as to learn by heart, so to speak, the subject that he wants to paint, and then gets at it with warmth. The method is excellent, from his point of view. I told him how Géricault used the model, that is to say freely, and yet exacting a rigorous holding of the pose. We fairly outdid each other in exclaiming over that immense talent. What force a great nature draws from itself! A new argument against the foolishness of resisting, and of modeling oneself on other people.

[32] M. Adolphe Moreau, stock broker, collector of paintings; his collection was given to the Louvre by his son, M. Etienne Moreau-Nélaton. A great admirer of Delacroix, he had acquired a number of his finest canvases.

February 21.

Today I closed my door, being driven to that by the tiresomeness of visitors. Took up the *Arab Comedians* again,[33] starting early, on account of Franchomme's concert, where I was to go at two o'clock. On my way, I met Mme Sand, who took me the rest of the distance in her carriage. It was with real pleasure that I saw her again: she was excellent. Music of the angels. Quartet by Haydn, one of the last that he wrote. Chopin tells me that experience gives to it that perfection which we admire in it. Mozart, he added, did not need experience; science, with him, was always on the level of inspiration. Quintets by him, which I had already heard at the house of Boissard.[34] The *Rudolphe* trio by Beethoven: commonplace passages together with sublime beauties.

Resisted a dinner invitation from Mme Sand, so as to go home and rest.

In the evening went to the house of M. Thiers.

February 22.

Continued the *Arab Comedians* and got ahead a great deal.

February 23.

Worked on the *Arab Comedians*. Préault came in.[35]

In the evening went to a small gathering at the house of Alberthe.[36] It was a great pleasure to see her again, that dear friend. She looked young again in her toilette and was indefatigable all evening; her daughter was very nice also; she dances gracefully, especially the insipid polka.

Mareste recounts to us the letter that Sophie Arnould[37] wrote to

[33] *Comédiens et Bouffons Arabes,* of the Salon of 1848; it is now in the museum of Tours, (Catalogue Robaut, 1044).

[34] Boissard de Boisdenier (1813–1866), painter, musician and writer.

[35] Antoine-Augustin Préault (1809–1879), the noted sculptor.

[36] Alberthe de Rubempré, his cousin.

[37] Sophie Arnould (1740–1803), celebrated actress.

Lucien when he was minister[38]: "Citizen Minister, I have lighted many fires in my life, I have not a stick of wood to put in my own. The fact is that I am dying of hunger." Signed, "An old actress who is not of your time." "Mlle de Châteauvieux, Mlle de Châteauneuf, who are all those ladies?" someone asked her. She answered "Just so many tumble-down châteaux."

February 25.

At the house of Mme de Forget in the evening, Mme H . . . played for me some infamous modern music; among other pieces, to give me a treat, the two compositions that my neighbors of the garden used to skin alive all last summer.

February 26.

Dauzats[39] had informed me the night before that Mme la Duchesse d'Orléans[40] would go to the exhibition in the Rue St. Lazare and desired to see me there. She was extremely kind to me.

On coming out, I went to meet Villot,[41] who had gone in the morning to an exhibition in the Rue Grange-Batelière: a magnificent Titian, *Lucretia and Tarquinius,* and the *Virgin Raising the Veil* by Raphael.[42] Awkwardness and magnificence in that Titian. Admir-

---

[38] Lucien Bonaparte.

[39] Adrien Dauzats (1803–1868), of Bordeaux; painter; the friend of Delacroix and one of the executors of his will.

[40] The Duchess of Orléans, widow of the duke, the oldest son of Louis-Philippe, who had been an admirer and protector of Delacroix.

[41] Frédéric Villot (1809–1875), a mediocre engraver; one of Delacroix's very early friends, and his teacher in the processes of etching. Appointed Curator of Paintings at the Louvre in 1848, he drew up that museum's catalogues of paintings, still a model of their kind. A controversy over the restoring of the Rubens from the Luxembourg palace caused him to be deprived of his position, but he was given administrative functions as "Secretary-general" of the Louvre in 1861; in which capacity he remained until his death. At first closely associated with Delacroix, he drew away from him later. For Mme Villot, Delacroix entertained sentiments which seem to have gone beyond those of mere friendship.

[42] Both the pictures seem to have been questionable as to their genuineness.

able balancing of the lines in that Raphael. I became completely aware today that that is beyond doubt the thing to which he owes his greatest beauties. Boldnesses and incorrect details, caused by the need to follow his own style and the accustomed direction of his hand. The execution, when seen under a glass, shows small brush strokes.

February 27.

Grenier came to make a study in pastel from the *Marcus Aurelius.*[43] We talked of Mozart and Beethoven. In the latter, he finds an active tendency toward misanthropy and despair, and more especially a painting of nature, which does not go to such lengths in the others; we compared him with Shakespeare: he does me the honor of placing me in the class with these wild contemplators of human nature. One must confess that, despite his celestial perfection, Mozart does not open that particular horizon to the mind. Would that come from the fact that Beethoven appeared only later? I think one can say that he really reflected more fully the modern character of the arts, turned, as he was, to the expression of melancholy and of that which, rightly or wrongly, people call romanticism. Notwithstanding which, *Don Juan* is full of that sentiment.

Dreamed of Mme de L. . . . Certainly there is scarce a night when I don't see her or that I am not happy in her company, and I am very foolishly neglecting her: she is a delightful being!

February 28.

Drew in the Foscari and covered the canvas with grisaille, black and white. That should be a pretty good preparation to avoid pinkish and russet tones. The big copy of *Saint Benedict,*[44] which I made in that way, has a freshness difficult to obtain by other means. My composition

[43] The *Death of Marcus Aurelius* of the Salon of 1845, is now in the museum of Lyons (Catalogue Robaut, 924).

[44] Copy made in 1841 from the picture by Rubens, now in the Brussels museum (Catalogue Robaut, 736).

seems to me to offer difficulties of perspective which I did not expect.

In sum, a badly spent day, though I was not interrupted.

Dined with M. Thiers; I feel the same friendship for him and the same boredom in his drawing room.

At ten o'clock, went with D'Aragon to the house of Mme Sand: He tells us of a very interesting work, translated by a M. Cazalis, *La Douloureuse Passion de Notre Seigneur,* by Sister Catherine Emmerich, a German visionary. Read that. There are very singular details about the Passion which were revealed to that girl.

March 1.

After breakfast, I started to work over the *Christ au Tombeau:* this was my third session on the sketch: and, in my day's work, despite a little indisposition, I braced it up vigorously, and got it into condition for a fourth go. I am satisfied with this lay-in, but when one adds details, how can one preserve that impression of the whole which results from very simple masses? The majority of painters, and I did this formerly, begin with the details and work for the effect at the end. Whatever one's chagrin over losing the effect of simplicity in a fine sketch as one adds more details, there will still remain much more of that impression than one will attain if one proceeds in the opposite fashion.

Was planning all day to go and bury myself at the top of the house to see the *Mariage Secret.*[45] After dinner my courage failed me, and I stayed home reading *Monte Cristo,* which did not keep me from falling asleep.

March 2.

Dufay came in, also Colin. The former is struck by the need for a revolution. He believes in the coming of a state of things wherein the rascals will be kept in hand by the honest people.

[45] Comic opera by Cimarosa.

Feeling badly. I tried, very late, to work on the background of the *Christ*. Re-worked the mountains.

ED

One of the great advantages of the lay-in by tone and effect without bothering about the details, is that one is compelled to put in only those which are absolutely necessary. Beginning here by finishing the backgrounds, I have made them as simple as possible, so as not to appear overloaded, alongside the simple masses which the figures still are. When I finish the figures, the simplicity of the backgrounds will, by the same token, permit me or even force me to put in only what is absolutely needed. The real thing would be, once the lay-in is established, to push each section as far as possible, yet not allow the picture as a whole to advance: this of course presupposes that the effect and the tone of all parts have been determined. What I am saying is that the figure one would prefer to finish, as compared with the others — which are merely massed in — would necessarily preserve simplicity in the details, and so would not be too much out of keeping with its neighbors, even though they are still in the state of a sketch. Once the picture has, through a lay-in, reached a condition where it is satisfying to the mind as a matter of lines, color and effect, it is evident that if one continues to the end to work in the same manner, that is to say, to proceed with sketchy painting, one loses a large part of the profit of that great simplicity of impression which one attained in the beginning. The eye accustoms itself to the details which have gradually been introduced into each of the figures, and into all at the same time; the picture never seems finished. First defect of the method: the details stifle the masses; second defect: the work takes much longer to do.

March 3.

This day, Wednesday, repainted the rocks in the background of the *Christ* and finished the lay-in of the *Magdalen*, the nude figure in the foreground. *I regret that the paint in this lay-in is not applied heavily enough. Time smoothes out pictures to an incredible degree; my Sibyl* [46] *seemed to me already to have gone back into the canvas, so to speak. This is a matter to observe with attention.*

[46] The *Sibyl with the Golden Bough* (Catalogue Robaut, 918) appeared at the Salon of 1845.

Saw Bellini's *Puritans* Tuesday evening with Mme de Forget. That music gave me great pleasure. The moonlight scene at the end is magnificent, like those which the decorator of that theater paints. *They are obtained with very simple tints, I think, black, blue, and perhaps umber, only, they are well understood as to the planes and the way that one tint goes over the other.*

For the earthwork which represents the top of the ramparts, *a very simple tone, relieved with very vigorous strokes of white,* representing the lines of mortar between the stones. Tempera lends itself admirably to such simplicity of effect, the tints not mingling as in oil. Against the very simply painted sky, there are several towers or crenelated battlements, detaching one from the other by the mere intensity of the tone, *the reflections being well marked.* And it is sufficient to have a few touches of scarcely modified white to heighten the light passages.

March 4.

This morning Villot came in; I was glad to see him. M. Geoffroy, sent by Buloz, arrived. Villot never stops his argument when a stranger comes in; that is incredibly indiscreet.

Returned to the Chamber of Deputies and formed the resolution to do the hackwork of my painting myself; I was always able to do it perfectly well, and I shall be freer this way. Worked on the Orpheus especially.

These lay-ins with the tone and the mere mass are really admirable for this kind of work when it comes to parts like heads, for example, prepared by a single spot which you have just barely modeled. When the tones are exact, the features seem to draw themselves. The picture takes on largeness and simplicity. I think this is the best I have done of this type of work.

March 5.

Yesterday while working on the child, near the woman at the left in the *Orpheus,* I remembered those multiple small touches done with a small brush, and as if in a miniature, in the *Virgin* by Raphael which I saw in the Rue Grange-Batelière with Villot. In the objects where one sacrifices everything to style, the fine brushwork, free and proud, of men like Vanloo leads only to approximations. Style can result only from great research, and the fine brushing has got to stop when the touch is going well. I must try to see the big gouaches by Correggio at the Museum:[47] I believe they were done with very small touches.

Arnoux left this morning. We were talking of the artists who find themselves in the position of writing on their colleagues, and he cited the line of a certain M. Gabriel, a playwright, who says on this subject: "One can't at the same time be the groom who holds the stirrup and the man who shows his behind."

I have an invitation to dine on Monday with the Duc de Montpensier. Fatigued.

In the evening, fatigue and frightful humor; I stayed home. As a matter of fact, I am not sufficiently grateful for what Heaven does for me. In these moments of fatigue, I think that everything is lost.

March 6.

Got a good night's rest. Went back to my studio; it put me into good humor. I looked at the *Hunts* by Rubens. The one with the hippopotamus, which is the fiercest, is the one that I prefer: I love its emphasis, I love its forms — exaggerated and loose. I adore them with all my contempt for the sugary women and the dolls who swoon with delight over the paintings that are in fashion, and over the music of M. Verdi.

Mme Leblond, day before yesterday, simply could not understand my admiration for the two charming drawings by Prud'hon which belong to her husband.

[47] In the Catalogue of the drawings of the Louvre, 171 and 172.

Mme Guizot[48] asks me for a drawing for a lottery and assures me of her friendship.

I made some sketches from the *Hunts* by Rubens; there is as much to be learned from his exaggerations and his swelling forms as from exact imitations.

March 7.

On returning from the concert with Mme Sand I said that Beethoven moves us the more because he is the man of our time. He is romantic to the supreme degree.

The sight of the *Judgment of Paris* by Raphael, in a frightfully worn print, appears to me under a new light, since admiring, in the *Virgin with a Veil,* of the Rue Grange-Batelière, his admirable understanding of the lines. The interest in line, however, if one considers it for all pictures, is a quality which completely blots out everything that one sees after leaving the presence of Raphael. One must not indeed think too much about his quality, for fear of throwing everything out of the window. Is not the species of coldness toward Titian which I have always felt a result, possibly, of his almost constant ignorance as to charm of lines?

March 10.

I receive a letter announcing the funeral of Barye's[49] only daughter. That unhappy man is going to be very sad and very lonesome.

March 11.

Went to the funeral of Barye's daughter. Not one of the artists among

[48] Mother of the famous historian and statesman. Delacroix made a sketch of her which is not mentioned in the Robaut catalogue; it was bought at the posthumous sale of the master's works by the great critic, Théophile Silvestre, and was bequeathed by his widow to Elie Faure.

[49] Louis-Antoine Barye (1795–1875), the great sculptor. Delacroix, since early youth, had been one of his admirers. At this period, (1847), Barye was hard pressed to earn a living; since 1834 he had been kept out of the official Salon.

his friends whom I see with him ordinarily was there. From the church, I went to call on Vieillard, who is ill. We talked a great deal about the eternal question of progress, which we understand in such diverse fashion. I spoke to him about *Marcus Aurelius*, it is the only book from which he has drawn any consolation since his misfortune. I cited the example of the misfortune of Barye, who is even more alone than he: first his daughter, then the fact that he has certainly fewer friends. The reserve of his character, not to say more, prevents any expression of feeling. I told him that, all things considered, religion, better than all the systems, explains the destiny of man, which is to say, resignation. *Marcus Aurelius* says nothing else.

I saw Decamps's *Samson Turning the Millstone,* and with pleasure: there is genius in it.

At Mme de Forget's, saw David.[50] He paid me some compliments on the cupola which I just decorated at the Senate: but those compliments signify nothing.

Perpignan was telling me the anecdote of old Thomas Parr, who lived to the age of one hundred and forty. A man who wanted to see him met a decrepit old gentleman who was crying, and who said that he had just been beaten by his father for not having bowed to his grandfather; that was Parr. Perpignan remarks very justly that emotions wear out our lives as much as excesses; he cites the case of a woman who expressly forbade people to tell her the slightest circumstance which might affect her.

I do indeed feel how much I am fatigued by speaking emphatically, or even giving sustained attention to the thought of another.

March 12.

One of those days when you get nothing done. In the middle of the day tried to get at the *Valentin:* I had to give it up; I fell back on *Monte Cristo.*

[50] This may be David d'Angers, the sculptor, or Jules David, the son of the great painter.

After my dinner, called on Mme Sand. It is snowing frightfully and I was floundering about before I got to the Rue St. Lazare. That nice good-natured Chopin played for us a while. What a charming genius!

March 13.

Gaspard Lacroix came in for a moment. He praised me a great deal for the drawing of my *Christ*[51] of the Rue St. Louis. It is the first time that I get a compliment on that.

Yesterday Clésinger spoke to me about a statue of his which, he had no doubt, I should greatly like, on account of the *color*. Color, as it appears, being my only domain, I've got to find it in sculpture before I can be pleased with the work or before I can even understand the work!

March 14.

Gaspard Lacroix came to call for me and we went to Corot's studio. He affirms, like certain others who perhaps are not wrong, that in spite of my desire to systematize, I shall always be swept along by instinct. Corot is a true artist. One needs to see a painter in his own place to have an idea of his merit. I saw there, and appreciated in quite a different way, pictures which I had seen at the Salon and which had made but a moderate impression on me. His large *Baptism of Christ*,[52] full of naive beauties. His *trees* are superb. I spoke to him about the one which I am to do in the *Orpheus*. He told me to let go a little and allow myself to take what should come; that is what he does the greater part of the time. He does not admit that one can attain beauty by infinite labor. Titian, Raphael, Rubens etc. did their work easily. As a matter

[51] The *Pieta* in the church of St. Denis du Saint-Sacrement (Catalogue Robaut, 768).
[52] A picture ordered as a decoration of the baptismal fonts of St.-Nicolas-du-Chardonnet. Corot was very much contested at the time and had difficulty in getting into the Salon.

of fact, they did only what they knew well: the only thing is that their scope was more extended than that of a man who paints only landscape or flowers, for example. Notwithstanding this facility, there is still work, which is indispensable. Corot digs deep into a subject: his ideas come to him, and he adds them while he is working; that is the good way to do things.

With M. Thiers this evening. I came home feeling ill and in a frightful humor, after a short walk on the boulevard. This Paris is frightful! How cruel this dullness is! Why not see the good things that heaven has granted me? A bad state of mind darkens everything.

March 15.

At the Salon; my pictures don't look badly. The head of my *Cleopatra* was admired by M. Lefebvre, who considered that it was the only one there which had such strength: how does it come about that they did not see that ten years ago? I suppose that fashion must have its share in all ideas.

Grenier tells me that the violet tone in the upper part of the *Marocains Endormis* would just as well have represented the light of the lamp, since the latter is orange. I think he is right: for example the earth in the *Othello*, which was purplish, and which I laid in with an orange tone. Check up on this in the *Valentin.*

March 20.

Stayed at home all day to read the *Chevalier de la Maison Rouge* by Dumas, very entertaining, and very superficial. Melodrama the whole time.

March 30.

To the Théatre des Italiens with Mme de Forget: the first act of the *Mariage Secret*[53] the second of *Nabucco,* the second and third of *Othello.*

[53] Le *Mariage Secret,* comic-opera by Cimarosa; *Nabucodonosor* by Verdi; *Othello* by Rossini.

The *Mariage* seemed to me more divine than ever; it was perfection: One had to descend, and with what a fall, to get to *Nabucco!* I left before the end.

April 2.

Went to the Conservatory in the evening with Mme de Forget. Symphony by Mendelssohn which bored me extremely, save for a presto. One of the fine pieces by Cherubini, from the *Messe de Louis XVI*. At the end a Mozart symphony which delighted me.

My fatigue and the heat were excessive; but I had an experience there which never happened to me before: it was that the last piece seemed not only ravishing in every respect but that, apparently, it caused my fatigue to disappear while I was listening. That perfection, that completeness, those delicate shadings, all of that must be the despair of musicians who have any soul and any taste.

April 3.

I left early to call on Théophile Gautier. I thanked him warmly for his splendid article of the day before yesterday; it gave me great pleasure. Gautier suggested my holding an exhibition of all the pictures of mine that I could get together. He thinks that I can do that without a taint of charlatanism, and that that would bring in money. Called on M. de Morny.[54] His house displays a luxury such as I had seen nowhere else. His pictures look much better there. There is a magnificent Watteau. I was struck by the admirable art of that painting. Flanders and Venice meet in it, but the sight of a few Ruysdaels, especially a snow effect and a very simple marine where one sees no more than the sea in dull weather, with one or two boats, appeared to me the climax of art,

---

[54] M. de Morny (1811–1865), then a deputy, was the son of Queen Hortense and of General de Flahaut. In the magnificent Morny collection there were four pictures by Watteau; the one which attracted Delacroix's attention was certainly the *Plaisirs du Bal* now in the Wallace Collection in London. The Rubens, *Hercule et Omphale*, was one of the numerous copies of an original now lost.

because the art in it is completely concealed. That astounding simplicity lessens the effect of the Watteau and of the Rubens; they are too much the artists. To have such paintings under one's eyes in one's room, would be the loveliest of pleasures.

Called on Mornay.

On the quay I bought the *Lion* by Denon.[55] Called on Maindron. In his absence I was received by his old mother who showed me his group. That little garden has something agreeable about it, peopled, as it is, by the luckless statues which the unfortunate artist cannot dispose of. Cold, damp studio; piles of plaster, casts, etc. He came home, and was very appreciative of my visit. The marble alone for the group, which he has not been able to sell all these years, cost him three thousand francs.

April 4.

In the evening, with Mme de Forget, to the Conservatory: the *Pastoral Symphony; Agnus* by Mozart; Overture to *Leonore* by Beethoven, involved in style; and the *Credo* from the *Sacre* by Cherubini, noisy and not very moving.

April 23.

In the evening, Villot came to keep me company. He tells me that Titian, at the end of his life, used to say that he was beginning to learn his trade.

Tintoretto used to work at drawing tremendously, outside of his pictures; he copied certain heads of Vitellius hundreds of times, drawings by Michelangelo, etc.

April 25.

Riesener says a thing that is very precise concerning the exaggerated

[55] Vivant Denon (1747–1825), writer, engraver and wit, became Director of Museums under Napoleon. He engraved a drawing by Rembrandt, representing a *Lion Gnawing a Bone;* it is doubtless this very interesting engraving that Delacroix bought on the quay.

enthusiasm that the paintings of Michelangelo can inspire. I was speaking to him of what Corot had told me of the prodigious superiority of those works; Riesener very well says that the gigantic, the swollen quality, and even the monotony that such objects contain, necessarily crush what one sets beside them. The antique, when set beside Indian or Byzantine idols, appears shrunken, materialistic; how much more so is this the case with paintings like those of the Lesueur type, and even those of the Paul Veronese type. He is right in claiming that that should not trouble us, and that each thing in its place is right.

April 26.

In the evening, Pierret came to spend a while with me. He tells me of the evening at the house of Champmartin, where Dumas demonstrated the weakness of Racine, the nullity of Boileau, and the absolute lack of melancholy among the writers of the so-called grand century. I undertook their apology.

Dumas will not stop talking about that banal public square or that vestibule of a palace where everything takes place in the works of our tragic writers and of Molière. They[56] demand an art without prearranged conventions. But those so-called improbabilities shocked nobody. What shocks horribly is the mingling in *their* works, of an exaggerated fidelity — which the arts reject — and sentiments, characters, and situations of the falsest and most overdone kind. Why don't they say that an engraving or a drawing represents nothing, because it does not possess color? Were they sculptors, they would have painted their statues, and would have put springs in them to make them walk, believing that they had thereby come much nearer to the truth.

April 27.

Had a last look at the portrait of *Josephine* by Prud'hon.[57] Ravishing,

[56] By *they* Delacroix means Dumas and his group.
[57] This portrait, now in the Louvre, was at that time exhibited in the Durand-Ruel Gallery.

ravishing genius! That breast with its incorrectnesses, those arms, that head, that dress sown with little flecks of gold, the whole thing is divine. The grisaille is very apparent and reappears almost everywhere.

April 30.

I went to see the picture of *Suzanne,* attributed to Rubens. It is a Jordaens of the most fully characterized kind, and a magnificent picture. There were various modern pictures from the collection of Souty, and they cut a sorry figure alongside the Fleming. What gives this sad effect in all those unhappy canvases is the absolute lack of character. In each, one can see the character that they tried to assume: but not one has any distinction; I must make an exception for the *Allée d'Arbres* by Rousseau,[58] which is an excellent work in many of its parts. The lower part is perfect. The upper part is of a darkness which must come from some change in the paint; it is scaling off. There is a picture by Cottereau—deplorable; the head of a certain laughing sultan is the work of the silliest of men, and the painter is far from that. Why did he chose a profession in which his mind is of no use to him?

The Jordaens is a masterpiece of imitation, broad and well understood as painting. Here is a man who does well what he is made for! How differently men are constituted! The complete absence here of any ideal shocks one despite the perfection of the painting. The head of that woman is of a commonness of feature and expression which passes conception. How is it that he did not feel the need of rendering the poetic side of his subject, save through the admirable oppositions of color which make of it a masterpiece? The brutality of those old men, the chaste alarm of the honest woman, her delicate forms which, one feels, the eye of day itself should not see. All that would have been rendered by Prud'hon, by Lesueur, or by Raphael; here one feels that she and the men perfectly understand each other, and there is nothing animated among them save the admirable color of their heads,

[58] The picture mentioned is the famous *Allée de Châtaigniers,* now in the Louvre.

their hands, and their draperies. This painting is the best possible proof of the impossibility of bringing about a higher unity between truth of drawing and color on the one hand, and grandeur, poetry and charm on the other. At first I was overcome by the strength and science of this painting and then I saw that either to paint so vigorously or to imagine so poorly would be impossible for me. I need color, I need color as much as he, but for me it has a different purpose. And so I became reconciled with myself, after first having got the impression of an admirable quality which was denied me. That rendering, that precision, are a thousand leagues away from me, or rather I am a thousand leagues from them. This painting has not got a hold of me, as so many fine paintings have. A Rubens would have moved me more; but what a difference between those two men! With all the outspokenness of his colors and his heavy forms, he arrives at an ideal of the greatest power. Force, vehemence and splendor free him from the demands of grace and charm.

May 3.

I do wrong to utter my opinion so freely among people who are not my friends.

May 4.

Aubry, the picture dealer, was here this morning. What I saw at his place gives a very sad idea of the future of our school. Boucher and Vanloo are the great men on whom it sets its eyes, so as to follow in their path. But with those men there was real knowledge mingled with their bad taste. The pygmies of their present day — the insects, I ought to say — have neither sentiment nor the least feeling. Silly manual skill is the supreme goal.

May 5.

In the evening I went into Notre Dame de Lorette. Heard some music. Then went to see Leblond: Garcia was there. He sang for me a superb air by Cimarosa, from the *Sacrifice of Abraham*. Mme Leblond sang for me and gave me pleasure.

All I have in my head is the harmonies of Cimarosa. What a varied genius, supple and elegant! Decidedly, he is more dramatic than Mozart.

May 7.

Received a letter from Mme Sand. That poor friend writes me the most amiable letter, and her poor heart is full of trouble.[59] I went to see Clesinger's statue. Alas, I think that Planche is right: it is a daguerreotype in sculpture, except for the treatment of the marble, which is really very able. The proof of what I think is the weakness of the other pieces: no proportion, etc. Lack of intelligence as to the lines in the figure; one cannot see it as a whole from any angle.

I had a very agreeable visit to the Salon without meeting a soul. Couture's picture[60] gave me pleasure; he is very complete, in his own way. What he lacks, I think he will never acquire. On the other hand he is fully master of what he knows. I liked his portrait of a woman.

I saw my pictures without too much displeasure, especially the *Jewish Musicians* and the *Boat*. I was not too dissatisfied with the *Christ*.[61]

May 9.

At the house of Mme Marliani in the evening. She informs me of Chopin's illness. The poor lad has been ill for a week, and very gravely. He is a little bit better now.

May 10.

Went to see Chopin this morning without being received.

May 11.

Went to see Chopin about eleven o'clock.

[59] It was the moment of her break with Chopin.
[60] *The Romans of the Decadence.*
[61] *Shipwrecked Men Abandoned in a Boat* (Catalogue Robaut, 1010); *Jewish Musicians of Mogador* (Robaut, 1011), now in the Louvre; the *Christ au Tombeau* (Catalogue Robaut, 960).

Dined with J. About nine o'clock she took me to Chopin's house. I stayed there till after midnight.

May 12.

Read the *Three Musketeers* until just now, and found it very entertaining.

Champrosay, Monday May 22.

In the morning, sitting in the forest. I was thinking of those charming allegories of the Middle Ages and the Renaissance, those cities of God, those Elysian fields full of light, peopled with gracious figures, etc. Isn't that the tendency of periods when beliefs in higher powers have preserved their full strength? The soul rose ceaselessly above the trivialities and miseries of real life into imaginary dwellings which were embellished with everything that was lacking around you.

It is also the tendency of unhappy periods when dreadful powers weigh upon men and cripple the flights of the imagination. Nature, which had not been conquered by the genius of man at those periods, increased our material needs, and caused life to seem harsher, bringing about more eager dreams of an unknown well being. In our time, on the contrary, pleasures are more general, we are better housed, and distances are more easily traversed. Then, as always, desire poetized the existence of unhappy mortals, condemned as they are to disdain what they possess.

Action was directed solely to elevating the soul above matter. In our day, just the reverse is the case. The one purpose now is to entertain us with the spectacle of our miseries, whereas we should be eager to turn our eyes away from them. It was Protestantism which first disposed us toward this change. It depopulated heaven and the churches. The peoples with a genius for the positive embraced it with ardor. And so, material happiness is the only one for the moderns. The Revolution completed the process of pinning us down to the earth — that is to say, to material interests and to physical enjoyment. It abolished every kind of belief: instead of that natural support which a creature as weak as man seeks in a supernatural power, it presented him with abstract words: reason, justice, equality, rights. An association of brigands is just as well governed by those words as by a morally organized society. They have nothing in common with kindness, tenderness, charity, devotion. Bandits observe a certain justice toward one another, they possess a type of reason which causes them to prefer themselves to anyone else, they keep to a certain equality in dividing up their loot, which seems to them justice measured out to the insolent rich or to people who are fortunate — at their expense, as they consider it. Close examination is not needed for us to see that present-day society is governed on about the same principles and interprets things in the same way.

I do not know whether the world has yet seen such a spectacle:

that of selfishness replacing all the virtues which were regarded as the safeguards of society.

May 27.

Dined at the house of Chabrier with M. Poinsot, Marrast, Royer, David and Vieillard. Good day, delightful evening: conversation always interesting. There, then, is a full man. Genius, wit, finesse, simplicity, reason, common sense, all the rarest things. It's perfectly simple — he adores Voltaire: I found he had the right idea about everything.[62]

June 5.

Dined with Vieillard at the house of Mme de Forget. In the morning, Planet came with M. Martens, to daguerreotype the *Cléopâtre*.[63] Small success.

June 9.

With the majority of men, the intelligence is a field that lies fallow for almost all their lives. Seeing the multitude of stupid or at least mediocre people who seem to live only to vegetate, one has the right to be astonished that God should have given reason to his creatures, the faculty of imagining, of comparing, of combining, etc., to produce such small fruit. Laziness, ignorance, a passing situation, or chance throws them out of their course, and changes almost all men into passive instruments of circumstance.

We never know what we can get out of ourselves. Laziness is undoubtedly the greatest enemy to the development of our faculties. And so, *know thyself* would be the fundamental axiom of every society in which each of its members would perform his role exactly and would fulfill it to its limit.

[62] To which of the party is this compliment addressed?
[63] Delacroix was at once interested by the processes of photographic reproduction. The *Cléopâtre* (Catalogue Robaut, 691).

June 20.

At the home of Boissard. Had music again.

Robberechts not having arrived at first, they began with a trio by Beethoven, then Mozart supplied the whole program until the end. I found him more varied, more sublime, more full of resources than ever.

Before a picture by Boissard representing a *Christ,* I took good note of the decoration over the door of his studio. These paintings, although mediocre, offer an excellent lesson, which I applied at once, as to the principle which demands that an object, even a very light one, should almost always detach with a dark note against a darker object. To study this, it would be worth while to make sketches of these paintings.

For some time I have been in very good health, and go very often to the Chamber of Deputies.

June 25.

Today, probably at the hour of my dinner Grzimala came in. About my painting he told me things that pleased me, among others: that the *idea* always struck him, rather than the *convention* of painting; moreover that all pictures have something ridiculous about them which comes from fashion, etc. He never finds that in mine. Can he really be right? Could one infer from that that the less there is in pictures of the transitory element which most often contributes to present-day success, the more they fulfill the conditions of permanence and of greatness? Develop this.

July 1.

At the Chamber in the morning. At Chopin's house at three o'clock for a session.

He was divine. His trio was played for him with Fauchon, etc. Then he executed it himself and with a master hand.

July 10.

Cousin Delacroix came during the day:[64] it was a pleasure for me to see him. He is spending a week here. Chopin came in while he was here.

Painted the Magdalen in the *Christ au Tombeau*.

I must remember the simple effect of the head. It was laid in with a very gray and dead tone. I was uncertain whether I would put it more into shadow, or whether I would put on more vigorous lights. I gave to the latter a stronger accent as compared with the mass, and it was sufficient to color the whole shadow part with warm reflected tones; although the light and shadow are almost of the same value, the cold tones of the one and the warm ones of the other suffice to give accent to the whole. We were talking with Villot, the next day, about the fact that it needs very little work to produce effect in this manner. In the open air above all, this condition is of the most frequent occurrence. Paul Veronese owes to this method a great part of his admirable simplicity. A principle which Villot regards as most fruitful and most frequent, is that of making objects detach as a darker note against those which are behind them, doing this through the mass of the object and during the lay-in, when the local color is to be established from the first. I do not understand the application of this as well as he does. Look into this.

Veronese owes much of his simplicity, also, to the absence of details, which permits him to establish the local color from the start. His tempera painting almost forced him to that simplicity. Simplicity in the draperies will continue on into the rest of the picture to a remarkable extent. The vigorous contour, which he draws so appropriately around his figures, contributes to complete the effect of the simplicity he uses in his oppositions of light and shade, thus finishing and setting off the whole.

[64] Commandant Delacroix resided in the village of Ante-en Argonne, the place where the artist's father was born. He published a collection of verses.

Paul Veronese does not, like Titian, have any pretensions to making a masterpiece of each picture. That ability to refrain from *doing too much* everywhere, that apparent carelessness as to details which gives so much simplicity, is due to the habit of *decorating*. In this type of work one is compelled to subordinate many parts.

That principle of the small difference in value of the shadows in relation to the lights is to be applied especially to the representation of young persons. It is to be observed that the younger the subject is, the more the transparence of the skin establishes this effect.

July 11.

To be observed — how much our so-called civilization dulls natural feeling. Hector says to Ajax, book VII, as he leaves the combat: "The night is already advanced, and we must all obey night, which sets a limit for the works of men."

July 20.

Chopin came in the morning, while I was lunching after my return from the Museum, where I had received the commission for the copy of the *Corps de Garde*. He told me of the letter which he had received;[65] but he had read almost the whole of it to me since my return to Paris. There is no question but that it is atrocious. The cruelty of the passions, and the impatience so long repressed, come clearly to the surface in it: and, with a contrast which would be comic, if the matter were not such a sad one, the author, from time to time, assumes her role as a woman and goes off into long tirades which seem like borrowings from a novel or a lecture on philosophy.

September 1.

On the subject of distances in London I was writing to Vieillard:
"It is by leagues that one has to count: the mere disproportion

[65] The question was of the break with George Sand.

between the immensity of the place where those people dwell and the natural slightness of human proportions causes me to declare them enemies of that true civilization, which brings men together, enemies of that Attic civilization which built the Parthenon no bigger than one of our houses, and yet contained so much intelligence, life, force, and grandeur within the narrow limits of frontiers that bring a smile to our barbarous world, on which countries of enormous size hang loose like an ill fitted garment."

Worked at the Chamber.

September 2.

There were two nuns in the omnibus I rode in today: amid the general corruption, and the abandonment of all moral principles, their costume produced a strong effect on my mind; I like the sight of that costume which, at least on him or her who wears it, imposes absolute respect for the virtues and for devotion, respect for oneself and for others, even if this is a matter only of appearance.

September 5.

In the evening went to see Mme Marliani. There was an amiable woman there, Mme de Barrère, who speaks well on every subject without playing the pedant.

Leroux[66] has most assuredly found the great word, if not the thing itself, to save humanity and to pull it out of the mire: "Man is born free," he says, following Rousseau. Never has a heavier piece of foolishness been uttered, no matter how great the philosopher who spoke it.

There is the cornerstone of philosophy, for those gentlemen. Is there in all creation a being who is more of a *slave* than man? His weakness and his wants make him depend on the elements and on his fellows. But external matters are still a small part of the question.

[66] Pierre Leroux (1797–1871) philosopher and economist, one of the first followers of Saint-Simon, a friend of George Sand.

The passions that he finds within himself are the cruelest tyrants he has to fight, and one may add that to resist them is to resist his very nature.

Neither does he want a hierarchy for anything in his existence; that is the great reason why he finds Christianity odious; that is, to my thinking, precisely what constitutes its moral: submission to the law of nature, resignation to the sorrows of humanity, is the very last word of reason (and by the same token, submission to written law, divine or human).

September 18 .

M. Laurens came in this morning: he praises Mendelssohn very highly.

Painting is the trade that takes longest to learn and is the most difficult. It demands erudition like that of the composer, but it also demands execution like that of the violinist.

September 19.

I see in painters prose writers and poets. Rhyme, measure, the turning of verses which is indispensable and which gives them so much vigor, are analogous to the hidden symmetry, to the equilibrium at once wise and inspired, which governs the meeting or separation of lines and spaces, the echoes of color, etc. This thesis is easy to demonstrate, only one has need of more active organs and a greater sensibility to distinguish error, discord, false relationship among lines and colors, than one needs to perceive that a rhyme is inexact or that a hemistich is clumsily (or badly) hung. But the beauty of verse does not consist of exactitude in obeying rules, when even the most ignorant eyes see at once any lack of attention to them. It resides in a thousand secret harmonies and conventions which make up the power of poetry and which go straight to the imagination; in just the same way the happy choice of forms and the right understanding of their relationship act on the imagination in the art of painting. David's picture of *Leonidas* at *Thermopylae* is masculine and vigorous prose, I admit. Poussin almost never awakens his idea in you by other means than those of the more or less expressive pantomime of his figures. In his landscapes there is something that is more severely ordered; but most often with him as with the painters whom I call prose writers, it is chance that seems to have assembled the tones and controlled the lines of the composition. The poetic idea or expression does not strike you at the first glance.

September 25.

The Nymphs of the Sea let loose the Coursers of the Sun.[67]

September 26.

M. Cournault tells me that in Algiers he saw a workman who, when cutting pieces of leather or of cloth for ornaments, kept looking with great attention at a bouquet of flowers in order to guide himself. It is probable that they owe merely to observation of nature the harmony which they know how to obtain with colors. The Orientals have always had such taste. It does not appear that the Greeks and the Romans had it to the same degree, to judge by what remains of their painting.

October 5.

For the first time since September 12 I have resumed my decorations at the Chamber. I am satisfied with the effect of that figure of *Italy.* All day long I have been occupied, and very agreeably, with ideas and projects for paintings relative to this work. In a few moments I painted the figure of the man falling forward, pierced by an arrow.

That is the way one ought to do sketch-pictures, which would have the liberty and frankness of first notes. Little pictures enervate me, bore me, it is the same with easel pictures, even large ones, done in the studio. One exhausts oneself only to spoil them. One ought to put into big canvases, what Cournault tells me is in the *Battle of Ivry*

[67] Project for the ceiling of the *Galerie d'Apollon* in the Louvre.

by Rubens, in Florence: all the fire which, ordinarily, one gets only on walls.

The manner in which I treated the figure of *Italy* is very appropriate for work where the form is to be as completely rendered as imagination can desire, without ceasing to be in full color, etc.

Prud'hon's style was formed with a view to this need of coming back to the work ceaselessly, *yet with no failure in frankness*. In the ordinary manner of painting, one always has to spoil one thing in order to obtain another. Rubens is *loose* in his Naiades so as not to lose his light and his color. *In portraiture it is the same thing*: if one wants to arrive at an extreme strength of expression and of character, the frankness of the touch disappears, and with it the light and the color. One would obtain results very promptly and would never fatigue the work. One can always take it up again, since the result is almost infallible.

Wax was very useful to me with that figure in making the paint dry promptly and letting me return to the form at any moment. *Copal varnish* or ———— can take its place; one might mix wax with that.

What gives so much finesse and brilliance to painting on white paper is doubtless that transparence which is a matter of the essentially white nature of the paper. The brilliance of picture by Van Eyck and those by Rubens later on doubtless comes from the white of their panels.

It is probable that the first Venetians painted on very white grounds. Their dark flesh seems to be no more than a simple lacquer glaze over a ground which always shows through. In the same way, not only the flesh, but the backgrounds, the earth and the trees are glazed on over a white ground in the work of the early Flemings, for example. Let me recall, as regards the *Sleeping Nymph* which I began just lately, and at which I worked in the presence of Soulier and Pierret today, Sunday, what the effect was of the rock, behind the figure, and of the ground and also the depth of the forest, after I had glazed it with *yellow lacquer* and with *malachite* green etc., on a preparation of *white* that I had put over the horrible thing that the rock had been before, when I had painted it with *umber,* etc.

In the old Flemish pictures done on panels and therefore with a kind of glaze, the rusty color is very apparent. The difficulty then, consists in finding a proper compensation of gray, to balance the yellowing and the hotness of the tints.

I had an idea of all that in the sketch which I made, ten years ago, of the *Women Carried off by Horsemen*,[68] from an engraving after Rubens; as the sketch is, all that is lacking is a few tones of gray. It is not even possible that the background and the draperies should fail to have their part in the painting of the flesh, when one executes them with glazes on white grounds. When working in any other manner the incongruity between them is unbearable. It seemed to me, after having modelled that *Nymph* with *pure white,* that the background behind her, a background of rocks done with opaque tones such as would be used with a lay-in according to the system of the local halftone, was not the proper background, but that a light background, as of a drapery or a wall, was needed. I therefore covered that rock with *white:* and when, afterward, I decided to make another rock with tones as transparent as possible, the flesh could harmonize with that accessory: but I had to repaint the drapery, the earth, and the depth of the forest in the same way.

October 6.

I should certainly have reached a greater power, I should more quickly have produced small pictures with present-day or dramatic subjects, if I had made tracings of them with ink, in the style of my sketches for the Chamber, and then painted them with the technique of a sketch. When the dimensions are increased, the placing on the canvas becomes more difficult because of that very fact. Such a consideration would be of slight importance if one got a better picture in this way, but that is not the case; one takes trouble with the rendering in pictures where the rendering contributes to the effect. That is scarcely true in

[68] *The Rape of the Daughters of Leucippus,* in the Alte Pinakothek, Munich.

those small subjects. The *Desdemona,* the *Femme à la Rivière,* and the *Lélia*[69] will make a better effect as they are (in small size). As for the others, the larger size will be better.

The special charm of water color painting, beside which any painting in oil will appear rusty and pissy, comes from that continual transparence of the paper; the proof is that it loses this quality when one employs any body color; it loses it entirely in a gouache. The paintings of the Flemish primitives have a great deal of this charm. The use of turpentine contributes to it by getting rid of the oil.

October 7.

The nearer I keep to the original sketch in these little pictures, the more they will gain in energy. That shortens the time and obviates tiresome researches which take one away from the idea with which one started. The tracing on to the canvas is done with the pen. That is always best.

October 8.

To be remembered: the impression of a picture by Jacquand which I saw one of these days alongside a picture by Diaz, at Durand Ruel's. In the former, minute imitation from nature of the most insignificant objects: dryness, awkwardness; in the other, where there is a painter's imagination, but where his memories are faithful — life, grace, abundance. One would have said that Jacquand's picture was done by a man incapable of the memory of the slightest objects, a man for whom the detail under his eyes is the only one that could impress him.

October 9.

With Mme de Forget, saw a Chinese wall paper at Maigret's place. He told us that no art that we have could approach the solidity of their color. When he tried to put a patch on a part of the pink background,

[69] *Desdemona* (Catalogue Robaut, 698–700). *Lélia* (Catalogue Robaut, 1032, 1033).

it turned to a horrible color in a short time. All those charming birds are done by hand and also, as he told us, all the ornaments; these include whitish bamboos, touched up with silver, running over the whole field, which is a perfectly solid pink; the whole is sown with birds, butterflies, etc. of a perfection which does not derive its charm from a minute exactitude, from imitation, such as we always employ in our ornaments: on the contrary, for the bearing, the grace of the pose, and the contrast of the tones, it was the animal complete, but the whole thing done by a mind which had chosen and summed up the object in such a fashion as to make of it an ornament like those formed by the animals on Egyptian monuments and manuscripts.

(THE following lines were written on a loose sheet of paper. not dated, but found in the notebook of 1847.)

The public was evidently more enlightened at the periods when great talents, in order to please it, did not appeal to bombast and to bad taste.

The works it likes give the measure of its taste.

Talent itself is obliged to exaggerate effects, to hit hard. The savage in us always comes back. The most extreme civilization cannot banish from our cities the most atrocious crimes, which seem to belong to peoples blinded by barbarism.

In the same way, a human mind abandoned to itself always falls back into stupid childhood. It prefers toys to objects worthy of admiration.

A taste for simplicity cannot endure for long.

The human mind knows how to preserve nothing. Traditions are of no earthly use. Once the great man disappears, all is ended with him.

All the great problems of art were solved in the sixteenth century.

The perfection of drawing, of grace, and of composition, in Raphael.

Of color, and of chiaroscuro, in Correggio, in Titian, in Paul Veronese.

Rubens arrives, having already forgotten the traditions of grace and of simplicity. Through his genius he creates an ideal once more. He draws it up from his own nature. We get strength, striking effects, and expression pushed to its limit.

Rembrandt finds it in the vagueness of reverie and of the *handling?*

(The Notebook of the *Journal* for 1848 has not been preserved. Andrieu, Delacroix's pupil, related to M. Adolphe Moreau that Delacroix had lost it in a cab when driving home from the Gare de Lyon.)

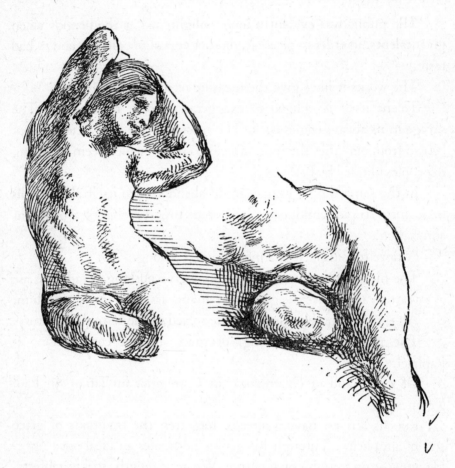

January 14.

APPOINTMENT for noon with the commission at the Palais Royal, to visit the places for the Exposition. Disgusting devastation, galleries transformed into storehouses for equipment. Paymaster's office established, etc. A clubroom with a platform; it smelled of pipe-smoke and of the barracks, etc. Then to the Tuileries for the same purpose: the same depressing spectacle, with this difference — that the palace no longer contains guests of the kind that we found in the Palais Royal; but everywhere there were traces of destructiveness, and ill-smelling dirt. The bed of the ex-King still has the mattresses and the bedclothes which he used, those of the Queen are there too. In the theater, a pile of remains from broken furniture, jewel boxes that had been forced open, wardrobes that had been smashed in, etc. Everywhere the portraits cut to pieces, with just one exception — those of the prince de Joinville; whence comes that preference? It is difficult to find a reply.

January 24.

To the Commission at nine o'clock.[1] Good day. It recalled to me the one which saw me begin the *Journal,* which I did just two years ago.[2]

January 29.

Alarms in the morning because of the revolt of the *garde mobile.*

In the evening, went to see Chopin; I stayed with him until ten o'clock. The dear fellow! We talked of Mme Sand, of her strange destiny, of her mixture of virtue and of vices. It was with reference to her *Mémoires.* He told me that it would be impossible for her to write them. She has forgotten all that: she has flights of sensibility and then quickly forgets. She wept for her old friend Pierret, and thought no more about him. I told him that I foresaw an unhappy old age for her. He does not think so. Her conscience does not reproach her with any of the things with which her friends reproach her. She has good health, it can stand anything. One thing alone would affect her deeply — the loss of Maurice,[3] or his turning to the bad entirely.

As to Chopin, his suffering prevents him from taking interest in anything, in work most of all. I told him that age and the agitations of the day would not be long about cooling me off also. He told me he

[1] Delacroix had been made a member of the Municipal Commission.
[2] This sentence is the proof that the *Journal* begins anew only in 1847.
[3] Maurice Sand, her son.

believed that I had strength enough to resist. "You will enjoy your talent," he said, "in a kind of serenity which is a rare privilege, and which is well worth the feverish search for reputation."

February 2.

In the evening with Chopin, Grzimala and Alkan; talked music. He thinks Beethoven was tormented by the idea of Bach. He based his work on Bach a great deal. Haydn, the man whose second and third parts, that is to say the pieces which follow the first, are the best, sometimes did them in three or four ways, all different. That astonishes me. Mozart, he says, worked a great deal also. Beyond a doubt; but not in that way. He must have been led by a view of the whole which did not permit him to make any sweeping changes in his original idea.

February 4.

In Rivet's collection I saw my sketch for *Sardanapalus*[4] again, and it did not displease me, despite certain eccentricities.

February 5.

M. Baudelaire[5] came in as I was starting to work anew on a little figure of a woman in Oriental costume[6] lying on a sofa, undertaken for Thomas,[7] of the Rue du Bac. He told me of the difficulties that Daumier experiences in finishing.

He ran on to Proudhon,[8] whom he admires and whom he calls

[4] Sketch for the *Sardanapalus (Catalogue Robaut, 168)* now in the Louvre.
[5] Baudelaire was one of the first writers to understand the genius of Delacroix. The admirable pages which he devoted to the master were collected in his *Curiosités Esthetiques.* An obituary article published in *Le National* was reprinted in his *Art Romantique.*
[6] Catalogue Robaut, 1045.
[7] A picture dealer.
[8] P. J. Proudhon (1809–1865), in his newspaper, *Le Peuple,* was at the time defending his socialistic ideas which, in public opinion, made of him the authentic representative of the Revolution of February.

the idol of the people. His views seem to be of the most modern, and altogether in the line of progress. Continued with the little figure after his departure.

Am in a very poor state of mind. To day it is public affairs which are the cause. Another day, it will be for some other reason. Must one not always be fighting against some bitter idea?

February 7.

At a picture dealer's, I see a so-called Rubens, the same being probably a Heemskerke or a Diepenbeck, very beautiful and very surprising in execution, purer probably than a Rubens would be: but no style, incorrectnesses of a poor kind, etc.

Looking at my picture of the *Women of Algiers,* I feel how agreeable and even how necessary it is to paint on the varnish. Only, one ought to discover a means of keeping the varnish underneath from being attacked at a later time when the varnish may be removed, or else one ought first to go over the sketch with a varnish which could not evaporate, like that of Desrosiers or of Soehnée, I think, or varnish with ——— in the first place, or else do the same in finishing.

February 9.

In the evening, to Chopin immediately after dinner. He gets indignant at seeing mediocrity appropriate to itself the inventions of the masters and spoil them or disgust people with them by its way of taking possession of them.

February 10.

A fool named Moreau whom I had not seen for a long time was at Pierret's house this evening; his toilette was most scrupulous, his gloves were hermetical. He appears to consider himself handsome, or interesting to the fair sex; that is why he has to rig himself out like that. I mention this only because this individual, who is nothing but a fop, made me think of certain lady-killers who are the victims of the obligation always to be handsome — which they think they have.

February 11.

I saw Thiers again: a bitter-sweet interview. He takes to heart my opposition to his desires. I was engaged in conversation, and that probably increased his bad humor. He did not tell me to come and see him again, and went off quite suddenly. I returned through the garden as far as the bridge, with M. Vallon and M. Bocher. I took the latter in a cab as far as the Place de la Concorde. For him the future of the Assembly looks pretty black. He thinks that Napoleon is more solidly established than his friends do; he is more popular than any of the rulers of the last thirty years. Republican ideas have penetrated more than people seem to think. I also believe that nothing like what was can come again; everything is changed in France, and everything is still changing. He pointed out to me the dull and neglected look of that crowd, although this is Sunday and the weather is of the most extraordinary, for all Paris seems to be out of doors.

Wednesday, February 14.

Thiers was very cold to me, more than I had as yet thought. I am beginning to think what Vieillard was telling me Monday at Cerfbeer's, that he has an elevated mind and a little soul. He ought really to esteem me for having opposed him in a thing which shocked my feelings. So much the worse for him, assuredly.

The Prince[9] made a compliment to Ingres on his beautiful picture of the *Capuchins*,[10] the said picture being by Granet; Napoleon told him that he himself owned the picture. Ingres' face was a study when he had to swallow his pill.

February 15.

Went back to work on my pictures of flowers and began with the basket of fruit.[11] I was feeling badly and did but little. That, however,

[9] Louis Napoleon, then president of France.
[10] Granet painted several versions of this subject; one of them is in the Metropolitan Museum, New York.
[11] Picture shown at the Salon of 1849 (Catalogue Robaut, 1072).

put me back into a good mood for work, and I think that if I soon finish the things that are not done at all, the parts which are already pushed ahead will immediately look finished.

February 16.

Worked on the *Flowers and Fruits.*

February 20.

Saw the *Gazza Ladra.*[12] I was in the box of the President with Mme de Forget. The masterpiece never gave me so much pleasure before.

February 22.

I met Pietri again who used to read Dante to me while I was working at my *Dante and Vergil.*

Monday February 26.

Did very little. Dined at the house of Bixio with Lamartine, Mérimée, Malleville, Scribe, Meyerbeer, and two Italians. I had a very good time. I had never been so long with Lamartine. Mérimée went for him at dinner about the poems of Pushkin, which Lamartine claims to have read, though they have never been translated by anybody. He gives the unpleasant impression of a man perpetually mystified. His self-esteem, which seems chiefly occupied with enjoying itself and with reminding others of everything he can attribute to himself, is perfectly calm amidst everybody's tacit agreement to consider him a bit cracked. His heavy voice has something rather unsympathetic about it.

Friday, March 2.

In the evening, went out to call on Chopin; I met Chenavard.[13] We

[12] *La Gazza Ladra,* comic opera by Rossini.

[13] Paul Chenavard (1807–1895), painter and theorist of painting, was one of the intimate friends of Delacroix who liked to exchange ideas on art with him. At this time, Chenavard had been commissioned to decorate the interior of the Panthéon, and was devoting himself entirely to the preparation of this great work. In 1851, when the government gave the Panthéon back to the Catholic Church, Chenavard's commission was annulled and, in his discouragement, he practically gave up painting.

talked for almost two hours, taking shelter for some time in the passage where servants wait, at the Opéra Comique.

He told me, when we were separating, that men are to be divided into two classes: the men who have one single law, the law of their interest; for those, the line to be followed is perfectly simple, and in every question they have only to consult that infallible standard. The men of the other class have the feeling for justice and the intention of following it. But the majority of them obey it only half way, or rather do not obey it at all, though reproaching themselves; or else, having for a time lost sight of that rule for their actions, they return to it and go to excesses which deprive them of the fruit of their preceding conduct, while still leaving them the blame for it. Thus they will, for example, have flattered the passions of a patron from whom they expect a favor, and then they will suddenly stop seeing him and will go so far as to become his enemies.

Petetin had told me that morning that, in order to have nothing to reproach himself with, he had put his ambition into his pocket. I said to Chenavard that I thought it impossible to be mixed up in other people's affairs and to remain completely honest. "How do you think it could be otherwise?" said he. "The man who takes justice as his rule is absolutely prevented from fighting against the man who thinks only of his interest: he will always be beaten in the career of ambition."

March 3.

Met Larrey[14] in the omnibus; he related to me that during the days of the Revolution in June they shot the wounded men that he was having transported on the stretchers.

March 4.

All day I have been reading *La Foire aux Idées (Vanity Fair)* in *La Revue,* translated and abridged by Chasles from Thackeray's book.

[14] Baron Larrey (1808–1896), military surgeon, professor, member of the Institute.

That interests me to the highest degree. It is to be hoped that everything this author produces will be translated.

Monday, March 5.

I went with Meissonier to his studio to see his drawing of the *Barricade*. His faithfulness in representation is horrible, and though one cannot say that the thing is not exact, perhaps there is lacking that indefinable thing which makes of an *odious object an object of art*. I say the same about his studies from nature; they are colder than his composition, and yet drawn with the same pencil with which Watteau would have drawn his coquettes and his delightful figures of shepherds. Immense merit, despite that. More and more I see, for my instruction and for my consolation, the confirmation of the thing that Cogniet told me last year with reference to the *Man Devoured by a Lion*[15] when he saw that picture alongside that of the cows by Mlle Bonheur,[16] which is to say that there is something else in painting beside exactitude and precise rendering from the model.

This morning I had an impression that was analogous but much more comprehensible, since the question was of a painting of a completely inferior order. Coming home after seeing the figure by Dubufe, the paintings in my studio and, among others, my poor *Marcus Aurelius*,[17] which I have accustomed myself to disdain, looked to me like masterpieces. What does that impression come from? From the fact, assuredly, noted in the presence of Meissonier's drawing, that the impression produced by my painting is infinitely superior to one produced by studies from nature.

[15] Doubtless Catalogue Robaut, 1017.

[16] Rosa Bonheur (1822–1899), pupil of Cogniet; the picture is doubtless her *Labourage Nivernais,* which got a medal of the first class at the Salon of 1848.

[17] The *Death of Marcus Aurelius* (Catalogue Robaut 924), the big picture which appeared in the Salon of 1845, was acquired in 1858 by the museum of Lyons for four thousand francs. "A picture that is splendid, magnificent, sublime, and not understood," wrote Baudelaire.

Made the acquaintance of Prudent;[18] he imitates Chopin closely. I was proud of that for my poor great man, who is dying.

Tuesday, March 6.

At the house of the Prefect in the evening. Very fine concert. Varcollier was so extremely kind as to have the choruses from *Idoménée*[19] performed instead of the *Ave Verum,* and he went so far in his courtesy as to send me word of the fact about six o'clock. That choir and the march which follows it are the sublime itself.

Thursday, March 8.

In the evening, Chopin. At his house, met an original who has come from Quimper to admire him and to cure him. For he is or has been a doctor and has a great contempt for the homeopaths of all colors. He is a rabid music lover: but his admiration is limited, practically, to Beethoven and Chopin. Mozart does not seem to him on their height; Cimarosa is old hat, etc. You've got to come from Quimper to have ideas like that and to express them with such nerve: that passes for the frankness of the Breton. I detest that kind of character. That so-called frankness which permits people to utter cutting or wounding opinions, is the thing for which I have the greatest antipathy. Relationships among men are no longer possible if frankness like that is a sufficient answer to everything. To speak frankly, one should, with a disposition like that, live in a stable, where relationships are established by thrusts of a pitchfork or by horns; that's the kind of frankness I prefer.

In the morning, at the studio of Couder,[20] to talk about the picture

[18] Racine Gauthier, called Prudent (1817–1863), pianist and composer.

[19] *Idoménée,* opera by Mozart.

[20] Louis-Charles-Auguste Couder (1790–1873) painter of history, pupil of Regnault and of David, presented himself in 1838 at the Institute in competition with Delacroix and was elected. The question discussed was of Delacroix's picture, *Liberty Guiding the People* which caused certain commercial difficulties at Lyons.

at Lyons. He is witty, and his wife is very good-looking. If we had been frank with each other, along the lines of my Breton, we should have had a fight before the end of the meeting; on the contrary, we parted in perfect agreement.

Saturday, March 10.

Saw Mme de Forget in the evening, M. Détrimont in the morning. I was struck by his Albrecht Dürers, and in a way I never was before; I observed, in the presence of his *Saint Hubert,* and of his *Adam and Eve,* that the true painter is the one who knows all of nature. Thus the human figures in his work have not more perfection than those of the animals of all kinds, or the trees, etc. He is consistent in everything he does, that is to say with the kind of rendering which the advance of the arts in his period carried with it. He is an instructive painter: everything he did is to be consulted.

Saw an engraving which I did not know, that of the *Chanoine Luxurieux* [21] who has fallen asleep near his stove: the devil shows him a nude woman, the latter being of a more elevated style than is usual with Dürer, and a lame cupid trying to guide himself on stilts.

M. Détrimont showed me a letter from my father; that gave me pleasure. What struck me most among his autographs is a piece of Leonardo da Vinci's writing on which there are sketches showing him taking note of the system which has come down from antiquity of *drawing with rounds;* [22] he discovered everything. These manuscripts are written backwards.

Sunday, March 11.

Went to the Sainte-Cécile concert and heard the divine *Pastoral Symphony* with happiness, but with something of distraction because of the lack of quiet among my neighbors. The rest of the program was devoted to virtuosi who wearied and bored me.

[21] Also known as *Le Rêve;* in England and America it is called *The Dream.*
[22] This process was also employed by Delacroix himself in drawings of horses.

I was venturesome enough to remark that Beethoven's compositions are in general too long, despite the astounding variety that he introduces in his manner of returning to the same motives. I do not recall that this defect ever struck me before in that symphony; be that as it may, it is evident that the artist diminishes his effect by demanding a too prolonged attention.

Painting has this advantage, among others, that it is more discreet; the most gigantic picture is seen in an instant. If the qualities that it contains, or certain parts of it attract the attention, that is quite as it should be: one can enjoy it a longer time, even, than one can a piece of music. But if the painting seems to you mediocre, all you need to do is turn your head to keep from being bored. On the day of Prudent's concert, the overture from the *Magic Flute* seemed to me not only ravishing, but perfect in proportion. Is one to say that, with the progress of instrumentation, it becomes more natural for the musician to be tempted into lengthening his pieces in order to bring about recurrent effects of the orchestra, varying each time that he shows them to us again?

One must never look on the time given to a concert as a chore, provided that there is at least one good piece. It is the soul's best nourishment. To prepare oneself, to leave home, to be taken even from important occupations in order to go and hear music adds value to the pleasure; to find oneself in a consecrated place and amid people whom a community of feeling seems to have gathered together so that they may have enjoyment in common, all that, even the boredom experienced on hearing certain pieces given by certain virtuosi, adds, unconsciously, to the effect of the beautiful thing. If that fine symphony had been executed for me in my studio, I should perhaps not have preserved the same memory of it at the present hour.

That also explains why the great and the rich are blasé at a too early age in the matter of pleasures of all kinds. They enter good boxes furnished with good carpets, are at a distance which assures them as much as possible against the noise and disturbance occasioned by people's coming and going, and by the minor troubles of all kinds which occur in a crowd if only — as it seems — to weary one's attention. They do not arrive before the exact moment when the piece is beginning and, as a merited punishment for their lack of devotion to the beautiful, they generally lose the best part of it through their lateness. The habits of society people cause their conversations on the most frivolous subject, or the sudden arrival of some importunate person, to destroy their whole peace of mind. It is a very imperfect pleasure to hear even the most beautiful music in a box with people of fashion. The poor artist seated in an orchestra chair and alone in his corner, or beside a friend as attentive as himself, is the only one who completely enjoys the beauty of a work, and by reason of that he carries away the memory of it without the slightest trace of the ridiculous entering in.

Monday, April 2.

This evening, saw *Athalie* with Mme de Forget in the box of the President.

Rachel did not give me pleasure in all the parts. But how I admired that high priest! What a creation! How overdone it would seem in a time like ours! and how well in place it is — with that ordered and convinced society which saw Racine and which made him what he is! That wild enthusiasm, that wordy fanaticism, is scarcely of our time: throats are cut and men are hurled to the ground coldly and without conviction. Mathan, in the scene with his confidant, says too naïvely "I am a rascal, I am an abominable being." Here Racine steps outside the truth, but he is sublime when Mathan, going forth deeply troubled to escape the imprecations of the high priest, knows not whither he is going and, unconscious of what he does, turns his steps in the direction of the sanctuary which he has profaned and which torments him by its existence.

Wednesday, April 4.

Man is always beginning everything anew, even in his own life. He cannot stop the forward movement of things. How should a people arrest that movement in its life? To speak only of the artist, his manner changes. After a certain time, he can no longer recall what means he used in the execution of his work. More than that, those who have systematized their style to the point where they do always things over in the same style, are usually the coldest and most inferior, through the very nature of art.

Dined at the house of Véron with Rachel,[23] M. Molé, the Duke of Osuna, General Rullière,[24] Armand Bertin and M. Fould,[25] who was near me and showed himself very courteous. Rachel is witty and very fine in every way. A man born and brought up as she was would with difficulty become what she is by nature. During the evening chatted with Rullière about *Athalie,* etc. He was very amiable.

People of every stripe came in. A certain Mme Ugalde, who is at present having success at the Opéra Comique, sang an air from the *Val d'Andorre;* I was not very sympathetic toward her; she has a rather low type of pronunciation, and has the map of Jerusalem painted all over her face: contrast with Rachel.

Talked a good deal about music with Armand Bertin. Spoke about Racine and about Shakespeare. He believes that in this country it's no use — people will always come back to what has been the beautiful for our nation, once and for all; I think he is right. We shall never be partisans of Shakespeare. The English are all Shakespeare. It is his influence that we see in all the things most characteristic of them.

Thursday, April 5.

A day of depression and of bad health. I went out about four o'clock to call on Deforge.

In the evening called on Mme de Forget who read me a part of

---

[23] Mademoiselle Rachel, the famous tragedian.
[24] General Rullière (1787–1863) was minister of war at the time.
[25] Achille Fould (1800–1867), statesman and financier.

the speech by Barbès[26] before his judges. In the speeches of those people, one sees all the falsity and the bombast that they have in their poor guilty heads. It's always that way with the race of bad writers, the wretched modern pestilence which calmly sacrifices a people to the ideas of a sick brain.

The goal, he says, is everything. Beyond a doubt, universal suffrage was something and had set up that Chamber; but both that Chamber and the provisional government which preceded it were the result, as they believe, of some kind of general demand; but the whole thing did not seem to him to deserve support, or rather he thought of it all as something to overthrow, from the moment that it departed from the goal which Barbès had established in his mind, without informing us, unfortunately, as to this admirable goal. And so he prefers imprisonment, a cell, to the suffering he would feel as a powerless witness to the sacrilege of deviating from the supreme goal of humanity toward which, whether we like it or not, that same humanity must finally advance — following the sublime aspirations of Barbès.

In the speech by Blanqui,[27] a few days before, poetic images in the modern style, as they claim to be, mingled with his arguing; he spoke of an abyss which the Revolution had to clear in order to pass from the ancient ideas to the new ones: our too feeble flight did not permit us to clear that fatal abyss, in which the future is near to drowning, but which does not slow up the rhetoric of Blanqui to the slightest degree. Everything is arduous in this style of speech, a matter of abysses and other bombast. Large and simple truths do not need, for their utterance and for impressing the minds of men, to borrow the style

[26] Barbès had taken an active part in the uprising of 1848 against national representation. Tried before the Haute-Cour at Bourges, he was condemned on April 17, 1849 to imprisonment for life.

[27] Blanqui, the politician, mixed up in all the conspiracies of the preceding régimes, led on into the attempt of 1848, in spite of his disagreements with Barbès; tried before the Haute-Cour of Bourges and condemned to prison for ten years.

of Hugo, who has never come within a hundred leagues of the truth and of *simplicity*.

Friday evening, April 6.

To the Conservatory with Mmes Bixio and Ménessier. The concert was not very fine. I had preserved a greater memory of the *Eroica*. Decidedly, Beethoven is terribly unequal. The first movement is beautiful; the andante, on which I was counting, completely disappointed me. Nothing beautiful or sublime at the beginning! All at once you fall down a hundred feet and find yourself amid things that are most singularly commonplace. The last movement lacks unity, also.

Saturday, April 7.

About half past three, accompanied Chopin on his drive. Although fatigued, I was happy to be of some use to him. The Avenue of the Champs-Elysées, the arch of the Etoile, the bottle of quinquina wine; being made to stop at the city limits, etc.

During the day, he talked music with me, and that gave him new animation. I asked him what establishes logic in music. He made me feel what counterpoint and harmony are; how the fugue is like pure logic in music, and that to know the fugue deeply is to be acquainted with the element of all reason and all consistency in music. I thought how happy I should have been to learn about all this — which is the despair of the common run of musicians. That feeling gave me an idea of the pleasure in science that is experienced by philosophers worthy of the name. The thing is that true science is not what is ordinarily understood under that term, that is to say, a department of knowledge which differs from art. No, science, looked upon in the way I mean, demonstrated by a man like Chopin, is art itself, and, obversely, art is no longer what the vulgar think it to be, that is, some sort of inspiration which comes from nowhere, which proceeds by chance, and presents no more than the picturesque externals of things. It is reason itself, adorned by genius, but following a necessary course and encompassed by higher laws. This brings me back to the difference between Mozart and Beethoven. As he said to me, "Where the latter is obscure and seems lacking in unity, the cause is not to be sought in what people look upon as a rather wild originality, the thing they honor him for; the reason is that he turns his back on eternal principles; Mozart never. Each of the parts has its own movement which, while still according with the others, keeps on with its own song and follows it perfectly; there is your counterpoint, 'punto contrapunto.'" He told me that the custom was to learn the harmonies before coming to counterpoint, that is to say, the succession of the notes which leads to the harmonies. The harmonies in the music of Berlioz are laid on as a veneer; he fills in the intervals as best he can.

These men so vehemently in love with style, who would rather be stupid than lacking in an *air of gravity*. This to be applied to Ingres and to his school.

Wednesday, April 11.

I think it was this evening that I saw Mme Potocka at the house of Chopin. The same admirable effect from her voice. I told her what I very sincerely think: that in music, as in all the other arts doubtless, as soon as style, character, the serious things, in a word, appear, everything else is forgotten. I like her much better when she sings the *Salice*[28] than in those charming Neapolitan melodies. She tried *Le Lac* by Lamartine with that melody by Niedermeyer, which is so common and so pretentious. That accursed tune tormented me for two days.

To Chopin in the evening; I found him almost in a state of collapse, hardly breathing. At the end of a certain time my presence restored him. He told me that boredom was his cruelest torment. I asked him whether he had not previously known that unbearable emptiness which I sometimes feel. He told that he always could busy himself with something. As unimportant as it may be in itself, a thing one

---

[28] The song of "The Willow"; in Rossini's *Othello*.

has to do fills one's time and drives away those vapors. Troubles are another matter.

Sunday, April 22.

Stayed at home, tired from last night. M. Poujade came in about one o'clock; he interested me but he stayed too long and fatigued me. Then Leblond. It was a pleasure to see him, despite my fatigue; I like him extremely. The presence of a friend is a thing so rare that it is worth all pleasures, or compensates for all miseries.

After dinner went to see Chopin, another man exquisite in heart and, needless to say, in mind. He talked to me of the people we had known together, Mme Kalergi, etc. He had dragged himself to the first performance of *Le Prophète*.[29] His horror at that rhapsody.

An idea comes to me: for someone to write the letters of a Roman of the century of Augustus or of the Emperors, demonstrating with all the reasons we can find today that the civilization of the ancient world cannot perish.

The leading spirits of the time attack the augurs and the pontiffs, thinking that they will stop in time.

Relationship with the present-day civilization of England, where abuses maintain the government.

Monday, April 23.

From knowledge which has been growing inescapable for a year, I believe one can affirm that all progress must necessarily carry with it not a still greater progress, but finally the negation of progress, a return to the point from which we set out. The history of the human race is there to prove it. Yet consider the blind confidence of this generation — and of the one which preceded it — in modern ideas, in the coming of some sort of new era of humanity. We are supposed to see a complete change in our destiny; but for that to occur, there ought first to be a sign of it, I think, in the nature of man himself. Nothing in the centuries which preceded us is offered as justification of the bizarre con-

[29] *Le Prophète*, opera by Meyerbeer.

fidence I mention, and it is in itself the only thing that hints at those future successes, those revolutions in human destiny which are so greatly desired. Is it not evident that progress, toward good or toward evil, has today brought society to the edge of an abyss into which it may very well fall, to make way for a state of complete barbarism; and the reason, the sole reason for this — does it not reside in that law which dominates all others here below, i.e., the need for change, whatever it may be? We must change. *Nil in eodem statu permanet.* That which ancient wisdom had discovered, before having made so many experiments, must necessarily be accepted by us, and we must submit to it. What is at present dying out among us will doubtless recreate itself, or will maintain itself at some other place, for a time of more or less duration.

The frightful *Prophète*, which its author doubtless looks upon as progress, is the annihilation of art. His submission to an imperious need to do something better or something different from what had been done, in a word the need to change, has caused him to lose sight of the eternal laws of taste and logic which govern the arts. Men like Berlioz and Hugo, and the rest of those so-called reformers, have not yet managed to abolish the laws which I just mentioned; but they have brought about a belief in the possibility of working along lines other than those of truth and reason. The same thing in politics. You can't get out of the beaten path save by returning to the infancy of society; and, after one reform has followed another, savagery is necessarily the state brought about by these changes.

Mozart said: "Violent passions should never be expressed to the point where they arouse disgust; even in situations of horror, music should never offend the ear and cease to be music." (*Revue des Deux Mondes*, March 15, 1849, page 892).

Friday, June 1.

Worked a great deal this morning and the preceding days to finish the small *Bride of Abydos*[30] and the *Bather*, rear view.[31]

To the Museum[32] about three o'clock, to retouch my picture a little.

In the big room of the French painters, Villot observed to me the superiority which is to be noted in such a school. I was very much struck by Gros especially, and above all by the *Battle of Eylau*. Everything in it pleases me at present. He is more the master in that than in the *Pest at Jaffa;* the execution is freer.

In the long gallery, admired the Rubens.[33] The figure of *Victory*

[30] Catalogue Robaut, 772.
[31] Catalogue Robaut, 1297.
[32] The Museum, that is to say the Louvre. The Salon of 1849 was held in the Tuileries.
[33] The pictures he discusses are those of the Marie de Médicis series. The *Sirens* are those in the episode of the *Landing at Marseille*, Delacroix had copied these figures (Catalogue Robaut, 260).

in Tears, in the next to the last picture. How that figure stands out from the others! even though the legs seem to have been painted by a hand other than that of the master; they show care; but the sublime head in tears and the folded arm, all that is genius itself.

Also the sirens never seemed to me so beautiful. Abandon and the most complete audacity can alone produce such impressions.

Saw the *Resurrection of our Lord* by Carracci. The dullness and coldness of that painting showed me what beauty there is in the subject.

Sunday, July 15.

I write Peisse,[34] with reference to his article of the 8th:

"I do not venture to say that everything you write there is exactly right, because I am reaping the benefit of it; what you say about color and the art of color has never been said very strongly. Criticism is like many other things, it drags along after what has already been said and does not get out of its rut. That famous element, the beautiful, which some see in the serpentine line, others see in the straight line, but they are all resolved that it is to be seen only in line. I am at my window, and I see the most beautiful landscape: the idea of a line does not come to my mind. The lark sings, the river sparkles with a thousand diamonds, the foliage murmurs; where are any lines to pro-duce these charming sensations? Those people refuse to see proportion and harmony unless they are between lines: the rest is chaos for them, and the compass alone is the judge. Pardon me my vigor as a critic in speaking against my critics. Note that I very humbly take shelter under the great names which you cite, even while I recognize in those masters qualities even finer than those usually attributed to them. Yes, Rubens draws, yes, Correggio draws. Not one of these men has broken with the ideal. Without the ideal, there is neither drawing, nor painting, nor color; and what is worse than lacking it, is to have that

[34] Jean-Louis Peisse (1803–1888) doctor, writer, curator of the collections of the Ecole des Beaux-Arts. Delacroix writes to thank him for an article of praise on his pictures at the Salon.

borrowed ideal which those people go to school to learn, and which is enough to cause hatred of the models. As several volumes might be written on the subject, I stop at this point, so as to speak once more of the pleasure that you have given me, etc."

Monday, July 23.

I dined at the house of Mme de Forget with Cavé, his wife, etc. In the evening M. Menneval[35] told me of the frightful conduct of the generals and marshals toward the Emperor, at Arcis-sur-Seine or sur-Aube. M. Fain,[36] lodging in another house than that of the Emperor, and crossing a square in order to join his master, came on a group of generals, among them Marshal Ney, who were deliberating among themselves as to whether they should not mete out to their benefactor the fate of Romulus: to kill him and to bury him there seemed to them as good a means as any other of getting rid of him and of getting back to their hotel, where they could enjoy themselves; he was, so they said, the scourge of France, etc. The Emperor, to whom M. Fain related the affair with emotion that will be imagined, contented himself with saying that they were mad.

Marshal Ney's greatest impropriety toward him occurred after the battle of the Moscova, when he complained that by sparing the guard, the Emperor had deprived him of the fruits of a more complete victory. Marshal Ney was the cruelest at Fontainebleau; he went to the point of threatening him with physical injury if he did not abdicate.

In the course of the Russian campaign, Berthier did not fear to tell him how terrible it was to see oneself endlessly dragged into new enterprises: "What good does it do," said he, "to have wealth, houses, and lands, if one has to go to war eternally and compromise everything?"

[35] Baron de Menneval (1778–1850), the former secretary of Napoleon I, who had accompanied him in the retreat from Russia; author of a book of memories of the Empire.

[36] Baron Fain (1778–1837), one of the secretaries of the Emperor, published historical memories of the Empire.

To their reproaches, which often were odious, Napoleon's only answer was patience; despite their ingratitude, he loved them as old comrades.

Before the last years, M. Menneval told me no one had dared to permit himself an observation when he gave an order. Confidence had partially abandoned him, but the sureness and firmness of his genius not at all, as the French campaign so well proved. If, at Waterloo, at the end of the battle, there had been at his disposal that reserve of the guard which he refused to engage at the Moscova, he would still have won the battle, despite the arrival of the Prussians.

I asked M. Menneval whether he had not been completely indisposed at the Moscova, according to generally accredited opinion. This is correct: he was sick, and attacked with a loss of voice, especially after the battle, so that it was impossible for him to give a spoken order. He was obliged to scribble his orders on bits of paper. Notwithstanding, he was completely master of his ideas. But after the battle of Dresden, the sudden indisposition with which he was seized paralyzed all the operations, carried with it the defeat of Vandamme, etc.

During the Consulate, he was very sick with malignant mange, which he had contracted at the siege of Toulon. He would lean against his table, pressing his side with his hand during crises of violent suffering. His paleness and his thinness, at this period, are explained by this sickly condition. Corvisart got him rid of his disease, at least in appearance; but it is probable that the disease of which he died had its original cause in this cruel malady.

Rouen, Thursday, October 3.

When I arrived at the museum my *Trajan*[37] was half covered by the scaffolding erected for the exhibition of Norman painters.

I do not recall that any of my pictures, seen in a gallery a long time after I had forgotten it, ever gave me as much pleasure as this one. Unfortunately one of the most interesting parts, perhaps the most

[37] *La Justice de Trajan* (Catalogue Robaut, 714), painted in 1840.

interesting, was hidden, that is, the woman at the feet of the Emperor. What I was able to see of it appeared to me to have a vigor and a depth which eclipse everything, without exception, that was around it. How strange it was that the picture should appear brilliant, for in general it is dark in tone.

For the first time I noticed two or three pictures by Lucas van Leyden, or some one of his type, which delighted me. Great delicacy in the rendering of the details which express the temperament, the fineness of the skin and the hair, the grace of the hands, etc. A broad treatment in painting cannot give this type of impression. Almost beyond these pictures, admired the *Shepherds* by Rubens. Alongside is a picture by Honthorst, representing *Christ before Pilate*. In the past I had admired it because of its naiveté and its fidelity to appearances. Beside the *Shepherds* of Rubens, it descends again until it is scarcely more than portraits of models.

Then to Saint Ouen: that place has always given me an impression of the sublime; there is no church that I compare with this one.

Saturday, October 6.

Went out late today; saw the Cathedral, which does not come within a hundred leagues of producing the effect of Saint Ouen; I mean the interior, for on the outside, and from all sides, it is admirable. The façade: forms magnificently piled up, irregularity which pleases, etc. The *Gate of the Booksellers* just as beautiful. What affected me the most are the two tombs[38] in the chapel at the rear, but especially that of M. de Brézé. Everything is admirable, above all the statue. The merits of the antique unite in it with the special quality of modern things and with the grace of the Renaissance: the shoulder-blades,

[38] The tomb of Louis de Brézé, Seneschal of Normandy, who died in 1531, was commissioned by his widow, Diane de Poitiers; she had her statue in alabaster placed beside the one of her husband. It is uncertain which of the statues of cardinals Delacroix refers to; several are by very great sculptors of the Renaissance, such as Jean Goujon.

1863

14

the arm, the leg, the feet, all of it is of a style and execution beyond all praise. The other tomb pleases me a great deal, but the ensemble has something strange about it; perhaps it is the effect of those two figures posing there as if by chance. The one of the cardinal, in particular, is of the greatest beauty, and of a style which one can compare only with the finest things of Raphael: the drapery, the head, etc.

To Saint Maclou; superb windows, carved doors, etc. The front of the church on the street has gained by being freed. Some years ago, a new modern street was cut through, leading down to the port.

Tuesday, October 9.

Through what sad fatality is it that man can never enjoy all the faculties of his nature at the same time, and that he cannot appreciate all the perfections of which it is capable, save at different periods of his life? The considerations which I am writing down here were suggested to me by a thought of Montesquieu's which I came upon just lately; he says that at the time when a man's mind has attained its maturity, his body weakens.

As to this point, I was thinking that a certain vivacity of impressions which comes from physical sensibility diminishes with age. On arriving here,[39] and especially after having lived here for some days, I have not experienced those movements of joy or of sadness with which this place used to fill me, movements which were so sweet to remember. I shall leave, probably, without experiencing that regret which I felt in other days. As to my mind, far more than at the time I speak of, it has sureness and the faculty of combining and expressing; the intelligence has grown stronger but the soul has lost its elasticity and its irritability. Why should not man, after all, be subject to the common fate

[39] Delacroix is writing at Valmont, near Fécamp, where his cousins of the Bataille and Bornot families lived. Their property contained abbey buildings of the eighteenth century and a church decorated in the sixteenth century with sculptures and stained glass. Delacroix had visited there since his childhood, and had painted decorations there in 1834, to make trial of his ideas for the work at the Chamber of Deputies.

of living beings? When we gather the delicious fruit, should we be so greedy as to breathe in the perfume of the flower at the same time? It needed the exquisite delicacy there is in the sensibility of youth to bring about that sureness, that maturity of mind. Perhaps the very great men, and I fully believe this, are those who, at the age when intelligence has its full strength, have preserved a part of that impetuosity in the impressions which is the characteristic of youth.

Spent the morning in reading Montesquieu.

To Fécamp, about two o'clock; the sea was magnificent. Fine views of the valley. After dinner, discussion of politics.

These last days, I have been comparing the paintings which are in my cousin's drawing room. I came to an idea of what separates a painting that is only naive from one that has a character such as will make it endure. In a word, I have often been led to ask myself why extreme facility and boldness of touch do not shock me in Rubens, and why they are merely detestable facility in a man like Vanloo,[40] I mean those of the present as well as those of the past. Fundamentally, my feeling is quite clear enough that facility in the great master is not his chief quality; that it is only the means and not the end, the reverse being the case with mediocre men. I had the pleasure of finding confirmation for this opinion on comparing the portrait I once painted of my old aunt[41] with those by uncle Riesener. There is already, in that work by a beginner, a sureness and an intelligence as to essentials, and even a quality of touch in the rendering of the whole which struck Gaultron[42] himself. I attach importance to his words only because they reassure me about my past; a vigorous hand, is what he said.

The weather is altogether fine; we have been to Saint Pierre, across the valley.

[40] This was Delacroix's general term for eighteenth century painting of the weaker kind.

[41] This portrait, signed and dated 1818 (Catalogue Robaut, 1460), is still preserved at Valmont, as are the other family portraits, those by uncle Riesener.

[42] One of Delacroix's pupils; he exhibited at the Salon from 1848 to 1861.

On the way, saw Angerville again, where I came, so many years ago, with my good mother, my sister, my nephew, and cousin Bataille — all of them are gone! That little house is still there, like the sea, which one gets a sight of from that point, and which will still be there when the house, in its turn, will be gone.

We went down to the sea by a road to the right, which I did not know. There is the finest greensward that one can imagine, it slopes gently downward. The stretch of sea which one surveys from the heights is very considerable. That great line of blue, green, pink, or the indefinable color which, simply, is that of the vast sea, always transports me. The intermittent sound which reaches one already from afar and the smell of the salt are simply intoxicating.

I perceive that my beautiful reflections on the preceding pages have prevented me from making a note on our first trip to Fécamp. I don't recall which day that was, but the weather was altogether different. The sea was rough, and was breaking splendidly against the jetty. We saw two little boats go forth.

Today, on the contrary, it is very calm, and I adore it like this, with the sun which has sowed the side whence it came with sparks and with diamonds, and has lent gaiety to that majestic sheet of water.

We visited the house of the priest, which belonged to good M. Hébert. Decidedly it is a bit sad; a person living alone there would end by turning to stone.

They are pulling down the charming ancient church of the place in order to build a new one. We were outraged by that.

Saturday, 13.

Spent the morning in finishing the reading of *Arsace et Isménie*, by Montesquieu. All the talent of the author is of no avail against the boredom of those stale adventures, those loves, that eternal constancy: fashion and, I believe, a feeling for truth also, have relegated that kind of writing to oblivion.

Before lunch, examined the pieces of stained glass in the charterhouse.[43] I must remember their fine character, it has to do with Raphael and even more with Correggio, in the beautiful and simple modeling and the boldness of indication. Black contours, strongly pronounced, so as to be seen from a distance, etc.

After lunch to the cemetery. Before that, towards Saint Ouen, to the house of a poor woman who works at making handkerchiefs. Poor people! They are paid twenty francs for twenty-four dozen of those handkerchiefs; that makes less than twenty sous for each dozen.

The chapel where the body of Bataille reposes does not please me. I regret that I was not consulted.

Killed time until dinner. Slept in my room, then took a turn about the park as night was falling. This park and these gigantic trees took on an aspect which is almost lugubrious; but in truth, if one could render such effects in painting, it would be the most sublime thing that I have seen in landscape. There is nothing that I can compare to it. That forest of the columns formed by the pines, the old walnut tree as one goes uphill, etc.

Monday, October 15.

I admired the door of the church at the cemetery. It is evidently a work of fantasy, done by a workman who had taste. It shows how much that last quality is the life of that art for which the books offer ready-made proportions, which engender works denuded of all character whenever one sees them. Drew. The sea still at low tide.

Tuesday October 16.

Before lunch I went out alone on the road to Fécamp. I wanted to climb to the little wood to the left, and to the pretty stretches of land where the pine trees are. Stopped by the hedges and the enclosures every little while. The people, who will always be in the majority, make a mistake in believing that the big estates are not a great utility.

[43] Delacroix reconstituted a stained glass window from these fragments; it is still in place in the chapel.

It is to the poor people that they are useful, and the profit they derive
from them in no wise impoverishes the rich, who let them profit by
the little windfalls which they find there. The openhandedness of
my good cousin gave happiness to the poor people who gathered fern
and dried branches. When the petits bourgeois get rich they close off
their property and barricade the avenues everywhere. The poor, completely shut out in this way, do not even profit by the ridiculous rights
which the Republican Government gives to them.

Coming back for lunch, I crossed the valley toward the mill. It
is astride the river, which one crosses on a plank. Saw the road behind
the wash house which we so often followed.

Bornot reminded me that it was at this wash house that I kissed
the mason's girl, that nice little thing who used to come from time to
time to pay her respects to our old cousin.

Thursday, October 18.

Delightful weather in the morning, before lunch. Drew the clumps of
trees in the garden; the morning sun gives charming effects there.

Friday, October 19.

From day to day I put off the moment of my departure. People are
kind to me, and this soft idling in a place that I love soothes me and
makes me postpone the time of resuming the ordinary pace of my life.

In the morning read Montesquieu, *Grandeur et Décadence*. Took
a walk in the garden before lunch. Afterward went boating with my
cousin and some of the little girls. I was fatigued by yesterday's walk
and also by the life that I am leading, especially by these meals, these
wines, etc.

Saturday, October 20.

After lunch, I learned of the death of poor Chopin. Strange, in the
morning, before getting up, I was struck by that idea. This is one more
time, after several others, that I have gotten that sort of a premonition.
What a loss! What miserable rogues fill the market place, while that
beautiful soul burns out!

Walks in the garden. Farewell to this beautiful place, the charm of which is really a delight. That charm is tasted to only the slightest degree by the inhabitants of this manor house. Amid all this, the good cousin talks to us of nothing but his acres, of repairs to the walls, or of quarrels with the municipal council. The result is that for the greater part of the time I remain mute and disheartened. At mealtime especially, when people usually tend toward joviality, you'd think we were sitting on ice. Are they happy this way?

Monday, October 23.

This morning in the *Description de Paris et de ses Edifices,* published in 1808 by Legrand and Landon, I read the terrifying list of the riches, of the monuments of all kinds which disappeared from the churches during the Revolution. It would be curious to write something on this subject in order to edify people as to the most evident result of revolutions.

1850

Friday, January 25.

I was thinking that the artists who have a sufficiently vigorous style are the ones to be most excused from exact imitation, witness Michelangelo. Arrived at that point, what they lose in literal truth they certainly make up in independence and pride.

January 30.

I was saying to Pradier that I eat full dinners since I cannot take lunch, on account of my work. And that in order to digest this dinner I take plenty of exercise afterward. He told me: "When one has an old carriage, one does not make it go long distances. One puts it into the shed, and takes it out only in time of need, and for easy riding."

This observation (recalled on February 20) causes me to overcome the annoyance of having to put myself out in order to make the trip to Belgium.

Came home at two o'clock in the morning, badly fatigued; this is the first time that I forget the lesson which I have just received.

January 31.

"Neglect nothing that can *increase your stature*," is what poor Beyle[1] wrote to me.

Thursday, February 14.

I am beginning to get out of humor entirely with the Schuberts, the dreamers, the Chateaubriands (it's a long time since I started to), the Lamartines, etc. Why will all that pass away? Because it is not true at

---

[1] Stendhal had died in 1842. Delacroix, who did not appreciate him very much at the beginning, came closer to him later on. Stendhal was indeed one of the first to recognize and to appreciate the genius of Delacroix whom he called, as early as 1824, "a pupil of Tintoretto."

all. Do lovers look at the moon when they have their mistress near them? . . . That's all right when she begins to tire you. Lovers do not weep together; they do not make hymns to the infinite, and do not go in very much for descriptions. Hours of real delight pass very quickly, and one does not fill them up like that. The sentiments of the *Meditations* are false, as well as those of *Raphael,* by the same author. That vagueness, and that perpetual sadness represent no one. It is the school of sickly love. That is a pretty poor recommendation, and yet the women seem to be crazy over that humbug. It is out of modesty; they know very well what to think about the thing on which love is based. They praise the makers of odes and invocations: but they draw to them and carefully seek out men in good health who are attentive to their charms.

Today Mme Potocka came in with her sister, Princess de Beauvau. The nudity of the *Femme Impertinente*[2] and that of the *Femme qui se Peigne*[3] made a certain impression on her. "What is it that you artists, you men, find so attractive in that? What is there about that which is more interesting than any other object seen in a state of nudity, or a state of crudity, an apple, for instance?"

Tuesday, February 19.

Went to hear Berlioz. The Leonore overture[4] produced the same confused impression upon me; I conclude from that that it is bad — full, if you like, of sparkling passages, but disunited. The same thing for Berlioz: the noise he makes is distracting; it is a heroic mess.

The beautiful is found only once in a given period. So much the worse for geniuses who arrive after that moment. In periods of decadence, the only chance to survive is for very independent geniuses. They cannot bring their public back to the good taste of former times because

[2] It was under this title that Delacroix designated one of his *Bathers* (Catalogue Robaut, 1246 or 1247).
[3] (Catalogue Robaut, 1165), now in the collection of M. David-Weill.
[4] By Beethoven.

it would be understood by no one; but there are lightning flashes in their work which show what they would have been in the time of simplicity. The mediocrity in those long centuries that forget the beautiful is far duller, even, than during the periods when it seems as if everybody could benefit by that taste for the simple and the true that is in the air. At such times dull artists set themselves to exaggerate the unconscious lapses of more gifted artists, which gives them the special platitude called turgidness; or else they go in for a superannuated imitation of the beauties of the good period, which gives the last word in insipidity. They go back even further in time. They assume the naiveté of the artists who preceded the great periods. They affect a contempt for that perfection which is the natural goal of all the arts.

The arts have their childhood, their virility and their decrepitude. There are vigorous geniuses who came too soon, just as there are others who come too late; in the one group and in the other, one comes on singular outbursts. Primitive talents do not arrive at perfection any more than talents that come in times of decadence. At the time of Mozart and of Cimarosa, one might count up forty musicians who seem to be of their family, and whose works contain, in varying degrees, all the conditions of perfection. From that moment on, all the genius of men like Rossini and Beethoven cannot save them from being *mannered*. It is through a manner that one pleases a public which is blasé, and therefore eager for novelties; manner is also the thing which so quickly renders old-fashioned the works of those artists who, even if inspired, are themselves the dupes of that false novelty which they thought to introduce into art. Whereupon it often happens that the public turns back to the forgotten masterpieces and takes new delight in the imperishable charm of beauty.

I absolutely must write what I think of the Gothic; the foregoing would take its place in that quite naturally.

February 22.

What the worthy Jacob, the father of Joseph, replied to Pharaoh ought certainly to strike those who can read. "What is your age?" said the King to him. "I am a hundred and thirty years old," said the old man, "and I have not yet had a happy day in that short pilgrimage." (Voltaire, *Encyclopédie*.)

Sunday, February 24.

In the evening to the divine *Mariage Secret*[5] with Mme de Forget. That perfection is met in very few human works.

For all fine works which have remained in the memory of men

[5] *Le Mariage Secret*, comic opera by Cimarosa.

one might do over what De Piles[6] does for the painters alone. I have questioned myself about this and, to speak only of music, I have successively preferred Mozart to Rossini, to Weber, to Beethoven, always from that point of view of perfection. When I reached the *Mariage Secret,* I found — not more of perfection, but perfection itself. No one has that proportion, that breeding, that expression, that gaiety, that tenderness, and beyond all else, the general characteristic which heightens all these qualities: that incomparable elegance, elegance in the expression of tender sentiments, elegance in making fun, elegance in the pathetic which, in its moderation, is appropriate to the piece.

One would be embarrassed to say in what respect Mozart can be inferior to Cimarosa, according to the idea of him that I have here. Perhaps something personal in my organization causes me to incline in the direction to which I do incline; yet an argument such as that would be the destruction of every idea of taste and of the really beautiful; every personal sentiment would be the measure of the beautiful and of taste. I even dared to tell myself that I found in Voltaire an aspect that is regrettable, disheartening, for one who loves his admirable mind; it is the abuse of that mind itself. Yes, that arbiter of taste, that exquisite judge, gets to the point of abuse in the matter of small effects; he is elegant, but too often witty, and that word is a frightful criticism. The great authors of the preceding century are simpler, have less of the recherché.

At four o'clock I went to see Rousseau's studies,[7] which gave me the greatest pleasure. Exhibited together, these pictures will give an idea of his talent, which the public is at a remove of a hundred leagues from understanding, and has been for the twenty years during which Rousseau has been kept from exhibiting.

[6] Roger de Piles (1635–1709), painter, art-critic, author of an *Abrégé de la Vie des Peintres.*
[7] Théodore Rousseau (1812–1867), the illustrious painter of Barbizon. The exhibition here mentioned is the one which preceded the sale, on March 2, 1850, of fifty-four canvases by the master.

Tuesday, February 26.

I was summoned by Durieu[8] to pass judgment on the process of Haro, of which we are to get a demonstration at Saint Eustache.

I learned there what no one in the world will believe: that the Cathedral of Beauvais lacks a wing which was never finished; the cathedral is a mixture of Gothic and of the sixteenth century. They are discussing seriously whether the part which remains to be done shall be rebuilt in the style of the rest or in that of the thirteenth century, which is the favorite style of the antiquaries at this moment. In this way, we should give a lesson in living to those ignoramuses of the sixteenth century who had the misfortune not to be born three centuries earlier.

Friday, March 1.

Saw the exhibition of pictures by Rousseau for his sale. Charmed by a quantity of works of an extreme originality.

Sunday, March 3.

To the *Union Musicale,* symphony in F by Beethoven, full of fire and of effect; then the overture of *Iphigenia in Aulis*[9] with the whole introduction, the airs of Agamemnon, and the choir for the arrival of Klytemnestra.

The overture, a masterpiece: grace, tenderness, simplicity and strength above all. But one must recognize the fact that if indeed all those qualities seize you strongly, the monotony wearies you a little. For a nineteenth century listener, after Mozart and Rossini, this sounds a bit like plain-song. The bass viols and their repeating of the theme pursue you like the trumpets in Berlioz.

Immediately afterward came the overture of the *Magic Flute;* this is in truth a masterpiece. I was convinced of this at once on hearing the music by Gluck's successors. Here, then, is where Mozart found

[8] Eugène Durieu (1800–1874) was at the time Directeur des Cultes; he had instituted a commission of arts and religious buildings and created the service of architects of the Diocese for the preservation of religious monuments.

[9] Opera by Gluck.

the art. And here is the step which it caused him to take. He is really the creator — I will not say of modern art, for now already, no more of it is being produced — but of the art carried to its summit, beyond which perfection does not exist.

I said to Princess Czartoriska, to whose house I went after leaving the concert: "We know Mozart by heart and everything that resembles him. Everything done in imitation of such music and in its style is inferior to it; we are wearied by it or sated with it. What can we do to be moved or, above all, to be surprised anew? Content ourselves with the bold, but not always happy attempts of the geniuses, sometimes very eminent ones, that our century produces. And what will these later men do when, as it seems, they consult their models only that they may know what to avoid? It is impossible that they should not fall into mere experiment."

Saturday, March 9.

I am overburdened with all the jobs that are piled up on me.

Several days — until Monday, the eleventh — passed without my getting anything done.

Monday, March 11.

Went back to work on the last picture of *Flowers*.[10]

In the evening went to see Mme Jaubert. Saw portraits and Persian drawings which caused me to repeat what Voltaire says somewhere, more or less like this: there are vast countries where taste has never penetrated; they are those countries of the Orient in which there is no society, where women are degraded, etc. All the arts are stationary there.

In these drawings there is neither perspective nor any feeling for what is really painting, that is, a certain illusion of projection. The figures are motionless, the poses awkward, etc.

One thing struck me above all — the character of architecture in

[10] The last of a series of four large pictures of flowers, now disappeared (Catalogue Robaut, 1070).

Persia. Although in the Arab style, everything is of the special character of the country. The form of the cupolas and the ogives, the details of the capitals, the ornaments, everything is original. On the contrary, one can cross Europe today, and from Cadiz to Petersburg, everything that is done in architecture has the look of coming out of the same studio. Our architects have just one procedure, and that is always to return to the original purity of *Greek art*. I don't speak of the craziest of them who do the same thing for the Gothic; those purists become aware every thirty years, that their immediate predecessors made a mistake in their appreciation of that exquisite imitation of the antique. Thus, in their day, Percier and Fontaine thought they had established it forever. This style, of which we see the remains in certain clocks produced forty years ago, appears today what it really is, which is to say, dry and mean, without a single one of the qualities of the antique.

Our moderns have found the receipt for those qualities in the monuments of Athens. They think themselves the first to have looked at them. As a result, the Parthenon is made responsible for all their follies. When I was at Bordeaux, I found the Parthenon everywhere: barracks, churches, fountains, everything derived from it. The sculpture of Phidias is honored by the painters in the same way. Don't even speak to them of the Roman antique or of the Greek before or after Phidias.

Among the drawings made by M. Laurens in Persia I saw a complete entablature, capitals, frieze, cornice, etc, entirely within the Greek proportions, but with ornaments which completely renew it, and which are a matter of invention.

To be remembered from the Persian drawings: those immense gates to buildings which are smaller than they; they look like a big operatic stage set erected in front of the building. I have never seen any other example of this anywhere.

March 16.

Mme Cavé came in and read me a few chapters of her book on drawing.[11] It is charming in its inventiveness and simplicity. It was a pleasure for me to see her and talk with her again.

Friday, March 22.

Voltaire exclaims in a letter about the *Père de Famille* by Diderot that everything disappears, everything degenerates; he compares his century with that of Louis XIV. He is right. The different types of art are confused one with another; miniature and genre painting take the place of clearcut styles, they become the substitute for grand effects and for simplicity. I add: Voltaire is already complaining about bad taste, and thus he is, one may say, still connected with the Great Century; in more than one respect he is worthy to belong to it. Meanwhile the taste for simplicity, which is no other thing than beauty, has disappeared. How do the modern philosophers, whose systems abound in all those beautiful things about the gradual development of humanity, reconcile this decadence of the works of the mind with the progress of political institutions? Without examining the question of whether the latter type of progress has as real a value as we suppose, it is incontestable that human dignity has been raised to a higher point, at least in written law; but is this the first time that men have perceived that they were not mere brutes and have therefore not allowed themselves to be governed? This so-called modern progress in the political world is therefore no more than an evolution, an accident of this particular moment. Tomorrow we may embrace despotism with all the fury that we have employed to render ourselves independent of every restraint.

What I would say here is that, contrary to those baroque ideas of continuing progress which Saint-Simon and others have brought into fashion, humanity goes on haphazard, let them say what they will. At the same time that perfection exists in one place, there is barbarism in another.

[11] *Le Dessin sans Maître* appeared in 1850. Delacroix devoted an article to it in the *Revue des Deux Mondes*. He had previously had a minor passion for Mme Cavé, who was then Mme Boulanger.

Champrosay, Saturday April 27.

I am sleeping an outrageous amount in the evening, and even during the day. The drawback to the country, for the man who fears much reading, is the boredom and a certain sadness inspired by the spectacle of nature.

I do not feel all that when I work; but this time I have resolved to do absolutely nothing, so as to get a rest from the somewhat abstract work of composing my ceiling.

Sunday, April 28.

In the morning, took a big walk in the forest. Entered by the lane of the marquis, saw again the lovelorn inscriptions on the wall of his park. Each year the rain and other effects of the weather carry off something of those words: by now they are almost illegible. I can't prevent myself, everytime I pass by — and I often do it on purpose — from being moved by the regrets and by the tenderness of that poor lover! He seems to be deeply convinced as to the eternity of his feeling for his Celestine. God knows what has become of her — and of his love? But who has not known that youthful exaltation, and the time when one has not a moment of repose, and when one takes delight in one's torments?

Tuesday, April 30.

Went out about nine o'clock. To the lane of the marquis and went as far as the hermitage. Opposite the hermitage, a great pile of wood that had been cut; every year I have this poignant regret at seeing a part of the forest cut down, and it is always the finest part, which is to say the richest and most ancient. There was a little covered path there which was charming.

Went to the right as far as the oak, called le Prieur. I saw there, along the whole path, a procession of ants which I defy the naturalists to explain to me. The whole tribe seemed to be defiling in order, as if to emigrate; a small number of those industrious creatures went upstream, in the opposite direction. Where were they going? We are all enclosed, pell-mell — animals, men, plants — in that immense box called the Universe.

We have the pretension to read in the stars, to conjecture as to the future and to the past, which are beyond the sight of our eyes, and we cannot comprehend a word of that which is right under our eyes. All these beings are forever separate, and indecipherable for one another.

Wednesday May 1.

On man's gifts of reflection and imagination. Fatal gifts.

It is evident that nature cares very little whether man has a mind or not. The real man is the savage; he is in accord with nature as she is. As soon as man sharpens his intelligence, increases his ideas and the way of expressing them, and acquires needs, nature runs counter to him in everything. He has to do violence to her continually. She, on her side, is not slow to respond. If for a moment he lets up in the work he has imposed upon himself, she resumes her rights, she invades, she undermines, she destroys or disfigures his work; it seems as if she were impatient at having to tolerate the masterpieces of man's imagination and of his hand. For the march of the seasons, for the course of the stars, of rivers and of winds, what importance is there in the Parthenon, St. Peter's in Rome, and so many other miracles of art? An earthquake, or the lava of a volcano will punish them: the birds will nest in their ruins; the wild beasts will drag out the bones of their founders from their half-open tombs. But man himself, when he gives way to the savage instinct which is the very basis of his nature, does he not conspire with the elements to destroy the works of beauty? Does not barbarism, like the Fury who watches Sisyphus rolling his stone to the top of the mountain, return almost periodically to overthrow and confound, to bring forth night after a too brilliant day? And that indefinable thing which has given to man an intelligence higher than that of the beasts, does it not seem to take pleasure in punishing him for that very intelligence?

A fatal gift, did I say? Beyond a doubt; amidst this universal conspiracy against the fruits of invention, of genius, and of the spirit which composes, does man have at least the consolation of wondering greatly at himself for his constancy, or of a rich and continued enjoyment of the various fruits which have issued from him? The contrary is most often the case. Not only must the man who is greatest through talent, through audacity, through constancy, be also the most persecuted, as he usually is, but he is himself fatigued and tormented by his burden of talent and imagination. He is as ingenious in tormenting himself as in enlightening others. Almost all the great men have had a life more thwarted, more miserable than that of other men.

Of what use then is that mind and all that effort? Does living according to nature mean that one must live in filth, swim across rivers for lack of bridges and of boats, live on acorns in the forests, or hunt deer and buffalo with bow and arrow, in order to preserve a wretched life a hundred times more useless than that of the oaks, which at least serve to feed and harbor some animals? Is Rousseau of this mind, when he proscribes the arts and the sciences, under pretext of their abuse? Is everything then a trap, a condition of misfortune, or a sign of corruption in what comes from the intelligence of men? Why does he not reproach the savage for ornamenting and bedecking his rude bow as best he can, for decorating with the feathers of birds the apron with which he hides his wretched nudity? And why should he hide it from the sun and from his fellow men? Is that not again a sentiment too elevated for that brute, for that machine made for living, for digesting, and for sleeping?

Tuesday, May 7.

Why not make a little collection of detached ideas which come to me from time to time completely molded and to which it would thus be difficult to attach others? Is it absolutely demanded that one produce a book, keeping within all the rules? Montaigne writes by fits and starts. Those are the most interesting works. After the effort needed by the author to follow the thread of his idea, to keep that idea warm, and to develop it in every part, one must realize that there is also the work of the reader who, having opened the book for his recreation, finds himself insensibly caught, almost as a matter of honor, by the task of deciphering, comprehending, and of retaining that which he would be only too happy to forget, so that at the end of his enterprise, he may profitably have followed all the roads which it has pleased the author to make him travel.

Thursday, May 9.

Feeling that I should not accomplish anything, I went to the forest about nine o'clock, going directly to the oak called *le Prieur*. Although the morning was magnificent, nothing could distract me from my black humor. I made a little sketch of the oak; the coolness which began to arise drove me away.

Without being cheered up, I was particularly struck by that always charming music of the birds of the spring: the maybirds, the nightingales, the blackbirds that are so melancholy, and the cuckoo whose cry I love in the wildest way, seemed to be doing their very utmost to please me. In a month at most, all those throats will be silent. Love makes them swell with its feeling; a little more, and it would make them speak. The strangeness of nature, always the same, forever inexplicable !

Saturday, May 11.

Today, like a child beginning its vacation, I took the greatest delight in my sudden resolution to stay here longer. How weak man is and easily changed in his emotions and his resolves! Last night I was mortally sad. Coming home in the evening, my whole thought was of catastrophes; this morning the sight of the fields and the sun, and the idea of avoiding for some time yet that frightful hubbub of Paris were heavenly for me. Whether happy or unhappy, I must nearly always go to extremes!

May 14.

Called on Mme Quantinet.

"Independence has isolation as its consequence." She cites to me that extract from *Adolphe* by Benjamin Constant. Alas, the alternative of being bored and harassed all one's life, as is the man caught in the bonds of a family, for example, or else of being abandoned by everything and everybody, because one would not submit to any constraint, that alternative, I say, is inevitable. There are men who have led the hardest of lives doing the imperious bidding of a shrewish woman, or enduring the caprices of a coquette with whom they had bound up their fate, and who at the end of their days cannot even console themselves that their eyes will be closed or their thin soup will be given them by that creature who could at least serve to soften their last moments. They leave you or die just at the time when they could render you the service of preventing your being alone. Children, if you have had any, after having caused you all the cares of their infancy or of their foolish youth, have abandoned you long since. You therefore necessarily fall into that frightful isolation in which your remainder of life and suffering burns itself out.

Friday, May 17.

Worked this morning at *La Femme qui se Peigne*.[12] Took a long walk in the forest.

I saw there the fight between a fly of a special kind and of a spider. I saw the two of them coming, the fly on its back and giving him furious blows; after a short resistance the spider expired under these attacks; the fly, after having sucked it, undertook the labor of dragging it off somewhere, doing so with a vivacity and a fury that were incredible. The fly dragged it backward across grasses and other obstacles. I looked on with a certain emotion at this Homeric little duel. I was the Jupiter contemplating the fight of this Achilles and this Hector. It may be noted that there was distributive justice in the victory of the fly over the spider; it was the contrary of what has been observed for so long a time. That fly was black, very long, and with red marks on the body.

[12] Catalogue Robaut, 1165.

Saturday, May 18.

In the morning worked at the *La Femme qui se Peigne,* which I am probably spoiling, then on the *Michelangelo.*[13]

About one o'clock, to the forest with my good Jenny.[14] I had an infinite pleasure in her expansive enjoyment of that charming bit of nature, so green and so fresh. I made her rest for a long time and she got back without any trouble. We went as far as Antin oak. While we were crossing the enclosure of Lamouroux, she said to me in a pained voice: "Look! Am I never going to see you in any more than a minor position, which is so little worthy of you? Shall I never see you owning a piece of land like this one, that you can live in and beautify?" She is right. In this respect I resemble Diderot who thought himself predestined to live in hovels, and who thought he was soon to die when he was installed in a fine apartment with splendid furniture, which he owed to the bounty of Catherine. But anyhow, I like moderate circumstances; I have a horror of luxury and display; I like old houses, old-fashioned furniture; things that are quite new don't appeal to me at all. What I want is that the place where I live and the things that I use talk to me of what they have seen, of what they have been, of what has happened to them. Am I more small-souled in that respect than my neighbor Minoret, who has just torn down part of the building that he had in order to construct a horrible chalet which is going to offend my eyes as long as I live here? When this Minoret came, as the successor of General Ledru, he hastened to tear down the latter's modest and ancient house; he prefers that perfectly new stone which he gets out of the quarry. Old lady d'Esnont has done the same thing. To

[13] Catalogue Robaut, 1184.

[14] Jenny Le Guillou (1801–1869). The friend and housekeeper of Delacroix; born at Brest in modest circumstances, she entered the service of Delacroix about 1835 and never left it; she cared for him till his last day with the greatest devotion. Delacroix had a great esteem and a real affection for her. Some people have reproached Jenny with having kept the relatives and friends of the master away from him in his last years; it is claimed she made it impossible to approach him.

tell the truth, the house was falling about her head. For me that amounts to two modern buildings that I must tolerate, and they are horrible. In Champrosay, moreover, there has been a perfect rivalry in putting up bad buildings, for some time. Gilbert had begun with his magnificent grill. The people who succeeded the Marquis de la Feuillade have had the house all plastered over, and had the awful idea of adding ornaments which render it ridiculous and take away all character and all proportion.

Monday, May 20.

I accompanied the Villots and Mme Barbier to the railroad station. I told Mme Barbier that the ignoble pantalettes of the women were an attack on the rights of men.

Saturday, June 8.

While considering my composition for the ceiling,[15] which pleases me only since yesterday, thanks to the changes that I made with pastel in the sky, I was saying to myself that a good picture was exactly like a good dish, containing the same ingredients as a bad one: it is all a question of the artist who produces it. How many magnificent compositions would be nothing without the grain of salt of the great cook! That power of the *indefinable thing* is astonishing in Rubens; what his temperament, his *vis poetica,* adds to a composition, without seeming to change it, is prodigious. It is no other than the turn of the style; the way he does it is everything, the matter he deals with is comparatively unimportant.

The new is very ancient, one may even say that it is always the most ancient thing there is.

Friday, June 14.

An architect who really fulfills all the conditions of his art seems to me a phoenix far more rare than a great painter, a great poet or a great

[15] The ceiling of the Galerie d'Apollon in the Louvre.

musician. It is absolutely evident to me that the reason for this resides in that absolutely necessary accord between great good sense and great inspiration. The details of utility which form the point of departure for the architect, details which are of the essence of things, take precedence over all the ornaments: and yet he is not an artist unless he lends fitting ornaments to the *usefulness* which is his theme. I say *fitting;* for, even after having established the exact relationship of his plan with every aspect of customary usage, he cannot embellish this plan save in a certain manner: he is not free to be lavish or sparing with ornaments; they are compelled to be as appropriate to the plan as the latter has been to customary usage. The sacrifices which the painter and the poet make to grace, to charm, and to the effect on the imagination, excuse certain things which exact reason would condemn as false. The only license which the architect permits himself may perhaps be compared with that which the great writer indulges in when, to a certain extent, he creates his own language. When he uses terms which are of the current speech of everybody, the special turn he gives them makes of them new terms; in the same way, by the employment, at once calculated and inspired, of ornaments which are within the domain of all in his profession, the architect gives to them a surprising novelty and reaches that form of the beautiful which it is given to his art to attain. An architect of genius will copy a monument and will be able, by variants, to render it original; he will render it fitting for its place, he will observe in distances and proportions such order that he will make it completely new. The common run of architects can copy only in a literal way, and so, to the humiliating confession of their impotence which they seem to make, they add lack of success even in imitating; for the monument they build, an imitation to the last detail, can never be in exactly the same conditions as the one which they imitate. Not only are they unable to invent a beautiful thing, but they spoil the fine original creation which, in their hands, becomes a flat and insignificant thing, as we are so surprised to discover.

Those whose procedure is not to imitate *en bloc* and with exactitude, work haphazardly, so to speak; the rules teach them that they have to ornament certain parts, and they ornament those parts, whatever the character of the monument and whatever its surroundings.

(Add to the preceding what I say as to the relationship between the proportions of the imitative monuments and those of the original works, for example the Parthenon or the Maison Carrée with the Madeleine, also the triumphal arch of the Place du Carrousel.)

Brussels, Saturday, July 6.

Set out for Brussels[16] with Jenny at eight o'clock and arrived there at quarter past five. That really tempts one to travel.

Badly installed at an inn, which puts me out of humor. In the evening took a walk in the park, which seems to me extremely dull. In any number of things I noticed the lack of taste in this country, and I dare say that when one compares all the other countries with France, one gets the same feeling. In the park, among other ornaments, there are figures issuing from the pedestal, and surrounding the basin. They are planted in the earth at the foot of each of the great trees which surround the basin: it was in the spaces between that they should have been placed! The uneven manner in which the trees grow renders them clumsy and out of place. They look as if placed there by chance. One sees statues there with pedestals *one foot* high. One can converse with these heroes and these demi-gods, and the statues are ordinarily more than life size; they are disproportioned, the enlargement in this case, having been calculated only for the distance at which, it was thought, the pedestal would place the figure.

[16] Delacroix was going to Belgium for the second time. His first trip dates from September 1838, just before his great works at the Chamber. On this trip he was not alone, but had as his companion the charming Elisa Boulanger, later on Mme Cavé, who had a passing caprice for the master, induced him to go with her, and suddenly deserted him at the Hague. The voyage of 1850 was undertaken because of ill health, his destination being Ems, where he was to take a cure.

Brussels, Sunday July 7.

In the morning went to Sainte Gudule.

Magnificent stained glass. I set down in my notebook the reflections which it suggested to me:

The part of the choir which faces you is the chapel of the Virgin.[17] It is the style of Rubens chastened.[18] The execution is very fine. An attempt has been made to use color as in pictures, but this attempt, although it is as able as possible, is an argument in favor of the stained glass of the earlier century. A system, and a convention for simplifying are absolutely necessary.

At the rear of the choir, there are windows from the designs by Navez, which partake of the defects of this mongrel style. In the last-named works, the product of bad artists in a bad period, what happens is that, when they try to avoid what they consider unpleasant effects by placing the leads in the manner of the ancient artist, they place them in such a manner as to give ideas quite the contrary of those that they want to express, or else their effects are directly ridiculous. The draperies and certain parts which they regard as less important look as if purposely surrounded with a black edging, because the heads, for example, silhouetting against the sky without leads to surround them, pretend to approach the effect of pictures. The effect is completely lame and miscarried. So also they seek to exaggerate the color of flesh. Whence comes the taste of certain periods and whence, again, that foolishness of certain others which renders them incapable even of reproducing what was well done in the past?

While I was looking at the stained glass of the chapel of the Virgin, I heard, among the works of music that were being very well played, the favorite psalm of Chopin, *Judah the Conqueror;* voices of choir boys, organ accompaniment, etc. For a moment I was entranced. This is an argument to be used against excessive rejuvenation of the Gregorian chant, or rather against the anathema so stupidly uttered against the efforts of modern musicians to speak to the imagination in church.

[17] The chapel of Notre Dame de Délivrance, now called Notre Dame de Lourdes. The windows were executed in 1556 at Antwerp, after cartoons by Theodore van Thulden, of the school of Rubens.
[18] "Rubens chastened," it was with these words that Gros spoke in 1822 of Delacroix's *Dante and Vergil.*

Antwerp, Monday July 8.

Left for Antwerp at eight o'clock.

The museum very badly arranged. The old one made a far better effect. Distributing the Rubens to different places causes them to lose greatly. And yet I had never before found in them, to such a degree, that superiority which crushes everything about them. The *Saint Francis* which I did not used to esteem so highly, was my favorite this time, and I also relished very greatly the *Christ on the Knees of the Father Eternal,* which must be of the same period. I read in the catalogue that the *Saint Francis* was painted when Rubens was forty or forty-two years old.

The Scourging of Christ from the church of Saint Paul is a masterpiece of genius, if ever there was one. It has a certain drawback: the big executioner to the left. It is really an incredible degree of the sublime that is needed to keep that ridiculous figure from spoiling everything. To the left, on the contrary, and scarcely visible, there is a Negro or Mulatto, one of the executioners, who is worthy of the rest of the picture. That bloodstreaked back, that head which tells so well of the fever of pain, that arm which one sees, all that is inexpressible in its beauty.

Brussels, Tuesday July 9.

I was to have departed: I have given myself one more day. I have had a long session at the Museum, where I shivered the whole time, in spite of the season.

The *Calvary* and the *Saint Lievin* are the climax of the maestria of Rubens.

The *Adoration of the Magi,* which I find superior to the one in Antwerp, has a certain dryness when one compares it with those two others. One sees in it no *sacrifices* whatsoever; what raises those two favorites of mine to such a point is, on the contrary, the art of appropriate negligences. The feet and the hand of Christ barely indicated. To these must be added an *Avenging Christ.* The fury of the brush and its verve cannot go further. The *Assumption* a little bit dry; the *Glory* seems to me to miscarry; I cannot believe that a great part of it is not accidental. There is a beautiful *Virgin Crowned,* to the right on entering. Vigor of effect; by no means the same freedom as in the fine ones. The clouds are carried to the point of blackness. That devil of a man denies himself nothing. His decision to make the flesh brilliant at all costs forces him to exaggerate in his vigor.

Still on Tuesday, went to the gallery of the Duke of Arenberg, about two o'clock. Fine Rembrandt, *Tobias Healing his Father.*

Sketch by Rubens, very coarsely drawn with the brush; color has been applied to some of the figures; allegory in the style of the one in Van Thulden's book.

Even on a ground rubbed in as a kind of grisaille, he frequently indicates the light passages with white. He generally begins his color with a local halftone, using a very light impasto. It is on that, according to my idea, that he places the lights and the dark passages. I noticed that localizing very clearly when studying the *Calvary.* The flesh tones of the two thieves are very different, without apparent effort. It is evident that he models or turns the figure in this local tone of light and shade, before applying the vigorous notes. I think that his lightly treated pictures like this one, and the *Saint Benedict* which resembles it, must have been done in this way. In his drier manner, each part has been painted in more isolated fashion. I must recall the hands of Saint Veronica: her linen all gray; the hands of the Virgin beside her, sublime in their negligence. The two thieves sublime from every point of view. The pallor and the terrified look of the old rascal in the foreground.

In the *Saint Francis* concealing the world with his robe, extraordinary simplicity of execution. The gray of the rub-in appears everywhere. A very light local tone for the flesh and a few touches of slightly heavier impasto for the light passages.

To be remembered frequently: the study of the *Woman in Bed* that I began about a month ago; the modeling was already established in the local color, without accents of shadow or of light. I hit on that a long time ago in a recumbent study, *Caroline*. Instinct guided me at that early time.

Ems, Saturday July 13.

Took my first glass of water.

Overture of the *Magic Flute* in the open air, executed by a little orchestra which is kept up to amuse the drinkers of the waters.

In the afternoon a short walk to the heights, crossing the bridge, and seeing the cemetery and the church. All that is charming, and yet I am living in the midst of insipidity. Isn't all that made to cause a certain sentiment of pleasure, or am I beginning to be less susceptible to such feelings? I don't know how I am to fill out my time. I have no engravings with me, and have no books except the *Homme de Cour*[19] and the *Extracts from Voltaire*. . . . Perhaps I shall be able to rent some.

Sunday, 14.

Today, Sunday, I may say that I am myself again: and so it's the first day that I find interest in all the things which surround me. This place is really charming. I went this afternoon, and in a good mood, to take a walk on the other side of the water. There, seated on a bench, I started to jot down in my notebook some reflections similar to those that I am tracing here. I told myself and I cannot repeat it to myself often enough for my repose and for my happiness (one and the other are but a single thing) that I cannot and must not live in any other way than through the mind; the food that it demands is more necessary to my life than that which my body calls for.

Why did I live so much, that famous day? (I am writing this two days afterward.) It was because I had a great many ideas which, at this moment, are a hundred leagues away. The secret of not having troubles, for me at least, is to have ideas. Therefore no effort is too

[19] *L'Homme de Cour*, by Gracian.

great if it gives me the means of bringing them into existence. Good books have that effect, and above all certain ones among those books. The first thing to have is health, to be sure; but even in a sickly condition, such books as those can reopen sources through which imagination can issue forth generously.

Took a delightful walk. To live in material fashion is not to live; in the three or four days since I came here, occupied as I have been with lodgings, with getting something for dinner, with running after the doctor, with obtaining a glass of water at the spring, I am a regular machine; I do not live, I am not in possession of my mind; the place is really beautiful and it means nothing to me. I take walks which would be delightful for a mind, and which are nothing but distance for a body and for legs which go on haphazard. What a shame for my *immortal soul!* Its whole ability is taken up with my quarrels with my host over getting a bed that I can sleep in, or it is taken up with my indignation against the Germans, who make the mistake of not being Frenchmen, which is to say that they understand nothing of the jargon of a man dropping from the clouds who, himself, understands nothing of their jargon. Most human beings live only such a life as that; but as they do not know the life of the mind, they do not feel themselves deprived of anything in the various kinds of limbo where they vegetate, nearer to the animal than to man.

July 15.

". . . How many pieces are there that are spoken of as Shakespeare's and that belong to him exclusively; and, at a period so distant when so many works of that time are lost, how can one distinguish that which is really of his composition from that which is not? The actors cut things off, transposed things, and even altered the text to please the spectators or for their own convenience: who knows how much rubbish they have cut off or added?" [20]

When one thinks that Voltaire could not get the text of his pieces played in the theater! The friends whom he charged with presenting them to the actors had already altered them, and those gentlemen of

[20] Extract from Captain T. Medwin's *Journal of the Conversations of Lord Byron*, 1824, of which Delacroix found a French translation in the reading room of Ems. He thus renews the deep interest in Byron which he had in his youth.

the theater did not fail to change, to transpose, etc. He complains of this all the time.

Thursday, July 18.

"In painting and especially in portraiture," says Mme Cavé in her treatise, "it is mind that is speaking to mind and not science speaking to science." This observation, a deeper one perhaps than she herself thought, is the arraignment of pedantry in execution. I have told myself a hundred times that painting, that is to say the material thing called painting, was no more than the pretext, than the bridge between the mind of the painter and that of the spectator. Cold exactitude is not art; ingenious artifice, when it *pleases* or when it *expresses,* is art itself. The so-called conscientiousness of the majority of painters is only perfection applied to the *art of boring.* People like that, if they could do it, would work with the same minute attention on the back of their canvas. It would be interesting to write a treatise on all the falsehoods which can add up to truth.

July 21.

During the day, I set seriously to work at the article on Mme Cavé's book, *Le Dessin sans Maître.*

I have made the resolve, a successful one, to drink the water before dinner. After the last glass, about five o'clock, I returned to those charming meadows along the Lahn, crossing the bridge and turning to the left. My head was full of ideas bred in me by the work of the day. Everything seemed easy to me. I think I should have done the article at one breath if I had had the strength to write for the time necessary.

I am writing this the next day, and that fine fire has cooled off. One ought to be able, like Lord Byron, to get back one's inspiration on command. Perhaps I am wrong to envy him for this, since, in painting, I have the same faculty; but whether because literature is not my element or whether I have not yet made it that,[21] when I look at this paper filled with little black spots, my mind does not catch fire as quickly as it does at the sight of my picture or just that of my palette. My palette, newly set and brilliant with the contrast of the colors, suffices to inflame my enthusiasm. However, I am persuaded that if I wrote oftener, I should reach the point of enjoying the same ability when picking up my pen. A little insistence is necessary, and once the machine gets going, I experience the same facility in writing as in painting and, what is singular, I have less need to go over what I have done. If it were only a question of sewing thoughts onto other thoughts, I should be quicker about finding myself armed and taking the right position in the field of battle; but the necessity of observing a continuity, of respecting a plan, of keeping oneself from getting mixed up in the midst of one's phrases, that is what makes the great difficulty, and what puts obstacles in the flow of the mind. You see your picture at a single glance; in your manuscript, you do not even see the whole page, which is to say that you cannot embrace it as a whole with your mind. It demands a singular amount of strength for you to be able to embrace the ensemble of the work and, at the same time, carry it on with the necessary abundance or sobriety, by means of the developments which succeed each other only one by one. Lord Byron says that when he writes, he does not know what is coming afterward and he does not bother much about it. In general, his poetry belongs to the style which I should call admirative; it is nearer to the ode than to narrative, he can therefore abandon himself to his caprice.

The task of the historian seems to me more difficult; he needs sustained attention to a thousand objects at once and, throughout his citations, his precise enumerations, and the facts which occupy only a

---

[21] Delacroix always wanted to express his ideas with his pen. In his youth he had passionately wished to be a poet, and he had hesitated as to which form—literature or painting—was best suited to the expression of his temperament. Late in life, we see that this preoccupation still haunts him.

relative position, he has got to preserve that warmth which animates the recital and makes it more than an extract from a gazette.

Experience is indispensable for learning all that one can do with one's instrument, but above all to avoid that which should not be attempted. The immature man throws himself into senseless attempts; by trying to make art yield more than it should and can yield, he does not even reach a certain sense of superiority within the limits of the possible. One must not forget that language (and I apply this to language in all the arts) is imperfect. The great writer ekes out this imperfection by the particular turn that he gives to his words. Experience alone can give, even to the greatest talent, that confidence in having done all that could be done. It is only the fools and the impotent who torment themselves to reach the impossible.

And yet one must be very daring! Without daring, and an extreme daring, there are no beauties. Jenny was saying to me when I was reading her that passage from Lord Byron where he praises gin as his Hippocrene, that this was because of the daring he drew from it. I think the observation is true, humiliating as it is for a great number of fine minds who have found in the bottle that *adjuventum* of talent which caused them to reach the top of the rocky crest of art. And so one must be outside oneself, *amens,* in order to be all that one can be! Happy is the man who, like Voltaire and other great ones, can find himself in that inspired state, even though he drink water and keep to a normal diet!

August 1.

". . . To bring a mediocre man to success! For a woman, as for kings, that is to give oneself the pleasure which so carries away the great actors and which consists of playing a bad piece a hundred times. It is the intoxication of egoism. In a word, it might be called the saturnalia of power. Power proves its strength to itself only by the strange abuse of crowning some absurdity with the palm of success, of insulting genius, the only strength that absolute power cannot attack. Caligula's giving the rank of commander to his horse, that imperial farce, has

been played and will always be played a great number of times."
(Balzac, *La Dernière Incarnation de Vautrin*).[22]

"... Woman is an inferior being, she obeys her organs too much."
(Idem.)

"... M. de Grandville, having reached the age of fifty-three years
without ever having been able to inspire love, admired tender natures,
like all men who have not been loved. Perhaps this despair, the lot of
many men to whom women do not grant their esteem or their friendship, was the secret bond of intimacy among MM. de Bauvau, de
Grandville and de Serizy, etc. . . ." (Idem.)

Cologne, Monday August 5.

Went to see the church of Saint Peter. After having asked directions in
vain, was carried past the difficulty by a colleague, a house-painter who,
brush in hand and so to speak taking off his hat at the name of Rubens
— whom everybody knows here, even the children and the women
who sell fruit — directed me as best he could. A rather mean church,
preceded by a cloister filled with little stations of the cross, a Calvary,
etc. People here are extremely devout. By paying my fifteen Silber-
groschen or one florin or two francs, I saw the famous *Saint Peter,*[23]
which has, on the back of it, an infamous copy. The Saint is magnificent; the other figures, which seem to me to have been done merely to
accompany him, and probably composed and invented as an after-
thought, are of the weakest, but they still have verve. In a word, I got
enough with one visit. And yet I still remember with admiration the
legs, the torso, and the head; it is of the finest quality, but the composition does not grip you.

Worn out, as I went home through the streets, but dined in good
humor.

[22] These precious extracts from Balzac throw a light on the psychology
of Delacroix.

[23] The *Crucifixion of Saint Peter* was executed by Rubens between 1636
and 1640 for the family of Jabach, the great financier, so many of whose
pictures are in the Louvre.

Tuesday, August 6. At Cologne.

Took the guide to go and see the cathedral. That unhappy building, which will never be finished,[24] is consequently encumbered for eternity with the wooden sheds of the workmen. Saint Ouen at Rouen, to which they thought they must add the spires which it lacked, could get along very well without them; but Cologne is in a curiously sketchy condition; the nave is not even covered. That is what they ought to apply themselves to finishing; the doorway would entail gigantic work, and the few poor devils whom one sees or whom one hears in those sheds, pecking away at pieces of stone, will not get a tenth of the work done in three centuries, even supposing that they get their money.

What is done is magnificent. One feels an impression of grandeur which recalled to me the cathedral of Seville. The choir and the transept have been finished since a long time. They have gone in for a foolish notion of gilding the capitals of the choir and painting them with red. The small pendentives are occupied by figures of angels in a so-called Raphaelesque style, producing an effect of complete meanness.

The more I witness of the efforts that are made to restore Gothic churches, and especially to paint them, the more set I become in the taste which makes me consider them most beautiful when they are least painted. It is no use proving to me that they were painted, for I know they were, since traces of it still exist, but I persist in thinking that we must still leave them in the condition that time has given to them; their bareness ornaments them sufficiently; the architecture has its full effect; whereas the efforts made by us — different men of a different time — to illuminate these beautiful monuments, cover them over with bad logic, make everything grimace, and render everything false and odious. The stained glass windows which the King of Bavaria has given to Cologne are again an unhappy example of our modern schools; the whole thing is full of the talent of men of the type of Ingres and Flandrin. The more such stuff tries to resemble the Gothic the more it turns to trumpery, to the trivial neo-christian painting of

[24] The cathedral was finished only in 1880.

the modern converts. The folly and the misfortune of it — when that fury which might expend itself harmlessly in our little exhibitions is used for the degradation of beautiful works like these churches! The one at Cologne is filled with curious monuments: of archbishops, and of warriors; there are altar screens, paintings or sculptures representing the Passion, etc.

On leaving, I saw the church of the Jesuits. There you have the exact opposite of what we are doing today: instead of amusing themselves with imitating the monuments of another period, they did what they could, mingling Gothic, Renaissance, and all the other styles in fact; and in the whole thing, artists who really were artists were able to bring about charming ensembles. In these churches one is dazzled with the profusion of riches, of marbles, statues and tombs covering the walls and spreading out beneath one's feet. Wooden stalls run the whole length of the wall; the organ ornamented, etc.

On my way home, saw the City Hall, a charming Renaissance building; opposite it, a house [25] probably of the time of Henri IV: very imposing rustic style.

This city is of the most interesting, animated, gay and, save for the Prussian uniforms which have a disagreeable effect on me, made for the imagination.

On our way to the railroad station, saw the exterior of the towers again, etc.

Left at ten o'clock; the heat extreme, and the route wearisome. The nuisance of the customs house after Pepinster and before Verviers or at Verviers itself.

Scribbled in my little notebook as we rode along.

Arrived at Malines at about six o'clock. Good little hotel of Saint Jacques and good supper which set me up. The great men who write their memoirs do not speak sufficiently of the influence of a good supper on the state of their mind. I am very close to the ground on that side,

[25] The *Spanische Bau,* a building of Flemish style, erected between 1611 and 1617.

provided that indigestion does not come to counterbalance the favorable effect of Ceres and of Bacchus. Even so, it would be true that the whole time you are at table and even for a certain while afterward, the brain sees things under a different aspect. This question of the fire born of the bottle is a great one, humiliating for certain men who think themselves far more than men, or who would like to be so. Wine carries you along much further along than you would have gone without it — a state of affairs to be accepted not only because the thing is that way, but also because it is a very agreeable way.

Antwerp. Saturday, August 10.

Went to the Museum. Made a sketch after Cranach. Admired the *Souls in Purgatory*, it is in the finest manner of Rubens. I could not tear myself away from the picture of the *Trinity*, from the *Saint Francis*, from the *Holy Family*, etc. The young man who is copying the large *Christ on the Cross* lent me his step-ladder, and I saw the picture in a different light. It is of the finest period; the halftone gives a frankly round modeling as a preparation, and then bold touches of light and dark are laid on with very thick impasto, especially in the light. How is it that I never noticed before now to what extent Rubens proceeds by means of the halftone, especially in his very fine works? His sketches ought to have put me on the track. The reverse of what we are told about Titian, he sketches in the tone of the figures which seem dark against the light tone. That also explains how it is that when he then does the background, having an extreme need to produce effect, he sets himself to render the flesh tones excessively brilliant by darkening the background. The head of the Christ, that of the soldier descending the ladder, the legs of the Christ and those of the other crucified man strongly colored in the preparatory work, with the lights laid on in small areas only. The Magdalen is remarkable for the following quality, that one sees clearly how the eyes, the lashes, the eyebrows, and the corners of the mouth are laid on over the underpainting, while it was still wet I think, contrary to the practice of Paul Veronese.

Le Coup de Lance. The soldier who is piercing the flank, darker in tonality than the thief who is behind him, by which means the figure is perfectly detached. The thief, of a golden tone, and his drapery of the same value, mingling it with the sky, which is of a warm gray. The neck of the horse is of a lighter color; there is a very vivid shine on the armor of the soldier with the lance, under his arm; the sky is very blue under the arm of the other man.

On the legs of the Christ there is a gradation of the light from the knees onward. The head, the arm, and the other hand of the Magdalen, very vivid. The feet of the Christ mostly rendered with halftones, but of an admirable likeness. The knee detaches marvelously against the arm and the hand of the Magdalen.

I must remember also the *Souls in Purgatory*. The modeling with halftone is evident in the figures of the lower part, as also the touches with which he draws the features anew. The sketch for the picture had to be good to permit him to do the picture itself with such certitude. One should make one's researches in the sketch, and then work with a sure hand in the execution of the picture.

In the evening, after dinner, started out in fine sunlight to call on Braekeleer; as I went up his street, I admired some magnificent Flemish horses, one yellow and one black.

Finally, saw the famous *Raising of the Cross:*[26] extreme emotion! A great deal of relationship with the *Medusa*.[27] He is young yet and is thinking of satisfying the pedants. Full of Michelangelo. Extraordinary loading on of the paint. Dryness that approaches that of Mauzaisse,[28] in certain parts, and yet it is not disturbing. Hair very dryly treated in the curly heads, in the old man with the red head and white hair who, below and to the right, is lifting up the cross, also in

[26] At the cathedral. The picture dates from 1610, soon after Rubens' return from Italy.

[27] The *Raft of the Medusa*, by Géricault.

[28] J. B. Mauzaisse (1783-1844), an academic painter who manufactured battle pictures for Versailles.

the dog, etc. Is this not prepared by the halftone? In the panel to the right, one sees heavily loaded preparations such as I often use, and a glaze on top of them, notably in the arm of the Roman who holds the staff, and in the criminals who are being crucified. Still more probable, although concealed by the finish, in the left-hand panel. The coloration has disappeared in the flesh, the light passages there being yellow and the shadows black. The folds are studied for stylistic purposes, the arrangement of the hair on the heads of the figures has been carefully considered. There is more freedom, though the brush is still that of a student, in the central picture; but he is completely free and returns to his own temperament in the panel containing the horse, which goes beyond everything. When I see this art, Géricault grows greater in my eyes: he divined this force and his work is in no respect inferior to what is here. Although Rubens has not yet reached the height of his knowledge of painting in the *Raising of the Cross,* it must be admitted that the impression is perhaps more gigantic and more elevated than in his masterpieces. He was steeped in sublime works, and one cannot say that he imitated. He had that characteristic, he and the other masters he bore in him. What a difference from the Carracci! When one thinks of them, one sees clearly that he did not imitate; he is always Rubens.

This will be useful to me for my ceiling.[29] I had that feeling when I began. Did I perhaps also owe it to others? The study of Michelangelo has exalted one generation of painters after another and lifted them all up above themselves.

The grand style cannot dispense with drawings established in advance. When you proceed by halftones, the contour is added at the end: that gives more of reality, but also a softer quality and perhaps less of character.

Sunday, August 11. At Antwerp.

About ten o'clock Braekeleer called for me so as to go and see the

[29] The ceiling of the Galerie d'Apollon in the Louvre, for which Delacroix had received the commission that same year.

pictures by Rubens which are being restored. That inexhaustible bab-
bler spoiled my second visit by hanging on to me and talking of nothing but himself. The impression of yesterday evening, at twilight, was
the right one.

I was so wearied that after having accompanied him to the house
of a collector who invited me yesterday to see his pictures, I went back
to my inn, and had a sleep instead of returning to the museum, which
would have completed my observations of the day before. And so I
stayed there lazily, listening to the chimes which always delight me,
and waiting for dinner.

We left at half past seven. At the railroad station found M. van
Huthen and a M. Cornelis, a major of artillery, who was very amiable
and very attentive, regretting that he had not been able to be useful
to me. My friends do not show me such interest as that. The personality
of a man in the public eye has got to be unknown for this feeling of
attentiveness to persist. When one has seen a prominent man several
times, one evidently finds him about the same as all the others! His
works had given us a greater idea of him and had idealized him. Hence
the proverb, "No man is a hero to his valet." I believe that with close
thought about that, one would arrive at a different conviction. The
really great man can be seen close by. That superficial people, after
having imagined him as something supernatural like the characters
in novels, very soon come to find that he is like everybody else, is by
no means astonishing. The characteristic of low persons is to go off
into false ideas the whole time, or at least to be beside the truth. The
fanatical and persistent admiration of all who came near to Napoleon
proves that I am right in this.

On Sunday evening, as we got back to Malines, it was with a
pleasant sensation that I found myself there again. All those good
Flemings were in holiday mood. These people are akin to us Frenchmen in their nature.

Drew from memory everything that had struck me during my
excursion to Antwerp.

Brussels, Monday August 12.

Left at nine o'clock on Monday. Hotel Tirlemont. Saw the cathedral again and its magnificent windows. Started drawing too early and had trouble with my stomach, which caused me a passing accident of which I felt the effects all day. It was while going to the Museum. Nevertheless I stayed there till three o'clock.

Took a walk in the park, to set myself right; the weather was gray. Went down into the hollow.

In the evening took a walk toward the theater and through the passages. I enjoyed seeing again all those places where I had such a pleasant time eleven years ago.[30]

Tuesday, August 13.

At Brussels, I read in the newspaper that experiments in photography have been made at Cambridge with an idea of getting an image of the sun, the moon and even the stars; of the star Alpha, in the Lyre, they obtained an impression the size of a pinhead. The letter which reports this result makes an observation as exact as it is curious: that since the light of the star which was daguerreotyped took twenty years to traverse the space separating it from the earth, the ray which was fixed on the plate had consequently left the celestial sphere a long time before Daguerre had discovered the process by means of which we have just gained control of this light.

I went to the Museum in a languid way; I was under the impression of my sick spell of yesterday. The place was so drafty that I had to leave. In the morning, I called for M. van Huthen at the other end of the city; he took me to the shops of some print dealers.

I have noticed more and more the extent to which the *Christ Bearing the Cross,* the *Christ Foudroyant le Monde (Christ as the Avenging Judge)* and the *Saint Lieven* characterize a manner apart in the work of Rubens. I believe that it is the last one. It is the ablest one. The contrast with the nearby pictures serves only to bring out this

[30] With Elisa Boulanger (Mme Cavé).

difference. The *Assumption* is very dry. The same is true of the *Adoration of the Magi,* by which I was so carried away the first day, doubtless because of its finish.

Saturday, August 17. Paris.[31]

A color for the halftone of gold or of neutral drapery, nicely suited to accentuating what surrounds it, by opposition: base, the lightest *chrome;* halftone, either *umber,* or *white Cassel earth; ochre* or something like it added according to the need.

Yellow tone for the sky after the very clear tone of *Naples yellow* and *white* which surrounds the Apollo: *white yellow ochre* and *chrome number two.* For gradation, raw *terre d'Italie* substituted for *yellow ochre.*

For the light passages in the mantle of Aeolus: raw *terre d'Italie* and *vermilion;* shadow: *burnt lake* and *burnt terre d'Italie.*

Light passages in the robe of Iris: *emeraude green, chrome yellow number two* — shadow: *emeraude green, raw terre d'Italie.*

For the sky the golden tone, beginning with the aureole, is made with raw *terre d'Italie* and *white* in the light part around the sun, the tone of *Prussian blue* and *white* comes next and marries with the foregoing, but is laid on dry.

[31] Immediately after his return to Paris, Delacroix gets back to the ceiling of the Galerie d'Apollon.

The following paragraphs are given as a specimen of the notes covering a large number of pages of the *Journal* here omitted, in which Delacroix sets down an almost endless variety of color combinations, partly as a matter of record for himself and partly for the guidance of the young painters who laid in the broad spaces of his decoration as a preparation for his own work later on in adding the complementary tones and in bringing the pictures to their completion. Even were the exact quantities of each color noted down, and were we sure of obtaining the same pigments as Delacroix used in his day, it is difficult to believe that the passages referred to could be of any assistance to a present-day painter, with his different subjects and vision and, above all, lacking the particular judgment through which Delacroix applied these colors to the passage in his painting on which he was at work. A careful study of the problem has been made by René Piot in his book *Les Palettes de Delacroix,* Paris, 1931.

August 23.

"Outside of the fact that he remained a bachelor, he completed his resemblance to the idler by his fear of the visits which keep the honest man at home when he would like to go out. He rarely enjoyed them, we are told, and never encouraged them." Sainte-Beuve, on M. Bazin, in the *Causeries du Lundi.*

Sainte-Beuve cites Villemain, who speaks of history in the following terms: "History is always to be written, and every distinguished mind, finding aid in the progress of ideas, which he adopts or he combats, discovers, in the events related by others, new lessons and views."

What Villemain says about history may be said about everything. Not only can I find in the recital of another man the material for new accounts, interesting from my point of view, but my own tale, just as I write it, is something that I could do over in twenty different ways. It is probable that God alone, or a god, can say about things only what should be said about them.

Tuesday, September 3.

Began work at the Louvre, for the ceiling. I helped Andrieu[32] to square off the cartoon.

Tuesday, September 17

Laurens informs me that Ziegler[33] is making a large number of daguerreotypes, among others some of nude men. I shall go to see him and ask him to lend me some of them.

[32] Pierre Andrieu (1821-1892), painter, pupil and collaborator of Delacroix. He worked, notably, at the decorations of the Hôtel de Ville, the Galerie d'Apollon and of Saint-Sulpice. After the death of Delacroix, he was commissioned to restore the ceiling of the Galerie d'Apollon and of the cupola of the Library of the Luxembourg. His own painting remained so strongly influenced by that of the master that it has not infrequently been mistaken for his, and even sold as such.

[33] Jules-Claude Ziegler (1804-1856), painter, ceramist, pupil of Ingres. Delacroix made numerous drawings from Ziegler's daguerreotypes.

Monday, September 23.

To prepare the figures in the picture: have good outlines as the point of departure, and when Andrieu has applied the color and begun to make the figure *turn*, give him new coaching in this elementary work and try to get him to the point of carrying it through with this amount of help. The retouching which I shall do will thus be easier. One ought to preserve the lines of the tracing and perfect them even before they are used, so that one could make a new tracing on the preparatory painting in case the drawing gets lost

In the whole thing one must follow the preparation of the decorators, particularly for distant figures; these must be modeled with flat tints, as we did in the cartoon; have the shadows cut sharp in them, and add light passages only to the smallest extent.

In Paul Veronese's *Susanna*,[34] I noticed how simply he handles the light and shadow, even in the planes of the foreground. In a vast composition like the ceiling, this is far more necessary. The chest, in the figure of Susanna, seems to be of a single tone, and it is in full light. The contours, also, are very pronounced: another means of getting clarity at a distance. I had the same experience with the cartoon, after having traced around the figures an almost characterless contour, omitting any accents.

September 24.

As to the prejudice that one is born a colorist and that one becomes a draftsman, or, let us say, *"nascuntur poetae, fiunt oratores."*

As to the poet-painters and the prose-painters.

Sunday, September 29.

Mme Cavé came in, to read me part of her treatise on water color; it is full of charming things.

While looking at the sketch which I colored from memory of the *Christ Bearing the Cross* by Rubens, I said to myself that that is the

[34] *Susanna and the Elders,* catalogue of the Louvre, number 1188.

247

way one ought to lay in pictures: using that intensity of tone, which may be somewhat lacking in light, but which establishes local relationships; after that one can return to it and put in the light and the accents with the necessary fantasy and verve. That would be the means of getting it (that verve) when it is needed, so as not to expend it uselessly, which is to say at the end. The opposite thing happens most often, and to me particularly.

One sees in Van Dyck's pictures (I don't mean his portraits) that he did not always have the boldness necessary to go back vigorously and with inspiration over his preparatory work, in which the halftone dominates a little too much. The two conceptions of painting which Mme Cavé was telling me about, that of color as *color,* and of light as *light,* have got to be reconciled in a single operation. If you make the light dominate too much, the breadth of the planes leads to the absence of half-tints, and consequently to discoloration; the opposite abuse is harmful above all in big compositions destined to be seen from a distance, like ceilings, etc. In the latter form of painting, Paul Veronese goes beyond Rubens through the simplicity of his local color and his breadth in handling the light. (I must remember the *Susanna and the Elders* in the Museum, which is a lesson to be pondered). Paul Veronese had greatly to strengthen his local color in order that it should not appear discolored when illumined by the very broad light he threw on it.

Wednesday, October 9, 1850.

Gave to M. Lacroix, for Debourge, the color-man who was burned out, a small pastel, *Tiger Licking its Paw.*[35]

Wednesday, October 16.

As to *pictorial license.* It is frequently to this that every master owes his most sublime effects: The unfinished condition in Rembrandt's work, the exaggeration in Rubens. Mediocre men cannot have such

[35] *Catalogue Robaut,* 1164 bis.

daring; they never get outside themselves. Method cannot govern everything; it leads everybody up to a certain point. How is it that not one of the great artists has tried to destroy that mass of prejudices? They were probably frightened at the task, and so abandoned the crowd to its silly ideas.

November 3.

Rubens frankly places the gray half-tint of the edge of the shadow between his local tone for the flesh and his transparent rub-in. In his work this tone reigns throughout. Paul Veronese lays on flat the half-tint of the flesh and that of the shadow. (I have noticed in my own experience that this procedure gives already an astonishing amount of illusion.) He is satisfied to bind one with the other by a grayer tone applied locally, when the underpainting is dry. In the same way, skimming over the surface, he lays on the vigorous and transparent gray tone which borders the shadow on the side where it is gray.

Titian probably did not know how he was going to finish a picture. Rembrandt must often have been in the same state of mind. His excessive giving way to his temperament is less an effect of his intention than one of the expedients he tried one after another.

[While taking a walk with Villot at Champrosay some two weeks ago,] we observed some astonishing effects. It was at sunset: the *chrome* and *lake* tones were the most brilliant at the side where the light was, the shadows were blue and cold to the last degree. It seems that the warmer the light tones are the more nature exaggerates the contrast with gray: witness the half-tints in the Arabs and in people of coppery complexion. The reason why that effect was so vivid in the landscape was precisely that law of contrast.

Yesterday, November 13.

I noticed the same phenomena at sunset: it is more brilliant, more striking, at noonday only because the contrasts are more clear cut. The gray of the clouds in the evening runs into *blue;* the part of the sky which is clear is bright *yellow* or orange. The general law is: *the more the contrast the more the brilliancy.*

Wednesday, November 27.

I spent the morning with Guillemardet.[36] He gives me this recipe of M. Dupin's [37] for getting ahold easily of what you want to say: don't think of the words when you are turning the matter over in your head beforehand — think only of the thing itself and imbue yourself with it thoroughly; the words will come automatically when the time comes for you to speak.

Saturday, December 28.

Called on Chabrier in the evening. Villemain the engineer was there, also an engineer from the school of roads and bridges. Those gentlemen considered that an invasion was impossible: in the first place our whole people would unite against the foreigner (a delightful safeguard in a divided country); then because the artillery was so perfected that no invading force was capable of overcoming it, any more than sharp-shooters with excellent rifles, fighting individually, could be beaten, the reason being that the army of invasion would have to move in heavy columns and that the inhabitants, by scattering and sniping them, would be sure to win. We objected in vain that in the first place artillery had been perfected for everybody, and that, on this score, the attackers would have an equal advantage; in the second place nothing prevented them from individual sniping either; there was simply no way of convincing those fellows.

---

[36] Félix Guillemardet, a friend of his boyhood.
[37] Dupin, senior (1783-1865), lawyer, jurisconsult, president of the Legislative Assembly in 1849.

Friday, June 6.

YESTERDAY, inauguration of the galleries at the Museum.[1] The profound impression made on me by the pictures of Lesueur does not prevent me from taking note of the degree of power which color can add to expression. Contrary to common opinion, I would say that color has a far more mysterious power and perhaps a stronger one; it acts, so to speak, without our being aware of it. I am convinced, even, that a great part of the charm of Lesueur is due to his color. He has the art which is completely lacking in Poussin, of giving unity to everything he represents. A figure by him is in itself a perfect ensemble of lines and of effects, and the picture, the sum of all the figures united,

[1] The Louvre had been closed for two years to permit considerable restorations. It was on this occasion that Delacroix's decoration for the ceiling of the Galerie d'Apollon was commissioned.

is harmonized everywhere. It is permissible, however, to believe that if he had had to paint the queen on horseback, of which subject Rubens has done such a magnificent picture, he would not have appealed to the imagination with a subject as devoid of expression as that one is. Only a colorist could imagine that bouquet — that horse and that transparent shadow of the hind leg which is connected with the mantle.

Poussin loses a great deal when his pictures hang near those of Lesueur. Grace is a muse of whom he has never caught a glimpse. Harmony of line, of effect, and of color is also a quality, or a union of the most precious qualities, which was completely denied him. Strength in the conception, correctness carried to the last degree, never any of those lapses or those sacrifices which bind things together, which give gentleness of effect and carry the eye along easily in the composition! He is strained in his Roman subjects and in his religious subjects; he is so in his bacchanals; his fauns and his satyrs are a little too restrained and serious; his nymphs are pretty chaste for mythological beings; they are very beautiful in person but have nothing mythological or supernatural about them. He was never able to paint the head of Christ; nor the body either, that body which must be treated with such tenderness; that head which tells us of His grace toward humanity and His sympathy with its suffering. When painting his Christs, he thought rather of Jupiter, or even of Apollo. He understood the Virgin no better; he did not catch a glimpse of that personality, full of the divine and the mysterious. He does not express the attention which the infant Jesus awakens in men when they are caught by His grace, and in the animals which the gospel tells us of as attending the birth of the divine child. The ox and the ass are not shown near the cradle of the God who has just been born on the same straw where they lie; the rustic appearance of the shepherds who come to adore Him is a bit touched up from memories of figures from the antique; the Magi have a little of the stiffness and the economy of draperies and accoutrements which one notices in statues; I do not find those mantles of silk or of velvet, covered with gems, worn by slaves and dragging on the floor of the stable at the feet of the Master of nature which a supernatural power announces to them. Where are those dromedaries, those censers, all that pomp? They are needed to give their admirable contrast with the humble refuge.

I am convinced that Lesueur did not use Poussin's method of arranging the effect of his pictures by means of little stage models lit up by the studio light. His so-called conscientiousness gives an extreme dryness to Poussin's pictures. It seems as if all the figures were without connection one with another; they seem cut out; hence those breaks and that absence of unity, of melting together, and of effect — qualities which are found in Lesueur and in all the colorists. Raphael falls into this fragmentary condition by reason of another practice, that of conscientiously drawing each figure nude, before draping it.

Although it is necessary to make acquaintance with all the parts of the figure, so as not to get away from the proportions which clothing may hide, I could not be a partisan of following this method in every case — one that he seems, from the studies by him which remain, to have conformed to scrupulously, at all times. I am very sure that if Rembrandt had held himself down to this studio practice, he would not have either that power of pantomime or that power over effects which makes his scenes so genuinely the expression of nature. Perhaps it will be discovered that Rembrandt is a far greater painter than Raphael.

I write this blasphemy — one that will make every school-man's hair stand on end — without coming to an absolute decision in the matter; but the further I go on in life the more I feel within me that truth is what is most beautiful, and most rare. Rembrandt has not, if you will, the absolute elevation of Raphael.

Perhaps that elevation which Raphael has in the lines, in the majesty of each one of his figures, is to be found again in Rembrandt's mysterious conception of his subjects, in the deep naturalness of expressions and of gestures. Although one may prefer that majestic emphasis of Raphael, which perhaps belongs to the grandeur of certain subjects, one might affirm, without causing oneself to be stoned by men of taste — by which I mean men of a genuine and sincere taste — that the great Dutchman was more natively a painter than the studious pupil of Perugino.

Saturday, June 14.

The execution of the dead bodies in the picture of *Python*,[2] that is my real execution, the one suited to my temperament. I should not paint that way from nature, and the freedom that I get in this way compensates for the absence of the model. I must remember the characteristic difference between this and the other parts of my picture.

Allegory of Glory.[3] Freed from terrestrial bonds and sustained by *Virtue, Genius* arrives at the dwelling place of *Glory,* its final goal: it abandons its remains to livid monsters, personifying envy, unjust persecution, etc.

[2] In the ceiling of the Galerie d'Apollon.
[3] This subject for a picture is one which always preoccupied Delacroix. Sketches for it exist; in particular, numbers 727 and 728 of the Robaut catalogue.

January, 26.

Saw the sublime tapestries of the *Life of Achilles* by Rubens at the Mousseaux sale.[1] His big pictures, or let us say his pictures in general, do not have the inexactitudes which are here, but neither do they have this incomparable verve. Here he is not *seeking*, and above all he is not *improving*. When he tries to chasten the form he looses the dash and the freedom which give unity and action; Hector's head is thrown back in a way that gives to it incomparable expression and even color; for it is to be observed that, faded as these tapestries are, they preserve the feeling of the color to an astonishing degree, especially as they must have been made from cartoons only slightly colored.

[1] These were tapestries from the estate of Louis-Philippe. Sold on January 28, 1852, all trace of them has been lost today. The catalogue of the sale had been drawn up by Viollet-le-Duc, who was at the time the architect of the Orléans family.

255

The *tripods brought before Achilles, with Briseis, whom the old men are returning to him.* What fine spun stuff, what small intentions would not the moderns have lavished upon this subject! As for him, he goes to the thing itself, like Homer. That is the most striking characteristic of these cartoons.

The decorations of these tapestries must not be forgotten: The children carrying the garlands; the terminal figures, at each side of the composition, and above all the emblem which characterizes each subject at the middle of the base. Thus in the *Death of Hector,* the cockfight, which is of an inexpressible energy; in the scene of the *Styx,* Cerberus lying asleep; under the *Wrath of Achilles,* a roaring lion.

In the last one, the Agamemnon is superb in his indignation mingled with fear. He is on his throne. On one side, the old men advance to halt Achilles; on the other, Achilles drawing his sword, but restrained by Minerva, who takes him by the hair, brusquely, as in Homer.

Achilles on the back of Chiron [2] seemed to me ridiculous: he looks as if he were in the riding school, and has the air of a horseman of the time of Rubens.

The Death of Achilles: the hero sinks to earth at the foot of the altar where he is sacrificing; an old man supports him as the arrow pierces his heel. Just at the gate of the temple, Paris, with a ridiculous little bow in his hand, and above him Apollo, pointing out Achilles to him with a gesture which avenges the whole Trojan war. Nothing could be more anti-French than all that. Everything else that was there, even the Italian things, seemed very cold compared to this.

I hope to return.

Tuesday, January 27.

Returned today to see the tapestries. I was feeling badly and that prevented my getting the benefit from them that I had hoped for; I made

[2] Delacroix had treated this subject, *Achilles and the Centaur,* in one of the pendentives, of the Chamber of Deputies.

Eugène Delacroix; from a Lithograph by Achille Sirouy

Dante and Vergil (1822). The Louvre. Photograph by Giraudon

The Massacre at Scio (1824). The Louvre

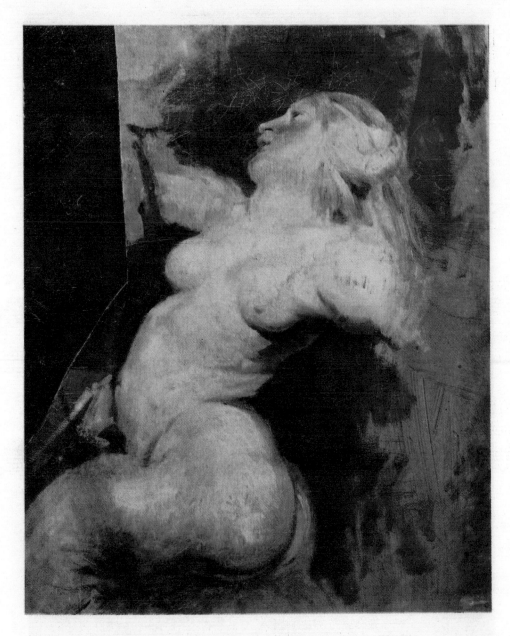

Sketch of a Figure in Rubens' Landing of Marie de Medici

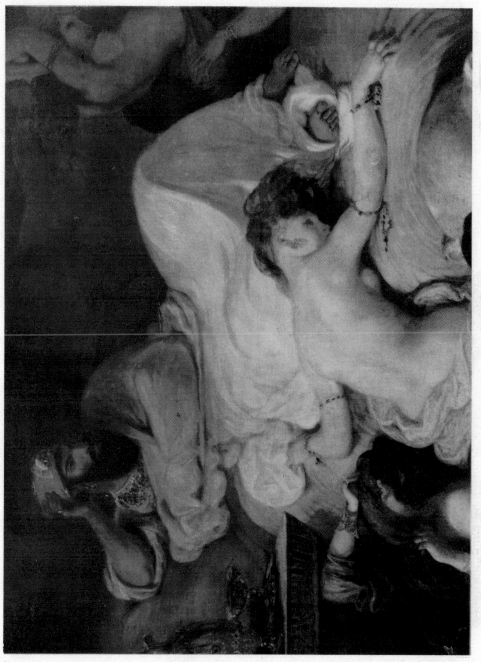

The Death of Sardanapalus, detail (1827). The Louvre

Liberty Guiding the People (1830). The Louvre. Photograph by Giraudon

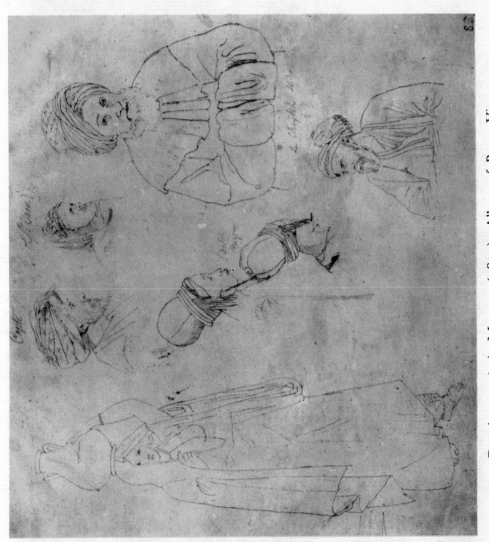

Drawings made in Morocco (1832). Album of Baron Vitta

Arabs of Oran, etching (1833)

Jewess of Algiers, etching (1833)

Women of Algiers (1834). The Louvre. Photograph by Giraudon

Mademoiselle de la Boutraye (1834). Collection of Mrs. Howard P. Eells, Cleveland, Ohio

Arab Chess Players (1835). Courtesy of Wildenstein and Company

At the Fountain. Courtesy of M. Knoedler and Company

Arab Comedians, water color (1836). Courtesy of Jacques Seligmann and Company

Chopin (1838). The Louvre

The Return of Columbus (1839). Collection of Dr. and Mrs. Harold M. Tovell, Toronto, Canada

a few sketches and experienced the same impression and the same impossibility of breaking away.

It is impossible to imagine anything superior to that *Agamemnon*. What simplicity! The beautiful head . . . with a mingling of apprehension, which dominates the indignation! The old man takes his hand, as if to calm him, and at the same time looks at Achilles. The head of the dying Hector is one of those things one never forgets; it is the truest in every respect and the most expressive that I know in the art of painting. The beard is simple and of admirable modeling. The way in which the lance strikes him, the iron already buried in his breast and carrying death with it, makes one tremble. There is Homer, and more than Homer, for the poet does not make me see his Hector save with the eyes of the mind, and here I see him with my bodily eyes. Therein lies the great superiority of painting: that is to say, when the image offered to the eyes not only satisfies the imagination, but fixes the object forever and goes beyond the conception.

The Briseis is charming: she displays a mingling of modesty and of joy; separated from her by the figures of the men who place the tripods on the ground, Achilles seems to feel an increase of his desire to satisfy his love by embracing her; the old man who presents her to him, advances bowing with a feeling of shame, mingled with the desire to please Achilles. In the *Achilles Discovered,* the group of girls is admirable: they are divided between the desire to busy themselves with the clothes and jewels, and their surprise at seeing Achilles, the helmet on his head, and already emancipated. Charming legs. I have already spoken of the gesture of Achilles, which is incomparable: his life and spirit shine in his eyes. The *Death of Achilles,* full of the same beauties. On further study, in order to make drawings, one is confounded by such science. That of the planes is what raises Rubens above all the so-called draftsmen; when they have to do with planes, it seems as if they were guided by luck: he, on the contrary, in his wildest passages, never fails with them. A superb figure; strength and truth; the acolyte crowned with leaves who supports Achilles at the moment when he is struck and sinks to earth, turning to his murderer with regrets which seem to say, "How did you dare to slay Achilles?" There is even something tender in that look, the intention of which may reach out to Apollo, who stands implacable above Paris and, almost pressed against him, indicates by a furious gesture where the blow is to be struck. The Vulcan is one of the most complete and most finished figures: the head is indeed that of the god; the weight of the body is prodigious. The Cyclops who brings the anvil and his two companions who beat upon the anvil, the Triton who receives from a winged child the fearful helmet — masterpieces of imagination and of composition!

The clearly formed decision manifest in the work, and certain exaggerated forms show that Rubens was in the situation of an artisan working at a trade that he knows well, without any of the endless search for improvement. He worked with the things that he knew, and consequently without disquietude as to his thought. The habiliment that he gives to his thoughts is always ready to his hand; his varied and sublime ideas are translated by forms which superficial people accuse of monotony, not to speak of their other grievances. That monotony does not displease the deep man who has sounded the secrets of art. This return to the same forms is at once the seal of the great master and the consequence of the irresistible swing of a sapient and practiced hand. From it there results the impression of the ease with which these works were produced, a feeling which adds to the force of the work.

Sunday, February 1.

Pierret informs me that the beautiful tapestries were sold for *two hundred francs* apiece: there were very fine ones among them, and Gobelins, with backgrounds of gold. A coppersmith bought them to burn them and get the metal.

Monday, February 2.

Mme Sand arrived about four o'clock. I have been reproaching myself since she got here, for not having been to see her. She is in very ill health; outside of her liver trouble, she has a kind of asthma similar to that which poor Chopin had.

I was talking to Mme Sand about the tacit agreement on cowardice and abasement that is evident among all those people, and they were so proud a short time ago![3] Their giddiness and boastfulness have been followed in the twinkling of an eye by utter cringing, in which the whole lot of them are as one. And yet we have not yet reached the level of the marshals of Napoleon in 1814; but that is only because the occasion for such conduct does not present itself. We are witnessing the greatest baseness in history.

Friday, February 13.

Occupied all these last days with my compositions for the Hôtel de Ville.[4] Went today to the Hôtel de Ville, where I felt myself singularly troubled when making a brief report on the paintings to be restored at Saint-Séverin and at Saint-Eustache;[5] I had a feeling of indisposition and a heaviness in the head which caused me to omit three quarters of it.

Summoned to see the designs of Lehmann.[6]

Sunday, February 15.

Symphony in G minor by Mozart at the Sainte-Cécile concert. I con-

[3] The opinion of Delacroix on the people who implored pardon from Louis Napoleon, after having opposed him at the moment of the *coup d'état*.

[4] The Salon de la Paix, including a ceiling and various panels (Catalogue Robaut 1119-1162).

[5] As it was a question of contemporary paintings for which Delacroix could have cared but little, his troubled mind and his scruples will be understood.

[6] Henri Lehmann (1814-1882), a German painter, pupil of Ingres. The question is doubtless that of the projects of the decoration for the Salle des Fêtes at the Hôtel de Ville, which were commissioned from Lehmann and which included twenty-eight pendentives dealing with the history of humanity. These pictures were destroyed by fire at the time of the Commune. The city had voted 80,000 francs to have these mediocre compositions engraved, and had neglected those of Delacroix.

fess that the whole business bored me a bit. The beginning (and I rather believe that the thing happened so because it was the beginning), independent of the real merit, gave me a great deal of pleasure. The overture and the finale from *Oberon*.[1] That fantastic quality in one of the worthiest successors of Mozart has the good fortune to come later than its sources in the work of the divine master, and its forms are more of today. They have not been pillaged and hammered over by all the musicians of the last sixty years. The *Chorus of Gauls* by Gounod seems very much like a fine thing; but it is necessary to hear music a few times before one can decide about it. It is necessary also for a musician to establish the authority or merely the comprehension of his style by a sufficiently large number of works. Pedantic instrumentation or a taste for archaism sometimes gives the idea of austerity and of simplicity when one hears the work of an unknown man. Ill-controlled verve, supported by reminiscences cleverly stuck together and by a certain brio in using the instruments, can give the illusion of fiery genius carried away by the ideas and capable of greater things. That is the history of Berlioz; the preceding example would apply to Mendelssohn. Each of them is lacking in ideas, and they hide that capital defect, as best they can, with all the means suggested to them by their ability and their memory.

There are few musicians who have not found a certain number of striking motifs. The appearance of these motifs in the first works of the composer gives an advantageous idea of his imagination; but these fleeting impulses are too often followed by a mortal languor. We are not in the presence of that happy facility of the great masters, who are prodigal of the happiest motifs, often in mere accompaniments; here is no longer that wealth of substance, always inexhaustible, always ready to burst forth, and offering to the artist everything he needs, so that he has it ready to his hand and does not spend his time over an endless hunt for the best, or with hesitations later on as to a choice amongst several forms of the same idea. This frankness, this abundance, is the

[1] Opera by Weber.

surest stamp of superiority in all the arts. Raphael and Rubens did not search for ideas — which came of themselves, and even in too great number. Their effort was scarcely to bring ideas to birth, but to render them in the best possible way, through the execution.

Thursday, February 19.

Dined at the house of Desgranges. Chance placed me beside Royer, the physician, once more: I was astonished at his sobriety: I must recall more frequently how important that virtue is, especially for a man who finds himself in such bad shape as I; eating only once a day, it is very difficult for me to keep from being swept beyond proper limits by an appetite that has been coming on for twenty-four hours.

Friday, February 20.

Dined at the house of Villot. These continual dinners trouble me a great deal. Dinners served in the Russian fashion, more than ever. The whole time it is being served, the table is covered with ring-biscuits and with sweetmeats; in the middle a display of flowers, but nowhere the smallest scrap of what a hungry stomach is demanding when one sits down to table. The waiters giving pitiful service, and handing about, according to their own whims, whatever they feel like giving you — in a word, what they disdain to keep for themselves. And people think all that is charming; farewell cordiality, farewell the amiable occupation of making a good dinner! You get up from table more or less satisfied, and you regret your bachelor dinners by your own fireside. That poor woman[8] has plunged into social habits which provide her with company made up of the most futile and tiresome people exclusively.

I escaped, avoiding the music, to call on my colleague at the municipal council, Didot.[9] The walk to his house, in the dry cold of

[8] Mme Villot.
[9] Ambroise Firmin-Didot (1790-1876), one of the most celebrated representatives of the family of publishers of this name; a distinguished Hellenist; he played an important role in the book business of France in the nineteenth century.

the air, did me some good. On arriving, a mob of guests; music still more detestable and, on the walls, bad pictures, except one, that nude man by Albrecht Dürer, which held me throughout the evening.

This unhoped-for find, and the singing of Delsarte, at Bertin's yesterday, caused me to reflect that one can get a great deal of good out of society, as tiring as it is and as futile as it appears. I should not have had any fatigue if I had stayed at my fireside; nor should I have had any of those sufferings which, because of contact with triviality and banality, are the price to be paid for pleasures which the common run of men seek in the drawing-room.

Villot was at Bertin's yesterday. He did not seem to be as much struck as I by the horrible painting we saw there, he is limited in his admirations; the reason is that his sentiment does not serve him after the moment when he has found a certain measure of talent; and this again he appreciates only in a certain number of artists, of a certain school: he is a fine person and serious in his conversation; but you never get warm with him. He is a man of merit to whom all the graces have been denied. We saw together the picture of David's old age, representing the *Wrath of Achilles;* it is weakness itself; idea and painting are equally absent. I thought at once of the *Agamemnon* and the *Achilles* of Rubens, which I saw hardly a month ago.

Saturday, February 21.

In the evening to the Jardin d'Hiver, where I took Mme de Forget to the ball of the ninth arrondissement, for which I had subscribed. The same thing happened with me as on the two preceeding days: I had prepared for a disagreeable time and I was relieved of my apprehensions. I was delighted by the sight of those exotic trees, some of them gigantic, lit by electric fireworks. The water, and the sound that it makes amid such surroundings, was wonderful in its effects. There were two swans that disported themselves in the water of a basin filled with plants, where they kept under the continual rain from a fountain which rose to a height of forty or fifty feet. Even the dancing entertained me, as also the commonplace orchestra; and the nerve of that orchestra leader, that bow, that thump of the drum, those cornets, that enthusiasm of the counter-jumpers fluttering about in their fine clothes excited in me a sentiment which, I am sure, is to be felt nowhere but in Paris.

Monday, February 23.

Painters who are not colorists produce illumination and not painting. All painting worthy of the name, unless one is talking about a black-and-white, must include the idea of color as one of its necessary supports, in the same way that it includes chiaroscuro and proportion and perspective. Proportion applies to sculpture as to painting; perspective determines the contour; chiaroscuro gives relief through the disposition of lights and shadows in their relationship with the background; color gives the appearance of life, etc.

The sculptor does not begin his work with a contour; with his material, he builds up an appearance of the object which, rough at first, immediately presents the chief characteristic of sculpture—actual relief and solidity. The colorists, the men who unite all the phases of painting, have to establish, at once and from the beginning, everything that is proper and essential to their art. They have to mass things in with color, even as the sculptor does with clay, marble or stone; their sketch, like that of the sculptor, must also render proportion, perspective, effect and color.

The contour is as much a thing of idea and convention in painting as it is in sculpture; it should result naturally from the right placing of the essential parts. The combined preparation of the effect (including perspective) and of color will approach more or less closely to its definitive appearance, according to the ability of the artist; but in this point of departure, there will be an unmistakable beginning of what is to come later on.

Tuesday, February 24.

Children's party at the house of Mme Herbelin; I noticed how horrible our clothing is by contrast with the dress of these little beings, who scattered notes of color wherever they were and who, because of their small size, were in no way to be confused with the grown people. It was like a basket of flowers.

Wednesday, February 25.

Mediocre people have an answer for everything and are astonished at nothing. They always want to have the air of knowing better than you what you are going to tell them; when, in their turn, they begin to speak, they repeat to you with the greatest confidence, as if dealing with their own property, the things that they have heard you say yourself at some other place.

As a matter of course also, the mediocrities I am speaking of are well provided with the kind of knowledge which everybody can obtain. The greater or less degree of good sense or of natural wit which they may have is the only thing that prevents their making perfect fools of themselves. The multitude of examples which occur to my memory all confirm me as to this ridiculous trait of all too many people. The only difference among them is, as I have said, in the degree of their foolishness. A capable and superior look is the natural accompaniment of this type of character.

Thursday, February 26.

Party at the house of Mlle Rachel. She was amiable. I met Musset[10] again; I was telling him that a nation has taste only in the things that it succeeds with. The French are good only for the things that are spoken or that are read. They have never had taste in music nor in

---

[10] Delacroix had known Alfred de Musset since the time of Nodier's parties at the Arsenal. He seems not greatly to have appreciated the talent of the poet. "He is a poet who has no color," as he said one day to Philarète Chasles. "He handles his pen like an engraver's tool; with it he cuts grooves into the heart of man, and kills him by pouring into it the corrosive of his poisoned soul. As for myself, I prefer gaping wounds and the bright color of the blood." *(Mémoires de Ph. Chasles).* Musset, on the contrary, manifested a great admiration for Delacroix and defended him against his detractors.

painting. Mincing and coquettish painting. . . . The great masters like Lesueur and Lebrun do not create a school. Manner is what captivates above all; in music, almost the same thing.

Monday, March 1.

The man who generally brings the coal and wood is a witty rogue. He talks a great deal. The other day he asks for his tip and says that he has a lot of children. Jenny says to him: "And why have you such a lot of children?" He answers her: "It's my wife who has them." It was the old Gallic humor at its purest. He gave us one last year, just as strong as that, but I've forgotten it.

Monday, March 8.

For the first time went to the monthly dinner, of the second Monday. On leaving, took a walk on the boulevard with Varcollier, and finished the evening at Perrin's. Saw again the lithograph by Géricault of the horses fighting. Great relationship with Michelangelo. The same power, the same precision and, despite the impression of power and of action, a slight immobility, because of the extreme study of details, probably.

Friday, April 2.

On coming out from the municipal council, saw the sketches for Sainte Clotilde at Varcollier's place: folly can go no further. Poor Préault forced to do a Gothic sculpture! What criticism can one make of contemporary works, after seeing this dirty stuff?

Monday, April 5.

I have been at Saint-Sulpice to lay in one of the four pendentives.

While taking a walk in the evening, just before being drenched by the rainstorm which came up suddenly, met Varcollier [11] in the Rue du Mont-Thabor; he told me with horror of the little samples of color by Lehmann at the Hôtel de Ville. He would have me constitute myself the avenger and the denouncer of that man's crimes. I objected

[11] Varcollier, head of the Bureau of Fine Arts in the Prefecture of the Seine.

that one would have to work oneself up into too great a wrath, and that the numerous misdeeds of this kind ought to have been repressed long since. I cited to him the works of his friends.

On the day following, on my way home from Saint-Sulpice, dropped in at Saint-Germain, where I saw the Gothic smears with which they are covering the walls of that unhappy church. Confirmation of what I was saying to my friend: I prefer the imaginary stuff of Lehmann to the counterfeits of Baltard, Flandrin and Co.

Wednesday, April 7.

Animals do not feel the weight of time. Imagination, which has been given to man so that he may feel beauty, brings him a host of imaginary ills; the invention of pleasures, and the arts that so completely fill the life of the creative artist charm the leisure of those who do no more than enjoy such productions. The hunt for food, for brief moments of animal passion, the nursing of the young, and the building of nests or of lairs, are the only works that nature has imposed on the animals. Instinct urges them to that; no calculation directs them in it. Man bears the weight of his thoughts as well as that of the natural miseries which make of him an animal. In the measure that he gets away from the state nearest to that of the animal, that is to say the savage state in its varying degrees, he perfects the means of nourishing that faculty of the ideal which is denied to the beast; but the appetites of his brain seem to grow in the measure that he seeks to satisfy them; when he neither imagines nor composes for his own account, he has to enjoy the imagination of other men, or he must study the secrets of surrounding nature, which offers him its problems. The man whose less cultivated or more obtuse nature renders him incapable of enjoying the delicate pleasures in which the mind has a part, gives himself up to material enjoyments to fill up his time, but, even so, they are a different thing from the instinct which urges the animal to hunt. If man hunts in a state of average civilization, it is as a pastime. There are plenty of men who sleep in order to avoid the boredom of idleness; it weighs upon them but they can not shake it off by occupations offering any attraction. The savage, who hunts or fishes in order to get food, sleeps during the moments that he does not put in on the making, in his own way, of his coarse tools, his bow and arrows, his nets, his hooks cut from fishbone, and his stone axe.

Friday, April 23.

First performance of the *Wandering Jew.*[12]

Thursday, April 29.

Goubaux came in during the day. We spoke of the negligence with which the classic pieces are performed. There is not a director of one of the boulevard theaters who would stand it in the modern pieces. The actors of the Français have gotten into a habit of singing their parts in a monotonous manner like children reciting a lesson. He cited an example to me, the beginning of *Iphigénie:* "Yes, it is Agamemnon, etc." He remembered having seen Saint-Prix, who passed for a talent and who had tradition beside, tranquilly get up from a corner of the theater, go and awaken Arcas and tell him, all in one breath: "Yes, it is Agamemnon, etc." What is the evident intention of Racine? That *yes* at the beginning evidently responds to the surprise which the servitor must exhibit on being awakened before dawn — by whom? by his master, by his king, the King of kings. Does his surprise not also tell that this king, this father, has watched anxiously, long before he came to his confidant to get some relief from his trouble by speaking of it? He must have walked about and then gone back to a tormented couch, before arising. In his preoccupation, which seems to be continual, he does not even answer the question of that faithful friend. He talks to himself; his agitation betrays itself in that glance at destiny rendered by the words: "Happy is he who, satisfied, etc."

"Yes, it is Agamemnon . . ." answers the surprise of Arcas. Those words should be punctuated by mute gestures and not strung out like

[12] Opera in five acts, words by Scribe and Saint-Georges, music by Halévy.

the beads of a rosary, or like what a man would speak if reading from a book. Actors are lazy fellows, who never even ask themselves whether they could not do better. I am convinced that they follow the road as laid out, and that they have no idea of the treasures of expression that so many fine works contain.

Goubaux was telling me how Talma used to say that he *made notes* on all his inflections, independent of the pronunciation of the words. Such a practice acted as a safety device, preventing him from going wrong when he was not fully inspired. It was a species of music which, once fixed in the memory, brought back in a circle all the intonations which he could not have omitted without danger of losing himself, and of being led too far or on a false track.

Wednesday, May 5.

One should lay in one's picture so that it was the look of representing the scene on a gray day, without sun, without clear-cut shadows. Speaking radically, there are neither lights nor shades. There is a color mass for each object, having different reflections on all sides. Let us suppose that, in this scene, in the open air and under gray light, a ray from the sun suddenly illumines the objects: you will have lights and shades as they are understood, but they are pure accidents. The deeper truth of this, singular as it may seem, contains the whole comprehension of color in painting. How strange it is that this truth has been understood by only a very small number of great painters, even among those who are regarded as colorists.

Champrosay, Thursday, May 6.

(Written as I lean my back against the fence, at the foot of the great oak in the alley of the Hermitage.) Arrived yesterday, Wednesday the 5th, at Champrosay to spend two or three days and install myself in my new lodging.

About four o'clock, started out on the road toward Soisy to get up an appetite. There, in the dust, I found the trace of water, spread about as if from the spout of a funnel, and it recalled to me my earlier observation, made at different places, on geometrical laws which preside over accidents of that type and which ordinary people think are the effect of chance. Cases in point are the furrows cut by the waters of the sea in the fine sand that one sees on the beaches, such as I observed last year at Dieppe, and such as I had seen at Tangier. In their irregularity, these furrows show the return of the same forms, but it seems that the action of the water, or the nature of the sand which receives these imprints, makes them take on different aspects, according to the place; thus, the marks at Dieppe, watery spaces on a very fine sand, scattered here and there or enclosed by very small rocks, gave a very good representation of the sea waves themselves. If one copied them with proper coloring, one would give an idea of the movement of the waves, which is so difficult to grasp. At Tangier, on the contrary, on a flat beach, the waters as they flowed back left their imprint in small furrows which represented almost to the point of deception the stripes in the coat of the tiger. The trace that I found yesterday on the road to Soisy represented exactly the branches of certain trees, when they have lost their leaves; the main branch was from the water which had flowed, and the little branches which interlaced in a thousand ways were produced by the spatterings which came out and crossed each other at the right and the left.

I have a horror of the common run of scientists: I have said elsewhere that they elbow one another in the antechamber of the sanctuary where nature hides her secrets, and are always waiting for someone more able than themselves to open the door a finger's breadth for them: let the illustrious Danish, Swedish or German astronomer Borzebilocoquantius discover a new star with his telescope, in the way I read about recently, and the race of scientists proudly records the new arrival; but no telescope has been constructed that will show them the relationships among things. Scientists ought to live only in the country, close to nature; they prefer to chat around the green tables of the academies and of the Institut about the things that everybody knows as well as they do; in the forests, on the mountains, you observe natural laws, you do not make a step without finding a subject for admiration.

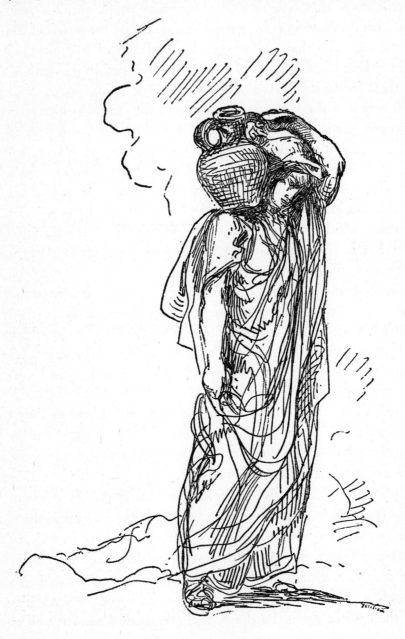

The animal, vegetable and insect worlds, the earth and the waters are food for the mind that studies and that wants to record the various laws of nature. But those gentlemen do not find such simple observation worthy of their genius; they want to penetrate deeper, they bring forth systems from the depth of their desks, which they look on as observatories. Besides it is necessary to frequent drawing rooms and to get *crosses* or *pensions;* the science which can put you on the track of such things is worth all the other sciences put together.

I compare writers who have ideas but do not know how to bring order into them, with those barbarian generals who led swarms of Persians or Huns into battle, where they fought haphazard, without order, without unity of effort, and consequently without results; bad writers are found as frequently among those who have ideas as among those who are devoid of them.

Delightful walk in the woods while my lodging is being arranged. A thousand various thoughts are suggested amidst this universal smile of nature. At every step in my walk, I disturb trysts — results of the spring season; the noise of my steps disturbs the poor birds who fly off, always in pairs. Oh! the birds, the dogs, the rabbits! Humble professors of good sense, all of them silent, all of them submissive to the eternal decrees — how far they all are above our vain and cold knowledge! Here is the awakening of the whole of this nature which has opened the door to love. New green leaves are coming out, new beings will be born, to people this universe grown young again. The sense of science awakens in me, and is more active than in the city. Those idiots (the scientists) live in their study rooms and look on them as the sanctuary of nature. They send for skeletons and dried grasses instead of seeing them bathed with dew.

Wednesday May 12.

I extract from a letter to Pierret my reflections on the interruption of my work during a week.

". . . One must not leave one's task; that is the reason why time, why nature, in a word everything that labors slowly and ceaselessly, does such good work. But we, doing things intermittently, never spin the same thread to the end. Before my departure, I was doing the work of the M. Delacroix of two weeks ago: now I am going to do the work of the Delacroix of a few moments ago. I have to find a new pattern in the weave: the knitting will be coarser or finer."

Dieppe, Monday, September 6.

In the railway carriage going to Rouen, I met a big bearded man who was very sympathetic to me, and who told me the most interesting things about the German emigrants, especially about certain of the colonies of that race, established in southern Russia, where he saw them. Those people descend in large part from the Hussites, who have become the Moravian Brothers. They live there communally, but are not communists in the way that term was understood in France, during our recent disturbances: the land alone is held in common, and probably also the tools of labor, since each one owes to the community the tribute of his labor; but some special industries get rich more than others do, since each one has its own treasury, which it manages with more or less of care and of ability. It is possible for a man to get a substitute to do his share in the communal work. They have taken the name of Meronites or Menonites.

Thursday, September 9.

In the evening I enjoyed the sea for an hour and a half; I could not tear myself away from it.

In truth, one must credit modern literature with having given a great interest to certain works, through descriptions which previously were not extended enough. Only, the abuse which has been made of this virtue, when the part has become almost the whole, has disgusted people with the style.

Saturday, September 11.

On waking up, I saw from my bed that the bay was practically at high tide and that the masts of the ships were swaying more than ordinarily; I concluded from that that the sea must be beautiful; I therefore hastened to the pier and I did have the finest spectacle to enjoy for nearly four hours.

Came home; in the evening read my beloved *Balsamo*.[13]

In the afternoon the sea was at low tide, which led me to go out a long distance on the sand, which was not too damp. I had the most delightful enjoyment of the sea; I believe that the greatest attraction of things is in the memory that they awaken in the heart or in the mind, but especially in the heart. I am always thinking of Bataille[14] and of Valmont, as it was when I went there for the first time, so many years ago. . . . The regret for time that is gone, the charm of our early years, and the freshness of first impressions have more effect on me than the scene itself. The smell of the sea, especially at low tide, which is perhaps its most penetrating charm, brings me back, with an incredible power, to the center of those beloved objects and those beloved moments which are no more.

Sunday, September 12.

Beautiful day, the sun rose early. Before my windows I had the ships hung with flags.

On the pier I met Mme Sheppard. She invited me to dinner for tomorrow. I slipped away from the young lady of yesterday, she is becoming unbearable; she and her crowd spoiled my evening again yesterday; impossible to avoid them at the pier. . . . In truth, I am the biggest fool possible: I am simply polite and considerate with people; it must be that there is something more than that in my look. They hang on to me, and I don't know how to get rid of them. Entered the pavillion for a time this evening because Possoz urged me to do so;

[13] *Joseph Balsamo* (1846-1848), novel by Alexandre Dumas, who is not accustomed to getting compliments from Delacroix.

[14] A cousin of Delacroix, the former owner of the Abbey of Valmont, near Fécamp, where Delacroix liked to spend his vacations.

he is completely at home there; the sea, which was at high tide, was breaking with a fine fury.

I am finding out pretty thoroughly here that too much freedom leads to boredom. One needs solitude and one needs distraction. The meeting with Possoz, which I was fearing, has turned into a resource at certain moments. The same applies to Mme Sheppard, for a short time. Without Dumas and his *Balsamo,* I should have started back for Paris, so that now these breaks in my solitude are what take up most of my time, and I am far from regretting my vague memories.

Everything that is great produces approximately the same sensation. What is the sea and its sublime effect? that of an enormous quantity of water. . . . Yesterday evening, I was listening with pleasure to the bells of Saint-Jacques, which ring very late, and at the same time I was seeing, in the shadow, the mass of the church. The details disappear, the object in itself was even greater; I had the sensation of the sublime, which the church seen in daylight does not give me at all, for it is common enough. An exact small-scale model of the same church would be still further from giving you that feeling. The vague look of things, which comes in the dark, adds much more to the impression of the sea: that is what I saw at the pier during the night, when one gets the merest half glimpse of the waves, near as they are, and when the rest loses itself in the horizon. Saint-Rémy produces far more effect on me than Saint-Jacques, which is however in better taste, more united and having a oneness of style. The former of these two churches is of a mongrel taste quite like that of the church of the Abbey of Valmont, one that is quite open to the criticism of architects. Saint-Eustache, which is in the same category, although more consistent in all its parts, is assuredly the most imposing church in Paris. I am sure that Saint-Ouen,[15] when it has been scraped off, will no longer produce any effect; the darkness of the windows and the blackened walls, the cobwebs and the dust veiled the details and made the ensemble seem larger. The cliffs produce their effect by their mass alone, and that effect is im-

[15] At Rouen.

mense, especially when one gets close by, which still further increases the contrast of that mass with the neighboring objects and with our own smallness.

Monday, September 13.

Look here! Fool that you are, you get a sore throat from discussing with idiots, you go arguing with silliness in petticoats for a whole evening, and you do that about *God,* about the *justice of this world,* about *good* and *evil,* and on *progress!*

This morning I got up tired, out of breath. . . . I have no head for anything, not even for taking a rest. O folly, folly thrice over! Persuade men! What a piling up of stupidities in the bigger number of those heads! And they want to give education to all those people born to labor and honestly to follow the furrow of their plough: and they want to make ideologists out of such as that! . . . All these reflections with reference to the dinner at Mme Sheppard's house.

This morning I found a jelly-fish at the pier. These people that I meet prevent me from enjoying the sea. It is time to get away. . . .

Act, so that you shall not suffer. Every time that you can diminish your boredom or your suffering through action, act — and without deliberating. That seems quite simple, at the first glance. Here is a trivial example: I leave my house, a garment bothers me, I continue on my way because I am too lazy to return and take another one. The examples are innumerable. This resolution applied to the common-places of existence, as to the important matters, would furnish the spirit with a spring of steel, and with balance, which is the state most fitted for the prevention of boredom. To feel that you have done what should be done raises you in your own eyes. After that, if you have no other reason for pleasure, you enjoy that chief of pleasures, which is self-content. The satisfaction of the man who has worked and made good use of his day is immense. When I am in that state, it is delightful for me, afterward, to enjoy my rest and even the mildest recreations. Indeed, I can find myself in the company of the most tiresome people, and feel no regret about it. The memory of the task that I have accomplished comes back to me and preserves me from boredom and sadness.

Tuesday, September 14.

I went to pay my last visit to the sea, about three o'clock. It was in a state of fine calm, and was as beautiful as I have ever seen it. I could not tear myself away. I was on the beach and I did not go to the pier all day long. The soul attaches itself with passion to the objects that one is about to leave behind.

It was from this side of the sea that I made a study from memory: golden sky, boats waiting for the tide so as to get back to port.[16]

Paris, September 15.

Sophocles, when asked in his old age whether he regretted the pleasures of love, replied: "Love? I have delivered myself of it wholeheartedly, as from a savage and furious master."

Monday, September 20.

On architecture. It is the ideal itself; everything in it is idealized by men. The straight line itself is of his invention, for it exists nowhere in nature. The lion seeks his cavern; the wolf and the wild boar take shelter in the depth of the forests; a few animals make homes for themselves, but they are guided by instinct alone; they do not know what it is to modify or to embellish them. Man, in his habitations, imitates the cavern and the aerial dome of the forests; in the periods when the arts are carried to perfection, architecture produces masterpieces: in all periods, the taste of the moment, and new departures in practice introduce changes which testify to the freedom of taste.

Directly, architecture takes nothing from nature, as sculpture or painting does; in this it approaches music, unless one affirm that, as music recalls certain sounds of the world, architecture imitates the

[16] Catalogue Robaut, 1245.

lair or the cavern, or the forest; but that is not direct imitation, in the sense understood when speaking of the two arts which copy the precise forms offered by nature.

Saturday, October 2.

This evening I am reading the *Mémoires de Balsamo*. The mixture of passages where he shows talent and that eternal effect of melodrama sometimes makes you feel like throwing the book out of the window; and at other moments, there is the attraction of curiosity which makes you keep on all evening with these singular books, for you cannot prevent yourself from admiring the verve in them, and a certain imagination, even though you cannot esteem the author as an artist. There is no modesty in them, and they address themselves to a century without modesty and without restraint.

Saturday, October 9.

I was saying to Andrieu that one is a master only when one brings to things the patience to which they are entitled. The young man compromises everything by his wild rush at his picture. For painting, maturity is needed. I was telling him, while retouching the *Venus*,[17] that young people have something *trembly, vague, confused*; age accentuates the planes in the execution of the masters, thus creating differences which vary the type of effect. The execution of Rubens, which is precise and without the mystery of Correggio or of Titian, always gives to his people a look of being older: his nymphs are fine strapping women of forty-five years of age; with his children, there is almost always the same drawback.

Monday, October 11.

I have applied high-lights of Naples yellow to my figures of the *Earth*,[18] because they were too red and, although that seemed to me

[17] In one of the compartments of the Salon de la Paix (Catalogue Robaut, 1144).
[18] In the ceiling of the Salon de la Paix.

against the natural effect, as I see it, of making the high-lights gray or violet, I noticed that the flesh immediately became luminous, which proves that Rubens was right. One thing is certain and that is that by making the flesh red or purplish, and by using high-lights of the same type, there is no longer any contrast, and you therefore get the same tone everywhere. If, into the bargain, the half-tints are violet also, as I have rather the habit of making them, it necessarily follows that everything is reddish. Therefore one absolutely must put more *green* into the half-tints, in this case. As to the golden high-light, I cannot explain why, but it has a fine quality: Rubens uses it every-where. . . . It is written into the Kermess.[19]

Tuesday, October 12.

Saw Mlle Rachel in *Cinna*. Beauvallet is certainly not bad as Augustus, especially at the end. There is a man who is making progress; and so he is getting wrinkled, and probably white haired, something that the wig of Augustus prevented my judging.

Consider this: the actor who, according to common report, has been bad or mediocre all his life, or at least throughout his youth — the age of strength and feeling — now becomes passable or excellent when he no longer has teeth or breath; and shall the same not be true in the other arts? Do I not write better and with more facility than in the past? Scarcely do I take up my pen, when ideas crowd in and fill my brain as in the past, and not only that, but what I formerly found very difficult — close relationship and measure — come to me naturally, and at the very time that I conceive what I have to say.

And in painting, does not the same thing occur? Whence does it come that nowadays I do not know a single instant of boredom when I have the brush in my hand, and that I feel that, if only my strength were sufficient, I should not stop painting save to eat and sleep? I

[19] The great picture by Rubens in the Louvre. M. Joubin considers that the word *written* is a misprint here; it does not seem an impossible reading to other students of the text.

remember that in the past, in that so-called age of verve and of the strength of the imagination, with my lack of experience in all those fine qualities, I was halted at every step, and frequently disgusted. It is a pitiful derision of nature that she should place us in the situation that age prepares for us. One's maturity is complete, and the imagination as fresh, as active as ever, especially because of the silence of mad and impetuous passion, which age carries away; but strength is lacking, the senses are worn down and demand repose more than movement. And yet with all these drawbacks what a consolation it is that comes from work! How glad I am no longer to be forced to find my happiness where I had to search for it in the past! From what savage tyranny have I not been snatched by this weakening of the body? What used to preoccupy me the least was my painting. And so one must do what one can; if nature rejects work for more than a certain number of moments, one must not do her violence, but count oneself happy over the things which she still has for us; we must not be so attached to the quest for praise — which is nothing but wind: we must get our enjoyment from the work itself and from the delightful hours that follow it, feeling to the full that this repose has been paid for with that salutary fatigue which maintains the health of the soul. And that reacts on the health of the body; it prevents the rust of the years from clogging the sentiments which are noble.

Monday, October 18.

All these last days I have been working with an extreme tenacity, before sending off my paintings which are to be glued to the wall tomorrow;[20] I have gone without resting for seven, eight, and nearly nine hours' work on my pictures.

I believe that my system of just one meal a day is decidedly the one that suits me the best.

Friday, October 23.

On the difference between the French genius and the Italian genius in

[20] At the Hôtel de Ville.

the arts: the former advances as the equal of the latter in elegance and in style, at the time of the Renaissance. How does it happen that that detestable style, soft and *Carracesque,* should have prevailed? At that time, unfortunately, painting had not yet been born.[21] All that remains of that period is the sculpture of Jean Goujon. Moreover, it must be that the French genius has a more pronounced leaning toward sculpture; in almost all periods there have been great sculptors, and that art, if one except Poussin and Lesueur, was more advanced than the other. When those two great painters appeared, there were no longer any traces of the great schools of Italy: I am speaking of those in which naturalness was united to great knowledge. The great schools which appear sixty to a hundred years after Raphael are mere academies for the teaching of recipes. There you have the models that Lesueur and Poussin saw prevailing in their time: fashion and habit led them on, despite that admiration felt for the antique, which characterizes above all men like Poussin, Lesueur, and all the creators of the Galerie d' Apollon.

I prefer to converse with things rather than with men: all men are tiresome; their obsessions, etc. The work is worth more than the man. It may be that Corneille was insufferable; Cousin[22] the same thing; Poinsot, etc. In the work there is a gravity which is not in the man. Poussin is perhaps the one who most of all stands behind his work. The productions in which one feels the labor, etc.

Monday, November 1.

To write treaties on the arts *ex professo,* to divide, to treat methodically, to summarize, to make systems for categorical instruction — all this is error, loss of time, a false and useless idea. The ablest man cannot

[21] The French Primitives had not yet come into men's consciousness, and the French school, according to the tradition accepted in the time of Delacroix, began with Vouet and Lesueur.

[22] Victor Cousin, the philosopher; Poinsot, the mathematician. Delacroix met them in society and does not seem to have been very well entertained when in their company.

do for others more than he does for himself, which is to say to note and observe, in the measure that nature offers him objects of interest. With such a man, the points of view change at every moment. Opinions must necessarily be modified; one never knows a master well enough to speak of him absolutely and definitively.

If a man of talent would set down his thoughts on the arts, let him give them forth just as they come to him; let him not fear to contradict himself; there will be more fruit for his harvest amid the profusion of his ideas, even if contradictory, than in the web of a work which has been combed, squeezed, and cut up, for the sake of concentrating on its form. . . . When Poussin, in a mood of caprice, said that Raphael was an ass compared with the antique, he knew what he was saying; he was thinking only of comparing the drawing and the knowledge of anatomy of the one man and that of the others, and he had a good chance to prove that Raphael was ignorant beside the ancients.

On that score, he might have said also that Raphael did not know as much as he, Poussin, did, but he would have said that in a different way. . . . In the presence of the miracles of grace and naturalness, bound together in union, the miracles of science and of instinctive composition pushed to a point where no one has equalled him, Raphael would have appeared to him what he really is, superior even to the ancients in certain parts of his art, and especially in those which were completely denied to Poussin.

Invention with Raphael, and by that I mean drawing and color, is what it can be; and I do not mean by that that it is bad; but such as it is, if one compare it with similar marvels from the hands of Titian, of Correggio, and of the Flemings, it becomes secondary, and it had to be so; it might have been so even more, and still not take away, seriously, from the merits which place Raphael not only in the front rank, but above all artists, ancient and modern, as regards the qualities in which he excels. I should even venture to affirm that these qualities would be reduced in value had he given more thought to the science of anatomy, to the handling of the brush, or to effect. One might almost say the same of Poussin himself, considering the things in which he excels. His disdain of color, and the somewhat harsh precision of his touch, especially in the pictures of his best manner, contribute to increase his sense of expression, and his judgment of characters.

Tuesday, November 17.

Man is a social animal who detests his fellows. Now explain this strange thing: the closer he lives to a foolish being who is similar to himself, the more harm he seems to desire for that other unfortunate. The household and its gentle pleasures, the friends traveling along his path, who were quite bearable when seen once a week, and who cause regret when they go far away, become the objects of mortal hate when circumstance forces them all to live together intimately for a long time.

The wilful and tormenting spirit which causes us to prefer ourselves and our opinions to those of our neighbor will not let us bear contradiction and opposition to our fantasies. If to this natural humor you add the one which sickness or troubles give to you to make the matter worse, the aversion inspired by a person to whom we are bound by fate can become a veritable torture. The crimes which we see committed by numbers of miserable men within present day society are more frightful than those committed by savages. A Hottentot or an Iroquois splits the head of the man whom he wants to despoil; among the cannibals, it is for food that the victim is killed, just as our butchers kill a sheep or a pig. But those perfidious traps, laid long in advance and hidden under all sorts of veils — friendship, tenderness, or small attentions — are to be found only among civilized men.

Friday, November 26.

Took a long walk with Jenny along the outer boulevards, Monceau, the Barrière de Courcelles, and the Place d'Europe; then across that great plain where we were almost lost; that is excellent for the health.

One ought to go out every day before dinner, dress, see one's friends, and get out of the dust of the studio.

It should be remembered that Montesquieu never allowed himself to be overcome by fatigue, after having given a reasonable time to composition. By rendering work easier and more orderly, experience can gain for us this faculty, which is denied to youth.

Saturday, November 27.

It is decided that my ceilings and other paintings are to be covered over with paper and that the room shall be open to the public: I am delighted with this arrangement. I shall have the time to return to the work at my leisure.

I have just examined all the sketches which served me in doing this work. How many of them there are that satisfied me hugely at the beginning, and that seem to me weak and insufficient, or badly ordered, since the paintings have been carried through! I cannot sufficiently remind myself that a great deal of work is needed to bring a picture to the degree of expressiveness of which it is capable. The more I look it over, the more it will gain, from the standpoint of expression. . . . There is no doubt but that the touch should disappear, and that the skill in execution should no longer be the principal merit of the work; and yet, how many a time does it not happen that after obstinate work has turned the thought about and let one study it from every side, the hand obeys more quickly and surely, and so gives to the last touches the necessary lightness!

(Entry without date).

Remember that the enemy of all painting is the *gray:* a painting will almost always appear grayer than it is, on account of its oblique position under the light. The portraits by Rubens, those women at the Museum — with the chain,[23] etc., where the panel shows through everywhere; Van Eyck, etc.

---

[23] The portrait of Anne of Austria and the portrait of Helena Fourment, each one with a chain.

Hence also the principle which excludes long processes of retouching, which is to say that one should make one's decisions at the beginning. . . . With that in mind, one ought to try to satisfy oneself fully with the figures painted in the background; by such a practice, it would afterward be easier to subordinate the background.

It is absolutely necessary that the half-tint in the picture, which is to say all the tones in general, be exaggerated. You may wager that the picture will be shown under a light that falls obliquely; and so, perforce, that what is true from a single point of view, i.e. with the light coming from in front, will be gray and false under all other aspects. The work of Rubens is exaggerated; that of Titian also; Veronese sometimes gray because of his excessive search for the truth.

Rubens paints his figures and does the background afterward; but then he does it in such a way as to make them tell: he must have painted on white grounds; as a matter of fact, the local tint ought to be transparent; although a half-tint, it imitates, at the beginning, the way the blood shows through the skin. Notice that in all cases, in his studies, the light passages are painted and almost finished over simple rub-ins for the accessories.

1853

January 2.

COLOR is nothing if it is not appropriate to the subject, and if it does not augment the effect of the picture through the power of the imagination. Let men like Boucher and Vanloo paint tones that are light and charming for the eye, etc.

Monday, January 10.

Halévy was relating to Trousseau[1] and myself at dinner, that having heard of an old man beaten by his son he found out that the so-called old man was fifty or fifty-two years old, but he seemed as if twenty years older; it was some retired saloon-keeper. Brutal natures give way quickly, when physical activity no longer keeps them going. On that score, we were saying that people who work with their minds hold together better. It very often happens to me that in the morning I am or think myself ill until the moment when I set to work. I admit the possibility that a boring work would not have the same effect, but what work is there that does not tie down the man who devotes himself to it? I was saying to Trousseau that I am not like those musicians who speak ill of music, etc. He told me that he passionately loved his profession, which is one of the most repugnant that one can follow. He is a man of pleasure, one who must like his ease. Every day, at this season of the year, his alarm clock makes him get up and hasten to his hospital, lift the dressing of wounds, feel the pulse and, what is worse yet, do so for disgusting patients in the foul air where he spends the morning. When he does not feel greatly disposed to do all this it is likely that pride drives him to it. Dupuytren was never once missing from his job, and it is unlikely that it was the assiduity which caused

---

[1] Dr. Armand Trousseau (1801-1867), a distinguished physician of the period, highly considered in society, deputy at the Constitutive Assembly in 1848.

him to die at his too early age. On the contrary, it may perhaps have combated some evil influence which would have ended by killing him sooner.

Thursday, January 27.

Dined at the house of Bixio[2] with d'Argent, Decazes, and Prince Napoleon. Afterwood, went to Manceau's house. From all that, I remember only two or three pieces from the *Magic Flute,* to which Mme Manceau treated us.

In writing, I do not experience anywhere near the difficulty that I find in painting my pictures. To reach the point of satisfying myself, in whatever I may be writing, I need far less attention to my composition than I must have to satisfy myself fully in painting. Unknown to ourselves, we spend our lives in practicing the art of expressing our ideas by means of words. The man who turns over in his head how he will speak, in order to obtain a favor, to get rid of a bore, or to work on the feelings of a fair ingrate, is studying the practice of literature, without a thought that he is doing so. Every day we have to write letters which demand our whole attention and on which, at times, our fate may depend. Such are the reasons why a superior man always writes well, especially when he treats of things which he knows well. That is why women write as well as the greatest men. It is the only art that is practiced by women of slight talent. . . . They have to feign, they must charm, touch, and get rid of people, coming and going. Their presence of mind, and their extreme lucidity in certain cases, find their application here, and marvelously. Moreover, what confirms all this is that, since they do not shine by a great power of imagination, it is above all in the expression of nothings that they are past mistresses.

[2] Alexandre Bixio (1808-1865), politician, founder, with Buloz, of the *Revue des Deux Mondes;* in 1848, Minister of Agriculture. Duke Decazes, the younger (1819-1886), occupied important diplomatic posts under the Restoration. Prince Napoleon (1822–1890), second son of King Jerome, cousin of the Emperor, had just been named hereditary prince, senator, and Councilor of State.

A letter, a note, something which does not demand a long labor of composition, is the field where they triumph.

Monday, February 7.

Today we had the insipid and indecent turmoil of the celebration at the Senate. No order, everybody pell-mell, and ten times as many people invited as the place can contain. Obliged to go there on foot and to return the same way and get the carriage at Saint-Sulpice. . . . What poor dogs! what rascals applauding one another in their embroidered uniforms! What baseness they all exhibit so eagerly!

Friday, March 4.

Cui lecta potenter erit res,
Nec facundia deseret hunc, nec lucidus ordo.[3]

Friday, March 18.

After the meeting of the Council,[4] saw the admirable *Saint Just*[5] by Rubens. The next day, when I tried to recall it by means of a sketch from the engraving, I was able to assure myself that the use of a fine pointed brush instead of a wide flat one determines the smooth and finished execution of Rubens, one in which there is no sharp contrast of planes. This manner leads to a rounder execution, like his; at the same time, it is quicker to give the sense of finish. Moreover, the use of panels almost compels the use of pointed brushes. The smooth and rather soft touch leaves less of roughness in the paint. With ordinary sables and brushes, one gets a hardness, a difficulty in blending the

[3] Horace, *Ars Poetica.*
[4] The Municipal Council where Delacroix wasted so much time.
[5] This picture, commissioned of Rubens about 1685, was taken from a monastery in Antwerp and sold for 1300 florins. It was bought in 1853 for 1600 francs by Napoleon III who presented it to the Museum of Bordeaux. Only the decapitated head of Saint Just is by Rubens; the rest is studio work. Delacroix's copy, made from memory, is now in the Museum of Freiburg, Switzerland (Catalogue Robaut, 1942).

colors, which is almost inevitable; the traces of the brush leave grooves which are impossible to conceal.

Sunday, March 27.

To those who are partisans of form and contour exclusively:

The sculptors are superior to you. When they establish the form, they fulfill all the conditions of their art. At the same time, like the partisans of contour, they seek the nobility of forms and of arrangement. You do not model, since you ignore chiaroscuro, which lives only through establishing the exact relationships of light and shade. With your slaty skies, with the dullness and lack of effect in your flesh tones, you cannot produce the sense of projection. As to the color, which is an element in painting, you pretend to despise it, and with good reason. . . .

Monday, March 28.

To Irene:[6]

"I am the one most punished by my horrible laziness about writing since it deprives me of receiving frequent news of you and, by converse with you, of renewing the charm of youthful memories. In this I am all the more guilty and the enemy of myself, because, isolated as I am, I much more frequently live, in my mind, through the past, than through what surrounds me. I have no sympathy at all with the present time; the ideas in which my contemporaries take such passionate interest leave me absolutely cold; my memories and all my predilections look to the past; all my study turns toward the masterpieces of the earlier centuries. At all events, it is fortunate that, with such a disposition, I have never dreamed of marriage: to a young and amiable wife I should certainly have appeared infinitely more of a bear and a misanthrope than I appear to those who see me only in passing."

To Andrieu:

"I do not deserve as much credit as might be thought for doing a

[6] A letter published in the *Correspondance.* It is addressed to Irene Cervoni, a childhood friend of Delacroix's.

great deal of work, for it is the greatest recreation that I can give myself. . . . Before my easel, I forget the annoyances and cares which fall
to everybody's lot. The essential thing in this world is to combat
ennui and vexation. I think that beyond a doubt, among the pleasures
from which one may choose, he who finds them in a field like painting
must discover charms in it which ordinary amusements do not present.
They are made up above all of the memory we retain of the time
spent on the work, one that remains with us afterward. In the case
of the commoner pleasures, the memory of them is not, ordinarily, the
most agreeable thing; more often it is regret that remains behind, or
even worse things sometimes. Therefore do all the work you can: that
is the whole philosophy of the good way of life."

April 1.

For the first time I have made use of my tickets for the Théatre des
Italiens. . . . How curious! I had all the trouble in the world in deciding
to do so and then, once I had gone there, I took great pleasure in it;
only, I met three people there, and all three of them asked to come and
see me. One of them is Lasteyrie,[7] who would like to bring me his
book on the stained-glass windows; the second is Delécluze,[8] who
tapped me on the shoulder with an amiability one would scarcely
expect from a man who, pen in hand, has flattered me but little
throughout the thirty years or so during which he has been offering
me up as a sacrifice at each Salon. The third personage who asked to
call on me is a young man whom I recall having seen, without knowing
where, and without knowing his name; that form of distraction is
frequent with me.

The memory of that delightful music *(Semiramis)*[9] fills me with
satisfaction and with gentle thoughts on this next day, April 1.

[7] Count Ferdinand de Lasteyrie, politician and archeologist.
[8] Etienne-Jean Delécluze (1781-1863), art critic, defender of the
tradition of David and the academy; it was he who, referring to the *Dante and
Vergil* of the Salon of 1822, treated the picture as a "spattering of colors."
[9] Opera by Rossini.

What remains in my mind is simply the impressions of the sublime, which abound in that work. On the stage, the padding, the transparent planning, and the routine of the master's talent chill the impression; but when I am away from the actors and the theater, memory melts the general effect into an ensemble, a few divine passages transport me and, doing so, remind me of the character I had in my youth.

The other day, Rivet[10] came to see me and, looking at the little *Desdemona at the Feet of her Father*,[11] he could not prevent himself from humming the *Se il padre m'abbandona*, and the tears came to his eyes. It was for our happy days together. I was not his equal, at least not in tenderness and for many another quality, and how much I regret not having cultivated that pure and disinterested friendship! He still sees me, and with pleasure, as I have no doubt; but too many things and too many years have separated us. A few years ago, he said to me, recalling that period of our intimacy at Mantes:[12] "I loved you as one loves a mistress."

At the Italiens, where they are playing to empty benches, there is a certain Cruvelli[13] about whom there is little talk in society, though her talent is far superior to that of La Grisi, who was enchanting everybody when the *Bouffes* were in fashion.

One thing that no one thought of, when Rossini appeared — and for which they forgot to criticize him after giving him so much of criticism — is the point to which he is Romantic. He breaks with the

[10] Baron Rivet, a friend of Delacroix's youth, and his studio comrade; he entered politics, was a deputy in 1848, protested against the coup d'état, and returned to private life during the whole duration of the Second Empire.

[11] Catalogue Robaut, 698, or a repetition of it.

[12] The Rivet family had an estate at Mantes. Delacroix was a visitor and painted there, notably some water colors where one sees the old bridge of Mantes.

[13] Sophie Cruvell called Cruvelli, a well known German singer who made her Paris début in 1853 and entered the Opera in 1854. She became Baroness Vigier and left the stage. Giulia Grisi (1811-1869), celebrated Italian singer who had a great success in Paris between 1840 and 1850.

ancient formulas which, down to his time were illustrated by the greatest examples. It is only with him that one finds those pathetic introductions, and those passages, often very rapid, but which summarize a whole situation for the soul, and do so outside of all the conventions. It is indeed a part, and the only one in his talent, which is shielded from imitation. He is not a colorist in the style of Rubens. I am still speaking of those mysterious passages. Elsewhere he is more crude or more banal, and then he resembles the Fleming; but everywhere, with him, there is Italian grace, and even abuse of that grace.

Sunday, April 3.

Returned to the Italiens: the *Barber*. All those charming motifs, those from *Semiramis* and from the *Barber* are with me continually.

I am working to finish my pictures for the Salon,[14] and all those little pictures for which I am asked. Never has there been so much eagerness for what I do. It seems as if my paintings were a novelty, recently discovered.

Friday, April 8.

Started out quite early to call on the artists who had requested me to visit them. What wretched sores, what incurable diseases of the brain! I had only one compensation, but it was complete: I saw a genuine masterpiece, the portrait that Rodakowski[15] has painted of his mother and has just brought back. This work confirms the preceding one with which I was so much struck at the Exposition.

[14] At the Salon of 1853 Delacroix exhibited the *Saint Stephen* (of the Museum of Arras), (Catalogue Robaut 1211), the *Disciples at Emmaus,* (Robaut, 1192), and the *African Pirates* (Robaut, 1194). As for the small pictures asked for by dealers and collectors after Delacroix had come into fashion, they may be grouped under three chief headings: memories of Morocco, religious pictures (notably a whole series of *Christ on the Lake of Genesareth*), and animals (lions, tigers, etc.).

[15] Henri Rodakowski (1823-1894), a Polish painter who had exhibited a fine portrait of Dembinski at the Salon of 1852; it is now in the Museum of Cracow.

Wednesday, April 13.

One always has to spoil a picture a little bit, in order to finish it. The last touches, which are given to bring about harmony among the parts, take away from the freshness. In order to appear before the public one has to cut away all the happy negligences which are the passion of the artist. I compare these murderous retouchings to those banal turns in music which terminate all melodies, and with those insignificant spaces which the composer is forced to place between the interesting parts of his work, in order to lead from one motif to the other, or to accentuate them. The retouchings, however, are not as harmful to the picture as one might believe when the picture is well thought out and has been done with deep feeling. By effacing the touches, the first ones as well as the last ones, time gives back to the work its definitive ensemble.

Thursday, April 14.

The *Moniteur*[16] would like to have a specimen of my prose: that comes at the wrong time, with all my other occupations.

Went to the house of R. to end the evening by hearing the rehearsal and the choice of pieces that Delsarte is making for his concert. That eternal primitive music, without interruption, is pretty monotonous; a melody of Cherubini's, that he ventured to put amidst all that, seemed to me a thunderbolt of invention.

Friday, April 15.

I went to see the paintings by Courbet.[17] I was astonished at the vigor and the relief in his principal picture; but what a picture! What a subject! The commonness of the forms would do no harm; it is the commonness and the uselessness of the thought which are abominable;

[16] The article on Poussin appeared in *Le Moniteur* in June, 1853.

[17] First meeting of Delacroix and of Courbet, the new star that is rising. If capable of appreciating his talent, Delacroix could not love him. Indeed he had a horror of him, as he had for Balzac, and for the same reasons. They were of profoundly different genius. The principal picture referred to is the celebrated *Bathers,* acquired by Bruyas and now in the Museum of Montpellier. The picture created a scandal.

and if only his idea, common and useless as it is, were clear! What are those two figures doing? A fat bourgeoise is seen from the back, completely nude save for a carelessly painted bit of cloth, covering the lower part of her buttocks; she comes out of a little strip of water which does not seem deep enough for even a foot-bath. She makes a gesture which expresses nothing, and another woman, whom one may suppose to be her maid, is seated on the ground, taking off her shoes and stockings. One sees stockings that have just been taken off, one of them only halfway, I think. Between these two figures there is an exchange of thoughts which one cannot understand. The landscape is of an extraordinary vigor, but Courbet has done no more than enlarge a study exhibited there, near his large canvas; the conclusion is that the figures were put in afterward and without connection with their surroundings. This brings up the question of harmony between the accessories and the principal object, a thing lacking in the majority of great painters. It is not the biggest defect in Courbet. There is also a *Spinner Asleep*,[18] which presents the same qualities, both of vigor and of imitation. The wheel, the distaff — admirable; the dress, the armchair — heavy and without grace. The *Two Wrestlers*[19] show lack of action, and confirm the artist's impotence in the matter of invention. The background kills the figures; it would be necessary to cut off more than three feet all around.

Oh, Rossini! Oh, Mozart! Oh, geniuses inspired in all the arts, who draw from things only such elements of them as are to be shown to the mind! What would you say before these pictures? Oh, *Semiramis!* Oh, entry of the priests to crown Ninias!

Saturday, April 16.

In the morning, someone brings Millet in for a visit. He talks about

---

[18] One of Courbet's sisters, Zélie; now in the Museum of Montpellier.
[19] The *Two Wrestlers* (Hirsch Collection, at Chenonceaux), two academy figures against a background of landscape—the big oval of the Champs Elysées.

Michelangelo and about the Bible which is, he says, the only book that he reads, or practically that. This explains the somewhat ambitious look of his peasants. Moreover he is a peasant himself, and boasts of it. He is certainly of the constellation or squadron of artists with beards who made the Revolution of 1848, or who applauded it, apparently believing that there would be equality of talents as of fortune. As a man, however, Millet seems to me to be above that level; in the small number of his works that I have been able to see, works differing but little one from another, a deep but pretentious feeling evidently struggles against dry or else confused execution in an effort to reveal itself.[20]

Wednesday, April 20.

Called on Princess Marcelline.[21] I arrived in time for a little music. Mme Potocka was there, and looked extremely well. Returning with Grzimala, we talked about Chopin. He told me that Chopin's improvisations were far bolder than his finished compositions. They would doubtless stand in the position of the sketch for the picture as compared with the picture when finished. No, one does not spoil a picture in finishing it! Perhaps there is less room for the imagination when the work is in a sketchy condition. A building which is going up and where the details are not yet indicated gives one an impression that is different from what one gets from the same building when it has received its complement of ornamentation and finish. The same is true of a ruin, which is the more striking because of the lost parts. Its details are effaced or mutilated, just as in the building that is going up one does not yet see more than the rudiments and the vague indication of moldings and of the ornamented parts. The finished building encloses the imagination within a circle and forbids it to go beyond

[20] A judgment, lacking perhaps in good will, but that remains definitive, in Delacroix's mind.

[21] Princess Marcelline Czartoriska and Countess Potocka, women of fashion celebrated for their beauty, and forming with Grzimala and others a group of admirers of Chopin.

that. Perhaps the sketch of a work gives so much pleasure just because each one finishes it to his liking. Artists gifted with very marked senti-ment, when looking at even a fine work and admiring it, criticize it not merely for the faults which are actually there, but with respect to the way in which it differs from their own feeling. When Correggio said his famous *Anch'io son' pittore,* he meant: "There is a fine work, but I should have put into it something which is not there." And so the artist does not spoil the picture by finishing it; only, when he renounces the vagueness of the sketch, he shows himself more completely in his own personality, thus unveiling the whole direction of his talent, but also its limits.

Thursday, April 21.

Went to the sale of pictures by Decamps. . . . I had a deep impression at the sight of several works and sketches by him; they gave me a better idea of his talent than I had before. The drawing of *Christ in the Pretorium,* the *Job,* the small *Miraculous Draught of Fishes,* some landscapes, etc. When one takes up one's pen to describe such ex-pressive objects, one feels sharply, before one's inability to give one's idea in words, the frontiers which separate the arts. One feels a kind of ill humor against oneself at not being able to set down one's memor-ies, which, however, remain just as vividly in the mind after an im-perfect description in words. And so I shall say no more on the subject, save that at this exhibition, as at Delsarte's concert in the evening, I felt for the thousandth time that, with the arts, and even with the best works in them, one must content oneself with the few gleams representing the moments when the artist was inspired.

The *Joshua* by Decamps displeased me at first; when I looked at it closely it was a confused mixture of slighted and twisted forms; at a distance, I understood what made up the beauty of the picture: the distribution of the groups and of the light approaches the sublime.

In the evening, with the trio by Mozart for viola, piano and clarinet, certain passages gave me a delightful sensation, but the rest seemed to me monotonous. When I say that works like these can give only certain moments of pleasure, I do not mean, assuredly, that that is always the fault of the work; in the case of Mozart, I am convinced that the fault was my own. In the first place, certain forms have grown antiquated and have been spoiled by continued repetition at the hands of all succeeding musicians: that is the first thing to impair the freshness of the work. One cannot help being astonished, indeed, at the fact that certain parts have remained so delightful after all the time that has passed (time moves fast for our concepts of the arts), and after so much music, good or bad, has simply made tracings from the lines invented by the enchanting originator. There is another reason why a creation of Mozart's should be less arresting than the brusque novelty which we find today in Beethoven and in Weber: in the first place, they are of our time and, in the second place, they have not the perfection of their illustrious predecessor. The effect is exactly the same as the one I was speaking of on the preceding page: it is the one produced by the sketch as compared with the finished work, the one you get from the ruin of a monument or from its first rudiments as compared with the monument when complete. Mozart is superior to all others in the way he carries his form through to its conclusion. Beauties like those of Racine do not shine in the proximity of works marked by bad taste or spoiled effects; the apparent inferiority of the poet and the musician, however, consecrates them for all time in the admiration of men, and raises them to the height that is most rarely attained.

After these works, or alongside them if you will, are those which, in reality, show considerable negligences, or defects that make them unequal in merit perhaps, but do not reduce the sensation they produce, save to the extent in which the parts are only relatively successful. Rubens is full of these negligences or hasty work. The sublime *Flagellation* at Antwerp, with its ridiculous executioners; the *Martyrdom of Saint Peter* at Cologne, where one finds the same drawback, that is to say an admirable principal figure, and all the other ones bad.

Rossini is a little bit of that family. After the period of novelty which frequently causes everything an artist does to be accepted, as was the case with him, after the time of lassitude and of reaction when almost nothing is seen save his faults, the moment comes when distance consecrates the beauty of his art and renders the spectator indifferent to imperfections. That is what I experienced at that performance of *Semiramis*.

April 26.

Yesterday, at the Tuileries ball, when we were talking about the marriage of an august person, I said that one of the drawbacks of the French character, the one that has perhaps contributed more than any other to the catastrophes and breakdowns in which our history abounds, is the absence in everybody of the feeling for duty. There is not a man here who keeps appointments punctually, who considers himself absolutely bound by a promise; hence, in any number of cases, that elasticity of conscience. We imagine that obligation resides in the thing that pleases us or that is to our interest. With the English race, on the contrary, while it has not to same degree that power of impulse which sweeps us along at every moment, the need for duty is felt by all. Nelson, at Trafalgar, instead of speaking to his sailors of glory and of posterity, simply said to them in his proclamation: "England expects every man to do his duty."

On leaving Boilay's house at half past twelve this evening I hastened to the Théatre des Italiens to get an ice, for all the cafés were closed. I did get one at the café of the Passage de l'Opéra, on the boulevard, and there I met M. Chevandier, who walked home with me. Among other details as to Decamps, he tells me, first, that it is impossible for the latter to use a model when working on his pictures and, in the second place, what seems to me the consequence of this disposition, that he is extremely timid when he works from nature. Independence of imagination before the picture should be entire. The living model, as compared with the figure that you have created and harmonized with the rest of your composition, disturbs the mind and introduces a foreign element into the ensemble of the picture.

Wednesday, April 27.

Dined at the house of Princess Marcelline with Grzimala. Delightful trio by Weber, which unfortunately preceded a trio by Mozart: the order should have been reversed. I had a strong inclination to fall asleep, which was kept within the bounds of respect by the first piece; but I could not hold out when it came to the second one. The form in Mozart, less unforeseen and, I venture to say, more perfect, but above all less modern, got the better of my attention, and digestion triumphed.

Thursday morning, April 28.

A host of *sacrifices* are needed to bring painting to its full effect, and I believe I make a good many. I can't stand it when the artist exhibits himself. There are however very fine things which are conceived with an over-done sense of effect: among such are the works of Rembrandt and, among us, of Decamps. Exaggeration is natural to them and not at all shocking when they employ it. I make this reflection as I look at my portrait of M. Bruyas;[22] Rembrandt would have shown no more than the head; the hands would have been barely indicated, as also the clothing. Without saying that I prefer the method which allows all objects to be seen according to their degree of importance — for I admire Rembrandt exceedingly — I feel that I should be clumsy if I tried those effects. In that respect I am on the side of the Italians. Paul Veronese is the *nec plus ultra* of rendering, in all parts of the picture; the same is true of Rubens, and perhaps he has the advantage over the glorious Paolo in subjects of pathos, where he knows how to attract attention to the principal object by certain exaggerations, thus increasing the power of the expression. On the other hand, there is something artificial in this manner, and it is felt as much or perhaps even more than the sacrifices in Rembrandt's work and the vagueness that he employs so noticeably in the less important passages. Neither the one nor the other satisfies me, as regards myself. I believe that I have

[22] At the Museum of Montpellier, Bruyas is shown seated in an armchair; a half-length portrait, the left hand holding a handkerchief.

noticed quite often that my own desire is that no artifice be felt but that, none the less, one's interest be directed to the proper place; but that result, again, is to be obtained only by sacrifices; they would have to be infinitely more delicate than those in Rembrandt's style, in order to respond to my feeling.

My recollection of the great painters does not present me at this moment with an absolute model of that perfection which I ask for. Poussin never sought it and did not desire it; his figures are planted one beside the other like statues; does that come from the habit he had, as we are told, of making small models in order to get his shadows exactly? If he does obtain this latter advantage, I am less grateful to him for it than if he had given a more unified relationship among his personages, even if with less of exactitude in the observation of the effect. Paul Veronese is infinitely more harmonious (I am speaking here only of the matter of effect), but there is a scattering of one's interest in looking at his picture. On the other hand, the nature of his compositions, which are very often conversation pieces, or subjects centered about an anecdote, does not make so great a demand for concentration of interest. In pictures by him where the number of actors is more limited, his effects have something of the banal and conventional. He distributes the light in a practically uniform manner and, with him as with Rubens and many other great painters, one may observe, while on this point, that he repeats certain habits of execution to an exaggerated degree. They were doubtless led to this by the great number of commissions which they received; they were workmen to a far greater extent than we think, and it was as such that they regarded themselves. The painters of the fifteenth century painted saddles, banners, and shields; the same was done by the makers of the great church windows. The profession of the latter men fused with that of the painter as, today, it does with that of the house-painter.

It is to the glory of the two great French painters, Poussin and Lesueur, to have sought — and successfully — to escape from this banality. In this respect, not only do they recall the naiveté of the primitives of Flanders and of Italy, among whom frankness of expression is never spoiled by any habit of execution but, even more, they open up a whole new path to the future. Although they were immediately followed by schools representing a decadence, in which the domination of habit — especially that of going to study the contemporary masters of Italy — soon arrested the impulse toward the study of truth, Poussin and Lesueur nevertheless prepare the way for the modern schools, which have broken with convention and sought at the very source of things the effect on the imagination which is proper to the realm of painting. If these later schools did not follow exactly in the steps of those great men, they at least recognized in the masters an ardent protest against academic conventions and, consequently, against bad taste. David, Gros, and Prud'hon, whatever differences one may notice in their style, kept their eyes fixed on those two fathers of French art; in a word, they consecrated the artist's independence of tradition by teaching him that, whatever its utility, he must have the courage to stand by his own sentiment, and prefer that to everything else.

The numerous writers who have treated the history of Poussin have not considered him sufficiently as an innovator of the rarest kind. The style of painting amid which he was brought up and against which he protested by his works held sway over the entire domain of the arts; and despite the long career of Poussin its influence survived him. The decadent schools of Italy clasped hands with the schools of men like Lebrun, Jouvenet and, at a still later time, with men like Vanloo and those who succeeded them. Lesueur and Poussin did not arrest that torrent. When Poussin arrived in Italy, he found the Carracci and their successors carried to the clouds and *dispensing glory*. There was no complete education for an artist without the visit to Italy, but that did not mean that he was sent there to study true models, like the antique and the masters of the sixteenth century. The Carracci and their pupils had got a monopoly of all possible reputation, and they were the dispensers of glory, which is to say that they exalted only what resembled themselves; they played politics, with all the authority they could derive from their temporary success, to crush everything which tended to get out of the beaten track. Domenichino, who had himself come forth from that school but who was led by the sincerity of his genius to seek true expression and effect, becomes the object of universal hatred and persecution. They went so far that his life was threatened, and the jealous fury of his enemies compelled him to hide and almost to disappear. This great painter added to the true modesty almost inseparable from great talents the timidity of a gentle and melancholy character; it is probable that this universal conspiracy contributed to shorten his days.

At the height of this bitter war waged by everyone against a man who did not defend himself, even by his works, Poussin, still unknown, a stranger to all cliques. . . .

This independence of all convention appears again strongly with Poussin, in his landscape, etc. As a scrupulous and poetic observer both of history and of the movements of the human heart, Poussin is a unique painter! [23]

Monday May 2.

Dined at the house of Pierret with Riesener, his friend Lassus, Feuillet and Durieu. I brought away the unhappy impression, which still lasts today and which my work cannot diminish, of the secret enmity of those men toward me. Underneath it are a host of sentiments which, at times, do not even take the trouble to wear a mask. . . . I am isolated among these former friends! . . . There is an infinite number of things

[23] In this passage, Delacroix rapidly notes the ideas which he will develop in his articles on Poussin for *Le Moniteur* of June, 1853. These articles have been collected in the *Œuvres Litteraires* of Delacroix (Paris, Cres, 1928). A difference in tone, as to Poussin, is to be noted here, if one recalls his thoughts on the master in earlier pages. His reading of history, as a preparation for his articles, had probably made him see a parallel between the treatment of the masters by the academies of the seventeenth century and those of his own day.

for which they cannot pardon me, most prominently, the advantages over them that chance has given to me.

"Voltaire," says Sainte-Beuve,[24] "considering Gui Patin from the ensemble of his letters, judged him severely and without real justice. 'He serves to show,' writes Voltaire, 'how unfaithful as guides to history are the contemporary authors who hastily write down the news of the day. Such news is often found to be false or disfigured by malignity; moreover, this multitude of small facts is rarely precious save for small minds.' *Small minds,*" adds Sainte-Beuve, "I do not like people to say that about others, especially when those others compose an entire class, a natural group; it is too condensed and easy a manner of indicating that one is oneself of a different group."

For my own part, I think that Sainte-Beuve, who belongs in that group of anecdote writers which Voltaire so strongly disliked, is wrong in reproving him for attacking a group, as he calls it. To be sure, fools form a group which is none the more respectable for being so numerous. It is natural to attack what one does not like, without considering whether that something forms a group or not. As for me, I am of the opinion of Voltaire: I have always detested the collectors and retailers of anecdotes, especially those of the day before, which are precisely of the type that displeased Voltaire. Poor Beyle had a weakness for feeding on such stuff. Mérimée is the same way, and it is one thing that makes him tiresome to me. An anecdote must come into the conversation like anything else; but to center interest on that alone is to imitate the collectors of curiosities, another group that I cannot stand: they disgust you with beautiful things by tiring your eyes with their abundance and confusion instead of giving accent to a small number of objects through their choice and their placing in a light which suits them.

[24] Article on Gui Patin, of April 25th, 1853, published in the *Causeries du Lundi.*

Tuesday, May 3.

Invited by Nieuwerkerke[25] to the Louvre for a discourse on art or the progress of art by a certain Ravaisson. Big reunion of artists, of semi-artists, of priests, and of women. After having waited a proper length of time for the arrival first of Princess Mathilde and then, for a very long time beside, that of M. Fould, the professor began, with a dry voice and a slightly Gascon accent. There is no one like the men of that country for having a blank mind and for making a speech like this one, of which, however, I heard only half. He gave us Neo-Christian ideas in all their purity: the Beautiful is only found at a given point which is situated — almost exclusively — between the thirteenth and the fifteenth century; Giotto and, I believe, Perugino are the culminating point; Raphael declines almost immediately after his first trial pieces; the Antique is to be esteemed only in about half of its attempts; we must detest it in its impurities; he arraigns it because of the abuses of it made in the eighteenth century. The saturnalias of Boucher and of Voltaire who, according to the professor, certainly preferred no other than immodest paintings, sufficed to make us hate the whole of that phase of the Antique — unhappily not separable from it — consisting of satyrs, nymphs pursued, and all the other erotic subjects. There is no great artist without the friendship of a hero or of a great spirit of some other kind. If Phidias is so great it is only because of the friendship of Pericles. . . . Without Dante, Giotto does not count. What a queer type of affection! Aristotle, he says at the outset, puts at the head or the end of his treatise on aesthetics a statement that the most beautiful reasonings on the Beautiful have never caused anyone and will never cause anyone to discover the Beautiful. Everyone must have wondered, then, what the professor was doing there. After having spoken of Voltaire's opinion on the arts, he hails poor baron S. before

---

[25] Count de Nieuwerkerke (1811-1892) sculptor and director of fine arts from 1849 to the end of the Empire. He was hostile to Delacroix, first as an artist and then as a man, because of the cordiality that Princess Mathilde felt for the master.

his tribunal, and would have got a good answer from him, if the accused could have answered. That poor baron, according to him, sees the modern coming of the Beautiful only at a time when a government by the two Chambers shall have spread all over Europe and when the National Guard shall have been installed among all peoples. That was the capital joke of the lecture and it caused an explosion of priestly gaiety such as is peculiar to the men of the Church, whose black robes were to be seen here and there in that very mixed audience.

I went away, perhaps a little scandalously after that first part, of which I give only a pale résumé. I was encouraged to do so by the example of a few people who, like myself, found that they had been sufficiently edified on the Beautiful.

From there, I went on foot to meet Rivet, enjoying the magnificent weather and the fact that I could move my legs in freedom, after the captivity I had just endured.

Sunday, May 8.

Man is capable of the most diverse things. . . .

La Bruyère says: "It is an excess of confidence in parents to hope for everything from the good education of their children, it is a great mistake to expect nothing from it and to neglect it. . . ." Further on: "Even were it true, as some say, that education does not give to man a different heart or a different complexion, that it changes nothing in his fundamental nature and touches the surface alone, I should not cease from saying that it is not useless for him."

I am completely of his opinion, and I add that education continues throughout our lives; I define it as the cultivation of our spirit and of our mind as a result of our own fostering and of outer circumstances. Intercourse with decent or bad people is the good or bad education which goes on throughout one's life. The mind lifts up upon contact with honest minds; it is the same with the spirit. We harden in the society of hard and cold people, and if it were possible for a man of merely ordinary virtue to live among scoundrels he must come finally to resemble them, however little he did so at the beginning.

Tried all day long to clear up my article on Poussin. I am coming to the conclusion that there is only one way to succeed with this, if indeed I can reach such a result: it is to keep my mind off painting until the article is finished. This devil of a trade demands a greater intensity than I am accustomed to give to painting, and yet I write with great facility; I could fill whole pages with hardly any corrections. I believe I noted in this very copy-book that I find more ease in writing than in my own work. The trouble I am going through comes from having to do my work within certain limits, and within them I am obliged to do many different things; I lack a fixed method for coördinating the parts, for arranging them in their order, especially when I have made so many notes in order to remember what I determined to emphasize in my prose.

Therefore, only assiduous application to the one purpose can help me in this work. And so I do not dare to think of painting for fear of sending the whole business to the devil. I am constantly meditating a work in the manner of the *Spectator*:[26] a short article, of three or four pages or even less, on the first subject that comes to mind. I will take the responsibility of thinking out as many as are demanded, for I have an inexhaustible quarry of them.

Monday, May 9.

A delightful morning. Reached the oak of Antin, which I did not recognize — it seemed so small to me; jotted down some new observations, similar to those which I have noted here, on the effect produced by unfinished things: sketches, lay-ins, etc.

I get the same impression from disproportion. Perfect artists do not astonish us so much through their perfection itself; what we feel, with them, is that there is no incongruity in their work, to reveal how perfect and well-proportioned a whole they have produced. When, on the contrary, I approach this magnificent tree and stand beneath its immense branches, perceiving parts only in their relation with the ensemble, I am struck by its grandeur. And so I am led to infer that some of the effect produced by the statues of Michelangelo is due to certain disproportionate or unfinished parts which augment the importance of the parts which are complete. If one can judge of his paintings through engravings, it seems to me that they do not present this defect to the same degree. I have often told myself that, whatever he himself thought, he was more of a painter than a sculptor. In his sculpture, he does not proceed as did the ancients, which is to say by the masses; it always seems as if he had drawn an outline in his mind and then set himself to fill it in, as a painter does. One would say that his figure or his group presents itself to him from one angle alone; that is the painter. Hence, when one must change one's position as sculpture

[26] Addison's *Spectator;* its essay form pleased Delacroix, who had always read it with interest.

demands, there are twisted limbs and planes that lack exactitude, in a word everything that one does not see in the antique.

Monday, May 9. [Second entry].[27]

I am at Champrosay since Saturday. I take a solitary walk in the forest while waiting for my room to be arranged so that I can get back to the famous Poussin. Noticing the Antin oak from a distance, I did not recognize it at first, finding it so ordinary, and my mind went back to an observation I had set down in my notebook about two weeks ago, as to the effect of the sketch in its relation to the finished work. I said that the sketch of a picture or a monument — and the same is true of a ruin or, in a word any work of the imagination in which parts are lacking — ought to react on the soul in just the proportion that we have to add to the work, while it is producing its impression on us. I add that perfect works, like those of a Racine or of a Mozart, do not, at the first moment, produce as much effect as those of less correct or even careless geniuses, who give you salient parts standing out in all the stronger relief because others, beside them, are vague or completely bad.

Standing before this fine tree (the Antin oak) which is so well proportioned, I find a new confirmation of these ideas. At the distance necessary for the eye to seize it as a whole, it seems to be of ordinary size; if I place myself under its branches the impression changes completely: perceiving only the trunk which I almost touch and the springing-point of the thick branches which spread out over my head like the immense arms of the giant of the forest, I am astonished at the grandeur of its details; in a word I see it as big, and even terrifying in its bigness.

Can it be that disproportion is one of the conditions which compel admiration? If, on one side, Mozart, Cimarosa, and Racine cause less

---

[27] This passage comes from a notebook of 1857 in which Delacroix — re-reading what he had written four years previously — amplifies his ideas, which are here given as a sequel to the original note.

of astonishment by reason of the admirable proportion in their works, do not Shakespeare, Michelangelo and Beethoven owe a part of their effect to an opposite course? In my own opinion, that is the fact.

The antique never surprises, never gives that gigantic and exaggerated effect. One finds oneself at ease with those admirable creations; reflection alone makes them seem big and places them on their incomparable height. Michelangelo astonishes,[28] and brings into the soul a troubled sentiment which amounts to admiration, but one is not long in perceiving shocking incongruities which are, in his art, the consequence of too hasty work, caused either by the fire with which the artist engaged upon it or else by the fatigue which probably seized him at the end of a labor impossible of completion.

That last cause is evident in his statues, as we should know even had his historians not taken care to inform us that he was almost always seized with disgust when finishing, because of the impossibility, as they say, of rendering his sublime ideas. One sees clearly, from the parts left in a sketchy condition, from feet not yet cut from the block, and others where the material was lacking, that the vice of the work comes rather from the manner of conceiving and executing than from the extraordinary demands of a genius made for higher attainments and arrested before he could content himself. It is more probable that his conception was vague, and that he counted too much on the inspiration of the moment for the development of his thought; if he often stopped in his discouragement, the reason is that he could really do no more.

Friday, May 13.

Jenny and I followed the alley of the Ermitage as far as the big oak, at the foot of which we took a rest; before that we had entered the Ermitage, of which a part is for sale. There is a manor such as I ought to have! The garden, which is only a vegetable garden, is charming; it is still full of old trees which have given their fruits to the environs.

[28] At an earlier time, in the *Revue de Paris* of 1830, Delacroix had published a study of Michelangelo where these ideas are developed.

Those knotty trunks, twisted by the years, still cover themselves with magnificent fruits and flowers, amidst those buildings ruined not by time but by the hand of man. One is saddened before this inhuman spectacle at the stupid rage for demolishing which has marked our periods of discord. To tear down, to tear out, to burn, that is what the fanatics of liberty know how to do quite as well as the fanatics of religion; that is the starting-point for the one group as for the other when it is unchained; but that is also where the brutal impulse stops. To erect something durable, to mark its passage with anything but ruins — that is what the blind proletariat is impotent to do. I observed, likewise, how steadily works due to the spirit of continuity, conceived in a great idea of duration and executed with the necessary care, bear the seal of strength even in their remains, and that it is almost impossible to make these fragments disappear completely. Those ancient corporations, above all the monks, believe themselves to be eternal, for they seem to have laid their foundations for centuries of centuries. What remains of the old walls puts to shame the shoddy work of the more modern and ignoble buildings that have been added to them. The proportion in these fragments has about it something gigantic when compared with what private individuals are doing under our eyes every day.

I was thinking, at the same time, that it was somewhat the same for the work of a man of talent. In sculpture, this is beyond dispute, for the clumsiest restorations still let one see what belongs to the original; but in painting itself, fragile as it is, and sometimes quite massacred by unskilful retouching, the disposition, the character, and a certain ineffaceable imprint show the hand and the conception of a great artist.

Monday, May 16.

Spent the whole day in my room in delightful idleness, writing a little in this book, and reading the *Revue Britannique,* especially the part about the white niece of Uncle Tom when Jonathan, the American, crosses Africa on a dromedary, seeking his Arab mistress at the center of that continent.

Girardin[29] still believes firmly in the attainment of universal well-being, and one of the means of producing it, one that he returns to with predilection, is the ploughing, by machinery and on a large scale, of all the lands of France. He thinks he is contributing greatly to the happiness of mankind by dispensing with work; he pretends to think that all those unfortunate beings who wrest their food from the earth, painfully — as I admit, but with the feeling of their energy and of their well-employed perseverance, will be very moral and well satisfied with themselves when this land, which was their fatherland at all events, where their children were born and in which they buried their parents, should no longer be anything more than a place for the manu-facture of products, exploited by the great arms of a machine, and yielding up the greater part of its production to the impure and god-less hands of speculators. Will steam stop before churches and ceme-teries? And will the Frenchmen, returning to his fatherland after some years, be reduced to asking where it was that his village stood, and where the grave of his fathers was? For villages will be as useless as the rest; villagers are those who cultivate the soil, for they have to stay in the place where their care is required at every moment. It will be necessary to build cities on the basis of this workless and disinherited mass of people, who will no longer find anything to do in the fields, it will be necessary to construct for them immense barracks where they will lodge pell-mell. And when they are there, the Fleming beside the man of Marseilles, of Normandy and of Alsace, what will they have to do but read the quotations in the newspaper, not to see whether the harvest has been good in their beloved fields, not to see if they can advantageously sell their wheat, their hay, or their grapes, but to see whether their stocks in the unanimous universal property are going up

[29] Emile de Girardin (1802-1881), the famous publicist, at that time director of *La Presse*. Exiled after the coup d'état, he had returned to France at the beginning of 1852, thanks to his relations with Prince Napoleon.

or down? They will have paper instead of land! They will go to the billiard-rooms to gamble with this paper against that of their unknown neighbors, different in customs and in speech, and when they are ruined, will they at least have the chance they once had, when hail had destroyed their fruits or harvest, of repairing their misfortune by dint of work and constancy, or at least of drawing some consolation from the hope of a better year, from the sight of that field which they had watered so often with their sweat?

O unworthy philanthropists! O philosophers without heart and without imagination! You think that man is a machine, like your other machines; you degrade him from his most sacred rights, under pretext of saving him from labors which you affect to look on as vile and which are the law of his being, not only the one which commands that he himself create resources against need, but the one which at the same time raises him in his own eyes and employs the short span of time given him in a way that is almost sacred. O wretched journalists, scribblers and cracked-brained schemers! Instead of transforming the human race into a vile herd, let it have its true heritage — its attachment, its devotion to the soil! And then when new invasions of barbarians threaten what they still call their fatherland, they will rise with joy to defend it. They will not fight to defend the property of the machines, any more than those poor Russians, those poor regimented serfs would work for their masters and their emperor, when they came here to avenge their quarrels. Alas, poor peasants, poor villagers! The hypocritical preaching you have offered them has already borne its fruits all too well! If your machine does not do its work on the earth, it is already working in their abused imagination. Their ideas of a general dividing-up, of leisure and of continual pleasure, are realized in these unworthy projects. They are already abandoning the work of the field in haphazard fashion and with the most ill-founded hopes; they are rushing headlong to the cities, where nothing but disappointment awaits them; there they complete the perversion of those feelings of dignity offered by the love of labor, and the more your machines feed them the more they will become degraded! What a noble spectacle in this best of centuries — human cattle fattened by the philosophers!

Friday, May 20.

While at lunch, read the article by Peisse, who surveys the Salon as a whole and who inquires into the present-day tendencies into the arts. Quite correctly, he sees them in the *picturesque,* which he believes to be an inferior tendency. Yes, if it is only a question of creating an effect for the eyes by an arrangement of lines and colors, in other words an arabesque; but if, to a composition which is already interesting through the choice of subject, you add a disposition of lines which augments the impression, if you add chiaroscuro which seizes the imagination, and color adapted to the characters, you have solved a more difficult problem you have entered a realm of superior ideas, doing what the musician does when, to a single theme, he adds the resources of harmony and its combinations. Peisse calls *musical* that tendency of which he speaks; he uses the word in disparagement, while I, for my part, consider it as praiseworthy as any other.

His friend Chenavard has insinuated into his mind his own theories of the arts, and Chenavard considers that music is an inferior art; he has that French type of mind which needs ideas that can be expressed in words; as to those before which speech is impotent, he cuts them off from the domain of the arts. Even if we admit that drawing is everything, it is not, evidently, a matter of pure and simple form. Within the contour which suffices for such a purpose, there is coarseness or there is grace: a contour drawn by Raphael will have a different charm from what it would have if drawn by Chenavard. What could be vaguer or more inexplicable than the impression it produces? Are we to establish degrees of nobility among the feelings? That is what is done by the learned and unfortunately too cold Chenavard. He puts literature in the first rank; painting comes next, and music is only last. That would perhaps be true if one of them could contain the others or replace them; the trouble is that if words can easily give a general idea of a painting or a symphony, the reader is still at a loss to understand them because they are themselves so lacking in exactitude. One must see the things that are made for the eyes; one must hear the things that are made for the ears. When one writes things that are to be spoken, they will produce more effect coming from the lips of an orator than they will if merely read. A great actor will transform a piece, so to speak, by his accent. . . . I stop here.

Saturday, May 21.

All morning I worked at pastels of the lions and the trees which I had studied the day before at the Jardin des Plantes; at about quarter past two, I went to call for Pierret and Riesener; I found Pierret very much changed. Why is it that when I meet two such old friends here in the country, under the open sky and amidst the beauties of the spring, the sight of them does not give me the complete happiness that I should not have failed to get in the past? I felt myself irresistibly moved by feelings which they did not have: I was in the presence of witnesses and not of friends. I took them to the house, and then to the forest. Riesener began again with his criticism of this search for a certain finish in my small pictures, which seem to him to lose heavily as compared with what I get from the sketch or from things done in more rapid fashion and at a single go. Perhaps he is right, and perhaps he is wrong. Pierret said, probably to contradict him, that things ought to be the way the painter feels, and that the interest of the work takes precedence over all those matters of touch and of frankness. I answered him with the observation that I set down in this book a few days ago regarding the unfailing effect of the sketch as compared to the finished picture, which is always somewhat spoiled as to the touch, but where the harmony and depth of the expression become a compensation.

At the oak called *le Prieur,* I showed them how much more striking the isolated parts appeared; in a word, the old story of the comparison between Racine and Shakespeare. They reminded me of my warmth, some months ago, when I was correcting myself by re-reading, or by reseeing at the theater, *Cinna* and certain pieces by Racine; they confessed to remembering the emotion which I had communicated when I spoke to them of those matters.

After dinner, they looked over the photographs which I owe to the kindness of Durieu. I made them try the experiment which I had made myself, without thinking of it, two days before: which is to say that after having examined these photographs of nude models, some of them poorly built, overdeveloped in places and producing a rather disagreeable effect, I displayed some engravings by Marcantonio. We had a feeling of repulsion, almost of disgust, at their incorrectness, their mannerism, and their lack of naturalness; and we felt these things despite the virtue of style: it is the only one to be admired in that artist, but we were not admiring it at that moment. As a matter of fact, let a man of genius make use of the daguerreotype as it is to be used, and he will raise himself to a height that we do not know. It is especially when one is looking at these engravings which pass for the masterpieces of the Italian school and which have wearied the admiration of all painters, that one feels the exactitude of Poussin's saying that "Raphael is an ass compared to the ancients." Down to the present this machine-art has rendered us only a detestable service: it spoils the masterpieces for us, without completely satisfying us.

Sunday, May 22.

At Villot's house. Talked at dinner about *table-tipping:* Mme Villot has seen and made experiments; she has almost come to believe that there is something supernatural about it. As a matter of fact, after dinner I myself had an experience through my eyes, if not otherwise, of that famous discovery. Genevieve, the housemaid, caused a hat to turn; a center table turned visibly and tilted up a foot on one side; but after having seated ourselves for half an hour around the big dining table, it was impossible to budge it from its natural immobility. Those ladies pretended that I was not a good subject; the same applied to one or two other persons present.

Man makes progress in all directions: he takes command over matter, as is incontestably shown, but he does not learn how to command himself. Build your railroads and your telegraph lines, cross lands and seas in the twinkling of an eye, but let us see you direct the passions as you direct gas balloons! Above all, let us see you abolish the evil passions, which have not lost their detestable power over men's hearts despite the liberal and fraternal maxims of the period! Therein lies the problem of progress, and even of true happiness. But it seems, quite on the contrary, that our instincts of covetousness and of selfish enjoyment are infinitely more excited by all these materialistic advances.

The desire for a happiness which is impossible because it would be obtained without regard to the peace of the soul always manages to place itself beside each new scientific conquest, and seems to render more distant the chimera of that happiness of the senses which people always have in mind. Rascality and treachery, ingratitude and venal baseness still keep watch in men's hearts! Even for the inventors of your ingenious modern appliances, you do not have the gratitude which it seems you should owe them, if in reality you consider yourself happy by means of their effort. Instead of raising statues to them and making them the first to enjoy that well-being which is so longed for, you let them die in obscurity or, under your very eyes, you permit people to try to take away the merit of their inventions.

Sunday, May 29.

All these last days have flowed away rapidly, half occupied with work and half with going out; but there has been much less of the latter thing, because of the rain that we are having these last two or three days. Sometimes I want to throw Poussin out of the window, sometimes I pick him up again with fury or, at other times, in a more reasonable way.

Mme Barbier, who came to spend the day, despite this frightful weather, has invited me to dinner; I got pleasure and my usual satisfaction from conversation out of the talk of this witty woman; beside wit, however, one asks for the small amenities of human society — which the rustics of our day may criticize, but which add to talk the flavor that is necessary. Our fathers must have had a prodigiously good time, for those amenities were infinitely more general, and what still remains of politeness in our nation, despite the coarseness which is invading everything, proves what society must have been. For those who feel this kind of charm, there is no material progress that can compensate for it. It is not astonishing that present-day society is looked on as insipid. The revolution that is taking place in the masses is continually filling it up with parvenus; or rather we are not seeing society as it was: what is given the name is indeed the most tiresome thing. What pleasure can you find among tradesmen who have gotten rich, and who today constitute practically the whole of the upper classes? The very limited ideas of the counting-house in conflict with the ambition to appear distinguished offer the silliest of contrasts. What shall I say to M. Minoret, for example, who has neither education, nor any desire to talk?

One ought to cultivate amiable people, there are few enough of them; with amiable people, frivolity is charming, but frivolity in the drawing-room of people who have fixed up their counters and put their ledgers in order so as to give a ball, who have dressed up their clerks in Sunday clothes so that they may offer their hand to the ladies? I prefer being in the company of peasants!

Came home about ten o'clock; the rain gave a delightful odor to all the leaves in their freshness; the stars were brilliant — but above all, that odor! Toward Gibert's vegetable garden, and as far as Quantinet's, an odor that reached back to my youth, so penetrating, so delicious, that there is nothing I can compare it with. I walked back over the ground five or six times; I couldn't tear myself away. It reminded me of the odor of certain little plants in the vegetable garden

I used to see at Augerville,[30] on the grounds of M. Castillon, Sr. — plants that have a kind of fruit which bursts in your hand.

In her conversation of this evening, Mme Barbier spoke to me of Pauline Villot;[31] although she gave me a glimpse of the animosity which she possibly has a right to feel, as she clearly indicated, she caused me to think deeply of her virtues, of her devotion — as she understands it, of the affection she has for me and that I, in turn, can trace in myself with respect to her; there are beings who are born to mean much to each other: the memory of her pleases me and always moves me.

There are few people in whom I cannot take pleasure; and when one has the desire to please them, there are but few who do not make you some return for your effort; it is vain for me to search my memory for the least entertaining people, it seems to me that through one's mere desire to be on the best possible terms with them, their warmth, as much of it as they have (and I am speaking of the coldest and most crabbed of them), comes to the surface, shows itself to you, answers you, and keeps up your good humor. The fact that you forget them quickly and that the memory of them does not awaken in you the least spark of sentiment should not make you conclude that you are an ingrate, nor that they are any the more interesting. It is the case of two metals, two bodies of whatever kind, which are inert, each taken separately, and which yet send forth a little fire when they come into contact with each other. Keep them apart, and they simply remain in their state of insensibility.

When I think of Pierret and of Riesener without seeing them, I am like the metal, insensible. When I am with them, after the first moments needed to warm up that ice, I get back the movements of former times: I melt when I am near them. Perhaps they themselves are astonished to feel themselves softening, but I will wager that I retain for a longer time than they the shock from that spark of memory.

[30] Near Malesherbes, where the property of Berryer was situated.
[31] Her sister-in-law.

No base interest separates me from them. When, in my dreams, I see the people who are my enemies, the sight of whom offends me during my waking hours, I find them charming; I chat with them then as if they were my friends, and I feel quite astonished at finding them so amiable: with the simplicity of the somnambulist, I tell myself that I had not appreciated them enough and that I did not do them justice; I promise myself to look them up and to see them. Is it that when I dream I divine their qualities, or is it that, when awake, my malice — if I really have as much of it as they — insists on seeing only their defects; or again, is it simply that I am better when I am asleep?

Tuesday, May 31.

Rain or fog all day long. I did not leave my room, but made good use of my time by working at the article. Certain fables of La Fontaine's enchanted me.

Went out while it was still daylight and took a walk on the road to Soisy, still in the same state of mind. Fog and bad weather count for nothing in the sadness of the mind; it is when there is night in our soul that everything seems to us either lugubrious or unbearable, and it is not enough to be free from real causes for sadness, the state of one's health is enough to change everything. That infamous thing called digestion is the great arbiter of our feelings.

Wednesday, June 1.

On opening the window of the studio in the morning, always with this same misty weather, I am as if intoxicated with the odor exhaled by all this verdure, drenched with raindrops, and with all these flowers, bent over and ravaged, but still beautiful. Of what pleasures is the city man not deprived, the miserable employee or lawyer who breathes no other odor than that of dusty papers or of the mud of that miserable Paris! What compensation for the peasant, for the man of the fields! What perfume there is in this damp earth and in these trees! That strong odor of the woods, how penetrating it is, and how immediately it awakens gracious and pure memories, memories of one's earliest youth and of feelings which belong to the depth of the soul! O beloved scenes where once I saw you, dear people whom I am to see no more, beloved days that delighted me and that are gone! How many times has the sight of this verdure and this delightful odor of the woods awakened memories which are the asylum, the blessed refuge to which the spirit takes wings, so as to withdraw from daily cares! This affection which consoles me and which alone gives my heart a movement like that of the past, for how long a time will fate let me keep it?

Sunday, June 5.

All these last days, practically the same life. Worked, and almost finished the article; went out about three o'clock usually, twice or thrice to the alley of the Ermitage, among other walks. Ravishing view: the garden of Armide. The new greens, the leaves, now being full grown, give a grace, a richness of foliage which is superb. Rounded luxuriance is the dominant note. Trunks have a decoration of leaves: the walnut with its yellowish tone against patches of bluish distance. The whole has a look of fairyland and enchantment.

This evening, after dinner, went out in the twilight; instead of going to the Barbiers', took a walk along the road to Soisy. A charming star above the great poplar trees of the road on the way out. Delightfully cool weather.

The day before, took a walk before dinner with Jenny; I was so happy at the pleasure which she had, sick as she was.

Monday, June 6.

On opening my window this morning to taste the most delightful weather in the world and to regret that one must ever plunge into miserable papers, I see two swallows alight in the alley of the garden; I noticed that they walked very slowly with a waddling gait. When they want to clear a space of no more than two feet, they use their wings. Nature, which has endowed them with such big wings, has not given them nimble feet.

The spectacle one has from these windows is delightful at every hour of the day: I cannot tear myself away from it. The odor of the leaves and of the flowers and the garden adds even more to this pleasure.

Tuesday, June 7.

Finished the article.

At about four o'clock, took a walk in the forest. I saw again the same things as the other day, in that alley which goes to the Ermitage; they were illumined in the same way, and yet they did not give me the same pleasure.

Dined at Mme Barbier's; all evening, the talk was only of love and its singularities. She had the drollest idea in the world when we were speaking of the number of children that one finds at Soisy. "As a matter of fact," said she, "what could they do in such a dull place? There is no view: they have got to amuse themselves somehow."

On returning in the evening, the stars, which had not been seen for some days, shone with their full brilliance. What a spectacle, above those black masses formed by the trees, or perceived through the branches! I went to Gibert's garden, and again I got that divine odor which had already charmed me, but a little bit weakened. I left there with regret.

And now finally, I think I shall get off tomorrow. Perhaps I am experiencing a little less pleasure at this moment, not because I have been here for a long time, but because I have decided to leave. I often ask myself, thinking of the bitterness that always follows upon every pleasure: can one be really happy in a situation which must end? That apprehension as to the rapidity of time and the coming void always manages to spoil every enjoyment.

Saturday, June 11.

Finally got to work at a pretty good pace. It seemed to me that I should never be able to paint any more.

Sunday, June 26.

This morning, the article on Poussin appeared. Even yesterday I was writing to Mérimée that I had no news of it, and in the evening, as I was having dinner, they sent me the proofs of it to correct in haste.

I did my days' work at the Hôtel de Ville; I returned on foot. Stopped a long time at Saint-Eustache to hear vespers: that made me understand for a few moments the pleasure there is in being devout. I saw all the people connected with the church passing and repassing, from the cripple who gives you holy water, muffled up like a personage in a Rembrandt, to the priest in a canon's hood and with his cope of ceremony.

Wednesday, June 29.

Delightful music at the house of the amiable Princess Marcelline.[32] The memory of the *Fantasia* by Mozart, a grave piece, at moments touching on the terrible, one whose title is lighter than the character of the piece would require. A sonata by Beethoven that I knew already, but admirable. Undoubtedly I like it a great deal, especially in the part where the imagination shares his grief. The man is always sad. Mozart is a modern also, which is to say one who does not fear to touch on the melancholy side of things, like the men of his time (French gaiety, with its demand that we deal only with attractive things, banishes from conversation and the arts anything that saddens and recalls our unhappy condition); but Mozart unites the hint of delightful sadness that we need, with the serenity and the easy elegance of a mind that has the happiness of seeing the agreeable side of things also. I took issue with their friend R., who does not love Cimarosa, who does not feel him, as he said, with a certain self-satisfaction. What a different man Chopin is! Just see, I told them, how he is of his time, how he makes use of the progress that others have made in his art! How he adores Mozart, and how little he resembles him! His friend Kwiatkowski often reproached him with certain Italian

[32] Princess Czartoriska.

reminiscenses which, in spite of him, smell of the modern productions of men like Bellini, etc. That is a thing that I don't quite like either. But what charm! And what novelty!

July 1.

There is something to be written on Romanticism.

M. Menneval related to Vieillard, who repeats it to me today, this detail about Emperor Napoleon I: he was visiting a monument which was under construction and for which, doubtless, he had examined the estimates; while walking over a place covered with plaques of marble, he tapped with his foot. Then he repeated the experiment he seemed to be making with a cane that he asked for; he then inquired the thickness of each marble plaque. On receiving his reply he caused a workman to be summoned and, in his presence, had the man raise up one of the pieces of marble, which was found to be of half the thickness that he had been told.

Sunday, July 10.

After my work at the Salon, I went to examine the pictures from the standpoint of the distribution of medals. The way they are given seems to me most vicious. All who have, like myself, been commissioned to make this choice will have been struck with the same difficulty. It almost always happens that every painter who seems to me to deserve a third class, a second, or a first class medal has already obtained it. Here, for example, is a man who has already had the second; is he to be given the first because he deserves the second, which can not be given him? It thus happens that an artist rarely receives a reward for that one among his works which deserves it the most. It is at the moment when he has produced a masterpiece that there is nothing left to offer him as an award or an encouragement. The man who has done well twice is more meritorious than the man who has done well once. If the women gave the medal, they would be of that opinion. Mlle Rosa Bonheur has made an effort this year that is superior to those of the preceding years;[33] you are reduced to encouraging her by voice and by gesture. M. Rodakowski who has done a masterpiece this year,[34] is obliged to console himself with the medal that he obtained last year for an inferior work. M. Ziem, with his *View of Venice,* keeps to the height of his pictures of last year; but it is forbidden to the jury to testify to him as to their satisfaction. On the other hand, here is an *Annunciation* by M. Jalabert, which is a picture for the medal of the second class. Now, M. Jalabert has already obtained that; is he therefore to be given the first, which is a higher award than his picture of this year deserves? If you are exact and follow the regulations, you will give him nothing, and yet he deserves something. Should artists who exhibit at the Salon be put on a level with the pupils in the primary schools where the teacher, so as to encourage the parents even more than the pupils, gives prizes to everybody? If the purpose of awards is to reach what is best in an exhibition, one ought to give a prize to everything outstanding, but in the exact proportion of the merit of the work, and if the exhibit of an artist shows the amount of talent entitling him to a medal of the third, second or first class, it is right that he should obtain it even if he has had it already; that would be a better means of keeping up emulation and yet of giving prizes; in this way any man gifted with a reasonable modicum of talent can count on getting prizes when his turn comes.

Tuesday, August 16.

Jenny has left for Dieppe; I miss her here a great deal.

Sunday, August 28.

Came home with Fleury. The heat has fallen off completely. The day when I last saw him, a few days before the election, when he con-

---

[28] She had exhibited a *Horse Fair,* which had a great success and was popularized by the engraving. The picture was sold in 1887 at the Stewart sale in New York for 268,500 francs.

[34] A portrait of his mother.

fessed that he did not vote for me, he was full of protestations for the next time; here he is today, loaded with all the honors of war, member of the Institut, professor, etc.; he no longer has any but the weakest opinions of the unfortunates who are still on the same footing as everybody else.

Wednesday, September 28.

Seven o'clock in the morning, as I get up. No one imagines to what degree mediocrity abounds: Lefuel, Baltard, a thousand examples press in on one, of men having heavy commissions in the arts, in the government, in the armies, in everything. Those are the people who everywhere block the machine set in motion by the men of talent. Superior men are naturally innovators. They appear, and on all sides they find fools and mediocrities fastening on everything — only to show what they are in whatever they do. The natural impulse of the better men urges them to reforms, to try new roads, so as to escape from platitude and silliness. If they succeed and end by getting the upper hand in matters of routine, they in their turn have the incapables on their shoulders, men who take special pride in following out to the limit the stupidity natural to them, and who spoil everything they touch.

Saturday, October 8.

Yesterday I read the excellent passage on old age in the *Spectator*.[35] I am thinking of copying it entire.

I think I remember his placing tranquillity in the first rank among the advantages which age gives us over youth. Indeed, that is the true wealth which the old man should enjoy, if he lives according to the position at which he has arrived. Although it is said that old age is the time of ambition, it is perhaps only the time of legitimate ambition, the kind that is comparatively easy to satisfy. In fact, when one sees a mature man aspire to honors, they cannot — save in the case of

[35] *The Spectator* of Addison.

complete folly on his part — be other than those which he has the right to hope for as a result of the work of his whole life. Certainly, one does not create a career for oneself when fifty years old. One then enjoys the fruits of the career that one has pursued; honors naturally come to the man who already possesses respect. Consider the old man in what I shall not call the pursuit — for that word has too much the sound of youth about it — but in the calm search for the prerogatives to which he has a right; what he needs is tranquillity, which I regard as the sovereign good at his age. If fortune has not favored the efforts of his youth, and I am still speaking here of the man who has given proof of merit and of constancy, if his position is mediocre, long experience with that mediocrity should render it easier for him to endure it, even if that means a perspective in which the same state will continue till the end of his life.

Is there anything more ridiculous than agitating oneself at the age when everything invites us or forces us to repose, than being the competitor of people doubly encouraged by the strength of their years and by the interest which attaches to youth? The man of merit whom circumstances have not favored should still, in the situation where his declining years are passed, enjoy the calm which that situation brings with it; only extreme poverty can render that position intolerable; and the foregoing does not apply to those who, through very rare chance and despite notable qualities, have fallen so low. It is spiritual strength then, and a very rare strength, which is necessary for such an unfortunate in keeping up his fight. In the case of such a man, there would still be reason for consolation in the feeling of his own merit and of the injustice of fortune.

Youth sees everything before it and would aspire to everything; that is what makes its continual unrest and agitation. The idea of repose is as incompatible with that age as is the idea of agitation for the latter part of life. The old man, on the contrary, would be inexcusable in keeping up that feverish agitation. He has measured that strength and he knows the value of time; he knows how much of it would be needed to reach his goal, an uncertain one at best. At his age, he should have touched the goal which he has set himself, and not be reopening the question of the future. All these are reasons which should lead him to calmness and cause him to draw from the position he has acquired all the fruit which it can reasonably yield.

Sunday, October 9.

Painted the *Christ in the Bark,*[36] from my old sketch, and worked until two o'clock.

I am writing to my cousin:[37]

"The rarity of the visits which I make to this place (Champrosay) causes me to find it charming when I return here. The secret of happiness is not to possess things but to enjoy them; I should certainly be less happy if I were the owner of a great château, where I should be bored or where others would bore me. But those who do not love solitude cannot feel the pleasure which I experience in being king in a cottage! Freedom, but with busy leisure and a mind ceaselessly at work, causes all possible places and times to be enchanting. During these rainy days I have not, so far, been bored."

Monday, October 10.

To compose a *Dictionary of the Arts and of Painting:*[38] a simple program. Separate work for each article.

Authorities: the ruin of great talents, and almost the whole talent of mediocrities. They are the leading-strings which help everybody to walk at the beginning of his career, but on almost everybody they leave ineffaceable marks. People like Ingres never get out of them. They do not make a step without such aid. They are like people who would eat pap all their lives; and so on.

[36] Catalogue Robaut, 1214—1220.
[37] Mme Lamey, at Strasbourg.
[38] Delacroix was, throughout the whole latter part of his life, preoccupied with the writing of this *Dictionary*, its fragmentary form suiting him better than a didactic work.

Wednesday, October 12.
Dined at Mme Barbier's. Mme Villot returned this evening; I spoke

imprudently, with certain regrets, of the restorations of the pictures at the Museum: the great Veronese, which that unhappy Villot has killed with his attentions,[39] was a text upon which I did not wax too emphatic when I saw the warmth with which she defended the science of her husband. That is probably the only virtue she finds in him, and she considers it his chief ornament, as she should. She told me that when it came to restoration, not a stroke of the brush was applied unless M. Villot took up the palette himself. A grand recommendation, as we see so very clearly.

On the use of the model. The question is as to effect, and how to obtain it when using the model, or when working from nature in general; true effect is also the rarest thing in the majority of pictures where a big role is played by the model, who concentrates all thought upon himself, so that nothing remains of the painter. In the case of man both very learned and very intelligent, a well-understood use of the model permits the suppression of details which the painter who works from his head always includes too prodigally for fear of omitting something important, and that is what prevents him from touching really characteristic details in a free way and from showing them in their full light. For example in the painting one does out of one's head, the shadows always have too much detail, in the trees particularly, in the draperies, etc.

Rubens is a remarkable example of the abuse of details. His painting, in which imagination dominates, is everywhere super-abundant; his accessories are too much worked out; his picture is like an assembly where everybody speaks at once. And yet, if you compare that exuberant manner — I will not say to the dryness and poverty of modern work — but to very beautiful pictures where nature has been imitated with sobriety and greater exactitude, you very quickly

---

[39] The restorations made by Villot of certain pictures in the Louvre aroused so much adverse opinion that Villot was obliged to resign his post as Curator of Paintings in 1860, when he was given a purely administrative position as secretary of the Louvre.

feel that the true painter is the one in whom imagination speaks before all else.

When we were in the forest yesterday and I was praising to Jenny the forest-painting of Diaz, she said, with her great good sense, "The closer the imitation the colder it is," and that is the truth! Continual caution about showing only what is shown in nature will always make the painter colder than the nature which he thinks he is imitating; moreover, nature is far from being always interesting from the standpoint of effect and of ensemble. If each detail offers a perfection which I shall call inimitable, these details collectively, on the other hand, rarely present an effect equivalent to the one which results, in the work of the great artist, from the feeling for the ensemble and the composition. That is what made me say just now that if the use of the model gave to the picture something striking, it could do so only in the case of very intelligent men: in other words, the only ones who can really benefit by consulting the model are those who can produce their effect without a model.

How do things stand, now, if the subject contains a large element of pathos? See how, in such subjects, Rubens triumphs over all others! How the frankness of his execution, which is a consequence of the freedom with which he imitates, adds to the effect he wants to produce on the mind! Consider such an interesting subject as the scene taking place around the bed of a dying woman, for example; seize and render that ensemble by photography, if that is possible: it will be falsified in a thousand ways. The reason is that, according to the degree of your imagination, the subject will appear to you more or less beautiful, you will be more or less the poet in that scene in which you are an actor; you see only what is interesting, whereas the instrument puts in everything.

I make this observation and I corroborate all those which precede —— on the need for a great deal of intelligence in using the imagination, as I look again at the sketches I made at Nohant for the *Sainte Anne:* the first one, made from nature, is unbearable when I look at the second which, however, is almost a tracing of the preceding one, but which shows my intentions in a more pronounced way, and eliminates useless things, while at the same time introducing the degree of elegance which I felt to be necessary if I was to render the impression of the subject.

It is therefore much more important for the artist to approach the ideal which is in him, and peculiar to him, than to record, even in a strong way, the transitory ideal which nature may present — and she does present such aspects; but I repeat once more that it is only a certain type of man who sees them in nature, and not the common run of men, which is a proof that it is his imagination which creates the beautiful, and precisely because he follows his genius.

This work of idealization, indeed, takes place within me almost without my knowing it when I make a tracing of a composition which has come from my brain. This second edition is always corrected, and nearer to a necessary ideal; thus there comes about something that seems to be a contradiction and that yet explains how a too-detailed execution, like that of Rubens for example, is saved from injuring the effect on the imagination. That execution is applied to a thoroughly idealized theme; the superabundance of the details which slip into it, by reason of imperfect memory, cannot destroy that peculiarly interesting simplicity which was first discovered in the exposition of the idea; and, as we have just seen in the case of Rubens, the frankness of the execution absolutely compensates for the difficulty caused by the prodigality of the details. So that if, into such a composition, you introduce a passage carefully painted from the model, and do so without producing a complete discord, you have accomplished the greatest feat, that of harmonizing what seems unreconcilable; it is, so to speak, the introduction of reality into a dream; you will have united two different arts, for the art of the really idealistic painter is as far from that of the cold copyist as the declamation of Phèdre is from the letter some little shopgirl writes to her lover. The majority of painters who are so scrupulous in their use of the model generally get from such work no better result than badly digested compositions, devoid of all interest. They think they have done everything when they have reproduced heads, hands, and accessories, imitated with servility and lacking any relationship among themselves.

Took a walk with Jenny toward the Prieur oak. We went out by way of the edge of the forest and returned through the big alley. The heather, the ferns, and the fine, green grass recall to the poor woman her country and her youth.

As to the *imitation of nature,* that great point of departure for all the schools, the one on which they divide profoundly as soon as they interpret it; the whole question seems to come down to this: is the imitation made with a view to pleasing the imagination, or is it merely intended to satisfy a singular sort of conscience, one which permits self-content in the artist when he has made a copy, as exact as possible, of the model before his eyes?

Saturday, October 15.

Dined at Mme Villot's. The conversation turned on painting with olive oil. If that invention had been made thirty years ago, as also that of the daguerreotype, my career might perhaps have been more completely filled out. The facility of painting at every moment without having to bother about the palette, and then the instruction that the daguerreotype affords to a man who paints from memory, are inestimable advantages.

Sunday, October 16.

Read an article on Trouville, in the *Mémoires* of Dumas; there are some charming things in it. . . . What is it that those people lack? taste, tact, the art of choosing among all the things before them, and of knowing how to stop at the right time. It is probable that they do not work; would it suffice them to work in order to acquire what they lack? I do not think so.

Monday, October 17.

Still on the question of the use of the model and on imitation.

Jean-Jacques says rightly that the best way to paint the charms of

331

liberty is to be in prison, that the best way to describe a pleasant bit
of country is to live in a wearisome city and to see the sky only from
an attic window and amongst the chimneys. With my nose to the
landscape, surrounded by trees and charming spots, my landscape
painting is heavy, too much worked out, more truthful in detail perhaps, but lacking harmony with the subject. When Courbet painted
the background of his woman bathing,[40] he copied it scrupulously
from a study I saw beside his easel. Nothing could be colder; it is a
piece of inlaid woodwork. I didn't begin to do anything passable in my
trip to Africa until the moment when I had sufficiently forgotten
small details, and so remembered the striking and poetic side of things
for my pictures; up to that point, I was pursued by the love of exactitude, which the majority of people mistake for truth.

In spite of the bad roads, I took a little turn before dinner in the
forest as far as Bayvet with my poor good Jenny, whose health seems
better, as I am delighted to see. What profound common sense there
is in this daughter of nature, and what value there is at the depths
of her very singular prejudices!

At Mme Barbier's, Véron's book[41] was lying on the table. A
woman who is no fool, and who was there, considers it a bore; that
is one way of saying that it didn't please her, and it will not please
anybody at all who has the least idea of what constitutes a passable
thing. Here is no philosophy (there is a big article to write on that
word as regards the arts in general: without the kind of philosophy
I mean a book or a picture does not last, or rather it has no existence);
here is a mass of anecdotes, some of them interesting, others silly and
fit only to amuse lackeys, lists of names, word by word repetition of
historical facts that one can look up anywhere if one takes the trouble
— all that does not add up to a book. It is an anonymous collection of fragments of all colors from which he takes the color away

[40] *The Bathers* of the Salon of 1853, now in the Museum of Montpellier.
[41] The *Mémoires d'un Bourgeois de Paris,* which had just appeared, and
which contained particulars about Delacroix furnished by himself.

in fitting them together. What? not one reflection to glue one fact on to the other, or rather what reflections! For I am making a mistake: he does put something of his own in from time to time, but what common stuff it is! The poor man has given his measure prematurely. After taking pains to get rid of any idea we might have that he was capable of writing something possessing common sense, he even spends his time in destroying the feeble prestige that surrounded him, namely the idea that he had some capacity for business and that his way of dealing with people had at least made him prosperous. Not at all; he shows that all his business schemes were upset by chance, and that it was chance also which brought him success, often in the most unexpected ways, and the ones that were most contrary to what he foresaw.

In the judgment that I am passing, I have no animosity; on the contrary, I like him very much, in spite of his cavalier manner; but that is the thing that is inseparable from the parvenu. I think he is going to lose a great deal through this ill-conceived book. He would have gained a great deal, on the contrary, by not publishing it and just letting people think he was writing it. Unfortunately he confirms everything that people above the commonest level could expect from him. I always thought him more important through his manners than through his real qualities.

A certain tact has rarely deceived me; I was writing here, a short time ago, about the great number of mediocre men; but what degrees there still are in mediocrity! Here is one in the lowest class of it! I mean among men who think themselves capable of intellectual work. He serves to bring out the value of those who are the chiefs of the tribe, like Dumas, for example, about whom people are talking, these last days. Alongside of Véron, Dumas looks like a big man, and I have no doubt but that that is his own opinion; but what is Dumas and almost everything that is written today in comparison with a prodigy like Voltaire, for example? Alongside that marvel of lucidity, of brilliance and of simplicity altogether, what becomes of this disordered gossip, this endless stringing out of phrases and of volumes sown with things that are good and that are detestable, without restraint, without law, without sobriety, without consideration for the good sense of the reader! And so this man is mediocre in his use of faculties which are still above the ordinary; all those people resemble one another. Poor Aurore [42] herself joins him in her possession of similar defects, along with qualities of much value. Neither one of them works, but that is not because of laziness. They don't know how to work, that is to say to prune, to condense, to summarize and bring order into things. The need to write at so and so much a page is the fatal cause which would undermine an even more robust talent. They make capital of the volumes they pile up; the masterpiece is impossible today.

Thursday, October 20.

What an adoration I have for painting! The mere memory of certain pictures, even when I don't see them, goes through me with a feeling which stirs my whole being like all those rare and interesting memories that one finds at long intervals in one's life, and especially in the very early years of it.

Mme V. was recalling some of the Rubens' that she saw at Windsor. [43] She spoke of a big equestrian portrait, one of those big figures in full armor, with a young man near by. It seemed to me as if I saw it. I know a great deal of what Rubens has done, and think I know everything that he can do. The mere memory of a little woman who certainly did not, when she saw the picture, feel the emotion which I experience when just imagining it, when I have not seen it, awoke in me the great images of the pictures by him that so struck my youth in Paris, at the Musée Napoléon, and in Belgium, on the two trips that I have made there.

[42] George Sand.

[43] Mme Villot's indications are lacking in exactitude. The picture referred to is probably the *Saint George,* which is not at Windsor but at Buckingham Palace; it was painted in 1629 by Rubens for Charles I, whose features he has given to his *Saint George* in armor and on horseback.

Glory to that Homer of painting, to that father of warmth and of enthusiasm in the art where he blots out everything — not, if you like, through the perfection which he has brought to one part or another, but through that secret force and that life of the soul which he has attained everywhere. How strange! the picture which perhaps gave me the strongest sensation, the *Raising of the Cross*,[44] is not the one most brilliant through the qualities peculiar to him and in which he is incomparable. It is neither through color nor through the delicacy nor the frankness of the execution that this picture triumphs over the others but, curiously enough, through Italian qualities which, in the work of the Italians, do not delight me to the same degree; I think it is appropriate for me to take note here of the quite analogous way I have felt before Gros' battle pictures, and before the *Medusa*, especially when I saw it half finished. The essential thing about these works is their reaching of the sublime, which comes in part from the size of the figures. The same pictures in small dimension would, I am sure, produce quite a different effect on me. In the effect of Rubens and in that of Géricault there is also an indefinable something of the style of Michelangelo, which adds again to the effect produced by the dimension of the figures and which gives them something terrifying. Proportion counts for very much in the greater or lesser power of a picture. Not only, as I was saying, would these pictures, executed in small size, be ordinary work for the master, but, were they merely life-size, they would not attain the effect of the sublime. The proof is that the engraving after the picture by Rubens does not at all produce that effect on me.

I ought to say that the matter of dimensions is not everything, for several of his pictures in which the figures are very large do not give me that type of emotion which, for me, is the most elevated one; neither can I say that it is something exclusively Italian in style, for Gros' pictures, which do not present a trace of it and which are completely his own, transport me to the same degree into that state of the soul

[44] At the Cathedral of Antwerp.

which I regard as the most powerful that painting can inspire. The impressions produced by the arts on sensitive organisms are a curious mystery: confused impressions, if one tries to describe them, clear-cut and full of strength if one feels them again, and if only through memory! I strongly believe that we always mix in something of ourselves with feelings which seem to come from the objects that strike us. It is probable that the only reason why these works please me so much is that they respond to feelings which are my own; and since they give me the same degree of pleasure, different as they are, it must be that I find in myself the source of the effect which they produce.

The type of emotion peculiar to painting is, so to speak, *tangible;* poetry and music cannot give it. You enjoy the actual representation of objects as if you really saw them, and at the same time the meaning which the images have for the mind warms you and transports you. These figures, these objects, which seem the thing itself to a certain part of your intelligent being are like a solid bridge on which imagination supports itself to penetrate to the mysterious and profound sensation for which the forms are, so to speak, the hieroglyph, but a hieroglyph far more eloquent than a cold representation, a thing equivalent to no more than a character in the printer's font of type: it is in this sense that the art is sublime, if we compare it to one wherein thought reaches the mind only with the help of letters arranged in an order that has been agreed upon; it is a far more complicated art, if you will (since the font of type is nothing and thought seems to be everything), but a hundred times more expressive if one consider that, independently of the idea, the visible sign, the speaking hieroglyph, a sign without value for the mind in the work of the writer becomes a source of the liveliest enjoyment in the work of the painter. And so, looking upon the spectacle of created things, we have here the satisfaction given by beauty, proportion, contrast, harmony of color, and everything that the eye looks upon with so much pleasure in the outer world —one of the great needs of our nature.

Many people will consider that it is precisely in this simplification of the means of expression that the superiority of literature resides. Such people have never considered with pleasure an arm, a hand, a torso from the antique or from Puget; they care for sculpture even less than painting, and they are strangely deceived if they think that when they have written: *a foot* or *a hand,* they have given to my mind the same emotion as the one I experience when I see a beautiful foot or a beautiful hand. The arts are not algebra, in which the abbreviation of the figures contributes to the success of the problem; success in the arts is by no means a matter of abridging, but of amplifying, if possible, and prolonging the sensation by all possible means. What is the theater? One of the most certain witnesses to man's need for experiencing the largest possible number of emotions at one time. It gathers together all the arts so that each may make us feel their combined effect more strongly; pantomime, costume, and the beauty of the performer double the effect of the word that is spoken or sung. The representation of the place in which the action occurs adds still further to all these types of impression.

It will now be clearer why I have spoken as I have about the *power of painting.* If it possesses but a single moment, it concentrates the *effect* of that moment; the painter is far more the master of that which he wants to express than is the poet or the musician, who is in the hands of interpreters; in a word, if his memory is directed toward fewer aspects of things, he produces an effect which is absolutely one and which can satisfy completely; in addition, the work of the painter is not subject to the same variations, as regards the manner in which it may be understood at different periods. Changing fashion and the prejudices of the moment may cause its value to be looked upon in different ways; but in the end it is always the same, it remains as the artist wanted it to be, whereas the same is not true of things that must pass through the hands of interpreters, as must the works of the theatre. Since the feeling of the artist is no longer there to guide the actors or the singers, the execution can no longer respond to the original intention of the work: the accent disappears, and with it the most delicate part of the impression. Indeed it is a happy author whose work is not mutilated, an affront to which he is exposed even during his lifetime! The mere change of an actor changes the whole physiognomy of a piece.

Tuesday, October 25.

I have not been writing all these last days because I have too much to write. The time is so filled up by work and a little walking, that when I start to write too long in this notebook, I do not get into the swing of my work again.

I kept to the small *Sainte Anne* this morning, varying the work with little walks in the garden. I adore this little vegetable garden: this yellowing grapevine, these tomatoes along the wall, and this gentle sunlight over the whole of it infuse me with a secret joy, with a well-being comparable with what one feels when the body is in perfect health. But all that is fugitive; any number of times I have found myself in this delightful condition during the twenty days that I am spending here.

It seems as if one needed a mark, a special reminder for each one of these moments, for this sun pouring the last rays of the year over these flowers and these fruits, for this beautiful river which, yesterday and today, I watched as it flowed along so tranquilly, reflecting the sunset sky; one needs something to recall the poetic solitude of Trousseau's place, and to bring back those stars that I see on my walk every evening, shining like diamonds above and amidst the trees of the road.

In the evening, went to Mme Barbier's; she read from the *Mémoires* of Véron. Was I too severe in speaking about the book two or three days ago? Even though all I know of it as yet is these detached passages, I do not think so.

What are the memoirs of a living man when he writes of men still alive, as he is? Either he must set everybody against him by saying what is to be said about each individual (and doing anything like that would get him into pretty deep water), or he must take the course of saying only pleasant things about all the people he rubs elbows with, and whom he may meet at any moment. Hence the tiresome necessity of resorting to the anecdotes that are bandied about everywhere or that are sent in to him, without being at all the more interesting on that account — the whole thing not holding together in the least— in a word, these are not his memoirs, which is to say *genuine* and *sincere* judgments on the men of his time. Add to that the absence of all composition and the banality of his style, which Barbier admires very much, however.

Wednesday, October 26.

The *Spectator*[45] speaks of what it calls *geniuses of the first order,* such as Pindar, Homer, the Bible — confused amidst sublime and un- finished things — Shakespeare, etc.; and then of those in which it sees more of art such as Vergil, Plato, etc.

A question to be resolved! Can Shakespeare, mingling passages of surprising naturalness with interminable and tasteless conversations, offer us better subject for admiration than Vergil and Racine, in whose work all inventions are in their place and appear in the form that befits them? It seems to me that the latter case is the one that offers most difficulties; for you do not make exceptions in favor of the men, among these diverse geniuses, who are more in conformity with what the *Spectator* calls the rules of art, of truth and of vigor in their descriptions.[46]

What use would there be in the finest and most finished style if the thought is formless or common? The former among those remark- able men are perhaps like bad boys whom one forgives for big mistakes because of certain good impulses. We always get back to the matter of the finished work compared with the sketch for it, of which I spoke before — of the monument which shows only its big directing lines,

---

[45] The *Spectator* of Addison.
[46] M. Joubin observes here that obscurities in the above passage in the *Journal* are due to difficulties in reading the manuscript.

before the finishing and the coördinating of all the parts has given to it a more decided aspect and has consequently limited its effect on the imagination, that faculty which delights in vagueness, expands with ease, and embraces vast objects of which it has had a mere hint. Again, in the sketch for the monument, as compared to what it will look like when finished, the imagination cannot conceive the thing in a form too different from what the finished work will have, whereas in the production of geniuses like Pindar one stumbles on monstrosities, right alongside the finest concepts. Corneille is full of such contrasts; Shakespeare also. Mozart is not at all that way, nor is Racine, nor Vergil, nor Ariosto. In presence of their work, the mind feels a continual joy, and even while it delights in the spectacle of Phèdre's or Dido's passion, it cannot help being grateful for the poet's divine work in polishing the style which renders these touching thoughts. The author took such care as was needed in order to clear from the road he makes me cover, or from the perspective he shows me, all obstacles that might hamper or offend me.

If geniuses like Homer and Shakespeare present aspects that are so disagreeable, what shall we say of the imitators of their school, when they let themselves go and sacrifice all precision? The *Spectator* is right in trouncing them, for there is nothing more detestable; of all the types of imitation this is the stupidest and clumsiest. I have not said that it is particularly as *original geniuses* that the *Spectator* exalts men like Homer and Shakespeare; that would be the object of another analysis, in which they would be compared to men like Mozart and Ariosto, who do not seem to me to show the slightest lack of originality, although their work is so regular.

There is nothing more dangerous for young minds than confusion between these types, for young people are always more given to admiring what is gigantic than what is reasonable. A swollen and incorrect style seems to them the summit of genius, and nothing is easier than the imitation of such a style. We never convince ourselves sufficiently that the greatest talents do only what they can do; when they are weak or puffed up, the reason is that inspiration could not follow them, or rather that they were not able to awaken it, and above all confine it within due limits. Instead of dominating their subject, they have been dominated by their fire or by a certain inability to chasten their ideas. Mozart might say of himself, though he would probably have said it in less swollen terms: *Je suis maître de moi, comme de l'univers.* Mounted on the chariot of his improvisation, and like Apollo at the zenith of his course, whether at the beginnings or at the end, it is with a firm hand that he holds the reins of his racers, as he sheds light everywhere. And that is what men like Corneille, sweeping on with irregular leaps, cannot do, and they surprise you as much by the suddenness with which they fall as by the flights with which they clear sublime peaks.

In the case of singular geniuses, one must not too greatly spare what are called their negligences, and what ought rather to be called the breaks in their work; they could not have done other than what they did do. Often they have sweated heavily over very weak or very disturbing passages. This state does not seem to be at all rare with Beethoven, whose manuscripts are often as full of corrections as those of Ariosto. It must frequently happen with these men that beauties come as a surprise to themselves, and that, on the contrary, they spend a considerable time in attenuating the effect of these passages by repetition and misplaced amplifications.

Friday, October 28.

Got up this morning as usual; but filled with the idea that I did not have to pack my baggage, I again savored the pleasure of doing nothing.

After walking up and down a hundred times and looking at my paintings, I settled down in my armchair at the fireside in my bedroom; I got my nose into the *Nouvelles Russes;*[47] I read two of them: the *Fatalist* and *Dombrowski,* which gave me some delightful moments. Aside from the details about customs with which we are not acquainted, I suspect that they are lacking in originality. One feels as if one were

[47] The *Nouvelles Russes* of Nicolas Gogol.

reading the short stories of Mérimée, and as they are modern, there is no difficulty in imagining that the author knew them.[48] This slightly mongrel style gives one a strange pleasure, which is not the same pleasure one feels when reading great authors. These stories have a perfume of reality which astonishes; it is the feeling which surprised everybody when the novels of Walter Scott appeared; but good taste cannot accept them as accomplished works. Read the novels of Voltaire, *Don Quixote, Gil Blas.* You do not in any way imagine that you are witnessing completely real events, such as you would get from a story of an eye-witness. You feel the hand of the artist and you are meant to feel it, in the same way that you see the frame of every picture. In these works,[49] on the contrary, after the description of certain details which surprise by their apparent naïveté, like the exact name of the people in the story, unusual customs, etc., one is forced to see that what is offered is a more or less romantic fable which destroys the illusion. Instead of giving a true account under the names of Damon and of Alceste, you write a novel like any other novel, and it seems all the more so because of the attempt at illusion, expended on secondary details alone. All of Walter Scott is like that. The apparent novelty contributed to his success more than all his imagination, and what is making his works seem old-fashioned today and is placing them lower than the famous ones I have cited, is precisely his abuse of truth to detail. (This would connect with the article on imitation, above).[50]

Saturday, November 5.

As to the plague of long articles. The men who know what they have to say write well.

On the facility that women have in writing. See previous entries in this notebook. As to the greater difficulties that painting presents, consider the saying of Chardin and of Titian: *The whole of life for*

[48] In 1867, Mérimée did in fact translate Turgenev's *Nouvelles Moscovites,* which have a relationship with those of Gogol.

[49] i. e. those of Gogol and writers of his type.

[50] See entry of October 12, 1853.

learning. Moreover, the difficulties are to be considered in relation to the particular character of each mind.

Friday, November 11.

Love is like those sovereigns who fall into a doze in times of prosperity, and I do not mean by that that it burns out when its favors are too easily obtained, etc.

Monday, November 14.

I came home through the Faubourg Saint-Germain in order to buy some gloves; I bought the engraving by Piranesi, a big church interior that is very striking. Also, going by the Tour Saint-Jacques,[51] I saw men digging up a quantity of bones that were in their original position. The mind likes such spectacles and cannot get enough of them. While walking past Hetzel's shop, Silvestre[52] picked me up and made me enter.

Before dinner, Mme Pierret and Marie came to call on me: it is the famous day for offering me congratulations.[53] In the evening, after my dinner, Riesener came in and stayed fairly late. He advises me to publish my sketches by means of photography; I had already formed that plan, which might be fruitful. He told me of the seriousness with which good Durieu[54] and the friend who is helping him in his operations are speaking of the trouble they take, and how they attribute to themselves a large part of the success in the said operations, or rather in their result. It was only very timidly that Riesener asked them if he

[51] The cutting through of the Rue de Rivoli had brought about the disengaging of the tower of Saint-Jacques and the demolition of the surrounding houses. In this way bones were dug up in the cemetery which used to lie close to the ancient church of Saint-Jacques de la Boucherie.

[52] Théophile Silvestre (1823-1876), a remarkable writer and art critic, a great admirer of Delacroix; in 1856 he published his precious work entitled *Les Artistes Français,* in which there is an important essay on Delacroix.

[53] Saint Eugène's day.

[54] Durieu was at that time Director of Cults and was taking an intelligent interest in parochial buildings, which he had undertaken to have photographed.

might indeed without indiscretion and without being accused of plagiarism, make use of their photographs in order to paint pictures from them. At Pierret's, last Monday, I was a witness myself of the good humor with which he took credit for the success, on hearing me exclaim with admiration, which he imagined was for himself.

Tuesday, November 15.

For a week I have been having trouble with my stomach, and I am doing nothing. This morning, I am better and I am still enjoying a delightful laziness today, at my fireside, as if to indemnify me for my regrets over the time lost. I am surrounded by my notebooks of previous years; the nearer they get to the present moment, the rarer I find that eternal complaint against the boredom and the emptiness which I used to feel in the past. If age really gives me more gaiety and tranquillity of mind, it will be, rightly enough, a genuine compensation for the advantages of which it deprives me.

In my notebook of 1849 I was reading that poor Chopin, during one of those visits to him which I used often to make at that time when his disease was already terribly advanced, told me that his suffering prevented him from taking interest in anything, and especially in his work. On this score, I said to him that age and the troubles of the period would not be long in cooling me off also. He answered that in his opinion I had the strength to resist. "You will have the enjoyment of your talent," he said, "in a sort of serenity which is a rare privilege and which is worth far more than the feverish search for reputation."

Thursday, November 17.

Good Alberthe sent me a ticket for *Cenerentola*.[55] I spent a really delightful evening; I was full of ideas, and the music and spectacle helped with that.

[55] Opera by Rossini; it is an interpretation of *Cinderella*.

In the theater I noticed, from observing some satin, how much the tone of the object itself is to be found only just alongside of the glossy part; the same is true of the hide of a horse.

Listening to that charming piece, with its delicately wrought passages and its music that I know by heart, I saw indifference on almost all those faces of bored people; they come there only as a matter of form, or just to hear Mme Alboni.[56] The rest is a side issue, and they yawn while they stick it out. I was enjoying everything. I said to myself: "It is for me that they are playing this evening, I am all alone here; a sorcerer has even had the kindness to place near me some phantom spectators, so that the idea of my isolation shall not decrease my pleasure; it was for me that those decorations were painted and those costumes were cut and, as for the music, I am the only one to hear it."

The reform of the costumes has gone to the point of suppressing everything that means ingenious caricature, inherent in the very nature of the subject. The costumer thinks himself exact when he gives to Dandini a carefully dated costume of a lord of Louis XV's time; the same thing for the prince; you think that you are witnessing a piece by Marivaux. With Cinderella, we are in fairyland. Yet Alidor has a black costume like that of a lawyer.

Saturday, November 19.

I met Fleury this morning, then Halévy, and then Gisors.

This evening, at Gihaut's place, I was looking at the photographs after works by Marcantonio in the Delessert collection. Are we forever to admire as perfect these images full of incoherences and incorrections, not all of which are the work of the engraver? I still remember the disagreeable way in which I was affected, this spring when I was in the country, and was comparing them with photographs from nature.

[56] Marietta Alboni (1826-1894), the celebrated Italian singer had made her début at the Opéra in 1847, and sang all the pieces in the repertory there.

I saw the *Feast in the House of Simon*,[57] an engraving that is reproduced and highly esteemed. Could anything be colder than the action in it! The Magdalen, planted in profile before the Christ, literally wiping his feet with the big ribbons that hang from her head and that the engraver offers us as hair. Nothing of the unction that such a subject carries with it! Nothing of the wanton repenting her luxury and her beauty, which she lays at the feet of Christ, who ought, at least by his manner, to show her some appreciation, or at all events to look upon her with indulgence and kindness; the spectators as cold, as dull as the two capital figures. They are all separated from one another, as if such an extraordinary spectacle would not bring them together in a group, to see from closer by, or to communicate to one another what they think. There is one of them, the nearest to the Christ, making a gesture that is ridiculous and without purpose. He seems to be embracing the table with just one of his arms. His arm seems wider than the whole table, and this incorrection, which nothing explains and which occurs in the most conspicuous part of the picture, increases the stupidity of all the rest. Compare this foolish representation of the most touching subject in the Gospel, the one richest in tender and elevated sentiments, in picturesque contrasts arising from the different natures that are brought into contact — that beautiful creature in the flower of her youth and her health, those old men and those mature men, in whose presence she does not fear to humiliate her beauty and to confess her errors — compare, I say, what the divine Raphael has made of all that with what Rubens made of it.[58] He did not fail with any element of the characterization. The scene takes place in the house of a rich man: numerous servitors surround the

[57] Engraving by Marcantonio (Bartsch No. 23); the original plate has been spoiled by successive reworkings; the proofs of it are very bad. There also exist numerous copies of it which are quite mediocre.

[58] The picture by Rubens, the *Feast in the House of Simon* has been in the Hermitage Museum in Leningrad since the eighteenth century; it formally belonged to Walpole. Delacroix therefore knew it only from an engraving, since he never went to Russia.

table; the Christ, in the most prominent place, has a befitting serenity. The Magdalen, in the effusion of her feeling, drags in the dust her brocaded robes, her veils and her jewels; her golden hair streaming over her shoulders and spread in confusion over the feet of the Christ is not an accessory, vain and without interest. The vase of perfumes is the richest that he could imagine; nothing it too beautiful or too rich to be laid at the feet of the master of nature, who has become an indulgent master toward our errors and toward our weaknesses. And can the spectators look on with indifference at the sight of such beauty, prostrate and in tears, at such shoulders, at such a bosom, at such eyes, glistening and gently raised? The people speak to each other, they point to each other, they look upon the whole scene with animated gestures, some with an air of astonishment or of respect, others with a surprise in which malice is mingled. There is nature, and there is the painter! We accept all that tradition presents us as consecrated, we see with the eyes of others; the artists are the first to be caught, and are carried away more than the public which is less intelligent, which contents itself with what the arts present it at every period, as it does with the bread that comes from the baker. What have you to say for those pious imbeciles who stupidly copy the inadvertencies of the painter of Urbino, and magnify them as sublime beauties, those luck-less wretches who, unmoved by any sentiment, cling to those phases of the greatest talent wherein it lays itself open to criticism or ridicule, who imitate such things interminably, not understanding that these weak or neglected details are the regrettable accompaniment of the beautiful things that they can never attain?

Sunday, November 20.

Rubens is not simple because he is not labored.[59]

Tuesday, November 22.

Did not feel like work.

[59] In other words: What is so baffling about Rubens is that you are una-ware of any effort in his prodigious painting.

About three o'clock I went to the Museum. Vividly impressed by the Italian drawings of the fifteenth century and the beginning of the sixteenth century. Head of a nun, dead or dying, by Vanni; drawing by Signorelli; nude men. Small torso in front view: early Florentine school. Drawings by Leonardo da Vinci.[60] For the first time I noticed the ones by Carracci for the *grisailles* of the Farnese Palace: the cleverness in them overpowers the feeling; the handling, his touch, carry him along in spite of himself; he knows too much of such things and, since he does not study, he no longer discovers anything new or interesting. There is the pitfall of progress in the arts, and it is inevitable. That whole school is the same way. Head of Christ and other heads by Guido, where, despite the expression, his great cleverness with the pencil is even more surprising than the expression. What then are we to say of those present-day schools whose sole concern is with that lying cleverness, and who seek for it? In Leonardo's drawings above all, the touch is not seen, the sentiment alone reaches the mind. I still remember the time, not long ago, when I harassed myself endlessly for not being able to reach that dexterity in execution which the schools unfortunately accustom the best minds to consider the last word in art. The tendency to imitate naively and with simple means has always been my own, and I used, on the contrary, to envy the ease of the brush, and the coquettish touch of men like Bonington: and in him, I am mentioning a man filled with sentiment, but one who was swept along by his mere skill; it is such sacrifice of the noblest qualities to an unhappy facility which causes his works to sink in our esteem today and stamps them with a seal of weakness, like those of the Vanloo type.

There is great food for thought in that visit which I made yesterday, and it would be a good thing to repeat it from time to time.

[60] Italian drawings in the Louvre; see the *Catalogue Reiset,* 1879, the last one published: Nos. 362 (Vanni); 340, 343, 347 (Signorelli); 419 (Florentine school, fifteenth century); 1452-1519 (Leonardo da Vinci); 153 et seq. (Annibale Carracci); 291, 294, 297 (Guido).

Thursday, November 24.

Took a walk during the evening in the Galerie Vivienne, where I saw some photographs at a bookseller's. What attracted me was the *Raising of the Cross*[61] by Rubens; it interested me very much: the incorrections, no longer being saved by the handling and the color, are more clearly seen.

The sight, or rather the remembrance of my emotion before that masterpiece occupied me in a delightful way throughout the rest of the evening. I am thinking, by way of contrast, of those drawings by Carracci that I saw the day before yesterday: I have seen drawings by Rubens for that picture; certainly they are not conscientious, and in them he shows more of himself than of the model he had before his eyes; but that is of the nature of that secret force in men like Rubens; the feeling of the artist himself dominates everything and is borne in on the spectator. At first glance, the forms in Rubens are as banal as those in Carracci, but they are of a different order of significance. With Carracci, a big mind, a big talent, a big ability — I speak only of what I have seen — but nothing of that which transports you and gives you ineffaceable emotions!

Friday, November 25.

Visit from Fortoul, the minister, and from the prefect, at the Hôtel de Ville.

In the evening, that terrible Dumas, who will not let go his prey, came and got me up at midnight, his notebook of blank paper in his hand. God knows what he is going to do with the details that I was fool enough to give him![62] I like him very much, but I am not made

[61] In the cathedral of Antwerp.
[62] Dumas came for the notes that he utilized in his *Mémoires.* Delacroix, always distrustful of writers, newspaper men, and men of letters in general, does not much like to get into their hands even when they are favorable to him. Here is what Alexandre Dumas wrote: "Delacroix, with his *Massacre at Scio,* around which the painters of all parties gathered in discussion, Delacroix, who, in painting, like Hugo in literature, was to find only blind zealots or fierce detractors, Delacroix, who was already known by his *Dante Crossing the Styx,* and who was, throughout his life, to preserve the artist's rare privilege

of the same stuff, and we are not moving toward the same goal. His public is not mine; there must be one of us that is crazy. He leaves me the first numbers of his diary, which is delightful.

Saturday, November 26.

In the evening, went to hear *Lucrezia Borgia:*[63] I enjoyed it from one end to the other, even more than I enjoyed *Cenerentola,* the other day. Music, actors, setting, costumes, the whole thing interested me. I made reparation, that evening, to the unhappy Donizetti, now dead, to whom I do justice—thereby imitating the common run of mortals, alas! and even the best among them. They are all unjust toward contemporary talent. I was enthralled by the chorus of cloaked men, in the charming setting of the garden staircase under the moon. There are reminiscences of Meyerbeer amidst that Italian elegance, and they marry very well with the rest. Especially delighted with the aria which follows, sung by Mario[64] in his delicious fashion: another injustice repaired; today I find him charming. That resembles the way you suddenly fall in love, after years, with a person whom you are accustomed to see every day and to whom you thought yourself indifferent. Here we have the good school of Rossini; among the best things that Donizetti has borrowed from him are those introductions which bring the soul of the listener into the state that the musician wants. Like Bellini, he also owes to Rossini those mysterious choruses of the type I mentioned, and he does not spoil them (I think back to the chorus of the priests in *Semiramis,* etc.).

of awakening hatreds and admirations with each new work: Delacroix a man of wit, of science and of an imagination which has only one oddity — that of obstinately wanting to be the colleague of M. Picot and of M. Abel de Pujol, and who, happily, at least so we hope, will not be that. "He was," adds M. Joubin, in his laconic note, (i. e. a member of the Institute).

[63] Opera by Donizetti.

[64] The Marquis de Candia, called Mario (1808-1883) entered the theater in 1838; he was one of the most illustrious tenors of his time; he married Giulia Grisi, the celebrated singer.

Monday, November 28.

First performance of *Mauprat*.[65] All Mme Sand's pieces exhibit the same composition, or rather lack of composition: the beginning is always intriguing and promises to have interest; the middle of the piece drags on in what she thinks are development of the characters and which are only means to work up action.

It seems that in this piece, as in the others, from the second act till the end — and there are six acts! — the situation does not make a single step; the character of her young man, from whom the mud cannot be scraped off and who is told in every fashion that he is beloved, does not cross the borders of despair, of rage and of nonsense. It is just as it was with the *Pressoir*.[66]

The poor woman! she struggles against an obstacle of a kind that should forbid her to write plays; the thing is below the level of the most ill-founded melodramas, in this respect; there are phrases filled with charm; therein lies her talent. Her virtuous peasants are deadly; there are two of them in *Mauprat*. The lord is equally virtuous, the young person irreproachable, the rival of the young man full of propriety and moderation when it comes to machinations against his rival. The violent young man himself is, in reality, of excellent character. There is a poor little dog who brings about ridiculous situations. She is lacking in the sense of the theater, as she lacks the sense of certain proprieties in her novels; she does not write for the French, although she writes excellent French; and yet in the matter of taste the present-day public is not very difficult. It is the same thing as with Dumas, who tramples on everything, who goes about with a slouchy suit and thinks himself above the things that everybody is accustomed to respect. She undoubtedly has a big talent, but she is even less aware than the majority of writers of what is best suited to her. Am I unjust again?

[65] The novel had appeared in 1837 and had had a great success, which it did not repeat when transported to the stage of the Odéon. It has just been adapted for the cinema, but has no more success there (1928).

[66] An allusion which I do not understand, unless it is a misreading of the manuscript — note by M. Joubin.

I like her, but one has got to say that her works will not last. She lacks taste.

Came home after one o'clock in the morning. I met my old friend Ricourt again. He talked to me and still remembers the sketch of the *Satyr in the Nets:*[67] he talked to me about what I already was at that far-off time. He remembers the green coat,[68] the long hair, the exaltation over Shakespeare, over novelties, etc. . . . .

Dined at the Hôtel de Ville. Didot took me home with him and showed me some interesting manuscripts with vignettes.

Wednesday, November 30.

Dined at the house of Princess Marcelline. Duet of bass fiddle and piano by Mozart, in which the beginning recalls: *Du moment qu'on aime.* Duet of the same instruments by Beethoven, the one that I know already and which they have played.

What a life I am leading! I was making that reflection while hearing the beautiful music, especially that of Mozart, who breathes the calm of a well-ordered period. I am in that phase of life when the tumult of the mad passions does not mingle with the delightful emotions which works of art give to me. I don't know the meaning of dusty papers and hateful occupations, which is what almost all human beings must devote themselves to; instead of thinking of business, I think only of Rubens and of Mozart: my great business, for a week, is the memory of an aria or a picture. I go to my work as others hasten to their mistress, and when I leave it, I carry away into my solitude or amidst the distraction which I go to seek, a charming memory which has but little resemblance to the troubled pleasure of lovers.

At the house of the princess I saw the portrait of Prince Adam[69]

[67] Robaut thinks that this is an allusion to a sketch by Delacroix after Rubens.

[68] Allusion to the green vest of the portrait in the Louvre (Catalogue Robaut, 295).

[69] Prince Czartoriski, portrait by Paul Delaroche, the *bête noire* of Delacroix.

by Delaroche; one would say it was the ghost of the poor man, so completely does he seem to have had all the blood drawn from his veins, and so much has his face been elongated. That is, indeed, following the expression of Delaroche himself, what may be called *serious* painting. I was talking to him one day about the admirable Murillos of Marshal Soult,[70] which he was good enough to let me admire; only, said he, *that is not serious painting*.

I came home at one o'clock in the morning. Jenny told me that when one has listened to music for an hour it is all that one can stand. She is right: it is even a great deal. An aria or two like the duet by Mozart, and the rest causes fatigue and impatience.

Wednesday, December 7.

Insipid dinner at Casenave's. Bethmont[71] sat opposite me. He is a personage with a very sugary manner of saying things. With his mild eyes, he laid Véron out, after dinner, in quite a spicy way; he did so with a good deal of malice, and then rounded off his piece with the most charming sweetness. In that honeyed philippic against the champion of the presidency in 1851, one clearly felt that the former member of the provisional government was letting some of his secret rancor escape. He was a great deal of the churchman in his speech and even in his attitude: the artificial eloquence of the lawyer comes out as a matter of course in everything that he says, but with a certain hesitation as to the terms, which indicates that there is something rebellious in that mind, despite the way he must have cultivated it and despite his practice in the profession of the speaker, which he has followed throughout his whole life. I remember that Vieillard, with all his candor, spoke to me of Bethmont in contrast with his other colleagues, fiery or intolerant republicans, saying: "What a charming man! what

---

[70] The famous collection of Marshal Soult contained fifteen Murillos, more particularly the *Assumption of the Virgin,* now in the Louvre. It had been sold at auction in May, 1852.

[71] Eugène Bethmont (1804-1860), a politician who was Minister of Justice and then Counselor of State under the provisional government.

gentleness!" I remember that he displeased me at once when I saw him in the past, at the house of good M. N——, who was not so critical: a certain fashion of listening to you while saying nothing himself, or of answering you with reticence, gave me the impression of him in which I have been confirmed the two or three times that I have met him. I noticed that he showed great feeling over the death of poor Wilson. It seemed to me that he was shedding real tears for his friend. What am I to conclude from all that? that I was mistaken in my judgment? Not at all! He is, like all men, a bizarre and inexplicable composite of contraries; that is what those fellows who turn out novels and plays refuse to understand. Their men are all of one piece. There are no such creatures. There are ten men in one man, and often they all show themselves within one hour, under certain circumstances.

Thursday, December 8.

I was invited to call on Mlle Brohan,[72] and after having taken my walk in the stinging but agreeable cold (when I should have been at her house), I stayed home to read Dumas's second article on me;[73] it gives me rather the look of the hero in a novel. Ten years ago, I should have gone and hugged him for his amiability: at that time I was very much concerned about the opinion of the fair sex, an opinion that I hold today in complete contempt, though not without thinking with pleasure, sometimes, of the days when everything about the ladies seemed to me charming. Today, I recognize one charm in them, and it is no longer for me. It is reason, more than age, that gives me another point of view. The former one is the tyrant that dominates all the rest.

That Brohan was certainly charming in her earlier days! What eyes! what teeth! what freshness! When I met her again at Véron's house, two or three years ago, she had lost considerably but still had a certain charm. She has a good deal of wit, but is rather given to striving

---

[72] Augustine Brohan (1807-1877) had had the greatest success at the Théâtre-Français and at the Vaudeville. She had not acted since 1842.

[73] In his *Mémoires,* from the notes furnished by Delacroix.

after effect. I remember that she kissed me that day because of what they had told her I was: I believe there was some question of her portrait. All through the dinner Houssaye,[74] who was her manager at the time, though not the manager of her conscience, for he was her lover also, maintained the somber attitude of a jealous lover, which was funny enough on the part of a theatrical manager, a person who is supposed to be pretty familiar with the ways of the feminine part of the declaiming and singing, croaking and bellowing herd of which he is the shepherd.

I didn't go there this evening for fear of meeting too many of those compromising figures, which would have made me flee to the antipodes.

Friday, December 9.

The best way would be to write it in the form of letters.[75] One goes from one subject to another without transition; one is not forced to go in for developments. A letter can be as short or as long as you like.

Saturday, December 10.

At Chabrier's this evening. Lefebvre[76] was talking with Jomini. I am making a note that I should read his two books, *Napoléon au Tribunal d'Alexandre et de César* and the *Grandes Opérations Militaires*. He gives high praise to the style of Ségur, in the campaign of 1812. I should read the Battle of Dresden. Fine things also in the French campaign. During that Dresden campaign, the Emperor was really like a thunderbolt, a man of the type of the Rolands and the Rinaldos, so often did his glance or his presence give birth to miracles; and it was after that battle, which was to be decisive, that eating the wing of a chicken gave him an indigestion which paralyzed his faculties and

[74] Arsène Houssaye (1815-1896), writer and art critic, at that time administrator of the Comédie Française.

[75] Delacroix is thinking of the form that he could give to his writing on art.

[76] Probably not Charles Lefebvre, the painter (1805-1882); Baron Jomini, (1779-1869), French historian and general.

therefore the movements of his army, bringing on the defeat of Vandamme.

The good admiral [77] who was there, has kindness and benevolence clearly marked in his face. He told me that when he woke up in the night, he would be seized with horrible discouragement. That surprised me in a man who has not the look of being nervous. It is a state that is general with almost all men. Lefebvre is the same way. I had gotten into a state of terrible misanthropy, which I left behind on entering (although I did not have an especially good time there), but I fell into it again during the whole time that I was going home.

It seemed to me splendid to be hated by everybody and to be at war with the human race. They talked about working excessively; I said that there was no excess along that line, or at least that it could do no harm, provided that one took the exercise that the body demands and above all if one did not try to carry on with work and pleasure at the same time. As to this, they said that Cuvier had died of overwork: I don't believe it for a second. He looked so strong, someone said. Not at all! he was very thin and put one garment over another like the Marquis de Mascarille and the Vicomte de Jodelet in the *Précieuses*. He wanted to keep perspiring the whole time. It isn't a bad system; I am beginning to lean toward that habit of wearing a great deal of clothes; I think it is very healthy for me. Cuvier had the reputation of making love with little girls and of procuring them at any cost; that explains his paralysis and all the troubles to which he succumbed, more than his excesses with work.

I have heard *Norma*.[78] I thought I was going to be bored, and the contrary was the case; that music, which I thought I knew by heart and that I was tired of, seemed to me delightful. The piece is short, another merit. Mme Parodi gave me more pleasure than in *Lucrezia;* perhaps it was because I read afterward in my newspaper that she was

[77] Admiral Casy (1787-1862), who had been Minister of Marine, was at that time a senator.

[78] Opera by Bellini.

a pupil of Mme Pasta, whose features she recalls very much. The public seems to regret la Grisi and refuses her its favor. Quite often my applause was the only one to break that universal coldness.

December 14.

In the evening, I stayed in my studio where I made a charcoal drawing from a Renaissance torso, to try out a fixative that Riesener uses. That unhappy man [79] is wearing himself out with his eternal Niobes. He is always making schemes to get rich with small pictures. He is lost. He is beginning to say: "Now it is too late," like all the lazy men who have forever been saying with assurance: "I have plenty of time." The attitude toward me of that excellent lady, my cousin, is very curious. The first part of the conversation is marked by a certain hatred, or some rancor or other, that resides in the depth of her small heart. She stares hard at me and throws out stinging words which would upset a man less obstinate than I in remaining calm. I answer her in the same way that she speaks to me, but minus the anger. Little by little she softens up and, at the end of the evening, she is solicitude itself.

I came home with Pierret in the freezing weather that began in the afternoon; there was lovely moonlight. I recalled to him, in the Champs Elysées, that at this same place, more than thirty years earlier we were returning together at about the same hour from Saint-Germain, where we had gone to see Soulier's mother, on foot, if you please, and with the weather far below zero. Was it the same Pierret with whom I was going arm-in-arm? What fire there was in our friendship! what ice there is now! [80] He told me about the magnificent projects they are making for these Champs Elysées. Lawns in the English style will replace the old trees. The balustrades of the square have disappeared; the obelisk is going to follow them, to be deposited I don't know where. Man simply has to depart, so fragile a being is he, if he does

[79] The relationship between Delacroix and the Rieseners had grown cold, beginning with the time that Jenny had taken her place as the watch-dog in Delacroix's household.

[80] Still on account of Jenny, who had formerly been a servant of the Pierrets.

not want to witness the ruin of all the objects that were contemporaries of his momentary passage. Here I am no longer recognizing my friend, because thirty years have passed over my feelings. If I had lost him fifteen years ago, I should have regretted him eternally; but I haven't yet had the time to lose my taste for the sight of the trees and the monuments that I have seen all my life. I should have liked to see them until the end.

Sunday, December 18.

In the evening went to hear *William Tell,* sitting next to Saint-Georges,[81] who made me lose several pieces with his various remarks. With all that, I got back more clearly than ever my impressions of this fine work, which one cannot admire enough.

Saturday December 24.

Dined at the house of Buloz. I came home on foot and entered Saint-Roch's for the midnight mass. I don't know whether it was because of all the people crowded in there, or the lights, or because of that kind of solemnity, but the whole thing did give me the impression that all the paintings on the wall there were even colder and more insipid than I had thought them.[82] How rare talent is! What a lot of labor is expended in smearing up canvas, and yet what finer opportunity could one have than these religious subjects! From all those pictures so patiently or even so ably manufactured by every kind of hand and every kind of school, I asked for only one touch, for one spark of feeling and of deep emotion, which it seems to me I should have got into such work almost in spite of myself. At that moment, which had some solemnity, they seemed to me worse than usual; but, in the reverse case, how a beautiful thing would have delighted me! That is what I have felt every time that a fine painting was before my eyes in church, while religious music was playing; and in the latter art it is not necessary that the piece be so carefully chosen in order to produce its effect,

[81] Vernoy de Saint-Georges, publicist and writer of librettos for opera.

[82] Many modern paintings, by L. Boulanger, Henri Scheffer, Devéria, Chassériau, etc., which could scarcely please Delacroix.

since music doubtless addresses itself to a different part of the imagination, one that is more easily captivated. Thus I recall having seen, and with the greatest pleasure, a copy of Prud'hon's *Christ* at Saint-Philippe du Roule; I think it was during the funeral of M. de Beauharnais.[83] Never, I am positive, did that composition, which is open to criticism, seem to me better. The part of it which is a matter of feeling seemed to free itself, and came to me on the wings of the music. The ancients were acquainted with something like that and put it into practice: it is told of a great painter of antiquity that when he showed his pictures he had music played for his audience, of a kind that would bring them into the state of mind appropriate to the subject of his paintings; thus he had a trumpet sounded when showing the figure of a soldier in arms, etc. I remember my enthusiasm when I was painting at Saint-Denis du Saint-Sacrement[84] and when I was hearing the music of the services; Sunday was doubly a feast day; I always had a good session on that day. The best head in my *Dante* picture[85] was swept in with the greatest speed and spirit while Pierret was reading me a canto from Dante which I knew already but to which he lent, by his accent, an energy that electrified me. That head is the one of the man behind the boat, facing you and trying to climb on board, after throwing his arm over the gunwale.

They were talking at the table about *local color*. Meyerbeer was saying, rightly, that it depends on an indefinable thing, which is not at all the exact observation of usages and costumes: "Who is there who has more of it," he said, "than Schiller in his *William Tell?* And yet he had never seen anything of Switzerland." Meyerbeer is a master of that kind of thing: the *Huguenots, Robert,* etc. Cousin did not find the slightest local color in Racine, whom he does not like at all; he imagines that Corneille, whom he is mad over, is full of it. I said what I thought about Racine and what ought to be said, which is that he

[83] François de Beauharnais, the father of Mme de Lavalette, the grandfather of Mme de Forget; he died in 1823.

[84] The *Pietà* (Catalogue Robaut, 768), painted in 1843.

[85] The *Dante and Vergil,* of 1822 (Catalogue Robaut, 49).

is too perfect; that that perfection and the absence of breaks and incongruities deprive him of the spice that one finds in works full of
beauties and defects at the same time. He told me again and again that
Racine's ideas were picked up everywhere and were no more than translations. He cited to me I don't know how many copies of Euripides
or Vergil annotated by Racine so that he might extract verses from
them, ready made. How many people have annotated Euripides and
all the other ancients, without drawing from them the least scrap of
anything that could be said to resemble a verse by Racine! Mme Sand
was saying the same thing to me: those are the curiosities of the profession! The language of a great man, spoken by him, is always a
beautiful language. One might just as well say that Corneille, who
arrives at great beauty in his use of our language, would have been
finer yet in Spanish! The men of a profession are more acute in criticism
than other people are, but they are headstrong when it comes to the
things of the profession. Painters worry about nothing else. The
interests, the subject, and even picturesqueness disappear before the
merits of execution, I mean execution as the School understands it.

In re-reading what I have said of Meyerbeer, under the head of
local color it just occurs to me that he is too much taken up with it.
In the *Huguenots,* for example: the increasing heaviness of his work,
and the bizarre quality in the singing derive in large part from this
exaggeration in his interest. He wants to keep his feet on the ground,
even while seeking the ideal; he parted company with the graces by
seeking to appear more exact and more learned. The *Prophet,* which
I do not recall, scarcely having heard it, must be a new step along this
road; I have retained nothing of it. In *William Tell,* if he had composed
it, he would have wanted to make us recognize the Swiss and the
passions of the Swiss in his slightest duet. As for Racine, it is with
broad strokes that he paints a few landscapes in which, if you like, one
feels the air of the mountains, or rather that melancholy which seizes
upon the soul in the presence of the great spectacles of nature, and
against this background he has thrown men, passions, grace and

elegance everywhere. Racine has done the same thing. What matter if Achilles is a Frenchman! And who ever saw the Greek Achilles? Who would dare to make him speak as Homer has done, in any language but Greek? "What tongue are you going to use?" asks Pancrace of Sganarelle. "Good Lord! the one I have in my mouth!" One can speak only with one's tongue, but one can also speak with the spirit of one's time. You have to be understood by those who hear you, but above all you must understand yourself. Produce the Greek Achilles! Why, bless you! did Homer himself do that? He produced an Achilles for the people of his time. The men who had seen the real Achilles were gone, long since. The old Achilles must have been more like a Huron than the hero in Homer. Those oxen and sheep that the poet describes him as putting on the spit with his own hands, were perhaps eaten raw by him after he had knocked them on the head. The luxury with which Homer adorns him comes from the poet's imagination; the tripods, the tents and the vessels are no other than those that Homer had before him in the world where he lived. They are a joke, those vessels with which the Greeks went to the siege of Troy! The entire host of the Greeks would have surrendered to the flotilla that goes forth from Fécamp or from Dieppe for the herring fishing. That has been the weakness of our time, in its poets and its artists — that idea that they had made a great conquest with the invention of local color. It was the English who began the march, and, following them, we had to make our effort to take by assault the masterpieces of human genius.

(Insert here everything I have said above as to the unreality of Walter Scott's fables, and of modern novels, in their seeking for truth to detail.)

Tuesday, December 27.

Worked but little and felt rather badly, the thing getting worse at dinner-time.

Good Alberthe had sent me an opera ticket in the morning. And so I went to the Italiens, and going out, which was hard for me, made me feel better rather than worse. They were playing *Lucia*. The other day, at *Lucrezia,* I did justice to Donizetti; I repented my severity toward him. Today, stooped over and weary as I was, the whole thing seemed to me very noisy, of very little interest. Nothing of the subject, nor of the passions, except perhaps the famous quintette. Ornament takes up all the room there is in this music; you get nothing but festoons and astragals: I call it sensual music, and only that; it is designed just to tickle the ear for a moment.

I met my friend Chasles[86] in the lobby. With that way of his — honeyed and stiff at the same time, characterizing that lack of frankness in his nature — he began to grovel with a humility that he did not even mean me to think real. I told him that one ought not to say either good or evil of oneself. As a matter of fact if you speak evil, everybody takes you at your word; if you speak too well of yourself or only a little bit well, you weary everybody. He got through with all his compliments, and we talked about the theater, about the art of the drama, about Racine, and Shakespeare. He prefers the latter to everything else, "But," as he said to me, "he is for me less of an artist than a philosopher. He does not seek unity, the epitome, the type, as artists do; he takes a character: it is something that he has seen and that he studies, making you see it as natural as life." That explanation seems to me exact. I asked him if, with all his entrances and exits, and that continual changing of places and of characters, Shakespeare's plays are not tiring even for a man who grasps all the merit of his speech. He agreed to that.

Friday, December 30.

Someone told me, speaking of my *Venus,*[87] that when one looked at it one saw the whole thing at once. That expression struck me: that is, as a matter of fact, the quality that ought to dominate; the other ones ought merely to follow.

[86] Philarète Chasles, a writer, a boyhood friend of Delacroix's.

[87] The *Venus* which decorates one of the panels of the Salon de la Paix at the Hôtel de Ville (Catalogue Robaut, 1144).

1854

January 5.

"Thus, in all our resolves, we must decide which is the line of conduct that presents the fewest drawbacks and then follow it out as being the best one, because one never finds anything perfectly pure and unmixed, or exempt from danger." Machiavelli.

January 17.

Literary men pretend to believe that the enjoyment of the ear and the eye in music and in painting is like that of the palate in the action of eating and drinking.

January 29.

During the morning, Riesener came to bring me some news, and he had to go out in the most horrible mud and rain to do so; what he had to tell me was that, last night, my ceiling had been a complete fiasco. What a good heart he has! What a kind relative he is![1] Finding me very cold about his remarks, due to the fact *that I consider my work good,* he went off without having accomplished his purpose. And what he took with him was anxiety over having counted too much on the kindness of my disposition; the way his face got long and green told of his fear that he would see orders for pictures and ceilings fly away.

March 11.

A long interruption in these poor notes of daily happenings: I feel very badly about it; these trifling things written down in such a fugitive way seem to me all that is left to me of my life, the more it flows away. My lack of memory makes them necessary for me; since the beginning of the year, the steady work needed for finishing at the Hôtel de Ville has been distracting me too much; since I finished it, and that will soon be a month since, my eyes are in a bad state, I am afraid to read and to write.[2]

March 15.

Dined at the house of Hippolyte Rodrigues[3] with Halévy, Boilay, and Mirès; the last named is a very original man, very sensible and very witty; he gives one proof that it is the mind that makes the man. Speaking of the fact that nowadays the people believe that prosperity

[1] On January 28th there had been a celebration at the Hôtel de Ville, and Delacroix must have finished and uncovered his ceiling for that date (see a letter from Delacroix to Théophile Gautier, published in *l'Artiste,* December, 1904). M. Joubin remarks that Riesener was certainly not pleasant about the affair, but he considers that underneath it there must be some more of Jenny's work.

[2] Delacroix had contracted an affection of the retina while working at his ceiling in a very dark hall.

[3] Hippolyte Rodrigues, stockbroker and writer; he was the father-in-law of Halévy, the composer; Boilay, publicist; Mirès (1809-1871), celebrated financier and wild speculator; at this time he was one of the most prominent men in the field of finance.

is its due, independently of the mind and the industry employed in obtaining it, in a word, speaking of the rage for equality and happiness which possesses everybody and which I was deploring, he said that it was a source of action which appeared when the time was ripe for it and which would last a certain length of time, like all the others that have aroused men over periods of greater or less duration; the wars of religion are another example of this.

He said that however strong your business judgment, you need a partner, someone who will act as your other self, who will clear your mind and will sometimes put your finger on the falseness of a calculation on which you were building your hopes.

Mirès said that the artist was a variety of madman. But the artist, unlike the men of other professions, does not need that presence of mind, that fixity of resolution, without which neither the general in the army nor the administrator nor the financier can do anything good.

The thought comes to me next day that part of the superiority of Louis-Napoleon doubtless comes from the fact that he has about him *nothing of the artist*.

March 22.

As to landscape. As to types in the arts. On the imitation of the antique: everyone has imitated it. *As to composition:*[4] criticism of various compositions by great masters: *Entrance of Alexander into Babylon,*[5] by Lebrun. The false picturesque preferred to good taste, as in Lebrun, or insignificance and platitude, as in the *Christ at the Tomb* by Titian; the same thing applies to the *Crowning with Thorns.* In the work of Paul Veronese, the arrangement is preferable by far, but there is no dramatic interest whatsoever: whether he paints the Christ or a middle-class Venetian, he always gives us the same indoor clothing, the same blue background, and the same little Negroes carrying little dogs; the

[4] Subjects of a whole series of essays on art, noted here by Delacroix for future study.
[5] One of the most celebrated paintings in the series of the *Battles of Alexander,* painted between 1662 and 1668; now in the Louvre.

whole thing is, to be sure, arranged with harmonious lines and color.

March 23.

Ball at the Tuileries: the same feeling of being bored with other people and with myself. This gilded abjectness is the saddest of all.

As to sculpture: the art *princeps*. Modern sculptors do nothing but make *pastiches*.

Literature. It is everybody's art: one learns it without being aware that one does so.

The commissions. At the last session[6] I was struck by the way that matters have to be submitted to specialists. Memorandum on this subject: everything that commissions do is incomplete and, more especially, incoherent; at that session, the artists voted together; they had reason on their side; the others understand only in a confused fashion; they have no clear ideas.

That is not to say that, if I had governmental power, I would turn over questions of art, for example, to commissions of artists. The commissions would be purely consultative, and the able man who would preside over them would follow his own ideas entirely, after having listened to them. When they are gathered at a meeting and are thinking of their profession alone, each one promptly goes back to his narrow point of view; when opposed by completely incompetent people, the sure and general advantages are clearly visible to their eyes, and they will succeed in making them visible to others.

I am speaking here against republics. You object on the ground that some of them have achieved splendor; I see the reason for that in the spirit of tradition which has survived everything in certain bodies entrusted, in these republics, with the managing of affairs. The most celebrated republics are the aristocratic ones. A noble, like a plebeian, provided that he has sense, will understand the interest of the country; but the plebeian is a member of a body which is nowhere; the noble, on the contrary is something only by virtue of tradition, and of the

---

[6] i. e., of the Commission of the Universal Exposition, of 1855.

conserving spirit which renders only the dearer to him a fatherland at the head of which he is placed by those institutions which it is his mission to defend: Venice, Rome, England, etc., are examples in point.

National spirit will be recovered by the people only when it finds itself directly confronted by the interests of foreign nations. It is like that in commissions where artists, when opposed by manufacturers, vote like a single man. Send to a European congress a certain number of English plebeians (I speak of the ones who, at home, make up the opposition, who are for progress and change) — they will be Englishmen before anything else when dealing with the Germans, the French, etc.; without giving way to the extent of one syllable, they will maintain those English privileges which make up the strength of England, and which a secret instinct tells them of as the principle of that strength.

March 24.

Worked on the lay-in of the *Lion Hunters,*[7] for Weill.

At half past two, meeting of the Commission. Discussion of the rule concerning the exhibition of works produced since the beginning of the century. Aided by Mérimée, I successfully fought that proposition, which was shelved. Ingres was pitiful; his brain is all warped; he can see only one point. It is the same as in his painting; not the slightest logic, and no imagination at all: *Stratonice, Angélique,* the *Vow of Louis XIII,* his recent ceiling with his *France* and his *Monster.*[8]

[7] One of the variants of the big picture at Bordeaux, perhaps 1278 in the Robaut Catalogue.

[8] *Stratonice ou la Maladie d'Antiochus,* at the Musée Condé, Chantilly; *Roger Délivrant Angélique;* the *Vow of Louis XIII,* in the Cathedral of Montauban; the ceiling mentioned is that of the Salon de l'Empereur at the Hôtel de Ville, representing the *Apotheosis of Napoleon I,* which had just been inaugurated, in the month of February; this ceiling was destroyed in the fire of 1871, and is known to us only by the painted study in the Louvre. It shows Napoleon in a golden chariot drawn by four horses, guided by Victory to the temple of Immortality. To the left, below, France with a veil of crêpe; to the right, Nemesis pursuing Crime and Anarchy (what Delacroix calls the *Monster*). It is simply an antique cameo on a large scale.

March 26.

Went to the Sainte-Cécile concert. The only thing I gave attention to was the *Heroic Symphony*. I found the first part admirable. The andante is the most tragic, the most sublime thing that Beethoven has written, though that applies only to the first half. Then came the *Marche du Sacre* by Cherubini, which I listened to with pleasure. As to the *Preciosa*,[9] the heat of the concert-hall, or a brioche that I had eaten before going there, paralyzed my immortal soul, and I slept the whole time.

I was thinking, as I listened to the first piece, of the way that musicians seek to establish unity in their works. The return of the motifs is, in general, the thing that they look on as the most efficacious: it is also the thing that is most accessible to men of mediocre talent. If, in certain places, this return is the cause of a great satisfaction for the mind and for the ear, it seems like a secondary means, when too frequently used, or rather a pure artifice. Is memory so fugitive that one cannot establish relationships amongst the different parts of a piece of music unless the principal idea is affirmed almost to satiety by continual repetition? A letter, a piece of prose or of poetry presents a deduction, an ensemble, arising from the development of ideas born one from the other, and it does not do so through the repetition of some phrase, which might be regarded as the capital point of the composition. In this respect, musicians resemble those preachers who take the phrase which serves as the text of their discourse, repeat it to satiety, and stick it in everywhere.

At this moment I am recalling several arias of Mozart which are admirable in their logic and deduction, without the principal motif being repeated: the aria *Qui l' odio non facunda,* the chorus of the priests from the *Magic Flute,* the trio of the *Window* from *Don Giovanni,* the quintet from the same opera, etc. These last are extended selections, a fact that increases the merit of the composer. In his symphonies, he sometimes repeats the principal motif to the point of satiety; it may be

[9] Opera by Weber.

that in that respect he is simply conforming to established usages. The art of music more than the others, it seems to me, is dominated by the pedantic habits of the profession, things that give a certain satisfaction to purely musical people, but which always weary the listener who has not gone far in his curiosity about technique, as represented by such things as fugues, learned repetitions, etc.

These repetitions of the motif occasionally seem to me a source of enjoyment, as I said; but that is the case only when they are employed in an appropriate manner. Their effect, when unity is not arrived at naturally, is less that of causing you to feel the oneness of the work than of causing you fatigue; real unity derives from elements of which genius alone has the secret. The mind is so imperfect, it has such trouble in concentrating, that even in the presence of a fine work the man most sensitive to the arts experiences a kind of disquietude, a certain difficulty in arriving at complete enjoyment; and this difficulty is not to be overcome by petty means of producing a factitious unity, such as by repetitions of the motifs in music, or by concentration of the effect in painting; those are the little tricks easily seized upon and employed by the common run of artists. A picture is a thing that seems as if it should satisfy this need for unity the most completely and easily, since one has the impression of taking the whole thing in at once; yet it will not succeed more than anything else if it be not well composed, and indeed I will add that, should it offer a great unity of effect and carry this to the highest point, the spirit will not, even so, be completely satisfied. It is necessary that when the work which has aroused the activity of the spirit is no longer present the work may, none the less, be enjoyed again in memory: in that case, what dominates is the unity of the work, if indeed the quality be really present. Then it is that the mind seizes the ensemble of the composition, or takes note of the incongruities and the breaks. These remarks made apropos of music lead me to recognize more particularly how poor professional people are as connoisseurs of the art which they practice if to the exercise of that art they do not add superiority of mind or fineness of feeling, qualities that cannot be acquired from the mere habit of playing an instrument or of using a brush. All that such men know of an art is the rut in which they drag themselves along, and the examples that the *schools* hold up for admiration. Never are they struck by the elements which mean originality; on the contrary, they are far more disposed to speak ill of such matters; in a word, the *intellectual* element is a source of sentiment which escapes them completely, and since they are, unfortunately, the most numerous group of judges, they can mislead public taste for a long time and even delay the real judgment that is to be passed on fine works. Hence, doubtless, the condescension with which great talents look down upon the narrow and mean taste which is, in general, the rule in conservatories and schools. Hence that return to technique which claims to be *learned* but which does not satisfy any need of the soul; when shallow people keep applying the accepted banalities to certain masterpieces, they reduce the effect of such work, and quickly mark them with a seal of decrepitude.

Fine works of art never grow old because the one thing that stamps them is true feeling. The language of the passions, the movements of the heart are always the same; what most surely stamps things as ancient, and what sometimes ends by causing their greatest beauty to be neglected, are the ready-made formulas within the reach of everybody at the moment when the work was composed; certain ornaments, accessory to the idea and commended by fashion, are what cause the success of the majority of works. Those who, as very rare *prodigies,* have been able to do without these accessories, have been understood only at a very late time and with great difficulty or by generations which have grown insensible to the charms of convention.

There is an *accepted mold* into which ideas good or bad are thrown, and the greatest talents, the most original ones, involuntarily bear the trace of it. What music is there that, after a certain number of years, can hold out against the appearance of being old-fashioned as a direct result of the cadenzas and the grace-notes which, in many cases, were what made its fortune at the time when it appeared? When the modern Italian school substituted ornaments of a style that seemed new for those that we were accustomed to in the music of our fathers, that novelty appeared to be the pinnacle of distinction; but that impression did not last as long as the fashion in clothing and in buildings. At most it had enough power to weary us, temporarily, of the ancient works, which it caused to appear old-fashioned; but what has already aged in the most prodigious way are these ornaments, this indiscreet decorating that a magnificent genius[10] did not disdain to add to his happy conceptions, and that a host of imitators has used as the very substance of works devoid of invention.

And this is the place to deplore that unhappy characteristic of certain inventions which charm us in original minds. The very felicities, the ornaments added by the hand of genius to expressive and profound ideas are demanded, so to speak, and genius naturally yields to them. They are intervals, almost necessary moments of repose, which give the mind a rest and lead it to new ideas.

As to the new sonorities, the combinations of Beethoven: they have already become the heritage or rather the loot of the slenderest beginners.

April 4.

As to the difference that there is between literature and painting in the matter of *the effect that may be produced by the sketch of a thought,* in a word, as to the impossibility of sketching in literature in such fashion as to describe a thing to the mind, and as to the strength that the idea may present, on the contrary, in a sketch or first note by a painter. Music is perforce in the same category as literature, and I believe that the difference between the arts of design and the others derives from the fact that the latter develop the idea only by offering impressions *one after the other.* Whereas four strokes of the brush or the pencil are enough to sum up for the mind the whole impression of a pictorial composition.

[10] Rossini —— note by M. Joubin.

Even when the literary or musical piece is completed, as to its general composition, which is supposed necessarily to render an impression on the mind, lack of finish in the details will be a greater drawback than in a marble or a picture; in a word, approximations are unbearable, or rather, what in painting is called the *indication* or the *sketch* is impossible in music: whereas in painting, a fine indication or a sketch filled with great feeling may be the equal of the most finished productions in the matter of expression.

April 7.

Concert by the princess.[11] I sat beside Mlle Gavard and her brother; the heat was unbearable there, as was also the smell of a dead rat. The concert was extremely long. The finest part was at the beginning; although that necessarily spoiled the rest, we at least had the pleasure of enjoying without fatigue the whole of Mozart's beautiful symphony in C minor; my poor Chopin has weaknesses, after that. The good princess insists on playing the big works; she is encouraged in that by her musicians, who have no idea what it is all about, real professionals though they are. These compositions are somewhat lacking in the breath of life. It must be granted that the texture, the invention, and the perfection are all in Mozart. Barbereau was telling me, at the house of Boissard, after that beautiful quartet which I shall discuss later, that Mozart, even more than Haydn, has simplicity and frankness in his ideas; one appreciates him more especially when remembering him later on. Barbereau attributes this very largely to science, not omitting inspiration; he says that it is science which permits the composer to profit by ideas.

April 8.

The happy man is the one who has conquered his happiness or the moment of happiness that he feels at a given time. The thing they talk so much about and call progress tends to suppress the effort be-

[11] Czartoriska.

tween desire and its accomplishment; its effect would doubtless be to render man more unhappy, in reality. Man accustoms himself[12] . . . to a perspective of happiness easy to attain: suppression of distance, suppression of labor in every field.

After having suppressed space, after having brought down to low cost all sorts of substances which are employed for the luxury and the pleasure of a decadent generation, the one thing that remains to be done is to make the earth decide to spread forth more generously her ancient gifts, the very source of our life. It is more difficult to regulate the course of the seasons than to hollow out mountains and to lay out pieces of iron in long lines over stretches of country, thereby bringing places close together and saving time.[13] Philanthropists have imagined indeed that mechanics would one day make up for the caprices of the wind and the difficulties of the soil, and thus give freely to the human race the food that it has been wresting from the earth by hard labor ever since it was cast, naked, upon the face of the earth, and since the time when it gave up the procuring of a miserable subsistence through bows and arrows and at the expense of other miserable creatures who get their food without the same trouble, and yet with work that is hard enough.

April 11.

I was doing my packing all morning and then, at two o'clock, went to the house of Boissard. Divine quartet by Mozart.

Chenavard was telling us about Rossini: they used to treat him as a *perrucone* (old hat) already in 1828. He bursts with jealousy over the successes of the most unimportant musicians. The philosopher quoted to us the remark of Boileau, already a very old one, to Louis Racine: he told him that *he had never heard praise for the merest shoemaker without feeling the tooth of envy in his heart*. He said that emulation was necessary.

[12] Some words are omitted here.
[13] A great deal of railroad building was in progress at the time.

Champrosay, April 12.

I brought with me the end of Silvestre's article on me.[14] I am very well pleased about it. Those poor artists! They perish if people do not take notice of them. He puts me in the category of those who have preferred *the opinion of posterity to that of their period.*

April 22.

In bad humor all morning, the result of a bad cigar. And as a consequence, bad work; fixed up or spoiled the *Clorinde;* that is the thing I've got to do now, and I shall have to make a heroic effort to get it going again.

April 23.

Got ahead with the picture of the *Little Arab Seated beside his Horse.*[15] Took up the *Clorinde* again, and believe I have brought it to an effect entirely different, one that leads me back to my original idea, which had escaped me little by iittle. Unfortunately it often happens that the execution, or difficulties, completely secondary considerations, throw one off from one's intention. The original idea, the sketch, which is so to speak the egg or embryo of the idea, is usually far from being complete; it contains everything, if you will, but it is necessary to free this everything, which is simply a mixing together of all parts. Just the thing that makes of this sketch the essential expression of the idea is not the suppression of details, but their complete subordination to the big lines which are, before all else, to create the impression. The greatest difficulty therefore is that of returning in the picture to that effacing of the details which, however, make up the composition, the web and the woof of the picture.

I do not know whether I am mistaken, but I believe that the greatest artists have had great struggles with that difficulty, the most

[14] This is the study published at the time by Théophile Silvestre and included, the following year, in the work entitled: *Les Artistes Français,* in the edition of Crès et Cie, Paris, 1926.

[15] Unknown; variant of the picture at Bordeaux (Catalogue Robaut, 1046).

serious one of all. Here one sees more than ever the drawback of giving to the details, through grace or coquetry in execution, so much interest that later on one mortally regrets sacrificing them when they are injurious to the ensemble. It is here that that breed of painters who are prodigal of easy and witty touches, fellows who go in for expressive torsos and heads, run into confusion through the very thing which they considered to be their great success. The picture, composed of *separate pieces,* each finished with care and placed next to its neighbor, one after another, looks like a masterpiece and the climax of cleverness, as long as it is not finished, which is to say as long as the field is not covered: because finishing, for those painters who finish each detail as they put it on the canvas, is to cover that canvas. In the presence of such work, proceeding without a halt, as it does, in the presence of those parts which seem the more interesting since you have nothing but parts to admire, one is involuntarily seized by a somewhat thought-less astonishment; but when the last touch has been placed, when the architect of that whole heap of separate parts has placed upon them the pinnacle of his motley edifice and said his last word, one sees nothing but breaks and encumberment; one sees that in no place has he at-tained order. The interest that one gives to each object disappears in the confusion; what seems like precise and proper execution becomes dryness itself through the constant absence of *sacrifices.* From this putting together as if by accident of parts having no necessary connec-tion, will you demand that penetrating and rapid impression, that original sketch giving the impression of an ideal which the artist is supposed to have glimpsed or caught in the first moment of inspira-tion? With the great artists, this sketch is not a dream, a confused cloud, it is something other than a mixture of barely perceptible lineaments; the great artists alone have a fixed point of departure, and it is to that pure expression that it is so difficult for them to return in either a pro-longed or rapid execution of the work. Will the mediocre artist, con-cerned with his craft alone, arrive at such a result with the help of those extraordinary feats of strength in the matter of details which mislead as to the idea, instead of bringing it to the light? It is incredible to what point there is confusion concerning the first elements of composition in the minds of the majority of artists. How indeed should they be disturbed about returning through their *execution* to the idea, when they never had one?

April 27.

The study I made of the trees along my road has helped me to brace up the picture of the *Lion Hunters*[16] which, in my bad state of yesterday, I had got into an unfortunate state, although it had been going well the day before. I was seized with an inspiring rage, like the other day when I reworked the *Clorinde,* not that there were changes to be made, but the picture had suddenly gotten into that languishing and dull state which simply points a finger at lack of ardor in working. I am sorry for the people who work tranquilly and coldly. I think that everything they do can be no more than cold and tranquil, and cannot fail to bring the spectator into a still worse condition of coldness and tranquillity. There are some of them who glory in this cool composure, this absence of emotion; they imagine that they are mastering their inspiration.

We have had a heavy rain; it was impossible to go out in the evening, so I spent it sleeping and walking about the house and making plans. I am turning over in my head the two pictures of *Lions*[17] for the Exposition; I am thinking also of the allegory of *Genius Attaining Glory.*

Delicious sensation, on going to bed at a very late hour, of the freshness of the evening when I opened my windows and there entered

---

[16] Catalogue Robaut, 1019. That same year, 1854, Jules Gérard, the "Lion-Killer," published his book *La Chasse aux Lions,* which all Paris was reading.

[17] Doubtless the picture, since partly destroyed by fire, at the Museum of Bordeaux (Catalogue Robaut, 1242), and the variant (Catalogue Robaut, 1278). The project for the *Genius* never went beyond the preparatory sketches (Catalogue Robaut, 727 and 728).

all the *diamonds* of the song of the nightingale. If it were possible to paint this song for the mind by means of the eyes, I would compare it to the splendor sent forth by the stars when you see them through the trees on a fine night; those notes, light, or vivid, or fluted, or full of an energy inconceivable in that little throat, for me represent those fires, now sparkling, now slightly veiled, scattered unevenly, like immortal diamonds, in the deep vault of the night. The meeting of these two emotions, which is a very frequent occurrence at this season, and the feeling of solitude and of freshness and, in addition, of coolness, the odor of plants and above all of the woods, which seems more intense in the evening, are one of those spiritual feasts to which the imperfect thing that is creation rarely invites the soul.

April 28.

On waking up, my thoughts turn to those moments, so agreeable and so sweet to my memory and my heart, that I spent with my good aunt[18] in the country. I am thinking of her, of Henry, of that unfortunate Léon Riesener, who has been ruined by his household for feelings like these, if ever he had them, his married life having turned him into a drudge instead of an artist. When I call him that, I mean that all he is interested in is the material thing, and in the unhappiest way; he is really dragging the saddest burden that one can possibly bear, that of his marriage and the household he has to support; there is no longer in him a single spark of aspiration toward the pleasures of the mind or of his profession; but his present situation is taking me away from my thoughts of this morning.

Reflecting on the freshness of memories, on the color of enchantment that they assume in a distant past, I was wondering at that involuntary work of the spirit which, passing pleasant moments in review, separates from them and suppresses anything that lessens the charm of the time when one was in their midst. I was comparing that kind of idealization, for it is one, with the effect of fine works of the

---

[18] Mme Henri Riesener, the mother of Léon.

imagination. The great artist concentrates interest by suppressing details that are useless or repellent or foolish; his powerful hand disposes and establishes, adds or suppresses, and thus makes its own use of the objects which are its own; he moves about within his domain and there spreads forth a feast for you; in the work of a mediocre artist, one feels that he has not been the master of anything; he exerts no influence whatsoever upon the borrowed materials that he heaps up. What order should he establish in that work where everything dominates him? All he can do is to invent timidly and copy with servility; now, instead of acting as does the imagination when it suppresses repulsive elements, he gives them an equal and sometimes a superior rank through the servile manner with which he copies. And so everything in his work is confusion and insipidity. Even when a certain degree of interest or indeed of charm appears, by reason of the personal inspiration he may infuse into his compilation, I compare it to life as it is, and to that mixture of pleasant gleams and of disgusts which compose it. In the same way, in the motley composition of my semi-artist, where the evil chokes the good, we barely feel the current of life offering us its fleeting moments of happiness, so completely are they spoiled by the commonplace troubles that we meet every day.

Can a man say that he has been happy at a given moment in his life which memory causes him to look on as charming? He is so, assuredly, in the memory itself, he notes the happiness that he must have felt; but at the instant of that so-called happiness, did he really feel himself to be happy? He was like a man who possesses a piece of land in which there lies buried a treasure of which he is unaware. Would you call such a man rich? no more than I would call happy the man who is so without imagining that he is, or without knowing the extent of his happiness. The vulgar call the monarch happy, because he has everything at his disposal, everything — especially — that the vulgar lack; but the latter do not see that he is besieged by the annoyances attaching to his exalted position, just as the common man is besieged by the enemies of his mean estate. These annoyances darken all pleasures, for him as for the monarch; and how many things there are that he enjoys, scarcely aware of them indeed, though they are inestimable and, for the great whom he envies, forbidden or even unknown! These advantages are so numerous, they are so certain, that they amply suffice, I will not say to console, but to render delightful the lot of that part of humanity that stands between riches and poverty.

The pure enjoyment that I find here, not to speak of the fact that I have little taste for the pleasures of the great, permits me to let this note go without more emphasis.

April 29.

Went back to my picture of the *Women Bathing*.

Since I have come here, I have gone on to a better understanding of the *principle* of the trees, although the foliage is not very far advanced. One should model them with a colored reflection, as when one is treating flesh: the same principle seems even more practical for the present case. This reflection should not be entirely a reflection. When one comes to finishing, one adds to the reflection in places where that is necessary, and when one paints on top of passages that are light or gray, the transition is less brusque. I notice that one should always model with masses that turn, as would be the case with objects not composed of an infinitude of little parts, such as leaves: but as they are extremely transparent, the tone of the reflection plays a big role in the treatment of the leaves.

Therefore:

1st, this general tone which is not entirely a *reflection, nor yet shadow, nor yet light,* but is *transparent almost everywhere:*

2nd, that the edge is colder and darker, marking the passage from this reflection into the *lighter part,* which should be indicated in the lay-in;

3rd, and the leaves completely within the cast shadow from those above, which have neither *reflections* nor *lights,* and which it is better merely to indicate;

4th, the *mat passages in the light* which are the last that should be painted.

One must always argue the thing out like this and, above all, keep in mind the direction from which the light comes. If it comes from behind the tree, the latter will be almost all reflection. It will present a mass of reflection in which a few touches of *mat tone* will be barely visible; if on the contrary the light comes from behind the spectator, which is to say that it is facing the tree, the branches on the other side of the trunk, instead of having reflections, will be massed in a tone of *shadow that is unbroken* and *completely flat*. To sum up, the more flatly the different tones are laid on, the more lightness the tree will possess.

The more I reflect on color, the more I discover how much the reflected half-tint affords us the principle that must dominate, because it is what gives the true tone, as a matter of fact, the tone that constitutes the value, and the one that counts in the object and causes it to exist. Light, to which the schools teach us to attach equal importance, and which they place on the canvas at the same time as the half-tint and the shadow, is only a pure accident: without understanding that, one cannot understand true color, I mean color that gives the feeling of thickness and the feeling of that radical difference which should distinguish one object from the other.

April 30.

I write to Mme de Forget:

. . . .

"Have you read about the funny lawsuit against Dumas that is being brought by Mme Balzac, the widow?[19] She is absolutely set on erecting a tomb for her husband, according to her own ideas but of course with the subscriptions of the public. She is right if she really has built this tomb; but if after four years, it still remains to be built,

[19] There had been scheduled for May 15, at the Ambigu, a performance to raise funds for a monument in honor of Balzac.

Dumas is right in wanting to render this small honor, which will cost him nothing, to the dead colleague, that Balzac whom he detested when alive."

And now comes poor Lamartine who takes up his pen to give to a public of children an *expurgata* edition of his own works.[20] The preface that he puts at the head of this volume of his selected works seems itself to be badly in need of a purge and, above all, of abridgement. It contains sentences like this one: "The more of abundance there is in a writer, the more river-slime he must deposit along his course . . . the thought of man does not spout forth on the *first* wave nor on all waves. Limpid, rapid, incorruptible, *worthy of being* envasée[21] *in the urns of the centuries so as to be given to the human race and to quench its thirst,* the thought of *the man most favored with the gifts of heaven* is a torrent flowing from a more or less elevated point and hollowing out for itself a more or less deep bed in the memory of men, etc., but which, in its flow, carries with it froth, dregs, and sand, that one must be careful not to gather up with *the water from heaven.*"

We are going to see that *water from heaven* which M. de Lamartine distills on days when he is feeling good. If the style of the selections he is publishing has the flavor of what we have just read, people may indeed be of the opinion, as he himself confesses, that the collection is still too voluminous. Is it not strange that an author exhibits and confesses in this way to the eyes of all that he is full of *that slime,* of that sand which he speaks of, something that attests only the haste of his writing and at the same time his contempt for the kind public that he is addressing! Thus, with the intention of giving his wares another form, he himself engages in the trade of writing a criticism on his own books, and he takes the trouble to show us all that is bad in

[20] It was a work entitled *Lectures pour Tons* etc., Paris Grasset, 1854. M. Joubin notes that Delacroix did not appreciate Lamartine's genius at all, and is harsh with him.

[21] The literal meaning of *envasée* is *choked with mud;* Lamartine evidently made a slip which caused him to use the word in the sense of *enclosed in a vase,* as would befit "water from heaven."

them. He goes so far as to rewrite passages, he *suppresses the strophe,* he *purifies the image,* he corrects the word. It is probable that this is the last book that he intends to publish; for who will want to buy the others henceforth? It is clear that he will do them over in another fashion every ten years, purifying them, we may be quite sure.

May 5.

At nine o'clock, committee meeting for the Collège Stanislas.[22] In France, and I may say in other countries, there is no longer any middle ground: either be a Jesuit or a Septembrist; one régime or the other has got to be suffered. This introduction of ecclesiastics into education, a thing confessed and invited by the government, is a tendency in which one cannot stop without necessarily falling into the opposite extreme.

May 10.

Insipid morning and a bad state of mind at the Hôtel de Ville. Discussion in the committee on the Stanislas project.

As I was leaving I saw the hall decorated by Ingres.[23] The proportions of his ceiling give one a real shock: he did not calculate the loss that the perspective of the ceiling brings about in the figures. The emptiness of the whole lower part of the picture is unbearable, and that big solid blue in which the horses — quite nude also — are swimming, with that nude emperor and that chariot going through the air, produce the most discordant effect, for the mind as for the eye. The figures in the panel are the weakest that he has done: awkwardness predominates over all the merits of the man. Pretension and awkwardness, with a certain suavity in details that have charm, in spite of or because of their affectation — and that, I think, is what will remain of this for our descendants.

[22] The Collège Stanislas was a private ecclesiastical institution which it was proposed to attach to the University.
[23] The Salon de l'Empereur, in which Ingres painted his ceiling, the *Apotheosis of Napoleon I,* which was mentioned on page 368.

I went to look at my Salon:[24] I did not get back a single one of my impressions, everything in it seemed to me garish.

I found the Place de la Concorde all upset again. They are talking about taking away the obelisk. Perrier was pretending this morning that it blocked the view! They are talking of selling the Champs-Elysées to speculators! It is the Palais de l'Industrie that has given them such ideas. When we resemble the Americans a bit more, the Jardin des Tuileries will be sold as open lots that are good for nothing.

May 20.

Started for Augerville[25] with Berryer, Batta and M. Hennequin. A sad departure; I am growing young again in the way I am sad over everything that happens. The state of my health has some bearing on the matter.

The arrival was charming: this place was especially arranged for him, it is full of ancient things that I adore. I do not know any impression more delightful than that of an old country house; in the cities one no longer finds even a trace of ancient customs: the old portraits, the old woodwork, the turrets, the pointed roofs, everything pleases the imagination and the heart, even to the odor that one breathes in these ancient houses. One finds there quantities of forgotten picture-books such as delighted our childhood and that were new at that time. There is a room here which was dwelt in by the great Condé, and where the paintings in distemper still exist. These paintings are of an astounding freshness; the burnished gilding is intact.

The Bishop of Orleans has arrived this afternoon, on his tour of confirmation. He is very fine, very distinguished, and has a great deal of wit.

[24] The Salon de la Paix at the Hôtel de Ville.
[25] The estate of Berryer, the famous lawyer, Delacroix's cousin; Augerville was situated near Malesherbes. Alexandre Batta (1816–1902), celebrated Dutch cellist; Amédée Hennequin (1817-1859), writer, a friend of Berryer's. As to these visits to Augerville, one may read the *Souvenirs* of Mme Jaubert, a cousin of Berryer's.

Hamlet and Horatio (1839). The Louvre. Photograph by Giraudon

Lion Devouring a Horse, lithograph (1844)

The Education of Achilles, drawing (about 1844)

The Education of Achilles, mural painting (about 1844). Chamber of Deputies
Paris. Photograph by Vizzavona

Numa and Egeria, study for or after the mural painting at the Chamber of Deputies (about 1844). Courtesy of M. Knoedler and Company

LA CAPTIVITÉ
A
BABYLONE

The Captivity at Babylon, mural painting (about 1844). Chamber of Deputies,
Paris. Photograph by Vizzavona

The Sibyl with the Golden Bough (1845)

The Abduction of Rebecca (1846). The Metropolitan Museum, New York

Perseus and Andromeda (1847). Collection of Mr. Leo Stein

Flowers (1848). Courtesy of Wildenstein and Company

Arab Mounting his Horse (1849). Courtesy of Wildenstein and Company

Morning (1850). Collection of M. D. David-Weill, Paris

Sketch for the Ceiling of the Galerie d'Apollon (1850). Museum of Brussels

Ruth and Boas (also known as A View of Tangier). Courtesy of Messrs. Durand-Ruel

Daniel in the Lions' Den (1853). Courtesy of Messrs. Durand-Ruel

Christ on the Lake of Genesareth, sketch (1853). Courtesy of Messrs. Durand-Ruel

I like that bishop very much. I must have some wax in my nature: I melt easily as soon as my mind gets heated up with some spectacle, or because of the presence of a person who has something imposing or interesting about him. I talked about the original sin in a way that must have given those gentlemen a great idea of my convictions. And so the evening went off very well indeed.

May 22.

Before going to church in the morning, to see the confirmation ceremony, Berryer took me into his office, which is next to his room, and read me some fragments from manuscripts of his father's, wherein he relates the first service that my father rendered him. My father[26] was so placed that he could do anything, under Turgot: his waiting-room was filled with men covered with decorations, with great ladies, and with people seeking favors of every kind. This position made him subject to a great many attacks because, said Berryer the father, of his austere probity. He had begun as a lawyer and regretted leaving that profession; hence, quite naturally, his advising Berryer to adopt that calling, rather than bury himself in government offices. Later on, under the Convention, Berryer, who was badly compromised, was saved by my father.

About ten o'clock the people came in procession to call for the bishop. The ceremony touched me very much.

Berryer's father and wife are buried in the church. The idea came to me of doing a *Saint Peter* for them; he is the patron of the parish and

---

[26] Charles Delacroix, the father of Eugène, had been, in his early days, the secretary of Turgot, at that time governor of the *généralité* of Limoges. He was then promoted to be first clerk in the Marine and to the *Contrôle général*. He had retired in 1779. Then came the Revolution. Appointed administrator of the Department of the Marine, he was elected to the Convention, and then became Minister of Foreign Relations from 1795 to 1797, then Minister to Holland and, finally, from 1805, prefect at Marseilles and at Bordeaux.

and he was the patron of Berryer's father; this plan will perhaps disappear with my Catholic sentiments of the present moment.[27]

After the ceremony and Monseigneur's exhortation, we witnessed the benediction of the graves in the cemetery: that was really beautiful. The bishop, bare-headed, and in his robes of ceremony, the crozier in one hand and the aspersorium in the other, walks with long steps sprinkling the holy water right and left over the humble sepulchers. Religion is a beautiful thing when it is like this. The consolations and the counsels that the prelate gave in the church to these simple men, burnt by the work of the countryside and chained to hard necessities, went to their true goal. On returning, and before re-entering the house, he blessed the children that the mothers presented to him.

May 23.

Weather as in the time of the Deluge. We had been told that the princess[28] would arrive today: a nice story to believe, with that frightful rain! And yet she did come. She was proof against everything: she showed neither fatigue nor a wry face. We took the ladies about for a long walk. The good princess was perhaps a bit bored by having to inspect the whole estate. She had taken my arm very amiably, and I didn't have a dull moment. She has a character of the same type as my own; she has the desire to please. She would be gracious with a cow-herd, and she does not have to make any effort in following out that propensity. What there is of a really good or an obliging nature under all that, heaven knows better than I or better than she herself does perhaps . . . I am like that; you remain the way you were made.

While we were waiting for those ladies, the other time we took a walk (it was on Monday), Berryer, seated at the end of the alley of linden trees where he has built a walk, was telling me that he advised

[27] That is what really happened. The *Saint Peter* was never executed.
[28] Czartoriska.

Villemain[29] to be gentle in his judgments of men and their passions, in what he is writing about the men of our time: it is a matter of adopting a point of view suited to the passions and the prejudices of the present day. Martignac, the gentlest of men, wanted to have him and his father hanged, after 1815, because of the famous lawsuit in which the two of them[30] had taken the part of the men proscribed.

May 24.

Batta and the princess played us some delightful things in the evening; there was a sonata by Beethoven, of which I already knew the piano part. Very great and very rare pleasure.

May 25.

Saw two copies of London *Punch*. I must try to get it in Paris: there are some types of caricature in it that contain very fine drawing.

Went upstairs to bed before the rest of the company, which kept on with its game until midnight.

. . . .

They think that they will be truer when they vie with nature in her aspect of literal truth; it is the reverse that occurs; more literal their way of representing, the flatter their work is and the more it shows the absolute failure of rivalry. The only thing that one can hope to arrive at is an equivalent. What we are called upon to make is not the thing itself but the semblance of the thing: moreover it is for the mind and not for the eye that we must produce our effect.

May 29.

A bad day. I did scarcely any work; took a solitary walk in the evening.

[29] Villemain, who had played a very brilliant role under the monarchy of July, had been back in private life since 1848 and was busying himself exclusively with his position of *secrétaire perpétuel* of the Académie Française.

[30] Berryer and his father. The matter referred to was the trial of Marshal Ney, who was defended by Berryer Senior, assisted by his son and by Dupin aîné.

Painted a short time on the *Christ on the Sea:*[31] impression of the sublime and of the light.

June 7.

Went back to the small sketch for the *Lion Hunt.*

In the evening went to *La Vestale;*[32] although I got impatient at the length of the intermissions, I was very much interested. Mme Cruvelli has something of the antique in her gestures, especially in the scene with the tripod. She is not squeezed into her clothes as ordinary actresses are when they wear Greek or Roman costumes. The music, also, has character. I remember that Franchomme smiled when I put that above Cherubini. Perhaps he was right in the matter of technique; but I believe that the same opera treated by the famous master of counterpoint would not have had those bursts of passion and at the same time that simplicity. Berlioz, to whom I was talking, tells me that Spontini was a man who had flashes of genius.

During the day I went to the World's Fair Commission. They had been bothering us with a question as to which of us wanted to go to London for the opening of the Crystal Palace. Despite the presence of that kind Lord Cowley[33] and despite pressing invitations, all they could find was two members who were willing to go. When questioned on the subject, all the rest of us declined the commission. The English have again produced one of their marvels, which they do with a facility most astonishing to us, thanks to the money they can raise up to any amount, and thanks to their commercial audacity, on which score we imagine we are imitating them. They triumph over our inferiority, a thing which will not cease until we undergo a change of character. Our Exposition and the place in which we are going to hold it are pitiful; but, once more, our type of mind will never bend in that direc-

[31] Robaut has grouped in the year 1853 (Numbers 1214-1220) several pictures with or without date representing Christ on the Lake of Genesareth. The picture referred to is doubtless one of these or a similar work.
[32] Opera by Spontini.
[33] At that time the British ambassador in Paris.

tion, one in which the Americans already surpass the English themselves, gifted as they are with the same steadiness and the same energy when it comes to carrying out a plan.

June 12.

The Monday dinner. Delaroche seemed to me to act like a very good fellow. Everybody, except Dauzats, was against me in maintaining that animals alone have instinct, and that man has none. Although the terrible Chaix-d'est-Ange[34] was in the opposing camp, I supported my opinion with the warmth that I thought it deserved, and afterward I thought of a hundred arguments, each one stronger than the others, that I had left unspoken.

June 16.

Gave Haro, for cradling, the cardboard panel of the small Andromeda.[35] Went to the Council, where I had missed several of the last sessions. Ottin,[36] whom I meet on my return, relates to me how Simart[37] once made a figure of *David* and how Ingres, whom he had got to come to his studio, made him destroy it on account of the subject. It seems all one could permit oneself was a Greek subject: to do a *David* was a monstrosity. What would he say of poor Préault, who does things like *Ophelia* and other eccentricities, English and Romantic?

Dined at the house of Mme de Forget, with young d'Ideville. Played billiards with him.

. . . .

On the fragility of painting, especially among the moderns.

[34] Chaix-d'est-Ange (1800-1876), the celebrated lawyer.
[35] Catalogue Robaut, 1001 and 1002.
[36] Auguste Ottin (1811-1890), sculptor, pupil of David d'Angers, author of the group on the Medici Fountain at the Luxembourg.
[37] Pierre Simart (1806-1857), sculptor, winner of the Prix de Rome, author of the decoration on the tomb of Napoleon at the Invalides. The scene described must have taken place at the Villa Médicis at the time when Ingres was the director there.

June 17.

Dined at the house of Chabrier with Poinsot, Admiral Casy, d'Audiffret, Beauchesne, etc. At dinner, Poinsot relates to me an incident at which he was present and which shows Napoleon's intentions as regards the Madeleine; he says that the Emperor intended to have prayers said for the soul of Louis XVI, in celebration of the 21st of January; he said he would make them swallow that pill, no matter how bitter it would be for them (he meant the men like Cambacérès, Fouché, etc.).

June 18.

At eight o'clock, went to Durieu's place. Until nearly five o'clock, we did nothing put pose. Thévelin[38] made as many sketches as Durieu made prints: a minute or a minute and a half at most for each.

Huet[39] took me home with him and then I noticed that I had forgotten my spectacles and I returned, in haste and tired out, to get them at Durieu's place, on the seventh floor. That poor Huet has not the least talent: he paints like an old man, and there is no longer a vestige of color in his work.

June 24.

Went to see Mercey,[40] to show him my sketch: he cooled me off with his remarks, some of which, however, are well founded.

---

[38] Thévenin (1819-1869), engraver. Delacroix certainly wrote Thévelin; he was probably referring to Jean-Charles Thévenin.

[39] Paul Huet (1804–1869), a landscape painter eminent in the Romantic School. One need not accept literally the severe judgment on him here set down by Delacroix—who had great esteem and affection for the comrade of his youth. He was evidently upset by the loss of his glasses and having to climb seven flights of stairs again to get them, after the long session of posing for Durieu.

[40] The Director of the Beaux-Arts at the time. The question was doubtless as to a sketch for Saint-Sulpice.

June 25.

Went to see Durieu. Photographs and drawings from the *Bohémien*.

During an interval, I went to Saint-Sulpice to see what Andrieu has been tracing. Everything is adjusted to perfection, and I think the work is going to go very well; the start is excellent.

From time to time I rather enjoy those parties that get me away from home: they drive away old thoughts and give you new ones. Here, by the way, are two Sundays in succession that I have been to them; both times I had lunch there, and I am the man who, as a rule, can't swallow a thing even in the accustomed surroundings of his studio. It is just the same thing that I noticed with such surprise during my visit to Berryer. Diversions, conversations, and getting the mind out of its usual rut have an influence on the body.

June 27.

Dined at Riesener's with Vieillard. During the day, almost finished the *Arab Horseman and the Tiger*[41] for Weill. Arnoux dropped in during the day. He told me about a scheme for an exhibition that is being considered by Delamarre.[42] He says that the *Massacre*[43] did not gain from the removal of the varnish, and I am almost of his opinion, without having seen it. The picture will have lost the transparence of the shadows, in the same way that that occurred when they worked on the Veronese,[44] and the same as will almost inevitably happen every time. Haro says that he takes off varnish by washing and not by rubbing with his finger. If he has done that, he has overcome a great difficulty. In the meantime, he has spoiled the portraits of my two brothers as children by Uncle Riesener that I entrusted to him.

June 28.

In the morning worked on the *Arab Teaching his Son to Ride.*[45] Boissard dropped in. Then Villot; I was glad to see him. They are all surprised to see how much I am getting done. I tell them that instead of running around like most of the artists, I spend my time in my studio.

I must remember to ask Riesener for my study of trees on paper. I want to borrow his sketches and some landscape studies of Frépillon and other places, because of the cool tones they have. Also the one from Valmont to use in the picture of the *Two Knights and the Nymphs,* from the *Jerusalem.*

[41] A picture that has not been identified.

[42] Delamarre (1796-1870), journalist, deputy, owner of the newspaper *La Patrie* after 1844; he had undertaken to solve the insoluble problem of the sale of artists' works without having recourse to the dealers, and he had planned to build a gallery for that purpose. The plan seems never to have been realized.

[43] The *Massacre at Scio.*

[44] The Veronese of the Louvre, restored by Villot. The matter has been discussed before.

[45] Catalogue Robaut, 1237.

June 29.

Dined at Poinsot's.

On the fragility of painting and of everything that our arts produce. As to pictures: *canvases, oils, varnishes,* while the chemists are boasting of progress. It is like social progress, which consists of starting a war among all classes by means of the silly ambitions excited in the lower classes: a way of reaching *sociality,* if you like, but not *sociability.* The best-made lithographs by Charlet, dating from twenty years ago, are crumbling into dust. Progress, in its own opinion, has perfected paper, and not one of our books, of our writings of the rules that serve to regulate our business relations, will exist any more, half a century hence. Sociality means that each one should work for himself and not bother about other people. We are supposed to make merry during our short journey through this life, and let the people who come afterward make the best of whatever state they are in. What used to be called the *family* is today a vain word. In our present code, veneration, even fear of the father, has been abolished through the familiarity that custom now permits; we see what the chief thing is that is dissolving all the bonds which once united the members of a family. The equal division of estates adds the last step to this process. The place of birth, the paternal habitation, thus falls easily into the hands of strangers after the death of the father. Someone may reply that we are sacrificing to different gods: the welfare of humanity has become the sole passion of men who cannot live with their brothers, the men in whose veins their own blood runs. There are charity organizers who relieve us of the care of giving the right destination to the offerings we make to the unfortunates of the whole world, whom one thus assists without knowing them or without ever meeting them. These professional philanthropists are all fat and well fed: they live happily from the money that they are entrusted to spend. How happy, then, are all these benefactors and this century, thinking they have suppressed all evils because they can keep them out of sight; happier yet the adroit dispensers of everybody's charity, having solved the problem of depriving themselves of nothing, while giving to everyone.

Went to Boissard's place at two o'clock to hear some music. They don't yet grasp the Beethoven of the last period. I was asking Barbereau whether he had quite gotten to the core of the last quartets: he tells me that a magnifying glass is still needed to get everything, and perhaps it will always be needed. The first violinist told me that it was magnificent, and that there were always obscure passages. I had the boldness to tell him that what remained obscure for everybody, and especially for the violinist, had doubtless been obscure in the mind of its author. However, let us not pronounce judgment yet; the thing on which we should always lay our wagers is genius.

June 30.

Went to Saint-Sulpice, which is getting along well. My heart beats faster when I find myself in the presence of great walls to paint.

Dined with Mme de Forget, to whom I went at five o'clock to look at the decorations over her doors; they are out of proportion, and she is replacing them with hangings; I finished the evening there.

July 1.

A day of uninterrupted work. Great and delightful sentiment of solitude and tranquillity — of the deep happiness that they give. There is no man more sociable than I. Once I am in the presence of people who please me, even if some of them come in merely by chance — unless some irritating trait of theirs inspires me with aversion, I always yield to the pleasure it gives me to be cordial with people: I act as if everybody was my friend, I go more than half way in meeting people on the grounds of amiability, I have the desire to please them, to be liked. This peculiar disposition has probably given a wrong idea of my character. There is nothing that so much resembles falseness and flattery as this desire to be on friendly terms with people, which is simply a natural inclination. I attribute to my nervous and irritable constitution this peculiar passion for solitude, which seems so strongly in opposition to an inclination to be amiable that I carry to almost ridiculous lengths. I want to please the workman who delivers a piece of furniture for me; I want the man thrown in my path by chance to feel satisfaction as he leaves me, whether he is a peasant or a nobleman; and with the desire to be agreeable and live with people on good terms, there is in me an almost silly pride which has almost always made me avoid seeing people who could be useful to me, fearing, as I do, that I may seem to flatter them. The fear of being interrupted when I am alone generally comes, when I am at home, from the fact that I am engaged in my one occupation, which is painting: I have no other that possesses the least importance. This fear, which also pursues me when I am taking a walk by myself, is an effect of that very desire to be as sociable as possible in the company of my fellow-men. The nervousness of my temperament causes me to feel anxious over the fatigue that I should feel from meeting a given person, even though amiable; I am like that Gascon who said on going into battle: "I tremble at the perils to which my courage will expose me."

July 2.

The horses that I drew in the meadow on Berryer's estate, with a Greek shepherd seated, and a girl or some other figure.[46]

July 3.

Repetition, by Andrieu, of the *Christ*[47] in the collection of Grzimala for B———. My good Jenny was saying to me, on seeing the disorder in which my drawings are heaping up, scattered and unclassified as they are, that it was absolutely necessary *to give to things the time that they demand.*

[46] This is probably the picture entitled *Halt of Greek Horsemen,* (Catalogue Robaut, 1389), now in the Museum of the City of Cleveland, Ohio.

[47] *Christ on the Lake of Genesareth* (Catalogue Robaut, 1219). We see that Delacroix entrusted Andrieu with repetitions of his pictures, which he himself finished later on.

July 4.

I must send my *Justinian* [48] to the Exposition of 1855.

. . . .

I got up before five o'clock. Noted some ideas that had come to me for the article on "The Beautiful," [49] and went back to bed until eight o'clock; a certain indisposition had seized me. Got to work again until dinner time, almost without stopping, except to sleep for a few minutes. I had to make as big an effort as that in order to get this work into a state where I could finish it within two or three days more: it's the devil's own job.

After dinner, rather against my habit, I did the best part of the work by making an examination of the subject as a whole; a few of the pages were written with a certain verve. I am writing this on Wednesday morning, and I have not re-read what I put down previously. I should be curious to see whether, as I think, the state of mind I was in after dinner puts me into the best disposition for producing. At this moment when I have just gotten up, I am really fatigued by my excessive work of yesterday, and I haven't an idea in my head: body and mind are simply asking for rest.

All these evenings I have been taking walks by myself.

July 5.

Returning home, my eyes fall on the picture of *Lot* by Rubens,[50] of which I made a small copy. I am astonished at the coldness of that composition and at the smallness of the interest that it presents, apart from the talent for painting the figures. It is not really until you get to Rembrandt that you see the beginning, in pictures, of that accord

[48] The big canvas of *The Emperor Justinian Composing his Statutes*, painted in 1826, used to decorate the great hall of the Council of State (Catalogue Robaut, 153). The picture was destroyed by fire in 1871.

[49] The article entitled "Questions sur le Beau" appeared in the *Revue des Deux Mondes* for July 15, 1854.

[50] In the Louvre.

between accessories and the chief subject, which seems to me one of the most important elements, if not the most important one. On this point, one might draw up a comparison among the famous masters.

July 6.

Write something about the antique. As to false embellishments: the cartoons of Rubens for the *Life of Achilles,* the passages from Homer and the Greek tragic poets in which one hears the cry of nature: Vulcan in his forge, in the *Iliad*. Comparison with David.

July 19.

Andrieu tells me that the weather necessary for grapevines is the contrary of what one needs for wheat: for the latter fresh clear weather is the thing; for the grapes what is needed is stifling weather, the hot winds of the South. Relate this with my reflection on *necessary misfortunes*.

Not only do we see this apparent contradiction in nature, which seems to satisfy one group of men at the expense of another, but we ourselves are full of contradictions, of fluctuations, of inconstant movements, which give an agreeable or a hateful quality to the position we are in, one that does not change: it is we who change. We wish for a certain state of happiness, which ceases to be one when we have obtained it. The situation we have been desiring is often worse, as a matter of fact, than the one in which we were before.

Man is so bizarre that he finds in misfortune itself reasons for consolation and almost for pleasure, like this one, for example, to feel oneself unjustly persecuted and to have within oneself the consciousness of merit too good for one's present fortune; but it far more frequently happens that man is bored in the midst of prosperity, that he even considers himself unfortunate while possessing it. La Fontaine's shepherd, when he had become prime minister and was surrounded in his elevated position by jealousy and intrigue, must have been an object of pity and must have felt himself to be one; he must have experienced a vivid moment of happiness, when he had donned his simple shepherd clothes once more and when they gave him his standing in the eyes of all men, so that he could return to the scenes and the life where, with this costume, he tasted the happiness the most genuinely suited to man, that of a simple life devoted to work.

It is almost never that man sees his happiness as resting upon true values; almost always he thinks that it resides in the causes of vanity, in the silly pleasure of getting oneself looked at, the thing that brings envy with it. But in that vain career, he does not usually attain his object at all; the moment that he begins to rejoice at holding the center of the stage and drawing all eyes to him, his own glance goes to a still higher goal; his desires mount in the measure that he himself rises, he himself envies as much as he is envied; as to the true values, he is forever drawing further away from them: tranquillity of mind, independence based on modest desires, easy to satisfy, such things are absolutely denied him. His time belongs to everybody; he wastes his life in foolish occupations. Provided that he feels the ermine and the watered silk over his shoulders, provided that the wind of favor carries him along and sustains him, he swallows down the annoyances of his position, he wears out his life among dusty papers, he gives it, without regret, to other people's business. To be minister, to be president, is to be in a slippery situation which not alone compromises your tranquillity, but also your reputation; it imposes severe tests on the character, and if one's conscience is not well assured of itself, it is exposed to shipwreck on the reefs that keep coming into view.

The great majority of men is composed of unfortunates deprived of the things most necessary for life. The chief of all satisfactions for them would be the possibility of obtaining what they lack; their crowning happiness would be to add thereto that degree of ease and of superfluity which rounds out enjoyment for the physical and moral faculties.

July 21.

Dined today with Mme de Forget, who is leaving tomorrow for Ems.

Mme de la Valette[51] told her that the seasons were not as they used to be.

This is to be connected with Wednesday's reflections on necessary misfortunes. I was saying in those reflections that everything around man must change and undergo revolution, but that his mind was changing also and saw the same objects with a different eye. To the extent that his body is modified by age and accidents, he no longer feels in the same manner. The morose character of old men is one effect of this beginning of the destruction of their machine; they no longer find relish or interest in anything. To them it seems that nature is declining, and that the elements are becoming confused, because they no longer see and no longer feel, because they are offended by the things that formerly gave them pleasure.

There are accidents which, in certain countries, are looked on as frightful misfortunes, and which in other countries create no impression whatsoever. Public opinion places honor and dishonor in the most diverse things. An Arab cannot bear the idea that a stranger should see the face of his wife, even by chance. An Arab woman will make it her point of honor to hide herself carefully: she would be quite ready to pick up her robes, thus baring the rest of her body, in order to veil her head.

It is the same thing with the accidents upon which people base happy or unhappy auguries. In France and, I think, among the other European peoples, it is one of the most unhappy auguries for a man and above all a soldier to mount a horse whose four feet are marked with white: the famous General Lasalle, who held religiously to this prejudice, never wanted to ride such a horse. The day which was to be the day of his death was marked by several unhappy auguries which had been striking him all through the morning: a broken mirror, a broken pipe, the portrait of his wife also smashed just at the moment when he was going to give a last look at her, and then he mounted a horse belonging to someone else without taking heed of the feet of his

[51] The mother of Mme de Forget.

mount. The horse had this fatal mark: it was while seated on this horse that, a few moments later, he was struck by the shot which caused his death not long after; it had been fired at a moment when the fighting was suspended. The shot came from a Croatian, I think, who was one of the prisoners that had just been taken after Wagram. These four white feet are, on the contrary, a mark and sign of consideration among Orientals, who do not fail to mention the thing in setting down the genealogies of horses; I am looking at the proof of this in the authentic document, certified by the ancients of the country, which accompanies the present that Abd-el-Kader has just made to the Emperor of a certain number of valuable horses. I pass over a thousand other examples of the kind.

How many men have desired death itself as a refuge and a thing of value, when it is the object of universal terror and is considered the one misfortune most surely without remedy, so that it is the cause of fairly permanent affliction in the generality of lives. And even when it is looked on as a misfortune, should not every effort be made to accustom oneself to that necessary solution, to that liberation from the other ills of which we complain, and which really are ills — since we feel them, whereas with death, which is to say the end, there is no longer consciousness or feeling? We ourselves owe our lives solely to that innumerable multitude of deaths which we heap up around us. Our well-being, which is to say our happiness, has as its sole foundation the ruin of those living beings which we sacrifice, not only to our needs but often to a passing pleasure, like that of hunting, for example, which is a mere recreation for most men.

July 22.

Arnoux dropped in to see me. He tells me that Corot is quite enchanted with my ceiling.[52] He quoted to me certain other words of approbation, of the same kind.

[52] The ceiling of the Hôtel de Ville.

July 24.

What Raphael and Michelangelo would have been in our period.

July 28.

I am thinking of the novels of Voltaire, of the tragedies of Racine, of a thousand and again a thousand masterpieces. How now! I am to believe that all those things were produced so that every quarter of a century men should be forever asking themselves whether there is some thing to amuse them in the works of the mind! Is not this incredible consumption of masterpieces, produced for the human herd by the most brilliant minds and the most sublime geniuses, enough to terrify that part of our sad human race which preserves some sense of delicacy? Shall not this insatiable thirst for novelty make anyone want to look back and see whether, by chance, the aging masterpieces are not more new, more young than the rhapsodies which flatter our idleness, and which it prefers to the masterpieces? What? these miracles of invention, of wit, of good sense, of gaiety or of pathos have been produced by those great minds, at the cost of sweat and of midnight vigils, so rarely recompensed, alas! by even the banal praise of the moment that saw their birth — and would you now tell me that all these things, after a short existence and a few eulogies, are to fall back into the dust of the libraries and into the unfertile and almost dishonoring esteem of the men called savants and antiquaries! What! the pedants in the colleges are to be the ones to pull us by the sleeve and warn us that Racine is at least simple, that La Fontaine saw as much in nature as Lamartine, that Lesage painted men as they are, when the so-called leaders of civilization are the men who, starting as mere pedants, are created ministers, or shepherds of the people, because they once had a quarter-hour of *inspiration suited to the intelligence of the day,* and these are the men who are to produce a literature, something new, in a word! A fine kind of novelty! . . .

July 29.

On the portrait. On landscape, as an accompaniment to a subject. *Of the contempt by the moderns* for this element of interest. On the ignorance of almost all the great masters as to the effect that one may draw from this: for example, Rubens, who did landscape very well, did not trouble to get it into relation with his figures so as to render them more striking, I mean striking for the mind, because for the eye, his backgrounds are usually calculated to over-intensify the color of the figures, this being done principally through contrast. The landscapes of Titian, of Rembrandt, and of Poussin are, as a rule, in harmony with the figures. With Rembrandt even — and he carries this to perfection — the background and the figures are absolutely one. Interest is everywhere: you do not divide off anything, any more than you do in a beautiful scene that nature offers you and in which everything contributes to your delight. With Watteau, the trees are a *matter of formula:* they are always the same trees, and recall theatrical scenery more than the trees of the forests. A picture by Watteau placed beside a Ruysdael or an Ostade loses greatly. The artificiality is all too plain. You quickly tire of the convention which they present, whereas you cannot tear yourself away from the Flemings. The majority of the masters got into the habit, of which their schools were servile imitators, of exaggerating the darkness of the backgrounds of portraits; they thought thus to render the heads more interesting; but those dark backgrounds, when we see them beside the illumined faces, deprive such portraits of the simplicity which ought to be their chief characteristic. The objects supposed to be shown in relief appear to be under the influence of very extraordinary conditions. Is it natural, as a matter of fact, that an illumined face should cut out against a background so very obscure that one feels that light could never penetrate it? Should not the light, after falling on the subject, logically reach the wall or the tapestry against which the person is seen? Unless one suppose that the figure is seen, by chance, against an extremely dark drapery — and that condition is very rare — or against an entrance to a cave or a cellar where no light enters, a circumstance that would be even rarer, the scheme must be considered most artificial.

What gives to portraits their principal charm is simplicity. I do not count as portraits those pictures in which the artist seeks to idealize the features of a celebrated man whom he has not seen but whom he paints from traditional likenesses; invention has the right to enter into such representations. True portraits are those that one does from one's contemporaries: we like to see them on the canvas as we meet them around us, even in the case of illustrious persons. Indeed it is as regards the latter class of men that fullness of truth in a portrait constitutes its greatest attraction. When such persons are far from our sight, our mind takes pleasure in aggrandizing their image, as it does with the qualities which distinguish them; when that image is fixed and before our eyes, we find infinite charm in comparing the reality with the thing which we imagined. We like to find the man alongside the hero, or in place of him.

Exaggerating the darkness of the background causes a strongly lighted face to stand out well, if you like; but that big light becomes almost crudity: in a word, it is an extraordinary effect that we have before our eyes rather than a natural object. Figures so singularly detached seem more like phantoms and apparitions than like men. The effect is only too apt to come about by itself, as a consequence of the darkening of the colors in the course of time. The dark colors become darker yet in relation to the light colors, which hold their own better, especially if the pictures have frequently had their varnish removed and then been revarnished. The varnish sticks to the dark parts, from which it is not easily detached; and so the blacks in the picture always go on increasing, and a background which appeared only middling dark when the work was new, turns to complete darkness in the course of time. When copying a Titian or a Rembrandt we think that we are getting the lights or shades into the relationship in which the master held them; we piously reproduce the work or, as I prefer to say, the insult of time. The great men would be very painfully surprised to come upon smoky daubs instead of their works, thinking how they did them. The background of the *Descent from the Cross* by Rubens, which must in truth have been a very dark sky, but such as the painter could imagine in representing the scene, has become so dark that it is impossible to distinguish a single detail in it.

We are sometimes astonished that nothing is left of the painting of antiquity; what we should be astonished at is that we still can find some vestiges of it in the third-class scrawls which still decorate the walls of Herculaneum; the chances for their preservation were slightly better, since they were executed on walls and were not exposed to as many accidents as the pictures of the great masters, painted on canvas or on panels and hence, from the fact that they could be carried about, exposed to more accidents. We should be less astonished at their destruction if we reflected that the majority of pictures produced since the renaissance of the arts, which is to say very recent things, are already difficult to recognize, and that a great number of them have already perished from a thousand causes. These causes go on multiplying, thanks to the progress of *rascality* in all branches, whether it falsifies the materials which enter into the composition of colors, of oils, and of varnishes, or whether a manufacturer substitutes cotton for hemp in canvases, and woods of bad quality for the tested woods which were formerly used for panels. Unskillful restorations finish this work of destruction. Plenty of people imagine that they have done a great thing for pictures when they have had them restored; they think that it is the same with painting as it is with a house that is repaired, and which is always a house, or like everything else that we use, that time destroys, but which our industry causes to last and serve for a longer time when we replaster and repair it in a thousand ways. Even if one go so far as to admit that a woman who knows how to make up can conceal a few wrinkles and so produce the illusion of seeming younger than she is, the case of pictures is a different one: each so-called restoration is an injury a thousand times more regrettable than those of time; it is not a restored picture that you are given, but a different picture, that of the miserable dauber who has substituted himself for the author of the real picture, which has disappeared under his retouching.

Restorations in sculpture do not have the same drawback. As to new (or renewed) Gothic.

July 30.

Get Durieu photographs to take to Dieppe, and also the sketches after Landon[53] and Thévelin. Photographs of heads. Animals and anatomy.

August 3.

In the morning, had an appointment with Abbé Coquant to ask him to let me work on Sundays (at Saint-Sulpice). Impossibility upon impossibility. The Emperor, the Empress, and Monseigneur conspire to keep a poor painter like myself from committing the sacrilege or expressing, on Sundays as on other days, the ideas that he brings forth from his brain to glorify the Lord. And yet I used to like particularly to work on Sundays in the churches: the music of the services quite exalted me. I did a great deal in this way at Saint-Denis du Saint-Sacrement. Took lunch at the Place de l'Hôtel-de-Ville; read an article in the *Indépendance Belge* on a translation of the *Inferno* made by a certain M. Ratisbonne. This is the first time that a modern ventures to speak his opinion of that illustrious barbarian. The article says that this poem is not a poem, that it is not what Aristotle calls a *unity,* which is to say something having a beginning, a middle, and an end; that it could just as well have ten cantos as well as twenty, or thirty-three; that interest centers in no part of it: that it is nothing but episodes sewed one to the other, that at times it has real fire through the wild descriptions of torments, but that often it is more bizarre than striking, there being no gradation in the horror which these episodes inspire, and none of these inventions of torture or punishment having any relationship with the crimes of the damned. What the article does not say is that the translator still further spoils, by the fantastic quality of his words, what may appear singular in the imagina-

---

[53] Paul Landon (1760-1826), painter, author of numerous works on the museums and on the artists; they contain line drawings after the pictures.

tion of the poet; he does, however, criticize certain exaggerated expressions, even while approving the system by which the translator follows the author word for word, so to speak, and glues himself to tercet after tercet and verse after verse.

How could the author be other than completely baroque, with so foolish a pretension? Since he must use a language so different in its form and its genius, one that is impregnated with our modern ways, what makes him add to the difficulty of translating an ancient author, only half intelligible even to his compatriots, concise, elliptical, obscure, and scarcely understanding himself? I consider that translating, if we look on the matter merely as the majority of translators do — which is to say a rendering into speech that is human and acceptable to the men one is addressing — is a work quite difficult enough. To get the genius of a language, especially when rendering the ideas of a completely different period, is a feat that I regard as almost useless to attempt. M. Ratisbonne flays the French language and our ears, and he gives us neither the spirit nor the harmony of his poet, and consequently no true sense of him either. This thing is to be classed with the translations by Viardot and others, who write Spanish French when translating Cervantes, or else English French when translating Shakespeare.

August 5.

It is to be noted that every original talent shows the same phases in its development as art in general goes through in its various evolutions, to wit: timidity and dryness at the beginning, and breadth or negligence as to details at the end. The *Count Palatiano*[54] compared to my recent paintings.

How singular this law is! What occurs here, occurs in everything. I might be lead to infer that every object is in itself a complete world. Man, it has been said, is a *little world*. Not only is he in his unity a complete whole, with an ensemble of laws consistent with those of the

[54] Dated 1826 (Catalogue Robaut, 170).

great whole, but even a part of an object is a species of complete unity; thus a branch detached from a tree presents the conditions of the tree in its entirety. Thus it is that the talent of an isolated man, in the continuity of his development, presents the different phases to be seen in the history of the art which he practices (the above, again, is to be connected with Chenavard's theories on the childhood and the old age of the world). Plant the branch of a poplar tree, and soon it will become a poplar. Where have I seen it said that there are animals — and this is probable — which, cut into pieces, give you as many distinct creatures, each with its own existence, as there are fragments?

I find this note relating to what has gone just before in a sketch-book in which I wrote the words in the forest at Champrosay on September 16, 1849.

Nature is singularly consistent with herself: at Trouville, at the seaside, I drew some fragments of rock in which the accidents of the form were so proportioned as to give, on the paper, the idea of an immense cliff; all that was lacking was an object suited to establish the scale of size. At this moment, I am writing alongside a big anthill, partly the result of small accidents in the surface of the ground at the foot of a tree, and partly due to the patient work of the ants; there are slopes, and parts that overhang and form little gorges, through which the inhabitants go back and forth with a busy air, like the little people of a little country, which the imagination can magnify in a moment. What is only a molehill, I can see at any time as a vast expanse cut across by precipitous rocks and steep declivities, because of the tiny size of its inhabitants. A fragment of coal or of flint or of any other stone may present in reduced proportion the forms of immense rocks.

At Dieppe I noticed the same thing in the rocks at the water level which the sea covers at every tide; among them I saw gulfs, arms of the sea, frowning peaks suspended above abysses, valleys which by their windings divided up a whole country that showed the accidents we observe about us. The same thing is true as to the waves of the sea, which are divided, themselves, into little waves, again subdividing, and individually presenting the same accidents of light and the same drawing. The great waves of certain seas, those of the Cape for example, which are said to be half a league wide at times, are composed of a multitude of waves, among which the greater number are as small as those that one sees in a garden pool.

I have often noticed, when drawing trees, that a given branch, taken separately, is a little tree in itself: for one to see it so it would be sufficient if the leaves merely had the right proportion.

Just after this observation, in the same sketchbook, are notes on certain phenomena which repeat themselves in extremely different objects, such as the designs that the sea engraves in the sand and that recall the stripes on tigers. As to the grace of sinuosities, of roads, etc. The booklet is the one in which I drew up plans at Champrosay in 1848 and 1849. It is bound in red.

Flee the wicked, even when they are agreeable, instructive, and charming. It is curious: blind impulse, as much as chance, often makes you draw close to a perverse nature. This inclination must be combated, since one cannot flee from the hazard of meeting certain persons.

August 9.

Read in the *Revue* an article by Saint-Marc Girardin on the *Lettre sur les Spectacles* of Rousseau.[55] He discusses at length the question of the danger that may lurk in the theater. I believe there is some, but not more than in all our other pleasures. Everything that we devise to take us out of the constant spectacle of our misery and the ills engendered by our life as it is, turns the mind toward things that are more or less forbidden by strict morality. You obtain interest only by exhibiting the passions and the agitation they cause: that is scarcely the means of inspiring resignation and virtue. Our arts are constantly making passion attractive. All those nude women in pictures, all those

---

[55] *Rousseau et le Théatre,* in the *Revue des Deux Mondes* for August 1, 1854. Saint-Marc Girardin (1801-1873), of the Académie Française, professor at the Sorbonne.

women in love in novels and in plays, all those husbands or guardians deceived are at the poles from being incentives to chastity and to family life. Rousseau would have been a hundred more times revolted by the modern theater and the modern novel. In the past, with few exceptions in the one art or the other, the triumph or defeat of the passions turned to the profit of morality, at least to a certain degree. The theater rarely showed a picture of adultery *(Phèdre*, the *Mère Coupable)*. Love was a passion thwarted, but one whose goal was lawful, according to our idea of what is right. People were a hundred leagues from those romantic eccentricities which afford the usual theme of modern dramas and the food for idle minds. What seeds of virtue or of mere visible propriety can be left in the heart by the Antonys, Lélias and all the others among whom it is hard to choose, for one thing because of their exaggeration, and for the other because of their cynicism?

August 11.

Weigh together the advantages in the life of the man who reflects and of the man who does not reflect. Take the country gentleman, born amidst the rural abundance of his fields and his manor, spending his life in hunting and in visits to his neighbors; then take the life of the man who seeks for pastimes; he is modern, he reads, produces, he lives according to the dictates of his self-esteem; can his infrequent delights, those which he derives from art, be compared with those of the other man? Unfortunately, he feels keenly the thing that he lacks: at the heart of the aridity which he sometimes finds in his abstract happiness, he has a vivid feeling of the delight that it would be for him to live in the open air, amidst a family, in an old house within an antique domain, where he can trace the life of his ancestors. On the other hand, the man of the country who is no more than that, has coarse pleasures, gets drunk, lives on gossip, and has no appreciation of the noble and really happy side of his existence.

The above is to be placed with the contradictions in the opinions of men as to what constitutes misfortune: see the chapter on necessary misfortunes.

The real misfortune for the countryman, whose only refuge from boredom after a hunt is to go and sleep like his dogs, is suffering, sickness, even as it is for the philosopher who sighs for the happiness of the fields: neither the one nor the other, when he is sick, thinks himself unhappy in the life that he is forced to lead; and whether they suffer from boredom or from real ills, the one no less than the other has the same horror of death, which is to say of the end of that boredom or of that suffering.

Habit dulls all the sentiments: the daily stings of family life, etc. Mme Sand ought to be happy, and I know that she is not.

It is a happy man who contents himself with the surface of things. I admire and envy the men like Berryer, who seems to dig deep into nothing — you give it to me, I take it: let us not weigh anything: let us always be attentive to the desires of the world, to appearances, to what is superficial — and who are satisfied with that.

How many times I have wanted to read people's hearts for the sole purpose of knowing what there was of happiness behind those contented faces! When I look at all those sons of Adam, heirs to the same trouble that I bear, I ask myself how men like Halévy and Gautier, weighed down by debt and by demands of family or of vanity, can have a calm and smiling look, amid all their troubles. The only way that they can be happy is by keeping up a headlong speed, hiding from themselves the dangers amidst which they steer their boats, often in desperation, and where shipwreck awaits them one time or another.

August 12.

I called on Berger this afternoon to bring him my picture of the *Women Bathing.*[56] At his place I saw a picture by de Keyser,[57] who is very much esteemed by collectors. My own, of which I have a pretty slight opinion — having painted it under unsympathetic conditions — seemed to me to be a masterpiece by comparison.

I went to the Hôtel de Ville on account of Vimont's affair.[58] M. Perrier[59] asked me, with all the discretion that one can use in committing an indiscretion, to give him a drawing, *"a trifle,"* as he said, *"in order that I may have a keepsake from you, one of those things that you do so lightly, when your thoughts are off somewhere else."*

My health is better, I am more cheerful these last days, though I

[56] Catalogue Robaut, 1246. M. Berger was the prefect of the Seine.
[57] Nicaise de Keyser (1813-1887), of Antwerp, one of the earliest representatives of Romanticism in Belgian painting.
[58] Painter, pupil of Delacroix; the matter was doubtless one of some commission.
[59] A member of the Municipal Council.

have some rumblings in my stomach and feel the effects of that. This evening, while taking a walk, enjoyed the feeling that I am getting back my strength. I am happy to leave Paris: I am in a hurry to do so in order to get my poor Jenny out of this wretched atmosphere as soon as possible.

August 13.

Lay-figure at Lefranc's, for 350 francs. Rue des Fossés-Saint-Germain, 23. See if he rents them, when I come back, and whether that would be cheaper. I shall tell Andrieu to find out about this.

The Academy of Moral and Political Sciences had announced for the competition of 1847 the following question: what influence do progress and the taste for material well-being exercise upon the morality of the people? I find the above in my little notebook of '47. I should be curious to know the conclusions which won the prize of the learned Academy. It is composed almost exclusively of the moralists we know so well, those who made the revolution of 1830 and the one of 1848; the prize, which was offered before the outbreak of the latter revolution, was unquestionably meant to glorify progress and that taste for well-being which is only too natural in my opinion, and has no need to be encouraged in people's hearts, whence, on the contrary, it would be very difficult to dislodge it. What a masterpiece of philosophy it is to discover that man, whether on an upper or a lower rung of the ladder, wants to be better off than he is! It would be a different matter if they were discovering, at the same time, a way of rendering him content when he has climbed one or more steps toward the objects of his ambition.

Unfortunately, ambition is insatiable and what happens is that after a man, through his resistance to misfortune or difficulties, has kept alive the vigor of his soul amidst a life of poverty, he loses the sense of duty when in a position that he improves with ease and that he wants to improve without limit. (See the chapter on plowing by machinery, etc. Girardin, etc.)

Dieppe, August 18.

I had a streak of idling; had a sleep on a couch, despite the beautiful sunlight; and yet I had gone for a walk; I even entered the church of Saint-Jacques.

If, for our poor mind that is so eager for change, there is an undeniable charm in seeing new objects, it must also be confessed that the gentle pleasure of getting back to objects already known is a very great one. In the presence of such objects, we remember the pleasures we once felt, to which imagination adds the charm of distance.

I have difficulty in overcoming the sense of languor and of emptiness which weighs upon me when, in a place where I arrive, I have not yet got back to my habits. The only pleasures that I find here, these first days, are just those of seeing once more a place that I like and where I have been happy. My past happiness seems to me greater than that of today. The cause of this is the lack of occupations that could interest me, except seeing the things round about, and these do indeed possess considerable interest.

More than I had done until this time, I have observed the fidelity to expression in the *Saint-Sépulcre* [60] at the church of Saint-Jacques. I don't know where I wrote, just lately, that seeing that work also confirmed in me Chenavard's idea that Christianity loves the picturesque. Painting, better than sculpture, allies itself with the pomp of the Church, and harmonizes more intimately with the feelings of the Christian.

August 19.

A thousand difficulties in installing ourselves in lodgings: we think the thing horrible and unbearable, and we end up by getting used to it. The smallest events of my life and the most important things that have happened to me present the same phases and the same accidents. A scheme presents itself with all its attractions: hardly is one embarked on it, when a thousand contrary things arise and seem as if they must

[60] This *Sépulcre* is modern.

arrest everything, and render everything detestable. Either volition or chance causes the difficulties to flatten out, whereupon the situation becomes tolerable at first, and sometime excellent. Has every man his destiny really written out and traced for him, as he has his face and his temperament? As for me, and up to the present time, I have no hesitation about saying that I am convinced that such is the case. On the whole I am a very fortunate man, but I have always had to buy each advantage through combat. Thereby I have gathered up some of destiny's favors, granted with a miserly hand, it is true, but also presenting something that is surer; it is the same as with those trees that sprout up from thin soil where they grow slowly and with difficulty, their branches twisted and knotty as a result of their struggle for existence; the wood of such trees is considered harder than that of the beautiful trees that grow in a short time from rich soil, their straight, smooth trunks seeming to have shot up without effort.

The fate of my poor Jenny offers a similar fixity (it has never varied); yet it is hardly to be called worthy of the fate that her virtues have deserved. Never was so noble and firm a nature put to such cruel tests. May heaven give to her now, at least, some days of happiness, and less of cruel suffering, as a recompense for the noble poverty she has borne with so calm a brow and out of motives so generous! Should not the moral laws, like those that govern merely the physical, have the privilege of being invariable?

August 23.

I think that it was this morning that I went with Jenny, who is benefited by these walks, for a good swing, the whole length of the cliffs, in the direction of the baths; it was there that I noticed those rocks at the level of the water, and that I had so much pleasure in seeing the tide invade them.

About four o'clock, took a walk with Jenny in the direction of Le Pollet. We went into the new church. It is all built according to an Italian model that the architects are very fond of nowadays. It presents an aspect of the most complete bareness; those fellows see austere simplicity in what was mere barbarism with the inventors of this type of architecture; it would be perhaps better suited to Protestants, who have a horror of Roman pomp; but these great walls, all bare, and these ungenerous windows which manage to distill just a little light in this country where the sky is dark for three-quarters of the year, are scarcely suited to a Catholic church. I cannot sufficiently protest against the stupidity of the architects, and I *except no one here on this score.* Every one of the caprices that fashion has sanctioned in its turn, in every century, becomes sacramental for them. It would seem that only those men who preceded them had been gifted with the freedom to invent what pleased them and decorate their dwellings therewith. They forbid the production of anything save what they find elsewhere, ready-made and approved by the books. The beavers will invent a new way of building their houses before an architect permits a new method and a new style in his art which, in parenthesis, is more a matter of convention than any other, and which, consequently, is the one that most permits caprice and change.

August 24.

Today, was at last able to rent a novel by Dumas, so as to get out of the boredom caused in me by the absence of any occupation. All the preceding days, took walks; also made drawings from Durieu's photographs.

I made a large-scale drawing of the fore part of the ship which is under my window. The mind, refreshed by work, communicates to the whole being a sense of happiness.

August 25.

During my walk this morning, I made an extended study of the sea. The sun being behind me, the face of the waves rising before me was yellow, and the side turned toward the distance reflected the sky. Shadows from the clouds rippled over the whole scene and produced

charming effects: in the distance, at the place where the sea was blue
and green, the shadows seemed violet; a violet and golden tone extended also over the nearer parts when the shadow fell upon them.
The waves were like agate. In these shadowy passages, one got again
the same relationship of yellow waves — looking in the direction of
the sun, and of the blue and metallic parts reflecting the sky.

Letter to Mme de Forget, from which I copy, and which is related
to what goes before.

"I am sorry that you have already ended your excursion, since I
am at the beginning of my own: but Paris pleases you more than it
does me. Outside of Paris, I feel myself more of a man; in Paris, I
am only a *Monsieur*. All one finds is gentlemen and ladies, which is
to say dolls: here, I see sailors, plowmen, soldiers, fish-mongers.

"The grand toilet of those ladies, all in the latest fashion, makes a
contrast with the big boots of the fishermen of Le Pollet and the short
skirts of the Norman women, who are not lacking in a certain charm,
despite their headdress, which resembles a cotton bonnet.

"I am getting some excellent cooking. In my lodgings I found a
stove similar to yours and I have developed a passion for everything
that comes out of that stove. As for the fish and the oysters, the crabs
and the lobsters, they are incomparable. You, in Paris, are eating only
leavings, by comparison. As you see, I am wallowing in materialism;
everything — the very cider — tastes good here. There are moments,
indeed, when I yearn to have something consecutive to do. The little
drawings that I make here and there do not suffice to occupy my mind;
and so I pick up my novel again, or I go to the pier to see the boats
coming in or going out.

"This is the life that I am going to lead for some time yet; I shall
doubtless make a few excursions in the neighborhood; but my head-
quarters will always be on the Quai Duquesne. One has to drive away,
however one can, the ghosts of that devil of a life that has been given
us — I don't know why — and that so easily becomes bitter when
one does not turn a brow of steel to boredom and botherations. In a

word, one has got to shake up one's body and one's mind which get to gnawing each other when we are stagnant in our indolence — which is really no more than torpor. One has absolutely got to change from rest to work, and then the other way around: in that way each seems equally agreeable and healthy. The unfortunate who is loaded down with heavy work and who labors without relaxation is doubtless horribly unfortunate, but the man who is obliged to amuse himself the whole time, finds no happiness in his recreation, nor even tranquillity; he feels that he is combating the boredom that grips him by the hair: The ghost is always there alongside the pleasure, and looks over its shoulder. Do not think, dear lady, that because I have my hours of work I am exempt from the attacks of this terrible enemy: my conviction is that with a certain turn of mind, one needs an inconceivable energy if one is not to be bored, and if one is to use one's will sufficiently to escape from that languor we are forever falling into. The pleasure that I find at this very moment, in talking out this feeling with you, is a proof that I eagerly seize the chances to occupy my mind when I have the strength to do so, even when it comes to discussing this boredom that I seek to drive away. All my life I have found my free time too long. In large part, I attribute this disposition to the pleasure that I have always found in work itself: the real or pretended pleasures that followed it did not perhaps offer a great enough contrast with the fatigue that the work gave me, fatigue which most men feel very harshly. I can very perfectly imagine the enjoyment that is derived from repose by that mass of men that we see weighted down with hateful work; and I am not speaking only of the poor people who work for their bread everyday: I speak also of lawyers, of men in offices, swamped in dusty papers and continually occupied with tiresome affairs, or things that do not concern them. It is true that the majority of such people are tormented but little by imagination: indeed they find in their mechanical occupations a way as good as any other, of filling up their time. The stupider they are, the less they are unhappy.

"I end by consoling myself with this last axiom that it is because

I have a mind that I am bored, not at this moment, however, when I am writing: on the contrary I have just spent an agreeable half-hour, turning my thoughts toward you, dear lady, and talking to you, in my own way, of this subject which interests everybody. These ideas, in their turn, will perhaps cause you to spend five minutes with a certain pleasure when you read them, especially if they recall the true affection that I bear you."

August 26.

Going out, about half-past ten, I walked as far as the Customs House, on the quay, to shake off all the insipidity of the people with whom I had spent the evening. I saw those English steamboats that are so mean in their forms. Great indignation against those races that know no more than a single thing: *to go fast;* let them go to the devil then, and faster yet, with their machines and all their inventions that make of man just another machine!

August 27.

At noon they were to launch a big ship that they call a *clipper.* Here is another American invention that will let people go faster: always faster. When they have got travelers comfortably lodged in a cannon, so that that cannon shall make them travel as fast as bullets in any direction they may care to take, civilization will doubtless have taken a long step: we are marching toward that happy time; it will have suppressed space but will not have suppressed boredom, as one sees if one considers the always increasing need of filling up one's hours, in which matter going and coming occupied at least a part.

I was to have met Chenavard to view the spectacle with me; I did enjoy it perfectly and it was fine to see. I picked up my companion only afterward. We went for a stroll, sat down, ass on the grass, and then on chairs at the seaside. Lots of conversation, very good and very interesting, on politics and on painting. Finally I got tired and I went home, pretty late.

Monday, August 28.

Had a date with Chenavard on the beach at one o'clock, to take him to see my sketches: he always seems to me to have the less esteem for the talent of the great masters in proportion to the decadence amidst which they live. It is the contrary that one ought to say. Perhaps it is true that amidst general indifference, talent does not bear all its fruits: it is agreed that to do the little I have done, I have had to expend a thousand times more energy than those men like Raphael and Rubens who had only to show themselves to the surprised world — which was, however, prepared to admire—for them to be crowned with encouragement and applause.

August 31.

In the evening, endless conversation with Chenavard, on the beach and all along the streets. He told me of the difficulty that Michelangelo often had in working, and cited a saying of his: Benedetto Varchi[61] said to him *"Signor Buonarrotti, avete il cervello di Giove"*; he is supposed to have answered: *"Si vuole il martello di Vulcano per farne uscire qualche cosa."*[62] At a certain period he had burned great quantities of studies and of sketches so as not to leave traces of the labor that his works had cost him, when he turned them back and forth, as a man does in producing verse. He often carved from drawings; his sculpture bears witness to this procedure. He used to say that *good sculpture* was the kind that *never looked like painting,* and that *good painting,* on the contrary, was the kind that *looked like sculpture.*

It was today that Chenavard talked to me again of his famous idea

[61] Benedetto Varchi (1502-1562), Florentine historian and poet. Delacroix had always been preoccupied with Michelangelo. He had devoted an essay to him in the *Revue de Paris,* in 1830; more recently, in 1852, he had painted *Michelangelo in His Studio* (in the Museum of Montpellier, Catalogue Robaut, 1184); it is often thought that he was representing himself in the picture.

[62] "Signor Buonarrotti, you have the brain of Jove." "It needs the hammer of Vulcan to get anything out of it."

as to decadence. He pigeon-holes things too much. And he has the
fault of not esteeming at their true value all the qualities that are to
be esteemed. Although he says that the men of two hundred years ago
are not on a level of those of three hundred years ago, and that the men
of today are not on a level with those of fifty or a hundred years ago,
I believe that Gros, David, Prud'hon, Géricault, and Charlet are men
admirable in the way that Titian and Raphael were; [63] I believe that
I myself have painted certain passages that would not be disdained by
those gentlemen, and that I have had certain conceptions that they did
not have.

September 1.

This morning and yesterday I got up early and went to the beach with
Jenny.

Worked during the day. Before dinner, looking out of my window,
I drew some boats.

In the evening, I put Chenavard off: my mind was fatigued by his
diatribe of last night. Naively or knowingly, he makes a practice of
enervating your mind as a surgeon practices cutting and bleeding.
What is beautiful is beautiful, I don't care in what period it was done
or for whom: as soon as there are two of us to admire Charlet and Géricault, you have the proof, in the first place, that they are admirable,
and in the second, that they can find admirers. I shall admire what
deserves it to the day of my death, and if I am the last of my race, I
shall tell myself that after the night which is to follow me on the hemi-
sphere that I inhabit, there will be daybreak again somewhere, and
that man, still having a heart and a mind, will get his enjoyment from
those two things.

September 2.

Scientists do no more, after all, than find in nature what is there. The
personality of the scientist is absent from his work; it is quite a dif-

[63] On all these modern masters, except David, Delacroix had published
essays which have been collected as his *Œuvres Litteraires* (published by Crès
et Cie, Paris).

ferent matter with the artist. The seal that he imprints on his production is what makes it the work of an artist, which is to say of an inventor. The scientist discovers the elements of things, if you like, and the artist, with elements having no value in the place they chance to be, composes, invents a unity, in one word, creates; he strikes the imagination of men by the spectacle of his creations, and in a particular manner. He summarizes, he renders clear the sensations that things arouse within us, and which the great run of men, in the presence of nature, only vaguely see and feel.

September 3.

To the pier in the morning. I saw two brigs, one of them from Nantes, weighing anchor. That interested me a great deal, from the point of view of study. I am getting a complete course in yards and pulleys, etc., so as to understand how all those things work; probably I shall never get any use from this, but I have always wanted to understand such mechanisms, and anyhow I can't think of anything more picturesque. My observations, although superficial, have led me to see how clumsy all these matters still are, what heaviness and inefficacy there is most of the time in all that rigging; until the time of steam, which is changing everything, the art has not made a step in two hundred years. Those two poor boats, dragged out of the port with great effort by every kind of towing, got to the outside waters, but without being able to move a foot ahead. I drew them first in the motionless state they were in; and when I left them, tired by the length of time I had been waiting, they were still in the same position. The bookseller informs me that the two volumes of *Bragelonne*,[64] which unfortunately will contain the most interesting part of the book, are lacking from his shelves, and he proposes to have them sent from Paris. Here is one of the tribulations of Dieppe that I went through years ago already, when

[64] *Le Vicomte de Bragelonne,* sequel to the *Three Musketeers* and to *Twenty Years Later,* had appeared in twenty-six volumes between 1848 and 1850.

reading the story of *Balsamo*. I have taken out the *Provincial à Paris*[65] by Balzac: it's enough to make you furious; it does nothing but describe the small details in the life of the roués of the years 1840 to 1847: little backstage stories; what a '*rat*' is, the story of the *châle Sélim* that was sold to an English woman. In a very famous preface, the publisher places Balzac beside Molière, saying that if he had lived in the seventeenth century, he would have written the *Femmes Savantes* and the *Misanthrope,* and that Molière, in our time, would have written the *Comédie Humaine.* The thing that seems to him to give Balzac a place apart in our time is that, unlike the majority of writers in our period, his works bore the seal of permanence; and he tells us so at the beginning of that rhapsody, which keeps turning around the minor slang words of the day, and around every sort of contemptible figure wrapped up in the little problem of the moment, both the figures and the moment being things of which history will remember nothing.

September 6.

In the morning, abandoned the pier in order to climb up to the left, behind the château; followed the road as far as the cemetery; before reaching it, delightful sensation at the top of the ravine that we crossed the other day; small path mounting on the other side, lit by the rays of the morning and disappearing in the shadow in the beech trees. Entered the cemetery, less forbidding than that frightful Père-Lachaise, less silly, less limited, less bourgeois. Forgotten graves overgrown with grass, clumps of rosebushes and clematis perfuming the air in this sojourn of death; perfect solitude, moreover, ultimate conformity with the object of the place and with the necessary purpose of what is there, which is to say silence and forgetfulness.

After lunch, Chenavard dropped in; I took him to see the *Mariani*

[65] It had appeared in 1848 under this title. The preface, signed "The publisher," ended on that comparison with Molière which seems to have shocked Delacroix so much. It is reproduced *in extenso* by Lovenjoul in his *Histoire des oeuvres de H. de Balzac.*

weigh anchor. He tells me, and it is true, that among the moderns, by which he means since the time of Christ, men of talent must either be flat, in the style of Delaroche, or outlandish and incomplete. Michelangelo is a man of a single moment, after which he repeated himself; few ideas, consequently, but power that, undoubtedly, no one has equalled. He has created types: his *Almighty God,* his *Devils,* his *Moses* — and yet he cannot do heads, indeed he abandons them; that is the sin of the moderns: Puget and so many others. With the ancients, on the contrary, how many types do we get: *Jupiter, Bacchus, Hercules,* etc.! Returned in the frightful heat along the quay, very much overcome and fatigued by this second excess, after the one this morning. I had overtaxed myself.

Speaking of Meissonier, Chenavard said that what characterizes a master is his recognizing of the essential thing in the picture, the thing that must absolutely be reached. Mere talent thinks only of details: Ingres, David, etc.[66]

September 7.

Went out early with Jenny, who is going to bathe. Not finding the sea interesting, I gain the Cours Bourbon, which I find iust as charming at this early morning hour.

Returning by way of the church of Saint Jacques, I see a poster announcing that the mountain singers would chant the mass this very day; I came just at the right time, and my surprise was no greater than my pleasure.

They are peasants, all from the Pyrenees, with magnificent voices; you see no sheets of music paper, nor anyone beating time; however, it appears probable that one of those men, gray-haired and seated, is directing them. They sing without accompaniment. On leaving, I could not refrain from following them and complimenting one of them. In general, they have serious faces. I was touched by the children. The

[66] It may be observed that Delacroix, in his weariness, is simply setting down what Chenavard had said. Allusions to David, at other places in his writings, do not at all agree in treating that master as a "mere talent."

voice of the man-child is far more penetrating than that of women, which I have always found shrill and poor in expression; and then in that naive artist, eight or ten years old, there is something almost sacred; those pure voices lifting up to God, from a body that is scarcely a body and from a soul that has not yet been soiled, must carry straight to the foot of His throne and speak to His unending goodness, to intercede for our weakness and our poor passions.

It was a very touching spectacle for a simple man like myself to see, those young people and those children in their poor and uniform clothes forming a circle and singing without written music while they looked at each other. I sometimes regretted the absence of accompaniment. To some extent it was the fault of the music, beautiful in itself and bearing the stamp of Italian elegance, but containing pieces that were too long and too complicated for that unaccompanied chant of the simple artists, who seemed to sing from inspiration. My final impression was still a very strong one, completely recalling to me the one made by the singers of the bas-relief by Luca della Robbia, even to the costume worn by all of them, a blue blouse fastened by a belt. These poor folk have sung at the *Etablissement,* in real concerts. I should regret to see them there, singing fashionable airs, and doubtless as much rigged out in finery as the damnable modern music that is demanded by the moderns of such places.

Came home after the mass; did a small unfinished water color of the port filled with curious green water; I was in a bad mood caused by an infernal cigar that I had picked up. Noted the contrast, on that water, of the very black ships, the red flags, etc.

Read that dull book, *Eugénie Grandet:* such works do not stand up well against the test of time; the messiness and inexperience which tell all too clearly of the incurable lack of perfection in the author's talent, will place all such things among the rejected by-products of the centuries. No measure, no ensemble, no proportion.

Before dinner, went back to the Cours Bourbon, of which I never grow tired: the view from the end of it, especially the one that continues the promenade to the foot of the mountain, is ravishing. I had sent Jenny and Julie to the theatre. There was no staying on the pier, because of the wind, and the sea offered nothing of interest, save for the grandeur of the proportions given to the pier and the sand of the beach by the seaward sweep of the water.

I went and picked up Chenavard; we kept away from the beach, on account of the wind, and went through the streets to the quay of the last basin, where we stayed in the moonlight until eleven o'clock.

I felt his sensitiveness, and his esteem for me. He is unhappy; he feels that he has wasted his faculties. Philosophy is a meat without substance which, pretending to give knowledge to man, has not increased his resignation in the face of inevitable evils, and of the contradictions and imperfections of our nature. It always seems to me that being a philosopher should include, with the habit of more attentive reflection upon man and upon life, the habit, also, of taking things as they are, and of turning our life and passions toward the good or at all events toward the best that is open to us. But no! All those dreamers are as much agitated as other people; it seems as if their contemplation of the mind of man, something more to be pitied than admired, takes from them that serenity which is often the lot of men bound to more practical work and, in my opinion, work that is more worthy of their effort. I asked the poor fellow whom I respect so much why he was at Dieppe, why he had gone to Italy and to Germany, and why he had returned there. What was he fleeing and what did he seek, amid all his agitation? A mind turning toward doubt must surely doubt the more, after having seen everything.

He considers me happy, and he is right, and I see myself as even more happy, since witnessing his miserable situation. His devastating doctrine as to the necessary decadence of the arts is perhaps true, but it is necessary to forbid ourselves every thought of such a thing.

We must do like Roland, who casts into the depths of the sea, and forever, the terrible firearm invented by the perfidious Duke of Holland; it is necessary to keep out of men's consciousness those debatable truths which can render them only more unhappy or more cowardly in their pursuit of the right. A man lives in his century and does well to speak to his contemporaries in a language which they can understand and which can touch them. That is what he does, moreover, when he seeks his principal appeal to the imagination within the depths of his own mind. The thing that holds attention in his works is not conformity with the ideas of his time: that advantage, if it is one, is to be found in all the mediocre men who swarm so miserably in every century and who chase after favor by miserable flatteries of passing taste. Using the language of his contemporaries, he should teach them, so to speak, the things which that language did not express before; and if his reputation deserves to last, it will be because he has presented a living example of taste in a period when taste was too little esteemed.

The day when Chenavard and I were talking on the wooden pier, I told him that taste was the thing that gave each talent its rank. What constitutes the superiority of La Fontaine, of Molière, of Racine and of Ariosto over men like Corneille and Shakespeare and Michelangelo, is taste. It remains to be seen, as I do not deny, whether strength or originality carried to a certain point do not, despite everything, chiefly compel our admiration. But here we get back to the possibility of discussion, and to personal inclination.

I adore Rubens, Michelangelo, etc., and yet I was saying to Cousin that I thought the defect in Racine was his very perfection; the one reason why people find him so beautiful is because, in reality, he is too beautiful. An object that is perfectly beautiful carries with it perfect simplicity which, at first sight, does not cause the emotion that one feels in the presence of things that are gigantic, their very disproportion being an element of beauty. Would objects of this kind, whether in nature or in art really be more beautiful? Doubtless not, but they may cause a stronger impression. Who will dare to say that Corneille is more beautiful because his work presents rough and neglected passages? One has to say that with men of that family, there are passages so strong that one does not think of the defects, and so the mind gets used to them; but do not say that Racine or Mozart is less spirited because these same beauties are found in every point of his work, where they form its woof, its very tissue. I have said elsewhere that sublime men filled with eccentricity are like those rakes that women are mad about: they are just so many prodigals with whom people are thankful for certain generous exceptions to their licentious conduct. What is to be said of Ariosto, who is all perfection, who unites all tones and all images, the gay, the tragic, the decorous, the tender? But I stop.

September 8.

A perfect work, as Mérimée said to me, should not require notes. I am tempted to say that a piece of writing that is really well written, and above all well deduced and thought out, does not require interruptions. If the thoughts are well connected and the style is well linked together, no break will be needed until the thought, forming the basis of the subject, is completely developed. Montaigne is an illustrious example of that need for *genius* in this *special case*.

Began this day very well, which is to say with the desire to do something; I have been writing at this book until eleven o'clock. I was wearied by my walk of last night and by my conversation with Chenavard. I have a great need for rest, and mental work has indeed rested me.

After lunch I set to work with extreme eagerness, drawing the horses yoked by fours to the carts, and their very picturesque harness. After that, I made a drawing, large size, of the whole fore part of the ship which is under my window. The mind, refreshed by work, communicates a feeling of happiness to one's whole being.

It was in this mood that I went to the pier and then returned along the waterfront and went to the Cours Bourbon for my dinner with Chenavard. I thought in the first place that we were going to have a good dinner, and then that the dinner would be gay. The dinner was detestable, and the lugubrious predictions of my companion did not bring any gaiety into the time we spent together.

I think that the fatality which, according to him, sweeps things along, has its connection also with the possibility of a bond between ourselves. One day I am drawn toward him, the next day, the unsympathetic side of the man prevails. He tells me of the domestic misfortunes of that poor, cracked Boissard. He tells me that Leibnitz did not leave his working table, and often slept and ate without leaving his chair. He informs me that, contrary to general opinion, Fénelon wrote with a marvelous facility, and that the *Télémaque* was produced in three months. He compares Rousseau with Rembrandt, a comparison that seems to me exact.

That devil of a companion of mine never praises anything but what is beyond our powers. Kant, Plato, those are the men! They are almost gods! If I mention a modern who stands within arm's reach, he strips him bare immediately, makes me touch his sores and leaves nothing of him. He does not have the gift of admiring, as he says — and as certainly appears. He is interesting — and he repels. Can repulsion be the result of perfect virtue or of perfect good faith? Can a finely balanced soul dwell in a sordid envelope? If he picks up a drawing to examine it, he handles it and turns it about carelessly, and puts his finger on the paper as if it were a thing of no value.

I believe that there is affectation in that kind of disdain for things that demand careful treatment; the inner revolt in the proud soul of this cynic shows through, despite him, in this apparent contempt for common decency; his mind has had some deep wound: perhaps, since he cannot bear himself because of his feeling of impotence, he tries to fool himself into seeing impotence everywhere. He has all kinds of talents, and the whole thing is dead; he composes, he draws, and people are coldly just to him: that is all that they can do. Listening to his conversation, one is astonished at how much he knows and how much he seems to add to the ideas of others. He does not like painting, and he admits it. Why doesn't he write, why doesn't he produce books? He believes himself capable of doing it and, as he says, has at times succeeded with it; but he confesses that he is forced to take too much trouble if he wants to express his ideas. That excuse betrays his weakness. Why does he not do like his admirable Rousseau? The latter, unquestionably, had something to say, and he said it very well, despite his difficulty in doing so, a matter of which he was almost vain.

Did I write the above under an impression more unfavorable than I generally get? Not at all, for he pleases me; I am almost fond of him and should prefer to find him more likable; but I always come away from him with the ideas that I express here.

September 9.

You should be an epicure as to your work.

Spanish ship captured by American pirates.

September 11.

Took a walk through the main street and looked with pleasure at the
shops, something I do not do in Paris. Everything acted on me as a
pleasant stimulant. Going near Saint-Remy and seeing the door open,
I went in and enjoyed the most grandiose spectacle, that of the dark,
lofty church lit by half a dozen smoky candles placed here and there. I
challenge the opponents of the *vague* to produce for me a sensation that
can be compared with this one and to do so with the preciseness that
results from sharply defined lines. If we classify the various feelings in
an order of nobility, as Chenavard does, we may decide at will for an
architectural drawing or for a drawing by Rembrandt.

Left the church enchanted and yet badly worried over the difficulty of working without getting from nature more than mere sentiment: in addition one needs all the complicated lines and perspectives,
projection of shadows, etc., which turned the thing I just saw into the
most magnificent picture.

September 13.

In the evening entered Saint-Remy a second time.

September 14.

As to the use one can make of one's friends: such, I believe, is the
title of one of Plutarch's treatises. A courtier or merely a man of the
world intent on pushing himself, and on making his career, would
doubtless not look into the point that the good Plutarch intended to
make in his treatise. For a man like that, there is only one way to profit
by one's friends: the first thing is to be on good terms with the powerful; then you must get them to intrigue for you or you must hook
yourself into their fortune. Of what importance is the respect — as

distinguished from material prosperity — that they may deserve? Of what importance is self-respect? Why should one think of such a matter as being accepted and loved by men of great virtue and great character? And yet it is to that type of utility that one should attach oneself with all one's strength, in every kind of relationship. Contact with honest men does more than confirm us in our feeling as to what is right: but it teaches us that there is no esteem whatever to be given to the benefits one may acquire only by some departure from strict integrity. In this way one learns that not a single essential duty is to be neglected.

September 15.

David said to that man who was wearying him by his talk about processes, methods of every kind: "I knew all that when I didn't yet know anything."

Chenavard dropped in on me while I was drawing some boats, and Isabey came almost immediately after him. It was a queer business, having those two men together. I went on with my drawing so as to be more at my ease.

Going out with the first of them and listening to him explain his system of *Paris as a sea-port,* the soldiers at their firing practice took my attention, and I am glad that for the moment I gave up the conversation of my companion to go and look at those unlucky fellows.

I had never conceived, for the profession of the soldier, the idea that I formed of it at that moment. It is one of contempt mingled with indignation at the brutes who have called slaughtering an art, it is one of profound pity for those sheeps dressed as wolves whose trade as Voltaire says so well, is to kill and be killed so as to earn their living. That mechanical operation of loading a gun, of launching that terrible thunderbolt that explodes as it leaves their hands, without their appearing to have any idea of what they are doing, offers a pitiable spectacle to a man whose heart is not entirely of stone. In another way, it would have disgusted men like Alexander or Caesar if you told them that those automatons, methodically lowering their guns and firing them at random, are fighting men. Where is the strength, where is the skill in that stupid game: the strength, the courage to attack, to press and overcome a ferocious enemy, the skill to preserve yourself from his blows? What! you go and plant yourself in front of another animal quite as much intimidated as yourself and, at a proper distance, you philosophically shoot balls of lead and of iron at each other, without any defense against the shots that are fired back at you, and you persuade your plumed and epauletted herd that that's the way for them to cover themselves with glory! That unhappy profession is rendered false in its principal object. Heroism consists in approaching the enemy in such a way that personal courage counts for something. To stand up passively before artillery fire is the act of a coward quite as much as that of a brave man: the latter is indignant at being treated like a wall or a piece of earthworks: he feels entitled to no more credit for that than there is for the crowd of tremblers near him who are waiting for their death or the end of a fight which shall also put an end to their fear. That intimidated mass, firing or fired upon, thus becomes, through a reversal of their role, the one strength of modern armies; it is through their mass that they are effective. The courage of men of action becomes almost useless. On the contrary, it turns to ice in this humiliating situation: what use is there in that anger which naturally seizes upon an impetuous heart at the sight of a comrade falling near by, or at the sound of the trumpets and the noise of the artillery calling aloud for vengeance? I am sorry I cannot form a clear idea of what is called a cavalry charge. I have always heard that kind of movement spoken of as something of a joke, in which, so to speak, the roles are fixed in advance, which is to say that if the infantry, or other body against which the charge is made, seems too resolute, only a feint at attacking is made: you save up your courage for a better occasion or for enemies less disposed to resist.

The sight of that platoon-firing, shooting hastily from double ranks in a way that must hinder accuracy, seemed to me a bad means

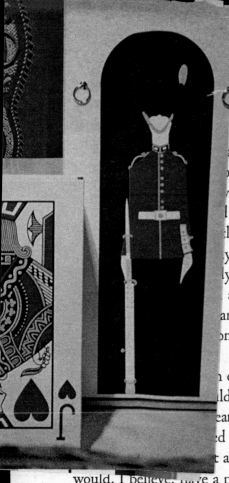

...ot to mention, as I was saying, the way in ...become useless in this type of fighting. It ...acting in small groups, men who are accurate ...in ranks promptly in making a fierce attack ...e more effect than those walls of flesh with ...l inaccurate shooting. They will unquestion- ...chines, the action of which will be more cal- ...y: already a whole swarm of inventions is ...ly to crush an entire corps in a few minutes, or ...and cowards in the twinkling of an eye. All ...and more to the same end, the abolishing of ...omplete change from the trade of the soldier to

...order to utilize individual courage, bodies of ...ld be needed, the selection not being made ...earance of the men, as is usually the case, but ...d courage. A corps like this, making a sudden ...t and supported by musket fire from a distance would, I believe, have a prodigious effect.

What a strange thing painting is, pleasing us by its resemblance to objects which could not please us in themselves!

September 17.

Chenavard dropped in about eleven o'clock. He spoke with assurance, at least so I think, about the direction of his thinking, about the contrasts between the esteem which he believes to be denied him and the merit he believes himself to possess, and which I genuinely recognize in him. He knows that he is not well liked; people reproach him with being too hard on others, when he himself gives few proofs of talent and of activity. His lack of confidence and the discouragement that he confesses seemed to me, as they do to him, the cause of his small success: he is so quick to give up. How can he have for people the interest that attaches to men gifted not alone with elevation, but also with energy, drawn from the desire to reach the first rank, and with confidence in that energy? He does not consider that Géricault is a master; he sees something muscle-bound in him. "He is a very brilliant young man," and he does not believe that he would ever have been more than that. He supports his idea with good reasons, based on the insignificance of Géricault's talent when he had the problem of making a picture, based also on the way that posed figures predominate, as details also do, even though they are treated with force.

(I am re-reading what concerns Géricault above, six months afterwards, which is to say on March 24, 1855, during my state of languor before the Exposition; yesterday I looked again at lithographs by Géricault, horses, a lion even, etc.; the whole thing is cold, despite the superior way in which the details are treated; but there is never any feeling of ensemble anywhere. There is not one of those horses but has some parts that are askew, either too small or else badly connected; there is never a background that has the least relationship with the subject.)

Had a pretty poor time at dinner. On the beach I was repaid for this by seeing the sun set amid bands of clouds, red and with sinister gilding, as they reflected in the sea, which was dark at every place that did not catch this reflection. I stayed motionless on the sand for more than half an hour, watching the waves and never tiring of their fury and their rolling and their sweeping along of the foam and the pebbles.

Then I went to the pier, where the devil's own wind was blowing. Roamed about the streets after taking some tea; went to bed at ten o'clock.

September 18.

I lay awake for part of the night, but it was not a disagreeable condition to be in. The mind has an incredible power at night. I thought about yesterday's conversation on mind and matter.

God put mind into the world as one of the necessary forces. It is not everything, as those famous idealists and Platonists would have it;

it is like electricity, like all the imponderable forces which act upon matter.

I am composed of matter and of mind: those two elements cannot perish.

Met Chenavard at seven o'clock in the evening. He took me home with him to give me back the photographs that I had lent him. He is forever insisting on the pre-eminence of literature. And of metaphysics. He tells me that I am of the family of men like Napoleon, people who see no more than ideologies in those who are not men of action. Conversation on style. He has a certain belief in it, or so it seems if one takes his words in their ordinary sense. He considers me partial.

September 20.

We visited the château at Eu. It is impossible for me to express my aversion for the frightful bad taste there: painting, architecture, ornaments, the very posts in the courtyard, all were mean and wretched. The garden is as poor as the rest. The château and the church with its cold, bare restorations, and the narrow entrance between it and the commons offered a spectacle revolting to taste and to common sense. May God pardon the poor king, admirable man that he was, for his predilections in matters of art. Everything here tells of Fontaine,[68] the Institute, Picot, etc. When I got back to Dieppe, it was like getting back to one's native land.

When studying the sculptures in the vaults at Eu, I noticed that the headdress of one of the countesses in the carvings there was like that of the women of Tréport, save for the pearls and the quality of the cloth: it is a kind of skullcap, but very gracious. The costume of the women at Tréport is charming: a simple bodice and a double skirt; one sees the inner one extending below the outer one; the sleeves of their blouses are wide as far as the elbow. They have the easy move-

[68] Fontaine (1762-1853), architect. François-Edouard Picot (1786-18-68), painter, continuator of the Davidian tradition.

ments that I noticed among the Jewish women of Tangier in their homes.

September 22.

This night, I was turning over in my head the *Cogito, ergo sum,* of Descartes.

September 23.

On silence and the silent arts. Silence is always imposing: even fools might often borrow from it a respectable look. In business, in every kind of relationship, men wise enough to keep silent at the right time owe a great deal to that. Nothing is more difficult than such restraint for those who are swayed by their imagination, for men of subtle mind who easily see all the aspects of things, so that it is hard for them to forbear expressing what takes place in them: they utter rash propositions, imprudent promises made without reflection, stinging words hazarded as to personages who are more or less dangerous and to be feared, confidences into which they are swept while in a state of enthusiasm and that they frequently speak out to the first person who happens along; it would be a long list that one might draw up of the difficulties and dangers which result from all sorts of indiscretions. By listening, on the contrary, you can only gain. You know the thing that you wanted to say to the other person, you are full of it; what he has to say to you is something of which you are doubtless ignorant: either he will teach you something that is new to you, or he will recall to you something that you have forgotten.

But how can one resist giving a favorable idea of one's mind to a man who is surprised and charmed, in appearance, at what one is saying? Fools are much more easily carried along by the vain pleasure of listening to themselves talk to others; incapable of profiting by an instructive and substantial conversation, they think less about informing their hearer than of dazzling him; it is with self-satisfaction that they come forth from conversation in which all they have earned, as payment for the boredom they have caused, is the contempt of sensible men. Taciturnity in a fool would already be the sign of a mind.

I confess my predilection for the silent arts, for those mute things of which Poussin made profession, as he said. Words are indiscreet; they break in on your tranquillity, solicit your attention and arouse discussion. Painting and sculpture appear more serious: it is you who must seek them out. The book, on the contrary, is importunate; it follows you, you find it everywhere. You have to turn the pages, follow the reasoning of the author, and go to the end of the work in order to judge it. How often has one not regretted the attention one has had to give to a mediocre book for the small number of ideas scattered here and there in its pages, ideas that one extracted with difficulty! The reading of a book not wholly frivolous is work: it causes a certain fatigue at least; the man who writes seems to be trying his strength with the critic. He discusses and one can discuss with him.

The work of the painter and the sculptor is all of a piece like the works of nature. The author is not present in it, and is not in communication with you like the writer or the orator. He offers what might be called a tangible reality, which is, however, full of mystery. Your attention is not treated as a dupe; the good parts of the work are instantly visible; if unbearable mediocrity should appear, it doesn't take you long to turn your eyes away, whereas the sight of a masterpiece holds you despite yourself, fixes you in a contemplation that only invincible charm can explain. This mute charm operates with the same force and seems to grow, everytime that your eyes fall on the work.

It is not quite the same thing with a book. Its beauties are not sufficiently detached to excite the same pleasure constantly. They are too much bound up with other parts which cannot offer the same interest; the good and the bad are chained together, often without transition. If the reading of a good book awakens our ideas, and that is one of the first conditions of such reading, we involuntarily mingle the author's ideas with ours; his images cannot be striking enough to keep us from forming a picture of our own, alongside the one which he presents to us. Nothing proves this better than the slightness of our inclination for books of great length. An ode, a fable will present the virtues of a picture that one takes in at a glance. What tragedy is there that does not become wearisome? And how much more is this the case when we come to works like *Emile* or *L'Esprit des Lois*.

Returned to Saint-Remy, which I drew, though I had forgotten my spectacles.

Dined at six o'clock; night falls at that hour. In the evening, took a walk and wandered about.

September 26.

Departure from Dieppe. In the morning I went to make my adieu to the pier; I sketched the view of the beach and the château. The weather was magnificent and the sea calm and azured.

Arrived at five o'clock. Paris always arouses in me the same antipathy.

September 27.

Spent the day in beginning to bring order into the mass of engravings and drawings.

September 28.

This morning, looking at the small *Saint Sebastian* in pastel on paper, compared with heavily loaded pastels on dark paper, I was struck by the enormous difference in the matter of luminosity, and by the absence of heaviness. In the same way, Flemish painting when compared with that of Venice easily produces in you an appreciation of its lightness.

October 2.

Varcollier is amiable toward me, and I am touched by his attentions. Unfortunately, what I used to call friendship is a passion I no longer feel to the same degree; moreover it is very late now for it to be born anew. Except for *just one being* [69] in this world, one who really makes my heart beat, the rest quickly fatigue me and leave no trace after them.

October 4.

It was early in life that I understood the fact that a certain fortune is indispensable to a man in my position. It would be just as bad for me to have a very considerable one as it would be to have none at all. Dignity, and respect for one's character must be accompanied by a measure of secure ease. That is the thing that I appreciate and that is absolutely necessary — far more than the little conveniences that are to be bought with a small amount of wealth. What comes immediately after this need for independence is tranquillity of mind, freedom from those anxieties and those ignoble shifts to which one is put by money embarrassments. One has to have a great deal of prudence if one is to reach this indispensable state and maintain oneself in it; one must unremittingly keep before one's eye the need for that calm, that absence of material cares, which permits one to give oneself entire to high enterprises, and which prevents the soul and the mind from going downhill.

These reflections result from my conversation of this evening with Riesener, who came to see me after my dinner; they derive also from what he told me about the situation of the Pierrets. His own does not seem to me much better, his future situation and perhaps his present one. He has behaved in a mad way all his life; there is a foundation of good sense in his mind, and he has always gone against it in his conduct.

This good sense, which is so rare, serves me as a transition in speaking of my visit to Chenavard, this morning. There is a fellow who is or who seems filled with sense, when he speaks, when he demonstrates, when he compares or deduces. His compositions on one hand, and his

[69] This is Jenny — note by M. Joubin.

predilections on the others, are the refutation of this wisdom. He loves Michelangelo, he loves Rousseau: those talents and certain others of very imposing aspect are of the kind that young men especially admire. Men of the type of Racine and Voltaire are admired by mature minds, to which they appeal always more strongly.

The one explanation I can give for this differing esteem in which one holds these authors at different times in one's life is the lack of reason one must observe in their many inflated passages, even when one is doing justice to the great qualities that they possess. In Rousseau, there is something which is not natural, which tells of effort, and which points to a mind where the false and the true are struggling with each other. I maintain that a really great man does not contain an atom of falsity: falsity, bad taste, absence of true logic — those things are all one.

In support of his theories, and to justify his intention in composing the *Deluge*,[70] Chenavard showed me an immense portfolio containing all the engravings after Michelangelo that he had been able to obtain. He confirmed me in my feeling instead of changing it. I told him that the *Last Judgment*,[71] for example, played a very small role in my thoughts. All I see in it is striking details, striking — like a punch in the head; but interest, unity, and continuity are all absent. His *Christ on the Cross*[72] does not give me any of the ideas that such

---

[70] Chenavard, a mind befogged with dreaming on social questions and aesthetic theories, had had the idea of decorating the interior of the Pantheon with a series of grisailles, summarizing the history of humanity and of its moral evolution: what he called the *Palingénesie Universelle*. The Provisional Government of 1848 accepted his plan. Chenavard worked for three years to execute it, after which, the Pantheon having been returned to religious uses in 1851, he had to give up the project. The *Deluge* mentioned here is the first of the forty compositions which Chenavard planned, and which were never executed.

[71] In his article on Michelangelo in the *Revue de Paris* of 1830, Delacroix had already developed these ideas.

[72] This is certainly an error in the reading of the text. It is the *Christ as a Judge*, the figure dominating the whole scene of the *Last Judgment*, that is referred to.

a subject should arouse. It is the same thing with his Biblical subjects.

Titian — there is a man whose qualities can be savored by people who are getting old; I confess that I did not appreciate him at all in the time when I had such admiration for Michelangelo and Lord Byron. It is not, in my opinion, either by the depth of his expression or by a great understanding of the subject that he touches you, but by his simplicity and by the absence of affectation. The painter-qualities are carried to the highest point in his work: what he does is done — through and through; when he paints eyes, they see, they are lit with the fire of life. Life and reason are everywhere. Rubens is quite different and has a quite different turn of the imagination, but he really paints men. Neither of these artists loses his sense of proportion save when he imitates Michelangelo and tries to take on a grandiose quality that is only swollen pretense, and that usually drowns out his real qualities.

The claim that Chenavard makes for his blessed Michelangelo is that he has painted man above all, and I say that all he has painted is muscles and poses, in which even science, contrary to general opinion, is by no means the dominant factor. The least of the ancients has infinitely more knowledge than there is in the whole work of Michelangelo. He did not know a single one of the feelings of man, not one of his passions. When he was making an arm or a leg, it seems as if he were thinking only of that arm or leg and was not giving the slightest consideration to the way it relates with the action of the figure to which it belongs, much less to the action of the picture as a whole.

You are forced to admit that certain passages treated in this way, things that resulted from the artist's exclusive absorption in them are of a character in which the only passion is their own. Therein lies his great merit; he brings a sense of the grand and the terrible into even an isolated limb. Puget, with a different character, is analogous to him in this respect. You will stand for a day looking at an arm by Puget, and that arm is part of a statue which, on the whole, is mediocre. What is the secret reason for this type of admiration? That is something that I will not take the responsibility of explaining.

We talked about the rules of composition. I told him that an absolute truth can give an impression contrary to the truth, at least contrary to that relative truth with which art deals; and when you stop to consider this thoroughly, there is logic in the exaggeration which causes the important parts, the ones which must create the impression, to project at the right moment; the question is one of guiding the mind in the right direction. As to our subject, *Mirabeau at the Protest of Versailles,*[73] I told him that Mirabeau and the Assembly ought to be on one side and the envoy of the King all alone on the other. He shows arranged and balanced groups, varied poses, men talking among themselves in a natural manner, as may well have happened at the time; his design is well distributed as regards the eye, and follows the material rules of composition; but the mind gets no idea of the National Assembly protesting against the injunction of M. de Brézé. That emotion which animates a whole assembly as it would animate a single man ought to be expressed in absolute fashion. Reason demands that Mirabeau be at the head of the group of men who crowd behind him, attentive to what is taking place: all minds, like that of the spectator, are fixed upon the event. When it took place, Mirabeau was doubtless not at the exact place which would make him the center of the picture; the arrival of M. de Brézé was perhaps not announced in such a way as to bring the Assembly together in a single group in order to receive him and, in a certain way, to oppose him; but the painter cannot otherwise express this idea of resistance: it is indispensable that the figure of Brézé be isolated. He doubtless came with followers and servants, but we must show him stepping forward alone and leaving them at a distance. Chenavard commits the incredible mistake of making them arrive from one side, while Brézé comes from the other and is lost in the

[73] *Mirabeau Replying to the Marquis de Dreux-Brézé,* such was the subject which the government of Louis-Philippe had announced for the competition of 1831. Delacroix, Chenavard, and other artists competed. Delacroix did not receive the award. His picture (Catalogue Robaut, 360), is today at the Museum of Ny-Carlsberg at Copenhagen; that of Chenavard is in the Museum of Lyons.

group of his adversaries. In a scene having so much character, where the throne is on one side and the people on the other, he places Mirabeau at random on the side where one sees the throne, upon which — mistake number two — workmen are climbing up to take down the draperies. The throne should have been as isolated, as abandoned as — morally — it then was by everyone and by public opinion; and above all the Assembly should have been shown facing the throne.

October 5.

To feel oneself surrounded by papers that have a voice, I mean drawings, sketches, souvenirs; to read two acts of *Britannicus,* feeling more astonishment each time at that pinnacle of perfection; the hope, I dare not say the certitude, of not being disturbed; a little work or a great deal, but above all security in solitude, therein lies a happiness which, at many a moment, seems superior to all others. It is then that you have the full enjoyment of your existence; nothing hurries you, you are solicited by nothing among all those things that lie outside a circle of study where, satisfied with little, (I mean *little of what pleases the crowd*), but on the contrary aspiring to the things that inward contemplation sees as the greatest, or that appear so in the light of the masterpieces of all time, I feel myself neither borne down by the weight of the hours nor terrified at their swiftness. Here is a voluptuous pleasure of the mind, a delicious mingling of calm and of ardor that the passions cannot give.

(Relate this with what I wrote at Ems on the need, beyond all others, of finding one's enjoyment in one's own existence.)

October 7.

I do not know whether I have mentioned hearing *Semiramis* at the Italiens with Mme de Forget, on Tuesday. The abundance of grace-notes and the padding are an injustice to that magnificent wealth of imagination that Rossini scatters everywhere. They are incomparable decorations painted on paper: their texture lets one see the parts that were filled in at random, and that weakens the impression.

October 12.

Worked with *frenzy* the whole day, until after three o'clock. I couldn't break away from it. I pushed ahead the grisaille of the *Moroccan Mounting his Horse,*[14] the *Fight Between a Lion and a Tiger,* the small *Woman of Algiers with a Greyhound,* and applied color to the cartoon of the *Hamlet Killing Polonius.*

Taking a walk after such a spell of work is a real delight. The weather is still very fine. I simply have to refrain from enjoying the landscape in the morning, except from my windows; going out for even a short time distracts my mind from work and condemns me to boredom for the rest of the day, on account of the difficulty of getting back afterward into a working mood.

I went down to the river and had another look at Trousseau's view, which I had done on cardboard: it isn't the same thing at all. The landscape that I need is not the absolutely real landscape; but then again, is absolute truth to be seen in the work of the landscapists who have painted true and yet have remained in the class of the great artists? There is nothing to equal the truth of the Flemings, or so it seems; but how much of man there is in the work of that school! Painters who simply reproduce their studies in their pictures will never give to the spectator a lively feeling of nature. The spectator is moved because nature reappears in his memory even while he is looking at your picture. It is necessary for your picture already to have received its properties of grace and idealization, if the ideal, which recollection implants whether we like it or not in our memory of all things, is not to find you inferior to what it regards as a representation of nature.

Today we had the famous capon with garlic, a thing to cause hesitation in a whole company of English grenadiers.

In the evening, took a walk with Jenny. The sight of the stars shining through the trees gave me the idea of doing a picture in which I might use that highly poetic effect; it is difficult in painting because it makes the whole canvas dark: it might be appropriate for a *Flight into*

[14] Catalogue Robaut, 1076, 1304, 1045, and 766.

Egypt. Saint Joseph leading the ass and throwing the light of his lantern on the water of a little ford; that weak illumination would suffice in the matter of the contrasts; or again the *Shepherds going to adore Christ in the Stable,* its doors wide open, and seen from a distance; or again the *Caravan of the Magi.*

Conversation with Jenny le Guillou about Chenavard's assertion that in a poor period talent is of less avail. What I should have been in the time of Raphael, I am today. What Chenavard is today, which is to say dazzled by the gigantic in Michelangelo, he would most certainly have been in the time of that master. Rubens is still Rubens even if he did come a hundred years after the immortals of Italy; if today someone is Rubens or any other master, he is so only the more. He adorns his century simply by his own existence, instead of being one of a company of other talents that contribute to its splendor. As to success at the time, it may indeed be doubtful; as to the people who approve, their number may indeed be limited; but a single admirer lost in the crowd is quite as moved as those who hailed Raphael and Michelangelo. That which is done for men will always find men to recognize its value.

I know perfectly well that Chenavard, forever intent on the importance of his famous *style,* does not admit that superiority may be found in every type of art. The beautiful which a given century accepts as suited to its needs will seem to him an inferior quality of the *beautiful;* but even if one grant him the right to that idea, does he think that a really superior man will not carry into any type of art whatsoever enough strength, enough novelty, to turn the work he pursues into an art as superior to the things around him as he is himself?

October 15.

I am complying with my rule, and it is a good one, of not allowing myself to finish until the effect and the tone are completely seized; I keep on redrawing and correcting things, and do so *in whatever way my feeling of the moment demands;* and as a matter of fact, is there anything more foolish than working in any other way? Can my feeling of yesterday be my guide today? I do not know how other men work. This way is my way. When everything has been carried along according to this principle, finishing is nothing, especially when one has tones that fit in immediately with those already set down. Without them, the execution would lose its frankness, and one would lose the vivacity of the touches applied as a reaction to sentiment; in this way the touches scarcely seem modified.

Before repainting, one must scrape down any passages of thick color.

October 21.

Racine's handling of the roles is almost perfect. He thought of everything and never resorted to padding: Burrhus, a leading role if there ever was one; the same applies to Narcisse Britannicus, the naive, the ardent, the imprudent Britannicus; Junie, so loving, but delicate and prudent amidst all her tenderness, and prudent with her lover alone. I will not say a word about Néron and Agrippine, because in the theatre, with two roles like those, or with one alone when it is played by a passable actor, one goes forth content; one feels that one has seen a piece by Racine even when one has allowed to pass unnoticed, through the delivery of bad actors, all those shades which make up the whole of Racine.

There are pieces in which the principal character, the one who is the pivot of the piece, is sacrificed; these parts are always given to minor players. Is there a role comparable with that of Agamemnon? One sees in him ambition, tenderness, the different positions he is in as regards his wife, in a word his perpetual agitations; yet one may not impute these to weakness of sentiment, which would take from him the esteem of the spectator, since their origin resides in the situation best calculated to test a great character. I do not say that the role of Achille which is usually played by the leading man of the company, is inferior to that of Agamemnon; it is what it must be, but that is not the role that establishes the interest of the piece. Clytemnestre, Achille, Iphigénie, all are striking characters through their passion, and their position in the piece; yet to a certain extent they are only instruments to act upon Agamemnon, urging him on and driving him toward one point or another.

How many people are there who think about all this when they go to the play? And of those who are capable of such reflection, I would ask whether it is the work of the actors which has led them to awareness of these diverse impressions?

October 22.

Worked a little at the *Odalisque* I am doing from the daguerreotype, but without much enthusiasm.

In the evening, went to Barbier's house; Villot was there. We did not say a word to each other.

Augerville, October 23.

We are at dinner; there was a good deal of talk about cooking, and I said that it was degenerating. Berryer, taking up my idea, cited the preface of Carême, in which he calls as his witness to this decadence which he deplores the spirit of his immortal master, Lavoypiere. That illustrious artist had been chosen by Murat to follow him to Naples when he was made king. The great Lavoypiere exclaimed against the barbarism of the country to which he was being brought: "I am given two sets of kitchen utensils, ye gods! two sets of kitchen utensils to do the cooking of a king!"

October 27.

Mme Berryer, the daughter-in-law, wants to abstain from meat, in spite of the dispensation from the Bishop of Orléans for the whole diocese. She is like the peasant who, during a sermon which drew tears from everyone else, remained indifferent. To the people who reproached him for his coldness he said that he did not belong to the parish.

On this score I said that, leaving aside all personal sentiment, I considered Protestantism an absurdity. Berryer tells me that Thiers had said precisely the same thing to the Prince of Wurtemberg. "You are going against the tradition of the human race, against the compendium of all the philosophies, the one that contains everything, etc."

In the evening, Berryer reads proverbs to us.

October 29.

Berryer relates to us the anecdote about Napoleon going to the marriage of Maret[75] at Saint-Cloud or at Versailles. He had Talleyrand in the carriage with him; he said that his youth had ended at Saint-Jean-d'Acre; by which he doubtless meant his confidence in his star. The English, said he, had stopped him there when he was engaged in getting to Constantinople. "At that," said he, "what I was prevented from doing in the South, I shall perhaps do some day in the North." Talleyrand, surprised, wrote a few days afterward to an old woman very well known at the time of the former régime: "I don't know whether that man is mad (this was still at the beginning of the Consulate); but here is what he told me the other day." Later on this letter fell into the hands of Pozzo;[76] this was at the moment of the campaign of 1812. Pozzo, who was going everywhere to gather together enemies of Napoleon, goes as far as the Sublime Porte, since Turkey was at war with Russia; and at the moment when a Russian army was advancing, he shows the letter and achieves his purpose of having the two empires conclude the treaty which permitted Russia to turn all her forces against France.

Came home today by way of some very beautiful bits of country, among others the one containing that curious pit that one can see from the outside. I regret very much that I did not make a sketch of it.

[75] Maret, Duke of Bassano, was, at the time, the secretary-general of the First Consul.

[76] Pozzo di Borgo (1764–1842), the famous adversary of Napoleon, a member of the Separatist government in Corsica with Paoli; later, at the court of Russia, where he had taken refuge, he combatted the policy of Napoleon.

Rocks in the foreground, etc., as also a clump of trees that made me think of *Norma*.

October 30.

Mme de Caen was here for dinner looking her best: my heart is in my mouth when she is present, but only when she is in evening dress and shows her arms and shoulders; I become quite reasonable again during the day, when she wears street clothes. She came this morning to see the paintings in my room and unceremoniously took me to see the ones in her own, letting me pass through her dressing-room. What reassures me as to my virtue is the thought which came to me that, in other days, that dressing-room and that bedroom had seen the piquant Marcelline, who has neither such arms nor such a breast as I suspect Mme de Caen to have, but who pleases by an indefinable something, by her wit, by her clever eyes, by everything that makes her stay in your memory.

November 1.

Went out in the boat for a short time during the day, which passed quietly like the others: but frankly, I am getting tired of this renouncing of all exercise of the imagination. Good Lord, what kind of a life is it that these people lead, living all the time the way I am doing at this moment! All these elegant gentlemen, and all these dainty little ladies do no more than drag themselves along from one hour to the other, without the slightest occupation for body or mind.

November 2.

I was greatly struck by the mass on the Day of the Dead. It made me reflect on all that religion offers to the imagination, and how at the same time it addresses itself to man's most intimate sense. *Beati mites, beati pacifi:* when was there ever a doctrine which thus made gentleness, resignation, and simple virtue man's one goal on the earth. *Beati pauperes spiritu:* Christ promises heaven to the poor in spirit, that is, to the simple: the saying is less designed to abase the pride in which the human mind delights when considering itself than to show that simplicity of heart is a greater thing than brilliance of intellect.

Champrosay, November 7.

In the evening I called on the ladies: Mme Barbier is ill, and I spent the evening in very friendly conversation with Mme Villot.

The reaction I get from all such recreation is not of the type that I would wish. For a solitary man who wants to remain solitary, a dangerous element still comes into the matter. Youth may divide itself among all the emotions: one's treasury closes its gates tighter with age; at that time the muse is a jealous mistress; she abandons you upon the slightest infidelity.

1855

January 20.

At the house of Viardot. Music by Gluck, admirably sung by his wife. Philosopher Chenavard no longer said that music is the least of the arts! I told him that the words of those operas are admirable. Broad, clear-cut divisions are necessary. The verses, adapted from those of Racine and disfigured in consequence, produce a far more powerful effect when sung to music.

The next, Sunday, went to the house of Tattet. Membrée sang some pieces of his composition. The one from the *Etudiants* would be bad even with the finest music. It is a small opera without recitatives. Which is to say that the story and the singing are merged in one. That is fatiguing for the mind, which follows neither the music nor the story, having to jump from one to the other all the time. A new proof that one must not step outside the *laws* that were found in the beginning for all the arts: relate whatever you like with the recitative, but with song let only passion sing — and with words that my mind guesses before you speak them.

The attention should never be divided. Fine verse is in its place in spoken tragedy; in opera, music alone should occupy me.

Chenavard agreed, without my having to beg him to do so, that there is nothing to compare with the emotion given by music. It expresses incomparable nuances. The gods, for whom earthly fare is too coarse, doubtless converse by no other means than music. For the well-deserved honor of music, one should invert Figaro's saying: "That which cannot be sung, is spoken." A Frenchman had to say the thing that Beaumarchais said.

What places music above the other arts (great reserves are to be made for painting, and precisely because of its great analogy with music), is that it is completely a thing of convention, and yet it is a complete language. All one needs is to enter its domain.

January 24.

Went to Morny's ball, in the evening.

Again I noticed the astounding perfection of the Flemings, no matter what may hang along side them. There was a pretty Watteau,[1] which became completely artificial, as I had already observed in the past.

January 28.

Called on Thiers in the evening. He talks to me of the prodigious resources that Napoleon found in his genius and in his indefatigable audacity during the memorable campaign of 1814.[2]

February 2.

Called at the house of Cerfbeer; it was stifling there. I chatted with Pontécoulant and with his wife. He told me quite rightly that the

[1] *Les Plaisirs du Bal*, now in the Wallace Collection, London; Delacroix has already spoken of this picture in the *Journal*, April 3, 1847.
[2] Thiers was at that time occupied with his *Histoire du Consulat et de l'Empire.*

taking of Sebastopol would be an irremediable obstacle to peace; that the Emperor, in 1812, had not re-established the kingdom of Poland because he did not want to cut off all possibility of restoring peace, since he was well persuaded that Russia would never abandon her claims to Poland but would always adhere to them as a matter of pride, if nothing else — the same feeling with which today she looks upon the Crimea, the real talisman which opens to her the road to the domination of the Orient.

On leaving that house I strolled along the boulevard, and with delight: I breathed in the coolness of the evening, as if it were a rare thing. I asked myself, and I had reason to do so, why men crowd into unhealthy rooms instead of walking about in the pure air, which costs nothing. All they talk about is insipid, and their words teach nothing and correct nothing; they bury themselves in card games or give solitary yawns amid the rush of people when they find no one whom they can bore.

February 6.

Dined at the house of the princess.[3] She always pleases me: she had a dress which she did not know how to manage; the material of it was so magnificent that it looked like a cuirass made of twenty yards of stuff; as a result of this ridiculous width, all women look alike because they all look like wine-vats.

After dinner I dropped in at Fould's for a moment and then came back to hear the princess with Franchomme; but the pleasure of the evening was two or three pieces of Chopin's which she had played for me before I left to call on the Minister.

Grzimala was asserting to us that Mme Sand had accepted money from Meyerbeer for the articles she has written in his praise. I cannot believe it, and I protested against the statement. The poor woman really needs money: she has written too much, and for money; but that she should descend to the trade of the hired publicity agent is something that I cannot believe!

[3] Czartoriska.

Berryer called at the house of the princess.

February 19.

Berryer writes me this evening to ask whether I shall be able to get a place for next Thursday, the day of his election. I reply:

"My dear cousin, I hasten to tell you that it is only from you that I can hope for a place at a session which will be so interesting for me. I have almost nothing but enemies at the Palais Mazarin. They want to keep me outside that door on every possible occasion; receive me at least for that day, which is dear to me on more than one account. Affectionately yours."

In reply to this letter, all Berryer could send me was a ticket for the upper part of the amphitheater of the Institute. Arriving at half-past twelve, amidst snow and cold, I found people waiting in a line that extended down to the street door, which is to say that all the staircases and passages leading to that amphitheatre were full, as was the place itself. Among those good people there were some who claimed that that side was excellent, but all were waiting for some lady to faint, or for some other prodigy, in order to slip into the interior; and there were two hundred of them there!

I am a bit put out with Berryer. Had our positions been reversed, I should have insisted on finding a place for my cousin. All his friends from Frohsdorf[4] and others were, I am sure, well installed, and had brought along specially big ears to listen with. . . . I am mistaken: they were there in order to say that they had been there.

M. Stevens[5] asked me for the Turkish vest which he got at the Decamps sale, and which he had loaned me about two months ago; I have returned it to him.

March 5.

Concert by the amiable princess. Chopin's concerto produced little

[4] Residence of the Count de Chambord, the Legitimist claimant of the throne of France. Berryer, as is well known, belonged to the Legitimist party.
[5] Joseph Stevens (1819–1892), the Belgian animal-painter.

effect. People keep on insisting on playing that instead of his delight-ful short pieces. The poor princess and her piano were lost in that theater. When la Viardot,[6] as a prelude, sang Chopin's mazurkas arranged for the voice, one felt the artist; Delaroche said just that to me; he was seated near to me in the place that I had to take after having had to offer my own to the Vaufreland ladies.

The short fragments of a Haydn symphony that I heard yesterday enchanted me as much as the rest repelled me. I have come to the point where I can no longer lend my ears or my attention save to what is excellent.

As to immoderate respect for the masters: cite the coldness of certain Titians, the *Christ at the Tomb,* etc.

Oculos habent et non vident, they have eyes and they see not. Hence the rarity of good judges of painting.

As to *style.* It is not to be confused with *fashion.*

March 15.

Dined at the house of Bertin;[7] that nice Delsarte said to me that Mozart had pillaged Galuppi outrageously, doubtless in about the same way that Molière pillaged anywhere when he found something to take. I told him that *what was Mozart* had not been taken from Galuppi nor from anyone else. He places Lulli above everyone else, even Gluck, whom he admires very much, however. He sang some light little songs of the old time, that were charming when sung with the taste that he puts into things. I called his attention to the fact that if he took pains to sing with the same care the music of the great musicians whom he does not love, it would produce as much effect, and perhaps more. He sang the beautiful air from *Telasco* and again it had its enchanting effect upon me.

With certain artists one must overlook their eccentricity on some point or other, without diminishing one's esteem for their talent:

[6] Pauline Viardot, *née* Garcia.

[7] Edouard Bertin, painter, director of the *Journal des Débats* from 1854 on, a boyhood friend of Delacroix's. François Delsarte, musician, teacher of singing.

Delsarte is a bit mad in the way he acts; his plans to make humanity happy, his tremendous perserverance for a while in his attempt to become a homeopathic doctor, and finally his ridiculous and exclusive preference for old music, which is the pendant for his eccentricity in behavior, put him in the class with Ingres, for example, who is said to act like a child, and who has preferences and antipathies which are equally silly. There is something lacking in those people. Neither Mozart nor Molière nor Racine could have had silly preferences, or silly antipathies; their *reason,* consequently, was on a level with their *genius,* or rather was *their genius itself.*

The stupid public is today abandoning Rossini for Gluck, as it once abandoned Gluck for Rossini; some little song of the year 1500 is placed higher than anything that Cimarosa produced. We need not bother about that stupid herd which has always got to find something else to go crazy about, because it has not taste or discernment about anything; but men in the profession, artists or practically that, who are looked on as superior men, are inexplicable when they are so cowardly as to lend themselves to all this silliness.

March 22.

M. Janmot,[8] who came to see me this morning, told me, when we were discussing the question of good lay-ins, that Ingres says: "One applies finish only to what is finished already."

March 23.

This morning, on examining some sketches which I made from the figures in the Galerie d'Apollon (sculptures on the cornices) and copied from the book of engravings that Duban had lent me, I noticed the incorrigible coldness of those things.[9] Despite the breadth of the execution, I can attribute it only to the excessive timidity which will

[8] Louis Janmot (1814-1892), a painter of religious subjects.

[9] In 1849, when Delacroix was making studies for the ceiling of the Galerie d'Apollon, he had made drawings of the architectural order established by LeBrun, in order to maintain a perfect unity between his painting and its frame. One of these drawings is reproduced as No. 1117 in the Robaut catalogue.

never permit the artist to get away from the model;[10] and this timidity appears in the crouching figures on the cornices,— in just the kind of work in which fantasy would be more than permitted. It is through love of perfection that these figures are imperfect.

There is a little of the reflection of that exaggerated exactitude in the whole school that begins with Poussin and with the Carracci. Prudence is doubtless a virtue, but it does not add charm. I compare the grace of the figures of a Correggio, of a Raphael, of a Michelangelo, of a Bonasone, or of a Primaticcio with the grace of a ravishing woman who enchants you without your being able to say why. On the other hand, I compare the cold correctness of the figures in the French style with those big, well-built women who are devoid of charm.

Saturday March 24.

The pleasure that I experience in re-reading my reflections, as noted in these little books in earlier days, or merely in seeing the mentions of what I did on a given day, whom I saw, and where I was, ought to be a corrective of my laziness and make me write oftener. In my state of languor, shall I really continue when I notice the rapid passing of the time that is left me to finish my pictures? Being greatly vexed on seeing how little good will there is among the people at this Exposition who might be useful to me, I still take pleasure in being useful, I feed on the memory of my own sentiments, since I can draw no great profit from the feeling of other people. . . . I feel myself very isolated, and that state of affairs worries me even more regarding the future. Why is it that things go badly with me? Because, at certain moments, I cannot stand the least unpleasantness; I like any number of people and see them with pleasure, but they have got to come at the right time: there is no magician who can arrange the moments for meetings, and for the most part they occur at inconvenient times.

Young Armstrong[11] told me about Turner, who bequeathed a

[10] That is to say, from the living model.

[11] Thomas Armstrong, an English painter, came to study in the schools of Paris in 1853.

hundred thousand pounds sterling to found a retreat for poor or infirm artists. He lived an avaricious life, with one old servant. I remember having received him at my studio just once, when I was living on the Quai Voltaire.[12]

He made only a middling impression on me: he had the look of an English farmer, black coat of a rather coarse type, thick shoes—and a cold, hard face.

Toward half-past five, Haro informed me that a new arrangement has been made regarding the panel that I had been promised at the Exposition, and that it has been given to Ingres. Chennevières,[13] who was so affectionate with me the other day, appeared not to remember the rights which those gentlemen had given me regarding that place. I am going to go today, Saturday, to the Minister.

March 25.

Yesterday, Saturday, continued to feel ill, but with some improvements. I am still reading Dumas's novel, *Nanon de Lartigues:*[14] in between times I fall asleep. The novel is charming at the beginning; then, as usual, come the tiresome parts that are badly digested or emphatic. In this one I don't yet very well see the dawn of those so-called dramatic and passionate parts that he introduces into all his novels, even when they are most comic.

That mixture of the comic and the pathetic is in decidedly bad taste. The mind ought to know where it is, and even where it is being led. We Frenchmen who have been for so long a time familiar with that way of looking upon the arts would have great difficulty, unless for example we had read a great deal of English, in getting to an under-

[12] Delacroix lived at 15 Quai Voltaire from January, 1829 until October, 1835.
[13] Philippe de Chennevières (1820-1899), was at that time Inspector of Museums and one of the organizers of the Exposition of 1855. Later on he was the Directeur des Beaux-Arts.
[14] First part of the novel entitled *La Guerre des Femmes,* published in 1844 in *La Patrie,* and later on in two volumes.

standing of the reverse effect in Shakespeare's plays. We cannot imagine a piece of buffoonery coming out of the mouth of a high priest, of an Athalie, or even the slightest attempt, in such a character, at the familiar style. In most cases, Comedy presents only very serious passions in the man who feels them, but the effect of them is to provoke laughter rather than tragic emotion.

I think that Chasles was right in what he told me in a conversation on Shakespeare, of which I have spoken in one of these notebooks: "He is neither a writer of comedies nor of tragedies, properly so called; his art is his own, and it is an art of pyschology as much as of poetry. He does not paint the ambitious man, the jealous man, the consummate scoundrel, but a certain jealous man, a certain ambitious man, who is less a type than a nature with its particular nuance. Macbeth, Othello, Iago are as far as the poles from being types; the particularities or rather the singularities of those characters can make them seem to be individuals, but do not give the absolute idea of each of their passions. Shakespeare possesses such a power of reality that he makes us adopt his personage as if it were the portrait of a man we had known. The familiarity that he puts into the speeches of his personages does not shock us any more than that which we might encounter in the men about us, not in a theater, but among men now in sorrow, now in exaltation, now rendered ridiculous, even, by the situations which life-as-it-is brings about from time to time; hence the spicing of the piece through unrelated scenes which, in Shakespeare, give us not at all the shock they would in our theater. Hamlet, in the midst of his grief and his schemes for vengeance, indulges in endless buffooneries with Polonius and with the students; he amuses himself with lessons to the actors who are brought to him to play a bad tragedy. Moreover, through the whole piece something like a strong wind seems to be blowing: a progression and a development of passions and events which, although irregular if judged by our habit, assume a character of unity which enthrones that virtue in our mind when we think back to the play. For if that sovereign quality were not there, amid all the drawbacks which we have just discussed, Shakespeare's plays would not have deserved to hold the admiration of the centuries. There is a secret logic, an unperceived order in those accumulations of details, which would seem to add up to nothing more than a shapeless mountain, but in which one still feels distinct parts, passages well planned to afford relief, and at all times continuity and consistency."

My poor Dumas, of whom I am so fond and who doubtless thinks himself a Shakespeare, does not present to the mind details as powerful, nor yet an ensemble which, in our memory, shall constitute a well marked unity. The parts are never well balanced; his comedy, which is the best thing in his writing, gives one a sense of being pent up within certain sections of his works; then, all of a sudden, he makes you enter the realm of sentimental drama, and those same characters who were making you laugh turn into weepers and declaimers. Who would recognize in those joyous musketeers of the beginning of the work, those creatures of melodrama at the end of the story, busying themselves with a certain milady who gets a formal trial and is executed amid storm and darkness? And here one sees the customary defect of Mme Sand. When you have finished reading her novel, your ideas about her characters are completely mixed up. The one who entertained you by his sallies can now do no more than make you shed tears over his virtue, over his devotion to his fellow men, or else he speaks the language of magical incantations. I could cite a hundred examples of the disappointment thus prepared for the reader.

March 31.

I am feeling better: I have started work again. The princess came about four o'clock to see my pictures; she recommends me to come on Monday and hear Gounod. She had a green shawl which was horribly unbecoming for a woman like her, and yet she preserves her charm. The mind is a big element in matters of love; one could fall in love with that woman, who is no longer young, who is not at all pretty and who lacks freshness. How strange is the sentiment I have in mind!

The thing at the bottom of it is always possession, but possession of what, in a woman who is not pretty? Possession of that body which is by no means pleasing? For if it is the mind with which one is in love, one can enjoy it quite as well without possessing that unattractive body: we can find a thousand pretty women who don't mean a thing to us. The desire to have everything in a person who has moved us, a certain curiosity which is a powerful motive force in love affairs, and perhaps the illusion of penetrating deeper into that soul and into that mind, all these feelings unite to form a single feeling; and who shall tell us that at the moment when our eyes imagine they see only an exterior object devoid of attraction, certain charms responsive to our inner nature are not driving us onward without our knowing it? The expression of the eyes suffices to charm.

May 2.

Called this evening on that insipid Paiva.[15] What society! What conversation! Young men with beards or without beards; gay young creatures forty-five years old, German barons and dukes, journalists, and new faces every day! Amaury Duval was there. It was only with him that I could open my mouth. I was petrified at all that uselessness and insipidity. The worthy Dumas thinks himself in society when he is there. As he is a little god for all of them, as he gets an excellent dinner there every week and can bring along any girl he happens to have at the moment, as they consult him even about the talents of the cook and he decides whether to keep that one or get a new one, he is planted there like the Mondor that you sometimes found in certain salons in the old days; he yawns or sleeps while people are talking to him; but all in all, he is really a good fellow.

When, at half-past eleven, I got out of the stupor of that pest-laden atmosphere, it was simply a treat to breathe the air out of doors. I walked for an hour communing with myself, pretty dissatisfied none

[15] A woman of easy virtue, well known in society during the Second Empire.

461

the less, morose, returning to a thousand disagreeable objects, and mentally placing myself amidst all those dilemmas that are prepared for us by life-as-it-is; there is one especially that forms the basis of all our thinking along these lines: the various elements composing it are solitude, boredom, torpor, society with or without a hold on you, a permanent state of rage, and then, above all, aspiration toward solitude. Conclusion: to remain in solitude, without submitting to any of the other tests, since the supreme desire, finally, is tranquillity, even if that tranquillity means a kind of annihilation.

May 15.

Seventh visit from the doctor. Inauguration of the Exposition. After that I went, and imprudently, to the exhibition of pictures, Dauzats accompanying me and returning home with me. I felt the cold in that place very badly. I saw Ingres's exhibition. The dominating thing in it, to a great degree, is the ridiculous; it is the complete expression of an incomplete intelligence; effort and pretension are everywhere; there is not a spark of naturalness in it.[16]

May 22

Dumas sends an inquiry in the morning as to whether I am at home; I answer that I shall be there at two o'clock. He asks me for notes on things that are perfectly useless for the public to know, how I go about my painting, my ideas on color, etc. So as to prolong the session, he asks to dine with me: I seize the opportunity, which I know will give me some pleasant moments. He goes out to do an errand and comes back after seven o'clock, when I was about to dine alone, having gotten terrifically hungry.

After dinner, we take a cab, pick up one of those little girls of his, and go to see the Italian tragedy and comedy. There is only one reason for going to such a theater as that: the desire to strengthen one's knowledge of Italian. Nothing could have been more of a bore.

[16] A little later, Delacroix will put down a second impression of Ingres's work, modifying the severity of the one above.

Dumas was telling me that he was in the midst of a lawsuit which should take care of his whole future, something like 800,000 francs as a beginning, without counting the rest. The poor chap is beginning to find it too much to write night and day and never have a cent. "I can't go on," he told me, "I am leaving two novels half finished. . . . I am going away, I am going to travel, and on my return I shall see whether an Alcide has turned up to finish those two unsatisfactory jobs." He is persuaded that, like Ulysses, he will leave behind him a bow that no one else can bend; meanwhile he doesn't see that he has grown any older, and in various matters he acts like a young man. He has mistresses and indeed overworks them; the girl we called for to take to the theater wanted to beg off; she said she would die of lung trouble at the rate she was going. The worthy Dumas pays a fatherly call on her every day, takes care of the essentials of the household, and does not bother about the way his protégée may amuse herself! Lucky man! lucky state of being carefree! He deserves to die, like the heroes on the field of battle, without having to know the miseries of the end, hopeless poverty and abandonment.

He told me that for all he had two children he might as well be alone. The two of them attend to their own affairs and leave it to his Isabelle to console him. On the other hand, Mme Cavé was telling me next day that her daughter complained of having to live with a father who brought his mistresses to see her, and who was never at home. . . . Strange world!

May 26.

Dined at Mme Villot's; Mme Herbelin, Rodakowski, Ferré and Nieuwerkerke were there. Another outburst of indignation against the flowers that strewed the table, etc.

In the evening, at nine o'clock, Nieuwerkerke takes me to the house of Prince Napoleon for the first of his soirées. . . . What a crowd! What faces ! Barye, the republican, Rousseau, the republican, [17]

[17] Théodore Rousseau, the landscape painter; François-Louis Français, the painter.

Français, the republican, Mr. So-and-so, the royalist, Mr. Such-a-one, the Orleanist; the whole lot of them squeezing in together and rubbing shoulders. There were some charming women there; among others, there was Mme Barbier, looking her best. I left there late, and went to take an ice at the Café de Foy: the ones served by the Prince were detestable.

I had a bad night, the first part of it; I got up just as day was breaking and took a walk; that set me up again. I had the enjoyment of that solemn moment when nature gets back her strength, and royalists and republicans all lie wrapped in the same slumber.

May 29.

Today I had as guests at dinner: Mérimée, Nieuwerkerke, Boilay, Halévy, Villot, Viel-Castel, Arago, Pelletier and Lefuel; [18] they seemed to have a good time and to be at their ease. I looked forward apprehensively to the evening, thinking it would be a mere task, and it turned out to be a pleasure. I wish I had a place where I could often have such parties.

June 1.

Went to the meeting of the Council which is still held in the Salle des Cariatides; the question of ball tickets was discussed. I raised my voice against the practice of demanding them only for persons well known to the applicant; it is a funny thing to see all those grocers, all those bad painters, all those dealers in paper and all those rich fellows feeling more at home and more at ease in society than this shoemaker or that tailor who was probably invited by mistake and with whom they fear to rub shoulders. I told them that in our day French society was all

[18] Pelletier held an important post in the Ministère d'Etat. Count Horace de Viel-Castel (1798-1864), a writer, entered the administration of the Beaux-Arts and became curator of the Musée des Souverains, a position which he held until 1862. It is Alfred Arago, Inspector-general of Fine Arts, who is referred to, and not his father, the famous astronomer. The other personages have been met before.

made up of these bootmakers and grocers, and that they had better not look into such matters too closely.

After that I went to the Exposition. The group of Ingres' things seemed to me better than it did the first time, and I am thankful to him for many fine qualities that he gets. I met Mme Villot there with a friend of hers.

This was the evening when I saw the kind Alberthe again and she was as nice to me as anyone could be. For a long time nothing could be talked of but a big dog that filled up the whole room; they couldn't find words to express their admiration for him. I hate it when people spend a lot of time over such episodical personages as *dogs* and *children,* who never interest anybody but their owners or the people who brought them into the world.

June 7.

I went to the Hôtel de Ville for the banquet given to the Lord-Mayor; not having been properly informed, I missed the ceremony of the morning which, they tell me, was very imposing; it was a matter of the Lord-Mayor's presenting the address of the corporation of London to the municipality of Paris. The costumes of the Lord-Mayor and the aldermen were worth seeing. The banquet given in the Salle des Fêtes was splendid; the lights made a magnificent effect. I sat alongside a poor Englishman who didn't know a word of French; I have almost forgotten my English; I had to stop and hunt for every word. We both kept up a pretense of understanding what the other was saying, and at that we didn't say much.

Champrosay June 14.

After dinner, took a walk in the park with young Rodrigues, a babe at the breast of painting, getting his milk from Picot,[19] and tiring me a little with his naive conversation; but thanks to his good will, I got some fresh air amidst the most beautiful trees in the world.

[19] François-Edouard Picot (1786-1868), pupil of Vincent and of David, elected to the Institute in 1836; he decorated a number of churches in Paris.

June 15.

In *La Presse* I read a passage from Mme Sand's *Histoire de sa Vie.*
Today she is telling about her relationship with Balzac. The poor
woman is forced to pay a tribute of admiration to everybody. In this
prose, printed during her lifetime and addressed to contemporaries,
she speaks of him in pretty admiring terms. She is forced to make much
of all those celebrities of her time so as not to be reproached with envy
— she who is still alive: it is one of the thousand drawbacks to her
work. She talks a good deal of the paternal sentiment that Latouche[20]
has for her, and of the way that she and Arago are like sister and
brother. What an enterprise, and especially for a person in her place —
talking about herself, when the need to do it during her lifetime does
not permit the frankness which alone would give interest to her work,
if not for its own sake at least for that of the originals of whom she
aspires to leave portraits for posterity. She has the weakness to speak
of her theory in the matter of novels, to talk of that *need for the ideal;*
and that favorite phrase of hers expresses her way of representing men
as they should be. Balzac, she says, encourages her in that attempt,
proposing to himself that in his own work he will paint them *as they
are,* a claim for which he thinks he has furnished justification, or more
than that.

June 16.

Dined at the house of Parchappe. Deadly dullness; not the slightest
interest and, to wind it up, *lotto,* with old women and adolescents. I
must confess that in the end I took an interest in it because I won. Man
is a queer animal!

June 17.

The next day, Sunday, as I get up I think of the special charm of the
English school. The little I have seen of it has left memories with me.

[20] Henri de Latouche (1785-1851), writer, journalist, dramatist; in 1819,
he published the works of André Chénier; he was the first to discover the literary value of George Sand and, in 1831, got her first novel published.

With the English painters, there is a real finesse, dominating all the tendency toward unoriginal work, which does crop up here and there, as in our dull school. With us, finesse is the rarest thing: everything has the look of having been done with clumsy tools and, what is worse, by obtuse and commonplace minds. Take away Meissonier, Decamps, one or two others, and some of the early pictures by Ingres, and everything is banal, spiritless, without intention and without warmth. You have only to give a glance at that silly and banal paper, the *Illustration,* that our pinchbeck artists slap together, and then compare it with a similar collection published by the English, in order to get an idea of the degree of commonness, softness, and insipidity that characterizes most of our production. This so-called draftsmen's-country doesn't really show a trace of draftsmanship, nor is there the least bit more of it in the most pretentious pictures. In those little drawings, every object, almost, is treated with the interest that it demands: landscapes, maritime views, costumes and military scenes, the whole thing is charming, touched in exactly, and above all — drawn. I don't see who there is among ourselves who can be compared with Leslie,[21] with Grant and with all those men of the school that descends partly from Wilkie and partly from Hogarth, with a little of the suppleness and the facility introduced by the school of forty years ago, that of the men like Lawrence and those about him, who shone by their elegance and lightness.

If one considers another phase of English painting which is quite new, what is called the Dry School — and that looks back to the Flemish primitives — one finds, under its apparent reminiscences and its aridity of treatment, a feeling for truth that is real and completely local. What good faith they have, amid their so-called imitation of the old pictures! For example, compare the *Order for Liberation* by

[21] Charles Robert Leslie (1794-1859), genre painter; Delacroix got inspiration from him for the small historical pictures of his youth. Francis Grant (1803-1878), portrait painter. These two artists were represented at the Exposition of 1855.

Hunt[22] or by Millais, I don't now remember which, with our primitives,[23] our Byzantines, obstinately attached to style and, with their eyes fixed on the images of another time, getting only the stiffness of them without adding any qualities of their own. That mob of dull mediocrities is enormous; not a dash of truth, the truth that comes from the soul; not one painting like that child sleeping in its mother's arms, with its silky baby hair, its so truthful understanding of sleep, and all its other parts — even to the redness of the legs and feet — so singular in its observation and, above all, in its sentiment. And now look at men among ourselves like Delaroche, Janmot and Flandrin: there is the grand style for you! What is there in the pictures of such fellows of the real man that painted them? How much of Giulio Romano there is in this one, how much of Perugino there is in that one — or of Ingres, his teacher; and everywhere pretension to seriousness, to being a great man, to the thing that Delaroche calls serious art!

Leys[24] the Fleming, seems to me very interesting also: but, for all the look his execution has of being more independent, he does not have that completely good-natured quality of the English; I see effort, manner, something that disquiets me as to perfect good faith on the part of this painter, and the others stand below him.

Gautier has several articles on the English school:[25] he began with that. Arnoux, who hates him, told me at Delamarre's place that Gautier is writing these to flatter the *Moniteur*, which is publishing them. For my own part I would willingly credit him with enough good taste to have that kind of marked predilection for the work of men whom we

[22] William Holman Hunt (1827-1910) was with John Everett Millais (1829-1896) the chief of the Pre-Raphaelite school, that new school under discussion here. The *Order for Liberation* which Delacroix speaks of was by Millais. At the Exposition of 1855, Hunt had exhibited three pictures among which the *Lost Sheep* will astonish Delacroix (see below) and will be widely noticed by critics and artists.

[23] Ingres and his school.

[24] Baron Henri Leys (1815-1869), one of the chiefs of the Romantic school in Belgium.

[25] Published under the title *Les Beaux-Arts en Europe*, two volumes, 1855.

are to treat, in any event, with the courtesy due to foreigners; and yet it was not his remarks which put me on the track of the sentiments that I express here. It is by comparison with other pictures by painters of our own, supposed to have parallel qualities, that he should have had the courage to demonstrate the merit of the Englishmen; I find nothing of that in his articles. He takes a picture, describes it in his own way, and so makes a charming picture of his own; but he has not done the work of a true critic. Provided he can find words that will tickle his reader, that will dazzle him with the macaronic expressions he discovers (with a pleasure that is sometimes contagious), provided he can make allusions to Spain and to Turkey, to the Alhambra and the Atmeidan of Constantinople, he is satisfied, he has achieved his purpose as a curious author, and I don't believe that he sees any further than that. When he reaches the French, his articles will do for each one of them what he has done for the English. There is neither instruction nor philosophy in such criticism.

It was in the same way that he made his analysis, last year, of Janmot's very interesting pictures. He did not give me any idea of that really interesting personality which will be smothered in the vulgarity, in the *chic,* that dominates everything here. How interesting it would be for a critic possessing some penetration to compare these pictures, imperfect as they are from the standpoint of execution, with these English pictures which are just as naïve, but so different in inspiration! Janmot has looked at Raphael, Perugino etc., as the English have looked at Van Eyck, Wilkie, Hogarth and others; but the English remain just as original after having made that study. With Janmot there is a remarkable Dantesque perfume. When I look at his painting I think of those angels of Purgatory in the poem of the famous Florentine; I like those robes, green as meadow grass in the month of May, and those heads, the result of his inspirations or his dreams, which are like reminiscences of another world. A naive artist like that will not get a tithe of the justice to which he is entitled. His barbarous execution unfortunately places him in a rank which is neither second, nor third, nor last; he talks a language which no one else can come to use; it isn't even a language; but one can see his ideas amidst all the confusion and the naive barbarism of his rendering. His talent is curious and solitary in our country and in our time; the example of Ingres, his teacher, so often resulting in mere technical imitation and thus breeding a horde of followers devoid of any idea of their own, was impotent before the task of imparting a sense of execution to this man of natural talent who still cannot get out of his swaddling clothes, who will remain throughout his life in the state of a bird still dragging about with it the shell from which it was born, and dragging itself about all smeared with the mucus amid which it was formed.

Dined at the house of Halévy with Mme Ristori,[26] Janin, Laurent Jan, Fouché and Bayvet's son, who is a handsome lad (I mention this because of the homeliness of his father and his mother).

La Ristori is a big woman with a cold face: no one would ever say that she had a talent like hers. Her little husband has the look of being her elder son. He is a Roman marquis or prince.

Laurent Jan was pretty unbearable, as he usually is, with his fashionable manner of being witty, which he achieves simply by saying the opposite of every reasonable opinion. His verve is inexhaustible, once he gets started. Janin was silent, and I regret it: I like his type of mind very much; the same applies to Halévy. And yet, despite my small sympathy with his continual railing and that loud voice of his which leaves you mute and regretful, I had pleasure in seeing him.[27] At my age, there is no greater pleasure than that of finding oneself in the company of intelligent people who understand everything before it is half spoken. I told that blond little Roman prince, who sat beside him at the table, that Paris, whose opinion puts the seal on reputations,

---

[26] Mme Adelaide Ristori (1829-1906), the celebrated Italian actress; she appeared in Paris at the Théâtre-Français in 1855, where she became the rival of Rachel. Her extraordinary success continued for years. In 1849 she had married Marquis Capranica del Grillo.

[27] Laurent Jan.

was composed of five hundred persons who have minds and who judge and think for the mass of two-legged animals who live in Paris, but who are Parisians in name only. It is with a man of the former type, thinking and judging, above all judging for himself, that it does you good to find yourself, even if you have to dispute with him throughout the quarter of an hour or the day that you are to spend with him. When I compare the company I had on Sunday with what I had the day before at the Parchappe's, I promptly pass over the eccentricities of my Laurent Jan, I think only of the unexpected quality of his talk, his artist-quality in everything, which makes of him a precious original.

The people who pride themselves on being high society are practically unaware of the extent to which they are deprived of real society, which is to say, the extent to which they miss the social pleasures. Take away from them their talk about the weather, their gossip about the neighborhood and their friends, and there is nothing left but whist to console them for the long hours that they spend facing each other. But it is doubtless less of a deprivation for them because they can have no idea of the pleasure I was speaking about just now. It is a rare thing to find people with minds, and those who do in high society as it is called, become vain enough to accept boredom or dull enough to be like the people surrounding them. [What is one to say, for example, about a man like Berryer whose only recreation, after his fatiguing work, is found among these society people, almost everyone of whom seems more of a bore, if that were possible, than all the rest! He is a singular man, hard to make out, especially at the beginning. In reality, the lawyer in him dominates everything else; the man has disappeared, he is just the same in society as he is at his office or at the bar; he undergoes boredom in the same way that he wears his robe, because of the needs of the cause].[28] One sees certain society people who have the capacity for enjoyment that is found among artists — I use that word to sum up my idea — and who make a great effort to

[28] The lines between brackets were specially added later on, in 1860, when Delacroix was re-reading his *Journal*.

have artists around them, really finding pleasure in their conversation.

The good princess[29] is like that: after she has received or visited her society acquaintances, she has less formal days when she likes to see painters and musicians. Several of those ladies have a lover of every type possible, so as to be acquainted with talent of all kinds.

June 19.

At dinner this evening, I get the letter from Eugène de Forget announcing the death of Mme de Lavalette.[30]

Paris, June 20.

Left at half-past six. I told the driver to take me to the house of Mme de Forget, not knowing at what hour the funeral would take place. I find her very sad. I tell her how unbecoming it seems to me to have the ceremony in a little church which is only a kind of annex. Neither Eugène, to whom I talk, nor she has a clear grasp of the reason why public homage should have been given with a certain splendor; but to so small an extent was it a public matter that I was ashamed at the lack of feeling and the distant manner of the people present.

The service being at noon, I return home until that hour. In the middle of the church service, or rather at the end, there arrives M. de Montebello, *aide de camp* of the Emperor, not in a government carriage, and in every-day uniform. The irregularity on this point is so considerable that he feels that he must excuse himself to Eugène, alleging delay as his reason. To tell the truth, the Emperor was not properly notified, according to what I think is a dependable report; it was his daughter or his grandson who ought to have given that noti-

[29] Czartoriska.

[30] The mother of Mme de Forget, Delacroix's intimate friend, whose son was Eugène de Forget; Delacroix was related to the Lavalettes. Mme de Lavalette had become famous through the help she gave her husband when he escaped from prison after the Restoration had condemned him to death for having seized possession of the postal system when Napoleon made his return from the Isle of Elba.

fication, and it was possibly not given at all. In brief, even fewer persons accompanied the body to the cemetery, and among these persons, not one of the former friends of M. de Lavalette. I cursed and still curse the timidity which prevented me from speaking up and saying what anyone of decent spirit has to feel at such a time; but in truth, before that frigid and even profoundly indifferent audience, that was almost impossible; only a lawyer could have found inspiration under such circumstances.

The memory of men is short indeed: the memory of events is as quickly buried as that of the personages who take part in them. Among all the people these last days to whom I told that I had been in Paris for the burial of Mme de Lavalette, not one had any idea about the lady to whom I was referring. How much there was to say of the woman who had just died, and who had been dead for forty years, a stately phantom in the low estate to which we had seen her condemned!

I went to take another look at my poor graves,[31] which I found to be well kept; but with a wild idea that I might be able to escape and get back that same day, and even at an early hour, to my peaceful retreat, I did not take the time to go and see the grave of my good aunt[32] and that of dear Chopin.

When I got home, where I went as quickly as possible, I found Guillemardet's letter[33] telling me that the next day he was to accompany his poor mother to her last resting place. After that, I was more tranquil about the use of my time and I did not think of Champrosay any longer.

I went out for dinner and then returned home with the same tranquillity, not allowing my mind too much meditation; I had closed the door on emotion, between what I went through in the morning and what awaited me next morning. The weather was incredibly cold: after a few turns on the boulevard, I went back and got to bed.

Champrosay, June 21.

Got up before six o'clock. As I didn't bring anyone to Paris with me and have to do everything myself, I'm kept so busy that I am fatigued by that alone.

I arrived at Passy a little before nine o'clock. I met and embraced

[31] His mother was buried at Père-Lachaise.
[32] His aunt Riesener.
[33] Edouard Guillemardet, the comrade of his childhood, son of the former ambassador of France at Madrid, and brother of Félix, the intimate friend of Delacroix; he had died in 1840.

poor Caroline.[34] The ceremony was sad, and yet there was about it something more touching than what you find in all matters of the sort in Paris. The air in that place is fatal to all true emotion; the formality of a funeral, the priests who perform the ceremony and all the rest of it make of that act of grief an act no different from any other. In Passy, half an hour away from that pestiferous Paris, the funeral, the service and the faces of all who take part in the affair are completely changed; everything is decent and serious, even to the attitude of the people who come to their windows to look on.

I went into the sacristy with that excellent friend, that excellent son, to sign the act of decease; when he had placed his name on the register, he added below, *her son*. I signed in my turn, and it seemed to me that I had almost the right to do the same thing; that kind-hearted friend had had the same thought and, as we went back to our places, he said to me with an anguished expression: "I was thinking, don't you see, that you, my poor friend, at this moment, you are Félix!" Those were his exact words.

He took me to the railroad station[35] with one of his friends. I had made up my mind, during the morning to do some necessary errands; I had even thought of going to see that famous *Myrrha*[36] as a matter of conscience. I had counted too much on my strength or on my lack of sensibility. I had to give in to the effects of all the emotion I had gone through.

Paris, June 29.

Othello. A noble and complete pleasure; the tragic force, the linking together of the scenes, and the gradation of the interest fill me with an admiration that is going to bear fruit in my mind. I see again that Wallack,[37] whom I saw in London just thirty years ago, perhaps day

[34] The sister of Félix and of Edouard Guillemardet.
[35] From Passy.
[36] Tragedy by Alfieri, played by La Ristori.
[37] James William Wallack (1794-1864), celebrated Anglo-American actor who played in the classic tradition.

for day (for I was there in the month of June), in the role of Faust. Seeing that piece, which was very well arranged, although changed in character, inspired me with the idea of producing compositions in lithography.[38] Terry,[39] who played the part of the devil, was perfect.

Champrosay, June 30.

At nine o'clock in the morning, I went to serve on the jury. There I met Cockerell again[40] and Taylor, old acquaintances both; I stayed there until about noon examining the pictures by the Englishmen, whom I admire very much; I am really astounded at the sheep by Hunt.

Contrary to my habit, I made a very good lunch on a piece of ham and a jug of Bavarian beer. I feel perfectly happy, absolutely free and expansive in this low pot-house, seated at a table in the open air and watching the few idlers pass by as they go to the Exposition.

July 1.

All these interruptions are injurious even to the minor work I am doing; I have no very clear idea of what I am getting done as the days go by. I am trying to recall my impressions from the performance of *Othello*. I add color to the drawings that I made there. I am still sleeping an outrageous amount, and that is a mistake.

July 2.

In the morning, I could not resist taking a turn in the forest, which

[38] He refers to the seventeen lithographs illustrating Stapfer's translation of Goethe's *Faust,* which appeared in 1828.

[39] An English actor, certainly not the celebrated Edward Terry, born in 1844.

[40] Charles Robert Cockerell (1788-1863), English architect and archaeologist, known through his excavation at the temple of Aegina and at the temple of Phigalea in Greece and his works on Greek architecture. Baron Taylor (1789-1879), writer, senator, member of the Institute, author of the famous *Voyages Pittoresques et Romantiques dans l'Ancienne France,* creator of societies for mutal help among artists and writers.

did not prevent me from working during the day at the *Hamlet*,[41] at the *Lions*, etc.

At six o'clock I called on Mme Barbier. Took a turn in the garden with those ladies before dinner; after dinner had a chat in the park; in brief I had a good time. The company of women, despite my retreat, always has an infinite charm for me; when we went back, I found myself with six women seated in a circle, and I among them.

July 5.

Natural gifts unsupported by culture may be said to resemble that honeysuckle, charming in its grace, but without odor, that I see hanging from the trees in the forest.

July 13.

Augerville. In the rocks with forms like those of men and animals, I notice new types, more or less clearly defined.[42] I even draw a kind of wild boar and a kind of elephant, a number of bodies of centaurs, of bull's heads, etc.; from such things one might get some excellent types of fantastic animals; in such a way these bizarre forms would take on verisimilitude. A strange coincidence! What caprice presided over the formation of this rock, the only one of its kind in this region?

July 15.

Took a walk in the direction of the rocks; again I admire the figures of men and of animals; I made some new and astonishing discoveries among them.

In a pathway higher up, I came upon an unfortunate beetle struggling against the ants, who were resolved on his destruction; I stood

[41] *Hamlet and Polonius* (Catalogue Robaut, 943).
[42] Whenever he visited Augerville, Delacroix made drawings from these bizarre rocks.

observing him for a long time, overthrowing his enemies and dragging them after him, held back by his feet, to which two or three of those pitiless workers were clinging. Attacked on his antennae, sometimes covered by the ants, he finally succumbed. Having gone off for a while, I found him motionless and completely conquered when I returned; I moved him about a little, but death had come in the end. As it seemed to me, the ants were engaged in dragging him to their anthill, which, however, was not to be seen near by. For a time I left the whole tragedy and established myself in the little pavilion with the copper ball over it, and got a few minutes of sleep there. At the end of about half an hour, I went back to my ants. To my great surprise, I found neither ants nor insect!

At lunch Berryer told me that the ants usually cut prey of this sort into little pieces which they carry off one at a time. In the case that I had just seen, I can't understand how they managed to get away with the creature in such a short time.

July 16.

We work out the *Gazza.*[43] I was still full of the *Don Juan* of the other day and couldn't possibly get up any more admiration for Rossini's masterpiece. Once again I saw that one must take nothing away from works of art — even more, that one must not compare them one to another. The parts treated carelessly by Rossini in no way impair the impression that he leaves on your memory. That father, that daughter, that tribunal — the whole thing is living. Those sorry musicians, the *croque-notes* of the princess,[44] who swear only by Mozart, and do not understand Mozart any better than they do Rossini. That vital element, that secret force, which is the whole of Shakespeare, doesn't exist for them. They simply cannot get on without the alexandrine and counter-point: all they admire in Mozart is his regularity.

[43] *La Gazza Ladra,* opera by Rossini. They had a great deal of music at Augerville.
[44] Princess Czartoriska.

July 26.

I go to see *Myrrha* with Cousin Delacroix. That Ristori is really full of talent; but how tiresome those pieces are!

I suffer horribly from the heat and from boredom. The fatigue from my days spent in the church is more or less the cause of this discomfort in the evening. I have had everything scraped and I am plastering — troweling, so to speak — not only the hollow part, but all the parts of the figures that are to be luminous, such as flesh and draperies. The pictures will be the better for it, but I came near to catching painter's colic at the job.

August 3.

I went to the Exposition; I noticed that fountain which spouts gigantic artificial flowers.

The sight of all those machines makes me feel very bad. I don't like that stuff which, all alone and left to itself, seems to be producing things worthy of admiration.

After leaving, I went to see Courbet's exhibition;[45] he has reduced the admission to ten cents. I stay there alone for nearly an hour and discover that the picture of his which they refused is a masterpiece;[46] I simply could not tear myself away from the sight of it. He has made enormous progress, and yet that made me admire his *Burial*. In the latter work the figures are one on top of the other, the composition is not well understood. But there are superb details: the priests, the choir boys, the vase of holy water, the weeping women, etc. In the later work (the *Atelier*) the planes are well understood, there is atmosphere and there are some parts that are important in their execution: the haunches, and the thigh of the nude model and her bosom; the woman in the front plane, with a shawl. The only fault is that the

[45] Courbet, whose *Burial at Ornans* and *The Atelier* had been refused by the jury, organized a special exhibition of his works at No. 7 avenue Montaigne, near the Exposition.

[46] The picture referred to is *The Atelier*, which had been refused with the *Burial at Ornans*.

picture he is painting offers an ambiguity: it looks as if it had a *real sky* in the midst of the picture. They have refused one of the most singular works of this period; but a strapping lad like Courbet is not going to be discouraged for so small a thing as that.

I dined at the Exposition, sitting between Mercey and Mérimée; the former thinks as I do about Courbet; the latter does not like Michelangelo!

Detestable modern music by those singing choirs which are in fashion.

August 11.

I must think about getting a palette that could be put into water.

August 15.

I write to Mme de Forget:[47]

"You ask me where happiness is to be found in this world. After many experiments, I have convinced myself that it resides only in self-content. The passions cannot give this contentment; we always desire the impossible: what we obtain does not satisfy us. I suppose that people gifted with solid virtue must possess a great part of that contentment which I see as the condition of happiness: not being myself sufficiently virtuous to please myself in that respect, I get my recompense in the real satisfaction that work gives. It affords a genuine sense of well-being and increases our indifference to the pleasures which are pleasures in name only, the things that society people are obliged to content themselves with. And there, dear lady, you have my little philosophy and, especially when I am feeling well, it is certain in its effect. It should be no bar to the small amusements that one may snatch from time to time: a little affair of the heart at the right moment, the sight of a beautiful countryside, and traveling, in general, may leave charming traces in one's memory. One recalls all those emotions, when

[47] The letter is published in the *Correspondence* of Delacroix.

one is far away or when one can no longer have such experiences; it is therefore laying up a small store of happiness for the future, whatever that may be.

"And so I work, save for the interruptions caused by the time I have to give, now, to the festivities that are in progress or in preparation. But even these jobs do not bother me too much. They are a rest for my mind, though they are fatiguing in other ways. It is a different fatigue from what painting causes. I put on full dress for occasions when the *Te Deum* is played; I attend banquets, I have just as good a time with imbeciles as with thinking men: mingling together in that crowd, all men look alike: a single sentiment animates them, the idea of pushing ahead and of stepping across the body of your neighbor. It is a spectacle full of interest for a philosopher who has not yet left behind him all of the vanities.

"I certainly hope this letter is long enough; I am writing you under the impression of my official visits of yesterday. We are awaiting the Queen of England, who will give me other subjects for meditation. *Apropos,* I am having a pair of knee-breeches made: it is the greatest event of the week.

"Good-bye, dear lady, remember me frequently to M. Laity, etc."

August 18.

Arrival of the Queen of England.[48] I leave the church[49] about three o'clock to go home. No cab! Paris has gone mad today. One meets nothing but guilds of workmen, market women and girls dressed in white, the whole lot of them carrying banners and jostling one another

[48] Queen Victoria, accompanied by Prince Albert, arrived at the Gare de Strasbourg (Gare de l'Est) and drove in an open carriage across all Paris and to Saint-Cloud, where she resided. The welcome which Paris gave her was triumphal. The visit of the English sovereigns, from the 18th to the 27th of August, 1855, was the occasion for splendid festivities; the one at the Hôtel de Ville was, it appears, never equalled.

[49] Saint-Sulpice, where he was working.

in their desire to make this a good reception. The fact is that nobody saw anything, the Queen having arrived at night. I regretted it, for all those good people who had put their whole heart into this business.

August 25.

Went to Versailles, this evening. Illuminations in front of the château, etc. It is not with the pleasure I had expected that I am seeing the *Battle of Aboukir*[50] again. The rawness of the tones is extreme; the tangling up of men and horses is pretty near to inexcusable.

August 30.

This morning I did a good deal of work at the church,[51] inspired by the music and the chanting. There was an extra service at eight o'clock; that music puts me into a state of exaltation that is favorable to painting.

August 31.

Went to call on Schwiter.[52] At his place, when looking at his own painting, at the portrait of West by Lawrence[53] and at engravings after Reynolds, I was struck by the unhappy influence of all mannerism. Those Englishmen, with Lawrence the first among them, have blindly copied their grandfather, Reynolds, without taking note of the twists that he gave to the truth. Those licenses, which have contributed to give to his painting a kind of originality, but which are far from being justifiable in all cases, the exaggeration for effect and indeed the

[50] By Baron Gros.

[51] Saint-Sulpice.

[52] Baron Louis Schwiter (1809-1865), painter, a childhood friend of Delacroix's who had made his acquaintance through Pierret, a cousin of Schwiter's. In 1826, Delacroix painted a full length portrait of him; it is now in the National Gallery. He had named him as one of the executors of his will.

[53] The portrait of Benjamin West by Lawrence is now in the National Gallery.

completely false effects which are the consequences of that, have decided the style of all his followers, and that gives to the whole school the look of artificiality which is not compensated for by certain virtues. Thus the head of West, which is painted in the most vigorous light, is accompanied by accessories such as clothing, a curtain, etc., which are in no way touched by that light; in a word, it is devoid of all explanation; as a consequence, it is false and the ensemble is mannered. A head by Van Dyck or by Rubens, if set beside a thing like this, immediately places it in a completely secondary rank. (Connect the above with what I am writing at Dieppe as to naive imitation and the influence of the schools: it might be incorporated or added on).[54]

Real superiority, as I have said somewhere in these brief memories of the masters, admits no eccentricity. Rubens is carried away by his genius and plunges into exaggerations which take the direction of his idea and are always founded on nature.

The so-called geniuses that we see today, full of ridiculous affectation and marked by bad taste as much as by pretension, are beclouded in whatever ideas they possess; even in their personal conduct they continue the bizarre manner which they look on as a sign of talent; they are mere phantoms of writers, painters, and musicians. Neither Racine, nor Mozart, nor Michelangelo nor Rubens could be ridiculous in such a way. The great genius is simply a being of a more highly reasonable order. The Englishmen of the school of Reynolds believed that they were imitating the great Flemish and Italian colorists, painting pictures that have the look of being smoked, they thought they were doing vigorous pictures; they imitated the darkening which time brings to all pictures, and more especially they imitated that false brilliance deriving from successive removals of the varnish, operations which darken certain parts while others are given a brilliance which was not in the intention of the masters. These unhappy deteriorations caused them to think, as is shown by the portrait of West, that a head could

[54] Note added, later on, by Delacroix, when he is writing similar reflections during his stay at Dieppe, see entry of September 30, 1855.

be very brilliant when the clothing in the picture received no light whatsoever, and that backgrounds can be in complete darkness when the objects in front of them are illuminated: that is an absolutely false idea.

September 11.

On my way to Croze,[55] arrived in Limoges at about eleven o'clock and installed myself for the day at the Hôtel du Grand Périgord. I got a lunch that I stood in need of after the unbearable journey. I went to see the city, the museum, the church of Saint Pierre, the cathedral, and Saint-Michel. The cathedral is unfinished, the nave is lacking. In general, the churches in this country are lugubrious in their darkness. I fell asleep in the cathedral. At Saint-Michel, near the museum, where I went last, I did the same thing. These short rests set me up again completely. I got shaved by a frater and went to dinner about half-past four. Mushrooms that were excellentissimi; we don't know them in Paris.

I start out at six o'clock for Brive. In the coupé, *tête-à-tête* with a brigadier in the gendarmerie, a very decent chap; superb head. He leaves me about nine o'clock. I spend a good night, now sleeping, now seeing by the light of the train lamps the curious country that I'm going through — Uzerche, etc. — and that I regret not seeing by daylight.

As I looked out upon really bizarre objects, I was thinking of *that little world* which man bears within him. People who say that man learns everything through education are idiots, and that includes the great philosophers who have maintained that theory. As singular and unexpected as the spectacles offered to our eyes may be, they never surprise us completely; there is within us an echo which replies to all impressions; either we have seen a given thing at some other place, or else all possible combinations of things are prepared in advance within

[55] The château of Croze, between Brive and Souillac, in the department of Lot, belonged to the Verninac family, related to Delacroix through his sister, Henriette.

our brain. When we encounter them in this passing world, we do no more than open a compartment of our brain or of our soul. How can one explain otherwise the incredible power of the imagination and, as a final proof, the fact that this power is, relatively speaking, incomparably strong during childhood? Not only did I have as much imagination during childhood and youth, but when objects created deeper impressions within me than now, or offered me incomparable delights, my surprise was no greater than any I now experience. Whence could I have derived all those impressions at that earlier time?

September 15.

The state of neglect that is everywhere in this poor Croze and that shocked me in the beginning, ended by pleasing me: nothing here resembles our present-day houses. The grass grows wherever it likes, the house is preserved without any outside assistance.

The church of Turenne remarkable because of a grand look that it has; its simplicity and its very bareness do it no harm.

September 16.

Started out at seven o'clock for Brive with François and Dussol. On our way we met the doctor who gives massage, and then the servant of François with her charming sister, the girl I saw in rags and barefooted near the horses, the day of the race at Turenne. This time she was coquettishly dressed and was going to Brive to buy some things for her wedding, which is to take place in a week. Her husband will be a lucky dog at certain times. She is of the most delicate and piquant type, the blond armed with all the special, incomparable attraction of such women. I had perfectly divined her quality that first time when I saw her.

Traveling toward Périgueux, I go through the richest and most smiling country, but keep feeling the weight of the heat or else the force of the sharp wind.

I arrive at Périgueux just at sundown; a most appetizing young woman has been granted me as a prison companion, entering the comfortless box where I am, one station before reaching the city. I cross that pretty town amidst the transparencies and the illuminations that celebrate the good news from Sebastopol.

I get information about the railroad and find myself compelled to change my plan. I shall go to Montmoreau and take the train, proceeding by way of Ribérac, which I shall reach in the post-chaise; I shall dine at the Hôtel de France, opposite the carriage station. The rather poor meal, served by a girl of lively though already full-blown attractiveness, did wonders for me. This place is not too badly spoiled by commercial travelers, who speak the same language everywhere: it is a curious mixture of ineptitude and fatuity; already at Brive, when I arrived there from Limoges and was waiting to start out for Croze, I had lunch in the company of some of those fellows.

At Périgueux, after dining and paying my 3 fr. 50 to the good hostess, I admire the rotundity of her fashionable dress and the rest of the magnificent clothes that she wears on her way from the courtyard to the kitchen and the dining room. I go out of doors delighted with everything I have seen and especially with the beauty of the women of this country, who are not less than exciting. I walk about until quite late on the big promenade which is filled with strollers of every station, hucksters from the fair, musicians, wandering acrobats, and lottery-people. I even find *real beauty,* the piquant quality uniting with a grace and a correctness not to be found in the North and never seen in Paris.

September 17.

Made a joyous departure from Montmoreau. Woke up in the morning at Ribérac and perched myself in the coupé with a young soldier and a good Périgourdin who told me about his wine, etc. Everything that I see enchants me. The rising sun gives to this rich and charming landscape an attractiveness which is beyond expression. The way this country resembles my beloved forest awakens delightful memories once more. As we go through wooded places I imagine myself again with my dear Charles and my good Albert, in the days when we used to go hunting in the morning dew, under the trees and amidst the grape-vines. There is no way to describe memories as sweet as these! The very strength of such feelings ends by dulling them and causes me a sort of fatigue or rather, a sort of insensibility.

Going from Ribérac to Montmoreau, I notice the vines clinging to the trees or to perches that support them in the Italian manner. That is very pretty and very picturesque, it would look well in a painting; my neighbor, the soldier, a good-looking young man who returns without much enthusiasm from the Crimea where he had his feet frozen, tells me that this method is not the best, not so much for the grapevine itself as for the things around it, because of the shadow result-ing from such an arrangement. My young infantryman tells me that the English are *parade-ground soldiers who quit too easily,* despite the way they are famed for tenacity. Perhaps, as good allies, we treat them, in the matter of their bravery, in the way that people treat misers when they try to get something out of them by praising their generosity.

September 20.

Strasbourg.[56] While I was having an early lunch with my cousins, Schuler,[57] the engraver, came in; I used to meet him at Guérin's studio in the days when I was finishing up there: He had heard of my arrival from one of the members of the *Société Rhénane des Amis des Arts* where I was taken yesterday; he places himself at my disposal. We go to the house of M. Simonis to see the superb Correggio:[58] *Venus Dis-*

---

[56] This is one of a number of trips to Strasbourg, where Delacroix used to visit his cousins.

[57] Charles-Auguste Schuler (1804-1859), a romantic painter and engrav-er.

[58] The picture may have been a copy of the one in the National Gallery, *Mercury Instructing Cupid in the Presence of Venus,* or of some other picture not by Correggio.

arming Cupid; I did not esteem it at first as much as I should. I very much regret that it is only three weeks later that I am writing down the impression that I got from it: knowledge, grace, balance of lines, charm of color, bold freedom — all work together in that charming work. Certain harsh outlines alarmed me; I have realized since that they were perfectly justified by the need to make certain parts stand out in a vigorous manner.

Other fine pictures at that house also, but they are confused in my memory: they are Flemish works, and that tells everything about them. A fine head by Van Dyck, a man in armor.

We go to the museum and to the city hall; I see a pretty good copy of my *Dante,* the work of Brion,[59] a young man who has done good pictures of Alsatian subjects. I see some quite interesting things: a male nude by Heim,[60] among others; that man had in his work a type of feeling that was not unlike that of the Italian masters. This picture is in very bad condition; I see here his last big picture, exhibited two years ago, and since then rolled up and left in a corner just the way it was delivered. That is how the provincial museums treat pictures.

Baden, on my arrival, September 25.

Yesterday [at Strasbourg], when I was with my good cousin [Mme Lamey], I went to see the tomb of the Maréchal de Saxe in the church of Saint Thomas: it is the perfect example of a defect that I had been thinking about. The execution of the figures is wonderful, but they almost scare you by the closeness with which they are imitated from the living model. The *Hercules,* although it is of the school and under the inspiration of Puget, has not that breath in its lungs, that boldness and, I will venture to say, those partial incorrectnesses that one sees everywhere in the works of the master; the proportions of this Hercules

[59] Gustave Brion (1824-1877), an Alsatian painter; he illustrated *Notre-Dame de Paris* and *Les Miserables.*
[60] *Berger Buvant à une Fontaine,* by François-Joseph Heim (1787-1865), author of the celebrated picture *Charles X Distribuant des Récompenses aux Artistes à la fin de l'Exposition de 1824,* now in the Louvre.

are very exact; every part is correct in its planes and shows a strong feeling for the treatment of flesh, but the pose is insipid: this is a wandering showman, and not the son of Alcmene; he is here — he might as well be anywhere else. That *Sorrowing France* facing Death, her face marked by a very faithful expression of grief, is the portrait of a Parisienne; the figure of *Death,* which evidently ought to be an ideal figure, is simply a jointed skeleton such as is to be found in every studio: the sculptor simply has thrown a big drapery over it, and then copied that carefully, making you feel very exactly, under the folds and at the open places where you can see through, the heads of the bones, the hollows and the projections. Barbarous as our ancestors were in their naive allegories, of which the Gothic is full, they represented symbolic figures in a very different way.

I remember, again, that little figure of *Death* which struck the hours on the old clock on the church at Strasbourg which I saw in the storeroom with all the others of the set, the old man, the young man, etc.; it is a terrible object but not merely hideous; when those men produced figures of devils or of angels, the imagination grasps, amid the awkwardnesses and the ignorance of proportions, what the artists wanted to do.

I do not speak of the monument[61] from the standpoint of unity of impression and of style: it is entirely lacking in that respect; the mind does not know which way to turn when faced with those dispersed figures, those broken flags, and those animals that have been thrown to the ground. And yet what a subject for the imagination of a true artist, when he hears the mere mention of it! That armed hero descending to the tomb, holding in his hand the baton of the commander, that figure of France, whom he has served, and who throws herself between him and the pitiless monster who would seize him, those trophies of his glory — vain ornaments for his tomb, those emblems of the subjugated powers — that eagle, that lion, and that dying leopard!

[61] Of the Maréchal de Saxe.

Here at Baden, on the 25th of September, still considering this matter, I notice from my window the great similarity that Shakespeare has to external nature; I am thinking of the scenery that appears before my eyes, for example, and I would note especially that heaping up of details, the ensemble of which none the less contrives to suggest a unity to the mind. The mountains that I crossed when coming here form the simplest and most majestic lines when seen from a distance; when seen from nearby, they are not even mountains any more, but rocky spaces, meadows, trees — in groups or separate, the works of man, houses and roads occupying the attention by turns.

That unity which the genius of Shakespeare establishes for the mind in the midst of his irregularities, is a quality peculiar to himself.

September 27.

In the morning, I feel like a new man again, as I usually do. I start out early. I begin with the church, a Gothic monument, restored a century and a half ago, and one in which, following the fashion of the time, there has been lavish use of ornaments in the style of Vanloo, as in the church at Brive, with plenty of flutings and panels in the Greek style as it was understood at the beginning of the present century. Two magnificent tombs in the choir: there is the one of the recumbent bishop in armor with the skeleton under the table on which he lies, but above all, the one of the old margrave, armed and erect, fixed to the wall, his baton of command in his hand and his helmet on the ground beside him — the whole thing in a Renaissance arrangement of the finest style. I set down at once, in my notebook, the difference between this style and that of another tomb, the most important of all, which is in the style of Vanloo. Despite the confusion and the bad taste, the weak allegories and the raw color, it is still superior to everything bearing the mark of our dull period, when coldness, insignificance, and meanness do away with every species of interest.

Climbing the very steep steps, I reached the palace of the grand duke;[62] I had taken it for some farm or convent; I went up through an avenue where the sun could pour in, and then I entered a pinewood which I had admired; I climbed, always thinking that it was for the last time, and finally I arrived at the old castle. Ruins patched up in the German fashion to make pretty views for a sketchbook; in the midst of it all, broken bottles and kitchen refuse; the pantry was in the hall of the knights. I noticed the granite rocks, resembling those in Corrèze. They were usually of a reddish color, like the earth and the stones of these regions.

Now and again I set things down in my notebook. On going down hill again I admired a great rising perspective under the pine trees. I notice the color, like that of *coal,* of the distance and of the trees. It was very hot as I was descending and my vigorous appetite made me hurry. At the end of the descent, I got off my track and become worried, feeling fatigue and seeing a delay with my lunch. I arrived finally all dusty and bristling, and sat down to the table. So that there have been all kinds of happenings which should not have come my way in Paris, the result being that I ate my lunch with an appetite that I never get up at home.

After lunch I slept almost all the rest of the day; another man would have made it his duty to go and see the waterfalls.

At six o'clock, called on Mme Kalergi, who had invited me; at her house I meet a Prince Wiasimski and his wife, the former a Kalmuk according to his features, the latter a charming and gracious Russian lady who looked even better next day in her morning toilette. There was, beside, a lady from Russia or from Berlin, a sentimental person, with whom I made the trip to Eberstein next day, in company with Mme Kalergi. The latter talked to me a great deal about Wagner;[63]

---

[62] The Neue Schloss, the summer residence of the Grand Duke.
[63] Richard Wagner, born in 1813, was still totally unknown in France; yet he had already written *The Flying Dutchman, Tannhäuser* and *Lohengrin.* Delacroix had never heard him spoken of and was distrustful — on principle — of the innovator in music as in politics. Wagner, who had been forced to leave Dresden after the revolutionary events of 1849, had retired to Zurich, where he

she was perfectly foolish about him, as she was about the Republic. This Wagner wants to be an innovator; he thinks that he has reached the truth; he suppresses a great many of the conventions of music, believing that conventions are not founded on necessary laws. He is a democrat; he also writes books about the happiness of humanity, books that are absurd, according to Mme Kalergi herself.

I started out fairly early; despite the stinging cold, I was going to take a long walk to the avenue of trees that goes to Lichtenthal. Delightful spots along the way. Coming back, I met Winterhalter,[64] a nice sort of devil, but a bore. He absolutely insisted on going for a drink of beer, and I followed him. He gave me the address of a dealer in ale and porter in Paris, Harris, Boulevard de la Madeleine 17, and Rue Basse-du-Rempart 24, and also one of a dealer in the raw ham of Mayence, Rue Richer, probably No. 10.

September 28.

I got under way early and without the precaution of taking my over-coat, going in the direction of the convent of Lichtenthal. A delightful walk, such as one can have only in the air and light of the morning; in the church of the convent the divine surprise, at the moment when I was going to leave, of hearing the chant of the nuns; in all France, one couldn't get a thing like that in a hundred years. I was saying to Mme Kalergi, who is a strong partisan of the Germans, that among them music has its roots in the earth, so to speak; with us, it is an artificial product.

A great Christ of painted wood, very expressive and terrifying, hanging beside and under the eyes of those poor nuns when they are in their gallery.

was then residing. The work to which Delacroix alludes is entitled *Die Kunst und die Revolution* and was published in 1849 at Leipzig.

[64] François-Xavier Winterhalter (1806-1873) was, under Louis-Philippe and under the Empire, the fashionable portraitist of the royal and aristocratic families of Europe.

What expression there was in those pure, silver toned voices ! What singing, and what simple harmony; the voice, that emanation of the temperament more than of the soul, seemed to betray repressed desires: at least I imagined that. I came away charmed.

I go to a little outdoor bazaar to make some purchases. I return for lunch and make ready to call on Mme Kalergi; from her place I go to see her prince, who shows me an *Auguste* Delacroix,[65] that he had been sold as a *Eugène. (A Rowland for an Oliver,* that is the title of an English play.) [66]

Walked under a hot sun as far as Eberstein, talking sentiment, politics, arts, etc. Castle like all the German residences: false Gothic, ornaments in all styles, but always detestably and awkwardly arranged. Awkwardness is the muse who most often looks over the shoulder of German artists. A semi-awkwardness is almost all the grace that their women have.

Fatigued on my return, I left those ladies and went home to sleep for an hour. Then had dinner.

Took another walk through the open thickets near the river, and then the always charming walk under the oaks of Lichtenthal. Horrible music played by the Baden men this evening. That of the Austrians, the first day, was better played; but with all their talents, they give nothing but the music suited to the great crowd of listeners who are here.

Strasbourg, September 29.

Spent part of the day drawing at the *Maison de l'œuvre* of the cathedral.[67] (I regret that I am writing these impressions ten days afterward, here at Dieppe: I was greatly struck with what I saw there. I should have liked to draw everything).

[65] Auguste Delacroix (1809-1868), a contemporary who misused his name to have his painting passed off on unsuspecting people such as Mme Kalergi's prince as work by Eugène Delacroix.
[66] Delacroix gives the words in English, as printed here.
[67] See Catalogue Robaut, 1399 to 1402, and 1912.

The first day, I was attracted by the works of the fifteenth century and the beginning of the Renaissance of the arts. The somewhat stiff, somewhat Gothic statues of the preceding period did not attract me; I did justice to them the next day and the one following, drawing ardently for three days, although interrupted by the cold and the unsuitability of the place, due to the lack of light or to the difficulty of getting a good position for work. The first day I drew the so-called statue of Erwin,[68] for Erwin is everywhere here, as Rubens is at Antwerp, and as Caesar is everywhere that you find a circular strip of grass resembling a camp. The head and hands are superb, but the draperies are already fussy and done according to a formula. The same applies to the statue opposite of the man with the mantle split at the shoulder, putting his hand over his eyes and raising his head in the air. More naive are the figures of the man in the robe and cape, kneeling, of the old judge seated in the antechamber, and the figures of the armored soldiers, unfortunately mutilated, and also in the antechamber; but they are of an earlier period.

September 30.

Returned to the *Maison de l'œuvre,* in spite of its being Sunday. Before that, we had been on some sort of errand with my good cousin; she didn't want to go away until she saw me enter the building. Immediately I was hard at it with the figures of angels of the thirteenth and fourteenth centuries: The Foolish Virgins and the bas-reliefs are still somewhat primitive in their proportions, but they are full of grace or of strength. I was struck by the force of the sentiment. *Science* is almost always fatal to it; manual skill or merely a more advanced knowledge of anatomy or of the proportions immediately gives the artist over to excessive freedom; he no longer reflects the image with the same purity; his possibility of rendering with facility or in con-

[68] Erwin von Steinbach (1240-1318), architect and sculptor who, beginning in 1277 built the façade of the cathedral of Strasbourg, which was begun about 1250.

densed fashion seduces him and carries him on to mannerism. The schools teach scarcely anything else: what master can communicate his personal sentiment? All that can be obtained from him is his *recipes;* the student's inclination promptly to appropriate for himself the facility of execution which — in the man of talent — is the result of experience, violates the nature of his own art and does no more, so to speak, than graft one tree on to another tree of a different species. There are robust artist temperaments that absorb everything, that profit by everything; although trained in styles which their nature would not have inspired in them, they get to their own road through the tangle of precepts and examples contrary to their temperament, profit by what is good and, although sometimes marked by a certain school imprint, they become men like Rubens, Titian, Raphael, etc. It is absolutely necessary that at some moment in their career they reach the point, not of despising all that is not themselves, but of stripping off the whole of that almost always blind fanaticism which urges us all to imitation of the great masters and to swear by their works alone. One has got to say to oneself: this is good for Rubens, this is good for Raphael, Titian or Michelangelo. What they do is their own affair; there is nothing to chain me down to one or the other of them. One has got to learn to be grateful for what one has found one-self; a handful of *naïve inspiration* is preferable to anything else. Molière, they say, one day closed his Plautus and Terence; he said to his friends: "I have had enough of these models: now I look within me and about me."

October 1.

My cousins and I went to call on good Schuler. I thanked him for his engravings. We went there especially to see the little portrait he is doing of my cousin as a frontispiece for his works; I left them to go to the *Maison de l'œuvre.*

The *naïfs* captivate me more and more. Among the heads, like that of the old man with the long beard and the long draperies, in the two somewhat colossal statues of an abbot and a king which are in the court, I notice how well they knew the procedure of the ancients. I draw them in the manner of our medals after the antique — by the planes only. The study of these models from a period supposed to be barbarous — and I was in the forefront of those who thought so — seems to strike from me the last chains by which I was bound, and confirms me in the opinion that *the beautiful* is everywhere, and that every man not only sees it but is absolutely constrained to render it in his own fashion.

Where do you find here those Greek types and that regularity which people have been accustomed to accepting as the invariable type of *the beautiful?* The heads of these men and these women are the ones that they had under their eyes. Will anyone say that there is no connection between the impulse which leads us to love a woman who pleases us and the impulse toward beauty in the arts? If we are so fashioned as to find in that creature who charms us the type of attraction fit to captivate us, how do you explain the phenomena of our remaining cold in the presence of the same traits and the same special graces when we find them rendered in pictures or in statues? Will anyone say that, not being able to prevent ourselves from loving, we love whatever we meet, for lack of anything better, and however imperfect it may be? The conclusion to be drawn from such an argument would be that our passion should be strong in the exact proportion that our mistress resembled Niobe or Venus, whereas the fact is that when we do come upon such women they do not make us love them in the least.

Women do not please by mere regularity of feature; there are women who do possess that advantage and who do not interest us at all. The charm which makes us love them resides in a thousand things. That word charm says everything.

This evening we went to make our farewell to the charms of Strasbourg, and to see the Promenade des Contades. I regret infinitely that I did not make its acquaintance before: I regret also not making a sketch or two of it.

I note the effect of the mountains of Germany, of a very solid and vigorous tint contrasting with the golden green of the trees and the meadows around the fortifications.

October 3.

On my way to Dieppe I meet Nieuwerkerke, who gets into the compartment where I am. There is a queer couple there; the woman is a Belgian, she flirts with Nieuwerkerke; I take the maid, who has the most beautiful features in the world, for a friend or a relative. Happily it is only within myself that the mistake occurs, and I do not commit the unpardonable crime of saying a kind word to a poor creature, beautiful as the angels and despised by her mistress, whose snub nose and vulgar little face seem, on the contrary, to put her in the servant-girl class.

After Rouen, where my charmer gets off, I travel on with the Englishman and his wife. I chat and keep up the acquaintance; I meet them next morning on the beach; they invite me to come and see them, which I promise to do and which I have not yet done.

I cannot express the pleasure that I had in seeing my Jenny again. Poor dear woman! Her little face was thin, but her eyes sparkled with happiness at finding someone to talk to; I go home with her on foot in spite of the bad weather; for several days and probably for the rest of my stay at Dieppe, I am and shall be under the charm of finding myself once more with the only being who gives me her heart unreservedly.

Dieppe, October 4.

I have not been bored a single moment. I look out of my window, I walk about in my room. The boats come in and go out; complete freedom, absence of hostile or tiresome faces; I find once more the view I had last year; I do not read a line.

I go to the beach this morning, and it is there that I meet the Englishman and his wife again.

I still feel the effects of not having kept to my diet these last days.

In the evening, after dinner, I cannot go out; I keep to my couch. I re-read with pleasure the little book of extracts that I have made from the correspondence of Voltaire. He says that lazy men are always mediocrities. I am forever devoured by the passion for learning, but not, like fools, for learning useless things; there are people who will never be musicians and who study all the subtleties of counterpoint; others learn Hebrew or Chaldean and set themselves to decipher the hieroglyphs or the cuniform characters of the palace of Semiramis. The worthy Villot, who can't get a thing out of his sterile attainments, has decorated his mind with the most varied and the most useless knowledge. Thus he has the satisfaction of always considering himself superior to those rarest or most eminent men, who deserve such a description only because each of them excels only in a single subject. It was long ago that I rejected all pedantic satisfactions. When I left college, I too wanted to know everything; I went to lectures; I thought I was becoming a philosopher with Cousin, another poet who was forcing himself to be a learned man: I went to the late Thurot, at the Collège de France, to write commentaries in Greek on Marcus Aurelius; but today I know too much to want to learn anything outside my own sphere; I am insatiable about knowledge which can make me great; I remember, and because of a quite natural inclination follow, the advice that Beyle sent me in a letter: "Neglect nothing that can render you great."

October 5.

It was this day, I think, that I went alone toward the cliffs near the bathing place. In the evening, to the pier in company with Jenny.

I spend hours without reading, without newspapers. I pass in review the drawings that I have brought along; I consider, with passion and without fatigue, those photographs of nude men,[69] that admirable poem, that human body from which I am learning to read and the sight of which tells me more than do the works of the scribblers.

[69] Durieu's photographs, of which we have heard before.

October 6.

Yesterday or today, sketches from the photographs.

Paris, November 5.

This morning I wrote to Berryer that I should certainly not go to Augerville: I have a horrible cold that I caught while working on the jury.

This evening I went to see Cerfbeer; I had taken dinner at his house a week before; he had very kindly invited me in order to talk over the awarding of medals, especially on hearing the report that I had better qualities than those which people sometimes grant me, and which place me fifth on the list. I told him that I was constrained to offer thanks to the gods at the idea that our country should have found four citizens more virtuous than I. ·

Horace[70] was telling me, one of these last days when we were on the jury, about what he did with Ingres, who had written to refuse the medal because he felt deeply insulted at coming after Vernet, and even more, according to what I was told by several people who are above suspicion in this — insulted at the insolence of the special jury on painting which had placed him on the same line as myself in the preliminary classing of the candidates.

Augerville, November 7.

What have I done in the last month? I have been busy with that jury; I have seen stupidities enough and I have permitted myself a certain amount of indulgence toward some poor devils. I want to remember the warmth shown by M. Français[71] when, having consistently voted to give the first medal to M. Corot, he was roused to indignation when they forgot that artist and could no longer find a place for him.

[70] Horace Vernet.
[71] François-Louis Français (1814-1897), landscape painter.

Dauzats and I did remember him and voted for him, and we were the only ones to do so.

Paris, November 14.

Left Augerville at nine o'clock with Berryer. We returned together to Paris by way of Etampes; his conversation is of the most interesting.

When one is agitated by the thousand vexations in life that one mistakes for real troubles, one is not sufficiently clear in mind regarding the genuine and irremediable losses which reach the seat of our feelings. But there are rock-like natures that, more promptly than other people, console themselves for even these things. Berryer was telling me on our trip home that one of the signs of progress in the United States is that you get your father insured when he starts on one of those trips where one is constantly in danger of being smashed to bits on the ships or the railroads. Once you have confidence that, in case of an accident, the father will be restored in terms of bank notes, the family is easy in its mind; the father can go to the moon and stay there if he feels like it; I do not doubt but that we shall attain the same degree of perfection.

Delamarre's idea, proposed to Berger when he was prefect, of sending the bodies of our relatives and friends to be turned into fertilizer for the arid plains of Sologne was of the same kind. That was an un-suspected manner of utilizing one's fellow-men when, because of death, they seemed to be of no more use.

November 20.

I go to *Il Trovatore* with a ticket from Alberthe. I suffer and am bored there, and catch another cold. Nothing equals the sterility of that music; everything in it is noise, and not one bit of the singing is clear in its character.

November 25.

Nothing can surmount reigning prejudices: when students were sent to Rome, from the time of Lebrun to that of David, the whole thing that was recommended to them was the study of Guido; nowadays, *the beautiful* is a matter of reproducing the technique of the old frescoes, but it is only the academic side of them that they are going to study. These two methods, seemingly so opposed to each other, meet at the point which will always furnish the watchword to all the schools: imitate the technique of this school or that school. Drawing upon one's imagination for the means of rendering nature and its effects, and rendering them according to one's own temperament: these are chimeras, vain study not leading to the *prix de Rome* and to the Institute; what you must do is to copy the execution of Guido or of Raphael, depending on which one is in fashion.

December 11.

I have just been examining Géricault's lithographs; I am struck by the constant absence of unity. Absence from the composition in general, absence in every figure and in every horse. Never are the horses modeled in the mass. Each detail is added on to the others, and they form only an ill-connected ensemble. It is the contrary that I observe in my *Christ at the Tomb* [72] for Count de Geloës, which I have before me. In general, the details are mediocre and, to some extent, will not stand examination. On the other hand the ensemble inspires an emotion at which I myself am astonished. You can't get away from the thing, and not a detail tries to get itself admired separately, or to distract your attention. The perfection of such an art resides in producing a simultaneous effect. If painting produced its effects after the manner of literature, which is merely a sequence of successive pictures, the detail would have a certain right to stand out in relief.

— I re-read this in December, 1856. It reminds me that Chénavard told me, two years ago at Dieppe, that he did not consider Géricault a master, because he has no *ensemble;* it is his own criterion for the title of master. He refuses it even to Meissonier.

[72] Catalogue Robaut, 1034 and 1035.

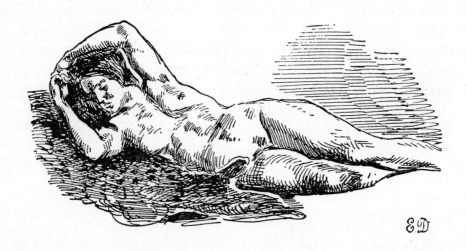

January 12.

(The prefect's dinner.)[1] Instead of dining with the prefect, I went with Mme Sand to see her piece, *Favilla*. An excellent subject, which my poor friend did not thoroughly develop. In spite of the fine things about her talent, I think she will never manage to produce a play. The situations die under her hand: *she does not grasp the interesting point.* The interesting point, therein lies the whole matter; she drowns it in details and is continually dulling the impression which ought to result from the stage and the characters. That situation of an amiable lunatic who thinks himself the master of a château where he is tolerated ought to be an excellent occasion for the comic or the pathetic. She hasn't the least idea in the world about what she lacks. Her obstinacy in pursuing a talent which appears to be denied her, to judge by the number of fruitless attempts she has made, classes her, however you look at it, in an inferior rank. It is very rare that great talents are not borne, in an almost invincible manner, toward the objects which are within their

[1] Baron Haussmann.

domain. It is to this stage, more particularly, that experience leads. Young people may be mistaken for a time as to their vocation, but not talents that have been ripened and practiced in a given type of work.

January 13.

At dinner, Mérimée was talking to me with the greatest esteem about Dumas: he prefers him to Walter Scott. Perhaps as he gets older, he gets better; perhaps he distributes praise so freely out of fear that he will have enemies.

January 14.

The dinner of the second Monday. Trousseau[2] tells us quite rightly that doctors are artists. With them as with the painters and the poets there is a scientific element; but it produces only mediocre doctors and artists. It is inspiration, it is the very genius for the profession which produces the great man.

January 17.

Mme Viardot, Bertin, Moreau. At the house of Mme Viardot: she sang once more the aria from *Armide: Sauvez-moi de l'amour!*

Berlioz was unbearable; he kept up his outcry against what seems to him barbarism and the most detestable taste, the trills and other ornaments especially prevalent in Italian music. He does not even spare them in the ancient authors, like Händel; he turns his wrath against the grace notes of the great aria of D. Anna.

January 18.

At the Hôtel de Ville, and then complete freedom; I love thus to roam around for a whole day in this old Paris. Two weeks ago I had been in

---

[2] Dr. Armand Trousseau (1801-1867), distinguished physician of the period, well known in society; he had been a deputy at the Constitutive Convention of 1848.

the Marais to call on General C., at the Place Royale, and I returned along the boulevards. Today I called on Guérin, who was not home, and so I went into Notre Dame.

In the morning I had been to the house of my dear Guillemardet. He delivered to me a package of letters that I wrote to Félix in the old days. It is easy to see in them how many years the mind needs in order to develop according to its true character. He told me that in those letters he already sees me as the man that I am to day. What I see in them, along with a certain vivacity, is that I had more bad taste and impertinence than brains: but that's the way things have to be. The strange discord between the power of the mind that age brings with it and the weakening of the body which is the consequence of age always impresses me and seems to me a contradiction in the decrees of nature. Are we to see in that a warning that we should turn to the things of the mind above all when the body and the senses begin to fail us? At all events it is incontestable that there is compensation here: but how necessary it is to watch ourselves so as not to give free rein at times to deceptive renewals of strength that make us think that we can be young, or make us act as if we were so. That is a trap which would mean ruin for everything.

January 19.

Dined at the house of Doucet. I walked home with Dumas, who talked to me about his amours with a widow who remained a *virgin* with her first husband and who is so still with a second one.

February 21.

As to masterpieces: Without the *masterpiece,* there is no great artist; yet those who have produced only one during their lives have not become great men through that. The things of that type are usually the product of youth. A certain precocious strength and a certain warmth which is in the blood as much as in the mind, have sometimes given a curious brilliance to men; but confidence as to talent aroused by early works has to be confirmed by other works which maturity, the age of genuine strength, should add, and nearly always does add when the talent is really strong.

February 25.

Admirable article by Gautier [3] in to day's *Moniteur* on the death of Heine.

I am writing him: "My dear Gautier, your funeral oration on Heine is a real masterpiece, and I cannot refrain from offering you my compliments on it. The impression it makes on me is constantly before my mind, and it will become part of my collection of *excerptae celebres*. How does it come that your art, possessing so many resources denied to our own, is still, under certain conditions, more ephemeral than painting, with all its fragility? What will become of four charming pages published in a newspaper between a catalogue of the virtuous actions performed in the eighty-six departments of France and an account of some comedy of the day before yesterday? Why was no notice given to a few men who are zealous on behalf of true and great talents? I did not even know of poor Heine's death: I should have wished to stand before the bier which deprived all of us of such fire, of such a mind, and have felt there what you felt so well. I send you this small homage, less for the obligations that I owe you than for the sad and gentle pleasure that your article has given me. Sincerely your friend."

April 6.

Dinner at the house of M. Fould. For some days I have been reading with great interest Baudelaire's translation of Edgar Poe. [4] In those conceptions, which really are *extraordinary*, which is to say *extra-human*, there is the fascination of the fantastic which is attributed to certain natures of the North or of some such region, but which is denied, very

[3] The article was reprinted at the head of the *Reisebilder*, in the edition of the *Œuvres Complets de Henri Heine*, published by Lévy in 1858.

[4] *Histoires Extraordinaires*, which had just been published by Michel Lévy.

certainly, to the nature of us Frenchmen. Men of that type take their sole pleasure in what is outside of nature, or extra-natural: for our part, we cannot lose balance to such a degree. Reason always has to have its share in even the wildest things we do. The most that I could imagine for things of this kind would be a debauch, but all these tales are of the same tone. I am sure there is not a German who would not feel at home in them. Although there is talent of the most remarkable kind in these conceptions, I believe that it is of an order inferior to the one that consists of painting things in the light of truth: I admit that the reading of *Gil Blas* or *Ariosto* does not give sensations of this order, and if the question is merely one of finding a means to vary our pleasures, this type of writing has its merit and keeps the imagination on edge; but one may not take such things in strong doses, and the author's continued use of the horrible, or the impossible which he renders probable, is something that goes against our mentality. One must not believe that such writers possess more imagination than those who content themselves with describing things as they are, and certainly it is easier to invent striking situations by such means than by going along the beaten path that intelligent minds have followed throughout the centuries.

April 9.

Called on Mme d'Haussonville.[5]

Yesterday on my way to Saint-Sulpice, I thought of writing something on the course necessarily followed by all the arts as they go on refining more and more: the idea had its origin in the impression made on me yesterday, at the house of the princess, by the works of Mozart which Gounod reviewed. My impression was confirmed this evening, at the house of Mme d'Haussonville, when I heard the aria from the *Nozze* as sung by Mme Viardot. Bertin was saying to me that such music was too full of delicacy and of expression carried to the final limit to be suited to the public. That is not the thing to be said:

[5] Mme la Comtesse d'Haussonville, daughter of the Duke de Broglie; her great portrait by Ingres is in the Frick Collection, New York.

in periods like ours, the public arrives at a love of details because of works which have given it a taste for refining on everything. But on the other hand, the public of our time does not like painting with broad strokes; that is reserved for infinitely rare minds which rise above vulgar demands and which still draw their nourishment from beauty as it was known in the great period; in a word, it is for those who love the beautiful, which is to say, simplicity.

And so, pictures done with broad strokes are needed; in the early ages of humanity the arts have that character. The basis of my idea was the need of being of one's time: Voltaire, in the *Huron*, makes that character say: *The tragedies of the Greeks are good for the Greeks*, and he is right. Hence the ridiculousness of trying to return up-stream and of producing archaism. Racine already appears refined in comparison with Corneille: but how much refining has been done since Racine! Walter Scott and Rousseau, to begin with, set themselves to work out a sense of vague impressions and melancholy which the ancients barely suspected. And now our moderns paint feelings alone; they describe externals, they analyze everything.

In music, the perfecting of the instruments, or the invention of new instruments brings about the temptation to go on to certain imitations. People will get to the point of giving a material imitation of the sound of the wind, of the sea, of a waterfall. Mme Ristori, last year, in *Pia* gave a rendering of the death struggle of one of the characters in a very faithful but very repulsive manner. The objects about which Boileau said that we must *offer them to the ear* and *hide them from the eyes*, are now of the domain of the arts: what we feel it necessary to perfect in the theater is the setting and the costumes. It is even evident that to do so is by no means to show bad taste. We need to refine on everything, we need to satisfy all the senses: the day will come when we shall execute symphonies at the same time that fine pictures will be shown to the eyes to complete the impression of the music.[6]

[6] M. Joubin notes that Delacroix foresees what has been done in the cinema.

It is said that Zeuxis or some other celebrated painter of antiquity had exhibited a picture representing a warrior or the horrors of war: he had a trumpet blown behind the picture to excite the good spectators even more. One can no longer paint a battle picture without burning a little powder near by in order to edify the emotions completely, or rather to awaken them. (See also my notes of Wednesday, April 16th on the same subject).

To get closer to the truth, some twenty years ago they had already gotten to the point of building real stage settings, as in the operas of *La Juive*[7] and *Gustave*.[8] In the former one, there were real statues on the stage and other accessories that are usually imitated by painting. In *Gustave,* there were real rocks, artificial ones it is true, but made up of projecting blocks. Thus through the love of illusion you reach the point of suppressing it completely. It will be understood that columns or statues set upon the stage under the conditions in which one ordinarily sees backdrops, and illuminated by lights coming from all sides, lose every kind of effect; it was at the same period that real armor, etc., was introduced on the stage, and so by our perfecting we got back to the childhood of art. When children, in their games, imitate the production of a play, they use real branches of trees to represent trees; that is the way things must have been done in the periods when the theater was invented. We are told that Shakespeare's plays were generally given in some sort of a barn, and no great pains were taken about the production. The constant change of setting which, as I may say in passing, appears to be a sign of an art already perverted rather than advanced, were rendered by a placard on which was written: This is a forest, this is a prison, etc. Within this conventional frame, the imagination of the spectator saw characters animated by passions drawn from nature, and that sufficed. Poverty of invention is fain to help itself out with these pretended innovations. Description, with

[7] Opera by Halévy and Scribe, first given in 1835.
[8] *Gustave III or Le Bal Masqué,* opera by Aubert and Scribe, given in 1833.

which modern novels bristle, is a sign of sterility: it is unquestionably easier to describe the dress, the externals of things, than to follow with delicacy the development of the characters and the painting of the heart.

April 16.

I must call on Mme d'Haussonville again.

On the need for refining in times of decadence. The great minds cannot escape it: people think a new class of works is being discovered when details are inserted at places where the ancients put none. The English, the Germanic peoples in general have always pushed us along this road. There is a great deal of refining in Shakespeare. By painting with great profundity sentiments which the ancients neglected or did not even know, he discovered a whole little world of sentiments which, with all men in all times, exist in a confused state and do not seem destined to reach our consciousness and be analyzed — until a particularly gifted genius has thrown the light of his torch into the secret corners of our soul. It would seem that the writer needs a prodigious erudition; but one knows how easy it is to be deceived on this point, and what there is in reality under this appearance of universal knowledge.

May 6.

In the evening I read to Jenny several scenes from *Athalie.*

May 12.

You consider that you are never sufficiently learned.

The drawing of Ingres.

Decamps's bottle of crude oil and of refined oil.

Not one false touch in the work of men of feeling.

Keep on studying without a halt; once you are in action, make mistakes if necessary, but execute freely.

May 20.

As to the soul after death. I find the following in an article on *Natural Religion,* by M. Jules Simon, in *La Presse:*

'For any person who does not subject his reason to authority, pretending to be infallible, the way that we shall exist after death is an absolutely unknown thing. If the soul is immortal, says Hume, it must have existed before our birth, and if our previous existence has not interested us, our subsequent existence should not be of more interest for us. Without going as far as Hume, one may believe that just as before our birth we were not what we are now and that these two ways of being are not bound together in such fashion as to leave the least vestige of our passing from one state to the other, so also, after death, we shall become new beings, under conditions which will have no more relationship with those of our present state than the latter have with the conditions preceding our birth.''

M. Simon existed for several months in his mother's womb; what idea has he of that existence? And since that existence, which forms a part of his present state, is unknown to him, how can his reason know what will become of him when death will carry into another state?

May 30.

"As to the beauty of her face, no woman ever equaled it . . . and yet her features were not cast in that regular mold which we have been falsely taught to revere in the classic works of Paganism: *There is no exquisite beauty,* says Lord Verulam, speaking truly of all types of beauty, *without a certain strangeness in the proportions.*" (Edgar Poe, *Ligéia.*)

I went during the day to invite F. Leroy to come and dine on Monday with Bouchereau: I had great pleasure in seeing him again.

On coming home, I continued my reading of Edgar Poe. His book awakes in me anew that sense of the mysterious which used, in former times, to be a greater preoccupation for me in my painting; it fell away, I believe, because of my work from nature, with allegorical subjects, etc. Baudelaire, in his preface, says that I bring back to painting the feeling for that so singular ideal which delights in the terrible. He is right: but the disjointed and incomprehensible qualities which mingle with his[9] conceptions do not suit my mind. His metaphysics and his researches into the soul and the future life are most singular, and give one a lot to think about. His Van Kirck, talking about the soul during a hypnotic sleep, is a bizarre and profound piece of writing which throws you into a state of contemplation. There is the same monotony in the fables as in all his stories; to tell the truth it is only the phantom gleam with which he illumines those confused but terrifying figures that makes up the charm of this singular and very original poet and philosopher.

June 6.

On leaving the Hôtel de Ville yesterday I went to see the famous agricultural exposition. All eyes are fastened upon it; people stand in admiration before these beautiful works of the imagination: machines for exploiting the earth, animals from all countries brought for a fraternal competition of all peoples: there is not one little bourgeois who, on leaving the place, is not infinitely grateful to himself for having been born in such a precious century. For my own part, I felt the greatest sadness amidst that bizarre mixture of things: those poor animals can't make out what that stupid crowd wants of them; they do not recognize the chance keepers who have been furnished to them. As to the peasants who have accompanied their beloved beasts, they lie there near their charges, casting anxious glances at the idle passers-by, and keeping watch to forestall the insults or the impudent teasing which they are by no means spared.

On entering that exposition of machines designed to plough, to sow and to reap, I thought myself in an arsenal amidst the machines of war: this is how I picture those ballistas and catapults, those coarse instruments bristling with iron points, and those chariots armed with

[9] i. e., Poe's.

scythes and steel blades: these are engines of Mars and not of blonde Ceres.

The complication of those frightful instruments is in singular contrast with the innocent nature of their employment; What! that frightful machine armed with tusks and points, bristling with sharp blades, is destined to give to man his daily bread! The plough, which I am astonished not to see placed among the constellations, like the lyre and the chariot, will now be no more than an instrument fallen to contempt! The horse has had his day, as well: new means are demanded by our insatiable desires.

Those little steam engines with their pistons, their balance wheel and their flaming throat are the horses of the future. The fearful and lugubrious jingling of their wheels and . . . Don Quixote would have laid lance in rest, etc.

Poor abused peoples, you will not find happiness in the disappearance of labor! Look at those idlers condemned to drag the burden of their days and not knowing what to do with their time, which the machines cut into still further. In other times, travel was a recreation for them: getting out of their daily torpor, seeing other regions and other customs beguiled the ennui which weighs upon them and pursues them. Nowadays, they are swept along at such speed that they can see nothing; they count the stages of their journey by the railroad stations — which all look alike. When they have crossed the whole of Europe, it seems as if they had not left those insipid stations which appear to follow them throughout their idleness and their incapacity for enjoyment. The costumes and the varied usages that they have sought at the ends of the earth will not be long in looking the same everywhere.

Already the Ottoman who used to walk about in robes and slippers under his always laughing sky has imprisoned himself in the ignoble clothing of our so-called civilization: he wears tight garments, as in countries where fresh air is an enemy against which one must protect oneself: he has adopted those monotonous colors which belonged to the peoples of the North, living as they do amid mud and hoar-frost.

Instead of gazing upon the Bosporus as it smiles beneath its sun —
and it was with tranquillity that they used to contemplate it — they
shut themselves in to see French comedies in little theaters; you find
the same comedies, the same newspapers and the same profitless noise
in every part of the world, as you find the eternal railroad station, with
its cyclops and its savage whistles.

One won't be able to go three leagues without that barbarous
accompaniment: the fields and the mountains will be furrowed with
it: we shall meet as the birds meet, in the plains of the air. Seeing no
longer counts for anything: the object of arriving is to start out again.
People will go from the Paris stock exchange to the St. Petersburg
stock exchange: business will demand the services of everybody, when
there are no longer any harvests to be reaped by willing hands, no more
fields to look after and improve by intelligent care. The thirst for
acquiring riches, which give so little enjoyment, will have made of this
world a world of brokers. They say that this is a fever as necessary to
the life of societies as, according to physicians, an actual fever is to the
human body in certain maladies. What, then, is this new malady unknown to so many societies of the past, which nevertheless astonished
the world by their great and genuinely useful enterprises, by conquests
in the domain of great ideas, by true riches employed to increase the
splendor of governments, and to raise in their own esteem the subjects
of these governments? Why is that pitiless activity not employed in
digging vast canals to carry off the waters of those fatal floods of which
we hear with consternation, why is it not used in the raising of dykes
capable of stemming them? That is what Egypt did, disciplining the
waters of the Nile and setting up the Pyramids against the invasion of
the sands of the desert; that is what the Romans did when they covered
the world of antiquity with their roads, with their bridges and also with
their arches of triumph.

Who will raise a dike against evil impulses? What hand will make
the overflow of wild passions return to their bed? Where is the people
that will raise a dike against cupidity, against low envy, against the

calumny that flouts honest men in silence, or the impotence of laws? When will that other machine, the pitiless press, be disciplined? when will the honor and the reputation of the upright man or the eminent man — and consequently the envied man — no longer be the target of poisoned calumnies from the merest nonentity?

(Tag all this on to the observations of the month of May, 1853, occasioned by those that Girardin set down on the subject of a mechanically ploughed France.)

June 10.

Among the great, there are, quite certainly, fiery geniuses who are undisciplined even when they believe themselves to be correct, the explanation being that instinct is all that they follow, and it does deceive at times. That is what one may say of Michelangelo, Shakespeare, and Puget, men who do not guide their genius, but who are guided by it. Corneille is one of the most conspicuous examples of this: he falls into abominations when he comes down from heaven. Balancing this, however, such men are the initiators, the shepherds of the flock: their work forms monuments which, if often formless, are eternal, dominating the deserts as well as the most refined civilizations. They become, for these civilizations, the point of departure and the criticism as well, because of the eternal character possessed by the fine part of their work.

Quite as incontestably, there are divine geniuses who obey their nature, but who command it also. Men like Vergil and Racine never fall into enormities: they have entered on a road which had been opened by giants — they have left behind them the formless blocks and the too audacious attempts; they exercise a more uncontested sway over the heart of mankind.

When the men of the former category want to change their course and act methodically, they fall into coldness and remain beneath, or rather to one side of themselves. The men of the second class keep their imagination in check, they change their course or give themselves new directions at will, without falling into contradictions or shocking errors.

June 14.

I sit next to Aubert at dinner, at the Hôtel de Ville. He tells me that, despite a happy life, he would not want to begin again to live, because of those thousand bitternesses with which life is sowed. This is the more remarkable because Aubert is a complete voluptuary: at his present age, he can still take enjoyment in the company of a woman. The sovereign good would therefore be tranquillity. Why not begin early with giving to tranquillity its pre-eminent position? If man is destined one day to find out that calm stands above all else, why not give oneself a life which can afford that anticipated calm, while still containing some of those sweet enjoyments which are not the same thing as the fearful upheavals caused by the passions? But how one must watch oneself if one would be spared them, when they are so greatly to be feared!

June 24.

Visited Thiers this evening. I complimented him on his Cabinet.

Delaroche was there: he plays the gay one, the marquis.

Quite a burst of friendly remarks.

June 29.

Dinner today with Villot and his wife. We talked painting all evening: that puts me into a good frame of mind.

Yesterday, on my arrival, I was dissatisfied at my having left here the *Herminie*, the *Boisguilbert Carrying off Rebecca*, the sketches for Hartmann,[10] etc.

July 5.

Went to the house of Barbier. Very gay dinner and evening. Mme

[10] Sketches for the four large pictures now in the collection of Mr. Albert Gallatin, of New York.

Franchetti was there and helped make the company agreeable. Mme Barbier is not as much delighted as Mme Villot by the wit of Dumas fils. Barbier says rightly that nothing is more fatiguing than that perpetual play of wit and of words on every occasion.

August 8.

The finest products of the arts are those which express the pure fantasy of the artist. Hence the inferiority of the French school, in sculpture and in painting — it always gives precedence to the study of the model instead of to the sentiment which dominates the painter or the sculptor. The French, in all periods, have always fallen into styles, or into the schoolman's enthusiasm for styles, which offers itself as the only true approach, and which is the falsest of all. Their love for reason in all things has caused them to. . . .[11]

August 26.

Made a fresh start today on the picture of *Jacob*, at Saint-Sulpice. I got a great deal done today: I raised the tone of the whole group, etc. The lay-in was very good.

August 27.

I live the life of a hermit and one day is just like every other one. I work at Saint-Sulpice every day except Sundays, and I see no one.

September 7.

From my window I see a man at work laying a floor in the gallery; he is nude to the waist. When I compare his color with that of the outer wall, I notice how colorful are the half-tints of the flesh, compared with those of inert matter. I noticed the same thing, the day before yesterday, at the Place Saint-Sulpice, where a scalawag had climbed up on the statues of the fountain; I saw him in full sunlight: dull

[11] The manuscript, which is in pencil, suddenly stops here.

orange in the light, very lively violet tones for the passage from the shadow, and golden reflections in the shadows turned toward the ground. The orange and the violet dominated alternately or mingled. The golden tone had a tendency toward green. Flesh gets its real color only in the open air, and especially in sunlight. Let a man put his head out of the window, and he is quite different from what he was inside the room; hence the foolishness of studio studies, for they set themselves to render that false color.

This morning (September 11), I saw the singer at the window of the house opposite, which is what made me write the above.

October 5.

Difficulty of translations. On coming home, read the translations from Dante and other writers. I noticed how difficult it is for our practical language to bend to the translations of thoroughly naive poets like Dante. The need of rhyme or of *saving* the commonplace aspect of a word forces you to circumlocutions which rob the passage of its zest. And yet, the day before, we were reading fables from La Fontaine, who is just as naive, who is more ornate, and who says everything without parasitical ornaments and without paraphrases. One should say only the things that are to be said: there is the quality that should be joined to elegance. The two Deschamps [12] and other moderns who have felt, as I do, how flavorless is the poetry of ready-made formulas, like those of the eighteenth century, can write passages in which the feeling of the original appears once more: but the whole thing is as barbarous as a foreign language would be. In a word, this is not translating into French, and elegance is absent from the word. In Horace, whom we were reading afterward, the same elegance, but also the same strength. There is no true poet without that.

[12] Emile and Antony Deschamps, poets of the Romantic clan; the former translated plays from Shakespeare, the latter translated the *Divine Comedy* of Dante.

October 8.

We start out at seven o'clock for Givry. Fine sunlight. From the window to the north I make a last sketch of the rising ground.

Saw La Neuville-au-Bois, the country of La Valette.[13] Saw, I was about to say saw again, Givry.[14] This place, which I knew only from the stories of all whom I have loved, has awakened their memory once more, and gentle emotions with it. I saw the paternal house as it is but, as I suppose, without many changes. My grandmother's tombstone is still at the corner of the cemetery, which is to be expropriated, just like everything else. Her ashes will simply have to move on, like tradesmen who are sent to open their shops elsewhere.

On arriving, I meet an old Delacroix wearing a blouse, an ex-officer, who on hearing my name presses my hand several times and almost had tears in his eyes.

Paris, October 9.

Painted two views of my cousin's place, in oil and from memory. In the evening, I learned from Boissard of the death of poor Chassériau.[15]

October 10.

Poor Chassériau's funeral. There I meet Dauzats, Diaz, and young Moreau[16] the painter. I quite like him. I returned from the church with Emile Lassalle.[17]

[13] The La Valettes were cousins of the Delacroix. Mme de Forget, the great friend of Delacroix was, it will be remembered, a daughter of La Valette.

[14] Givry-en-Argonne, the birthplace of Delacroix's father.

[15] Théodore Chassériau (1819-1856), the painter.

[16] Gustave Moreau (1826–1898), the painter, then at his beginnings, had exhibited a *Pieta* at the Salon of 1852, and *The Song of Songs* at the Salon of 1853; his personal conception of form and color was already to be recognized in them.

[17] Emile Lassalle (1813-1871), lithographer, had reproduced Delacroix's *Dante and Vergil*, and *Medea*.

Augerville, October 12.

The complement of memory is needed if enjoyment is to be perfect, and unfortunately one cannot at the same time enjoy and recall enjoyment. That is the ideal added to the real. Memory extracts the moment of delight or creates the necessary illusion.

October 13.

As I look at these woods the song of a thrush awakens in me the memory of similar moments, and this memory pleases me more than the present moment.

Self-content is the greatest contentment and, in a sense which is not as roundabout as it may appear, one wants to be content with the opinion that others have of one. Only, some derive this sentiment from virtue, others from the external advantages which attract the eyes of envy.

I admire this multitude of little cobwebs which the morning mist, as it loads them with humidity, makes visible to the eye. What a quantity of flies or other insects will have to be caught in these nets to feed the spinners, and of these latter, what a multitude must be offered to the appetite of the birds, etc.!

October 15.

I come upon a slug marked exactly like a panther: broad rings on its back and flanks, becoming spots and points at the head and near the belly, which is light in color, as in quadrupeds.

October 19.

Berryer was telling me, in the evening, that Pariset had told him that apparently every discovery of any importance which was made in medicine did no more than explain to him or even cause him to understand some line of Hippocrates that was still obscure.

Every evening while those gentlemen are having their interminable game of billiards, I take a walk in front of the château. At the beginning of the week I had delightful moonlight. We had an almost total eclipse, which gave to the moon that color of blood of which one reads in the poets and which Berryer told me he did not know. It is somewhat the same thing in this question of Pariset and Hippocrates. The great men see what the vulgar do not see: that is what makes them great men. What they have discovered and many times cried from the roofs is neglected or uncomprehended by those to whom they speak. Time, but more often another man of their own temper, finds the phenomena once more and at last demonstrates it to the crowd.

I wish I could recall whether Vergil, in the description of his tempest, makes the sky turn around the heads of his sailors, as I saw it when I was on my way to Tangier, during that windstorm in the night when the sky was without clouds and when it seemed, because of the movements of the ship, that the moon and the stars were in a continuous and immense movement.

Champrosay, October 21.

Left Augerville with Berryer and Cadillan. Magnificent weather. I still feel that appetite for nature and that freshness of impressions which, as a rule, belong only to youth. I believe that the majority of men are unacquainted with such feelings. They say: Here is fine weather, here are big trees: but all that does not fill them with a particular ravishing contentment, which is a living poem.

From Etampes to Juvisy I travel with them; in the same train I saw that woman who was so beautiful, so strange in her beauty, and as if made to be painted. She even impressed my neighbors, among whom one, a great mind in many respects, was a Frenchman with respect to the feelings which I expressed above. Next day I made memory sketches of that beautiful creature.

December 7.

M. Mesnard tells me that the work with color which is performed by the eye and the brain contributes largely to the fatigue which painting occasions. The fact is that I have to be in a thoroughly good state of health if I am to work at painting. For writing that is not as necessary: ideas can come to me when I am ill, if I can still hold my pen: before my easel, when I have the brush in my hand, it isn't the same thing.

December 9.

I take a long walk, from four o'clock till six. Paris seems charming to me. From the place Louis XV, I cross the Tuileries to come home through the Rue de la Paix. The beautiful gardens are quite abandoned. How they recall the memories of my youth!

In the evening, I paid a visit to Thiers. Only Roger was there. I saw the portrait by Delaroche, a feeble work, without character and without execution. It is possible to say sensible things, reasonable things, or even interesting things without reaching the point of producing literature. In painting, the same way. That Flemish portrait which he showed me, of a man in black, standing, is admirable and will always give pleasure, and through its *execution*.[18]

December 12.

Mozart writes in a letter somewhere, speaking of the principle that music can express all the passions, all the sorrows, all sufferings: "Nevertheless, the passions, whether violent or not, should never be so expressed as to reach the point of causing disgust; and music, even in situations of the greatest horror, *should never be painful to the ear, but should flatter and charm it, and thereby always remain music.*"

December 16.

Galimard surprised and disgusted me by his account of the number of little machines that have been set in motion to prevent my election.[19]

[18] The picture is a full-length *Portrait of a Man*, attributed to Terburg, and now in the Louvre.
[19] To the Institute.

December 29.

Voltaire was once asked by a company of friends to tell them a story of a robber; he said: "Gentlemen, there was once a tax collector ——— Dear me, I have forgotten the rest." He had a store of philosophy and detachment. And that is certainly not a thing for which to criticize him.

December 31.

In the article on Charlet.[20] There are talents that come into the world fully prepared and armed at every point. Since the beginning of things, there must always have existed that kind of pleasure which the most experienced men find in work, which is to say a species of mastery, the sureness of the hand keeping time with the definiteness of the conception. Bonington was that way also, but in the matter of his hand, above all; that hand was so able that it ran ahead of his thought; when he repainted his pictures, it was with so great a facility that everything he put on the canvas was charming. Yet not all the details worked together in many cases: his gropings, as he tried to get back his ensemble, sometimes made him abandon a work that he had begun. As to this type of improvisation, it should be observed that an element enters which does not occur with Charlet, and that is the element of color.

[20] The work by Colonel de la Combe entitled *Charlet, sa Vie, ses Lettres* had just appeared. Later on, in 1862, Delacroix will publish, in the *Revue des Deux Mondes,* an article on Charlet. He notes here some indications which he will utilize later.

January 1.[1]

Poussin defines the beautiful as delectation. After having examined all the pedantic modern definitions, such as the splendor of the good, etc., or that beauty is regularity, or that it is what most resembles Raphael or the Antique, or all the rest of the stupidities, it was no great trouble for me to find confirmation in my own mind for the definition which I find in Voltaire in his article on "Aristotle, the Poetics" in the *Dic-*

[1] For two weeks, the time preceding his election to the Academy, Delacroix, who was seriously ill, was obliged to keep to his room. It was during these days of forced repose that his always active mind was occupied with these reflections on art.

tionnaire Philosophique. He cites the foolish reflection of Pascal, who remarks that one does not say *geometrical beauty* or *medicinal beauty,* and that one is wrong to say *poetic beauty,* because one knows the object of geometry and of medicine, but one does not know any such thing as the model in nature which one must imitate in order to obtain that type of pleasure which is the object of poetry. To that, Voltaire replies: "It is pretty clear that this passage from Pascal is pitiful. We know well that there is nothing beautiful in a medicine, or in the properties of a triangle, and that *we reserve the word beautiful for that which causes pleasure and admiration to our soul and to our senses.*"

As to Titian. Eulogy of Titian. One eulogizes a contemporary whose place is not yet designated. Often it is the men least worthy of praise who are made the object of eulogy. But a eulogy of Titian! You will tell me that I remind you of that devout lawyer who had written the *Memorial in favor of God.* . . .

He can get along without my eulogies . . . his glorious shade. . . .

It seems indeed that those men of the sixteenth century have left but little for us to do; they were the first to travel the road, and seem to have got to the boundary line of possibility in all types of art; and yet in every one of these types, there have been new talents bringing new achievement into existence. These talents, appearing during periods that were less and less favorable to great enterprises, to boldness, to novelty, and to naiveté, have met with certain successes, if you like, and so have not failed to please their century, which was less favored but not less athirst for enjoyment.

In that heptarchy, or government of seven,[2] the scepter of government is shared with a certain equality, except for Titian alone; for he, though a part of the government, is rather to be looked on as a sort of viceroy in the fair domain of painting.

[2] Delacroix is here inspiring himself from the ideas of his friend Chenavard, who considered that there were only seven great painters (whence the word *heptarchy*); they were for him Leonardo da Vinci, Michelangelo, Raphael, Titian, Correggio, Rubens and Rembrandt.

We may look upon him as the creator of landscape. He introduced into it that breadth which he applied to the rendering of figures and of draperies.

One stands confounded at the force, the fecundity, and the universality of those men of the sixteenth century. Our miserable little pictures painted for our miserable dwellings, the disappearance of those Maecenases whose palaces were, for a series of generations, the refuge of works of art — which families regarded as titles of nobility: corporations of merchants commanded works which would terrify the sovereigns of our days, and ordered them from artists great enough in stature to accomplish all tasks.

Less than a hundred years later, Poussin already does no more than small pictures.

We must renounce any attempt even to imagine what the works of Titian must have been when they were new and had their full freshness.

We see these admirable works after three hundred years of varnish, of accidents, and of repairs worse than their other misfortunes. . . .

January 3.

The extent to which civilization, as we understand it, dulls the natural feelings. Hector says to Ajax (*Iliad,* Canto VII) as he leaves the combat: "Already night arrives, and we must all obey the night — setting limits on the work of men."

January 4.

The Cyclops preparing the apartment of Psyche.

No one can deny that with Raphael elegance is more stressed than naturalness, nor can he deny that this elegance frequently degenerates into mannerism. I know well that he has charm, the thing which passes definition. It is as in Rossini; *Ah! si dei mali amici.* Expression, but above all elegance.

If one lived to be a hundred and twenty years old, one would prefer

Titian to all else. He is not the man for young people. He is the least mannered and consequently the most varied of painters. Mannered talents have but a single tendency, a single habit. They follow the impulse of the hand more than they direct it. The talent which is least mannered must be the most varied: at every moment it is obeying a genuine emotion. It is obliged to render that emotion: adornment, and vain display of its facility or its skill have no slightest interest for it: on the contrary, it despises everything which does not lead it to a more vivid expression of its thought.

He is the man who most conceals the execution, the one who, in appearance, is least concerned with it.

As to Titian, Raphael and Correggio.[3] See Mengs. Something might be written on this subject.

There are people to whom nature has given taste: but even with such persons it increases with age, and purifies itself. The young man is all for the bizarre, for the forced, for the swollen. Do not apply the word coldness to what I call taste. The taste that I mean is a lucidity of the mind which instantly separates that which is worthy of admiration from that which is only false brilliance. In a word, it is the maturity of the mind.

With Titian there begins that breadth of handling which cuts cleanly away from the dryness of his predecessors and which is the perfection of painting. The painters who seek for that dryness of the Primitives, which was quite natural in schools making new attempts and issuing forth from almost barbarous sources, are like grown men who, in order to assume a naive appearance, would imitate the speech and gestures of childhood. That breadth of Titian's, which is the goal of painting and which is as far removed from the dryness of the first painters as it is from the monstrous abuse of the touch and of loose style by the painters who arrived when art was in its decadence. . . .

Thus it is with the Antique. I am now re-reading the expressions

[3] This is the title of a section of the writings of Raphael Mengs (1728-1779), which are collected in his *Œuvres Complètes*, Paris, 1786.

of admiration of some of his contemporaries. Their eulogies have something incredible about them: What indeed must those prodigious works have been when no part of them bore the trace of later neglect but when, on the contrary, the fineness of the touch, the melting quality and the incredible truth and splendor of the tints possessed all their freshness, time and inevitable accidents not having as yet taken anything from them. Aretino,[4] in an instructive dialogue on the painters of this period, details with admiration a number of Titian's works, and ends with the words: "But I must restrain myself and touch lightly upon his praise, since I am a comrade of his and since one must be absolutely blind if one does not see the sun."

He says afterward what he might have placed first: "Our Titian is therefore divine and unequaled in painting, etc." He adds: "Let us say in conclusion that, though there have been various excellent painters before the present time, these three merit and hold the first rank: Michelangelo, Raphael and Titian." I know well that the title of colorist is more of an obstacle than a recommendation with the modern schools which look upon the study of drawing alone as a virtue, and sacrifice all else to it.[5] The opinion is that a colorist busies himself only with inferior and, so to speak, earthly phases of painting: that a fine drawing is much finer when it is accompanied by tedious color, and that the main function of color is to distract attention from the more sublime quality, which can get along very easily without any prestige that color can give. It is what might be called the *abstract* side of painting, contour being its essential goal; aside from color, such a conception would give only secondary rank to others among the needs of painting, such as expression, the true disposition of effect, and composition itself.

The school which uses oil-painting to imitate the ancient frescoes

[4] *Dialogue sur la Peinture* by Louis Dolce, entitled *l'Aretin*, Florence, 1735.
[5] These are the grievances of Ingres and the others who were combatting Delacroix at the Institute.

is guilty of a strange misunderstanding. The elements in such technique which are ungrateful from the standpoint of color, and the material difficulties which it imposes on a timid talent require from the painter a lightness, a sureness, etc. . . .

Oil-painting, on the contrary, leads to a perfection of rendering which is the reverse of that painting with broad strokes; but it is necessary that everything in it be in agreement, the magic of backgrounds, etc. . . .

It is a type of drawing which can more properly ally itself, through decorations, with the great lines of architecture than it can express the fineness and the preciousness of objects.

And so Titian, with whom the rendering is so prodigious despite his broad understanding of details, devoted himself but little to fresco. Paul Veronese himself, who seems more adapted to it through an even greater breadth of handling and through the nature of the scenes which he loved to represent, painted but very few frescoes.

It must also be said that at the period when fresco flowered and was preferred, which is to say in the earliest times of the renaissance of art, painting was not yet mistress of all the means which it has since controlled. From the time when oil-painting gave the secret of its prodigies of illusion in the matter of color and effect, fresco has been but little cultivated and almost entirely abandoned.

I do not deny that the grand style, the epic style of painting, if one may call it so, saw the decline of its reign at that same time; but geniuses such as Michelangelo and Raphael are rare. The technique of fresco which they had rendered illustrious and which they had employed for their sublime conceptions must have perished in hands less bold than theirs. Genius, moreover, can employ with equal success the most diverse means. When it flows from the brush of a Rubens, oil-painting has equaled, in strength and in breadth, the amplitude of the most celebrated frescoes, however different its means: and, not going outside that Venetian school of which Titian is the torch, the great pictures by that admirable master, those of Veronese and even of

Tintoretto are examples of verve united to power, quite as much as are the most celebrated frescoes: they simply show another aspect of painting; the perfecting of the material means, while it may perhaps lose on the side of simplicity of impression, discovers sources of effect, of variety, of richness, etc. . . .

Such changes are necessarily brought in by time and new inventions: it is puerile to try to go upstream on the current of the ages and to seek in the primitive masters. . . .

Those fellows seemed to believe that poverty in the means is masterly sobriety, etc. . . .

In our climates fresco is subject to more of accidents. Even in the South it is very difficult to preserve. It turns pale, it detaches from the wall.

Remarkable letter to Peisse,[6] on the beauty that is to be seen only in lines. (In my notebook under the date of July 11, '49).

The majority of the books on the arts are written by people who are not artists: hence the number of false notions and judgments, due to haphazard caprice and to prejudice. I firmly believe that any man who has received a liberal education can speak pertinently of a book, but not of a work of painting or sculpture.

January 7.

All you are doing are sepia drawings. David's picture is nothing else.

January 8.

Casanova heard from Malipieri: "If you want to make people weep, you must weep yourself. If you want to make people laugh, your face must remain serious."

January 10.

Lengthiness in a book is a capital defect. Walter Scott, all the moderns,

---

[6] This letter, which was published in the *Correspondence* of Delacroix, was copied by him in part in the notebook of 1849, on July 11.

etc. What would you say of a picture which had more open spaces and more figures in it than were needed?

Voltaire says in the preface to the *Temple du Goût:* "I find all books too long."

Comparison between the execution of the painter and of the actor. Mme Pasta, Mme Malibran. (Notebook of 1847, January 3.)

As to the importance of color; its forming part of the charm of Lesueur. The weak side of Poussin. (Notebook of 1851, June 6.)

There is pictorial license in the same way that there is poetic license. (See the notebook for 1850, October 16.)

As to the merits of a great architect. (Notebook of 1850, June 14.)

This could be connected with the passage on man's small importance when one considers the purposes of nature, another good passage in the notebook of 1850, May 1. As to the way that the mind of man stands in equal contradiction with those same purposes.

Sunday, January 11.[7]

MATERIALS FOR A DICTIONARY OF THE FINE ARTS.

A SMALL PHILOSOPHIC DICTIONARY OF THE FINE ARTS.

COMPENDIUM OF A DICTIONARY OF THE FINE ARTS.

EXTRACT FROM A PHILOSOPHIC DICTIONARY OF THE FINE ARTS, OF PAINTING AND OF SCULPTURE.[8]

[7] It was on January 10, 1857, that Delacroix was elected to the Academy. It will be noted that on the very next day, January 11, he began to draw up his *Dictionnaire des Beaux-Arts.* As he could no longer be a professor at the Ecole, he had the idea of making himself useful by a work which should make public his ideas and his doctrine; these he notes in these ardent pages written during the three months of his illness as inspiration comes to him; he left the house for the first time on March 17.

[8] Various projected titles for the work he was beginning.

Fresco. It is considered a great merit in the masters who have excelled in fresco, to have had the boldness in execution which permitted them to paint directly, their first strokes showing, etc. But all frescoes were retouched in tempera.

Handling. (in painting).

French. French style, in the bad sense of the term.

The French school of sculpture. See the notebook of '49, October 6, for what I say of the tomb of M. de Brézé. See the notebook of '52, October 20.

Execution.

Model. (The model who poses for you). Use of the model.

Effect. Chiaroscuro.

Composition.

Accessories.

Details.

Draperies.

Palette.

Oil-painting.

Grace.

Contour. It should come last, contrary to the present-day habit. Only a very experienced man can use it accurately.

Brushwork. Fine brushwork. Reynolds said that a painter should draw with the brush.

Colors. Coloration; its importance. Notebook of '52, January 3.

Colors. (materials) Employed in painting.

Drawing. By means of the inner masses or by means of the contour.

The Beautiful. Poussin's definition and that of Voltaire. What the latter says of Pascal. See the notebook of '55, October 1. As to the figures at Strasbourg.

Simplicity. Examples of simplicity, the final achievement of art, the Antique, etc.

Antique.

Parthenon. (Marbles of the Parthenon) or Phidias; the modern rage for this style, to the detriment of the other periods of the antique. The Roman antique.

Schools.

Academies. What Voltaire says of them: that they have by no means made the great men.

Shadows. There are no shadows properly so-called. There are only reflections. Importance of establishing the limits of shadows. They are always too strong. Notebook of '47, June 10. The younger your sitter is, the lighter the shadows are.

Half-tints. Tempera renders them more easily.

Local tone. (Importance of the local tone).

Perspective or *drawing.*

Sculpture. Modern sculpture. Its difficulty after that of the ancients. French sculpture.

Manner.[9]

Master. He who teaches.

Master. He who possesses mastery.

Taste. It applies to all the arts.

Flemings. (Dutch).

Albrecht Dürer, Titian, Raphael, etc.

Panels. (Painting on panels).

The school of David.

The Italian, Flemish, German, Spanish, and French schools. Comparisons among them.

[9] At various places in the text of this book, Delacroix employs the word *manner* in a sense that clearly calls for its translation as *mannerism*, a more recent form which his conservative spirit did not fully accept. The reader evidently needs to use some imagination and his memories of the rest of the book in order to expand the present list of titles. M. Paul Flat, the editor of the first edition of the Journal, considered this study for the Dictionary as the most interesting section of the master's writings, for we see him here passing in review the phases of his art which have meant most to him and deciding what to include in a work that he had meditated for years.

Expression.

Cartoons. Preparatory studies for execution.

Sketch.

Copy.

Method. (Is there such a thing for drawing, painting, etc?)

Tradition. (Is followed until the time of David).[10]

Masters. Exaggerated respect for the men to whom this name has been given. Notebook of '55, September 30, at Strasbourg.

Pupils. (Difference in attitude between the students of the old time and the modern time).

Technique. (Is demonstrated when you have the palette in your hand). The small amount of light that the books throw on this subject. Adoration for false technique in the bad schools. Importance of genuine technique in bringing works to perfection. It is in the greatest masters that the most perfect technique in the world is found: Rubens, Titian, Veronese, the Dutch; the special pains they took, grinding colors, preparations, the drying of the different layers of paint. (See *Panels*). Among the moderns, this tradition is completely lost. Bad products, negligence in the preparations, canvases, brushes, abominable oils, lack of care on the part of the artist.

David introduced this negligence through his affectation of contempt for the material means.

David, from another standpoint, is completely materialistic. His respect for the model and the lay figure, etc., is always found again in the men of the Vanloo type.

Varnishes. (Their deadly effects). Their very judicious employment on old paintings. Cite the passages from Oudry.

Varnishes ought to be a kind of cuirass for the picture, and at the same time a means of restoring its brilliance.

Boucher and *Vanloo.* Their school: mannerism and the abandon-

[10] This idea, to which Delacroix returns a few lines later, was exactly that of Renoir, who may very well have derived it from the Journal.

ment of all investigation and of all naturalness. Remarkable methods of execution. A vestige of tradition.

Watteau. Greatly despised under David, restored to honor at a later time. Admirable execution. His fantasy does not hold up when he is placed in contrast with the Flemings. He appears scarcely more than theatrical when placed beside men like Ostade, Van de Velde, etc. He possesses the art of holding his picture together.

January 13.

Mme Barbier sends me some verses by Dagnan [11] written on the occasion of my entrance to the Academy.

Daguerreotype.

Photography.

Illusion, optical illusion. This term, which ordinarily is applied only to painting, could be applied as well to a certain type of literature.

Foreshortenings. As to the fact that there always are some, even in a figure that is quite erect, with the arms hanging at the sides. The art of foreshortenings or of perspective and drawing are all one. Certain schools have avoided them, really believing that they would not have to use them because they did not attempt violent foreshortenings. In a head seen in profile, the eye, and the forehead, etc., are foreshortened; the same applies to the rest.

Frame, border. They can have a good or bad influence on the effect of the picture. The gold so freely used in our day. Their form as related to the character of the picture.

Light, luminous point or high-light. Why is it that the true tone of the object is always found at the side of the luminous point? It is because this point is accentuated only on the parts which receive the full illumination, those which do not recede under the light. In a rounded part, the ovoid for example, this is not the case, everything recedes under the light.

The more polished or shiny an object is, the less one sees its

[11] Isidore Dagnan, (1790-1873), landscape painter.

particular color: as a matter of fact, it becomes a mirror reflecting the surrounding colors.

Vague (the). There is something from Obermann on *the vague* in my little blue notebooks. The church of Saint-Jacques at Dieppe, in the evening.[12] As to the fact that painting is vaguer than poetry, despite the definite appearance that it offers to our eyes. One of its greatest charms.

Binding-together (of pictures). The air and the reflections create a whole out of the objects most incongruous in color.

Lay-in. As to the possibilities which it opens to the imagination. Unfinished buildings, etc. Notebook of '55, March 23.

Decoration — theatrical.

Decoration — of monuments. Notebook of '47, June 10.

Inspiration.

Talent. Talent or genius and the possession of talent without genius. With regard to talent, see what I say on the subject in one of the little blue notebooks.[13] See also what I say about that little world which man bears within him. Notebook of '55, September 11.

Reflections. Every reflection partakes of green, the edge of every shadow partakes of violet.

Criticism. As to the insufficiency of most criticism. As to its lack of any use. Criticism follows the productions of the mind as the shadow follows the body. See the Encyclopedia for articles on the above subjects.

Proportion. The Parthenon perfect; the Madeleine bad. Grétry used to say that one made an aria of one's own by giving it a movement better suited to the situation; in the same way one changes the character of a monument, etc. Too perfect proportions are detrimental to the impression of the *sublime.* Notebook of '53, May 9.

Architect. Notebook of '50, June 14.

Backgrounds. The art of painting backgrounds.

[12] In his notebook of 1854, on September 14, Delacroix speaks of the impressions he had on an evening visit to Saint-Jacques.

[13] The notebook is lost.

Theatrical Art. See March 25, notebook of '55, on Shakespeare.
Skies.

Air. Aerial perspective, surrounding air.

Costume. Exactitude of costume.

Style. As to the art of writing. The great men write well. See notebook of '53, May 17. Charles V, etc. See same notebook May 8.[14] One is never long-winded when one says the thing that one should say.

Ideal.

Preface of a small *Dictionary of the Fine Arts*. See notebook of '52, Nov. 1. No man, however talented, can grasp the whole of art. All he can do is to set down what he knows, etc. One must not be too absolute; Poussin's words about Raphael.

Lay-in. The best kind is the one which gives to the painter a sense of security as to the result of the picture.

Distance. To establish the distance of objects, they are ordinarily grayed: it is the touch, etc. Flat tints also.

Landscape.

Horse, animals. These should not be treated with the perfection of drawing of the naturalists, especially when the painting or sculpture is in the grand style. Géricault too learned. Rubens and Gros superior. Barye mean in his lions. The antique is the model for this work as for all others.

Young people. I said somewhere that shadows on them were lighter. I find in the notebook of '52, October 9, what I was saying to Andrieu when painting the *Venus* of the Hôtel de Ville: Such shadows have about them something trembling and vague, which resembles the vapor rising from the earth on a fine summer day. Rubens, whose painting is very methodical, makes his women and children older than they are.

Gray and *Earth Colors*. The enemy of all painting is the gray. Painting will always appear grayer than it is because of its oblique

[14] This is the moment when Delacroix was writing his article on Poussin.

position under the light. Banish all the earth colors. See my note on a separate sheet of paper, notebook of '52, September 15.

Proportions. In such arts as literature or music, it is essential to have broad and firmly established proportions among the parts composing the work. Beethoven's pieces are too long. He causes fatigue by occupying the listener with the same idea for too long a time. Notebook of '49, March 11.

Albrecht Dürer. The true painter is the one who knows all nature. Human figures, animals, landscape, treated with the same perfection. Notebook of '49, March 10. Rubens is of that family.

Accessories. Notebook of '55, October 10. If you are negligent in your treatment of the accessories, you bring me back to the handicraft, to the impatience of the hand, etc.

Dramatic Art. The example of Shakespeare leads us to believe that the comic and the tragic may be mingled in the same work. Shakespeare has an art of his own, etc. Notebook of '55, March 25.

In many modern French novels, the mingling of the comic and tragic in certain parts is unbearable. *(Same note.)*

What Lord Byron says of Shakespeare, that only *German or English taste* can take pleasure in him. What he says in addition, about Shakespeare, same notebook June 19.[15]

Binding-together. The art of binding together the parts of the picture through the effect, color, line, reflections, etc.

Lines. Lines of the composition. To *bind them together,* to *contrast* them, to avoid artificiality notwithstanding.

Touch. Many masters have taken care not to permit the spectator to feel it, doubtless thinking that they thereby came closer to nature which, to be sure, does not show it. Touch is one of the many means which contribute to render the thought in painting. A painting can doubtless be very fine without showing the touch, but to think that one gets close to the effect of nature by such avoidance is puerile: one might just as well put real colored reliefs onto one's picture, on the

---

[15] Delacroix is inexact in referring to this date.

theory that bodies have projection! In all the arts there are means of execution which are accepted and agreed upon, and one is but an imperfect connoisseur if one cannot read the language that expresses these indications of the thought; the proof is that the vulgar prefer to all other pictures those which are smoothest and show the touch to the smallest extent, and that such people prefer them for that very reason. Moreover, everything in the work of a true master depends on the distance from which it directs you to consider the picture. At a certain distance, the touch melts into the ensemble, but it gives to the painting an accent which the tints, melted together, cannot produce. When on the contrary you look from very close by at the most finished work, you will still discover traces of touches and of accents, etc. . . . The logical conclusion would be that a sketch well touched in cannot give as much pleasure as a very finished picture, that is to say, one in which the touch is not felt; for there is a considerable number of pictures from which the touch is completely absent, but which are far from being finished. (See the words *to finish, finishing;* what that consists of, in the matter of a picture.)

Touch, employed in the proper way, affords a more fitting accentuation of the different planes of objects. When applied vigorously, it makes them come forward: the reverse manner sends them back.

Even in small pictures, touch is not displeasing. One may prefer a Teniers to a Mieris or a Van der Werff.

What are we to say of the masters who give a dry accentuation to the contours while abstaining from the touch? Contours no more exist in nature than do touches. In every art, we have always got to come back to the means agreed on, for they are the language of that art. What is a drawing in black and white, if not a convention to which the spectator is accustomed, and one which does not prevent his imagination from seeing in that translation of nature a complete equivalent?

The same thing applies to *engraving.* It does not need a very piercing eye to perceive that multitude of incised lines which, through their crossings, bring about the effect which the engraver wants to produce. They are touches, more or less ingenious in the way that they are placed, now widely spaced so as to bring the paper into play and so give more transparence to the work, now brought close together so as to dull the tint and give it the appearance of continuity, but always doing their work by means of conventions — which sentiment has discovered and consecrated; thus the whole wealth of nature is expressed without employing the magic of color — not for the purely physical sense of sight, but for the eyes of the mind and the soul; they behold the fresh splendor in the skin of the young girl, the wrinkles of the old man, the soft depths of cloths, the transparence of waters, the faraway look of skies and of mountains. If one argues from the absence of touch in certain pictures of great masters, one must not forget that time tends to conceal the touch.

Many of those painters who avoid the touch with greatest care, alleging that it does not exist in nature, exaggerate the contour, which also is not to be found there. They think that they are thus attaining preciseness; but it is real only for the dull senses of the semi-connoisseurs. Such artists even dispense with a proper expression of relief when they resort to their coarse enemy of all illusions, for their contours, evenly accented and used to an exaggerated extent, annul projection by rendering too visible the parts which, in every object, are always furthest from the eye, which is to say the edges. (See *Contour* or *Foreshortenings.*)

Exaggerated admiration for the old frescoes has contributed, in the case of many artists, to the maintaining of this inclination to overdo the contours. In this type of painting, the artist finds himself under the necessity of tracing the contours with certitude (See *Fresco*), and it is a necessity commanded by the material means used in the execution; moreover, in this type of work, as in painting on glass, where the means partake of convention more than do those of oil painting, the work has got to be done with broad strokes; the painter does not seek charm through the effect of color as much as through the large disposition of the lines and their harmonizing with those of the architecture.

Sculpture has its convention as *painting* and *engraving* have theirs. One is not shocked by the coldness which, it would seem, must result from the uniform color of the materials which it employs, whether they be marble, wood, stone, ivory, etc. The lack of coloration in the eyes, the hair, etc., is not an obstacle to the type of expression proper to this art. The isolating of the figures in the full round, lacking relationship as they do, with any background whatever, and the far stronger convention of bas-reliefs, are both equally far from creating any misunderstanding.

Sculpture itself includes the quality of touch: the exaggeration of certain hollows, or the way they are disposed, adds to the effect, as for example those holes bored into certain parts of the hair or of the accessories when, instead of using a continuous, incised line, the sculptor avoids the harshness it would give by the employment of these holes which from a distance, give softness and suppleness and a certain idea of lightness, especially in hair that is not too regular in its waves.

In the way that ornaments in architecture are touched in, we find once more how much of lightness and illusion the touch can produce. In the modern style, these ornaments are hollowed out to a uniform degree, so that, seen from nearby, they appear irreproachably correct: at the distance one must stand from the building, the impression is one of mere coldness and even of complete absence of effect. In the Antique on the contrary, we are astonished at the boldness and, at the same time, at the appropriateness of these studied artifices, this use of genuine touch to exaggerate the form along the lines of effect, or to soften the crudity of certain contours in order to bind together the different parts.

Schools. What they propose to themselves most of all: imitation of a certain reigning technique. See notebook of '55, November 25.

Decadence. The arts, since the sixteenth century, the point of perfection, show nothing but perpetual decadence. The change which has occurred in thought and custom is more the cause of this than the rarity of great artists: for neither the seventeenth, nor the eighteenth, nor the nineteenth century has lacked them. The absence of general taste, the gradual increase of wealth in the middle classes, the more and more imperious authority of sterile criticism, whose special work is that of encouraging mediocrity and of discouraging great talents, the temptation for men of strong mind to engage in the useful sciences, the emphasis on material knowledge, which frightens away the creatures of the imagination — all these causes, taken together, fatally condemn the arts to an ever greater subjection to the caprice of fashion and the loss of all elevation.

In every civilization there is just one precise point where it is given to human intelligence to show its whole strength: during these rapid moments, comparable to a lightning flash against a dark sky, it seems as though there were almost no interval between the breaking of that brilliant light and the last limit of its splendor. Following upon it comes night, more or less dark, but a return to the light is impossible. In order to get that, in the arts a rebirth of manners and morals would be necessary: for that is the middle ground between two barbarisms, one of them being caused by ignorance, the other one — for which there is far less remedy — coming from the excess and the abuse of knowledge.

It is in vain that talent rouses itself against the obstacles with which general indifference meets it. See the notebook of '55, September 25 (My walk to the church at Baden), as to the decline of art. Also what I say about the tomb of the Maréchal de Saxe.

English School. As to Reynolds and Lawrence. What I have said in the notebook of '55, August 31. The English School at the Exposition of 1855, June 17.

Exaggeration. Every exaggeration should take the direction of nature and of the idea. See the same note, notebook of '55, August 31.

Licenses.

The sea, marines. Look up what I say in the notebook of 1855 at Dieppe, on the manner of painting ships. Painters of marines do not represent the sea well, in general. The same reproach may be applied to them as to the painters of landscape. They want to show too much science, make portraits of waves, as the landscapists make portraits of trees, of the earth, of mountains, etc. They do not concern themselves enough with the effect on the imagination; the multiplicity of petty details — even true details — turns the mind away from the principal spectacle, which is the immensity or the depth to be rendered by any given art.

Interest. The art of concentrating it upon the necessary points. Not everything is to be shown. That seems difficult in painting, where the mind can imagine only what the eyes perceive. The poet has no trouble in sacrificing or of leaving in silence that which is secondary. The art of the painter consists in fixing attention only upon what is necessary, even while. . . .

Sacrifices. What must be sacrificed. A great art, unknown to novices. They want to show everything.

Classic. To what works is this name most naturally applied? To those, evidently, which seem destined to serve as models, as the rule, in all their parts. I call classic all works in which regularity predominates, those which satisfy the mind not alone by painting sentiments and things in an exact or grandiose or piquant manner, but also by unity and logical order, in a word, by all the qualities which increase the impression through the attainment of simplicity.

On this basis, Shakespeare would not be Classical, which is to say the right man to imitate in his processes, in his system. The admirable parts of his work cannot save and render acceptable his long-drawn-out passages, his continual playing on words, his ill-timed descriptions. His art, moreover, is completely a thing of his own.

Racine was a Romantic[16] for the people of his time. For all time, he is Classical, which is to say perfect.

Respect for tradition is nothing more than observation of the laws of taste, without which no tradition would be durable, etc.

[16] This was also the opinion of Stendhal who, in his work written in 1823, *Racine et Shakespeare,* did not hesitate "to maintain that Racine was Romantic."

The school of David has been qualified as the type of the Classical school. Although it was based on the imitation of the Antique, such a view of it is erroneous. Precisely that imitation, which is often unintelligent and exclusive, deprives this school of the chief *characteristic* of the Classical school, which is duration. Instead of penetrating the spirit of the Antique and connecting it with the study of nature, etc., one perceives that he was the echo of a period when there was a fancy for the Antique.

Although this word Classical implies beauties of a very elevated order, one may say also that there are hosts of very fine works to which this designation cannot be applied. Many people do not separate the idea of coldness from that of the Classical. It is true that a large number of artists imagine themselves Classical because they are cold. Reasoning in a similar way, there are some who think they have warmth because people call them Romantics. Warmth is real when it moves the spectator.

Subject. Importance of the subject. The subjects of fable are always new. Modern subjects difficult to treat because of the absence of the nude and the poverty of costumes. The originality of the painter gives novelty to subjects. Painting does not always need a subject. Géricault's painting of arms and of legs.

Knowledge. As to the necessity for the artist of being learned. How such knowledge is to be acquired independently of ordinary practice.

There is much talk of the painter's need to be universal. We are told that he must know history, the poets, even geography. That whole business is far from being useless, but is no more indispensable for him than for any other man who wants to adorn his mind. He has quite enough to do to be learned in his art and he never possesses knowledge of it in a complete way, however able or zealous he may be. Accuracy of the eye, sureness of hand, the art of carrying the picture on from the indications of the lay-in to the rounding out of the work, and so many other matters which are all of primary importance, demand application at every moment, and the practice of a lifetime. There are few artists, and I speak of those who really merit that name, who do not perceive, at the middle or decline of their career, that the time is too short for them to learn the things they do not know, or for them to begin again, with new expenditure of energy, the false or incomplete instruction which they have received.

Rubens, when past fifty years of age, used the time he did not give to the business of his mission to the king of Spain in copying the superb Italian originals he found in Madrid and which are still to be seen there. In his youth, he had copied enormously. This practice of copying, entirely neglected by the modern schools, was the source of immense knowledge. (See *Albrecht Dürer*.)

Flesh. Its predominating role among colorists: it is all the more necessary in modern subjects, in which the nude occurs but little.

Copies, copying. Therein lay the education of almost all the great masters. One first learned the manner of one's master, as an apprentice is taught the way of making a knife, without seeking to show his originality. Then one copied everything that came to hand among the works of contemporary or earlier artists. Painting began by being a mere craft. One made images as one stained glass or carpentry work. Painters painted shields, saddles, banners. Those primitive painters had more of the workman about them than we have: they learned the craft in superior fashion before they embarked on their own course. Today we get the opposite procedure.

Preface. The alphabetical order adopted by the writer has led him to give to this series of studies the name of DICTIONARY. The title would not really be proper save for a book as complete as possible, presenting in detail all the processes of the arts. Would it be possible for a single man to be gifted with the knowledge indispensable for such a task? Undoubtedly it would not.

These are studies set down in the form which has seemed most suitable for him, considering the distribution of his time, part of which he uses for other work. Perhaps he has also taken into account an insurmountable laziness about embarking upon the composition of a book. A dictionary is not a book: it is an instrument, a tool for making books or any other thing. The material, thus divided into articles, is thus extended or restricted according to the disposition of the author, and at times according to his laziness. It thus suppresses the transitions, the necessary connection among the parts, the order in which they should be disposed.

Although the author professes much respect for the book, properly so called, he, like a pretty considerable number of readers, has often experienced a kind of difficulty in giving the necessary attention to all the deductions and all the linking-together of a book, even one that has been well conceived and executed. We see a picture all at once, at least in its ensemble and its principal parts: for a painter accustomed to an impression like that, which is favorable to the understanding of the work, the book is like an edifice of which the front is often a sign-board, behind which, once he is introduced there, he must again and again give equal attention to the different rooms composing the monument he is visiting, not forgetting those which he has left behind him, and not without seeking in advance, through what he knows already, to determine what his impression will be at the end of his expedition.

It has been said that rivers are moving roads. It could be said that books are portions of pictures in movement, among which one follows the other without its being possible to grasp them at one time; to seize upon the connection among them demands from the reader almost as much intelligence as from the author. If the work is one of fantasy, addressing itself to the imagination alone, the attention demanded may become a pleasure; a well composed history produces the same effect upon the mind: the necessary sequence of events and their consequences forms a natural chain which the mind follows without trouble. But in a didactic work, the same cannot be true. The merit of such a work residing in its utility, it is to an understanding of all its parts and to extracting the meaning of them that the reader applies himself. The more easily he deduces the doctrine of the book, the more fruitful his reading will have been: now is there a simpler means, one that is more the enemy of all rhetoric, than this division of the material?

Although the author is himself of the profession and knows the things that long practice, aided by much special reflection, can teach him about it, he will not linger as much as might be thought over that part of the art which seems the whole of art to many mediocre artists, but without which art would not exist. He will thus seem to encroach on the domain of the critics of aesthetic affairs, men who doubtless think that practice is not needed for them to rise to speculative consideration of the arts.

He will treat of philosophic more than of technical matters. That may seem singular in a painter who writes on the arts: many semi-erudite men have treated the philosophy of art. It would seem that their profound ignorance of technical matters was looked on by them as a title to respect, persuaded as they were that preoccupation with this matter, so vital to every art, debarred professional artists from aesthetic speculation.

It would seem almost that they had imagined a profound ignorance of technical matters to be one reason more for rising to purely meta-physical considerations, in a word that preoccupation with a craft must render professional artists rather unfit to rise to the heights, which are forbidden to the people outside aesthetics and pure speculation.

In what art does execution so intimately follow invention? In painting and in poetry, *form is inseparable from conception,* etc, etc. Among readers, it is for instruction that some read, while others do so for amusement.

See the notebook of '50, May 7. "Montaigne writes by fits and starts. Those are the most interesting works. After the effort needed by the author to follow the thread of his idea, to keep that idea warm, etc., one must realize that there is also the work of the reader who, having opened the book for his recreation, finds himself insensibly caught, almost as a matter of honor, by the task of deciphering, etc."

Men of genius would not come to an understanding as to the production of a dictionary: on the other hand, if you had from each one of them a collection of their special observations, what a dictionary could be composed with such material!

This form must bring about repetitions, etc. So much the better! The same things repeated in another way often have. . . .

Romanticism. Notebook, '53, May 17.

Wednesday, January 23.

Notes for a DICTIONARY OF THE FINE ARTS:

Works on the arts.

Criticism. Its utility.

Flesh color. Flesh has its true color only when seen in the open air: (the effect noted from those scalawags who climbed on the statues of the fountain in the Place Saint-Sulpice, and that of the planers whom I saw from my window in the gallery: how strongly the half-tints of the flesh were colored when compared with inert matter. Notebook of 1856, September 7. Transparence of the half-tints. See the notebook of 1857, November 13.

Facile talents. There are talents that come into the world thoroughly prepared and armed at every point: Charlet, Bonington, etc. Notebook of '56, December 31.

Expression. It should not be rendered to the point of inspiring disgust. What Mozart says on this subject. Notebook of '56, December 12.

Execution. Same notebook, December 9th: "in the evening I visit Thiers etc."

The French are too much the slave of the model: tomb of the Maréchal de Saxe, at Strasbourg. Cariatides of the Galerie d'Apollon. Notebook of '55, March 23.

In Voltaire's *Questions Encyclopédiques,* in the article on *History,* I find the following which could serve as an epigraph for a dictionary of the fine arts: "The history of the arts is perhaps the most useful one of all, when, to a knowledge of invention and progress in the arts, it adds the description of their mechanism." (Champrosay, 1857, June 3.)

January 25.

Lithography, etching, the engraving of medals, impasto, scumbling, glazing.

Engraving. Engraving is an art which is disappearing, but its decadence is not solely due to the mechanical processes which are taking its place, neither to photography nor lithography, a thing which is far from replacing it, but which is easier and more economical.

The oldest engravings are perhaps the most expressive ones. Men like Lucas van Leyden, Albrecht Dürer, and Marcantonio are real engravers, in the sense that they seek above all to render the spirit of the painter whose work they are reproducing. Many men of genius, when reproducing their own creations, quite naturally yielded to their sentiment without bothering to translate an impression foreign to the work: others, when they apply themselves to the rendering of the work by another artist, carefully avoided the temptation to be brilliant in their own way, to display skill of the hand — which could only have turned the beholder away from the impression of the original work.

The perfection of the tool, which is to say of the material means of rendering, has begun.

Engraving is in reality translation (see *Translation*), that is to say the art of transporting from one art into another, as the translator does in the case of a book written in one language and which he transports into his own. The foreign language of the engraver, and it is here that genius is shown, does not solely consist of imitating the effects of painting by means of his own art, which is like another language. He has, if one may so speak, his own language; it marks his works with a peculiar stamp and, in a faithful translation of the work he is imitating, allows his special sentiment to shine through.

Color in engraving. To what extent.

Fresco. It would be wrong to suppose that this type of work is more difficult than oil painting because it has to be done at the first go. The fresco painter demands less of himself, materially speaking: he knows also that the spectator will not ask from him any of that finesse which, in the other type of work, is to be obtained only by complicated labors. He makes his plans in such a way that preparatory work abridges the definitive work. He must bring unity into something which is done like a mosaic and even worse than that, since each piece, at the moment when he paints it, is different in tone, etc. How is he to harmonize the one that was painted today with the one that was painted yesterday, if he has not previously established an exact scheme of the ensemble of his picture?[17] That is the office of the cartoon or drawing in which he studies in advance the lines, the effect and the very color that he wants to render. Neither must one take literally what we are told about the marvelous facility with which the fresco painters triumphed over these obstacles. There is hardly a morsel of fresco which satisfied its author so well that he did not have to retouch it. On the most renowned works, retouchings are numerous. And after all, what does it matter whether the work be done with facility? What is important is that it produce all the effect that one has the right to expect. Only, to the disadvantage of fresco, it must be said that these retouchings, made later on with a species of tempera and sometimes even with oil, can, in the course of time, be harmful to the unity of the work, and contribute to a lack of solidity in it.

Fresco turns dull and grows pale, more and more, as time passes. At the end of a century or two, it is difficult to judge what a fresco may have been and what the changes are that time has produced in it. The changes it undergoes take a direction the reverse of those which afflict

[17] Here, a passage struck out by Delacroix: "In mosaic, at least, the fragment that you plant next to another fragment is connected with it by the color of the ensemble; in fresco on the contrary one must strongly exaggerate the tone one lays on in order that the plaster, in drying, shall not grow dull to too great an extent.'

oil paintings. Blackness or an effect of somberness is produced in the latter through the carbonization of the oil, but even more through the dirt of varnishes. Fresco on the contrary, having lime as its base, is subject to a noticeable attenuation of its tints, because of the humidity of the place where it is located. All those who have worked in fresco have noticed that from one day to the other there appeared on the surface of the colors kept in separate jars, a sort of whitish film that looked like a gray veil. This effect, which is more pronounced when it appears over a considerable mass of the same tint, finally appears on the picture itself, veiling it, so to speak, and tending to make it discordant later on; for since this attenuation appears particularly on the colors in which the lime dominates, it follows that those which do not contain so large a proportion of lime remain more brilliant and, by their relative crudity, bring about an effect which was not in the mind of the painter.

We may easily conclude from the drawback just pointed out that fresco is not suitable to our climates, where the air contains a great deal of humidity; as a matter of fact warm climates are hostile to it for another reason, which is perhaps an even more cogent one. One of the great drawbacks to this type of work is the difficulty of making the preparation adhere to the wall (all this must be preceded by a summary explanation of the process of fresco). Along these lines, the great dryness of the south is an enemy impossible to combat. Every fresco tends in time to detach from the wall on which it was applied: that is its most frequent and inevitable end.

The thing is perhaps to be partly remedied, etc. (explain the process of mixing hair with the plaster).

It is not suitable for damp climates.

It is different from that of the ancients. Even the Gothic artists protected it in a better way.

Lay-in. It is difficult to say what was the lay-in of a man like Titian, for example. With him, the touch is so difficult to see, the hand of the workman escapes us so completely, that the paths he took to reach his perfection remain a mystery. There still exist preparations for pictures by him, but they point in different directions: some of them are mere grisaille, other ones are as if built up in big touches with almost raw tones; that was what he called making the bed of the painting. (That is what is particularly lacking in David and his school.) But I do not think that any of the preparations by Titian that remain can put us on the track of the means which he employed to bring them to that always consistent style which is to be noted in his finished works, despite such different points of departure.

The execution of Correggio offers practically the same problem, though what might be called the *ivoried* tint of his pictures with their softness of contrast rather leads one to think that he must almost always have begun with grisaille. (Speak of Prud'hon, and of the school of David. In that school the lay-in does not exist, for one cannot give the name to mere rubbings of color which are no more than a somewhat more completely defined drawing, immediately covered up by the paint.)

Woe to the artist who too quickly finishes certain parts of the lay-in. One must possess very great sureness if one is not to be led to modify those parts when the other parts are finished to the same degree, etc.

Thought. (First thought). The first outlines through which an able master indicates his thought contain the germ of everything significant that the work will offer. Raphael, Rembrandt, Poussin, — I mention these particularly because they are brilliant above all through the quality of thought in their studies — they make a few rapid strokes on the paper, and it seems that there is not one of them but has its importance. For intelligent eyes, the life of the work is already to be seen everywhere, and nothing in the development of this theme, in appearance so vague, will depart in the least from the artist's conception: it has scarcely opened to the light, and already it is complete.

There are accomplished talents which do not present the same vivacity or, more particularly, the same clarity in that matter of the thought's awakening to the light; with these latter, the execution is necessary in order to reach the imagination of the spectator. The presence of the model is indispensable to their progress. It is by another path that they reach one of the perfections of art.

In fact, if you take away from men like Titian, Murillo, or Van Dyck the astounding perfection of their imitation of living nature, if you take away their execution — causing one, as it does, to forget art and the artist, all you find, frequently, in the invention of the subject or in its disposition, is something quite denuded of interest for the mind, but something which the magician will surely know how to elevate by the poetry of his color and the prodigies of his brush. The extraordinary achieving of relief, the harmony of the nuance, the light and air, and all the other marvels of illusion will spread themselves across that theme, of which the sketch, cold and bare, told nothing to the mind.

Imagine what the first thought may have been for the admirable picture of the *Pilgrims at Emmaus*[18] by Paul Veronese: nothing could be more cold than that disposition of the canvas, cooled off even more by the presence of those characters foreign to the scene, the family of donors whose presence there is to be explained only as the most curious coinvention, permitting, as it does, those little girls in brocaded dresses and playing with the dog to be in the most conspicuous place in the picture, and also permitting so many other objects, costumes, architecture, etc. that are opposed to all probabilities!

And now, in Rembrandt, see the sketch[19] for this subject which he has treated several times and with predilection: it is before your own eyes that he flashes the light which dazzles the disciples at the moment when their divine Master is transfigured as He breaks the bread. The stage is empty: there are no importunate witnesses to the miraculous apparition. Deep astonishment, respect, terror are painted

[18] In the Louvre.
[19] He refers to the etching. One of the most celebrated pictures treating this subject is in the Louvre.

in those lines struck by feeling upon that copper, which, to stir you, has no need of the prestige of color.

In the first stroke of the brush that Rubens gives to his sketch, I see Mars or Bellona in their rage; the Furies wave their torch with sinister gleams, peaceful divinities hasten forward in tears to stop them or else flee at their approach; the arts and monuments are destroyed by the fire that has been set. In the barely traced indications of such a scene, it seems as if my mind outstripped my eye and seized the thought almost before it had taken form. Rubens traces with his brush the first idea of his subject, as Raphael or Poussin does with his pen or his pencil.

Repentances.

Transparence.

The Sublime. Notebook of '55, June 28. Effect of the vagueness at night, in the churches of Dieppe and upon the sea; the spectacle offered by a beautiful night.

The Supernatural.

The Terrible. The sensation of *the terrible* and, even more, that of *the horrible* is not to be borne for a long time. It is the same with *the supernatural.* For some days I have been reading a story by Edgar Poe about some shipwrecked people who, for an interval spread out over fifty pages, are in the most horrible and desperate position:[20] nothing could be more of a bore. Here one can recognize the bad taste of foreigners. The English, the Germans, and all the other anti-Latin peoples have no literature[21] because they have no idea of taste and measure. They tire you out even when treating the most interesting situation. Clarisse[22] herself, coming at a time when there was in England a reflection of literary understanding obtained from France, could have

[20] "Descent into the Maelstrom," in the *Strange Tales.*

[21] Recalling Delacroix's many admiring references to Goethe and Shakespeare (as in the paragraph after this one), it is evident that his irritation against "anti-Latin" writers in general is merely a momentary effect, due to Poe's longwinded description.

[22] *Clarissa Harlowe,* by Richardson.

been imagined only on the other side of the Channel. Walter Scott, and Cooper, to a far more exasperating extent, drown you in details which carry off all interest.

The terrible in the arts is a natural gift like that of grace. The artist who is not born to express that sensation and who wants to attempt it is even more ridiculous than the one who attempts lightness despite a lack of it in his nature. I have spoken elsewhere of the figure that Pigalle imagined as a representation of death, in the tomb of the Maréchal de Saxe. There, certainly, *the terrible* was in place. Shakespeare alone could make spirits talk. (1857, November 20.)

(Hunt up another example and add it to what I say of the coldness of the French schools, and of their too timid imitation of nature.)

Michelangelo. Antique masks, etc., Géricault.

The terrible is like the sublime: it is not to be abused.

The Sublime. Is most often due, curiously enough, to disproportion.

In a notebook (1853, May 9), I cite the fact that the Antin oak, seen from a distance, seemed mediocre. Its form is regular; the mass of its foliage is proportionate to the trunk and to the extension of its branches. When I get under the branches themselves, and see only parts, unrelated to the ensemble, I experience the sensation of the sublime. November 20, 1857.

Mozart and Racine appear natural, and astound less that Shakespeare and Michelangelo.

Pre-eminence in the arts. Are there any which are indeed superior? Notebook of '53, May 2). It is about Chenavard's system, resumed by Peisse in an article, that I speak at that date. (See what Cousin says, under *"The good, the beautiful,"* etc.)

Unity. Notebook of '57, March 22. From *Obermann:* "Unity, without which no work can be beautiful, etc.," to which I add that it is man alone who produces works without unity. Nature, on the contrary, etc. She establishes unity even in the parts of a whole.

The vague. Again the same page from *Obermann.* Again the church of Saint-Jacques at Dieppe.

The Model. Notebook of '57, March 5. Enslavement to the model in David. To him I oppose Géricault, who also imitates, but more freely, and brings in more of interest.

Preparation. Everything leads one to think that the preparations of the ancient Flemish schools were uniform. Rubens, in following them, for he changed nothing of the method of his masters in this respect, is in constant agreement with them. The groundwork for the painting was light, and as these schools used panels almost exclusively, it was smooth. The use of sable brushes was preferred to that of bristle brushes until the time of the recent schools. (Explain this difference.)

Effect on the imagination. (*See Interest.*) What Byron says of this. "The poems of Campbell[23] smell too much of the lamp. He is never content with what he has done: he has spoiled his finest productions by trying to finish them too much; all that was brilliant in the first out-burst is lost. What is true of poems is also true of pictures. They should not be too finished: the great art resides in the effect, no matter how it is produced." Notebook of '50, July 18.

"In painting, and especially in portraiture," says Madame Cavé, in her charming treatise,[24] "it is mind that speaks to mind, and not science that speaks to science." That observation, a more profound one than she herself thought it, perhaps, is the arraignment of pedantry in execution. A hundred times I have told myself that painting, from the standpoint of matter, was only a bridge spanning the space between the mind of the painter and that of the spectator. Cold exactitude is not art: ingenious artifice, when it pleases and expresses, is the whole of art. The so-called conscientiousness of the majority of painters is only laborious perfection in the art of boring.

One must be able to content oneself. Here is what Lord Byron says (Notebook of '50, July 18): "Experience is indispensable in teaching us all the advantages that we may derive from our instrument, but above all in permitting us to avoid that which should not be attempted. The immature man is always ready to rush into senseless attempts, as he tries to make art produce more than it can or more than it should; he does not arrive at even a certain degree of superiority within the limits of his possibilities."

(I remember that Decaisne[25] thought one ought to see smoke issuing from the nostrils of horses in order to give them more anima-

---

[23] Thomas Campbell (1776-1844), English poet. This whole passage is borrowed from the work by Captain Medwin, from which Delacroix had made an extract on July 15, 1850.

[24] *Le Dessin sans Maître.* Delacroix wrote an account of it for the *Revue des Deux Mondes* of September 15, 1850.

[25] Henri Decaisne (1799-1852), painter of historical subjects; pupil of David, Gros, and Girodet.

tion. I knew a very mediocre and cold painter who, on looking at the fiery horses of Gros, was not satisfied. He would have liked. . .) One must not forget that language (and I apply this to the language of all the arts) is always imperfect. The great writer makes up for this imperfection by the particular turn that he gives to the daily speech of everybody. Experience and, more especially, confidence in one's strength gives to talent the assurance that it has done all it could do. Only the mad or the impotent torment themselves about attaining the impossible. The superior man knows how to stop: he knows he has done what it is possible to do. Notebook of '50, June 25.

Without boldness and indeed without extreme boldness, there are no beauties. Lord Byron praises gin as his Hippocrene because of the boldness that he drew from it. And so one must almost be outside oneself, *amens,* in order to be all that one can be. A strange phenomenon which scarcely gives us a more favorable idea of our nature or of the opinion due those fine spirits who have sought in the bottle the secret of their talent.

(Add to this passage the part of the *blue book*[26] about the excitations of talent, about the intoxication of hashish, etc.) Happy are those who, like Voltaire and other great men, have been able to reach the state of inspiration while keeping to a simple diet, and water as a drink. (Lord Byron speaks of that Hippocrene. Notebook of '50, July 21.)

Church Music. Lord Byron says that he planned to compose a poem on Job. "But," said he, "I found it too sublime: there is no poetry that one can compare to that." I say the same thing about simple church music, etc.

Architect. Notebook of '50, June 14.

Authority.

Ancients and Moderns. See Thierry s article in the *Moniteur* of March 17, on Sainte Beuve's study of Vergil. Quarrel between simplicity and the modern urge toward other sources of the beautiful.

---

[26] This blue book is lost.

Beautiful. Vague. See *Obermann*, Vol 1, P. 153. See the extract in the notebook for 1857, March 22.

Binding-together. When we cast our eyes on the objects about us, whether in a landscape or an interior, we observe a kind of binding-together of the objects which meet our sight; it is produced by the atmosphere which envelopes them and by the reflections of all kinds which cause each object to participate to a certain extent in a sort of general harmony. The type of charm thus produced is one that painting cannot dispense with apparently; and yet the majority of painters, including great masters indeed, have not always paid proper attention to it. The greater number do not even seem to have observed in nature that essential harmony which establishes in a painting a type of unity which line alone does not suffice to create, despite the most ingenious arrangement. It seems almost superfluous to say that painters having little inclination for effect and for color have not taken it into account at all; but what is more surprising is that with many great colorists this quality is very often neglected, as a result, certainly, of deficient sentiment in this matter.

Michelangelo.[27] One may say that if his style has contributed to the corrupting of taste, the study of Michelangelo has exalted and raised above themselves all the generations of painters, one after another, who have come since his time. Rubens imitated him, but in the way that only he could imitate. He was imbued with sublime works, and he felt himself drawn toward them by what he had within him. What a difference between such imitation and that of the Carracci!

"In order *to succeed* in an art, one must cultivate it throughout the whole one of one's life" (Voltaire, discourse on tragedy, before his *Brutus.*) See the notebook of '50, May 22. After a long sojourn in England, he had grown unaccustomed to his own language; it took him a long time to get back to it; one has such need to keep in training . . . and it is Voltaire who is speaking!

[27] Delacroix had written a study of Michelangelo in the *Revue de Paris,* in 1830.

Painting for churches. Painted ornaments. Notebook of 1850, April 22. What Isabey said to me about it at Notre Dame de Lorette. In the same notebook, toward the end, there are other reflections on the same subject.

Difficulties as to gold backgrounds. Same note.

Monumental painting, as the moderns understand it, that which tolerates no rendering of distance, etc.

From all my notes, save those which apply to the *Dictionary,*[28] it would be well to produce a consecutive work by bringing together similar passages connected by insensible transitions. I must not, therefore, detach them and publish them separately. For example, I could bring together everything referring to the spectacle of nature, etc.

The form of *Dialogues* would permit great freedom; each character would speak for himself; there would be easy transitions, contradictions, etc. Extracts from a correspondence would serve the same purpose. Letters of two friends, one sad, the other gay, the two faces of life. Letters and critical observations.

Notes for a dictionary of the fine arts.

Short preface. . . . See La Rochefoucauld, vague titles. In La Bruyère, on certain judgments, etc.

Notes for a DICTIONARY OF THE FINE ARTS:

Preliminary notice.

The style of *Obermann.* Letters on all sorts of subjects.

Architecture of Christian churches. Article in the *Moniteur,* March 17, 1857, on M. Garnaud's idea of rendering this architecture by the Pyramid.[29]

[28] Paul Flat is surely correct in deciding from the above words that it was in Delacroix's mind to publish his journal, or at least the latter part of it. He observes that in the last years, especially in 1855, many pages which must have contained personal allusions, or judgments that appeared excessively severe, have been torn out, and that many proper names have been scratched out so energetically that it is impossible to read them.

[29] Antoine-Martin Garnaud (1796-1861), architect, had just published a book entitled *Essai sur le Caractère à Donner aux Edifices Religieux du Dix-neuvième Siècle.* It is this work that Delacroix refers to.

Homer. Rubens is more Homeric than certain antiques. He had a similar genius: it is the spirit that is everything. There is nothing Homeric about Ingres, save his pretensions. He makes tracings of externals. Rubens is a Homer, painting the spirit and indifferent to the garment, or rather using the garment of his period. (Tapestries of the *Life of Achilles.*)[30] He is more Homeric than Vergil: the reason is that it was natural for him to be so.

Polished objects. It would seem that by their nature they favor the effect suitable for their rendering because the lights on them are far more vigorous and the dark parts are far darker than is the case with dull objects. They are really mirrors: where they are not touched by a strong light, they reflect the dark parts with extreme intensity. I have said elsewhere[31] that the local color of the object is always to be found to the side of the most brilliant point, and this applies to glistening stuffs, and to the fur of animals, as well as to polished metals.

Sometimes it is almost impossible to tell what the tone of the object is: on an ovoid or on a globe where all the planes recede swiftly under the light, we notice this because there is only one point that faces the light and gets the high-light.

Execution. Good, or rather true execution is the one which, through practice, even when it seems most material, adds to the thought; without such execution, the thought is not complete. It is the same thing with fine verse. It is possible to express fine ideas in a dull way. David's execution is cold; it would chill ideas more elevated and more animated than his own, whereas execution should, on the contrary, enhance the idea and correct the commonplace or feeble elements that it may contain.

Imagination. It is the primary quality among the artist's needs. It is no less necessary for the art lover. I cannot conceive the buying of pictures by a man devoid of imagination: in his case, vanity replaces

[30] See entry in the *Journal* on January 26, 1852.
[31] See note in the *Journal*, under the heading of *light,* in the entry of January 13, 1857.

imagination, and does so to the extent that the latter quality is lacking. Strange as it may seem, the majority of men do lack the quality. Not only do they fail to possess the ardent or penetrating imagination which would cause them to see objects in a vivid manner — which would introduce them to the very cause of things — but they also lack any clear comprehension of works wherein such imagination is dominant.

It is not enough for the sensualists to offer us their maxim: *nil est in intellectu quod non fuerit prius in sensu;* they claim, as a consequence of this principle, that imagination is only a species of memory, but they are compelled to agree that although all men have sensation and memory, very few possess the imagination which, it is claimed, is composed of these two elements. In the artist, imagination does more than picture certain objects to itself: it combines them for the purpose which he seeks to achieve; imagination gives him images with which he composes at will. Where, then, is the acquired experience which can give that faculty of composition?

Impasto. True talent for execution consists of the ability to derive the greatest possible advantage from the material means. Every process has its virtues and its drawbacks: to speak only of oil-painting, which is the process nearest to perfection and most abundant in resources, it is important to study how it has been employed by the various schools and to see what advantage is to be derived from their various styles. But before going into the minutiae of each style one ought to grasp it *a priori.*

The advantages of oil-painting, which the great masters have brought to diverse perfection, are: 1. The intensity which the dark tones preserve at the time of execution, a thing not met with in tempera, nor in fresco, nor in water color, not, in a word, in any form of painting where water as the sole means of dissolving the colors leaves them far below their tone when it evaporates; oil has also the advantage of keeping the colors moist so that they may be blended; 2. The possibility of using, according to the character of the work, either thin passages or heavy impasto, a thing that favors the rendering in an incomparable way through the contrast of opaque and transparent passages; 3. The possibility of returning at will to the painting without its deteriorating; on the contrary, one can increase the vigor of its effect or attenuate the crudity of its tones; 4. The facility which the artist has in handling his brush, due to the fluid state in which the colors remain for a considerable time, etc.

Among the several drawbacks are: the effect of time on the varnishes; the need to wait before one can retouch.

It is necessary to calculate the contrast between impasto and glazing in such a way as to make this contrast felt, even when successive varnishings have produced their effect, which is always to render the picture smooth, etc.

Trees. Manner of painting them and of preparing to paint them.

In notebook (April 29, 1854) I have noted the natural development of this kind of lay-in.

Dust. The tone of dust is the most universal half-tint. As a matter of fact it is a composite of all the tones. The tones of the palette mixed together always give a dust-tone of greater or less intensity.

Interest, interesting. To bring interest into a work is the chief purpose which an artist should propose to himself; it is attained only by the union of many qualities. A subject interesting in itself cannot reach the point of arousing interest when it is treated by an unskilful hand: On the contrary, that which seems least apt to interest does interest and captivate when a learned hand answers to the breath of inspiration.

A kind of instinct allows the superior artist to penetrate the secret of the principal interest of his composition. The art of grouping, the art of appropriate lighting, of coloring with vivacity or sobriety, the art of sacrificing or of multiplying the means of effect, and a host of other qualities are necessary to the great artist in his exciting of interest, and to this result each contributes according to its own nature; exact truth or exaggeration in the matter of character, multiplicity or sobriety of details, the uniting of the masses or their dispersal, in a word, all these resources of art are like the keys of a piano, under the hand of the artist, as he draws certain tones from them while he allows others to sleep.

The principal source of interest comes from the soul, and it goes to the soul of the spectator in irresistible fashion: not that every interesting work strikes all spectators equally, because each one of them must have a soul of his own; only the person endowed with sensibility and imagination is to be stirred. These two faculties are indispensable to the spectator, as to the artist, though in different measure.

Mannered talents cannot awaken real interest: they can excite curiosity, flatter a momentary taste, or address themselves to passions that have nothing in common with art; but as the chief characteristic of mannerism is lack of sincerity, in the sentiment as in the imitation, they cannot strike the imagination, which is, with us, only a sort of mirror in which nature as it is stands reflected, in order to give us, by a powerful type of memory, the spectacle of things which the soul alone enjoys.

It is the masters, almost exclusively, who excite interest, but they do it by different means, according to the particular inclination of their genius. It would be absurd to ask of a Rubens the species of interest which a Leonardo or a Raphael knows how to excite by details like hands and heads in which correctness is united with expression. It is just as useless to ask of the latter painters those effects of the ensemble, that verve and that breadth which recommend the works of the most brilliant of painters. Rembrandt's *Tobias* [32] does not recommend itself by the same qualities as do the pictures of Titian, in which the perfection of the details is far from being hurtful to the beauty of the ensemble, even though the details do not carry into the imagination that emotion, indeed that trouble, which the naiveté and the vigor of the characters, the singularity and the depth of certain effects, cause the soul to feel in the presence of a work by Rembrandt.

[32] *The Angel Leaving Tobias,* in the Louvre.

David explained merit as a faithful copying of one's model, though this was to be amended by the aid of bits of the antique which should relieve its commonness, Correggio, on the contrary never glanced at nature save to prevent himself from falling into the monstrous. All his charm, everything in him that spells power and the effort of genius, issued from his imagination and awakened echos of it in imaginations fitted to comprehend him.

The schools see perfection in only one sort of merit at a given time. They condemn everything that the teachers then in fashion have condemned. Today drawing is in fashion, and again just a single type of drawing. David's drawing, as represented in the school which issued from him, is no longer true drawing.

Eclecticism in the arts. This pedantic word, introduced into the language by the philosophers of the present century, applies pretty well to the moderated purposes of certain schools. One might say that *eclecticism* is the French banner par excellence in the arts of design and in music. The Germans and the Italians, in their arts, have had clear-cut qualities among which certain ones are frequently hostile to others: The French seem always to have sought to reconcile these extremes by attenuating what appeared discordant among them. And so their works are less striking. They are addressed to the mind more than to feeling. In music, and in painting, they stand behind all the other schools, their works offering in small doses a compendium of qualities which exclude one another in other schools, but which the French temperament finds a way of allying.

Feeling. Feeling works miracles. Through it an engraving or a lithograph produces the effect on the imagination of the painting itself. In this grenadier by Charlet, I see the tone in every mark of the pencil: in a word I desire nothing more than what I see. It almost seems to me that coloration, painting would disturb me, and injure the effect of the ensemble.

Feeling is the intelligent touch that summarizes and gives the equivalent.

Masterpieces. As to the masterpiece, see the notebook for 1856, Feb. 21.

Actor. Diderot maintains that. . . .

Tragedy.

Originality. Does it consist in priority of invention as to certain ideas, certain striking effects?

School. Producing a school. Some mediocre men, or at best secondary men, have been able to *produce a school,* whereas some very great men have not had that advantage, if it is one. Eighty years ago, it was men like Vanloo who awarded the Prix de Rome, and whose style ruled in sovereign fashion. At this moment there arose a talent which had drunk from their principles and which was to become illustrious through entirely different principles. David, it may be said, is the renewer of art: but the credit for that is not to be found solely in his originality. Several attempts had been made: that of Mengs, and others. The discovery of the paintings of Herculaneum had urged many a mind to turn to the imitation and the admiration of the Antique. David, more vigorous than inventive in his mind, more partisan than artistic, imbued with modern ideas which were everywhere bursting forth in politics and which led to the exclusive admiration of the ancients, especially in political matters, summarized for the arts and . . . the enervated and artificial style of the Vanloo men had had its day. It was no more than mannerism, it was completely empty of ideas, etc.

A hundred and sixty years before, a far more original genius than that of David, unfolding at the moment when the school of Lebrun was in full force, did not have the same luck. All the genius of Puget, all his verve, all his strength, which had its source in inspiration from nature, could not produce a school (find a following) when faced with men like Coysevox and Coustou and all the rest of that school, in itself entitled to great consideration, but already marked by mannerism and the academic spirit.

Refining. As to the refining which takes place during the periods of decadence, notebook of 1856, April 9 and April 16.

Execution. The unhappy thing about David's pictures and those of his school is that they lack this precious quality, without which the rest is imperfect and almost useless. One can admire great drawing in them, sometimes a fine ordering of the work, as in Gérard; largeness, fire, or pathos, as in Girodet; true artistic taste in David himself, in the *Sabines* for example: but the charm which the worker's hand adds to all these merits is absent from their works, and that places them below those of the great masters whom time has consecrated. Prud'hon is the only painter of that period whose execution rises to equality with his idea and who pleases by that side of the artist's talent which people call material, but which is wholly a matter of feeling, whatever they say, wholly a matter of ideal, like the conception itself, which it should necessarily complete. In Davidian painting, the epidermis is everywhere lacking (December 15, 1857.)

The modern style (in literature). The modern style is bad. Abuse of sentiment, of the picturesque, on every occasion. If an admiral is telling the story of naval campaigns, he does it in the style of a novelist and almost of a humanitarian.[33] Everything is long-drawn out, everything is poetized. The writer wants to appear touched and penetrated by feeling, and mistakenly believes that his perpetual dithyrambics will win over the mind of the reader and give him a great idea of the author, especially as to the goodness of his heart. Memoirs and even history — detestable. Philosophy, the sciences, and everything written about these various subjects bear the imprint of this false color, of this borrowed style. I regret it for our contemporaries; in the things they will leave, above all in the portraits of themselves that they will have done, posterity will not seek its models of sincerity. Not even the admirable history by Thiers escapes the imprint of this lachrymose

[33] Sentimentality, for Delacroix, is a great defect, but *humanitarianism*, for him, is the worst of all. Witness poor George Sand, whom he adored as a woman and as a friend, but whose *humanitarian* ideas were unbearable to him.

style, which is always ready to pause midway for a sigh over the ambition of conquerors, over the rigor of the seasons, or over human sufferings. We get sermons or elegies. Nothing masculine[34]. . . to produce an effect which might merit a word no stronger than decorous, the reason being that nothing is in its place or else takes up too much space and is declaimed as if by a pedagogue, instead of being related in simple fashion.

Authorities. "The ruin of great talents, and almost the whole of the talent of mediocrities, etc. They are the leading-strings which help nearly everybody to walk, but on almost everybody they leave ineffaceable marks." Notebook of '53, Oct. 10.

Model. As to the use of the model. Notebook of '56, Oct. 13 and Oct. 4. See also Oct. 17.

Opera. As to the meeting of the various arts in this type of entertainment, as to the pleasure resulting from this meeting, and also as to the fatigue which must come over the spectator more quickly because of this superabundance of impression, see the blank book of Augerville, 1854.[35] In it I write also of sonority, which Chopin would not admit as a legitimate source of sensation.

Execution. We have said that good execution was of the greatest importance. One would go so far as to say that, if it is not everything, it is the one means for bringing the rest into the light and giving it its value. The schools of decadent periods have seen it above all as a matter of manual dexterity, as a certain dashing manner of expression, with what has been called frankness, fine brushwork, etc.

It is certain that after the great masters of the sixteenth century, there is a change in the material execution of painters. Studio painting, a kind of painting done at the first go, to which it is very difficult to return, is the successor of the execution which was a matter of sentiment and which each master carried out for himself, or rather which his instinct inspired in him according to the need of his genius.

[34] Three illegible words.
[35] This blank book has disappeared.

Certainly a Titian is not to be made with the means employed by a Rubens, etc. Stippling, etc. The Raphael that I saw in the Rue Grange-Batelière was done with small brush strokes. . . . A painter of the school of the Carracci would have thought himself dishonored if he had painted in such minute fashion. And with even stronger reason, those of the more recent and corrupt schools of the Vanloo type.

French style. As to the coldness of the French style: on that correctness, even in the great schools, like that of Louis XIV, which chill the imagination even while satisfying the mind. Notebook of '55, March 23. It is a singular thing that down to the school of Lebrun, of Poussin, etc., out of which came men like Coysevox, Coustou and the others, French sculpture unites fancy with fine execution and rivals the Italian schools in the grand style. M. de Brézé,[36] Germain Pilon, Jean Goujon. *The lay-in.* Notebook of '55, April 2.[37]

Color. On its superiority — or its exquisiteness, if you prefer — from the standpoint of the effect on the imagination. As to color in the work of Lesueur. Notebook of '51, June 6.

Oppositions. Granet said that painting consisted of putting white on black and black on white.

Artist.

Imitation. The term arts of imitation, is applied more particularly to painting and sculpture; the other arts, like music and poetry, do not imitate nature directly, although their purpose is to strike the imagination through the [feelings].[38]

As to the Antique and the Dutch schools. It will doubtless appear surprising that, under one heading, there should be a meeting of productions in appearance so diverse, diverse in time, but less diverse than is believed, if one considers the style and the spirit in which they were conceived.

[36] The tomb of Louis de Brézé (1536-1541) at the Cathedral of Rouen, one of the masterpieces of the Renaisssance.
[37] The page of this date has been torn out.
[38] The word *feelings* has been crossed out.

Antique. Whence comes that special quality, that perfect taste, which is found in the Antique alone? Perhaps from the fact that we compare with it everything that has been done with an idea of imitating it.

But again, what can one compare with it among the most perfect things that have been produced in the most diverse styles?

I do not see the least thing lacking in Vergil or Horace. I see well what I should like to find in our greatest writers, and also what I should prefer not to find in them. Perhaps it is also that, finding myself in what I shall venture to call a common civilization, as regards the latter men, I see more to the depths of them, I understand them better; above all, I see more clearly the discord between what they have done and what they have wanted to do. A Roman might have shown me in Horace and in Vergil blemishes or faults that I can not see in them.

But it is above all in everything that remains to us of the plastic arts of the ancients that this quality of taste and of perfect measure is found to the highest point of perfection. We can sustain comparison with them in literature; in the arts, never.

Titian is one of those who most approach the spirit of the Antique. He is of the family of the Dutchmen and, consequently, of the Antique. He knows how to work from nature: that is the thing in his pictures which recalls a type that is true, and consequently, a type that does not pass away, like that which issues from the imagination of a man who, having imitators of his manner, more quickly brings about a distaste for it.

One would say that there is a grain of madness in all the others; Titian alone has good sense, is master of himself, of his execution, and of his facility, which never dominates him and which he never parades.

We think to imitate the Antique, and therefore take it literally, so to speak, making our caricature of its draperies, etc.

Titian and the Flemings have the spirit of the Antique and not the imitation of its external forms.

The Antique does not sacrifice to grace, like Raphael, Correggio, and the Renaissance in general; it has no affectation, either of force or of the unforeseen, as in Michelangelo. It never descends to the low quality in certain parts of Puget's works, nor his too natural naturalness, etc.

In the work of all those men there are elements which go out of style; in the Antique there is nothing of that. With the moderns, there is always excess; with the Antique, always the same sobriety and the same contained strength.

Those who see in Titian only the greatest of the colorists are in grave error: he is so indeed, but he is at the same time the first of draftsmen, if one understand by drawing that which is in nature, and not the kind wherein the imagination of the painter is more important than the imitation of what we see. Not that Titian's imagination is servile: all one needs do is to compare his drawing with that of the painters who have applied themselves to render nature exactly, for example in the Bolognese or the Spanish school.

One may say that with the Italians style assumes more importance than anything else: by that I do not mean that all the Italian artists have a great style or even an agreeable style; I mean that they are inclined, each one of them, to abound in what one may call *their style,* whether one likes it or not: I mean by that that Michelangelo makes an abuse of his style, as much as does Bernini or Pietro da Cortona, keeping in mind with each one the elevation or the vulgarity of the style he uses, in a word, their special manner. What they think to add or unconsciously add to nature takes them away from any idea of imitation, and is harmful to the truth and to the naturalness of the expression. That precious naturalness is rarely to be found among the Italians from the time of Titian onward; Titian himself, however, preserves it amidst the overpowering temptation toward mannerism to be noted among his contemporaries, a mannerism which aims more or less at the sublime, but which the imitators very soon turn into the ridiculous.

There is another man to be mentioned here and placed on the same line as Titian, if one regards truth united with the ideal as the first of qualities: it is Paul Veronese. He is freer than Titian, but he is less finished. Both have that tranquillity, that calm temperament which indicates minds in possession of themselves. Paul seems more learned, less attached to the model, and therefore more independent in his execution. In exchange, the scruples of Titian have nothing about them which would incline to coldness: I speak especially about coldness in execution, for his own, on the contrary, suffices to give warmth to the picture; in the matter of expression, the one man and the other are less interested than the majority of the great masters. The rare quality possessed by both of these Venetians — animated composure if I may so express it — doubtless excludes the effects tending toward emotion. Here again are traits which they have in common with the Antique, in which the external plastic form takes precedence over expression. It is by the introduction of Christianity that people explain the singular revolution which, during the Middle Ages, takes place in the arts of design and brings about the predominance of expression. Christian mysticism, which hovered over everything, and the artists' custom of representing, almost exclusively, religious subjects which speak to the soul above all, unquestionably favored this general tendency toward expression. The necessary result for the modern periods was a greater degree of imperfection in the plastic qualities. The ancients do not show the exaggerations or lapses from correctness which are to be seen in men like Michelangelo, Puget, and Correggio; on the other hand, the fine calm of those beautiful figures does not awaken that side of the imagination which the moderns touch at so many points. That somber turbulence of Michelangelo, that indefinable quality of the mysterious and the aggrandized which lends its passion to his slightest work; that soft and penetrating grace, that irresistible attraction of Correggio, the profound expressiveness and the fire of Rubens, the vagueness, the magic, and the expressive drawing of Rembrandt, all that is of ourselves, and stands outside of everything conceived by the ancients.

Rossini is a striking example of the passion for pleasing, for exaggerated grace — and so the school he formed is unbearable!

February 4.

The following may form part of the preface to the DICTIONARY.

I should like to contribute to the teaching of a better way to read in the great works. In Athens, it is said, the number of judges of the Fine Arts was far larger than in our modern society. The greatness of taste so evident in the works of Antiquity confirms one in this opinion.

In Rome as in Athens, the same man was a lawyer, a warrior, a pontiff, an edile, an inspector of public games, a senator, and a magistrate. He had given himself the education belonging to each of these activities. Such a man could scarcely be a mediocre appreciator of knowledge along all lines pursued at the time. Among us a notary is only a notary and is acquainted with no more than the things of his office: do not speak to a cavalry colonel about judging pictures: at most he will have a knowledge of horses, and he will greatly regret that the horses of Rubens do not resemble English horses or those of the Limousin, such as he sees every day in his regiment or at the races.

It results from the above that the artist who works for an intelligent public blushes to descend to means of getting effects which taste would rebuke. Such taste perished among the ancients, not as a fashion changes — something which happens constantly among us and for no reason that could be called really necessary; taste perished among the ancients with their institutions and their customs, when they had to please barbarian conquerors such, for example, as the Romans were for the Greeks; above all, taste was corrupted when citizens no longer responded to the spring which moves men to great actions, when public virtue disappeared; and by that I do not mean virtue common to all citizens and inspiring men to do what is good, but at least that simple respect for morality which forces vice to conceal itself. It is difficult to imagine men like Phidias and Apelles governed by the frightful tyrants of the Late Empire, and amidst the degradation of soul which appears when the arts become willing accomplices of infamy. The reign of spies and scoundrels could not be that of the beautiful and, even less, that of the true. If these inestimable treasures are still to be found anywhere, it is in the noble protests of a Seneca or a Tacitus. Light graces and soft description make way for indignation and stoical resignation in their writings.

Are we to deduce a necessary connection between the *good* and the *beautiful?* Can a degraded society take pleasure in elevated things, of whatever type they may be? Probably not; and so, in the present state of our societies, with our narrow conception of manners and our mean little pleasures, the beautiful can be only an accident, and that accident does not play a role sufficiently important to change taste and bring the generality of minds to the beautiful. Afterward comes night and barbarism.

And therefore, incontestably, there are periods when the beautiful seems to flower more naturally: also there are nations which are priviledged as regards certain gifts of the mind, as there are countries and climates which favor the spread of the beautiful. The happy countries where nature . . . there is more leisure, etc. I will agree without difficulty that the Siberian. . . .[39]

Tuesday, February 17.

Fifth visit from the doctor.[40]

February 25.

Casanova[41] says somewhere:

"The gentle delights of peace are preferable by far to the charms of love: but one does not think so when one is enamored."

[39] These reflections will be utilized by Delacroix in his article on "The Beautiful" in the *Revue des Deux Mondes* for July 15, 1857.

[40] Doctor Rayer, consulting physician of the Emperor's household, was at the time tending Delacroix, who had been ill for two months.

[41] Delacroix, forced by his illness to keep to his room for two months, varies his occupations by reading a great deal and by making extracts from the books he read. He always had a great admiration for Casanova, whose experiences with women interested him very much.

"The work of getting my apartment finished[42] and the work of getting furniture for it use up my whole time: I am as completely surrounded by workmen as was Mme de Bernières. All this has had some effect on my miserable health. Yesterday I saw your brother who has at least spared me the embarrassment of choosing the stuffs for my new clothing and he took a load off my mind in doing so, for I am worth nothing at all in matters of detail." (Lettres Inédites de Voltaire.)

Vauvenard says of Voltaire:

"A rather curious thing, to which I can surely certify, is that, despite the homage he received, and the flattering things written or said to him, his modesty was extreme and sincere. Perhaps it is to his conviction in this matter that literature owes a large part of the works that he composed: he always worked as if he had to begin his reputation." (I think that there is really no great talent that is not of this disposition.) [43]

Thursday, March 5.

Today, while I was at lunch, two pictures attributed to Géricault were brought to me for my opinion. The small one is a very mediocre copy: costume of Roman beggars. The other, a No. 12 canvas, approximately (a study for an amphitheatre picture: arms, feet, etc., with cadavers), has a strength, a rendering of relief, that is admirable, with negligences which belong to the author's style, and add even more to its value.

Placed next to the portrait by David,[44] this painting takes on an even greater accent. Through it one sees everything that David always lacked, that power of the picturesque, that vigor, that daring which is to painting what the *vis comica* is to the art of the theater. Everything is even; there is no more interest in the head than in the draperies or the chair.

[42] Delacroix had for a long time been thinking of moving to a new apartment (it will be number six, Rue de Furstenberg); he applies Voltaire's reflections to his own case.

[43] Delacroix's own reflection on this passage.

[44] The portrait of his sister, Henriette de Verninac, by David, which Delacroix owned at the time.

His complete enslavement to that which the model offered to his eyes is one of the causes of this coldness: but it is more exact to think that this coldness was in himself: it was impossible for him to find anything outside the limit offered him by the imperfect means of the little piece of nature which he had under his eyes, and it seems as though he was satisfied when he had imitated it well: his whole audacity consisted in placing side by side fragments modeled on the Antique, such as a foot and an arm, and in bringing his living model as much as possible to that type of the beautiful, ready to hand, which the plaster cast offered him.

This fragment from Géricault is truly sublime: it proves more than ever that *there is no serpent nor odious monster,* etc. It is the best argument in favor of the Beautiful, as it should be understood. The lapses from correctness do not in the least take away from the beauty of this piece of painting: alongside the foot which is very precise and has more resemblance to nature (save that it is influenced by the personal ideal of the painter), there is a hand in which the planes are soft and as if done without consulting the model, as was the case, indeed, with figures that he used to do in the studio; and that hand does not take away from the beauty of the rest: it is raised by the power of style to the level of the other parts. This type of merit has the greatest relationship with that of Michelangelo, with whom incorrectitudes do no harm whatsoever.

I am reading with the greatest pleasure, in my notebook of 1852, for the month of January, what I say of the Rubens tapestries which at the time I saw at Mousseaux and which were sold by order of the civil list of Louis Philippe. When ever I want to speak of Rubens, or get myself to the right warmth for painting, I must re-read those notes. I still have a very vivid recollection of those admirable works. The idea came to me, on re-reading what I said of them, that I should do all the subjects over from memory (a series of the kind based on a different subject would be a fine theme). Devéria must absolutely get me the engravings of those subjects.

I note here what is to be entered under date of a day last month, when I was very weak and could not devote myself much to writing in this book: I refer to the unhappy impression which I received from the description of Thiers's character made to me by M. C. B.,[45] who came to pay me a little visit. He represented Thiers to me as the most selfish and insensitive of men, one whose interest centers on money, in a word the contrary of what I believed: a man quite incapable of affection. If I came to be convinced of all that, it would be one of the greatest disappointments that have ever fallen to my lot. Gratitude, in the first place, and the affection that I have always had for him, are feelings which fight in his favor. I know that although he always receives me affectionately he has never sought me out: his petty rancor, when I opposed him, as was my duty, in the matter of his senseless project to restore the Museum, executed in part according to his absurd ideas, spoiled him for me a little bit at the time of that adventure:[46] but since then I have again found him as he used to be, which is to say, full of that attractiveness which has always drawn me toward him.

To C. B. I said how sorry I was that Thiers had to live in such a household as he has made for himself, spending his life with such cold, insipid creatures. All that, according to C. B., makes absolutely no difference: he cares for no one and all he feels is what touches him directly in his person or in his self-love.

Monday, March 16.

Nowadays it is demanded that a writer be universal. The distinction between the savant and the poet or novelist is completely abolished. The slightest novel demands more erudition than a scientific treatise — what do I say? than twenty treatises, for a savant is either a chemist, or an astronomer, or a geographer, or an antiquarian. He may have a

[45] Probably Charles Blanc, who had been out of the directorship of the Beaux-Arts since 1852.

[46] See the entry for February 11, 1849. The question referred to was that of the big changes in the Louvre which were made in that year.

certain tinge of the learning related with that which he has made the occupation of his lifetime: but the more he concentrates on that special study, the more results he obtains in his research. It is not the same thing in the profession of the critic. The necessity for speaking about everything lays upon him the obligation to know everything; but who can know everything?

> *Si j'apprenais l'hébreu, les sciences, l'histoire.*
> *Tout cela, c'est la mer à boire.*

And so they don't learn all that; but they've got to look a bit as if they had done so.

I am terrified at the various books, digested or not, that can pass under the eyes of a man like Sainte-Beuve for example. Here he comes along today with an article on Livy: he tells the story of Livy's life, a matter that is but little known, and one about which his readers had never embarrassed themselves.

In an article, always too long, on Vergil, Thierry, of the *Moniteur,* speaks of the preference of our century for first hand works, those of primitives, etc, like Homer, and asks if Vergil could have produced an *Iliad,* had he come thirty or forty centuries afterward; he adds:

"If the ancients are our masters for all time, let us not for that reason disdain those of their followers who strive, however vainly, to become their equals. It is a great advantage to be the first on the scene: one gets the best things without even having to choose; one may be simple without even knowing what simplicity is; one is brief because one has no need to pad, or to exceed the pace of any other person; one stops in good time because there is no emulation urging one to go beyond that point. . . . Is it not frequently the absence of art that people imagine to be the culmination of art? If the development of art merely brings it to the point of producing artists of always smaller stature, I may be pardoned for feeling deep compassion over the periods which cannot exist without the complicated labors of art. I demand that we be not too much the dupes of a certain big word: simplicity, and that we do not make of simplicity the rule for periods when it is no longer possible."

That is the theme of all the pedants we have today. Chenavard is blind to everything that is not of the past. Delaroche used to bristle when people spoke of the Roman antique: Phidias above everything, just as, for Chenavard, it was Michelangelo above everything. And yet he puts Rubens in his famous Heptarchy.[47] He admires Rubens, and he uses him to crush to earth the hapless efforts of the men of our time. And yet Rubens appeared in a period of relative decadence: how can it be that, in such a system, we find him placed on the level of Michelangelo? He was great in a different way.

That simplicity which is exalted nowadays, and of which Thierry speaks often derives, in literature, from the rudeness of speech which

[47] The Heptarchy, or group of the seven great artists, the only great ones who ever existed, was, as previously noted, composed of Leonardo da Vinci, Michelangelo, Raphael, Titian, Correggio, Rubens and Rembrandt.

strikes us in primitive poetry: in a word, it is more a question of the clothing of thought than of the thought itself. Many people, especially at the present time, when it is imagined that language can be tempered anew and rejuvenated at will as a man shaves off a beard that has grown too long—many people, as I was saying, prefer Corneille to Racine merely because the former's language is less polished than the latter's. So it is for Michelangelo and Rubens: the technique of fresco, which was that of Michelangelo, forces the painter to a greater simplicity of means and of effect; the result it yields, independently even of the artist's talent — simply by reason of the material employed — is a certain grandeur, a necessity to renounce details. Rubens, with a different process, discovers different effects, which satisfy us for other reasons. Montesquieu well says: *Two beauties of ordinary value annul each other, two great beauties enhance each other.* A masterpiece by Rubens hanging beside a masterpiece by Michelangelo will not pale in the slightest. If, on the other hand, you study each of these works separately, what will doubtless happen is that, in the measure that you are impressionable, you will be possessed by the one you are looking at. A sensitive nature is easily seized and swept along by the beautiful: you will be completely within the grasp of that one of its expressions which is under your eye at the moment.

It is necessary to use the means familiar in the time when you are living, otherwise you will not be understood and you will not live. That instrument of another age that you want to employ in order to speak to the men of your time will always be an affected instrument, and the public of a later time, comparing that borrowed manner with the works of the period when it was the only manner known and understood — and therefore used with full effect — will condemn you to inferiority, and you will have already pronounced the condemnation yourself.

Chateaubriand was the father of a school.

As to the fact that Homer and the Bible are considered to possess very great beauty and that this beauty is more rarefied in Homer and Vergil.

I conclude with that quotation from Thierry about Vergil, which defines what I understand as the beautiful in modern art.

Wednesday, March 18.

Now it is three days since I started to go out, and it is doing me a great deal of good. Yesterday I had a drive to the Tuileries with Jenny. We went from the swing-bridge[48] as far as the gate of the Rue de Rivoli.

I must remember the ideas suggested to me by the contrast between the statues of the *Tiber* and the *Nile,* copies after the antique, and the groups of flowers and of nymphs of the time of Louis XIV. The ill-woven quality of the latter and the majestic unity of the former. Everywhere the same observation as to what was antique and as to what is modern.

I cannot tear myself away from Casanova.

Sunday, March 22.

In *Obermann,* I find the following on the beautiful:

"Regularity, proportion, symmetry, simplicity, according as one or another of these qualities is found to be more or less essential to the nature of the whole composed by these relationships. This whole is *unity,* without which there is no result, nor any work which can possess beauty, because, in such a case, there is not even what may be called a work. . . . A thing without ensemble is not beautiful; it is not a thing, but an assemblage of things, etc."

And I add, for later consideration: it is man alone who produces things that lack unity. Nature finds out the secret of bringing unity even into the parts detached from a whole. The branch detached from a tree is a little tree in itself.

Thursday, March 26.

I called today on Haro to go over the possibilities of making a studio

[48] At the entrance to the Tuileries, facing the Place de la Concorde.

of his place. He talked to me about the too considerable expense involved; the matter is not practical. On my way there, the sight of some young men whom I met in the street caused me to make various reflections of a different nature from those ordinarily made by old men. That age, which seems like the happiest one of a lifetime, does not excite my envy in the least; the only way it could do so would be by the strength one has at the time, for that offers the means of coping with great works; but I do not envy it at all for the pleasures which are its accompaniment. What I should desire — and it is a wish that is of course as impossible of realization as the thought of returning to youth — what I should desire would be to stop at the point where I am and there have a prolonged enjoyment of the advantages gained by a mind which I shall not call disabused, but genuinely reasonable. But the one thing is no more permitted than the other.

At Weill's Gallery, where I stopped for a moment, I just heard that poor Margueritte has died suddenly. Although older than I, he was still of an age to enjoy many things. Moreover, as I think he was not a man of distinguished nature, he may have been one of those who regret the pleasures of young men. The delights of the mind must needs hold a place of importance if they are to procure that calm happiness which I look to for a man who is arriving at the decline of life.

Just at this moment I come upon the following paragraph in *Casanova*, expressing sentiments very different from my own. It is during his trip to Holland. He recalls the caresses given him by the fair Esther.

"The happy days! When I recall them — and I love so well to let my thought return to them, despite the villainous old age that has rendered me so unfit for love — when I recall them, I feel myself grow young again and my existence resumes all the charms of youth, despite the reality which casts me so far from it."

Saturday, April 18.

Subjects for a library:

Augustus opposes the destruction of the Aeneid.

The Coronation of Petrarch or of Tasso.

The Sibyl proposing the volumes to Tarquinius and causing each one to be burned upon his refusal of it.

I must recall the *Life of Achilles* by Rubens.

April 22.

"I have just come by chance on a passage in Montaigne that is so similar in idea to what was occupying my mind that I have been struck and contented by it. In this conformity of thoughts there is a principle of secret joy: it is the one that renders man necessary to man, because it renders our ideas fruitful, *because it lends assurance to our imagination and confirms in us our opinion of what we are.*" (Senancour, *Obermann.*)

As to this passage, which has struck me, I want to add: this assurance which we are happy to give to our imagination is a need among all who work in the arts, especially when their inspiration is naive and sincere. I imagine that the painters or writers in whose work commonplaces are frequent have less need for that confirmation which, through the meeting with minds similar to their own, reassures them as to the value of their own thoughts. This is an imperious need for those whose inventions are accused of being bizarre, perhaps because of their originality, and who thus find the public stubborn and but little disposed to understand them.

"Memory of years past, things forever obliterated, places that one will see no more, men who have changed! The feeling of lost life ! What places were for me the thing they are for other men." (*Obermann.*)

April 25.

"Jacob divided into two troops his servitors, his sheep, his oxen and his camels. Thirty camels with their young were part of the presents sent to his brother in the hope of softening his heart." [49]

[49] The version of the Biblical story here referred to is not stated; it gives part of the scene which Delacroix represents in his mural of *Jacob Wrestling with the Angel,* at Saint-Sulpice.

May 3.

Expenses for my new lodging,[50] in July:
    One bas-relief: metope, with shipping   17 frs.
    Bas-relief of the Muses, and delivery   62.50
    Shipping for the two upright bas-reliefs   3.50

Champrosay, May 9.

Departed for Champrosay at quarter past one. Terrible rain as we were getting to the house; I was drenched, as was Jenny. We had stopped for a few moments, previously, at our old garden, now all torn up and ravaged because of the work that Candas is doing. I saw the little spring, which is now used only for washing clothes: the whole thing soiled with soap, and stagnant. The cherry trees that I set out when they were very small have grown to be enormous. One can still see the trace of the paths which I laid out. That gave me emotions more sweet than sad. I recalled the years that I had spent there. I still love this country; I attach myself easily to the places where I live: my mind and even my heart animate them.

May 10.

Day of idleness. Dined early. Went into the forest, which is to say in the opposite direction from Bayvet's path, to get back to the road. My poor Jenny is in very bad health.

May 11.

Took quite a long walk in the country, during the morning, and could not take my eyes off the verdure and the sunshine.

Returning home, worked a great deal on the article on "The Beautiful"[51] until dinner time.

In the evening, walked in the garden and in the country.

Weariness and sense of oppression before going to bed.

[50] 6 Rue de Furstenberg. Delacroix decorated his new studio with Greek bas-reliefs.
[51] The article, entitled "As to the Variations of the Beautiful" was to appear on July 15, 1857, in the *Revue des Deux Mondes*.

It is neither chance nor caprice which has determined the style of architecture and thereby the style of the other arts of the different lands; new proof that the Beautiful must vary according to climate.

With the severe, so to speak radical, style of Egyptian architecture, rather simple and elementary ornament and painting ally them-selves. . . . In that vast valley of Egypt, uniformly bounded by two almost symmetrical ranges, etc. Pylons, pyramids. . . .[52]

May 12.

Another morning walk. Seated under a charming bush in Bayvet's woods. The little white dog. Returned. Slept; at about half past one, took up the article again and worked till after four o'clock. I have almost finished. I have found in a rhapsody called *The Tribune of the Artists* a wretched decoction of 1849, a passage which I have just used, the one where I quote Texier, the traveler, as to the different materials which the ancients used in their buildings.

One ought always to have one's pen in hand when reading. There isn't a day when I don't find something interesting to note down, even from the worst newspaper.

I am getting great enjoyment from this charming place. In the morning it is with inexpressible pleasure that I open my window.

May 14.

I do not doubt but that if Alexander had known *Le Misanthrope,* he would have placed it in the famous casket alongside the *Iliad;* he would have had the casket enlarged in order to contain the *Misanthrope.*

People say of a man, in praising him, that he is a *unique* man.

Vain discussions and vain comparisons should be left to people who feel things weakly.

[52] These notes and those in subsequent passages will be used in the article on "The Beautiful."

Happy the periods which have seen, happy the artists who have found a public well prepared, encouraging *the efforts of the Muse.*

The real primitives are the men of original talent. If every man of talent bears within him a particular model, a new aspect, what is the value of a school which always brings back ancient types, since these types themselves were merely the expression of individual natures!

And does each one of these men please me in the same way ? Would not this simple observation condemn the school which recurs endlessly to consecrated types? In what respect are they more consecrated than others, since they are only the expression of individual natures such as appear at all periods?

Rossini said to B——: "I get glimpses of something different, which I shall not do. If I found a young man of genius, I could start him on a totally new path, and poor Rossini would be pretty well knocked out."

May 15. At Champrosay, in the green lane. One may compare the first version of the writer's or painter's work with platoon firing, where two hundred musket shots fired in the excitement of combat strike the enemy two or three times; sometimes two or three hundred shots are fired at the same moment, and not one of them hits the enemy.

You invite your friends to a banquet, and you serve them all the leavings of the kitchen.

In the Lane of the Ferns.

Sometimes similar geniuses appear at different periods. Originality of temper does not differ at all among these men of talent: it is only the forms of the time when they live that establish variety. Rubens, etc.

It is by no means the climate that produced a Homer or a Praxiteles. Go through Greece and its islands and you will not discover a poet or a sculptor. On the other hand, nature brought to birth in Flanders, and at a period near to our own, the Homer of painting.

There are privileged epochs; there are also climates where man has fewer needs, etc; but those influences do not suffice. Notebook of '57, Feb. 4.

The influence of customs is of more effect than that of climate. Doubtless among peoples with whom nature is clement; . . . but in the absence of a certain moral value, etc. A people must have self-respect if it is to be exigent in the matter of taste and if it is to hold in check its orators and its poets. The nations that deal with politics in terms of the fist or the pistol have no more literature than those devoted to gladiatorial combat.

May 16.

Jenny has gone to Paris. Seated under the big chestnut tree that was transplanted from the Hermitage.

That dear, gentle Chopin used always to get indignant against the school which attributes part of the charm of music to sonority. He spoke as a pianist.

Voltaire defines the *beautiful* as that which should charm mind and sense. A motif in music may speak to the imagination through an instrument which has but one way of pleasing the senses, but the combination of various instruments possessing different sonorities will give more power to the sensation. Otherwise what would be the use of employing now the flute, now the trumpet? The first will be associated with a tryst of two lovers, the second with a warrior's triumph; and so on. In the piano itself, why employ, at different times, muted tones or brilliant tones, if it is not to accentuate the idea expressed? Sonority is to be blamed when it is substituted for idea, and yet one must confess that in certain sonorities, independent of the expression itself, there is a pleasure for the senses.

It is the same thing with painting: a mere line expresses less and pleases less than a drawing which renders the shadows and the lights. The latter work will express less than a picture: I am supposing always the picture brought to the degree of harmony wherein drawing and color combine to form a single effect.

The moderns have invented a type of art which brings together everything which should charm the mind and the senses. It is opera. Declamation that is sung has more power than that which is merely spoken. The overture puts you into the frame of mind of the thing you will hear, but in a vague manner: the recitative clarifies the situations with more force than a simple declamation would have, and the aria, which is to some extent the point of admiration in each scene, completes the sensation through the combination of poetry and of all that music can add thereto. Add to that the illusion of the settings and the gracious movements of the dance.

Unfortunately all the operas are tiresome, because they hold you for too long a time in a situation which I shall call abusive. This performance, which holds the senses and the mind within its control, is the quicker to fatigue. You are promptly fatigued at the sight of a gallery of pictures: what then are we to say of an opera, uniting in a single frame the effects of all the arts together?

In this forest I notice not merely that my eyes are my one means of grasping objects, but also that they are affected agreeably or disagreeably.

May 17.

I have been in Paris for a meeting with Solar,[53] Barye and the architect.[54] Took the omnibus from the Lyons station. At Solar's place at a quarter to twelve. Then called on Madame de Forget. Had a prosaic lunch in a dark café at the corner of the Rue d'Aumale and took the omnibus back to the station. Agreeable trip. Fine weather. I enjoyed all this nature as if I were young. My health was good — that comes to almost the same thing.

Monday, May 18.

Finally got back to painting after being more than four and a half

[53] Félix Solar (1815-1871), writer, journalist and financier; his magnificent library was celebrated in the world of philosophy.
[54] The architect who was arranging the apartment in the Rue de Furstenberg.

months without it.[55] I began with the *Saint John* and *Herodias*,[56] which I am doing for Robert, at Sèvres. Worked with pleasure throughout the morning.

A walk in the forest in the middle of the day; despite the heat and despite that slightly fatiguing excursion, took up my palette again before dinner. In the evening, walked in the garden or in the little meadow of Bayvet's woods with Jenny. Every day Madame de Forget writes me a bulletin about the health of our poor Vieillard.[57]

May 19.

Day of our poor friend Vieillard's death — so clearly foreseen, these last days, and yet so cruel. I remember how deeply the poor man was always struck by the news of every death that reached him, even those which did not particularly concern him, because of that unexpected element there is in death, that cruel surprise which changes a being whom one has seen speaking and acting, into a thing without senses. What! laid low, motionless! there is no longer anything to awaken that clay! Poor comrade! the only time I ever saw him in good health, as it seemed, was this winter when he used to come and see me during my illness, when he would talk to me about Poinsot's condition or his anxiety over Cerfbeer.

May 20.

It was this morning that a note from Mme de Forget informed me of Vieillard's death. I was in a bad state of mind anyhow. At the end of the day, I have advanced the little picture that I was working on yesterday.

After dinner, I went into the forest with my poor Jenny. The death

---

[55] Delacroix had fallen ill at the end of December, and had employed his long captivity in making notes for the *Dictionary*.

[56] Catalogue Robaut, 858, theme of one of the pendentives of the Library of the Chamber of Deputies.

[57] Narcisse Vieillard (1791-1857), one of Delacroix's oldest friends. He had been the preceptor of Prince Napoleon Bonaparte, the brother of Napoleon III, and enjoyed great influence at Court. He was a senator at the time of his death.

of my poor friend Vieillard grieves me all the more when I think that I may lose this friend, who means far more to me.

Tuesday, June 2.

Paris. The day has passed rather well, save for my fatigue: I arrange with Joseph the errands that he is to do while I am at lunch for which I go to the little café at the corner of the Rue La Rochefoucauld. I stay more than an hour to give him time. I return; he has done almost nothing: and so he has to go off at the time when I need him, and I waste my time doing nothing, since I can not hunt up the things I need in my studio while he is away.

He comes back finally, but we have hardly the time to make ready for departing. I manage it however. I send him to get a carriage. At the end of half an hour, he comes to tell me that he could not find any; he was been set on getting a cab. I swear at him, I get furious. He finds one somehow or other. All the time we are driving along I beg the man to make haste: if my life were at stake, I don't think I should be more desperate. Finally, thanks to my cries and my urging of the coachman, I arrive at the very moment of departure and, finding myself installed, I take a joy that is almost childish, but complete. I have forgotten all my ills: I am enjoying everything that I see, and thus the evening is passed.

But twenty-four hours had not gone by before I got back to my most painful impressions, magnified, indeed, by the night and by solitude. Waking up after my first sleep, I remained for a long time a prey to all sorts of worries.

In brief, I woke up remembering what I had read in Montaigne during the day regarding the need for having nothing with which to reproach oneself. That is my position in regard to these ridiculous matters: it will be time enough for my lamentations when those mountains that I saw hanging over my head all night will finally have crushed me. During the day I went to bring the manuscript to Buloz: he promised to do his best for my good Lamey.[58]

I forgot to say that I met Ingres at Haro's place, and that he was very cordial and very courteous.

June 5.

Article on *the Sublime*.[59] Look this up in the notes for the *Dictionary*. Attributable most often to a strongly marked contrast or to a disproportion.

June 26.

In Paris. *On the sublime and on perfection*. These two words may seem almost synonyms. *Sublime* means all that is most elevated; *perfect,* that which is most complete, most fully realized and finished. *Perficere,* to completely finish, to place the crowning stone. *Sublimis,* that which is highest, that which touches the sky.

There are talents that breathe only in the highest regions and on the highest peaks. It seems as though Michelangelo would have stifled in the lower regions of art. It is to this continued and unbroken force that we must attribute the empire which he has exercised over the imagination of all artists. Titian stands in perfect contrast with him. (For great talents that were incomplete and sublime, see the notebook of 1856).

Lord Byron says somewhere: "Campbell's works smell of oil too much: he obliterates the traces of his first draft." Byron himself never fails to work over his verses with the greatest care: whatever may have been said about his facility, he himself tells that there were times when he composed two hundred verses without a break, and then reduced them to some twenty.

Those authors of ours, whose Muse is improvisation, will scarcely

[58] He is referring, probably, to a piece entitled *Hunyades,* by his cousin Lamey, who may have wanted to get it played in Paris.
[59] This article never saw the light.

arrive at perfection. They hope to save themselves through the occasional good luck that improvisation brings with it, and through accidental discoveries of the sublime; they certainly have my good wishes in their quest.

  Should one tell oneself that the means of finding the sublime is to refrain from polishing one's works? When one says that Racine is perfect and that Corneille is sublime, does one not seem to say that the one's writing is less worked over than the other's? What is certain is that one sees it clearly in Corneille when he is sublime. Racine is frequently so, and just as frequently: but the weave of his work is so sustained that the really sublime passages are joined one to another by insensible transitions: he does not shine like the lightning, which suddenly lights up the depths of the night. The sustained warmth of his diction and the accuracy with which he describes the feelings appear to come easy to him and do not reveal their prodigious quality until one penetrates deeper into his art, so profound and so sure of its strength. (See in Boileau, the *Treatise on the Sublime*.)

Sunday, June 28.

The first time that I went to the doctor[60] after having paid him. He seemed absent-minded, and more occupied with his own affairs than with my fever. He no longer remembered what he had prescribed for me.

July 3.

As to the mixture of the tragic and the comic in the theater and in novels, let us take as our watchword (the question which Maître Jacques put to the Miser in Molière's play): "Monsieur, is it to your coachman or your cook that you are speaking?"

  This morning I finished *David Copperfield*. At every moment the author falls into the trap of that accursed mixture. He goes from the grotesque to the sentimental and upsets the reader. Aunt Hetwood, so

[60] Dr. Rayer.

eccentric or rather such a burlesque at the beginning, does nothing but weep and exhibit her feelings at the end. The bad boy of the piece, David's friend, his model for what is comic and indeed almost for what is ridiculous at first, becomes the *Deus ex machina* who straightens out everybody's business.

Wednesday, July 8.

First visit from Dr. Laguerre.

Strasbourg, Sunday, August 3.

Towards seven o'clock we went to the Orangerie, amid miserable clouds of dust; but I was well repaid by the sight of the place, which is enchanting. There is nothing like that in Paris: moreover, very few people were there.

Everything is different here: these suburbs, these fields and meadows which adjoin the promenades and mingle with them have a rustic and peaceful air. The inhabitants do not have that giddy and impertinent look so common in our race. Decidedly it is a different race. It is in countries like this one that it is good to live when one gets old.

Nancy, Sunday, August 9.

Went out before lunch. Place Stanislas and cathedral. I admire the unity of style of all this building. Only one thing is defective, the statue of that good king Stanislas himself, who did everything here and is therefore the author of this unity. He is represented in a costume recalling that of the troubadours of the Empire, with soft boots and a mameluke's saber. You would look in vain for anything more ridiculous.[61]

The cathedral is entirely of its period:[62] I am very fond of these

---

[61] The statue is by Jacquot (1794-1874), a sculptor of Nancy; it was erected in 1831.

[62] The cathedral is of the eighteenth century.

pepper-box spires. The interior is a little cold, despite the harmony of style in all parts: it is like everything that comes out of the Vanloo camp: ordered, able, possessing unity, but cold and without interest. The author does not put his heart into what he does; he does not go to the heart of the man who sees his work.

The Place Stanislas with its fountains and the Hôtel de Ville[63] seem to be the work of a more gifted artist.

After lunch, visited a hundred curious things. Saw the statue of Drouot,[64] one of the heroes of Nancy, a real hero in every sense of the word, but pitifully represented, like all the heroes of our time, thanks to the poverty of sculpture; then saw the ancient walls of the city. Very fine and ancient gate with two great towers.[65] The turning passage-way, as in modern fortification. The part of the city that is in the Renaissance style: what grace, what lightness! How well suited to the lines of the architecture are all those little figures and those accessories! There is nothing more charming and capricious than these Roman costumes arranged in the style of Henri II.

The ducal palace, transition from the Gothic to the Renaissance.[66] The small objects of art, the paintings, the marbles, etc., are in a store-room awaiting the completion of repairs on the first floor. There is a Roman fragment which impressed me, a horseman with the cuirasse and the *peplum*. A copy[67] in gouache of the tapestry of Charles the Bold; I regret not being able to study it. Very remarkable staircase. The vault is supported by a huge pillar, from the foot of which rise the very low steps, thus arranged, as we are told, so that the dukes could ride their horses up to the great hall on the first floor.

Everything here speaks of Duke René II[68] or of Stanislas. They are the household gods of Nancy.

[63] The Hôtel de Ville is a remarkable building of the seventeenth century.
[64] By David d'Angers.
[65] The La Craffe gate.
[66] The Palais Ducal which contains the Musée Lorrain.
[67] By M. Vaultrin, a lawyer of Nancy.
[68] The conqueror of Charles the Bold.

We then went to see the church of the Cordeliers,[69] in which there is a round chapel, called the tomb of the dukes of Lorraine, although their bodies have been removed and the sarcophagi destroyed and replaced in modern style. Although spoken of as round, the chapel is octagonal: the vault alone, which seems to be of the period of the construction, is of a mongrel style, more or less Louis XIV. The choir of the church is adorned with beautiful woodwork; on both sides of the nave, and in the bays are various tombs of princes of the house of Lorraine; the most precious one is unquestionably that of the wife of René II,[70] who outlived him for many years and entered a convent at Pont-à-Mousson. The hands and the head in white stone, the robe and the veil in granite and in black marble. Here one sees the triumph of the art or rather of the character that an artist of talent can impress on an object: an eighty-year-old woman, her head surrounded by a hood, is of a really terrifying thinness, and yet represented in such a way that one never forgets the sight, and cannot take one's eyes from it.

After that, to the promenade, of which I have forgotten the name,[71] near the Prefecture. I know nothing so delightful, unless it is the Orangerie at Strasbourg, which is different in character. Here you find great trees and verdure, something that has none of the aridity of the Champs Elysées in Paris, nor of the symmetry of the Tuileries. The Prefecture is the palace where Stanislas lived.

After that, to the church of Bon-Secours, which contains the tomb of Stanislas. A charming work in its style: it is a great square room rather than a church. In the choir, to the right, the tomb of Stanislas, which I esteem more than did the author of the work himself, if tradition is correct. This author is Vassé,[72] a sculptor of whom Diderot speaks,

---

[69] Built by René II in memory of his victory over *le Téméraire* (1477), the *Chapelle Ronde,* of the seventeenth century, contains seven sarcophagi of black marble, set up in honor of the dukes of Lorraine.

[70] Philippe de Gueldres, second wife of René II, died in 1547; the statue is by Ligier Richier.

[71] La Pépinière.

[72] Louis-Claude Vassé (1716-1772), a pupil of Bouchardon.

and whom he often cites, to the best of my recollection. The unbearably loquacious sacristan who acts as cicerone and who showed me the church, relates that the poor sculptor blew out his brains in despair over seeing his work surpassed by the tomb of the wife of Stanislas which is opposite. In his work there is a recumbent figure, or let me say one that is struck down and overcome with grief, a figure of Charity which is very fine: the head is of an expression that one would call impossible for sculpture — it is so full of energy; she presses to her a child who nurses at her breast; the whole is of admirable rendering, as are also details like the hands and feet.

To the Museum,[73] where my picture is hung too high and badly lit. Even so, it did not displease me.

Fine works by Ruysdael. A big, uncouth picture in the style of Jordaens, not without a certain savage verve, representing the Transfiguration,[74] a lengthwise picture which reproduces and — by reason of the width — weakens the effect of the principal groups by Raphael.

Two pictures,[75] probably sketches by Rubens, which impressed me more than anything else, not that in all their parts they show the frankness of Rubens' hand, but they have that indefinable thing which belongs to him alone. The sea, of a black and tormented blue, is ideal in its truth. In the *Jonah Cast from the Bark,* the monster in the foreground seems to move and to beat the water with his tail. One makes him out with difficulty in the shadow of the foreground, amidst the foam and the black and pointed waves. In the other picture,[76] St. Peter

[73] *The Battle of Nancy,* which appeared at the Salon of 1834 and was given by the goverment to the Museum of Nancy (Catalogue Robaut, 355).

[74] *The Tranfiguration* by Rubens was part of a decorative ensemble commissioned between 1604 and 1606, by the Duke of Mantua for the church of the Santa Trinità at Mantua. This ensemble was broken up in 1797 when Mantua was taken by the French. The fragment at Nancy was placed there in 1801 by the government; it has been heavily repainted.

[75] These two fragments formed part of the predella (occupying the center of a triptych commissed from Rubens in 1618 by the Guild of Fishermen of Malines). The ensemble is a studio work retouched by Rubens.

[76] *Christ Walking on the Waters.*

poses coldly: but the admirable thing about that man is that such a circumstance does not in the least diminish the impression he creates. Before these pictures I feel that inner movement, that quiver, which a powerful piece of music gives: Oh, true genius, born for his art! always the sap, the marrow of the subject, with an execution which apparently cost him nothing! After that, there is nothing one can speak of, nothing that can interest one. When one has seen these pictures, which are only hasty sketches, full of a roughness of touch that upsets you in Rubens, there is nothing more that can be looked at.

And yet I must mention the great hall at the front of the museum, painted in fresco by the court painter of Stanislas.[77] The figures are not to be mentioned after those of Rubens: but the architectural ensemble, also painted in fresco is of a total effect that is no longer to be produced in our day.

To sum up, Nancy is a fine and large city, but dull and monotonous: the width of the streets and their alignment desolate me: I see the goal to which I am walking, a league away in a straight line. Only the West-End in London is more tiresome, because every house is like every other one, and because the streets are even wider and more interminable. Strasbourg pleases me a hundred times more, with its narrow but clean streets; there one breathes the atmosphere of the family, of order, of the peaceful life that, even so, knows no boredom.

Plombières, August 28.

For some days I have been taking pleasure in the Promenade de l'Empereur, for the evening, and even for the morning. The moon, at one of its quarters, rises over the wooded hills, awaits me, and retains me until I am driven away by the cold.

August 29.

Bade farewell to the church of Plombières. I like churches: I like to be there almost alone, and to sit on a bench where I can stay and fall into

---

[77] Jean Girardet (1709-1778), painter of François III of Lorraine, and afterward of Stanislas.

a good reverie. They want to build a new one here: if I return to Plombières when it is finished, I shan't go into it often. It is their age that renders them venerable: they are as if tapestried by all the vows that suffering hearts have exhaled toward heaven. Who can replace these inscriptions, these ex-votos, this pavement formed of worn tombstones, the altars, the steps worn by the feet and the knees of generations of men who have suffered there, and for whom the ancient church has murmured the last prayers? Briefly, I prefer the smallest village church as it has come from the hand of time, to Saint-Ouen at Rouen in its restoration, that Saint-Ouen which was so majestic, so somber, so sublime in its darkness of earlier days, and which today shines all over with its scraping, its new windows, etc.

I caught a cold today while taking my last bath. In the evening a final walk on the road to Saint-Loup. I cannot tear myself away from such beauty. On all sides, reapers and haymakers and well-filled hay carts drawn by the good oxen.

In the morning followed the Promenade de l'Empereur as far as the woods. On my way, a scene of reapers and haymakers: A charming and rustic effect. The flashes of the scythe,[78] etc.

(At the bottom of this page, a pencil sketch of men reaping and women tossing hay.)

August 31.

Left Plombières at seven in the morning. Traveled with four nuns: one of them had a charming face. Was ill with my cold all the way to Epinal.

Arrived about ten o'clock. Saw the church, dark and of a rather primitive Gothic: very much restored.

Terrible heat as I was getting back to the railroad. Reflections about the crowd which was squeezing into the station of this little city.

[78] "The Flashes of the Scythe" is the title of a chapter, taken from the above passage, by Raymond Escholier, in his admirable book on Delacroix; it is toward the end, looking ahead to the death of the master.

The railroad has hardly been laid out, the partitions in the waiting room have not yet been built, and already myriads of people squeeze in there on their way to and fro. Twenty years ago, it is doubtful if there was as much as one departure a day, carrying ten or twelve people who left the little town on indispensable business. As things are now, the travel, several times a day, amounts to five hundred or a thousand emigrants moving in every direction. The best places are occupied by people in blouses who look as if they did not have enough to buy a dinner. A singular revolution, a singular equality! What a most singular future for civilization! Anyhow, that word is changing its meaning. This feverish movement among classes whose material occupations seem as if they must keep people attached to the place where they get their livelihood, is a sign of revolt against eternal laws.

Arrived at Nancy toward one o'clock. We stay in the station until half past three. In our carriage we again meet two of our nuns of this morning; one, the superior of the community, is a woman of distinction. She converses with great amiability and without a shade of bigotry.

Rain and storm before Bar-le-Duc. It is with pleasure that I travel through the country that saw my father's childhood. In sum, an agreeable journey. In the carriage was a fat Englishman, a kind of Falstaff, with two abominable daughters; until almost the end of the journey, they looked the part of Lot and his daughters.

Arrived at half past eleven, more than an hour late.

Paris, September 3.

Visit from Dr. Laguerre.

One, *idem*, for Jenny.

I am writing to my good cousin:[79]

"Despite the solitary life that I lead here, as much as that is possible in Paris, I shall often regret our real tranquillity in Strasbourg and the good it did me in particular, with my badly impaired health and my

[79] Lamey, of Strasbourg.

restless, fatigued mind. In your peaceful city, everything seemed to me to breathe calm: here all I find on every face is burning fever: every place seems given up to perpetual change. This new world, good or bad, which is trying to reach the light across our ruins, is like a volcano under our feet, and lets no one catch his breath again save those who, like myself, begin to look upon themselves as strangers amid the things that are happening, and for whom hope is limited to a good employment of the passing day. So far I have gone out but once into the streets of Paris: I was frightened by all those faces of intriguers and of prostitutes."

Sunday, September 13.

I have been to the Museum. Two or three days before, I had had a session there. I hold in very high esteem the room of the modern French school. It seems far superior to what immediately preceded it. Everything that followed Lebrun, and especially the whole eighteenth century, is mere banality and professional skill. With our moderns, profundity of intention and sincerity shine forth, even in their faults. Unfortunately, our material processes are not on the high level of those used by our predecessors. All these pictures will perish before a very long time.

Augerville, Friday, October 16.

Superiority of music: absence of reasoning (not of logic). I was thinking all about that while listening to a very simple piece for organ and bass-viol which Batta played for us this evening, after having played it before dinner. The enchantment within me which this art creates; people think one's intellectual faculty has no part in this pleasure. That is why pedants give to the art of music an inferior rank.

During the day I tired myself out by following Berryer while he was measuring his land for the road around it. M. de Brézé called in the evening.

Before we went to bed, Berryer read us a letter of Nicole's[80] on prejudice, which he has done very well to insert in his *Essays on Morality*: it says that one can, that one should love one's friends without letting a querulous humor magnify the differences which may happen to exist between our origins and theirs. The whole thing said with that style of development, that prolongation — if one may so express it, which was in no way feared by the men of that century when they wanted to clarify their thought.

"The phrase-makers," as he was saying to me, quoting someone or other, "begin with Massillon." I am of his opinion. What breeding

[80] The famous Jansenist (1628-1695).

shows in every act of those men, who were capable of speaking at such length and with that care, that respect for the object treated or the person addressed, and who did all this with the absence of pretension and of effect, things that have gone on increasing ever since!

Thursday, October 29.

On Charlet.[81] See my notebook of 1857, February 8, for what I say about *feeling;* it is applicable to my article on Charlet.

"I wish that my weak voice might have the strength and authority it lacks, in order to speak to the public of France about the glory of certain great artists to which it accords no more than its esteem, at most." The merit of Charlet.

Happily, I have not been the only one to perceive it, and I shall not be the first to proclaim it. The book by M. de La Combe. For a public indifferent toward this great artist, it is not within my plan to speak of anything save his qualities as an artist. His pious biographer speaks more exactly than I could about the whole of one very special and rather intimate side of his life, about his letters, and about the character of his mind. I will merely say that that mind was of the finest and most original temper, and that under a soldierly and rustic exterior, etc., he possessed a strength and a good sense of the most rare and penetrating kind. The only example of this that I want to offer is the subject of almost all his compositions, in which, following the natural inclination of the French mind, he has put as much of the sense of comedy or sentiment as he has of his talent for painting.

That is a gift or a defect of our race: we always have to let something of our mind mix in with everything. You are free, if you like, to see in this a relative inferiority, when it comes to the question of painting. It is true that the life of painting derives above all from the

[81] Notes for an article on Charlet which was to appear in the *Revue des Deux Mondes* for July 1, 1862.

forms of the exterior of objects, from line, color, and effect, all of these being elements which have nothing in common with the literary idea — I have not said with the political idea, which is quite another matter. That word poetry, which one is forced to use even when discussing painting, reveals a poverty in language which has brought about a certain confusion as to the attributes and the privileges of each of the fine arts.

That the word is employed to signify the essential quality of all of the arts, and at the same time designates the art of painting with words, would seem to indicate that poetry is the art par excellence, since the dominant quality in the other ones is, to some extent, merely a matter of borrowing from poetry.

One asks in vain at the Library of the nation for the work of Charlet, the work of Géricault. The very insufficient funds are used for completing the work of masters who have often no merit other than rarity. It is the same way with the work of Prud'hon, the same way with Géricault. Those glories which touch us so nearly, those artists whom so many men still living have approached, do not possess the prestige of the old Italians or of the old Flemings. The work of Michelangelo is more complete than that of our admirable contemporaries.

If we cannot find enough marble to carve statues of them, I would have busts of them installed in the vestibule at least of those academies which, during their lifetime, managed so perfectly to get along without electing them to membership.[82]

I purposely associate these two names (Charlet and Géricault), not so much because they flowered at the same time as because a mutual admiration gave them an impassioned interest in each other; (tell about this).

Charlet placed Gros and Géricault higher than anyone else.

Géricault, who had gone to seek out Charlet in a tavern at Meudon for which he was painting the signboard, called him the *La Fontaine of*

---

[82] It is without resentment on his own account that Delacroix writes these lines in 1857, having been elected a member of the Academy in that year.

painting. He offers more than one similarity with that immortal painter of nature. Like him, he paints man not as a sentimental school would have him be, but as he is made, with his ridiculous sides and even his vices. Charlet is one of the greatest masters of the jest that the present time has produced. It was his pleasure to observe the poses of the naive figures whose ridiculous aspects and whose eccentricities he painted. He seemed to identify himself with them in all his admirable serious-ness. This penchant for the comic is frequently allied in him with touches of sensibility: *Giving Alms, The Return from the Frontier,* etc. *Jean Lapin, the Two Pigeons, France! Here Ends their Misery* (Describe).

His talent knew no dawn. A marvelous facility found itself from the first at the service of an inexhaustible imagination. He had that in common with Bonington, a charming talent too early lost to us, but one whose qualities, etc. . . .

But that facility was the reverse of the one needed to maintain him at all times at the height of his earliest works.

It seems as if talents more slowly formed, or should I say more laboriously, are destined to live longer, in their strength and in their amplitude.

In his last works it seems as if a prodigious facility were turning toward habit, or rather the intoxicating control by the hand makes itself felt too much.

Conceiving and executing were but a single act with him. He rarely made a separate sketch before beginning on his stone, and each detail was completed as the stone was covered.

Charlet was no man for the drawing-room: all through his life he was the son of the dragoon of *Sambre et Meuse* whose only bequest to that son, destined to render illustrious the name of a poor soldier, con-sisted of an old pair of leather breeches and a pair of boots.

One must be a bit the man of the drawing-rooms if one is to be adopted and pushed by the world of the drawing-rooms. For the major-ity of people who spend all their lives in candle light, who have never given a glance at nature save as it appears on the stage of the opera house, and who get enthusiastic (?) over a ballet-dancer, he has never been anything but a caricaturist, an artist of the pothouse.

A sentimental school which would like La Fontaine to have given to Master Wolf virtues instead of carnivorous instincts — and have made of Johnny Rabbit a preacher.

Charlet is Gallic like La Fontaine, like Rabelais, who seems the father of this whole line of masters of the jest.

I believe that a mere drawing permits you both to brood over a thing and to bring it to birth by the same operation. Within these narrow limits and with an execution that partakes of the summary, one may attain the highest emotion, even as one can with the complex execution of a picture in which it is impossible to grasp the composition and the rendering at one and the same time. Material execution. Its laws in painting. Time is just as indispensable for it as the training and the adroitness of the hand.

Charlet lived in the most modest circumstances, and the little he had was due, even so, to his assiduous labor of day after day: in the period of his masterpieces, he sold for trifling sums admirable plates which enriched only his publishers. . . . He was not the object of any favor whatsoever from the government. He had asked a small lodging for himself and his modest family; it is a favor that is granted to a horde of artists and obscure librarians: he could not obtain it, and was no more fortunate later on. The attempt that he made to be admitted to the Institute. He got only one vote, it was that of the sculptor David; I am not even quite sure about that, and if he did really get it, the cause is doubtless to be sought in the bad humor and the spirit of opposition which this celebrated artist felt as regards his fellow-members of the Academy.

He is simple everywhere. Never any pretension to effect. He does not go far to seek his ideas and does not torment himself to render them ingenious. He does not play the man with the big voice, as do almost all the moderns, who too often open their mouths when they have nothing to say. I should be tempted to say of him what Berryer told me about the littérateurs before Massillon: "It is with him." said he, "that the phrase-makers begin." Nothing foreign to the interest. The execution is what it must be. Regarding the interest which results from the ensemble of the drawing, it is not because the execution seeks to draw attention to itself. He is everywhere full of sentiment, but also of reason.

The fecundity of his thought, served by a hand of incomparable ability, could not stop. One composition led to another, and each of his days, as for all the men gifted with a happy inspiration. . . . Only, since he applied himself to works in which the execution was more rapid, his case reversed that of the painters of his period who grew pale by laboring over a single composition for years, etc.

And so, quite surely, it is not the number of his works that is to be counted, but the number of his masterpieces, and they are found by the hundreds.

Charlet presents one singularity of which there is perhaps not another example among the great painters. His first manner is the one which presents the greatest amplitude. In proportion as he advances in his career, his manner becomes wittier; the skill of his hand lets itself be felt a bit too much; he meets the comprehension of the public by a defter, cleaner touch — sometimes, it must be confessed, too deft and too clean, and giving only a superficial rendering of certain parts, though reserving for others a rendering of the most complete kind. In proportion as he goes on from his first period, whence date his finest things, he falls into what I will call the *French defect,* that of *having line everywhere.* In fact that is what may, perhaps more than other weaknesses be held against the French as compared with the other schools. The slightest details, the most insignificant ones, are studied with equal care and presented without any sacrifice or concern for the bad effect of such maladroit conscientiousness. In general, French painting shows us none of those happy negligences that have the merit of drawing interest to the parts which deserve to concentrate it. The

Flemings excel in this, not to mention Rembrandt, with whom this quality is as much a matter of calculation as of instinct, his capricious etching needle demanding of itself no more than a superficial rendering, even in essential parts. In the works of the Dutch and the Flemings, in their paintings as in their engravings, one notices that ease of execution which affords them the art of disguising sacrifices and thus charming the imagination. The latter faculty is quick to seize upon the intention of the artist, and understands even things that are not shown.

It is singular that that absence of lightness, that strained and repellent execution which arises from effort and takes away the charm of our paintings and our engravings, should be the defect for which we have the greatest antipathy in every form of literature. Grace and lightness form the principal attraction in verse and in prose — I will not say for the foreigners who are incapable of appreciating that precious quality: La Fontaine, Racine, Voltaire, not only in light poetry, but even, etc. . . . This art of taking from everything what is its flower, of not fatiguing the reader by idle details, in a word, the art of being brief which, in painting, corresponds to the art of showing nothing but essentials, is the quality which charms us, and its absence spoils for us works full of other qualities, but wherein the confused ordering and above all the indiscreet abundance dulls the imagination, which does not know where to pause.

It may be that Charlet was led on to details which, in the eye of connoisseurs, take away from the beauty of the works of the second half of his career. The demands of the publishers and of the public that wants to understand too much because it feels too weakly. . . .

Charlet offers the example of conceptions of an incredible unity, imagined and flung from him as swiftly as certain verses of Molière and of La Fontaine. Examples: *"Ah! quel plaisir d'être soldat,"* etc. Nothing is lacking.

The types that one does not forget, a characteristic of the great masters.

Paris, November 4.

One of these mornings, being in the sun which comes into my gallery, I was noticing the prismatic effect of the multitude of tiny threads forming the nap of my gray jacket. All the colors of the rainbow were shining in it as in a crystal or in a diamond. Each of these hair-like fibres being polished, reflected the most brilliant colors, which changed at each movement that I made; we do not perceive that effect when there is no sun, but. . . .

November 8.

Gave M. Haro the little Watteau which I got from Barroilhet; he is to restore it for me.[83]

In Thiers's *Histoire de l'Empire,* I find a note as to Napoleon's plan of 1813 to march on Berlin, which turned his mind away from the attention he needed to give to the position of Vandamme:

". . . When he wanted to realize fully what his ideas were, Napoleon set them down on paper, *knowing, like all men who have thought a great deal, that putting his ideas into words meant going into them more deeply.* He had therefore dictated his scheme in an admirable note, entitled: *Note on the general situation of my affairs on August 30,* one that is quite similar to the note he wrote at Moscow in October, 1812, and that reveals his whole thought at the moment when Vandamme was at Kulm. One feels the real cause of the negligence which brought about Vandamme's misfortune, etc. . . ."

November 9.

This morning I get a letter from my good Lamey. Curiously enough, ever since I woke up, I have been thinking of him continually, and of

[83] The picture in question, says M. Joubin, is one of the numerous copies from a well-known Watteau in the Hermitage at Leningrad. It was bequeathed by Delacroix to Baron Schwiter and was sold at the auction of the latter's collection on May 3, 1886, when it was No. 47 of the catalogue. In such reproductions of the work as I have been able to see, it appears to be a very fine thing, quite possibly an original, indeed.

the pleasure that I should have in news from him, and especially of the habit we ought to adopt of writing each other: that is exactly what he asks of me in his letter.

I write this because of the idea suggested to me by the beginning of that letter. *Si vales, bene est, ego valeo.* I got to reflecting on that word *valere,* which means in French, *se bien porter,* an expression or rather a locution which describes in several words one of the situations of the man who has his health, perhaps indeed the chief one, the one which is the surest indication of strength, which is to say that he is on his legs, for the sick man usually lies in bed. In French there is no single word to translate *having good health,* and very curiously the Latin word which expresses this has become part of our language: it is the word *valoir.* The English say of a man: *(Il vaut tant — He is worth so and so much),* it is as if they were saying: the health of his pocket-book is good or bad. We say *cette maison vaut cent mille francs* (that house is worth a hundred thousand francs), which is to say that it has the value, the strength, the probable duration — in a word the health of a house worth a hundred thousand francs. *Valeur* (valor) in the sense of courage comes from *valoir* and consequently from *valere.* From this we must conclude that in the mind of everybody, the first condition for being valorous is to be in good health. One has *valeur* (value or valor), *on vaut beaucoup* (one is worth a great deal): the health of the body adds to that of the soul and is often no other thing.

Valeur or courage in a weakened body is a rare thing: and again in a man who is capable of it, we must notice how much more he would be in possession of that *valeur,* if his health, as related to it, were in a better state.

Friday, November 13.

It is difficult to say what colors were employed by men like Titian and Rubens to produce those flesh tones which are so brilliant and have remained so, especially those half-tints in which the transparence of the blood under the skin makes itself felt despite the gray that every half-tint brings with it. For my own part, I am convinced that they mix the most brilliant colors in order to produce them.

When the tradition was interrupted with David who, like his school, introduced other mistakes, people got to the principle — so to name it — that sobriety is one of the elements of the beautiful. Let me explain: after the debauchery of drawing and the inappropriate brilliance of color which brought the decadent schools to outrage truth and taste in every way, it was necessary to return to simplicity in every department of art. Drawing was tempered anew in the water from antique springs: that opened a whole new horizon to the men who had a feeling for what is noble and true. Color partook of the reform; but that reform was indiscreet, since people believed that color could always remain attenuated and reduced to what was considered that it should be, i.e. to a simplicity which does not exist in nature. One finds in David (in the *Sabines* for example), the prototype of his reform, color that is relatively right: yet consider the tones that Rubens produces with frank, vigorous colors like the clear greens, the ultramarines, etc., and then see how David and his school think to recover them with black and white to make blue, black and yellow to make green, red ocher and black to make violet, and so on. Moreover he uses earth colors, umbers or Cassel earths, ochers, etc. Each of these relative blues and relative greens plays its part in that attenuated scale, especially when the picture is placed in a strong light which, as it penetrates their molecules, gives them all the brilliance of which they are capable; but if the picture is placed in shadow or if it recedes under the light, the earth becomes earth once more and the tones *no longer play,* so to speak. Above all, if it is placed alongside of a picture having full color, as do those of Titian and Rubens, it shows up as the thing it really is: earthy, dull, and without life. *Dust thou art to dust returning.*

Van Dyck uses more earthy colors than does Rubens, ocher, red brown, black, etc.

I extract this reflection, made at Champrosay on one of my walks from a book of sketches of the year 1853.

Friday, November 20.

I compare those writers who have ideas but who do not know how to bring order into them with those barbarian generals who led into battle hordes of Persians or of Huns, fighting haphazard, without unity of effort, and consequently without result. Bad writers are to be found among those who have ideas as among those devoid of them. It is the feeling for unity and the power to realize it in the work which make the great writer and the great artist.

November 21.

Swedenborg claims, in his theory of nature, that every organ is composed of homogeneous molecules composed of similar parts: thus the lungs are composed of a number of small lungs, the liver of little livers, the spleen of small spleens, etc.

Without being so great an observer, I perceived that truth a long time ago: I have often said that the branches of the tree were themselves small complete trees: fragments of rocks are like masses of rocks, bits of earth are like enormous masses of earth. I am persuaded that one could find such analogies in great number. A feather is composed of a million feathers.

Swedenborg's observation is taken from a certain Emerson who later says that if Napoleon could say: *"La France, c'est moi,"* it was because the men whom he governed were just so many small Napoleons.

The author claims that this great man was the representative of the modern genius, and particularly of democracy's tendency to material happiness, a thing that sees success in terms of the senses and subordinates to it intelligence itself, science, talent, etc. This point of view seems to me most questionable, but it carries with it the following true idea, that the ordinary man finds realized in Napoleon the ideal of the simple citizen who sees himself deserving to reach that high position where he can satisfy every kind of taste natural to a simple citizen, even if he must conceal his desires in cases where they cannot be satisfied. Every simple citizen in the nineteenth century wants to have the pleasures of good society, as Napoleon had them, to travel in comfortable carriages, have a well served table with plenty of servants, play the benefactor as regards those about him, enjoy the luxury of the arts, and accumulate titles and marks of distinction. He flatters himself with the thought that it is not impossible to attain all these pleasures, since one simple citizen did attain them. (*Revue Britannique*, vol. 2, 1850).

Monday, November 23.

How many degrees there are in what we have agreed to call civilization, how many there are between the Patagonians and men like those who sum up everything that moral and intellectual culture can add to a fortunate disposition. One may say that far more than three-fourths of the globe live in barbarism: the greater or less degree of it makes all the difference. Barbarians are not found among savages alone; how many savages there are in France, in England, in the whole of this Europe, so proud of the light in which it lives. Here we have the situation to be seen when, after about a century and a half of a rather refined civilization recalling the fine period of antiquity — I refer to the century of Louis XIV and a little beyond it — the human race (by which I mean the small number of nations which are carrying on the torch today) goes back into the shadows of a completely new barbarism. When we arrive at this state of mind, it is from mercantilism and the love of pleasure that the strongest impulses of the human soul derive. Young people are taught all the languages of Europe, and they will never know their own because of the systematic neglect of the ancient languages, which are ignored on account of their uselessness for money making. Our students are taught the sciences, not to enlighten their minds or to rectify their judgment, but to help them in calculations which lead to fortune.

One is terrified, when one looks at a map of the world and sees the mass of ignorance and brutalization which reigns on it surface. Of what interest can we be to that Providence that placed us in this strange world as its ornament, or so we are told? How can we justify the immortality of the soul when we look on all these souls filled with nothingness and with shadows? And they are more numerous than the leaves of the forest which the wind sweeps along to fatten the earth and make it bring forth new myriads of beings destined to the same annihilation. What merit or demerit is there in the end claimed as spiritual in so many creatures who are men only in name, who have no consciousness either of good or of evil, who are unconcerned whence they come or whither they go, who steal, deceive and at times cut the throats — not of ferocious enemies — but of other human animals made in the same image as themselves, and who do this because the interests of the latter cross their own and the presence in the world of these people offers a certain obstacle to their momentary desires.

How is it that this god, who wills that nothing be lost from the soul of a stupid Patagonian, takes so little interest in his passage over this earth? Why, if man is his work of predilection, abandon him to hunger, to dirt, to massacre, and to the terrors of a life of hazard beside which that of the animals is incomparably preferable, despite their anxiety, their fear, their lying in wait for prey, among similar torments which are, however, rendered lighter by that absence of the spark of intelligence whose light, even so, breaks through the most horrible human scum. Look! while in one part of the globe, men plough, sow, reap the fruits of the earth, gather in well-guarded cities and towns, and through such protection, concentrate all the instincts that make for perfection, there must eternally be countries where ignorance of the most elementary arts leaves man a prey to hideous abasement, not knowing how to gather his wheat, nor make clothes nor build a habitation that shall be anything more than a den or a warren? Guile, falsehood and theft make up the whole of the relationships of men among themselves: give your daughter to this man because he is a good stealer, or to that man because he'll pay you with more grease!

(Look up what is said as to their ignorance about everything, the way they make knives out of old iron bands. They know nothing of the use of the hammer, they do their iron-work by beating with flat stones on other flat stones that serve them as an anvil).

November 26.

No one showed less pretension than Kepler, and yet he could not refrain from complaining a little over the small amount of attention which, from the first, was given to his great discoveries. "I can perfectly well remain without readers for a century," he said, "since the Almighty spent six thousand years without getting an observer like myself." Men of the stature of Kepler are proud, never vain. Pride is born from an intimate consciousness of acquired superiority: it is a completely inner thing and has no need of outer stimulus: vanity, etc.

November 30.

I must ask the gardener for hollyhocks, syringas, lilies, zinnias, honeysuckle, nasturtiums, sunflowers, hyacinths, narcissus, tulips, renunculus, and marvels of Peru.

Sublime. I have said that in the case of the great men whose element seems to be the sublime, art appears to play a secondary role. They would need, what is impossible, inspiration at every moment: they would need to find a favoring wind everytime they spread their wings. The disjointed and unforeseen aspects which they present come from this intermittence. Like the great scenes in nature, there is about them a sort of indefinable abruptness. (On the same subject see the notebook of 1853, April 21, and August 18).

December 9.

I have always had too much esteem for people whom I see for the first time: I always imagine them to be superior.

Sunday, December 20.

I stay at home: I do not shave; this afternoon the beginning of a little cold gives me a pretext for not going out. Since the beginning of this month I have gotten back to work.

The studio is completely empty.[84] Who would believe it? This place, which has seen me surrounded by all sorts of paintings, among which several rejoiced me by their variety, and of which every one awakened in me a memory or an emotion, still pleases me in its solitude. It seems to be doubled. There are still about ten little pictures here which I am taking pleasure in finishing. As soon as I get up I climb hastily to the studio, scarcely taking time to brush my hair; I stay there till nightfall, without one empty moment and without one regret over the distractions which visits, or what are called pleasures, may afford. My ambition is bounded by these walls. I enjoy the last moments remaining to me to feel myself still in this place which has seen me for so many years, and in which was spent a great part of the latter period of my youth. I speak of myself in this way because, although getting along in years, my imagination and a certain something which I cannot define cause me to feel movements, impulses, and aspirations which still have a tang of the happy years about them. Unbridled ambition has not enslaved my faculties and has not made me sacrifice the pleasure of enjoying myself and my faculties to the vain desire of being admired in some prominent position by envious people, a vain bauble for one's last years, the use made by a fool — speaking from the standpoint of the mind and the heart — of those moments when a man of declining years should rather withdraw into his memories or into healthy occupations for his mind, in order to console himself for what is escaping him, when he should fill his last hours with other things than the sickening affairs with which the ambitious consume long days in order to be seen for a few moments, or rather to see themselves in the sunlight of favor. It is not without

[84] The studio in the Rue Notre-Dame-de-Lorette, which had just been dismantled.

lively emotion that I leave this humble place, where I have been now sad and now joyous for so many years.

Wednesday, December 23.

The day of Sainte Victoire.[85] I have let it pass without noticing, for I write this on the following day. How many years have passed, how many beloved objects have disappeared since we used to celebrate this dear anniversary !

Monday, December 28.

Made a quick change to the new studio[86] today. Worked in the morning at the *Horses Fighting.*[87]

Decidedly, my new place is charming. After dinner, I felt a bit of melancholy over finding myself transplanted. Little by little I got reconciled and was perfectly happy when I went to bed.

Woke up next morning and saw the most gracious sunlight on the houses opposite my window. The sight of my little garden and the smiling aspect of my studio always cause a feeling of pleasure in me.

Franklin defines man as the animal who knows how to make tools.

"Suddenly, the outer world appeared to him in a mirror. Men and things were admirably represented, but with that beguiling and yet indefinable difference which always causes a picture, an image, or a shadow to have more charm than the original." *(The Sign,* a story, by Hawthorne.) [88]

Tuesday, December 29.

I went as far as the Luxembourg in order to get into trim; I never saw finer weather.

---

[85] The saint's day of Delacroix's mother whose maiden name was Victoire Oeben.

[86] 6 Rue de Furstenberg, where he died in 1863.

[87] Catalogue Robaut, 1409.

[88] Nathaniel Hawthorne (1804-1864), American writer.

In the evening I had a visit from M. Hartmann,[89] who came to ask me for my copy of the man's portrait by Raphael. We talked theology the whole time. He is a fervent Protestant. Haro dropped in. In short, I was bored and tired when I got to bed.

Riouffe, at the end of his memoirs on his detention at the Conciergerie, terminates them with this cry of disgust: "I shall die ashamed of having been a man."

[89] M. Hartmann, banker, who had commissioned him to paint for his salon the *Four Seasons,* now in the collection of Mr. Albert Gallatin in New York.

February 5.

At the Council I see the model of a machine designed to transport the column of the Place du Châtelet a distance of some twenty meters further off. At the Place de la Bourse they have just planted some enormous horse-chestnut trees. Soon they will be transporting houses; who knows? perhaps cities.

February 16.

At three o'clock meeting of the committee at the Hôtel de Ville. I meet Flourens.[1] The prefect[2] told us some very interesting things about the

[1] Pierre Flourens (1794-1867), physiologist, perpetual secretary of the Academy of Sciences, was called in 1858 to membership in the Municipal Council.
[2] Baron Haussmann.

invasion of public education by the priests. They are monopolizing everything.

February 23.

The ancients are perfect in their sculpture: Raphael is not perfect in his art. I make this reflection with reference to the small picture of *Apollo and Marsyas.*[3] There you have an admirable work, one from which you can scarcely take your eyes. It is doubtless a masterpiece, but the masterpiece of an art which has not arrived at its perfection. One finds in it both the perfection of a special talent — and ignorance, a result of the time when it was produced. Apollo is glued to the background: this background with its little buildings is puerile: it is to be excused by the naiveté of the imitation and by the slight knowledge of aerial perspective which men possessed at that time. The Apollo has frail legs: they are weak in modeling: the feet look like little boards stuck on at the end of the legs; the neck and the collarbones are failures, or rather, they are not felt. It is about the same thing for the left arm which holds a staff: I repeat — individual sentiment and the charm peculiar to the rarest talent form the attraction of this picture.

Nothing of the kind is to be said about the small plaster casts which stood beside the picture at the house of its owner; they are probably casts from antique bronzes. In them some parts are neglected or rather less finished than the others; but the sentiment which animates the whole is inseparable from a complete knowledge of the art. Raphael is lame and graceful: the antique is full of that unaffected grace which we see in nature; nothing jars; nothing is to be regretted; nothing is lacking; nothing is in excess. There is no example among the moderns of such an art; in Raphael we see an art struggling with

[3] The attribution of this celebrated picture, now in the Louvre, is very much contested; the attribution to Raphael, at all events, does not seem probable. Delacroix had seen it in the house of Morris Moore, who owned it at the time.

its swaddling clothes; the sublime parts cause us to pass over the ignorant parts, the childish naïvetés which are but the promises of a more complete art. In Rubens there is an exuberance, a knowledge of the means of art and above all a facility in employing them which hurry the skilled hand of the artist along into exaggerated effects, into conventional practices designed to create more striking impressions. In Puget there are marvelous passages which, for truth and for energy, surpass the ancients and Rubens, but there is no ensemble: weak spots appear at every moment, defective passages brought together with great effort; the ignoble and the common appear at every step.

The antique is always even, serene, complete in its details and of an ensemble which is virtually beyond reproach. One would say that its works were done by a single artist: the nuances of style differ in the various periods, but do not take away from a single antique work that peculiar value which all of them owe to that unity of doctrine, to that tradition of strength with reserve and of simplicity which the moderns have never attained in the arts of design nor perhaps in any of the other arts.

Greek art was the son of Egyptian art. It needed all the marvelous aptitude of the people of Greece to reach all that perfection of their sculpture, even while following a sort of hieratic tradition like that of the Egyptians. It is the *liberality*[4] of their mind and spirit which animates and renders fertile those cold priestly images of a different art, one bound by inflexible tradition. But if one compare them with the modern man, torn by all the new things that the course of the centuries has brought in, through Christianity, through the discoveries by which the sciences have aided the boldness of imagination, and finally by reason of that inevitable revolution in human affairs which refuses to let one period be like those which have preceded it. . . .

[4] Delacroix underlines his word *libéralité*. Its dictionary meaning is evidently identical with the English word above, but the fact of his stressing it is a clear indication that his mind reached out to some idea such as the one implied by the term liberal arts, those that liberate us from the narrower requirements of the arts of utility.

The bold audacities of the great men have led to bad taste: but with these great men, the audacities I speak of opened the barriers to the men of the future — who resemble them. Even as Homer, among the ancients, appears as the source whence everything has issued, so, among the moderns, certain geniuses whom I shall venture to call enormous (and the word must be taken to denote the greatness of those geniuses and at the same time the impossibility of holding them to certain limits), have opened up all the roads that have been followed since their time, each of the great men doing so according to his special character, and in such fashion that not one of the great minds of the later time but is their tributary, necessarily finding in them the type of its inspiration. (Same subject, 1853, October 20.)

The example of these primitives is dangerous for weak talents and inexperienced men. Great talents, even at their beginnings, yield easily to the temptation to accept their own influence or the vagaries of their imagination as the effect of a genius similar to that of extraordinary men. It is to other great men like themselves, but coming at a later time, that their example is of most use: inferior natures are free to imitate at their ease the men like Vergil and Mozart. . . .

That mobility is so natural to men that the ancients themselves, whose greatness seen from afar appears monotonous to us, present analogies for it; their great masters of tragedy follow each other without resembling each other; Euripides has not the simplicity of Aeschylus: he is more poignant, he seeks effects, oppositions: the artifices of composition increase in the measure that men need to address themselves to new sources of interest which are discovered in the human soul.

It is like the work that we see taking place in modern art. To strengthen the effect of his sculptures, Michelangelo cannot draw upon the resources of the art of backgrounds and of the landscape which, in painting, augments the impression of the figures: but the pathos of movements and the finesse of planes become, together with expression, imperious needs of his passion.

The greatest admirers of Corneille and of Racine (they are rare today) have an unmistakable feeling that, in our time, works carved according to the model of those masters would leave us cold. The poverty of our poets deprives us of tragedies made for ourselves; we lack original geniuses: the only thing that men have thought up is imitation of Shakespeare mixed with what we call melodramas. But Shakespeare is too individual, his beauties and his exuberances are too intimate a part of an original nature for us to be completely satisfied by them when people try to produce, for our consumption, works along Shakespearean lines. He is not a man to be plundered, nor one whose work will bear the slightest reduction. Not only has he a genius of his own which nothing else resembles, but he is English, the beauties of his work are more beautiful for Englishmen, and it may be that his defects are no defects in the eyes of his compatriots. Even less were they so for his contemporaries; the latter were delighted by the things that shock us: what was to be beauty for every age, shining forth here and there in his work, was probably not what made people clap their hands in upper galleries frequented by sailors and fishmongers; and it is probable that the lords of Elizabeth's court did not have much better taste; to such beauties they preferred the playing on words and the conscious striving for witty expressions.

Some have thought they saw in Shakespeare all our fine modern inventions like lyricism and realism. From the fact that he makes valets talk like their masters, that he has Caesar question a shoemaker in his leather apron, and that the latter replies with the puns of the street-corner, people have concluded that truth was lacking in our plays, which have no knowledge of this new vein; and also, on seeing a lover in converse with his mistress spout two pages of dithyrambics to nature and the moon, or a man in the paroxysm of fury halt for interminable philosophic reflections, people have seen an element of interest in something that was no better than the worst of bores.

How much of pro and con are found in the same brain! One is astounded at the diversity of opinion among different men: but a man of healthy mind conceives all the possibilities, knows how to place himself — or unconsciously places himself at all points of view. That explains the fact that the same man frequently swings quite around in his opinions, a fact which should surprise only those who are themselves incapable of forming their own opinions.

In politics, where such change is even more frequent and sudden, it derives from entirely different causes, which I have no need to indicate: that is not my purpose.

It therefore seems that an impartial man should not write otherwise than as if he were uttering, so to speak, the ideas of two persons; just as there are two lawyers for a single suit. Each of these lawyers sees so clearly the arguments which militate in favor of an adversary that often he anticipates these arguments; and when he twists from their orbit the statements which are offered him as objections, it is by means of statements quite as good and which are at least plausible. Hence it follows that the truth in any question cannot be absolute: the Greeks, who are perfection, are not so perfect and the moderns, exhibiting more weaknesses or faults, are not as defective as is thought, for they compensate by their own qualities for the faults and weaknesses from which the Antique seems exempt.

In some old notes of mine, dating from four years ago,[5] I find my opinion on Titian. These last days, without remembering them, but working with different impressions, I have just been writing other opinions.

From which I conclude that a man of good faith would be almost wrong to write in a manner different from that used in judging a lawsuit: which is to say, the case being stated, one should have within oneself another speaker who plays the part of a lawyer employed to contradict, etc. . . . .

As to the instability of reputation among great men: it is explained by what precedes.

As to antique beauty and modern beauty.

[5] In the pages of the *Journal* beginning with the notes of July 29, 1854.

February 26.

The conversation that I had with J——[6] about the imperfect leg in the *Medea:*[7] as to how men of talent are struck by an idea to which everything must be subordinated. Hence the weak parts, which of necessity are sacrificed. It is good luck if the idea is clearly defined at birth, and if it develops itself. With the man of talent the difficult work is wholly directed to holding the weak passages to their proper place. As everything is weak in the work of men whose talent is weak, everything being the product of reflection or of reminiscences more than of inspiration, the deficiencies I speak of are less noticeable. Every part of their insipid work is the object of obstinate and sustained labor. Nature was miserly with them and made them pay dear for the least of their findings. To more gifted men heaven gives happy and striking ideas without cost; their labor is directed to bringing such ideas to the light in the best way possible.

February 28, 1860.

(I am re-reading this. It is to be related with what I wrote at the beginning of this year, in the notebook of 1860 on the same subject;[8] but I came to a different conclusion; it is not but that I still find the Antique just as perfect: but on comparing it with the moderns, notably in the medals of the Renaissance, in the works of Michelangelo, Correggio, etc., I find in the latter a peculiar charm which I do not venture to attribute to their lapses from correctness, but to a sort of piquant quality which is indefinable, and which is not found in the Antique, the latter affording you a more tranquil type of admiration. Among the ancients art embraced fewer objects.)

[6] Is this Madame de Forget or Jenny?
[7] He refers to the variant of the *Medea* (Catalogue Robaut, 1436 or 1437).
[8] See the *Journal* for January 16, 1860.

March 14, 1858.

The artists who seek perfection in everything are those who can attain it in nothing.

March 15.

For some days I have been having stomach trouble; perhaps I fatigued it a bit, and moreover I have been working very much, this last month and a half.

Here in my room I have under my eyes the small repetition of the *Trajan*[9] and the *Christ at Calvary*. The former is blond and light, far more than the latter. The little Watteau[10] which I have placed beside the two has once more completed for me the demonstration of the advantages of light backgrounds. In the *Christ,* the planes of the ground, especially those in the distance, almost mingle with the dark places in the figures. The most general rule is always to have backgrounds of a half-tint that shall be light, less so than the flesh, naturally, but calculated in such a fashion that dark accessories, such as clothing, beards and hair, shall stand out as dark, so as to give accent to foreground objects. That is one very remarkable thing about the Watteau; there are even several parts which have the same values as the background behind each; thus the stockings, the gray or yellowish shoes, etc., get contrast with the earth only through the parts, here and there, which are slightly darker.

One would need other pictures by Watteau in order to study the artful means by which he gets his effect.

In my Watteau, the trees of the background, although of a distant plane, are extremely light: there is not a single tone in them, any more

[9] He refers to the small sketch of the *Justice of Trajan* which remained in his possession until his death and was sold at the auction of the following year (Catalogue Robaut, 693). The *Christ at Calvary* is now in the Museum of Metz (Catalogue Robaut, 1378).

[10] As to this Watteau see the note on the entry in the *Journal* of November 8, 1857.

than in the tombs, to compete in even a slight degree with the vigor of those in the foreground. Indeed a lack of connection results from this, and it jars on me when I compare it with my *Trajan;* each little figure is isolated, and one sees all too clearly that it was painted in a leisurely way, independent of its neighbors.

It was today, after having thought the matter over in bed this morning, that I gave to Haro the idea which may put him on to the track of the painting of the Van Eycks. Since the problem consists, on the one hand, of the means to be adopted to avoid the great excess of oil in paints, and on the other, of the means for adding varnish in a corresponding quantity, I told him to reverse the problem: the pigments would be ground with a varnish which would permit one to keep the colors moist, and one would add the oil when painting. He is much impressed by my idea.

April 3.

I am re-reading several of my old notebooks on my hunt for the recipe for quinquina wine which I got from that worthy Boissel. I have turned up some certain matters of the past with a pleasure that is sweet and not too sad.

Why have I neglected this occupation,[11] which costs me so little when, from time to time, I dash off in these books a note of the things that happen in my existence, and especially in my brain? Necessarily, in notes of this type, set down from day to day, there are many things that one would not like to find in them later on. Commonplace details are not easy to treat, and it is natural to fear the use that could be made, at a distant time, of many things that had no interest and that were written without care.

[11] The *Journal* was written during the periods of relaxation which Delacroix could save from his professional work, that is to say during vacations or periods of illness. The *Journal* does not really continue between 1824 and 1847, which is to say during the period of Delacroix's great activity.

April 9.

From Voltaire to Cardinal de Bernis:

"I do not know, Monseigneur, if our *secrétaire perpétuel* has sent to Your Eminence the *Heraclius* by Calderon, which I turned over to him for the entertainment of the Academy. You will see which is the original, that of Calderon or that of Corneille. Such a reading may contain infinite amusement for a man of taste like yourself, and, in my opinion, it is quite funny to see the extent to which the gravest of all nations despises common sense.

"Meanwhile, here is the very faithful translation of the *Conspiracy against Caesar by Cassius and Brutus*[12] that is being played daily in London, and that is infinitely preferred to the *Cinna* of Corneille. I implore you to tell me how a people that has so many philosophers can have so little taste. You will perhaps answer me that that is because they are philosophers; but how now! should philosophy lead straight to absurdity ? and is not cultivated taste indeed a true element in philosophy ? "

Here is the reply of the Cardinal, who shows himself, in my opinion, more a man of genuine taste than Voltaire. The latter, as was natural, strongly biased by his habituation to our theater, in which, despite his genius, and whatever he may have thought of the matter himself, he had made no real innovation, sees taste only within the narrow limits of qualities which habit, more than a true understanding as to what pleases mankind, had established on our stage. I am far from taking any stand against the form of Corneille and Racine. It had at least had the virtue of novelty in their hands: that preference given to speech over action affords a complete system, and the inclination of our race is suited to it. Yet we must give consideration to the system of Shakespeare and of Calderon since it sufficed for the English and for the Spaniards, who preceded our great works by a century, and did so at the very time, we must admit, when our theater was struggling

[12] *Julius Caesar,* by Shakespeare.

amidst incredible darkness; their system, then, as open to criticism as it is, has perhaps more to say to the imagination, and does not so constantly make the author intrude between the spectator and the stage.

The real innovation (and I believe that at the time of Voltaire, and in the society in which he lived, it was impossible for Voltaire himself), that innovation would have been merely to bring about a species of order and reason in those complicated actions of the English and the Spaniards; but let us listen to the amiable cardinal, as his opinion is astonishing for the time in which he lived:

"Our *secrétaire perpétuel* has sent me the *Heraclius* of Calderon, and I have just read Shakespeare's *Julius Caesar*. These two plays have given me great pleasure, since they serve the history of the human mind and of the particular taste of nations. And yet one must agree that these tragedies, extravagant and coarse as they are, are by no means tiresome, and I will tell you, to my shame, that those old rhapsodies in which, from time to time, there are strokes of genius and very natural sentiments, are less odious to me than the cold elegies of our tragic writers of mediocre gifts. Look at the works of Paul Veronese, of Rubens, and of many another Flemish or Italian painter: often they will sin against truth to costume, they wound our sense of the proprieties and offend our taste: but the power of their brush and the truth of their coloring cause us to excuse these faults. It is about the same thing with dramatic works. Moreover, I am not astonished that the English people, which in certain respects resembles the Roman people, or which at least is flattered to resemble it, should be enchanted to hear the great personages of Rome express themselves like the middle class and, sometimes, the lowest orders of London. You seem to me to be surprised that philosophy, enlightening the mind and rectifying ideas, should have so little influence on the taste of a nation! You are quite right: and yet you will have observed that manners have even more empire over taste than have the sciences. It seems to me that in the matter of art and of literature, the progress of taste is more dependent on the spirit of society than on the philosophic spirit. The English nation is political and commercial, and by that very fact, it is less polished, but less frivolous than our own. The English talk about their business matters; the one and only occupation among ourselves is to talk about our pleasures; it is therefore not singular that we should be more difficult and more delicate than the English as to the choice of our pleasures and as to the means of procuring them for ourselves. Besides, what were we before the century of Corneille? From every standpoint, it behooves us to be modest."

April 12.

For the first time in more than fifteen months I have returned to the dinner of the second Monday. Also, on going out, I took a big walk along the boulevards, without feeling too great an emotion of regret. More than in the past, they entertained me, as if they were a theater.

April 13.

I have got to work again; retouched the *Hercules*[13] ordered by Chabrier.

At half past three, I called on Huet.[14] His pictures made a very strong impression on me. There is a rare vigor in them, although with vague passages, but that is part of his talent. One cannot admire anything without — beside that — regretting something. To sum up, great progress in the good parts. And that is enough to say about works which stick in your memory, and I find that to be the case with these. I have been thinking of them with great pleasure all through the evening.

After dinner, took turn after turn around my little garden. It is a great help to me. I am much in need of getting back my strength completely.

[13] Probably the *Hercules Resting* (Catalogue Robaut, 1351).
[14] Paul Huet.

May 7.

Today, for the first time, I take part in the dinner of the first Friday. I have a good time there and feel better the next day. One has to shake oneself up a bit. I leave the dinner in company with Villot, and then for an hour, take a long walk in an excellent frame of mind.

The next day I again took a walk: I entered the church of Saint-Roch for the music: what I heard mostly was the cruelest sermon on virginity. I came home in a state of extreme sadness that I have not gotten rid of today, Sunday, as I write these lines.

May 11.

Left for Champrosay at eleven o'clock; great happiness at finding myself there. I see my poor neighbors, whose grief is heart-rending.

One always finds something changed. There, under my windows, they are building a shed down in the plain and the roof of it hides from me a bit of the river. They are tearing down Villot's wall. Everything passes and we pass.

May 24.

Mme Villot invites me to call on her in the evening in order to meet a mysterious lady, a friend of Mme Sand. I go there despite my cold and a deluge of rain that I had to pass through. I meet Mme Plessis, a charming person who makes me promise to write to Mme Sand. She is about to kiss me, right before the company, when I tell her that I do not believe in that small person with whom we are supposed to be blessed and who is called *soul*.

May 26.

While laying in my *Christ Lowered into the Tomb*,[15] I think of a

---

[15] Catalogue Robaut, 1380; variant of a subject that Delacroix has treated several times. The *Entombment* by Baroccio (1528-1612); there exist several variants of it. The influence of Baroccio on the French painting of the eighteenth century is well known; he is one of those who contributed to the formation of the Vanloo style, against which Delacroix had such antipathy.

similar composition by Baroccio that one sees everywhere; and at the same time I think what Boileau said for all the arts: "Nothing is beautiful except the true." Nothing is true in that accursed composition: twisted poses, draperies flying without reason, etc. Reminiscences of the various styles of the masters.

The masters, and I speak of the greatest of them, those whose style is well marked, are true by means of that; otherwise they would not be fine. The gestures of Raphael are naive, despite the strangeness of his style; but what is odious is the imitation of that strangeness by imbeciles, who are false in gesture and intention, into the bargain.

Ingres, who has never known how to compose a subject as nature presents it, thinks that he is like Raphael because he apes certain gestures, certain manners habitual with the master; these have indeed, in the work of Ingres, a certain grace recalling that of Raphael; but with the latter one strongly feels that all such qualities emanate from himself and are not sought after.

July 3.

First day at the church[16] with Andrieu.

As to accessories. Mercey has said a fine thing in his book on the Exposition: the beautiful in the arts is truth idealized. He has cut through the question, dividing the pedants from the genuine artists; he has done away with the ambiguity that permitted the partisans of the *beautiful* to be forever masking their impotence to find the true.

As to accessories. They have enormous influence on the effect, and yet must always be sacrificed. In a well ordered picture, what I call *accessories* is an infinite subject. Not only furniture, small details, and backgrounds are accessory, but the draperies and the figures themselves, and in the chief figures, parts of those figures. In a portrait showing the hands, the hands are accessory: in the first place, they must be subordinated to the head: but often a hand ought to draw attention to itself, less than a part of the clothing, of the background, etc. The

[16] Saint-Sulpice, to finish the Chapelle des Saints-Anges.

reason why bad painters cannot attain the beautiful — *that truth idealized* of which Mercey speaks — is that, aside from the lack in their work of a general conception leading to *truth,* their accessories, instead of contributing to the general effect, misdirect it, on the contrary, through the almost invariable effort to bring out certain details which ought to be subordinated. There are several ways to reach this bad result: on one hand, excessive care in bringing out these details, as a means of displaying ability; on the other, the general habit of copying from nature all the accessories designed to contribute to the effect. When the painter copies all these fragments from actual objects, leaving them as they are and making no effort to modify them, how can he add or subtract, and give to these objects, inert in themselves, the power needed for the impression? [17]

Nancy, July 10.

Departed for Plombières at seven o'clock in the morning. Arrived at Nancy at two o'clock. Am in a bad state; it prevented me from dining; I go to bed at about eight o'clock.

I had gone to the Museum on my arrival to see the two sketches by Rubens once more; at first sight, they no longer seemed to me so fine; but soon the charm began to work, and I remained motionless before them, or nearly so, for I kept going from one to the other but without being able to leave them. There are twenty volumes to be written on the special effect of these works. It is the charm of the indefinable thing, an incredible savor amidst negligences; but the latter are due solely to the fact that these works are only sketches.

Plombières, July 14.

Today, after dinner, took a walk along the Epinal road. I made some

[17] It would seem that in thus defining the role of accessories, Delacroix is thinking of those astounding accessories which he was painting in the two compositions at Saint-Sulpice, notably Jacob's mantle and hat, which are treated with so great a simplicity and so marvelous a sense of the effect.

charming discoveries there, rocks, woods, and above all waters, waters of which one never tires, one feels an incessant desire to plunge into them, to be a bird, to be the tree that bathes in them, anything except an unhappy man, sick and bored.

July 27.

The Emperor departed at seven o'clock. I keep on with my walk, going as far as the delightful brook on the Saint-Loup road.

For three or four days I have been reading the *Paysans* by Balzac, after having been forced to give up *Ange Pitou* by Dumas, having been vanquished by its incredible badness. *The Queen's Necklace*, although full of the same faults and the same intemperance, did have some interesting passages, at least.

The *Paysans* interested me at the beginning: but as it goes on, it becomes almost as unbearable as the babble of Dumas. Always the same Lilliputian details, through which he thinks to give something striking to each of his characters. What confusion and what minutiae! What use can there be in full length portraits of miserable suppers so numerous as to take away all the interest of the work! As Mocquart said the other day, that isn't literature. It is like everything they are doing: they emphasize everything, they exhaust the material and, most of all, the curiosity of the reader.

In the *Débats*, the other day, I read an article on Rubens by a certain M. Taine[18] whom I have already judged from other writings of the kind to be a first class pedant, full of the faults that I have just mentioned. He also wants to say everything, and then he says it over again afterward.

[18] Hippolyte Taine (1828-1893) was already known through celebrated works, in particular *Les Philosophes Français du Dix-neuvième Siècle* (1857) and *Les Essais de Critique et d'Histoire* (1858). Delacroix's severe judgment has been struck out in the manuscript, perhaps by Delacroix himself, but at a later time.

Champrosay, August 12.

I start out through the country at six o'clock in the morning. Delightful walk. I go to the bank of the river and make a sketch looking toward Degoty's cabin. I bring back a sheaf of water-lilies and arrowhead plants: I flounder about for nearly an hour on the muddy banks of the river and have a grand time doing so in order to make my conquest of these humble plants. This debauch reminds me of Charenton, my childhood, and going fishing. I come home sunburned.

We have an abundance of fruits which we have not enjoyed previously; up to now, I have been eating them only at dinner, and they have not yet done me any harm.

August 17.

The last scene from *Roméo et Juliette;* the Capulets, the Montagues, Friar Laurence.[19]

August 19.

One works not only to produce, but to give value to time: one is satisfied with oneself and with one's day when one has stirred up ideas, made a good beginning of something or finished it well.

Reading memoirs and histories consoles one for the ordinary miseries of life through the picture drawn of human errors and miseries.

September 3.

I have been ill since Tuesday evening. Last night, dinner at the house of Barbier with Malakoff[20] and his fiancée, Mme de Montijo, etc.

All through this week-end I have been interrupting my painting

[19] M. Joubin observes that in the lists of subjects for pictures which appear in this part of the Journal, Delacroix returns to the romantic subjects of his youth inspired by Tasso, Shakespeare and Byron; some however are drawn from Racine.

[20] Marshal Pelissier, duc de Malakoff (1794-1864), had been the ambassador in London since April, 1858.

and reading Saint-Simon. All those everyday adventures take on an incredible interest under his pen. All those deaths, all those accidents that have been forgotten for so long a time console one for the nothingness in which one feels oneself to be.

Read, also, Lamartine's Commentaries on the *Iliad*. I intend to make some extracts from them. Reading those pages reawakens in me the admiration for everything that resembles Homer, among others Shakespeare and Dante. It must be confessed that our moderns (I speak of men like Racine and Voltaire) have not had acquaintance with that type of the sublime, those astounding naivetés which poetize commonplace details and make of them *paintings* which delight the imagination. It seems as if those men thought themselves too much the *grands seigneurs* to speak to us as if we were men, about our labor, about the simple movements of our nature, etc.

September 6.

I write to M. Berryer: "And so I have taken refuge here, where I have got back to a better state of health; but that is not all; here was what awaited me at Champrosay. The man who used to rent me my little place informs me in the most offhand way that he is going to sell his house, and that I must soon make other arrangements. So there I am, upset in my habits, and I was not any too well before; anyhow, I am here, and it is fifteen years that I have been coming to this country, that I see the same people, the same woods, the same hills. What would you have done in my place, dear cousin, you who have let yourself be walled up in the apartment that you have occupied for forty years, rather than seek another one? Probably, just what I did; which is to say that I have bought the house, which is not dear and which, with some small changes added to the purchase price, will make for me a little refuge suited to my humble fortune. And so, at this time of day, I have to return to Paris within two days and set myself for a month at the work I have constantly been postponing, and yet come here from time to time to see what is being done about the arrangements which I have mentioned.

"You will certainly have seen, on opening my letter, my dear cousin, that the only reason I was telling you so much about this was that I had nothing good to tell you, at least concerning myself. I wish I could reserve all this babble about my small affairs and pour it into your ears under the big trees at Augerville and along the banks of the Essonne. You see that I cannot do so, unfortunately, and you will well understand, I hope, that that is against my dearest wish."

September 11.

I return to work at Saint-Sulpice; I do a good deal with the *Heliodorus.* Next day, impotence. . .

September 14.

I go to the Louvre to see Masson's drawing in comparison with my picture.[21] Fine restorations of Spanish paintings. Black outlines in several parts of the Murillo: are they by him? Saw again the strange *Baptism of Christ* dating from the youth of Rubens.[22]

[21] He refers to the drawing made by the engraver Alphonse Masson (1814-1898) from the *Dante and Vergil,* for an engraving.

[22] This Rubens belonged to the same ensemble as the *Transfiguration* at the Museum of Nancy, of which Delacroix speaks on Aug. 9, 1857. The *Baptism of Christ,* which has been in the Museum of Antwerp since 1876, was then the property of M. Georges, an art official of the French government.

(Without date) Addresses of Models given me by Corot.

Madame Hirsch, Rue Lamée, No. 6. Superb dark head, of the type of la Ristori.

Adèle Rosenfeld, Rue du Marché-Ste-Cathérine, No. 5. A recumbent pose of hers seemed to me superb.

Joséphine Leclaire, Rue de Calais, No. 4, very elegant, fine ensemble, thin arms.

Rosine Gompel, Rue des Petits-Carreaux, No. 17.

January 3.

In Abbé Huc's account of his travels, page 146 — the charm of the journey through the desert and its influence on *health*. Page 96, influence on the temperament of the Tartars of this life in the desert.

January 9.

On the difficulty of preserving the impression of the original sketch. Of the necessity for sacrifices. Following this: of the artists who, like Vernet, finish immediately, and of the bad effect resulting therefrom. 1854, April 3 and 5.[1]

Walk in the forest and visit to the ruined convent of the Ermitage. Stupidity of the people who make such demolitions, whether they are religious fanatics or revolutionary fanatics. Solidity of the building that the monks left. 1853, May 11 and 13.

[1] Delacroix is referring to entries in earlier notebooks which concern him at the moment for his *Dictionary*. The entries of April 3 and 5, 1854, are lost.

Recipe for rice of a rather dry kind, of the type of pilaf. 1853, May 3.

Advantages of education according to La Bruyère. One gets one's education from honest people. 1853, May 8.

DICTIONARY.

Picture. To produce a picture, the art of leading it from the lay-in to the finished work. It is a science and an art at once; to carry it through in a really learned manner, much experience is indispensable.

Art is so long that, to arrive at the systematizing of certain principles which really govern every department of art the whole of a lifetime is needed. Men of born talent instinctively find the means for expressing their ideas; with them there is a mixture of spontaneous impulses and of gropings, across which the idea comes to the light with a charm that is perhaps more particular than the one offered by the production of a consummate master.

At the dawn of a talent there is something naive and bold at the same time, recalling the graces of childhood and also its happy freedom from care as to the conventions which govern grown men. That is what renders all the more surprising that boldness to be seen in the work of illustrious masters at a late period of their career. To be bold, when one may compromise one's past, is the greatest sign of strength.[2]

If I remember rightly, Napoleon places Turenne above all other captains, because he notices that his plans became more audacious the more he advanced in age. Napoleon himself has given the example of that extraordinary quality.

In the arts, particularly, very deep feeling is necessary if the originality of thought is to be maintained despite the habits to which even talent is fatally inclined to abandon itself. After having spent a great part of his life in accustoming the public to his genius, it is very difficult for the artist to keep from repeating himself, and to renew his talent, so to speak, in order not to fall, in his turn, into that very fault of banality and the commonplace which is characteristic of men and of schools as they grow old.

[2] Delacroix was deciding about his pictures for the Salon of 1859; they were roundly abused by the criticism of the day, and he did not exhibit again.

Gluck has given a most remarkable example of that power of the will, which was no other than the power of his genius. Rossini went on renewing himself down to his last masterpiece, which prematurely closed his illustrious career of masterpieces. Raphael, Mozart, etc.

Boldness. One should not, however, attribute this boldness, which is the seal of the great artists, solely to that gift for renewal, for the rejuvenation of talent by means of new effects. There are men who give their measure from the very start, and in whom a sublime monotony is the principal quality. Michelangelo never varied the physiognomy of that terrible talent, which in itself has renewed all the modern schools and given them the irresistible urge by which they are characterized.

Rubens was Rubens at once. It is remarkable that he never even varied his execution, that he modified it very little, even after receiving it from his master. If he copies Leonardo da Vinci, Michelangelo, Titian — and he copied unceasingly — it seems that he showed himself to be more Rubens than in his original works.

Imitation. One always begins by imitating.

It is well agreed that what is called *creation* in the great artists is nothing but a special manner possessed by each one in his seeing, coördinating and rendering of nature. But not only have these great men created nothing in the proper sense of the word, which means of *nothing* to make *something*, but, even more, in order to form their talent or to keep it healthy, they have had to imitate their predecessors, and imitate them almost unceasingly, whether voluntarily or unwittingly.

Raphael,[a] the greatest of painters, was most sedulous in imitating: imitation of his master, a thing that left in his style traces that were never effaced; imitation of the antique and of the masters who had preceded him, but freeing himself by degrees from the swaddling

[a] See the article by Delacroix on Raphael, published in the *Revue de Paris* in 1830, reproduced in the *Oeuvres Littéraires de Delacroix,* Crès et Cie., Paris.

clothes in which he found them wrapped, and finally imitation of his contemporaries such as Albrecht Dürer the German, Titian, Michelangelo, etc.

Rubens imitated unceasingly, but in such a way that it is difficult to. . . .

Imitators. It may be said of Rubens and of Raphaël that they imitated a great deal and, without offense, one may term them *imitators.* It will be more exact to say that they have had many imitators, who have been more occupied with transferring their style to mediocre works than in developing in their own work a style proper to it. The painters who have formed themselves by imitating their works but who have merely made a servile transfer of the style of these great men to their own works, reproducing only the weaker parts through lack of originality. . . .

August 8.

In the *Annuaire* of the Academy of Brussels for 1859 see page 139 for a note conceived as follows: "Moreover from a political standpoint, the trade of the painters occupied only a comparatively inferior rank. It could not compete with the trades of the butchers, the fish-sellers, the tailors, the blacksmiths, and the bakers." (For the article on the position of artists among the ancients and the moderns. To be written for the Dictionary of the Academy).

Strasbourg, August 23.

I am writing to Mme de Forget:

"I give you some news about my trip and my stay here.[4] I arrived

---

[4] This is Delacroix's last trip to visit his family. He was very fond of his cousin Lamey, of Strasbourg. From that place, he goes to Ante to call on Commandant Delacroix, his cousin. He no longer has the courage to note his impressions day by day.

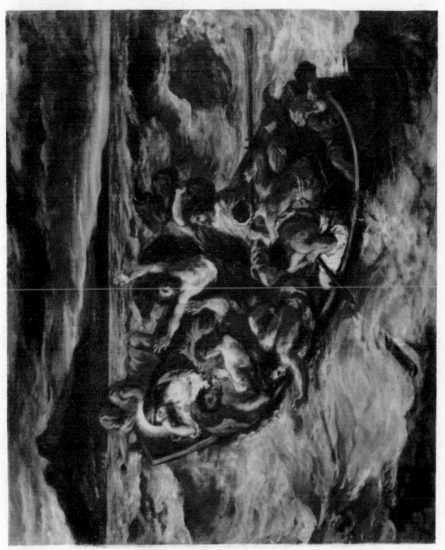

Christ on the Lake of Genesareth (1853). The Metropolitan Museum, New York

The Riding Lesson (1854). Courtesy of M. Knoedler and Company

Arabs on the March (1855). Museum of Providence, Rhode Island

Tiger Drinking. Courtesy of M. Knoedler and Company

Tiger Attacking a Woman (1856). Courtesy of Messrs. Durand-Ruel

The Feast in the House of Simon, by Rubens. Hermitage Museum, Leningrad

Heliodorus Driven from the Temple (1857-1861). Church of Saint-Sulpice, Paris Photograph by Giraudon

Jacob Wrestling with the Angel (1857-1861). Church of Saint-Sulpice, Paris.
Photograph by Giraudon

The Lion Hunt, by Rubens. Alte Pinakothek, Munich

The Lion Hunt (1861). The Art Institute of Chicago

Orpheus and Euridyce, or Spring (1862). Collection of Mr. Albert Gallatin, New York

Diana and Actaeon, or Summer (1862). Collection of Mr. Albert Gallatin,
New York

Bacchus and Ariadne, or Autumn (1862). Collection of Mr. Albert Gallatin, New York

Juno and Aeolus, or Winter (1862). Collection of Mr. Albert Gallatin,
New York

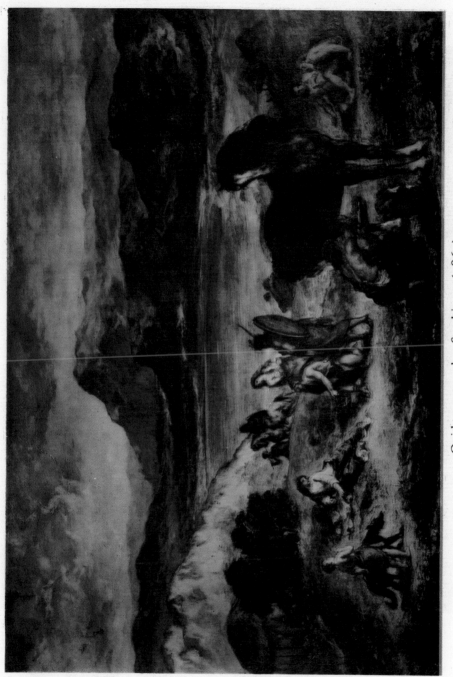

Ovid among the Scythians (1862).

Tiger

without too much dust and heat, indeed without too much trouble, although the stations were encumbered by the crowd of curious provincials who had come to Paris to admire our splendors, which I have fled as much as I could. The distraction and the locomotion have not yet sufficed to restore me; I hope that the profound repose which I enjoy here with my kind relative will cure my indisposition. Whatever the state of one's health, a mere change of place, in the absence of livelier pleasures, suffices to bring about far better feelings. This city seems quite primitive or, if you like, quite backward in comparison with Paris. I hear only German spoken; that reassures me a little as to the fear of being troubled on my walks by meeting importunate acquaintances; but where does one not meet the importunate? I read, I sleep a great deal, I walk about a little and I have infinite pleasure in a tête-à-tête with my cousin, whose mind and experience I like and who has precisely the same tastes as myself: and so this will continue steadily until I move on to join, for a few days only, my worthy cousin in Champagne, which is on my route for returning to Paris. All this will take until about September 10, and the Lord grant that by then I shall have regained my strength enough to resume my work, for I eagerly desire to push on, this fall.

"How are you? How do you govern your imagination? For that is the great point: one is happy when one thinks one is, and if your mind is elsewhere, on the contrary, all the distractions in the world will give you no satisfaction. I am sure that you would be refreshed by the view of the good countryside and the fine walks which begin at once as you get outside the walls of this city. No noise, few vehicles, and but little dressing; in a word, one goes a hundred years back; that would drive everyone away, and it enchants me.

"P. S. I am reading with delight a very old book that I had not read before, or that I no longer remembered: the *Bachelier de Salamanque* by Lesage. Read it or re-read it. You will see how far behind that leaves our men of genius."

At Strasbourg, August 25.

From the preface to the last edition of Boileau,[5] 1701:

". . . Starting out from the fact that a thought is beautiful only to the extent that it is true and that the infallible effect of the true, when it is well uttered, is to impress mankind, we conclude that that which does not impress men is neither beautiful not true, or else that it is badly uttered, and consequently that a work which is not enjoyed by the public is a very bad work. The greater part of mankind may indeed, for a while, take the false for the true and admire bad things: but it is not possible for a good thing to fail to please, in the course of time, and I defy all the authors most discontented with the public to show me a good book that the public has ever refused, unless they are thinking of their own books, of the merit of which they alone are persuaded. I admit nevertheless, and it is not to be denied, that sometimes, when excellent works appear, cliques and envy find the means to cause a low opinion of them and, in appearance, to render their success doubtful; but that can scarcely endure, and it happens with these works as with a piece of wood that one plunges to the depth of water with one's hand: it stays at the bottom as long as one holds it there, but soon, when the hand grows weary, it rises up and reaches the top. . . .

"Let us speak now of my new edition. It is the most correct that has yet appeared, and not only have I reviewed it with care but I have retouched several of my works anew. For I am by no means one of those authors who avoid labor, who think themselves no longer obliged to

---

[5] The reader will understand the importance of this extract from Boileau by recalling that in this same year, 1859, Delacroix's showing at the Salon, including eight pictures, among which were masterpieces like the *Abduction of Rebecca, Ovid among the Scythians,* and the *Christ at Calvary* of the Museum of Metz, aroused the most violent and unjust criticisms, as at the time of the *Massacre of Scio* or of the *Sardanapalus.* Delacroix suffered from this, as is to be seen from the fact that he exhibited no more; he said nothing about the matter, but the preface from Boileau contains the answer to his opponents, and calms his feelings.

repair anything in their writings once they have given them to the public. To excuse their laziness, they allege that they would fear that recasting their work too much would weaken it and deprive it of that free and easy look which, as they say, forms one of the greatest charms of discourse. But in my opinion that is too bad an excuse; it is the hastily made works, produced as the pen runs along, to use the current phrase, which are generally dry, hard and forced. A piece of writing should by no means appear to have been worked over; but it cannot be too much worked over, and frequently it is labor itself that, while polishing it, gives it that much wanted facility which charms the reader. There is much difference between facile verses and verses made with facility. The writings of Vergil, although extraordinarily worked over, are far more natural than those of Lucan, who wrote, it is said, with a prodigious rapidity. Ordinarily it is the pains that an author has taken to express his meaning and perfect the expression which causes the reader to have no pain on reading him. Voiture, who seemed so easy, worked over his writings extremely. One sees no end of people who easily produce mediocre things; but of people who produce very good ones, even with difficulty, one finds very few."

From Boileau's translation of the *Treatise on the Sublime*, by Longinus:

". . . For everything which is truly sublime has this special property, that when one listens to it, one's soul is elevated and is made to conceive a higher opinion of itself, so that it is filled with joy and with a certain noble pride: as if it had itself produced the things which it had merely heard just before.

August 29. Strasbourg, in the little garden.

At this very moment I am having a delightful pleasure. In my good cousin's little garden, I listen to the bells, which delight me, and I feel that a part of the pleasure that I have in hearing them comes because they recall to me those of Belgium. And so my enjoyment is composed both of the situation in which I am and the one that I recall.

August 30.

Strasbourg, in the little garden. There is a considerable number of Frenchmen, in this time of the so-called renewal of our language, who apply to Boileau the judgment that Byron passed on all our writers. That exactitude, which is true strength, that marrow of the imagination and of good sense is not at all poetry or imagination for them. Contrasts of words, surprises of style which are but a puerile or baroque music, conceal from them the emptiness or the swollen quality of the ideas in contemporary works. These works are, in this respect, like parade virtues, which create illusion in no one save strangers who see you in passing and have not the time to look into you more deeply. Solid virtue, that of the mind as that of the heart, is to be discovered only by daily and assiduous intercourse. Boileau is a man whose book should be under your pillow; he purifies and gives delectation: he creates love for the beautiful and the honest, whereas our moderns exhale only acrid perfumes, deadly for the soul at times, and falsifying the imagination by fantastic spectacles.

September 1. Strasbourg.

The most obstinate realist [6] is still compelled, in his rendering of nature, to make use of certain conventions of compositions or of execution. If the question is one of composition, he cannot take an isolated piece of painting or even a collection of them and make a picture from them.

[6] This passage is certainly a reply to the critics of the Salon of 1859, and to opinion that was hostile to Romanticism and favorable to the Realism that was triumphing with Courbet.

He must certainly circumscribe the idea in order that the mind of the spectator shall not float about in an ensemble that has, perforce, been cut to bits; otherwise art would not exist. When a photographer takes a view, all you ever see is a part cut off from a whole: the edge of the picture is as interesting as the center; all you can do is to suppose an ensemble, of which you see only a portion, apparently chosen by chance. The accessory is capital, as much as the principal; most often, it presents itself first and offends the sight. One must make more concessions to the infirmity of the reproduction in a photographic work than in a work of the imagination. The photographs which strike you most are those in which the very imperfection of the process as a matter of absolute rendering leaves certain gaps, a certain repose for the eye which permit it to concentrate on only a small number of objects. If the eye had the perfection of a magnifying glass, photography would be unbearable: one would see every leaf on a tree, every tile on a roof, and on these tiles, mosses, insects, etc. And what shall we say of those disturbing pictures produced by actual perspective, defects less disturbing perhaps in a landscape, where parts in the foreground may be magnified in even an exaggerated way without the spectator's being offended, save when human figures come into question? The obstinate realist will therefore, in his picture, correct that inflexible perspective which falsifies our seeing of objects by reason of its very correctness.

In the presence of nature herself, it is our imagination that makes the picture: we see neither the blades of grass in a landscape nor the accidents of the skin in a pretty face. Our eye, in its fortunate inability to perceive these infinitesimal details, reports to our mind only the things which it ought to perceive; the latter, again, unknown to ourselves, performs a special task; it does not take into account all that the eye presents to it; it connects the impressions it experiences with others which it received earlier, and its enjoyment is dependent on its disposition at the time. That is so true that the same view does not produce the same effect when taken in two different aspects.

What causes the inferiority of modern literature is the attempt to render everything; the ensemble disappears, drowned in the details, and ennui is the consequence. In certain novels, like those of Cooper, for example, one must read through a volume of conversation and of description in order to find one interesting passage; this defect takes away from the merit of Walter Scott to a singular degree, and renders his works very difficult to read; and so the mind strolls in languid fashion amid that monotony and that emptiness by means of which the author seems to take pleasure in talking to himself. Painting is fortunate in demanding no more than a glance in order to attract and to fix.

October 12.

Real beauty in the arts is eternal and would be accepted at all periods; but it wears the dress of its century: something of that dress clings to it, and woe to the works which appear in periods when the general taste is corrupted!

Truth is described to us as naked: I can conceive that only for abstract truth; but every truth in the arts comes about through means in which the hand of man is felt, and consequently with the form agreed on and adopted in the time when the artist lives.

The speech of his time gives a particular color to the work of the poet. That is so true that it is impossible, in a translation made at a much later time, to give an exact idea of a poem. That of Dante, despite all the more or less successful attempts, will never be rendered in its native beauty by the language of Racine and Voltaire. The same is true of Homer. Vergil, coming at a more refined period, resembling our own, even Horace, despite the conciseness of his language, will be rendered more happily in French; Abbé Delille has translated Vergil. Boileau might have translated Horace. And so it would be to a lesser extent the difficulty resulting from the diversity of languages than the different spirit of the period which presents an obstacle to genuine translation. The Italian of Dante is not the Italian of our day; the ideas of antiquity are suited to a language of antiquity. We speak of the ancient authors as elemental in their naturalness; it is their period which was so, and only by comparison with our own.

The usages of a period differ completely; the way to be expressive, to be humorous — to express oneself, in a word — is in harmony with the turn of the mind peculiar to the men of the time. We see the Italians of the fourteenth century only through the *Divine Comedy:* they laugh as we do, but about the things that were comic in their time.

October 25.

The saying of M. Pasquier, speaking of Solferino: "It is like confidence — a thing to be earned, and not to be commanded."

Hugo said to M. Berryer: "We are all like that." (He was alluding to the fear of becoming blind.)

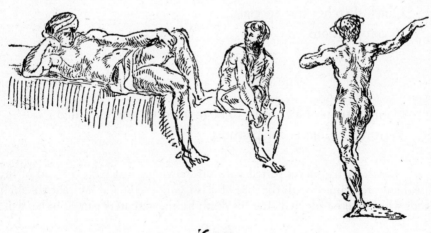

Addresses of models given by Riesener:
Sidonie, fine in her ensemble but not in her details.
Maria, blond, head like Juno.
Both of them, Rue du Roule, 16.
Mlle. Lucas, Rue Neuve-Coquenard, 26.

Principal divisions for classifying my drawings:[1]

Animals	Landscapes
Chamber of Deputies	Costumes and Architecture
Ceiling of the Louvre	Studies from Nature
Hôtel de Ville	Salon de la Paix
Saint-Sulpice	Masters
Antiques, Anatomy	Etchings and Lithographs by myself and by others
Quick sketches and Special compositions	Morocco

Compositions of all kinds, to be divided up and classified.
Writings, subjects for pictures.

[1] Delacroix had never parted with his drawings. Reaching the end of his life, he is preoccupied with the idea of classifying them, and lays out the divisions which will be adopted after his death by the executors named in his will.

January 4.

Extracts from the *Mémoires d'Outre-Tombe*.[2]

"We used to laugh at the enemies of M. de Fontanes who wanted to make out that he was a deep and dissimulating politician: he was simply an irascible poet, frank to the point of being choleric, a spirit that could brook no contradiction, and that could no more conceal an opinion than it could adopt that of another man. The literary principles of his friend Joubert were not his own. M. Joubert found something good everywhere and in every writer; Fontanes, on the contrary, had a horror of this or that doctrine, and could not bear to hear a mention of the name of certain authors. He was the sworn enemy of the modern style of composition:[3] to bring before the eyes of the reader a material act, the crime of the needy, or the gallows with its rope seemed to him an enormity; he maintained that one should never perceive the object in any but a poetic setting, as if under a globe of crystal. Grief exhausting itself mechanically, through tears, seemed to him only such a sensation as might be had from the Roman arena or the scenes of the guillotine; he understood tragic sentiment only in so far as it was ennobled by admiration, changed by means of art into pity, a thing that charms us. . . .

"It was M. de Fontanes, as I like to repeat, who encouraged my first attempts; it was he who foresaw *Le Génie du Christianisme;* it was his muse, filled with astonished devotion, who directed my own into the new paths toward which it had hastened; he taught me to conceal the deformity of objects by the manner of lighting them; to put, as much as was in me, Classical language into the mouth of my Romantic characters.[4] In those old days there were men who acted as

[2] Here follow 11 pages in the manuscript containing extracts from the *Mémoires d'Outre-Tombe* of Chateaubriand. The selections from them here given are based on the relationship to his own thoughts which Delacroix finds in them.

[3] This is exactly the position of Delacroix as regards Realism.

[4] The statement would apply to Delacroix's painting.

conservers of taste, like the dragons who guarded the golden apples of the Hesperides; they did not allow youth to enter until it could touch the fruit without spoiling it. . . .

"I was in the gallery when Napoleon entered:[5] he impressed me agreeably; I had never seen him save from afar. His smile was caressing and beautiful, his eye admirable, especially because of the way that it was placed under his forehead and framed by his lashes; there was nothing of the charlatan about his glance, nothing theatrical or affected. A prodigious imagination animated that politician who was so cold: he would not have been what he was, had the muse not been there; reason carried out the ideas of the poet. All those men in whom life is so strong are always a composite of two natures, for they must be capable of inspiration and of action: in the womb of the one nature, so to speak, the project is conceived, the other nature accomplishes it. . . .

"However, reflecting upon the idea of writing my *Mémoires,* I was conscious of the price set by the Ancients on the value of their name: it may be that there is a touching reality in that perpetuity attaching to the memories of our passage that we may leave behind. Perhaps, among the great men of antiquity, this idea of an immortal life in the human race stood for them in the place of that immortality of the soul which has remained a problem for us. If renown is but a small thing when it relates to ourselves alone, one must nevertheless agree that it is a fine privilege attaching to the friendship of a man of genius to give an imperishable existence to everything that he has loved."[6]

[5] Delacroix also had seen Napoleon only from afar, during his childhood; but he had seen him. We know, morever, how much the great figure of Napoleon always preoccupied him.
[6] M. Joubin remarks that this is the point of view of Delacroix respecting his *Journal* and also on the question of the soul, of which he speaks in the *Journal.*

January 15.

Dictionary:

Boldness. One needs great boldness if one is to dare to be oneself: it is above all in our time of decadence that this quality is rare. The primitives were bold in a naive fashion, without knowing, so to speak, that they were so; as a matter of fact, the greatest of boldnesses is to step outside of convention and of habits; now, the men who arrive the first have no precedents to fear; the field was free for them: behind them, no precedent to enchain their inspiration. But with the moderns, amid our schools corrupted and intimidated by precedents well calculated to enchain presumptuous impulses, nothing is so rare as that confidence which alone causes the production of masterpieces.

At Saint Helena, speaking of Admiral Brueys, the one who died so gloriously at Aboukir, Bonaparte said: "Brueys had . . . , but he did not have that confidence in the excellence of his plans, etc."

Neither genuine boldness, that which is founded on a native originality. . . .

It must be recognized that one too frequently finds with the common run of artists a blind confidence in forces which the vanity and mediocrity of such men cause them to see in themselves. Men devoid of ideas and of every kind of invention simply take themselves for geniuses and so proclaim themselves.

January 16.

For the preface to the *Dictionary*. A dictionary of this type will amount to practically nothing if it is the work of a single man of talent; it would be even better, or rather it would be the best possible, if it were the work of several men of talent, but on condition that each one of them treated his subject without the participation of his colleagues. Were it their common product, it would fall back into banality, and would not rise far above a work composed jointly by mediocre artists. Each article, amended by each of the collaborators, would lose its originality and assume, because of the corrections, an aspect of banal unity which could bear no fruit in the field of instruction.

It is the fruit of experience that should be found in a work of this type. Now, experience is always fruitful with men gifted with originality; in the case of commonplace artists, it is merely a matter of serving a somewhat longer apprenticeship to the recipes that are found everywhere.

In this manual, the reader will find articles on certain celebrated artists, but neither their character nor the events of their life will be treated. There will be an analysis, more or less long, of their particular style, the manner with which each one of them has adapted the technical side of art to this style.

What is important in a Dictionary of the Fine Arts is not to learn whether Michelangelo was a great citizen (story about the porter that he ran through with a spear in order to study the death struggle of a man expiring on a cross), since he was the greatest artist; what we want to learn is in what way his style was so suddenly formed after the gropings of schools that were scarcely out of the swaddling clothes of a timid childhood, and what influence this prodigious style has had on everything that has come since.

The reader will also find himself excused from listening for the thousandth time to the ridiculous story of Correggio, but perhaps it will be with pleasure that he will hear what the numerous historians of the celebrated artists have not sufficiently repeated, i.e. how surprising have been the steps which this great man caused painting to take, and how much, in this respect, he approaches Michelangelo himself, how much he has a right to the admiration of the centuries.

The principal purpose of a Dictionary of the Fine Arts is not pleasure, but instruction. To give or to illuminate certain essential principles, to enlighten inexperience with more or less success, and to show the road that must be followed as well as the pitfalls on roads that are dangerous or condemned by taste, such is the course that one may well propose to oneself for such a work; now where shall one find better application of principles than in the example of the great masters who have brought the different branches of the arts to perfection? What could be more instructive than the very errors of such men? For the admiration inspired by these privileged men, the first on the scene, must not be a blind admiration; to adore them for everything in their work would be, especially for young aspirants, the most dangerous thing possible; the majority of artists, even among those capable of a certain perfection, are inclined to base themselves on the weaknesses of the great men and to see therein a source of authority. Such passages in the work of privileged men are generally due to exaggerations of their particular sentiment, and easily become gross *misconceptions* when employed by weak imitators; whole schools have been founded on phases of the masters that have been badly interpreted, deplorable errors have been the consequence of the ill-considered zeal with which men have inspired themselves from the bad sides of remarkable artists, or rather, these errors have arisen because the aspirants have been power-less to reproduce anything of the sublime elements in their models.

Unfortunately, each man can suffice to only a limited task. As regards discussion of painting, or of the arts in general, which have been so superficially studied, it is possible that many men capable of writing excellent things have been restrained from writing by the idea of the insufficience of a single man, who will, moreover, be busy with the exercise of the profession itself (I speak of men engaged in professional work, and thus prepared to give instruction in it; I leave mere critics out of consideration).

To write a book is a work at once so respectable and so menacing that it has more than once chilled the courage of the man of talent ready to take up his pen and give a certain amount of leisure time to the instruction of those who were less advanced in their career. A book has, doubtless, a thousand advantages: it links things together, it de-duces principles, it develops, it resumes, it is, in a word, a monument; from such a standpoint, it flatters the self-esteem of its author as much as it enlightens its readers. But it requires a plan, and transitions: the author of that book imposes upon himself the task of omitting nothing that relates to the material.

The dictionary, on the contrary, suppresses a great deal. . . . If it has not the seriousness of the book, it does not cause the same fatigue; it does not oblige the panting reader to follow it in its course and its developments; although the dictionary is ordinarily the work of compilers, as they are called, it does not exclude originality of ideas and of observation: he would be an ill-inspired man who saw in the dictionary by Bayle, for example, nothing but compilations. It tranquilizes the mind in its trouble over plunging into long developments, over following them with proper attention, or over classifying or dividing up the material. One picks it up and one lays it down: one opens it at random, and it is not impossible to find in it, on reading a few fragments, the occasion for long and fruitful meditation.

A man like Michelangelo appears, he is a painter, an architect, a sculptor and a poet. Such a man would be the most prodigious phenomenon if he were a great poet at the same time that he is the greatest of sculptors and painters: but nature, happily for the artists who follow his traces from afar, and apparently to console them for being so inferior to him, did not permit him also to be the first of poets.[7] He doubtless wrote when he was tired of painting or of building; but his vocation was to give life to marble and bronze, and not to contest the palm with men like Dante and Vergil, or even like Petrarch. His writings are of brief compass, as befits a man with other things to do than to give long meditation to rhymes. Had he done no more than his sonnets, it is probable that posterity would not have occupied itself with him. That devouring imagination had need to spread itself forth without cease,

[7] Delacroix, in his youth, had imagined being a poet himself; it is with some satisfaction that he notices the inferiorty of Michelangelo as a poet to what he was as a painter. As for sculpture, it is known that Delacroix had thought for a while of working at it, and had written to Barye asking him for the address of the man who furnished him with modeling clay.

and although ceaselessly gnawed by melancholy and even by discouragement — his history tells of this at every moment — he needed to address himself to the imagination of men at the same time that he avoided their society, unwilling to have about him any but little men, subalterns, his workmen, whom he could push from his path at will, men whom he liked at moments and to whom he was hospitable when fatigued by keeping forced company with the great — those who stole his time and compelled him to observe the civilities.

The practice of an art demands the whole of a man; for him who is genuinely in love with it, devotion to the work is a duty. Painting and sculpture are almost the same art during these centuries of renewal, when encouragements are bestowed upon talent as they should be, and when the horde of mediocre talents has not yet scattered piecemeal the good will of the Maecenases and confused the admiration of the public. But when schools have multiplied and mediocre talents abound, each one claiming a part of the public munificence or that of the great, to whom shall it be granted to take the place of several men, if the claimant is the only one to carry on his work?

For if one can conceive a single man professing at the same time sculpture, painting, and even architecture, because of the bonds uniting these arts which are separated only in periods of decadence, we may not so easily recognize the possibility of bringing together. . . .

One must limit oneself. In our day, one who writes. . . .

January 25.

For the Dictionary:
As to the taste of nations. The English love of details, of the terrible. The monk. Italian taste in music, in art, etc.

January 26.

Charlet. I shall not follow the author[8] of the *Vie de Charlet* through

[8] M. de la Combe.

the anecdotes in his history. They take up a large part of the book; as a friend of the great artist, he got to know any number of minor matters, and he brings out, as he should, the honorable things in his character. He treats this as a pious duty, so to speak, and he deserves only praise for doing so, as well as for the parts of his work wherein he brings out the virtues of the illustrious draftsman.

Such is not the task of a contemporary of Charlet, an artist like himself, who undertakes to bring the public to an esteem of his works equal to their merit. In exhibiting to all eyes the intimate part of his life, he falls into contradiction with that opinion which has grown more and more firm, to wit, that this furor for biography. . . . History, biography itself, if it is possible to write one about a celebrated man whose name is the property of the centuries, has not the drawbacks. . . .

January 27.

Architecture. In our day, architecture has fallen to complete degradation; it is an art which no longer knows where it is; it wants to produce the new, and there are no new men. Bizarreness takes the place of that novelty which is so much sought for, and which is to so slight an extent novel and original precisely because it is sought for. The ancients arrived by degrees at the pinnacle of perfection, not all at once, not by telling themselves that they had absolutely to astonish, but by rising by degrees and almost without knowing they did so, to that perfection which was the fruit of genius supported by tradition.

What do the architects hope for when they break with all the traditions? People have grown tired, it is said, of Greek architecture, which the Romans, great as they were, respected — save for the modifications which their usages led them to adopt. After the darkness of the Middle Ages came the Renaissance, which was indeed a renascence of taste, which is to say of good sense, which is to say of the beautiful in every field; a return was made to those admirable proportions whose incontestable empire will always have to be recognized, despite all pretensions to originality. Our modern usages, so different on innumerable points from those of the ancients, are, however, marvelously adapted to the style of which I speak. Air, light, facility of movement for large numbers of people, grandiose aspect, all reply more and more to this gradual widening out of our cities and of our habitations. The enclosed and unquiet life of our forefathers, ceaselessly occupied with the defense of their houses, with keeping a sharp watch for attackers to be spied out through peepholes which let in scarcely any light, and the narrow streets, enemies of that development of lines native to the antique genius, were suited to a society that was oppressed and forced to keep constantly on the alert.

Therefore, what business have we with those constructors of buildings in the fashion of the Paris of the fifteenth century? Does it not seem that at each of those peepholes which they call windows, we must at any moment see men armed with arquebuses, or that we are to see a portcullis fall behind those gates swinging on formidable hinges and studded with menacing nails?

The architects have abdicated; there are some who distrust themselves and their colleagues to the point of telling you with a species of candor that there is no longer any invention, and even that invention is no longer possible. It is therefore necessary to fall back on the past and as, according to them, the taste for the antique has had its day, they get their inspiration from the Gothic, which seems to them something almost new, in their rejuvenation, because of the desuetude into which it had fallen; they plunge into the Gothic so as to appear novel. What Gothic! and what novelty! There are some who naively confess that the circle is closed, that Greek proportions are wearisome through their monotony; that there is no longer any return save to the proportions found in the monuments of the centuries of barbarism; even so, if they used the proportions of that art which was thought to be buried and added to them even a few gleams of true invention. . . . They do not invent, they make tracings from the Gothic.

January 30.

Dictionary:

Subjects of pictures. There are artists who can choose their subjects only from foreign works that lead to vagueness. Our authors are too perfect for us: the imagination of the spectator is guided by the impression of things so well presented and so perfect in execution.

Perhaps the English are more at ease when taking their subjects from Racine and Molière than from Shakespeare and Lord Byron.

The more perfect the work which gives the idea to the picture, the fewer chances a neighboring art will have to produce an equal effect on the imagination, if it inspires itself from such a book. Cervantes, Molière, Racine, etc.

January 31.

As to the soul. Jacques had difficulty in persuading himself that what is called *the soul,* that impalpable *being* — if the word *being* may be applied to something that has no body, that is not to be perceived by the senses, not even like the wind which, invisible as it is. . . .

. . . may continue to be that something which he feels, of which he can have no doubt, when the habitation formed of bones, and of flesh, in which the blood circulates and the nerves perform their function, has ceased to be that factory in movement, that laboratory of life which maintains itself amid opposing elements, amid so many accidents and vicissitudes.

When the eye has ceased to see, what becomes of the sensations reaching that poor thing, the soul, as it seeks a refuge I know not where, by means of that window, as we may call it, opened upon visible creation? You will say that the soul remembers what it has seen, keeping up its movement and consoling itself through memory; but if remembrance, after taking the place of sight as best it can, or of hearing, or of all the other senses that we lose in turn, then itself burns out, what will be the food of that flame which no one has seen? What becomes of it when, attacked in its last refuges by paralysis or imbecility, it is finally constrained, by the definitive cessation of life and by perpetual exile, to separate itself from those organs which are then no more than inert clay? Exiled from that body which some call its prison, is it a witness to the spectacle of mortal decomposition when priests, with their ceremony, come to murmur paternosters over that senseless clay, or when by chance a voice is raised to address to it a last farewell? At the brink of that tomb about to close, does it gather up its part of those funeral mummeries? What does it become at that supreme moment when, forced to exile itself completely from that body which it animated or from which it received animation, what condition does it assume in that widowhood of all the senses and at the moment when the blood stops and freezes, when it ceases to give impulse to this bizarre composite of matter and of spirit, approximately like the balance-wheel of a clock which, when it stops, stops all the other wheels and the movement?

Jacques grieved over this mortal doubt — and yet he sacrificed to glory. He spent days and nights in polishing a work or works destined, as he hoped, to perpetuate his name. This singular contradiction regarding the search for a vain renown to which his ashes would be insensible could not, on the one hand, correct his search, nor, on the other, give him the hope of survival and of feeling himself admired when he should no longer feel himself alive.

A friend of Jacques's was a thorough-going materialist: he was a man for whom that small domain which we call science did not have a corner that he would not have excavated and searched to its depths. It was with chagrin that he asked himself whence this immortal soul could have obtained the privilege of remaining all by itself amidst everything that we see. Unless one were quite positive about looking on this soul as portions of the great being, or emanations from it, he thought that it must partake of the common lot, be born (if something which is nothing can be born), develop according to its nature, and perish. Why should it ever have begun, he said to himself, if it is not to end? Are we to think that the innumerable souls of all human creatures, including those of idiots, Hottentots, and all the men no different from the brute, have existed for all eternity? For when you come down to the point, matter, save for its successive modifications, is in this situation: and so this immensity of nothings, destined, one day, to give intelligence to this, was necessary. . . .

Why, if the mind is not lost, do not the creations of the great souls participate in that privilege? A fine work seems to contain a part of the genius of its author. That fine picture, which is matter, is beautiful only because it is animated by a certain breath, which no more suffices to preserve it from destruction than our miserable soul suffices to make our miserable body endure. On the contrary, in the latter case, it is often that intemperate, mad, lawless soul which whirls its companion — I had almost said its inseparable companion — into a thousand dangers, into a thousand risks.[9]

February 3.

From the *Revue Britannique.* Thoughts of Samuel Rogers:

Do you want to get a cold article on your works? then have it written by one of your intimate friends.

From M. Vitet,[10] on "Pindare et l'Art Grec." *(Revue des Deux Mondes,* March 1, 1860).

"As a matter of fact such is the powerlessness of every speculative effort dealing with such a matter, so insurmountable is the difficulty of

[9] In matters of belief, observes M. Joubin, Delacroix remained a man of the eighteenth century, a disciple of the *Encyclopédie* and of Voltaire, whom he continued to read throughout his lifetime.

[10] An article entitled *Les Marbres d'Eleusis.* These penetrating pages define the character of Greek art as related to Roman art and, at the same time, Delacroix's position regarding the interpretation of antiquity, as compared with that of the school of David.

recovering in thought the lines and the contours, without the help of the eyes, that the leaders of this movement of renewal, all of them, in varying degrees, able, learned, ingenious, full of patience and of ardor — of genius even, in some cases, (I mention only Caylus, Barthélemy and Winckelmann), since they did not possess and could not know the real foundations of the art which they attempted to revive, were reduced to inventing ideas based on incomplete data and insufficient testimony; and so what could they do? what have they imagined? to what Greek art have they led us? to the one of which David was the publisher, not the father, the one which he accepted in its entirety from their science and wrote out with his able brush, under their dictation.

"They wanted to flee the influence of Rome, break away from the spirit of Vitruvius which weighed upon Lebrun, and seek, even in archaism, a remedy for decadence. They succeeded in avoiding the heaviness, the thickness, the indecision of lines, but they fell into dryness, thinness, and aridity. A strange system — that of suppressing life out of fear of its excesses! Its novelty, its very exaggeration blotted out its triumph: it was at first hailed almost with fanaticism, then allowed to drop, and ended by dying in a sort of lethargy, because that pretended purity was, in fact, death.

"Scarcely had it fallen, when we learned — almost without thinking of the matter, without any effort of genius, and without Winckelmann — what the real law was, the original condition which we had been pursuing for so long a time in our study of art. It was life, quite simply, life in its true measure, perfectly in balance with order and rule, but above all, life; and this is so true that any work of art from which life is absent, whatever its structure may be, and its forms and characteristics, is Greek only in name, or is not of the time of Greece, as may be affirmed with certainty. I do not know who it was who revealed to us that law, but the evidence for it was not well established and did not become incontestable until about the time of our expedition to Morea, and as a consequence of that. Already eight or ten years previously, however, people had got the first gleams of the truth.

Incomparable marbles, such as were possessed by no museum in Europe, suddenly appeared in London and in Paris. They were sculptures torn from the Parthenon itself; and there was a statue, less violently acquired and of less illustrious origin, but of similar style, our *Venus of Milo*. Is there still a clear memory of the astonishment, the disturbance into which these masterpieces threw men's minds? This type of beauty ran counter to all our traditions: here was no longer the stiffness of David, nor the noble amplitude of Lebrun; an unforeseen harmony of the most contrary gifts, an unbearable mixture of the ideal and of the real, of elegance and of force, of the noble and the natural, confounded our judgment. *The characteristic of true masterpieces is to cause this kind of surprises. They take us unawares and trouble us in the routine of our admirations; then, soon afterward, their ascendancy is triumphant, they seize upon us and turn to their profit our tendency toward habit: at that time, they make us see with new eyes, and bring down to a secondary rank everything that had reigned before them.*[11] Thus it was that the Elgin marbles and the Venus of Milo, when once accepted and understood, little by little dethroned the masterpieces we had preferred, not that there was with the latter the slightest decline but, as compared with these newly discovered things, they were of less noble birth and no longer had the right to first place."

February 8.

Balzac says in his *Petits Bourgeois:*

"In the arts, there arrives a point of perfection below which talent falls and to which genius alone attains. There is little difference between the work of genius and the work of talent, etc. . . . More than that, the vulgar are deceived by this. The mark of the genius is a certain appearance of facility. His work, in a word, must appear

[11] These lines, in which Delacroix recognizes the definition of his art and of his own work, were underlined in the manuscript by the painter himself.

ordinary at first sight, so natural is it always, even in the most elevated subjects."

From the above a deduction is to be drawn concerning the works of Decamps, of Dupré and, in a word, of all those who employ exaggerated means. It is very rare for the great men to resort to exaggeration in their works. A question to be examined.

Lawrence, Turner, Reynolds, and in general all the great English artists have the defect of exaggeration, particularly as to the effect, which prevents them from being classed among the great masters. Those exaggerated effects, those dark skies, those contrasts of shadow and of light — to which they have been led, however, by their own cloudy and variable sky, but which they have overdone to an unmeasured degree — make one hear the voice of the defects they borrow from fashion and prejudice in louder tones than the voice of their virtues. They have magnificent pictures, but the latter will never offer the spectacle of that eternal youth of the real masterpieces — exempt, all of them, I venture to say, from bombast and effort.

Extract from the *Mémoires d'Outre-Tombe*.

". . . That correctness in the representation of the inanimate object characterizes the spirit of the arts in our time: it announces the decadence of poetry and of true drama; it contents itself with the small beauties when it is impotent before the great ones; there is imitation, to the point of optical illusion, of armchairs and velvet, when there is no longer the power to paint the physiognomy of the man seated on the velvet and in the armchair. However, once people have descended to that truth to material form, they find themselves forced to continue with it, for the public, itself grown materialistic, demands that."

February 20.

From Sainte-Beuve, on M. Feydeau:[12]

[12] From an article in the *Moniteur* for February 20, 1860. (*Causeries du Lundi*).

"He says that people are altogether too anxious, and in a hypocritical way at that, about the morals and about the beauty that are forever being thrown at our heads. As he says, 'Outside of my duties as a professor and a professional critic, when I resume that role, I am impelled to do my hardest thinking as to the interests of talent. Is there novelty, is there still something new in this world? Is there somewhere, even today, still some verve, some ardor, some youth and some future? Is there anyone who tempts and who promises? I put these questions to myself, I remain open and attentive to the answers which, from time to time, come to me from the outside, and I do not let myself be turned aside from my interest by that special pleading which has been so fashionable these last years and is called *Morals* and *Beauty*.'[13]

"Morals, which these people constantly oppose to Art, should not it seems to me, be so constantly shown in contrast and in conflict with it. The great Goethe, the master of criticism, established the sovereign principle that we have above all to inquire into the execution in the work of the artist, and see whether he has done and how he has done what he wanted to do: 'There are many,' said he, 'who make their mistake by relating the idea of the Beautiful to the conception far more than to the execution of works of art; and so, doubtless, they must be embarrassed when the Apollo of the Vatican and other like figures, already beautiful in themselves, are placed in the same category of beauty with the *Laocoön,* with a *Faun* or other representations of the painful or the ignoble.'

"According to him, therefore, there is an essential part of the truth which entered into the works of the Ancients, into those that are most often admired and invoked, and it is that element of truth, of nature — often bare, hideous or low, less neglected by the Ancients themselves than it is said to be, and it is wrong to forbid the moderns to study and produce this same element of truth. 'Would that someone

[13] He refers to the prosecution of Baudelaire, in 1857, for the *Fleurs du Mal.*

might at last have the courage,' exclaimed Goethe, 'to withdraw from circulation the idea and even the word *Beauty* (he means abstract beauty, a mere idol) to which, once it is adopted, are indissolubly attached all kinds of false conceptions, would that he replaced it, as is only justice, by truth in its general meaning!'

"In France and in our society, it is even less the idea of beauty than that of morals that forms the great rock, with which people are forever arming themselves and that they hurl at the head of every new-comer with a readiness, a lightness of mind which one can scarcely refrain from calling curious, if one thinks of some of the men who make use of this weapon."

I add, on my own account, that as regards painting, it is with *beauty* that these people strike down everything that gets out of the rut. I am of the opinion of Goethe: one might say to oneself quite simply and gaily: "Let us crush the infamous."

From Captain Burton's journey in Africa:

"The wind was violent. The man called End-of-the-world took the occasion to quote to us the Somali proverb: 'Heat hurts but cold kills.' "

February 22.

Realism should be defined as the antipode of art. It is perhaps more odious in painting and in sculpture than in history and the novel; I do not mention poetry: for, by reason of the mere fact that the instrument of the poet is a pure convention, a measured language, in a word, which immediately places the reader above the earthy quality of every-day life, one sees how grotesque would be the contradiction in terms if anyone spoke of realistic poetry, admitting that such a monster could be conceived. What, in sculpture for example, would a realistic art be? Mere casts from nature would always be superior to the most perfect imitation which the hand of man can produce: for can one conceive a case in which the mind would not guide the hand of the artist and will anyone believe it possible, likewise, that, despite all attempts to imitate, he will not tinge his singular work with the color of his mind, unless one go to the point of supposing that the eye alone and the hand be sufficient to produce — I will not merely say an exact imitation — but even any work whatsoever?

If *realism* is not to be a word devoid of sense, all men would have to have the same mind, the same fashion of conceiving things.

(I must look up what I have said in the little blue notebooks[14] as to the contradiction shown by the theater between the system that tries to follow events as they are and the one which presents them and disposes them in a certain order, with a view to the effect.)

For what is the supreme purpose of every type of art, if it is not the effect? Does the mission of the artist include merely a disposing of the materials, leaving it to the spectator to draw from them, as best he can, a nondescript pleasure, each man after his own fashion? Is there not, independent of the interest that the mind discovers in the simple and clear carrying on of a composition, in the charm of situations ably controlled, a kind of moral sense attaching even to a fable? Who will bring it into clear view with more of success than the man who has disposed in advance all the parts of the composition, and in such a way that the spectator or the reader is led to perceive this, and to be seized and charmed thereby?

What do I find in a great number of modern works? An enumeration of everything that is to be presented to the reader, especially that of material objects, minute descriptions of characters, who do not describe themselves by their actions. It is as if I were seeing those building-sheds where each of the stones carved separately is before my eyes, but without relationship to its place in the ensemble of the monument. I detail them, one after the other, instead of seeing a vault, a gallery, or, even more, a whole palace, in which cornices, columns, capitals, even statues, combine only to form an ensemble either grandiose or merely agreeable but where all the parts are fused and coördinated by an intelligent art.

[14] These notebooks are lost.

In the majority of modern compositions, I see the author intent on describing an accessory character with the same care as the characters which should occupy the center of the stage. He exhausts himself in showing me under every aspect the super who is to appear only for a moment, and the mind is as much bound up with that character as with the hero of the story.

The first of principles is that of the need for sacrifices.

Isolated portraits, whatever their perfection, cannot form a picture. The special sentiment of the work is the one thing that can give unity, and the one way to obtain that is to show only those things which deserve to be seen.

Art, like poetry, lives through fictions. Propose to the professional realist the painting of supernatural objects: a god, a nymph, a monster, a fury, all those things of the imagination which transport the mind!

The Flemings (except Rubens, necessarily), so admirable in the painting of the scenes of familiar life, and who, curiously enough, have brought to this the sort of idealism demanded by this genre, as by all genres, have generally failed with mythological subjects or indeed merely historical or heroic subjects, those drawn from fable or from the poets. They trick out with ridiculous draperies or mythological accessories the figures they paint from nature, which is to say from simple Flemish models, and do so with all the scrupulous fidelity which they use at other times in representing a tavern scene. The result is bizarre incongruities which make of a Jupiter and a Venus, dressed-up citizens of Bruges or of Antwerp, etc. (recall the tomb of the Maréchal de Saxe).[15]

Realism is the great resource of the innovators at those periods when the schools are becoming languid and turning to mannerism; through it they awaken once more the blasé taste of the public, while the schools turn in the circle of the same inventions. The return to nature is proclaimed, some fine morning, by a man inspired, as he affirms. . . .[16]

The Carracci, and it is the most illustrious example one may offer, believed that they were rejuvenating the school of Raphael. They believed they saw in the master a weakening in the direction of material imitation. It is not very difficult, as a matter of fact, to see that the works of Raphael, that those of Michelangelo, Correggio, and their most illustrious contemporaries, owe to imagination their principal charm, and that the imitation of the model is secondary to it, and is even of a modest kind. The Carracci, very superior men, as one cannot deny, learned men gifted with a great feeling for art, told themselves one day that they must resume for the good of their own work the

[15] See the entry in the *Journal* on September 25, 1855.
[16] An allusion to Courbet.

thing that had escaped their illustrious predecessors, or rather the thing they had disdained; this disdain itself seemed to them perhaps a kind of impotence to combine in their works qualities derived from the variety of nature which seemed to them, the Carracci, an integral part of nature. They opened schools; it is with them, one must say, that we see the beginning of schools, as we understand them in our day, to wit, the assiduous and preferred study of the living model substituted almost entirely for the sustained attention given to all elements of art, among which this is only one.

The Carracci doubtless flattered themselves with the idea that, without abandoning the breadth and the deep sentiment of the composition, they would introduce into their pictures details which should be more perfect as to representation, and that they would thus raise themselves above the great masters who had preceded them. In a short time they had led their pupils, and themselves descended, to representation which was, it is true, more real, but one which detached the mind from the most essential elements in the picture — conceived as a thing whose first object is to please the imagination. As soon as the artists came to think that the means of obtaining perfection was to make of the picture a combination of faithfully imitated fragments. . . .

David is a singular composite of realism and the ideal. The Vanloo men no longer copied the model: although the triviality of their forms had fallen to the last abasement, they drew upon their memory and upon practice for everything. An art such as that sufficed for its time. Meretricious graces and enervated forms devoid of the accent of nature sufficed for those pictures, cast in the same mold, without originality of invention, with none of the naive graces which will make the works of the primitive schools endure. David began with abundant painting in this manner: it was that of the school from which he came. Devoid, as I believe, of any very live originality, but gifted with great good sense, and above all being born at the decline of that school and at the moment when the somewhat thoughtless admiration for the antique was appearing, thanks again to mediocre geniuses such as were possessed by men like Mengs and Winckelmann, he was struck, in a happy moment, by the languor, the weakness of those shameful productions of his time; the philosophic ideas which were then growing up, the ideas of grandeur and liberty in the people, ideas newly born, undoubtedly mingled with this disgust which he felt for the school whence he had come forth. This repulsion, which honors his genius and which is his principal title to glory, led him to the study of the Antique. He had the courage needed for a reformation of all his habits: he locked himself in, so to speak, with the *Laocoön,* with the *Antinous,* with the *Gladiator* and the other masculine conceptions of the antique genius: he had the courage to make his talent all over; in this he was like the immortal Gluck, who, at an advanced age, had renounced the Italian manner in order to temper himself anew in purer and more naive sources. He was the father of the whole modern school, in painting and in sculpture; his reform even continued into architecture, and to the very furniture for everyday use. He made Herculaneum and Pompeii the successors of the mongrel Pompadour style, and his principles had such a hold on the mind that his school was not inferior to him and produced pupils among whom some march on as his equals. He still reigns in some respects and, despite certain apparent transformations in the taste of what is the school today, it is manifest that everything still derives from him and from his principles. But what were these principles, and to what point did he confine himself within them, to what point was he faithful to them? Undoubtedly, the antique was the foundation, the cornerstone of his edifice. The simplicity, the majesty of the antique, the sobriety of composition, that of the draperies carried even further than with Poussin, but in the imitation of parts. . . .

To some extent, David immobilized sculpture, for his influence dominated that beautiful art as well as painting. If David had so complete an influence on painting, he had even more influence on the neighboring art, one that was not his own. After those years of fervor which. . . .

March 3.

I went out for the third time yesterday; for a long half hour I remained seated in the Luxembourg. Today the weather was sharp, and I came home earlier.

Through what singularity is it that the gravest literature is found to be the lot of the people that has passed and still passes for the lightest and most frivolous on the earth? The ancients themselves, who have laid down the rules for the things of the imagination in every field of art, present no examples of so sustained a feeling for order, clarity and seemliness as the French. There is a certain looseness in the works of the finest geniuses of antiquity; they like to wander. As they have the right to all our respect, we leave them free to go afield. We are stricter with our own men of talent. A book that is badly written in its ensemble is not allowed to save itself by the beauty of its details, nor even by the ingenious conception of the work itself. We demand that all the parts, ingenious or not, contribute in a certain measure to the connectedness of the whole; and on the other hand we demand that in a well ordered and logically built work, the details should not take away from the beauty of the conception. When a play had made the public hasten to the theater, the author had fulfilled his task only half way: it was necessary for the work to sustain itself, as the expression was, on being read.

It is probable that Shakespeare was but little concerned with this second part of his obligation toward his public. When the performance had achieved the effect that he had promised himself, above all when the gallery was satisfied, it is probable that he did not bother about the opinion of the purists; in the first place, the great majority of that public was unable to read, and could it have read, would it have had leisure for that, seeing that it was composed either of the young fops of the court, more occupied with their pleasures than with literature, or else of fishmongers, but little disposed to analyze the beauties of literature?

Who knows what became of the manuscript, the canvas upon

which the author had mounted his piece, of which scraps, distributed to the actors for them to learn their roles, fell into whatever hands were near and were gathered up at random by starveling printers, having full leave to piece them together according to their lights, and to fill up the gaps? Does it not seem that these plays so full of fantasy — I speak of what Shakespeare entitled comedies — or that those dramas, now lugubrious, now grotesque in their effect, I mean the tragedies, where heroes and servants mingle and speak each his own language, the action, capriciously led, taking place in twenty places at the same time or embracing an unlimited span of time, does it not seem, I say, that such works, with their beauties and their defects, must please only capricious minds, and that they can hold only a nation more frivolous than reflective?

For my part, I think that taste, the turn of mind of a nation, is strangely dependent on that of the celebrated men who, amidst that people, were the first to write or paint or produce works of any kind. Had Shakespeare been born at Gonesse, instead of at Stratford-on-Avon, and at a period in our history when, not yet having had either Rabelais or Montaigne, or Malherbe, or Corneille, there would have been far stronger reason for seeing the development in our country not only of a different theater (see Calderon, in Spain), but, even more, of a different literature. That the English character has added to such works some of its own rude quality, is a thing that I will believe without difficulty; as to the pretended barbarism that the English have shown at certain periods in their history and that people assign as one of the causes for the inclination of Shakespeare to go to extremes, as when he spatters blood over the whole stage, I do not believe, when I scrutinize our annals, that we owe much, in the matter of cruelty, to our neighbors the English, nor that the tragedies in action which threw so somber a tinge over the reigns of the Valois, notably, could have given us an education fitted to soften either manners or literature.

The fact that we banished massacres from our stage, which began to shine only at a gentler period, does not make our nation any more human in its history than the English nation: epochs still recent and of redoubtable memory have shown that the barbarian and even the savage still lived on in the civilized man, and that gaiety in the works of the mind could go hand in hand with pretty ferocious manners. The spirit of society, which is perhaps a more developed instinct in our French nature, could contribute to greater polish in literature; but it is more probable yet that the masterpieces of our great men came just at the right time to decry the bizarre or burlesque attempts of the preceding periods, and to turn men's minds toward the respect for certain eternal rules as to taste and seemliness which are no less those of every truly advanced social state than those of the works of the mind. We are often told that Molière, for example, could have appeared only among ourselves; I well believe it, he was the heir of Rabelais, not to mention the others.

March 8.

As to Rubens, as to his verve, as to the monotony of certain returns in his drawing. I copy here what I find in the notebook of 1852 following upon my observations upon the sublime tapestries dealing with the death of Achilles. "The conscious determination of Rubens in exaggerating certain forms shows that he was in the position of an artist who practices the trade that he knows well, without having to enter on that endless search to perfect it, etc."

In the same notebook, on February 15, speaking of a concert and of the music of men like Mendelssohn, etc.: "Here is not that happy facility of the great masters who are prodigal of the happiest motifs, etc."

Today I add the following, having acquired eight years of experience since the day when those reflections were written. It is good and appropriate to write down your ideas when they come to you, even if you are not occupied with a consecutive work into which these ideas can be inserted. But all such reflections take on the form of the moment. The day when they can be utilized in a work of a certain extent, one must refrain from too great attention to the form one gave them at the earlier time. One feels the patchwork quality in mediocre works. Voltaire must have noted down his ideas: his secretary tells us so. Pascal leaves us a proof of the same thing in his *Pensées,* which are the materials for a book. But those men, in pouring their material into the crucible, discovered whatever form they could and devoted themselves above all to the pursuit of ideas rather than to their form; and they certainly did not impose upon themselves the wearisome labor of hunting up the ideas that they had noted or of setting them, as a jeweler does his stones, in the form which they had first given them.

One must not be too difficult. A man of talent who composes should not treat himself as an enemy. He should suppose that what his inspiration has furnished to him has its value. The man who re-reads and who takes up his pen to correct himself is more or less another man than the one who wrote the first draft. There are two things that experience should teach: the first is that one must do a great deal of correcting; the second is that one should not do too much correcting.

March 14.

I have been to see the exhibition on the boulevard,[17] I have come home from it in a bad frame of mind. It was cold there. The pictures by Dupré and by Rousseau delighted me. Not a single Decamps gave me pleasure: it is antiquated, it is hard and soft, it is stringy; he still has imagination, but no drawing whatever; nothing becomes so tiresome as that obstinate finish over that weak drawing. He is as yellowed as old ivory, and his shadows are black.

[17] An exhibition of modern pictures at the gallery of Francis Petit, 26 Boulevard des Italiens. There were sixteen pictures by Delacroix. Among those by Théodore Rousseau was the famous *Allée des Châtaigniers,* now in the Louvre.

Mme Sand came to say goodbye to me in right amiable fashion. She wanted to get me to come to *Orpheus*[18] this evening.

March 29.

Extracts from the book of M. de Mercey,[19] *Etudes sur les Beaux-Arts depuis leur Origine jusqu' à nos Jours,* three volumes in octavo, 1855:

". . . Shall we get back to beauty properly so called, and to that ideal perfection of the form which gave so high a place to the great artists of antiquity? The present state of society permits us very little hope that we shall. Our customs which proscribe gesture and the nude are anything but favorable to the fine arts. The Greek artists lived under the happiest conditions; they could study beauty and reproduce it. Their religion looked upon the human form as divine, and the easy hand of morals together with the mildness of the climate permitted its exhibition to the eyes of the crowd. Men went naked in the gymnasiums and the public baths. The voluptuous ceremonies of a religion based on material things stripped women of part of their clothing *(and he might say that the tailor and the dressmaker did not have such a place among the Greeks).*[20] The painter and the statue-maker show their models among the athletes of Olympia, the priestesses of Cnidus and of Paphos, or the bare-armed virgins of the Panathenian processions.

". . . Indifference to matters of religion must necessarily bring with it indifference to matters of art; if art, as is claimed, can be nothing else than the expression of the dominant belief, the day on which

[18] Gluck's *Orpheus,* sung by Mme Viardot at the Théâtre Lyrique. At this period Delacroix made a sketch of *Hercules and Alcestis,* inspired by this opera (Catalogue Robaut, 1140).

[19] Extracts from the Introduction of the work. M. de Mercey, former director of fine arts, commissioner general of the Exposition of 1855, member of the Institute, died the same year.

[20] The words in parentheses are inserted by Delacroix.

that belief is shaken sees art totter with it; and later when incredulity comes to triumph, the artist and the priest succumb to the same blow. The history of art formally contradicts these systematic assertions. As we look over that history we see that if art is born and develops at the same time as religions, it is only at about the time of their decadence that it attains perfection. The works of these latest epochs are perhaps less striking, but because of the very fact that the lukewarmness of beliefs permits their being rendered less exclusive, they are more complete."

M. de Mercey doubtless means that during the Renaissance, for example, it is with men like Michelangelo and Raphael that the eye attains all of its perfection. But that is not the point of view of those theologian-artists who have come to us from Germany. It is not to be forgotten that they look upon the beautiful sixteenth century as the period of decadence.

He says that far from spiritualizing the form as the ancients did, Christianity has gone many steps toward humanizing it. In multiplying, indeed in exaggerating the poverty of the forms and the desolateness of expression, it thought to return to its very spirit, the adoration, that is to say, of a God who has become a man, laden with all our miseries and expiring in torment. For the martyrs, the same is to be said.

". . . Any man of good faith who can free himself from the yoke of passing fashions by admiring the mysterious grandeur [I deny the grandeur; physical height, yes: but there is something narrow in everything that is Gothic] [21] of the majority of these monuments of the second period of Christian architecture, will consider them rather as bold attempts than as the monuments of a complete art. He will discover in them strange analogies with the monuments which the Oriental peoples have left us; that same application of symbolism to the ensemble of the temple and to each one of its parts, that mingling of strength and of roughness, of triviality and of grandeur; those

[21] The words in parentheses are inserted by Delacroix.

infinite details applied to the most vast ensemble, without letting their delicacy, which is frequently puerile, take away from its majesty to the slightest degree. . . ."

On the contrary, I find that ill-considered details, the enfeebled quality of certain objects such as pillars carved with infinite detail, and the lack of proportion in the matter of height as related to width, take away enormously from the beauty of the Gothic.

". . . Conceived at different epochs and among different peoples, these edifices proceed from a single idea: the theological idea.

"The persistence of certain critics in finding the ideal of beauty in Christian art in what might more justly be called the deal of ugliness, has led them to strange aberrations, for example that of dating from the Renaissance the decadence of one of the finest epochs of modern art, and of considering Raphael, Michelangelo and all the rest of that generation of great artists only as painters quite inferior to those who had gone before, and who, as better Christians, had made a closer approach to their pretended ideal. . . ."

I must adopt this theme in order to fulminate against these real iconoclasts.

". . . In their opinion, from the time when art began to show some care for form, it became materialistic: through its search for beauty it became pagan. . . ."

He is wrong in his words, 'through its search for beauty'; he should have said in its search for life and expression: I certainly place Rubens and Rembrandt in the highest rank, but it is not from the standpoint of beauty that they are superior to the Gothic men.

"Creative power burned out completely; there could be great artists, skillful artists, even genius, but there no longer was art, according to the superior conception of that word. To pronounce such a sentence would be severe, if not completely unjust. The immortal artists of the fifteenth and sixteenth centuries may not all have been men of genius; they seem to us, however, singularly preferable to those creative spirits who had preceded them. The productions of their forerunners are not lacking, doubtless, either in vigor or in majesty; often indeed they bear the mark of a charming naiveté which belongs to the childhood of the arts as it does to the childhood of mankind; but these works, remarkable enough from such a standpoint, are far from offering that masculine and well-rounded beauty which characterizes the masterpieces of the succeeding periods. They were, in fact, only early and formless attempts; they proceeded, moreover, from an ideal that was to be modified by the great artists of later ages, an ideal to be rejected by all those who think that, to judge a work of art, taste is preferable to blind faith. Besides, is there in existence today, anywhere, such faith as this, the sole regulator of judgment among the apostles of the new doctrine? People may invoke it, make parade of it, and even persuade themselves that they possess it — and yet all of that does not really give them possession of it.

" 'What can be done by those who, in our day, are working, not without glory, to raise art up from these ruins?' exclaims the most eminent among them (Lamennais, *Esquisses d'une Philosophie*). 'They can do no more than the isolated man can do, the individual man; they cannot give to society that which it lacks, the consciousness of a faith which it does not possess! ' "

Are we to conclude from this that the new art must be postponed until that future period when "from a conception at once more extended and more definite, of God and the Universe, of humanity and of its laws, of its functions and of its destinies, there will come forth new types, which it will realize?" We do not think so; for that postponement until the great and future revolution, mystic and social, might very well be indefinite. Artists would run a great risk of letting their chisels and their brushes go to sleep for eternity if, before going to work, they were to await the realization of the marvelous period foretold by the modern precursors, the period when the dogma, which is still sleeping in the bosom of the infinite, will stand forth in all its shining splendor and rally to itself all the scattered and weakening religious beliefs of mankind.

April 3.

As to the fragility of painting and the other arts.

I am reading a *Life of Leonardo da Vinci* by a M. Clément *(Revue des Deux Mondes,* April 1, 1860). It is the pendant to a very good *Life of Michelangelo* by the same author, published last year. What strikes me in it particularly is his statement about the disappearance of almost all the artist's works, pictures, manuscripts, drawings, etc. No one has produced more and left so little. That reminds me of what Longchamps said of Voltaire: that he thought he had never done enough to assure his reputation. With a painter, every work is unique, it is exposed to far more chances of destruction or, what is perhaps worse, of alteration, and he has much more reason to try to produce many works in order that a few of them at least may survive.

What an interesting work it would be to write a commentary on Leonardo's treatise on painting. To embroider on its dryness would offer material for anything one would care to write.

In this Life of Leonardo, note the letter which he wrote to the Duke of Milan, in which he details all his inventions. I discovered in it that he had had an idea corresponding to the one which I had at Dieppe, in an article on the art of war, to wit, having chariots to transport small detachments of soldiers into the ranks of the enemy, etc. He says: "I make covered chariots *that are indestructible,* and with which the ranks of the enemy are penetrated and his artillery destroyed. There is no mass of armed men so great that it cannot be broken by this means, and behind these chariots, the infantry may advance without obstacles and without danger." He foresaw everything; he says, "In the case of naval combats, I can employ many offensive and defensive means, among others the *construction of ships that are proof against all bombardment,* etc."

The author of the article speaks of the various pictures of the Last Supper by the celebrated painters who preceded Leonardo: the *Cenacolo* of Giotto, that of Ghirlandajo, etc. These austere compositions are stiff, the characters do not reveal themselves by their expression, nor by their attitude, etc. More severe with the former of these masters, and already more lively with the other, they do not contribute to the action, which has nothing of that powerful unity and that prodigious variety which Leonardo was to put into his masterpiece. If one goes back to the time when that work was executed, one can do no less than wonder at the immense progress that Leonardo caused his art to make. Almost the contemporary of Ghirlandajo, the fellow student of Lorenzo di Credi and of Perugino, whom he had met in the studio of Verrocchio, he frees himself with one blow from the traditional painting of the fifteenth century; without errors, without weakening, without exaggerations, and as if with a single bound, he arrives at that judicious and learned naturalism, equally separated from servile imitation and from an empty and chimerical ideal. How singular it is that the most methodical of men, the one among the masters of this time who was most occupied with the processes of execution and who taught them with such precision that the works of his best pupils are confused with his own every day — this man, whose *manner* is so strongly characterized, is *without rhetoric.* Always attentive to nature, consulting her without cease, *he never indulges in self-imitation;* the most learned of the masters is also the one among them who is furthest from self-consciousness, and his two emulators, Michelangelo and Raphael, are far from deserving that eulogy to the same degree.

April 6.

Today I went to Saint-Sulpice. Boulangé[22] had done nothing and had not understood a word of what I wanted. I gave him the idea of the frames in grisaille[23] and of the garland, I did so, brush in hand, and

[22] Louis J. B. Boulangé (1812-1878), painter, collaborator of Delacroix at Saint-Sulpice; he had the work of laying in the backgrounds of the two big compositions. See the *Correspondence,* vol. 2, p. 140 and 141. Note that he is not Louis Boulanger.

[23] The ornaments in grisaille which bind together the oval ceiling and the panels in which the angels are painted.

with fury. The astonishing thing is that I came home merely fatigued and not enervated. It seems from this fact as if my health were coming back after all its small lapses.

April 7.

Went to Saint-Sulpice, where Boulangé was not awaiting me. The infamous rascal does not come, does not work, and blames me for these delays, pretending they are due to changes. He really was not there and I went home furious and wrote him a letter about it.

My evening walks are doing me good.

April 8.

Carrier[24] came at four o'clock, he is enthusiastic about the exhibition on the Boulevard des Italiens, especially about the *Interior*.[25] He took notice of the little Andromeda;[26] regarding that, I remember the one by Rubens that I saw a long time ago. I have seen two of them, moreover, one at Marseilles in the collection of Pellico,[27] the other in the collection of Hilaire Ledru in Paris, both of them very beautiful in color; but they make me think of this difficulty about the handling of Rubens: that he paints everything as if in the studio, and so his figures are not modified by different effects, appropriate to the scenes that he has to paint; hence that uniformity of the planes; it looks as if all the figures were models posing on the model stand, lit by the same illum-

---

[24] Auguste-Josephe Carrier (1800-1875), miniaturist, one of the executors of Delacroix's will.

[25] The *Interior of a Convent of Dominicans in Madrid* or the *Amende Honorable* (Catalogue Robaut, 351). It was in reality the great hall of the Palais de Justice at Rouen. The picture is now in the Pennsylvania Museum.

[26] Catalogue Robaut, 1001.

[27] If the *Andromeda* in the Pellico collection of Marseilles is the one now in the Museum of Arles, it is only a studio copy of the celebrated picture in the museum of Berlin.

ination, and at the same distance from the spectator. Veronese is very different in this respect.

April 12.

On Shakespeare, Molière, Rossini, etc.

I find the following in a notebook I kept at Augerville during my stay there in July, 1855 (Mme Jaubert was there): "Just now I saw those young ladies — blue, green and yellow — who were playing on the grass along the river. At the sight of those butterflies which are not butterflies, although their bodies present some analogy, whose wings spread a bit like those of locusts, and who are not locusts, I got thinking of that inexhaustible variety of nature, always consistent with herself, but always diverse, and affecting the most varied forms while using the same organs. The idea of old Shakespeare at once came to my mind: he creates with everything that he finds to hand. Each personage, placed in a given situation, presents itself to him all of a piece, with its character and its physiognomy. With the same human data he adds or subtracts, he modifies his material and produces for you men of his own invention, and yet they are true. . . . That is one of the surest characteristics of genius. Molière is like that, Cervantes is like that. Rossini, with all the alloy in him, is like that. If he differs from these men, it is through a more careless execution. Through a bizarre quality not often met with among men of genius, he is lazy, he has formulas and a habit of patching things together which give him a long-winded quality always evident in his handling but not marked with the seal of strength and of truth. As to his fecundity, it is inexhaustible; and when he wanted to be so, he is master of both the true and the ideal."

April 14.

Yesterday, and Friday, despite the presentiment I had, I went back to my studio after my long convalescence.

What I have done in the space of three weeks or a month and more, down to June 14 . . . is incredible.[28] I have greatly advanced the four pictures of the *Seasons* for Hartmann, etc, etc.

July 5.

Extract from the book of P. M. J. Flourens, *De la Longevité Humaine,* 1854. Preface.[29]

"From the physical side, I open to him great hopes for old age: a century of normal life and as much as two centuries of life in extreme cases, and all of that on one simple condition, but a rigorous one, that of a *well conducted, always busy existence,* work, study, moderation, *sobriety* in everything.

"The sobriety of Cornaro was extreme: twelve ounces of solid foods and fourteen ounces of wine per day made up his whole nourishment for more than half a century; during that time, he was never ill. 'I have always been healthy,' said he, 'since I have lived soberly.' "

I share his opinion that *minds perfect themselves in the measure that bodies grow old.* Each age has a strength which is peculiar to it, etc.

The mind of man is one in its essence, multiple in its faculties: their development is not simultaneous, but successive. Those which dominate at one age are not those which, etc.

Dieppe, July 19.

In the evening I go to the church of Saint-Remy; magnificent effect of that strange architecture illumined by two or three smoky candles planted here and there to render the shadows visible. Nothing more imposing could be seen.

Buffon liked only the verses of Racine; yet he said: "he would have been more exact in prose."

[28] A note written in retrospect on July 19 following.
[29] Because of his frequent illnesses, Delacroix was always preoccupied with the question of diet and of ways to take care of his weakening health.

Saturday, July 21.

It has been raining all day. After having tried to reproduce the effect of the setting sun that I saw yesterday evening, I take a walk under the arcades during the rain; I take a chance of getting to the pier when the weather clears up. I find the Rivet ladies there and their husbands. A terrible rain drives me away, and I go home drenched at about one o'clock.

At lunch, opposite that English family, the husband, the wife, and those three big boobies, their sons, each one uglier and more like his father than the others, I was thinking of the singular self-sufficiency of these automatons of money, and of their stupid pride in that famous constitution which guarantees no more liberty to them than to us, whom they regard as veritable slaves. In a land of equality, where there is an equal distribution of fortune among children, a strong, central-izing government is absolutely needed to do the important things. Private fortunes are too much divided up. The English aristocracy per-mits great efforts which have not, however, from any number of stand-points, the ensemble that may be obtained by a government which keeps a more special watch, and with greater power, over the great purposes which do honor to nations: great enterprises, unforeseen expeditions, etc.

The good middle-class Englishmen are so kind as to be very proud of their lords, who do not greet them, who draw all wealth to them-selves, and direct the government to the fullest extent.

July 22.

I have rented some books for a week. I have got my nose into a book by Dumas entitled: *Trois Mois au Sinai.* He is always using the cavalier tone of the comic theater that he cannot get rid of, even when speaking of the Pyramids; he uses a mixture of the most emphatic, most colorful style and studio jokes which would be more in place at a donkey party at Montmorency. It is very gay but very monotonous, I could not get half through the first volume.

I have taken *Ursule Mirouet,* by Balzac; always those pictures done from pygmies, of whom he shows all the details, whether the character be a principal or merely an accessory one. Despite the overdone opinion as to the merit of Balzac, I persist in considering that, in the first place, his conception of the novel is false, and then that his characters are false. He depicts his personages, as does Henry Monnier, through the technical words of the various professions, in short, through externals; he knows the words of the janitor and of the employee — in a word, the slang of each type. But what could be more false than these characters — prearranged and all of one piece? Look at his doctor and the friends of his doctor, that virtuous father Chapron, his face and even the form of his coat, which we are not spared, reflecting virtue, that Ursule Mirouet, the marvel of candor in her white dress and her blue sash, converting to the church her sceptic of an uncle!

No one is perfect, and the great masters of character show men as they are.

Champrosay, July 27.

In a corner of the railway carriage is a young lady whom I thought to be a ward of the silent and disagreeable man seated opposite her. In the local customs house the young person loosens up her tongue, to my great surprise, and addresses herself to me with an extreme amiability; my age and the Corbeil railroad line prevented my following up this charming adventure. She resembles Mme D.

I arrive at six o'clock and am delighted to get home.

August 1.

I am still reading Voltaire with delight. As to *Hamlet,* he says:

"Across the obscurities of this scrupulous translation, which cannot render the exact English word by the exact French word, one discovers the genius of the English language very easily, none the less;
one discovers its naturalness, which is not afraid of the lowest ideas nor
the most gigantic ones; also its energy, which the other nations would
take for hardness, its boldnesses, which minds little accustomed to
strange turns would think of as gibberish. But under these veils one
can discover truth, depth, and an indefinable thing that holds you and
stirs you far more than eloquence would. . . . He is a rough diamond
who has his blemishes; were one to polish him he would lose some of
his weight."

Does it not seem that the same thing may be said about Puget?
See him at the Louvre, surrounded by all the works of his time, conceived, as they are, in the style of classical and irreproachable correctness, if that correctness and a certain cold elegance are a merit. At first
approach, he shocks you by something bizarre, something ill-conceived
and confused in the ensemble; if you fix your eyes on one of the parts,
like an arm, a leg, or a torso, you will immediately be overcome by all
that power that is in the man; he crushes everything around him, you
cannot break away from him.

August 6.

I must do justice to Dumas and to Balzac. In his painting of the
remorse of the postmaster in *Ursule Mirouet* (it comes in the last part),
there are certain strokes that contain great truths. I write this at
Champrosay after the tragic death of Mère Bertin. The agitation that
I noticed in one of her heirs recalled to me certain movements of Balzac's
Mirouet and, strangely enough, it caused me, more than ever, to reflect
on the advantage of being honest, even when that advantage — that
of having a tranquil conscience — still takes second place in a noble
soul, as compared with the need to refrain from degrading itself
through the baseness demanded by self-interest. These sentiments have

recalled to me what I was reading lately in La Bruyère; I must look up the precise terms in which he speaks of the way a book can elevate you, and inspire sentiments of honor and of virtue; such a book is judged, it is good, etc.[30]

One may, however, make certain reserves: Balzac's book, false in a large number of its parts, is bad to that extent; it is good through the truthful description of that coarse nature which, devoid as it is of native delicacy, cannot bear the weight of remorse.

Dumas has pleased me also with his *Mémoires d'Horace,* inserted in *Le Siècle.*[31] His idea is a happy one, and the little I have read of his pages seemed to me delicately and ingeniously arranged.

October 2.

I write to M. Lamey:[32] "What have you to say about everything that is happening? Are chance and the passions of men not to cease bringing about the strangest combination in order to damn those who are their victims, and to occupy the leisure and curiosity of the ninnies, in which class I number myself because of the eagerness with which I devour those impertinent and lying newspapers that take advantage of our thirst for news?"

October 21.

That man Rubens is admirable. What an enchanter! I get out of sorts with him at times: I have words with him because of his heavy forms, because of his lack of research and of elegance. How superior he is to all those little qualities which make up the whole baggage of the others! There is a man, anyhow, who has the courage to be himself: he forces

[30] In La Bruyère's chapter, *Les Ouvrages de l'Esprit.*
[31] A newspaper serial embodying a fantasy on ancient Rome; it purported to be drawn from a manuscript found in the Library of the Vatican.
[32] The cousin at Strasbourg.

you to accept those so-called defects deriving from that force which sweeps along the man himself; they subjugate us despite the precepts which are good for everybody in the world — except him. Beyle[33] professed to esteem the earlier works of Rossini more than the last ones which, however, are regarded as superior by the crowd: he gives as his reason the fact that in his youth Rossini did not try to produce *great music,* and that is true. Rubens does not chasten himself, and he is right. By permitting himself everything, he carries you beyond the limit scarcely attained by the greatest painters; he dominates you, he overpowers you with all his liberty and boldness.

I take note also that his principal quality, if it is possible to make a forced choice, is the prodigious relief of his figures, which is to say their prodigious life. Without this gift, there is no great artist; the solving of the problem of relief and bulk is reached only by the greatest painters. I have said elsewhere, I think, that even in sculpture there were men who possessed the secret of not achieving relief; that will become evident for any man gifted with a certain sentiment who will compare Puget's work with all other sculptures possible, I do not except even the Antique. He attains life through relief as no one else has been able to do; the same applies to Rubens as regards the painters. Titian and Veronese are flat beside him; let us observe in passing that Raphael, despite his small store of color and of aerial perspective, is in general strong on relief in the individual figures. One would not say as much for the moderns among his imitators. There are good jokes to be made about the search for the flat, so esteemed by the arts now in fashion, including architecture.

October 22.

The gift of inventing powerfully, which is genius.
   Beati mites, quoniam ipsi possidebunt terram.

[33] Stendhal, in the *Vie de Rossini.*

November 13.

On reading Rémusat, a man of talent moreover, it is for the hundredth time that I make the reflection that modern literature smears weak sentiment over everything; this style, dragging in images on every occasion, and mixing in a pedantic and tearful seriousness that you never find in Voltaire, (Rousseau, by the way, being the inventor of it) gives to a treatise on centralization (that is what Rémusat is writing about) the tone of an ode or of an elegy.

"This figurative style of which they are so vain," etc.

Paris, November 25.

Yesterday we elected that insipid Signol[34] a member of the Institute. The most Meissonier got was sixteen votes. The only opponents he still had were the said Signol and the antique Hesse, both of them representatives or nurselings of the *Ecole*. These two factions, shuddering at the idea that an original talent should enter the Academy, united to overwhelm him. Doing so at the price of Signol's election, they did a deadlier thing than if Hesse had been the price, for he is an old man, leaving behind him no pupils to perpetuate the taste of the school of David, which I prefer, anyhow, to that taste compounded of antiques and mongrel Raphaelism which is that of Ingres and those who follow him.

I am writing, still on Sunday, to M. Lamey:

"We have within us something like a wheel that makes everything move as in a mill. It is absolutely necessary to make it turn, otherwise it rusts, and everything stops in our machine, body and mind. Your excellent regimen keeps you up in the fine state that you are in; as for me, I need exercise and work."

[34] Emile Signol (1804-1892), author of decorative paintings in the churches of Paris, notably at the Madeleine. Meissonier was elected to the Institute in 1861. Hesse himself, the antique Hesse, reached it in 1867.

Under the same inspiration I am writing to Mme. Sand:

"Please understand, my very dear lady, that a few excess years, though they release certain springs in the intelligence, give a singular heaviness to the ones that cause us to move and digest. I certainly believe in the perfecting of our mind as an effect of age; I am speaking of a good mind — healthy, naturally, and above all accurate. But, oh cruel condition of implacable nature! In a short time there is no body left, nor any circulation in that body to aid the mind; *man declines and departs just when he begins to work well, said Themistocles.*

In brief, there you are, out of your troubles, with a renewal of health. What a happiness, as you say so justly, to see around one everything one loves and to return to this daylight which shows you such beautiful things! What shall we find, beyond? the night, the frightful night. It will be no better than that; such, at least, is my sad presentiment: that sad limbo in which Achilles, already no more than a shadow, walked with regret, not because he was a hero no longer, but because he was the slave of a peasant since he had to bear the cold and the heat under that sun which, Heaven be praised, we still enjoy (on days when it isn't raining)."

January 1.

I HAVE begun this year by pursuing my work at the church[1] just as usual; I am paying my visits only by card, for that does not disturb me at all, and I have been at work all day; what a happy life! What a celestial compensation for my isolated state, as they call it! Brothers, parents, relatives of every kind and friends living together quarrel and detest each other more or less, without saying a word that is free from deceit. Painting harasses me and torments me, indeed in a thousand ways, like the most exacting mistress; for the last four months, I have been fleeing at daybreak and I hasten to this enchanting work as to the feet of the most cherished mistress; what had appeared easy, from a distance, now offers to me horrible and incessant difficulties. But how does it happen that this eternal combat, instead of breaking me down, lifts me up, and instead of discouraging me, consoles me and fills up my time so well, what I have left it? A happy compensation for the things that the good years of youth have carried away with them; a noble use for the moments of my old age which is besieging me from a thousand directions, but which still leaves me the strength to surmount bodily suffering and the ills of the soul!

As to *yellowish high-lights on flesh*. I find in the notebook of 1852, October 11, an experiment that I was making in this direction. On figures at the Hôtel de Ville, reddish or purplish in color, I risk some high-lights of *Naples yellow*. Although this is against the law demanding cold high-lights, putting yellow ones on a violet tone in the flesh brought about the effect successfully. In the *Kermesse,* etc.

January 7.

Among other things, I reply to Grzimala:

[1] Saint-Sulpice.

". . . When I shall have finished, I shall notify you and shall be seeing you again — with the same pleasure that I have always had, and with the sentiments that your good letter has revived. With what other man should I speak of the incomparable genius[2] for whom heaven was envious of the earth and of whom I think so often, no longer being able to see him in this world nor to hear his divine harmonies.

"If you sometimes see the charming Princess Marcelline,[3] another object of my respect, lay at her feet the homage of a poor man who has never ceased to be full of the memory of her kindnesses and of admiration for her talent, another bond with the seraph whom we have lost and who, at this hour, is charming the celestial spheres."

January 12.

I take pleasure in copying this letter which I am writing to Mme Sand, *currente calamo.*

"Dear Lady,

"I have learned, I no longer know from whom, that you are quite well, and that you are going to spend the winter I know not where, in order to make a complete recovery. Everything you do is well done, even though I am not edified as to your sojourn at the inns where you will recover your health. The good bed to which one is accustomed in the corner of the earth where Heaven has made us take root is like the milk of the nurse who brought us into the world. Thank Heaven, my health has been good so far; I find myself excused from the thing I have apprehended after two winters spent at my fireside, and that is running chances and going out to expose myself to adventures in order to preserve myself from fever. For the last four months I have been plying a trade which has given me back that health which I thought was lost. I get up very early, I hasten out of my house, and to work: I come home

[2] Chopin.
[3] Princess Czartoriska.

692

as late as I can and I do the same thing over next day. This continual entertainment and the ardor that I bring to working like a coach horse let me imagine that I have returned to that charming age when one is always on the go and when the going is, more particularly, to those false fair ones who pierce our hearts with their charming daggers. Now nothing charms me save painting and now, into the bargain, it gives me the health of a man thirty years old. It is my only thought, and the only intrigue I carry on is to give myself to it completely, which is to say that I plunge into my work as Newton (who died virgin) plunged into his famous research on gravitation (I think it was).

'My thoughts gravitate toward you, dear and good and faithful friend. I say that I do not intrigue, and yet I should perhaps not have written if I had not run across Bertin, who implored me to ask you what he could count on in the matter of the promise that you were good enough to make him about sending him a novel. He desires one eagerly and begs me to tell you so. I know that I am exposing myself to all the fury of our friend Buloz, if he happens to discover my request. He made a scene for me on this occasion, this summer; he apparently thinks me a vassal to the interests of the *Revue*. I treated him the best way I could and he calmed down. Tell me then, if you like (and you are speaking just to me), what your intentions are as regards the *Débats,* which, I repeat, has a very nice appetite, as I can well believe, for those pages which have a greater success than ever.

"Now there is no more room in this letter except to tell you that I shall always love you."

January 15.

Among other things I write to M. Berryer: *"To finish* demands a heart of steel: one has to make a decision about everything, and I find difficulties where I foresaw none. To keep on with this life, I go to bed early, doing nothing foreign to my purpose, and sustained in my resolution to deprive myself of every pleasure — most of all that of meeting the people I love — only by the hope of carrying my work through. I think I am going to die at it. It is in such a moment that one's own weakness becomes clear to one, as also the extent to which the thing that man calls a *finished* or *complete* work contains parts that are incomplete or impossible to complete."

As to taste in general, and in particular as to that of each people. On taste in general, and on that of each people in particular.

January 16.

On Charlet.

Seeing his picture of an Emperor on horseback, floundering in a swamp, unhappily finished up as compared with the sublime *Minuet,* and other works of his early period, which is incomparably his finest one, I take note that a talent is never stationary. If perforce it transforms itself we rarely may see a case where naiveté persists. Racine is an example of that, etc.

This very day, I am placing beside the finest sketches of Raphael that same *Minuet*. It loses nothing. That recalls to me the thought of Montesquieu: "Two beauties of mediocre value annul each other, two great beauties enhance each other and shine with the emulation that each has of the other." (verify the terms).

Augerville, October 9.

THURSDAY. Arrived on Tuesday.

We must not be unjust toward our nation. In our day, it has presented an art-phenomenon for which I know no other example elsewhere. After the marvels of the Renaissance when, more especially, our sculpture equaled or even surpassed Italian sculpture, France, we are obliged to say, underwent the decadence for which Italy had given her the example, as she had given that of her masterpieces. The reign of the Carracci, still a very glorious reign, had brought about for Italy, as for France, a series of mongrelized schools, among which the last word was furnished by the Vanloo school. It was reserved for our country, in its turn, to bring back the taste for the simple and the beautiful. The works of our philosophers had reawakened the feeling for nature and the cult of the ancients. David, in his paintings, summarized this double result. It is difficult to imagine what so bold a novelty, considering the period when it was produced, would have become in his hands if he had possessed the extraordinary qualities of a Michelangelo or of a Raphael. It was, in any event, of an immense influence amidst the general renewal of ideas and of politics. Great artists continued the work of David, and when that heritage, falling into less able hands, seemed to be stricken with the languor of which the finest schools have given examples, one after the other, there came a second renewal, similar in the fecundity of the ideas it stirred up to the one which David had set in motion; it showed phases of art that were quite new in the history of painting. After Gros, the issue of David, but original in such a number of ways, came Prud'hon, allying the nobility of the antique with the grace of men like Leonardo and Correggio, and then Géricault, who was more Romantic, and at the same time more in love with the vigor of the Florentines, and these two men opened infinite horizons and permitted new developments of all kinds.

[I hope the Ministry] will not consent to ill-considered eliminations nor take part in them. The pictures, very few in number, which had been designated for admission to the Louvre would have shed no great light, etc, and would be even more dispersed if sent to provincial museums. What is important to preserve is the instruction they could give if kept together; the question is far more of that than of any superior merit in the works themselves.

I will insist particularly upon the painters who have been the object of a large number of criticisms and whom people are proposing to eliminate to such an extent that the collection would be reduced almost to nothing; yet if we keep them together, they will give an idea of the connection among the Italian schools such as is to be found nowhere else in the collections of the museum.[1]

Augerville, October 12, 1862.

God is within us: it is that inner presence which makes us admire the beautiful, which rejoices us when we have done right and consoles us for not sharing the happiness of the wicked. It is that, beyond a doubt, which constitutes the inspiration of men of genius and which warms them at the spectacle of their own productions. There are men of virtue as there are men of genius; the one group and the other are inspired and favored by God. And so also the reverse would be true: there would thus be natures in whom the divine inspiration has no effect, who coldly commit crime, who never rejoice at the sight of the honest and of the beautiful. And so there are men favored by the eternal Being. Misfortune, which frequently, too frequently, seems to attach itself to these great hearts, does not, happily, cause them to succumb during their short passage: the sight of the wicked laden with the gifts of fortune should in no wise overcome them; what do I say? often they are consoled on seeing the trouble and the terrors which besiege evil beings and make bitter their prosperity. Their punishment, during the present life, is often to be witnessed. For the other group, the inner satisfaction of obeying divine inspiration is a sufficient recompense: the despair of the wicked, struck down in their unjust enjoyments, is. . . .

[1] Fragment of the first draft for a letter that Delacroix was preparing to send to the *Secrétaire perpétuel de l'Académie des Beaux-Arts* to protest against the dispersal of the Campana Collection, which had recently been acquired by France and which, within the Louvre, formed the *Musée Napoléon III*.

April 23.

I DINED at the house of Bertin, which was a pleasure as always; there I met Antony Deschamps;[1] he is the only man with whom I like to talk music because he loves Cimarosa as much as I do. I told him that the great difficulty with music was the absence of the unforeseen, due to the way one gets accustomed to the various pieces. The pleasure given by the fine parts is weakened by the absence of the unforeseen, and the waiting you are made to do by the weak parts and the long-winded passages that you know equally well can transform into a kind of martyrdom the hearing of a piece which delighted you the first time, whereas the neglected places were passed with the others and almost served to bind the composition together. Painting, which does not take you by the throat, and from which you can turn away your eyes whenever you like, does not present this difficulty; you see everything at once and, on the contrary, in a picture that you like, you accustom yourself to look only at the beautiful passages, of which one can not tire.

May 4.

The system, so strongly recommended by the Romantics, of mingling the comic and the tragic according to the practice of Shakespeare, may be as highly appreciated as you like. The genius of Shakespeare has the right to accustom the mind to that because of his strength, his frankness of intention and his grandeur of plane, but I believe this type of writing to be forbidden to a genius of secondary rank; to this clumsy conception, we owe a large number of bad plays and bad novels: the best of the latter, during these last thirty years, have been spoiled by the fury for this idea: I mean those of Dumas, those of Mme Sand, etc.

[1] Antony Deschamps, (1800-1869), poet and prose writer.

But this is not the only difficulty presented by modern literature along these lines; today people do not write a sermon, an account of travel, or even a report on some chance happening without assuming all the approaches to style, one after the other. Thiers himself, imbued as he is with the traditions and the great examples of our language, has not been able to resist, in his fine history, going in for all those perorations, chapter endings, and reflections, spotted with the tearful and sentimental style. A man who writes of a journey describes all the sunsets and all the landscapes that he sees with a comic style designed to touch your feelings, and thinks thereby to win the reader to him. This mixture of style in every piece is, so to speak, in every line. "And today," says Voltaire, "they write histories in the style of comic opera," etc. *It is well for every thing to be in its place.* When that astonishing man writes the *Pucelle,* he does not take the reader out of the light and bantering style, he does not depart from the tone of pleasantry; when, on the contrary, in the *Essai sur les Mœurs,* he devotes to the Maid an eloquent page, he shows nothing but admiration and regret for the heroine and yet without doing so in the style of an emphatic apology or of a funeral oration.

Nowadays one can not read a comedy or other light play without having one's handkerchief in hand, to wipe one's eyes over the passages in which the author has set himself to move the sensibility of his reader.

Friday, May 8.

I am writing to Dutilleux:

"My dear friend, the day before yesterday when I saw in your hands and under your eyes the little sketch of *Tobias,*[2] it seemed to me miserable, and yet, notwithstanding, I had done it with pleasure. Anyhow, be that impression what it may, I remembered after you had left that you had looked with pleasure at the little picture of the *Lion*[3]

[2] Catalogue Robaut, 1450.
[3] Catalogue Robaut, 1449.

which was on an easel. I trust indeed that I am not deceiving myself in thinking that it may have pleased you: I should have sent it to you at once had certain little touches not been necessary to finish it; I put them on yesterday. Receive it with the same pleasure that I have in sending it to you, and you will make me very happy.

It is still fresh in certain parts: avoid dust on it for two or three days."

Champrosay, June 16.

Returned to Champrosay after my two weeks of illness.

June 22.

The first merit of a picture is to be a feast for the eye. That is not to say that reason is not needed in it: the case stands as with fine verses, all the reason in the world does not prevent their being bad, if they shock the ear. The saying is: *to have an ear;* not all eyes are fitted to savor the delicacies of painting. In many people, the eye is false or inert; they see the objects literally, of the exquisite they see nothing.[4]

[4] This passage, written in lead-pencil, was not copied in the notebook, but was written in a sketchbook now lost. Delacroix died on August 13, 1863.

END OF THE JOURNAL

after 41 years, this remains first,

1863 died
1798 born
65

700

1822
1798
24 when he began the journal

SUPPLEMENT TO THE JOURNAL

SUPPLEMENT
TO THE JOURNAL

Undated. Envy has blackened every page of his history (1825).[1] While the Tartuffes and the Basilios of England were leaguing themselves against him, he laid down the lyre to which he owed his renown, he seized the sword of Pelopidas and lavished on the Hellenes his works, his fatigues, his nightly watching, his health, his fortune and finally his life. His enemies were numerous: but here is his tomb. Hate expires, envy pardons. The future, in its justice, will number him among those men whom passions and an excess of activity have condemned to unhappiness, through the gift of genius. One would say that he wanted to paint himself in his verses: misfortune, that is the lot of such great men. Such is the recompense of their elevated thoughts and of that great sacrifice which they consummate when, collecting into harmonious words the sensibilities of their organs, if I may so express it, adding to that the delicacy of their ideas, their strength, their soul, their passions, their blood, and their life, they give to their fellow men great lessons and immortal pleasures.

[1] Written after the death of Lord Byron.

Undated.[2] The question of the beautiful reduces approximately to this: which do you like better, a lion or a tiger? As between a Greek and an Englishman, each has his own way of expressing beauty, and those ways have nothing in common.

It is the moral idea of things that frightens us; in nature, a snake causes us horror, yet the boudoirs of pretty women are filled with ornaments of this kind: all the animals in stone that the Egyptians have bequeathed to us, toads, etc.

In nature, a thing is often full of character because of the slightness of accentuation or even of character itself that, at the first glance, it appears to have.

Dr. Bailly takes as a principle: "The proof that our ideas on the beauty of certain peoples are not false, is that nature seems to give more intelligence to the races that have most of what we look on as beauty." But this is not true of the arts; for if the Greek were more beautiful as a model than the Eskimo, the Eskimo would be more beautiful than the horse, which has less intelligence in the scale of living beings. But everything is so well arranged in nature that our pride is extreme. We build a world on every little point around us. The rage for explaining everything throws us into strange errors. We say that our neighbors have bad taste, and the judge in the matter is our own taste; for we know also that all the other neighbors condemn us.

Our painters are delighted to have a ready-made ideal of beauty in their pockets to hand out to their relatives and friends. To give an ideal quality to the head of an Egyptian, they make it resemble the profile of Antinous. They say: "We have done all that is possible, but if this is not more beautiful now because of the way we have corrected it, the thing to blame is nature, which is so baroque in turning up that nose and in making those lips so thick, when such features are intolerable to the sight." The heads that Girodet paints are an amusing ex-

[2] This fragment in the first edition of the *Journal,* is mistakenly assigned to the year 1823. It certainly dates from 1829. These are notes for the articles on art published by Delacroix in the *Revue de Paris* in May, 1829.

ample of this idea; such devilish things as nature makes, hooked noses, pug noses, etc., are his despair. What would it have cost her . . . to make everything straight? Why do those draperies take the liberty of not falling into the horizontal grace of antique statues? . . . Such was not the method of the ancients. On the contrary, they exaggerated in order to obtain the ideal and the great. What makes sovereign ugliness is our conventions and our mean arranging of the great and sublime thing called nature. . . . What is ugly is our way of embellishing heads and folds of drapery, of correcting art and nature by means of the transitory taste of a few dwarfs who rap the ancients over the knuckles, and do the same for the Middle Ages and for nature herself.

The earthy and olive colors have so overcome them that nature, with her vivid and bold tones, is discordant in their eyes.

The studio has become the crucible where human genius at the apogee of its development brings back to question not only that which is, but creates anew a fantastic and conventional nature which our weak minds, impotent to harmonize it with existing things, adopt by preference, because the miserable work is our own.

Notes for the article entitled "Art Critics" (*Revue de Paris*, 1829). The writers among the Romantics have defended themselves: but the poor painters. . . . Please permit. . . .

But the critics may be reassured. The artist will for a long time remain in their hands.

Beauty in art. Beauty! Where shall one begin on a subject so vast, one that has stirred so many celebrated writers? What a theme! An endless one; and let it be said in passing, just such questions as these are the most interesting, because with them, the last word is never said and because everyone can have a different opinion.

One of the maddest things about any system building on the ruins of another system is an affirmation that it has finally attained the beautiful: When the beautiful, as your grandfather saw it, is once for all condemned and put to flight, when it is in the pillory of the critics, will you still say that it is the beautiful?

And then, what kind of beauty are you talking of? for there are several kinds: what do I say? there are a thousand of them, there is one for every eye, for every soul, and each is appropriate to their inclinations, and to their special constitutions. Would it be too bold to affirm that, considering them only in their broad divisions, there are two types above all: the one belonging to people of delicate perceptions, people of a certain education and people of a certain standing to maintain before the world; and then the one of common people, coarse people, street-porters if you like, in a word those who have nothing more than a soul, if you can really call it one, which is to say a thing capable of feeling and of leaping with pleasure at the sight of any representation of nature.[3]

When one says such things, one is dealing in mere generalities. As long as you say: "The ugly is hateful, we must seek the beautiful," everyone is of your opinion. If you say: "This is ugly, that is not beautiful," then you find yourself at odds with any number of people, pursued by hatreds and never forgiven, unless. . . .

The difference, it will be understood, is a big one; for instead of being a species of savages ouside of all human laws, some kind of adorers of formless fetishes, the Romantics or frantics, as you please, really have a kind of good sense permitting them to distinguish a certain ugliness from a certain beauty; they will be recognized as really belonging to the family of bipeds gifted with more or less reason or a mania for reasoning. They distinguish accurately between the horribly tiresome work and the interesting work.

They really have a soul, passions, tastes. Consider Shakespeare,

---

[3] The above entry in the *Journal* and others in this section are given as examples of Delacroix's early speculations on questions of art. The reader will see that the subjects have been treated far better in his later years and will doubtless be grateful for the omission of many pages of material that is either immature or else repeated in better form as the painter advanced in years.

who makes his Jew say: "Has not a Jew hands, eyes, etc. . . ." and there you have exactly the claim of the Romantics.

People are always judging painting according to that of the old masters. It is what it must be, and they show the simplest and purest taste, etc. . . . but painting, etc. . . . And so, with the moderns, art dies as soon as it calls on the help of the Antique.

Do not confuse with the beautiful what other periods called the beautiful. Go further: be bold enough, in almost every case to say that what was the beautiful thirty or forty years ago is now the ugly. See whether you can bear the painting of men like Vanloo and of Boucher who delighted our grandmothers and who were the admiration of people who may well have been difficult to please, like Voltaire for example, and other great minds of the time. It will be necessary for another Revolution to change people's ideas once more before we can work out from all this material just the men who have true merit.

Notes written in an album dating from about 1840.[4]

Short articles on different subjects, on everything that strikes me. Published separately at first, and possible to collect afterward. On the ridiculousness of setting limits to the different types of painting; this narrows the mind; the man who, all his life, does nothing but make pin-holes. The greatest men have done something of everything when they felt like it. Caesar, Napoleon, Michelangelo, Rubens, Raphael, Leonardo da Vinci, Cellini, who was a goldsmith at first. Medals. Caradosso, Michelangelo — his sonnet on the block of marble, to the Marchioness: "I shall render thee immortal." Salvator Rosa, his satire better than his painting. He invented an instrument for improvising; a group of people used to gather in his studio and make improvisations;

---

[4] These notes were written in a small pocket notebook; they refer to the idea, so often in Delacroix's mind, that genius is not limited to a single expression, but should be universal; according to the character of the drawings in the album, it must date from about 1840.

his work lacks fineness but contains very vigorous passages. Engineer, painter and architect: the same thing.

François I advises Cellini as to the fortifications of Paris.

The mind is a pocket which distends the more things you put in it.

The born specialist — Agostino Carracci. His fine mind recognized. Gives all the ideas for the Galleria Farnese.

Hoffman.

Rossini writes very pretty verses, he arranges those for his operas according to his own ideas. It is well known what a capacity he has for everything.

Torrigiani, a soldier during the half of his lifetime, producing sculpture when occasion demanded.

Cervantes.

Verrocchio, painter and sculptor. In Leonardo da Vinci, he says: A man is not a painter if he is not universal.

Bonington superior to the genre painter. Such people never push back the limits of an art.

Nothing equals the landscapes of Titian and of Rubens. Those of the latter are the most admirable for the imagination. None of that studied detail which turns a landscape into a portrait. But the grandeur of nature and its fecundity.

Thus, not only is art divided into its different branches, but in addition, each type of art is divided up. Literature shows us examples of poets who do not write prose. The prose writer who does not write verse. The journalist, etc. There are some who write only novels, there are some who cut a novel into two or three sections and are so modest as to do only a part of one: thus we get the intimate novel, the maritime novel, etc.

The greatest portrait painters are the greatest painters.

Specialized men not progressive; they do not risk new forms. Men of vast brain having a need to express ideas, above all, do not attach importance to forms, or else invent them according to the needs of their work. Also they have less pretension, they make short work of processes in order to come at once to fundamentals. It is not a man in true possession of painting, music, etc., who will wait about expressing his ideas, who will go off hunting for curious rhymes and exquisite processes of painting. All that demands time which has to be taken away from essentials. Ideas, ideas. "But the rhyme, the rhyme," cries the professional poet.

Gluck, another specialty. He was able to make his fortune in the diamond business. And Diderot!

. . . At the moment when his picture lacked that last breath of life, that breath which causes a picture to cease being a picture and become a being, an *object,* and an object which takes its place in Creation, never again to die, possessing a name, a thing to be called transfiguration, etc. . . .

Gold is not often found in those smiling and fertile fields which bear peaceful harvests and fat pasturage. It is found in the entrails of the terrible rocks which terrify the traveler, *the lair of tigers and of wild birds.*

A great advantage about always composing the same tones is the facility one has in retouching and of being able to get back to what one has done before.

There is a great deal of the academic in Rubens: especially in his execution, especially in his systematic use of lightly painted shadow strongly marked at its edge. Titian is far simpler in this respect, and Murillo also.

Poetry does not possess that species of grandiose and abstract ideal which is found in painting and sculpture: there is nothing analogous to Michelangelo in poetry, which is not true and for which the natural is only a pretext, etc. . . . The group of the damned man and the devil biting his leg.[5]

Setting for the story of the sentiment in the heart and in the sick imagination of a man who, after having lived the life of the world, finds

[5] In the *Last Judgment* by Michelangelo.

himself a slave among barbarians, or thrown upon a desert isle, like Robinson, forced to wear out the strength of his body through his work — which brings him back to natural sentiments and calms his imagination. Or again, a painter, for example one of noble family, has become a monk. Impression of the paintings at the Invalides, in those cloisters. He decorates his magnificent monastery. His love affairs. His mistress is a nun. His disturbed heart. It seems to him frequently that he is still waiting — that it is possible for him to see her again.[6]

Ovid among the Scythians.[7]

"There is in nature a certain proportion of roundness and of sharpness: And it is upon observation of the middle ground between these two extremes that the perfect and true art of imitation depends. When the contours are too sharp, there results a hard and dry manner, and, in the same way, when one gets away from nature by giving too much roundness to the contour, one falls into what the painters call the cottony and the heavy, or into that kind of hardness that one finds in the works of Van der Werff." (Reynolds:)[8]

In my opinion, that is quite the rarest thing. Veronese often sins through hardness, Rubens and Correggio through softness. Perhaps if each one of them had set himself to the obtaining of relief through well understood planes rather than through melting or sharp contours, they would have avoided both defects. In Veronese, the draperies often lacking half-tints, are perhaps the principal cause for the dryness and the lack of relief, for the flesh is admirably understood with regard to the half-tint; far better than in Rubens, who is more academic, who has no dull, matt tones in the flesh. I believe that the brushwork of Rubens takes the place of a good many other things. But the best

[6] Idea for a novel.

[7] Words added later on in lead pencil. The preceding lines may have furnished a germ of the idea for Delacroix's picture of the great poet in exile.

[8] From Reynolds' *Discourses.*

example of the power assumed by a picture where the whole of the modeling is obtained by the planes, that is to say by modified half-tints rather than by the big academic masses of light and shadow is the contrast between the *Prodigal Son* by Murillo alongside of the *Saint Jerome* by Van Dyck or de Crayer in the collection of Maréchal Soult.[9]

Veronese's manner of painting everything with two more or less dark tints, as if everything were under a slight shadow, and later on strengthening the lights, seems like the best way of working in this system, which is the one that comes closest to nature. In relation to this, I must remember the men on the scaffolding in the Champs Elysées, who at first seem to be in full light. Then a ray of sunlight fell on only one of them and put all the others into a shade that then became apparent.

The method of glazing flesh passages, which is so good for imitating the transparence of the skin, leads to that absence of half-tints which is felt somewhat in Titian's pictures, where the light figures make a spot against the background and do not unite with it, as Murillo makes them do in his finer works.

The Carracci and Guercino seem to have been unaware of this principle. Their manner is wholly academic, they always present a collection of models each one copied separately, and all with their lights and their shadows, etc. . . .

You think that painting is a material art because it is merely with the eyes of the body that you see those lines, those figures, those colors. Woe to him who sees no more than a precise idea in a fine picture, and woe to the picture which shows to a man gifted with imagination nothing more than finish. The merit of the picture is the indefinable: it is just the thing which goes beyond precision: in a word, it is what the soul has added to the colors and to the lines, and that must go to the soul of the beholder. Line and color, in their exact sense, are the coarsely woven words on a coarsely woven canvas such as the Italians

[9] The collection of Maréchal Soult was sold in 1852. The catalogue does not mention the two pictures that Delacroix speaks of.

write in order to embroider their music on it. Painting is unquestionably that one among the arts in which the impression is the most material, coming from the hand of a commonplace artist, and I maintain that it is the one which a great artist carries furthest toward the obscure sources of our most sublime emotions; and it is the one from which we receive those mysterious shocks which our soul, freed, as it were, from terrestrial bonds and withdrawn into its most immaterial essence, receives almost unconsciously.

"There are but two roads that lead to an important goal and *to the doing of great things:* strength and perseverance. Strength is the lot of but a few privileged men; but austere perseverance, harsh and continuous, may be employed by the smallest of us and rarely fails of its purpose, for *its silent power grows irresistibly greater with time.*" (Goethe.)

Goethe forgets that perseverance itself is as rare a virtue as strength, and that it is indeed a part of strength. People think that it is within the power of everyone, *even the smallest of us,* according to what he says, to have perseverance. But the smallest man, which is to say the weakest man, is no more capable of perseverance than of strength.

Leda.[10] Her naive astonishment on seeing the swan at play in her bosom, surrounding her beautiful bare shoulders and the shining whiteness of her thighs. A new feeling awakens in her troubled spirit; she hides from her companions her mysterious love. Something divine that escapes definition shines in the whiteness of the bird whose neck passes softly over her delicate limbs and whose bold and amorous bill ventures to touch her most secret charms. The young beauty is at first troubled and seeks to reassure herself with the thought that it is only a bird. No witness beholds her transports. Lying in cool shadow beside the brooks which reflect her beautiful bare limbs while their crystalline waters gently touch the tips of her feet, she asks of the winds the object of her ardor, which she dares not remember.

---

[10] The subject of one of Delacroix's frescoes at Valmont.

In every object the first thing to be seized, in order to render it by drawing, is the contrast of the principal lines. Impress yourself well with this before letting your pencil touch the paper. In Girodet, for example, this rule is well observed in parts of his work, because of the tenseness with which he considered the model; he has somehow managed to seize something of her grace, but it gets into his work more or less by chance. He did not recognize the principle, even while applying it. X——[11] seems to me to be the only one who has understood and embodied the principle. Therein lies the whole secret of his drawing. The most difficult thing is to apply this to the entire body, as he did. Ingres has found out how to use it in details of hands, etc. Without artifices to aid the eye, it would be impossible to arrive at this point, such as prolonging a line, etc.; one should often draw with the glass.[12] All the other painters, without excepting Michelangelo and Raphael, have drawn by instinct, as a matter of inspiration, and have achieved grace by being impressed with it in nature; but they do not know the secret of X——; accuracy of the eye. It is not at the moment of execution that one should constrain oneself to measured studies, checking up with the plumb-line, etc; long before, one should have prepared oneself with that accuracy which, in the presence of nature, will by itself assist one in his impetuous desire to render the thing he sees. Wilkie[13] has the secret also. In portraits it is *indispensable*. When, for example, one has laid out one's ensemble with this understanding of the causes of things, when one knows the lines by heart, so to speak, one could reproduce them geometrically, as it were, in the picture. Portraits of women especially; it is necessary to begin with the grace of the ensemble. If you begin by the details, your work will always be heavy.

[11] Name crossed out.
[12] An ancient process, already employed by Leonardo da Vinci, Albrecht Dürer, and others. In it one uses a small panel through which holes are pierced at various levels; the panel is placed at a certain distance from a piece of reducing glass. The artist looks through one of the holes and draws the outlines of the object or of the landscape as they appear when seen through the glass.
[13] Sir David Wilkie (1785-1841), Scotch painter.

For example suppose you have a high-bred horse to draw, if you let yourself be caught by the details, your contours will never be sufficiently clear cut.

Make clear distinction among the various planes by marking each of them out by itself; classify each one according to the order in which they turn to the light; before proceeding to paint, decide on those which are of the same value. Thus, for example, in a drawing on colored paper, mark out the high-lights with white; then the illumined passages with white again but less vigorously; then those among the half-tints which may be represented by the paper, then a first half-tint with pencil, etc. When at the edge of a plane which you have firmly established, you put a little more light than in the center, you accentuate to just that much greater extent its departure from flatness, its relief. That is the chief secret of modeling. It would be useless to add black, no greater modeling would result. The conclusion is that modeling can be obtained by slight means.

There are lines which are monsters: the straight line, the regular curve, but especially two parallels. When man introduces them into nature, the elements gnaw them away. Mosses and other accidents break the straight lines of his monuments. One line alone has no meaning; a second one is needed to give it expression. This is a great law. Example: In musical harmonies a note has no expression, two together form a whole, express an idea.

Among the Ancients, harsh lines are corrected by the hand of the workmen. Compare the arches of antiquity with those of Percier and Fontaine.[14] There are never any parallels in nature, neither in her curved or straight lines.

It would be interesting to work out the question whether regular lines do not exist only in the brain of man. The animals do not reproduce them in their constructions, or rather in the attempts at regularity pre-

[14] Percier (1764 1838) and Fontaine (1762 1853), celebrated architects of the Imperial epoch, authors of the Arch of Triumph, of the Place du Carrousel, Paris.

sented by their works like the cocoon, and the honeycombs of the beehive. Is there a passage leading from inert matter to human intelligence, since the latter faculty conceives perfectly geometrical lines?

On the other hand, how many animals there are that work obstinately to destroy regularity! The swallow hangs its nest from the soffits of the palace, the worm traces his capricious path through the beam. Hence the charm of ancient and ruined things. That is what is called the varnish of time; in its ruins, the object once more approaches nature.

How many books there are that one does not read because they insist on being books! Their excess of length, of extent, fatigues. Nothing is more important for the writer than proportion in this matter. Since he presents his ideas in succession, the reverse of what the painter does, bad divisions of the material and an excess of detail fatigue the mind. Moreover, the predominance of inspiration does not carry with it the absence of all genius for combining things, and in the same way, the predominance of combining does not imply complete absence of inspiration. Alexander proceeded, according to the expression of Bossuet, by grand and impetuous thrusts. He cherished the poets and had only esteem for the philosophers. Caesar cherished the philosophers and had only esteem for the poets. Both reached the highest point of glory, the former by inspiration supported by combining, the latter by combining supported by inspiration. Alexander was great above all through his soul, Caesar through his mind.

Comparison between Puget[15] and Michelangelo (it might be introduced with reference to the drawing of Michelangelo). Extract and cite *in extenso* the judgment of M. Emeric-David[16] in the Ephémérides.

[15] Delacroix developed these ideas in an article on Puget published in 1845 in the *Plutarque Français*. These notes perhaps date from that year.

[16] Emeric-David (1755 1839), critic and historian of art; he was of the idea that the Greeks worked on a basis of a system of numbers which gave them their proportions.

This article could be a vindication of French art and a comparison between the merit of our masters and those of Italy, more particularly, since the critics claim that all beauty comes from there: Lesueur, his character, his angelic naiveté; Poussin and his gravity; Lebrun, although inferior, may be compared with the successors of the Carracci; he has not, in truth, the vitality of the latter nor the naive imitation of Guercino, but he is far superior to men like Cortona and Solimena.

Description of the marble sketch of *Alexander on Bucephalus*.[17]

Consult again the work by Cochin[18] on composition as used by French and foreign artists.

June 21 [1844].

As to the abuse of wit by the French. They bring it into their works everywhere, or rather they want the author to be apparent everywhere, they want the author to be a man of wit and with an understanding of everything; hence those personages in novels or in comedy who do not speak according to their characters, hence those endless reasonings to display superiority, erudition, etc.; in the arts the same is true. The painter thinks less about expressing his subject than of showing the brilliance of his ability, his skill; hence the beautiful execution, the learned touch, the remarkably rendered passage . . . well then, unhappy man! while I am admiring your skill, my heart is chilled and my imagination folds up its wings.

The truly great masters do not proceed after that fashion. No, without a doubt, they are not devoid of the charm of execution; quite the reverse; but it is not that sterile, material execution which can inspire no other esteem than that which is felt for a mere feat. Consider Paul Veronese, or the Antique. A real abnegation of vanity is needed

[17] By Puget.
[18] Charles-Nicholas Cochin (1715–1790), draughtsman, engraver and writer.

by men who would venture to be simple, if indeed they have the strength to be so; the proof, even among the great masters, is that they almost always begin by the abuse that I point out; during their youth, when all their qualities stifle them, they give preference to puffery and to wit . . . they want to shine rather than to touch; it is the author that they want to have admired through the characters he creates; when they are merely clear or touching, they imagine themselves to be flat.

If modern authors talk so much about duels, it is because people no longer fight them. It is the mainspring of their narratives; they give unconquerable bravery to their heroes; they seem to think that if they described poltroons, the reader would have a bad idea of the author's valor.

The heroes of Lord Byron are Hectors, mere lay figures, one would seek in vain for such types in nature.

This false style of writing has produced a thousand unfortunate imitations.

Yet nothing is easier than to imagine a completely ideal being, to be decorated at will with all the virtues or with all the extraordinary vices which seem the appanage of powerful natures.

September 22, [1844].

It would be more reasonable to say that those men in whom genius united with a great weakness of constitution, had a feeling, early in life, that they could not at the same time carry on study and the agitated and voluptuous life of the generality of men, organized in average fashion; thus men of genius have been led to moderation in order to conserve their strength, and this has been for them the equivalent of health, and with a number of them the system ended with a triumph over their weak constitution; I have not even mentioned the charms of study and the compensation they offer.[19]

[19] An allusion to his own manner of life.

Against rhetoric. The preface to *Obermann* and the book itself. A little rhetoric in that preface, I mean, of course, the preface that is not by Senancour.[20]

Rhetoric appears everywhere: it spoils pictures as it does books. What makes the difference between the books of literary men and those by men who write only because they have something to say, is that in the latter works, rhetoric is absent; on the other hand, it poisons the best inspirations of the professional writers.

Thinking again of that same preface by George Sand, why does it not satisfy me? In the first place, because of that trace of rhetoric which tangles up the subject itself with an ornate or conscious manner of expression. Perhaps if the author were less concerned about producing a piece of eloquence and had put her head between her hands more often to look straight at her own feelings, she would have represented for me a part of my own. I admire what she says, but she does not present my sentiments to me.

Another question. Is not the most desolating part of human work this incompleteness in the expression of sentiments, in the expression resulting from the reading of a book? It is only nature who creates complete things. On reading this preface, I said to myself: "Why this point of view and why not another, or why not both, or why not everything that may be said on the subject?" An idea serving as a starting point, and leading you on to another idea takes you away completely from the point of view which at first gave unity, from that general impression of an object which one conceives. In explanation, I would compare the state of an author preparing to describe a situation or to establish a system or to produce a piece of criticism, with that of a man on a hilltop who sees before him a vast countryside with woods, brooks, meadows, dwellings, and mountains. If he undertakes to give a detailed

[20] Senancour's *Obermann*, which had appeared in 1804, had just been republished in a third edition with a preface by George Sand (1844). This gives the approximate date of the above fragment. Extracts from *Obermann* in the *Journal* show what a favorite it was with Delacroix.

idea of all this, and if he enters one of the paths offered to him, he will arrive either at cottages, or at forests or at only a few parts of the vast landscape. He will often lose sight of the principal and most interesting parts, and will neglect them, because he made a bad decision at the start . . . but, I shall be told, what remedy do you see for that? I see none, and there is none. The works that seem to you the most complete are merely a matter of whimsical paradox. The point of view that one had at the beginning, and from which all the rest is to be the continuation, perhaps impressed you under its meanest aspect, the one in which it is least interesting! Verve, at times, or persistence in digging at an ungrateful soil, will cause us to find special or really beautiful passages; but again, you have made but an imperfect communication to the reader. Perhaps later on, when you see your work again and meditate upon your subject in a better frame of mind, you will blush to see how much has escaped you.

If one considered life as a simple loan, one would perhaps be less exacting. We possess actually nothing; everything goes through us, wealth, etc.

To whom have I lent the portrait of Fielding?[21]

One is never long-winded when one says exactly all that one has wanted to say. If you become concise by suppressing a *who* or a *that,* but become obscure or embarrassed by so doing, what advantage have you gained? Assuredly, you have not attained the purpose of the writer's art, which is above all to make himself understood.

It is always necessary to suppose that what you have to say is interesting; for if the matter did not stand so, there would be small importance to the question as to whether you were long-winded or concise.

The works of Hugo[22] resemble the first draft of a man who has some talent: he says everything that comes into his head.

[21] Portrait of Thales Fielding, his friend, dating from 1823 (Catalogue Robaut, 60).
[22] A paradox of Delacroix's that became celebrated; it was, however, a necessary consequence of the contrast between the genius of the two men.

On the falsity of the modern system in novels, that is to say that mania for optical illusion in descriptions of places and costumes, which at first gives an impression of severity, but only still more to falsify the impression of the work later on, when the characters turn out to be false, when they talk inappropriately and interminably, above all when the prearranged fable which is to bring them in and cause them to act offers no more than the commonplace or melodramatic tissue of all the well worn combinations used to produce effect. The characters make one think of children imitating the plays they have seen on the stage. The action is represented just as it was, which is usually an absurdity, like settings made up of real branches of trees to represent trees, etc.

To arrive at satisfaction for the mind, after having described the scene of the action or the externals of the actors, as Balzac and the others do, miracles of truth would be needed in the description of the characters and the speeches they are supposed to make; the slightest word indicating emphasis, the slightest prolixity in the expression of sentiments, destroys the whole effect of those preambles, in appearance so natural. When Gil Blas says that Señor ——— was a tall, thin esquire with cautious manners, he would not be amusing me if he told me how his eyes were, or all the details of his coat; or, if he missed one of these details, there will be one so characteristic as to describe the whole personage, and to such a point that accessory descriptions, if one added them, would produce no other effect than that of preventing the mind from seizing clearly the feature which decides the man's whole look.

Inspiration. Talent. (For the Dictionary).[23]
Ordinary people think that talent must be always on its own level and that it arises every morning like the sun, rested and refreshed, ready to draw from the same storehouse — always open, always full,

[23] This fragment is to be connected with the notes for the *Dictionary* written in 1857. It probably dates from the same period.

always abundant — new treasures that it will heap up on those of the day before; such people are unaware that, as in the case of all mortal things, talent has its increase and decrease, and that independently of the career it takes, like everything that breathes (a career consisting of feeble beginnings, growth, maturity, and gradual decline), it undergoes all the accidents of health, of sickness, and of the dispositions of the soul — its gaiety or its sadness. Outside of such matters, it is subject to vagaries in the full exercise of its strength, it frequently engages upon misleading roads; it then needs much time to get back from them to the point whence it started and, when there, it often discovers that it is no longer the same. As with our perishable flesh, as with our weak life which can be attacked on all sides and by all creatures, and which therefore is obliged to resist a thousand destructive influences and so demands either continual exercise or else incessant care to protect it from being devoured by the universe which weighs upon us, talent is obliged constantly to keep guard over itself, to combat, and to keep perpetually on the alert amid the obstacles that witness the exercise of its singular power. Adversity and prosperity are pitfalls equally to be feared. Too great success tends to enervate it, as non-success discourages it. Many a man of talent has known but a single gleam, which died away immediately after it had appeared. That gleam bursts forth in some cases immediately after these men have manifested themselves, and then disappears forever. Others, weak and tottering, or diffuse or monotonous at the beginning, have, after a long and almost dark career, shone with an incomparable splendor, as was the case with Cervantes; Lewis, [24] after having produced *The Monk,* never did another thing of value. There are some who have never undergone any eclipse, etc. . . .

The principal attribute of genius is to coördinate, to compose, to assemble relationships, and to see them with greater exactitude and in greater extension.

[24] Matthew Gregory Lewis (1775-1818), English novelist, friend of Scott and of Byron, author of *The Monk,* a novel which was celebrated in the time of Romanticism.

[*1846?*][25]

Every license as to unity of time and of place being given to the poet, Shakespeare's system is doubtless the most natural one; for with him, actions follow one another as they do in history: the personages announced, whether prepared or not, come upon the stage at the moment when they are needed, remain there but a few minutes if necessary, and are suppressed for the same reason which brought them on, which is to say the needs of the action. There you have indeed the way in which things happen in nature, but is that art? One might say that the French system, on the contrary, has overstepped the conditions necessary for art, and that, in order to remain faithful to these conditions, it has renounced being natural. The French system is evidently the result of very ingenious combination, designed to give an impression of greater nervous energy and greater unity, which is to say, something of greater art; but the result is that with the greatest masters these means become petty and puerile, and in their own way harmful to the impression, because they create a need for artificial springs of action, preparations, etc. Thus it is that this system brings about regularity and a kind of cold symmetry rather than unity. Shakespeare has at least the unity of a vast countryside filled with objects that are confused, it is true, one where the eye may perhaps hesitate to seize an ensemble from the myriad of details; yet that ensemble must finally appear, because the principal circumstances, thanks to the force of his genius, take a powerful hold upon the mind.

That a Greek temple, perfectly proportioned in all its parts, should seize the imagination and satisfy it completely is the easiest thing to conceive; the theme of the architect is immeasurably simpler than that of a dramatic poet: there is neither the unforeseen quality of events, nor eccentric characters, nor yet the wave-like movements of the pas-

---

[25] All the following fragments, which seem related with the year 1846, are from a notebook or several notebooks now lost. The reader will observe that the tone of these notes already announces the *Journal,* which will begin again to be regularly written in 1847.

sions, complicating the effects to be produced and the manner of expressing them in a thousand ways: yet I should not be far from believing that the inventors of the unity of time and place had imagined that only by means of certain rules could they introduce into a dramatic composition something of the simplicity of impression which the mind feels on seeing a Greek temple. Nothing would be more absurd, considering what I have just said of the immense difference.[26]

April 24, [1846?].

Yesterday evening I saw *Le Déserteur,* by Sedaine: here is a type of play that seems very near the perfection of dramatic art, if it is not perfection itself. It was still reserved for the French themselves to modify the grandiose but artificial system of their great geniuses, that of Corneille, of Racine, of Voltaire. Exaggerated love of the natural, or rather the natural carried into accessory details, as in the dramas of Diderot, of Sedaine, and others, has not prevented this form from making real progress: it leaves immense latitude for the development of characters and action, since it permits changes of place, and also great intervals between the acts; and yet the law of progression in the interest, the art with which the actions and the characters contribute to augment the moral effect, is here quite superior to that of the finest tragedies of Shakespeare: One does not find here those perpetual entrances and exits and those changes of setting, used to inform us of a word spoken a hundred leagues away, that crowd of secondary personages amid whom attention is fatigued, and in a word that absence of art. There are magnificent fragments, columns, even statues; but one is reduced to performing in one's own imagination the work necessary to recompose them and to give order to the ensemble. There is not a drama of second or even of third rank in France which is not thoroughly superior in

[26] M. Joubin complains that the reading of the text is doubtful in various passages hereabout. It would, indeed, seem more natural for Delacroix to have said, in the above sentence, "Nothing would be less absurd, etc."

interest to the foreign works: that derives from the art, from the choice among the means to effect, which is again a French invention.

The beautiful idea of a Goethe, with all his genius, if it is one, to go and begin Shakespeare over again three hundred years later! ... The beautiful novelty of those plays filled with digressions, with useless descriptions, and so distant, really, from Shakespeare, in the creating of characters, and in the strength of the situation. By following the French system of tragedies, it would have been impossible to produce the effect of the last scene of *Le Déserteur*, for example. That changing of place for five minutes, in order to show the scene where the deserter is prepared to submit to arrest, makes one shudder, despite one's expectation of seeing his pardon arrive. There you have an effect for which no recital could be a substitute. Goethe or some other writer of his school would doubtless have introduced this scene, but would have shown us twenty other ones of mediocre interest, beforehand. He would not have failed to bring into action the young girl begging the king for her lover's pardon: he might perhaps have considered that that introduced variety into the action. It is perhaps not even possible, with this system, to suppress very much of the material facts; otherwise, there is no longer any proportion between the facts shown to the spectators and those which merely recounted. Thus pieces of this kind progress in only a jerky fashion: you are as if on a rolling ship where you can walk only by leaning way over to one side and then to the other; hence fatigue and weariness for the spectator, who is forced to harness himself to the machine of the author and to sweat with him in order to get over all the difficulties of those evolving countries and characters. In an English or German play, the last scene of *Le Déserteur*, when the scene changes to produce a great effect, coming after twenty or thirty changes of lesser interest, must certainly find the spectator colder, more difficult to move. This fact about the genius of Goethe, that he could not draw any benefit from the progress of art in his period, and that he rather caused it to retrogress to the puerilities of the Spanish and English play, places him among the mean spirits who are touched with affectation. This man who always sees himself in action has not even the sense for choosing the best road when all the roads are laid out before him and around him and have already been traveled in admirable fashion. Lord Byron, in his dramas, has at least known how to preserve himself from that affectation of originality: he recognized the vice in Shakespeare's system and, although far from understanding the merits of the great tragic writers of France, the ripeness of his mind nevertheless showed him the superiority of taste and the sense there is in that form.

April 25.

Departing for Champrosay. In the *Meunier d'Angibault*,[27] I am reading the scene where a young man of the people refuses the hand of a marquise, pretending that there is too great a difference in caste. . . . They (the Utopians) do not consider that the *bourgeois* was not, in the past, a power; today he is everything.

May 22.

As to the preceding thought,[28] to wit, the facility that childhood has in imagining and combining — as regards this singular power, I have been led to this other idea, to this question which I have asked myself so often: where does the precise point lie in which our thought enjoys its full power? Here are children, Senancour and myself if you like, and doubtless many others, and we are gifted with faculties infinitely superior to those of grown men. I see, in some other place, people intoxicated by opium or by hashish, and arriving at terrifying exaltations of the mind, perceiving things totally unknown to a man in his ordinary senses, hovering above existence and looking upon it with pity as the

[27] By George Sand; it appeared in 1846.
[28] The thought mentioned is lacking. This proves that there is a break between the preceding paragraph and this one. Are they of the same period?

limits of our ordinary imagination seem to them like those of a little village, such as we might see lost afar off on a plain when we have reached immense heights that lose themselves above the clouds. In another direction, we see how the simple daily inspiration of a creative artist leads the mind to a lucidity, a strength, that has nothing in common with the simple good sense of ordinary life; and yet who is it who generally leads and decides all the events of this world, if it is not that man of simple good sense which, in so many cases is insufficient?

I shall be answered that, for the ordinary course of life, this natural light, exempt from intermittences, is sufficient; but it must also be confessed that in a very considerable number of other circumstances, these men so reasonably sufficient for the ordinary exigencies of life, are not merely quite insufficient, but may be considered perfect fools (that is what gives us bad generals and bad doctors), and the sole reason for this is that they are devoid of a superior kind of light. . . . That reasonable man who, with great effort of the brain, painfully composes bad works which render him an object of ridicule, is certainly as mad as the one who thinks he is Jupiter or that he is going to put the sun in his pocket; on the other hand, that inspired man whose conduct most often seems to all those commonplace sages to be that of a brainless man, of a maniac, becomes, from the moment he takes pen in hand, the interpreter of universal truth; he lends to the passions their language, he charms, he sweeps all hearts along, and leaves ineffaceable traces in the memory of men. Consider the effects of eloquence; consider a cause defended with all imaginable reason by a cold man who is gifted merely with what one calls good sense and compare his lagging progress, his dull expression, with the flight of a mind both impetuous and luminous which seizes upon all the resources that perish in nerveless hands; see how he carries conviction as he throws the light of his torch into the most hidden parts of the question, compelling attention by the animated language of truth or by something that seems like that because of his talent and his warmth of soul.

How does it happen that in a semi-intoxication, certain men, and

I am of their number, acquire a lucidity of glance far superior, in many cases, to that of their calm state? If, in that state, I re-read a page in which I could previously see nothing to change, I instantly and without hesitation perceive words that shock and bad turns of expression, and I rectify them with an extreme facility. It is the same with a picture; the mistakes and awkwardnesses at once leap into view; I judge my painting as if I were some other person.

And so there is childhood, when the organs, as it seems, are imperfect; there is the man who takes opium and who, for the man in cold blood, is a real madman, and then again the man who has eaten or drunk more than he is accustomed to, and whom we would therefore not ask for advice on an important affair; there, I say, are beings who seem to be quite out of the common state, who reason, who combine, who divine, who invent with a power, a finesse, a success, infinitely superior to what the merely reasonable man could flatter himself to draw out and obtain from his steady brain. Gros, at the time when he painted his fine works, had champagne with his lunch while at work. Hoffman certainly found his best tales in glasses of punch and burgundy; as to the musicians, it is recognized by universal consent that wine is their Hippocrene. . . .

What man is there, however cold he may be when the soup is served, who does not grow animated when the dessert is before him and who does not sometimes astonish himself by his way of astonishing the others with his verve, when the fruits are reached? Mr. Fox rarely took the platform in any state but that of intoxication, Sheridan and some others, the same; it is true that these are Englishmen. Yet one should not imitate that famous Swiss someone was telling me about who, seeing the good effects of a glass of wine taken in certain cases of illness, had become an inveterate drunkard in order to protect himself against illnesses of all kinds. We know many cases of musicians who, to preserve their divinity, which is to say their bottle, have been found dead on the highroad.

Boissard[29] when in a state of intoxication due to hashish played a piece on the violin as he had never done before, according to the testimony of the people present.

Champrosay, July 3.

Extracts from Rousseau on the origin of languages.[30]

The man who writes a book imposes upon himself the obligation of not contradicting himself. He is supposed to have weighed and balanced his ideas in such fashion that he will remain consistent with himself. On the other hand, in a book like that of Montaigne, which is nothing but the moving image of a human imagination, there is all the interest of the natural, and all the vivacity of impressions rendered and expressed as soon as felt. I write on Michelangelo: I sacrifice everything to Michelangelo. I write on Puget: his qualities alone appear to me; I can compare nothing with him. All that is to be demanded of a writer, which is to say of a man, is that the end of a page be consistent with the beginning. The lack of sincerity that any man of good faith will find in all the books or in almost all, comes from this so ridiculous desire to get the thought of the moment into harmony with that of the day before. "My friend, you were yesterday disposed to see everything blue; today you see everything red, and you are fighting against your feeling." *Mentem mortalia tangunt.* The finest triumph of a writer is to make those people think who can think; it is the greatest pleasure that can be afforded to that latter class of readers. As to the pretension to amuse those who do not think, is there a single noble soul who would consent to lower himself to the role of pander of the mind?

Little as I have done in literature, my experience has always been that, contrary to received and accredited opinion, especially among

[29] Boissard de Boisdenier, collector, painter and poet, founder of the "Club des Haschichiens" which was frequented by Baudelaire, Balzac, and Théophile Gautier.

[30] It may be that Delacroix was led to make the following entry by reading the extracts from Rousseau which he mentions.

men of letters, there is really more of mechanism entering in to the composition of literature and its execution than into the composition and execution of painting. It is understood that *mechanism* does not here mean *work of the hand,* but that it is a matter of the profession, one in which inspiration counts for nothing, as I would say, in passing to the literary gentlemen who think that they are not workmen because they do not labor with their hands. I will even add, as regards myself, and taking into consideration the few attempts at literature which I have made, that in the material difficulties presented by painting, I know nothing corresponding to the thankless labor of turning phrases and words back and forth, to avoid a consonance, a repetition, or else to add to the thought words which give no precise idea of it. I have heard all literary men say that their profession was diabolical, that they have to tear their work from them, and that there was a thankless side to it from which no facility could afford them relief. Lord Byron says: "The need to write boils within me like a torture of which I must deliver myself, *but that is never a pleasure; on the contrary, composition is for me a violent labor.*" I am very sure that Raphael, Rubens, Paul Veronese, or Murillo, holding his brush or pencil, never experienced anything like that. They were doubtless animated by the sort of fever that seizes upon great talents when they come to execute, and that does not go without troubled agitation; but such trouble of the mind, which is apprehension over not being as sublime as their genius demands, is far from being a torment; it is a spur without which nothing would be done and which is indeed the presage, for these privileged natures, of their realization of the sublime. For a true painter, the least accessories offer entertainment in executing, and inspiration animates the slightest details.

July 19.

Voltaire says very justly that once a language is fixed by a certain number of good authors, it is no longer to be changed. The reason, he says, is very simple: it is that if one changes the language indefinitely, these good authors end by no longer being understood. This is, indeed, an excellent reason; for let us suppose that amidst innovations in a language or by reason of them, new talents should arise, it would still be of only mediocre interest to add them to the ones already existing if for that it were necessary to sacrifice comprehension of the ancient masterpieces. Besides, what need has language for innovation? Consider all the men of mark in the same period; does it not seem that language diversifies itself under their pen? Consider a neighboring art, music: here the language is perforce not fixed; it is unfortunately true that the invention of a new instrument, or the seizing of certain harmonic combinations which had escaped earlier composers, may be the cause, I will not venture to say of progress in the art, but of a complete change, for the ear, in the meaning or the impression of certain effects. What is the consequence of this? It is that at the end of thirty years, the masterpieces have grown old and no longer cause emotion. What have the moderns to place beside men like Mozart and Cimarosa? And if we can suppose that Beethoven, Rossini and Weber, the latest to arrive, are not to grow old in their turn, must our admiration for them cause us to neglect the sublime masters who not alone are as powerful as they but, even more, have been their models and have brought them to the place where we see them?

September 23. On returning from Champrosay.
Constable said that the superiority of the green he uses for his meadows derives from the fact that it is composed of a multitude of different greens. What causes the lack of intensity and of life in verdure as it is painted by the common run of landscapists is that they ordinarily do it with a uniform tint.

What he said about the green of the meadows can be applied to all the other tones.

As to the importance of accessories. A very small accessory will sometimes destroy the effect of a picture: the brambles that I wanted to place behind the tiger for M. Roché[31] took away from the simplicity and expanse of the plains in the background.

[31] M. Roché, an architect at Bordeaux, had executed the tomb of Delacroix's brother at Bordeaux; out of gratitude, the master had sent him a *Lion* that was exhibited at the Salon of 1846 (Catalogue Robaut, 1019).

(END)

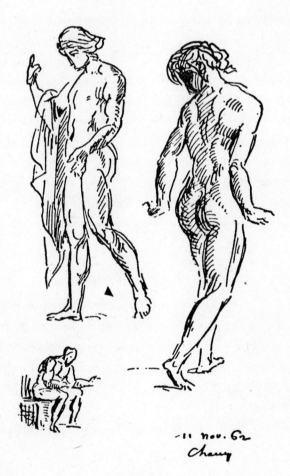

-11 nov. 62
Chassy

INDEX

INDEX

INDEX

745

About rocks like mountains & fragments like the whole pp 407

If the eye has the perfection of a magnifying glass -- pp 645

Real beauty is eternal -- pp 646

For classifying my drawings - , pp 648

To feast the eye -- Prime merit of a painting pp 700 - 1

Lack of the ensemble in Gericault - pp 501

" Facility in the great master is not his chief quality - " 204

Hear music, see a painting 313

as on the grass. 418

Michelangelo burned preliminary sketches p. 419

what is beautiful is beautiful p 420

understanding "yards & pulleys" 421

Peasants chart mass .423

p. 210